PROACTIVE POLICE MANAGEMENT

PROACTIVE POLICE MANAGEMENT

SIXTH EDITION

EDWARD A. THIBAULT, PH.D.
State University of New York College at Oswego

LAWRENCE M. LYNCH, M.P.A.
Onondaga Community College

R. BRUCE MCBRIDE, ED.D.
Utica College of Syracuse University

PEARSON
Prentice
Hall

Upper Saddle River, New Jersey 07458

Library of Congress Cataloging-in-Publication Data

Thibault, Edward A.
    Proactive police management / Edward A. Thibault, Lawrence M. Lynch, R. Bruce
McBride.—6th ed.
        p. cm.
    Includes bibliographical references and index.
    ISBN 0-13-112299-1
    1. Police administration. 2. Police administration—United States. I. Lynch,
Lawrence M. II. McBride, R. Bruce. III. Title.

HV7935.T47 2004
363.2'068—dc21   2003043859

Editor-in-Chief: Stephen Helba
Executive Editor: Frank Mortimer, Jr.
Assistant Editor: Sarah Holle
Marketing Manager: Tim Peyton
Editorial Assistant: Barbara Rosenberg
Managing Editor: Mary Carnis
Production Liaison: Brian Hyland
Production Editor: Janet Bolton
**Director of Manufacturing
  and Production:** Bruce Johnson
Manufacturing Manager: Ilene Sanford

Manufacturing Buyer: Cathleen Petersen
Creative Director: Cheryl Asherman
Senior Design Coordinator: Miguel Ortiz
Cover Design: Wanda España
Cover Photo: Jeff Haynes, AFP/Corbis
Interior Design: Janet Bolton
Composition: The GTS Companies, York Campus
Printing and Binding: Phoenix Book Tech
Proofreader: Maine Proofreading Services
Copy Editor: Judith Mara Riotto

10 9 8 7 6 5 4 3 2 1
ISBN 0-13-112299-1

CONTENTS

Preface xvii

Acknowledgments xxvii

SECTION I   Historical and Cultural Context

Chapter 1   Historical Perspective   1

The Industrial Revolution and Traditional Management,
1750–1900   2

Scientific Management, 1900 to Present   4

O.W. Wilson   5

William H. Parker   6

Other Contributors   7

Human Relations and Participative Management,
1925 to Present   8

Behavioral Management, 1945 to Present, and Systems
Management, 1960 to Present   10

Proactive Police Management, 1980 to
Present   11

William Bratton   12

Lee P. Brown   13

Female Police Executives   14

Conclusion   14

Questions for Review   15

Bibliography   16

Chapter 2   Police Culture   18

The Concept: Police Subculture   18
    Secrecy   19
    Solidarity   19
    Social Isolation   19
Characteristics of the Police Subculture   20
    Argot   20
    Esoteric Knowledge   21
    Cynicism   21
    Internal Sanctions   22
    Solidarity   22
    Social Isolation   23
    Perception of Violence and Psychological Distance   24
Informal Group Structures in Police Organizations   26
    The Hawthorne Study   27
    The Work Community   27
    The Effect of the Primary Group on Police Bureaucracy   28
Police Peer Norms   30
    Police Corruption and Internal Norms   31
    Corruption, Cliques, Meat Eaters, and Grass Eaters   32
Police Typologies   33
Minority Group Structures   35
    African-American Officers   35
    Female Officers   37
    Gay and Lesbian Police Officers   41
Conclusion   43
Questions for Review   44
Class Project   45
Bibliography   45

SECTION II   Basic Organizational Concepts

Chapter 3   Purposes and Principles of Police Organizations   50

Law Enforcement as Big Business   51
Civil Service and Promotions   52
    The Use of Civilian Employees   53
Traditional Purposes of Police Organizations   54
Traditional Measures of Police Effectiveness   54
Police Results and Performance Measures   55

Reality-Based, Proactive Purposes of Police Organizations   56
    Performance   57
    Preparedness   57
    Progressiveness   57
Management Principles   57
    Respond   57
    Regulate   58
    Restrain   58
    Recover   59
    Repress   59
    Reinforce   60
    Defining the Organization   60
The Concept of Organization   60
    Mechanical   61
    Humanist   61
The Traditional Concept of Bureaucracy from Max Weber   61
Conclusion   63
Questions for Review   63
Class Project   64
Bibliography   64

Chapter 4   Operating Principles   67

Administration   67
    Planning   68
    Organizing   68
    Staffing   68
    Directing   69
    Coordinating   69
    Reporting   69
    Budgeting   69
Supervision   70
    The RESPECT Approach to Supervision   71
Operations   74
    Line Functions   74
    Staff/Administrative Functions   76
    Auxiliary/Service Functions   76
Conclusion   77
Questions for Review   77
Class Project   78
Bibliography   78

Chapter 5   The Art and Style of Proactive Police Leadership   79

Proactive Leadership   80
    Talent   80
    Experience   82
    Ethics   83
    Training and Education   83
The Importance of Management Skills   84
Management Styles   85
    Managing in Chaos   86
    The Digital Nervous System   89
    Emotional Intelligence   90
    Total Quality Management   93
    Reengineering   96
    Herzberg's Eternal Triangle   98
    Katz's Three Skills Approach   99
    Maslow's Hierarchy of Needs   100
    Herzberg's Hygiene/Motivators Approach to Job Satisfaction   102
    McGregor's Theory X and Theory Y   104
    Theory Z   104
    Blake and Mouton's Managerial Grid   106
Conclusion   108
Questions for Review   108
Class Project   109
Bibliography   109

Chapter 6   Proactive Communication and Information Management   111

Communication Defined   112
Encoding and Decoding: The Meaning of Meaning   114
Feedback   115
    Who Communicates to Whom, and How?   115
Obstacles to Communication   118
The Johari Window   119
Operational Communications   122
    Types of Orders   122
    The Effectively Organized Directive   124
The Duty Manual   125
Proactive Organizational Communication Model   128
Conclusion   130
Questions for Review   130

Class Project   131
Bibliography   131

Chapter 7   Proactive Police Technology
for the Twenty-First Century   133

Computer Applications for Information Management   135
  Computer-Aided Dispatch   137
  Mobile Digital Communications   137
  Automatic Vehicle Monitoring   139
  911   140
  National Crime Information Center   141
  Automated Regional Justice Information System   142
  The Paperless Police Department   143
  New Technologies for Police Managers   144
  Proactive Management-Based Information System   145
  Crime Mapping   146
  CompStat   147
  Defending against Cyberterror and Cyberattacks   150
  Cross-Jurisdictional High-Speed Notification   151
  Law Enforcement at the Speed of Thought   152
Conclusion   153
Questions for Review   155
Class Project   155
Bibliography   155

SECTION III   Operational Considerations

Chapter 8   Patrol Operations and Community Policing   158

The Traditional Model   159
The Kansas City Studies   160
Rethinking the Traditional Model   161
  Preventive Patrol   162
  Calls for Service   163
  Administrative Tasks   164
  Directed Patrol   165
  Foot Patrol   167
  Bicycle Patrol   167
Team Policing   169
  History of Team Policing   169
  Positive Aspects of Team Policing   169
  Team Policing and Tactical Patrol   170

Problem-Oriented Policing   170

    Model Program and Examples of Excellence   172

Community Policing   174

    Traditional and Community Policing Compared   175

    The Implementation of Community Policing   175

    Recommendations for Implementation   177

    St. Petersburg: 911 Incident-Driven Service Police Officers
      Compared to Community-Service Police Officers   178

    Seattle: Successful Implementation of
      Community Policing   179

    Chicago: Community Policing   180

    Conclusion: Community Policing   182

Weed and Seed   183

Hot Spots   184

Police Pursuit Policies   185

    Pursuit Policy Recommendations   187

Conclusion   187

Questions for Review   188

Class Project   189

Bibliography   189

Chapter 9   Basic Line Functions   194

Generalist-Specialist Controversy   195

Traffic   197

    Effective Management in Traffic Matters   197

    Racial Profiling   198

Vice   201

    Drugs   201

    Prostitution   202

    Vice Units   203

Youth Services and Juvenile Aid Units   205

    Background   206

    The Role of Juvenile Aid   207

    Juvenile Record Keeping   208

    Personnel Selection for Juvenile Aid   209

    Organization of Juvenile Aid Operations   209

    Model Youth Programs   211

    School Violence and the Police   213

    Drug Abuse Resistance Education (DARE)   215

    Current Police Youth Programs   217

    Police Youth Program Potpourri   219

Investigation   222
    Preliminary Investigation   223
    Follow-up Investigation   224
    Traditional Structure   225
    The Rand Study   226
    Managing Criminal Investigations   227
    Investigative Issues and Concerns   229
Conclusion   231
Questions for Review   232
 Class Project   233
 Bibliography   233

SECTION IV   Managing the Police Organization

Chapter 10   Administrative/Staff Functions   237

Line/Staff Conflict and Cooperation   238
Community Relations   240
    Personnel for Community Relations   242
    Functions of the Community Relations Unit   242
    The Community Relations Officer   246
The Legal Adviser   247
Professional Standards   249
    Managing the Professional Standards/Internal Affairs Unit   251
    Disciplinary Actions   252
    Department Rules and Collective Bargaining Agreements   253
Proactive Control of Police Violence and Deviance   254
    Obstacles to Decreasing Police Deviance and Violence   255
    Early-Warning Systems to Identify Problem Officers   258
The Police Misconduct Model   259
The Internal Audit   261
    The Misconduct Review   262
    Using Proactive Community Policing to Decrease Police Deviance   263
Conclusion   266
Questions for Review   267
Class Project   268
Bibliography   268

Chapter 11   Auxiliary Functions   271

Communications   271
    Consolidation   273

Communications Personnel   273
Personal Attributes   274
Records   275
Computerization   276
Computer and Communications Administrator   277
Storage of Records   278
Security, Sealing, Purging, and Public Access to Records   278
Property Control   280
Inventory Control   280
Evidence Control   281
Found Property   282
Vehicle Maintenance   282
Personal Patrol Car   284
Building Maintenance   285
Temporary Detention Facility   286
Licensing   287
The Crime Laboratory   287
Computers and Fingerprints   292
Computer Crime Investigation Unit   292
Ancillary Public Safety Services   295
Conclusion   296
Questions for Review   298
Bibliography   298

Chapter 12   Human Resource Management   300

Personnel: The Major Cost   301
Police Civil Service Selection: Historical Background   301
Public Service Employment   301
Equal Employment Opportunity   304
Affirmative Action   305
The End of Affirmative Action?   307
The Role of the Police Human Resource Administrator   308
Personnel Selection: Issues and Concerns   309
Written Tests   309
Age   310
Physical Fitness   311
The Background Investigation   315
Residency   316
Psychological Testing   317
Lateral Entry   318

Polygraph Testing   318

The Interview   319

College Education Requirements   320

The Assessment Center   321

Recruitment Techniques   322

Toward a Rational Model of Police Selection   323

New Police Recruitment Selection Model   324

Other Personnel Issues   326

Sexual Harassment   326

Drug Testing   327

Public Police and Private Security   330

Contract Police Issues   331

Police Overtime   332

Stress Management   334

Fatigue Management   338

Employee-Assistance Programs   339

Conclusion   341

Questions for Review   342

Class Projects   343

Bibliography   343

Chapter 13   Training Policies   347

Historical Perspectives   347

General Need for Training   349

Location and Timing of Basic Training   351

Field Training for Police Officers   352

The Importance of Training to Police Managers   354

Historical Recommendations for Police Training   354

Project STAR   355

STAR Recommendations   356

Changes in the Training Curriculum, 1952 to Present   357

Topical Issues in Training   360

Terrorism and Emergency Management   360

AIDS and Other Blood-Borne Pathogens   361

Domestic Violence   361

Stalking   362

Tactical Operations   363

Diversity   363

Hate Crime   364

Americans with Disabilities Act   365

Computer and Video Simulation   *365*

New Technologies   *365*

Computer Crime Investigation   *366*

The Phase Approach to Training   367

Phase I: Recruit Training   *367*

Phase II: Intermediate Training   *368*

Phase III: Advanced Training   *368*

Phase IV: Developmental Training   *368*

Phase V: Specialist Training   *369*

Phase VI: Supervisory Training   *369*

Phase VII: Management Training   *372*

Summary   *374*

Civil Liability and Training   374

Conclusion   377

Questions for Review   378

Class Projects   379

Bibliography   379

Chapter 14   Proactive Planning: Operational and Fiscal   381

Planning Defined   382

The Significance of Planning   383

Accreditation for Law Enforcement Agencies   384

The Need for a Planning Officer or a Planning Unit   386

Steps in the Planning Process   387

Types of Plans   390

Long-Range Administrative/Management Plans   *390*

Fiscal Plans   *392*

Short-Range Operational/Tactical Plans   *401*

Policing Terrorism: Proactive Homeland Security   409

Criminal Groups versus Terrorist Groups   *411*

Hate Groups and Militias in the United States   *412*

Proactive Policies for Combating Terrorism   *413*

Critical Infrastructure Assessment and Protection   *414*

Summary: Police Planning for Terrorism   *415*

Compstat as a Planning Tool: A Reengineering,
  Data-Driven Approach   416

Conclusion   418

Questions for Review   419

Class Projects   419

Bibliography   420

SECTION V The Future: Collective Bargaining and Proactive Management

Chapter 15 Collective Bargaining and Police Management   423

Collective Bargaining Defined 424

History of Police Unionism 424

Police Unions Today 426

Major Police Union Organizations 430

Management Rights and Collective Bargaining: A Dilemma 432

The Collective Bargaining Process 433

Contract Administration 435

Fair Labor Standards Act 438

The Police Strike 439

Police Unions and the Political Process 440

Conclusion 441

Questions for Review 442

Class Project 442

Bibliography 444

Chapter 16 The Future of Proactive Police Management   446

A Scenario for the Future 446

Anticipating the Proactive Police Universe 447

The Proactive Police Response 448

Police Department Considerations 449

The Jurisdictional Dilemma 450

Technology 452

Personnel Practices 453

What Works and Evidence-Based Policing 455

Global Crime and the Need for a Global Police Organization 458

The Link between Global Terrorism and Global Crime Organizations 459

Obstacles to International Police Cooperation 460

Favorable Conditions for the Establishment of a Cross-National Police Service 461

The Global Investigation of Cross-National Crime 462

Conclusion 462

Questions for Review 465

Bibliography 465

Index 467

PREFACE

Our approach to police organizational management is proactive rather than reactive, with police managers anticipating events through planning, using police personnel and resources effectively, and delivering a whole range of police services to the community. This proactive concept is not new. In the preface of the 1829 duty manual of the recently organized London Metropolitan Police, Commissioners Rowan and Mayne wrote,

> It should be understood, at the outset, that the object to be obtained is the prevention of crime. To this great end every effort of the police is to be directed. The security of person and property, the preservation of public tranquility, and all other objects of a police establishment will thus be better effected than by the detection and punishment of the offender after he has succeeded in committing the crime.
>
> Every member of the police force, as the guide for personal and professional conduct should constantly keep this in mind. Officers and police constables should endeavor by such vigilance and activity as may render it impossible for anyone to commit a crime within that portion of the town under their charge.

Thus proactive policing is a grand and noble tradition of the first modern police force and policing throughout the ages.

Based on the authors' experience in education, policing, and management, three important considerations must be made before discussing proactive management for American policing. First, we believe that sound management is management based on a combination of theory and practice. Practice without analysis causes us to repeat the mistakes of history, so our theoretical analysis must be directed toward the practical for implementation into the day-to-day rigors of operating a police department.

Second, we reject complete adherence to the authoritarian as well as to the purely participatory styles of management. In the authoritarian model, which dominates many police organizations, important elements of planning and communications are eliminated or lost. In the full participatory model, response to emergency and life-threatening situations is hampered because too many people are involved, and decisions take too long. In crisis management, for example, one person has to be in charge of the crisis-management team, with subordinates responding to this top administrator.

Third, we rely to a great extent on the consultative style of management. As will be shown, the consultative style leaves room for change and "doors open" throughout all elements of the police organization. It can be an efficient and dynamic style of management, provided that the necessary elements of a well-run law enforcement agency are met. Consultation also includes discussions with the community on law enforcement and safety problems. It is one of the key ingredients for community-oriented and problem-oriented policing, which are being publicly advanced by police and community leaders. Proactive planning to deal with an infrastructure attack or activity by a "spree" sniper has to be done in consultation with private and public agencies and the community.

This new edition of *Proactive Police Management* provides a review, analysis, and synthesis of the various approaches to police management, including traditional scientific management, the behavioral/systems approach, and the human relations approach. There is enough detail concerning basic organization and management skills that police managers and students of police management will find the text useful. At the same time, major conceptual contributions from the behavioral sciences and human relations are explored in the context of police management. Most important is the constant theme of being proactive: planning ahead, anticipating the future, and attempting to establish some control by police managers over those future events.

Community policing is emphasized. Overall, community policing echoes the relationship between police and the community before automobiles and wireless radios. Much attention is also paid to evolving theories, such as total quality management and reengineering, along with new applications of computer technology, such as the spatial and time analysis of crime events. This combination of new proactive management concepts and the application of new technology continues to revolutionize policing as well as other private and public services in the United States.

In the first edition, we wrote that most police departments operate on traditional organization principles as stated in O.W. Wilson's classic police administration text from the 1950s. Since the 1990s, college-educated and professionally trained managers have become concerned with twenty-first-century proactive communication advances and organizational theories that can be readily applied to their departments.

Policing today remains in the limelight in terms of ethics, the use of authority and force, the crime problem as related to increased drug use and trafficking, and repeated calls by state and national leaders for dealing with crime and terrorism problems. Correspondingly, many police managers complain that they must do more with less under the burden of antiquated civil service and collective bargaining rules and reduced budgets. From the viewpoint of the general public, there is widespread support for police to contain crime. Communities will no longer tolerate corruption and brutality, as shown by the response to police brutality and racism in Los Angeles, New York City, and Cincinnati, along with the racial profiling issues in New Jersey and Maryland. The events of September 11, 2001, have had a profound impact on American policing. Departments of all sizes and types are now taking on additional responsibilities related to homeland security and emergency planning. It is against this background that we present the proactive style of management.

PROACTIVE POLICE MANAGEMENT HIGHLIGHTS

Proactive Police Management is widely used both as a textbook for college and university classes in police management and as a reference text for police managers in dealing with operational issues in their departments. It is also used for training police supervisors and administrators and is required reading for civil service promotional examinations.

Section I, "Historical and Cultural Context," places the skills and concepts needed to become a professional police manager in the context of the history of public administration and police management in Chapter 1 and as part of a police subculture in Chapter 2. Modern police management has a legacy from public administration, the social sciences, and traditional policing policies adapted throughout the United States and England. With few exceptions, the modern police organization is the result of an Anglo-Saxon heritage with a unique American contribution. This book concerns the American experience in modern police administration. The latest contributions owe much to the behavioral sciences, particularly psychology and sociology, and to advances in technology.

Most modern police administrators are promoted through the ranks. This increases the importance of the effect of the police subculture on police managers. The subculture shapes their everyday policies in ways that they may not even comprehend, especially in the crucial areas of internal discipline, training, personnel selection, and personnel management. Chapter 2 examines how the increasing numbers of African-American, Latino, female, and gay police officers are having an impact on the police subculture. Subcultural norms are presented in Chapter 2. For the police manager, an understanding of the police subculture is more important than all other administrative skills and knowledge combined.

"Basic Organizational Concepts," the next section, provides the fundamental conceptual framework for the structure of the police agency. For a department to operate effectively, both its formal and informal goals must be made explicit.

There are general purposes for any department, including community service, criminal apprehension, and crime prevention. However, a small department may wish to define its purposes in terms of community service, whereas a metropolitan police agency has to have more diverse goals, including traffic engineering, vice, organized crime, and so on. It is important for police managers to understand the specific purposes of their own departments to implement them effectively. Chapter 3 includes a discussion on the use of civilian employees.

For a department to progress from conceptual models to high operating efficiency, certain basic principles must be implemented. The concepts presented in Chapter 4, such as range and span of control, unity of command, and division of work, are basic to the operational knowledge of all police managers and supervisors, from the chief down to the supervising sergeants. With these concepts in place, it becomes possible to have an efficiently operating department whose internal policies permit consistency and cost-effective operations.

The review of basic leadership styles in Chapter 5 provides an understanding of how the implementation of authority by police managers can make or break a department. The style of leadership used by the police management team indicates the type of department being managed. The elements of democracy and hierarchy needed for an optimally efficient department demand a fairly complete knowledge of the styles of police leadership. Although many writers would like effective leadership to be scientific and cut-and-dried, it is still an art—the art of the possible. No matter how many books are written on leadership, the subject still concerns a human being leading other human beings. In Chapter 5, we introduce the concept of reengineering, which is often associated with restructuring and downsizing in large, complex organizations, and also the need for emotional intelligence.

Good communication skills, discussed in Chapter 6, are the very center of good management. Communication is more than having a radio, a cell phone, a beeper system, or a computerized communication center. Communication relates to how human beings understand each other. Policing and police management are human services made possible by communication between individuals. The implementation of first-class communication skills is the heart of the police organization.

Chapter 7 reviews how computers and advanced technology are revolutionizing police operations. This starts with 911, computer-aided dispatch, and vehicle monitoring and goes on to crime mapping, CompStat, and defending against cyberterror and cyberattacks. "Law Enforcement at the Speed of Thought" uses Bill Gates's futuristic scenario to show the maximum use of computer-based communication technology. We have to remember, however, that the proactive police manager must assume leadership and allow technology to assist police management, not drive policy decisions.

The next chapter presents the daily work of patrol operations and the newer approaches developed in the 1990s of community policing and problem-solving policing. After dicussing the traditional model and preventive and directed patrol, we explore the roots of community policing in team policing. Successful examples of community policing are given, along with a model that can be used to evaluate community policing programs. Today, community policing is the subject of much debate among police administrators since this philosophy offers much in delivering services to citizens. The chapter concludes with discussions of weed and seed, hot spots, and police pursuit policies.

Chapter 9 presents line functions other than patrol, including traffic, vice (organized crime and drugs), youth services, and investigation. Problem areas are examined, such as racial profiling in traffic stops and DARE and school violence. Following our earlier editions, we present a mix of new and old community relations programs that are offered in these areas.

The proactive approach is seen as a positive approach to increase the effectiveness for the delivery of line and patrol services. Advanced planning and analysis of a metropolitan or smaller area means that patrol activity is directed activity; in other words, the patrol is sent to do specific jobs in specific areas along with the normal activity of responding to citizens' phone calls.

Traffic is seen as primarily a planning/accident investigation activity. Traffic flow is basically an engineering problem where police pressure can be helpful but is not related to the core of the problem. Accident investigation is a technical function somewhat different from criminal investigation.

Vice, including organized and financial crime, is a place for specialists and officers who can work closely with a multitude of jurisdictions on the local, state, federal, and even international level. Youth services are seen as both preventive and useful for solving cases through youthful informants. Some specialized knowledge of youth culture and gangs is needed, and many departments are instituting or have instituted specialized youth officers or youth bureaus for this area.

Considerable time has been spent on investigations in many departments with no criteria determining when to end them. To make investigations functionally efficient, a management control system of specific responsibilities and the ability to stop them when necessary is vitally important.

The administrative functions covered in Chapter 10 deal with how uniformed police officers on the line relate to the basic administrative staff. Although primarily task oriented, this is also a function of two-way communication. Community relations personnel are seen as being part of the community they are policing rather than simply the speech makers of a special unit. Many departments have instituted a legal adviser, who, besides solving legal problems, can be an important link to the district attorney's office.

Internal affairs/police standards units and disciplinary problems are intertwined. The citizens' review board approach is rejected as being too political, whereas having the police protecting their own and hiding bad police work and corruption is also rejected. A positive approach between these two models is recommended. A department needs ongoing anti-misconduct efforts with clear-cut policies and an internal affairs officer or unit that will treat everyone fairly. This is one of the toughest problems in managing a police agency but one that must be met head-on with solid due process for officers but an over-riding concern with reducing misconduct.

The proactive control of police violence and deviance is emphasized. The impact of the police norms of secrecy, solidarity, and social isolation is discussed, along with how deviant police officers turn people into things to justify their misconduct. Proactive intervention policies are emphasized, along with due process procedures for police officers.

Chapter 11, "Auxiliary Functions," covers a variety of administrative activities. The communication function focuses on the actual carrying out of communications in the department and how the communication unit is organized. Other concerns discussed include records in the computer age and the role of security; property rooms; vehicle maintenance, turnover, and garage considerations; the maintenance of the police laboratory, either as a centralized regional laboratory or as a facility operated by the department; and computer investigation.

The next chapter, on human resource management, presents a wider focus on general personnel issues, including officer recruitment, affirmative action, the Americans with Disabilities Act, sexual harassment, drug testing, controlling police overtime, and police stress. Police fatigue and quantitative ways of measuring fatigue are also examined.

A major concern with training, the topic of Chapter 13, is providing curriculums that promote the full range of police services, with a major emphasis on human services. Training is an ongoing function. Society changes, innovations in police work are introduced every year, and new police management texts are published; a professionally trained and operational police officer must be aware of all this. The only way to have an aware and professionally trained police officer is to have a management team that allows for ongoing training for all of the officers over the duty year. Examples of some of the topical issues in training are stress management, terrorism and emergency management training, AIDS, domestic violence, stalking, tactical operations, diversity, hate crime, Americans with disabilities, new technologies, and computer crime investigation.

Chapter 14, which covers planning and research, is the core of the proactive approach. The basic idea is to plan ahead so that the police agency can deal with changing situations before they happen. Most police departments are reactive; that is, they wait for events to happen and then respond to them. This means that many departments do not do the operational planning or have the resources to meet emergencies and unforeseen situations. Planning is also related to fiscal affairs, and it is vital in this age of scarce resources for major police administrators to have top-flight budgeting skills. Homeland security and critical infrastructure assessment planning are becoming increasingly important.

Collective bargaining, discussed in Chapter 15, is one of the most important areas of police management. With police unions being adversarial, the collective bargaining process is important. It is vital for a chief and his or her management team to understand this process. The collective bargaining process can be an important management tool for creating innovations in the structural and personnel procedures of the department so that both management and the personnel "win" in the process. However, it has to be seen in this positive light; otherwise, collective bargaining can make enemies of management and the personnel who are being managed. In this chapter, attention is paid to the Fair Labor Standards Act, which has become an issue for police managers and unions and major court cases.

Chapter 16 looks to the future of proactive police management. The model for the future and the present is the proactive police agency that practices forward planning. A brief scenario showing what the future might hold for police managers is offered. Anticipating the proactive police universe looks to the immediate future of the next few decades to list what proactive police need to cope with. A description of future technology, Sherman's report on "what works," the meaning of evidence-based police management, and the future of global policing in the face of global crime are all examined. The chapter concludes with a proactive community-policing model.

HIGHLIGHTS OF THE SIXTH EDITION

Chapter 1 has been updated with proactive community policing as the management model for the twenty-first century. The last chapter in the book also expands on this model and adds issues of global policing. Short biographies of William Bratton and Lee Brown have been added, as well as an overview of female police executives.

Chapter 2, "Police Culture," describes the subcultural norms of secrecy, solidarity, and social isolation. It is a powerful chapter because it shows how police culture affects police organization, police deviance, and police violence. The challenges women face as they take their place as police officers and administrators have been documented with the latest studies. We added an additional section on the increased role of gay and lesbian officers in police departments.

Chapter 3 has additional sections on performance measures and accreditation.

The events of September 11, 2001, gave entirely new meanings to the concept of leadership. Accordingly, Chapter 5 on proactive police leadership has been updated with a discussion of leadership in chaos. Reengineering, which is an important part of the community-policing revolution, and total quality management (TQM), which is still important for customer service, are emphasized. The concept of emotional intelligence from corporate management practice will revolutionize police management in the twenty-first century. It works well with many clients, ranging from community leaders to subordinates.

Chapter 6 of the fifth edition, was divided into two chapters because of the increasing importance of technology to police managers. "Proactive Communication and Information Management" covers the basic materials and concepts for communication skills that every police manager needs. No matter how sophisticated the technology, police managers still need clear and effective communication skills. Internal and external communication must be organized and structured to be effective. With enormous amounts of data becoming accessible, the indexing and organization of records—locally, nationally, and globally—is crucial to usability. We must know specifically what information we need and for what purpose, and we must have a clear-cut display of that information. Good concepts are needed before technology can work effectively.

Chapter 7, "Proactive Police Technology," deals with the technology revolution and how police management can use the latest technology. Examples are described, from 911 and computer-aided dispatch (CAD), to global positioning, computer mapping, and CompStat. Strategies to defend against cyberterror attacks are discussed. Bill Gates's "communication at the speed of thought" idea is applied to police.

Chapter 8, "Patrol Operations and Community Policing," expands the community policing case studies with new examples of what works. Specific criteria for community policing are offered to clarify what is and what is not community policing, and specific examples are given. Seattle was an early success because it has rich resources and clear goals for working with organized community groups. A larger challenge and a success story for the twenty-first century is Chicago's community policing program. A model for the problem-solving approach to policing is given, along with successful examples. A section on police pursuits with policy recommendations deals with this historically significant police management problem. Useful weed-and-seed programs are also described.

The basic line functions presented in Chapter 9 have been revised to deal with racial profiling, school violence, and investigations. DARE is described and evaluated. We also include an overview of the Boston Gun Project, which was used successfully to reduce juvenile violent crime in that city.

Chapter 10, "Administrative/Staff Functions," has a major section on controlling police deviance and violence. Secrecy, solidarity, social isolation, and treating people as things explain why police deviance, violence, and cover-ups have been so persistent. Specific recommendations are given to deal with this major police management problem. The sixth edition added a section on police misconduct, including police misconduct review. An early-warning system is recommended to identify problem officers. It focuses on citizen complaints, use of force, reprimands, and discharge of firearms and describes the Miami Police Department's intervention policies.

Chapter 11 on auxiliary functions recommends that police departments that have the trained personnel and necessary computers establish a computer crime investigation unit. The variety of computer crimes is outlined. The process of creating a successful computer crime unit that works closely with the business community is described.

Chapter 12, "Human Resource Management," draws on a nationwide survey on overtime to document this problem and to recommend solutions. Overtime is a major police management problem that costs millions of dollars. A high percentage of police departments have no effective means of controlling and documenting overtime. Specific recommendations are made that can save police management much of the money spent on overtime. Police fatigue is another long overlooked problem. It is recommended that police managers institute an alertness assurance program to protect the department from lawsuits resulting from tired officers who make mistakes.

Chapter 13 on training policies has been updated to reflect changing topical issues in training. Some topical issues discussed in this edition are stress management, terrorism and emergency management, AIDS, domestic violence, stalking, tactical operations, diversity, hate crime, the Americans with Disabilities Act, computer and video simulation, new technologies, and computer crime.

Chapter 14, "Proactive Planning," has new recommendations on how to organize for emergency mobilizations and anti-terrorist planning.

The next chapter, on collective bargaining, has been updated to reflect the new police bargaining units and the political activism now associated with police unions.

Chapter 16, which covers the future of proactive police management, discusses the immediate future of the police universe. It reviews what works in proactive policing based on evidence-based policing. A major section here has been added on global crime and global policing. Terrorists have penetrated the United States through computer-based crime, drugs, violent terrorist acts, transnational extortion, money laundering, and international organized crime. Foreign governments have even sponsored all of these activities. The European Union is developing a continent-wide Europolice, which has recently conducted a successful multicountry drug raid and prosecution. The global approach to policing is examined in detail.

ACKNOWLEDGMENTS

In closing, we would like to acknowledge the hundreds of students we have taught over the past two decades. Today, many former students are police and public administrators, and their comments and questions on the topics in this book have been invaluable. We also thank the many faculty members who adopted this book and gave us critical comments.

We would like to thank the many police administrators who have used this book for administrative and educational purposes. Proactive administrators who continue to give us new insights into management issues include Chief Duane White, Lt. Tom Albergo, and Sgt. Robert Benton of the Escondido Police Department; the training and management staff at the New York State Bureau for Municipal Police; the police chiefs in the State University of New York System; and our friends and colleagues all over the world with the International Association of Chiefs of Police and the International Association of Campus Law Enforcement Administrators.

Special acknowledgement goes to Raymond Haines, assistant vice chancellor for labor relations at the State University of New York; Vivian Lord, University of North Carolina, Charlotte, NC; John Race, University of Pittsburgh, PA; and Thomas Whetstone, University of Louisville, Louisville, KY for their comments and contributions to this edition.

Lawrence Lynch gives thanks to Marilyn Lynch for her patience and support.

Edward A. Thibault gives thanks to Donna Hale for her materials on female police officers. To *The Great Uncaught*, combining the best of police practice and scholarship, David Owens, Donna Stuccio, Pat Faiello, Jim Ruiz, Jim Burnett, Lorenzo Boyd, and Jack Dempsey—for keeping me in touch with police culture and for their insights, police humor, and debate. Thanks to COTGU. Special thanks to my wife, Marianne Pampuch, for her love, support, and affection.

To my former department chair, Richard Loder, for his encouragement over these many editions. To Terry Hoffman for his close reading of the text and updating on community policing in Chicago. To Korni Swaroop Kumar, colleague, friend, and international scholar, who gave me permission to rewrite and use our work on global policing. Many thanks to the police supervisors and managers across the nation who have discussed issues in the text. Their contributions were invaluable.

R. Bruce McBride gives thanks to his loving family—Barbara, Robbie, Megan, and Brian McBride. He also says thanks to his colleagues and students at Utica College of Syracuse University, where he returned to teach and write in January 2001, for their constructive comments. This edition also acknowledges the memory of Al Cali, of the University at Albany, who was a kind teacher and friend.

We would also like to thank Frank Mortimer, Sara Holle for her patience and professionalism, and the staff at Prentice Hall for their continuing support and for publishing the sixth edition of *Proactive Police Management*. Finally, special thanks to Janet Bolton, lead project editor, and Judith Riotto for increasing the clarity of the writing and for her many fixes.

Edward A. Thibault, Ph.D.
Lawrence Lynch, M.P.A.
R. Bruce McBride, Ed.D.

PROACTIVE POLICE MANAGEMENT

HISTORICAL PERSPECTIVE

bureaucracy

common culture

empowerment

human relations

Law Enforcement Assistance
Administration (LEAA)

local control

Metropolitan Police Act

modus operandi

National Association of
Women Law Enforcement
Executives (NAWLEE)

Pendleton Act

proactive

scientific management

The origins of the modern police force can be traced to the creation of the Metropolitan Police in London, England, in the year 1829. The social and economic conditions created by the Industrial Revolution caused a great surge in the number of people migrating to the cities of England, and this largely uneducated and poorly trained population brought with it the chaos of poverty, unemployment, and crime. This, in turn, led to a proliferation of private and special police forces designed to serve the needs of the diverse interest groups prevalent at the time. The merchant police were hired to protect the individual store owners and shopkeepers, a parochial police protected churchgoers and church property, and special police were hired to protect the harbor front and shipping interests on the Thames, just to mention a few.

Organization of these special groups was at best haphazard and self-serving. The people of the big cities had no organized group to serve the general interests of the total population. The home secretary at the time, Sir Robert Peel, lobbied intensively in Parliament for a professional organized police force under government control. His Act for Improving the Police In and Near the Metropolis of London, commonly known as the **Metropolitan Police Act,** was approved in 1829. Its main purpose, as outlined in the first duty manual, was to prevent crime and to protect property.

Lieutenant Colonel Charles Rowan and Richard Maynes, Esq., the authors of the first instruction manual, adapted their text from the 1803 military manual of the Irish constabulary police, entitled *Military Training and Moral Training*. The force was organized into ranks of superintendent, inspectors, sergeants, and police constables (Reith, 1975: 135–36). Some 11,000 recruits were screened to attain the final 1,000 officers who made up the semimilitary structure of the forerunner of our modern police organizations.

Before we examine the historical development of police management theory, we should trace the main stages of development of the present managerial systems of law enforcement in the United States. The history can be divided into roughly six periods. As shown in Table 1–1, these periods are actually cumulative; that is, many characteristics from one era persist into subsequent periods.

THE INDUSTRIAL REVOLUTION AND TRADITIONAL MANAGEMENT, 1750–1900

One of the major management principles of the Metropolitan Police Act that appeared in the original 1829 duty manual was Principle 9 (Reith, 1975: 166), namely, *the test of police efficiency is the absence of crime and disorder and not the visible evidence of police action in dealing with them.* This principle should become increasingly important as police managers look toward the proactive management model and utilize more planning and research to provide a more efficient delivery of services to attain this principle.

The force's authorized strength of 3,295 men in 1829 was arrived at by attempting to determine, in as logical a fashion as possible, the relationship between disorder and crime in each section of London and the personnel necessary to deal with it. During its first four years of existence, this police force was not only engaged in all-night battles with rioting mobs, it was also under constant threat of being eliminated by the government. However, strong leadership coupled with an excellent command structure and a semimilitary organizational model brought order to the streets of London, along with diminished evidence of crime in general. This model, which continued to have a solid history of success in the later nineteenth and early twentieth centuries, was gradually extended to all parts of England.

Another important component of this fledgling force was the principle of **local control.** As Reith points out in his history of police (1975: 169), "In England, each separate police force in the provinces is established under local authority which in the boroughs is the Watch Committee of the town or city council and in the counties the Standing Joint Committee of the county council, comprising justices of the peace and county councillors in equal numbers. . . . There is no central headquarters, no minister or chief of police." The British were very proud of the local control of their police forces, and this concept was exported to America. As a result, the selection of constables and the

TABLE 1-1 *Periods of History in Police Management*

Years	Period	Major Leaders and Authors	Major Contributions to Police Management
1750–1900	Industrial Revolution, traditional management model	Sir Robert Peel, Charles Rowan, Richard Maynes, John Moore, Henry Fielding, John Fielding	Economic man, centralized administration, semimilitary model, ranks, strong leadership, crime prevention objective of policing
1900 to present	Scientific management	Max Weber, O.W. Wilson, Frederick Taylor, Henry Fayol, Raymond Fosdick, Elmer D. Graper, Bruce Smith, August Vollmer, V.A. Leonard, Dwight Waldo, William Parker	Modern bureaucracy, unity of command, civil service, division of labor, specialization, one-way authority, narrow span of control, omnipresent patrol officer, hierarchy
1925 to present	Human relations and participative management	Elton Mayo, Chester I. Barnard, Leonard Fuld, Frederick Herzberg, R.R. Blake, J.S. Mouton, Rensis Likert, W. Edwards Deming	Focus on personnel management, motivation techniques, morale, stress management, participatory and democratic management with team approach, communication models, TQM[a]
1945 to present	Behavioral management	Herbert Simon, Douglas Murray McGregor	PPB, organizational development, PERT, STAR[b]
1960 to present	Systems management	Patrick Murphy, James McNamara	Zero-based budgeting, interfacing of subsystems
1980 to present	Proactive police management	James Q. Wilson, George Kelling, Herman Goldstein, William Bratton, Lee Brown, Robert Trojanowicz, Larry Sherman	Emphasis on forward planning, consultative management, problem solving, high-technology information systems, data-driven departments, preventing crime, communities deciding the police agenda

[a]TQM, total quality management.
[b]PPB, programming, planning, and budgeting; PERT, program evaluation and review techniques; STAR, system training and analysis of requirements.

election of sheriffs in the United States have to this day been strictly controlled and zealously guarded by their respective communities. The political need for local control and the federal system of government severely curtailed the creation of countywide or metropolitan police agencies in the United States. This reluctance to consolidate or combine forces in light of modern-day economics is a major issue for proactive police managers.

Today, Great Britain's police have traded local control for centralized administration and services, especially in the area of supervisory and command-level policies. At present, it is the policy of most constabularies to transfer a newly appointed officer to a different constabulary after an appropriate training period. The policy of not promoting police managers to take charge in their local districts eliminates a great deal of local influence and control over the police force.

In the United States, the lack of lateral entry between agencies has created a career ladder within the agency that has had the opposite effect: increased local control. The American promotional system leads to some special management problems in the areas of both training and control. The demand for local control by communities in many areas continues to hamper a more efficient delivery of services. The result is an overlapping of jurisdictional authority and duplication of services.

With the passing of the **Pendleton Act** of 1870, federal employees were placed under a civil service merit system governing conditions of their employment in an effort to reduce the political interference that had prevailed in the Jacksonian era. Shortly thereafter, civil service reform spread throughout the states. The new era created by the scientific management writers and leaders after 1900 gave rise to modern bureaucratic techniques and civil service reforms in policing.

SCIENTIFIC MANAGEMENT, 1900 TO PRESENT

Nigro and Nigro, in their widely used textbook on public administration, refer to **scientific management** as the machine model, where the emphasis is on efficiency, orderliness, and output. They cite Frederick Taylor as providing the four basic principles of this approach (Nigro and Nigro, 1973: 92–96):

1. Division of labor and specialization
2. Unity of command and centralization of decision making
3. One-way authority
4. Narrow span of control

This, along with the monocratically organized bureaucracy developed by Max Weber (see Chapter 3 for a discussion of Weber's principles), became the basic conceptual structure for scientific management. As Nigro and Nigro (1973: 97) point out, the emphasis was on "rationality, predictability, impersonality, technical competence, and authoritarianism." This model fit well with the already existing semimilitary model of police organization, where the manager was definitely in charge of the organizational machinery.

In their study of **bureaucracy,** Blau and Meyer (1971: 34) give us three stages of developing bureaucracies that are also characteristics of police organizations. First, cash salaries replace unpaid work by family members. Then a clerical component is added, and the owners are separated from management. Finally, managers are expected to have professional qualifications. This has had further implications that are distinctly nondemocratic, namely, that "bureaucratic authority . . . prevents the group itself from conferring the position of leadership upon the member of their choice" (1971: 66). If the group itself cannot pick its leaders, then a rationale has to be developed for another selection process. This is also true of the surrounding political context. One of the thrusts of scientific management is to have professional police managers replace political appointees, whereby authority is then conferred by expertise and professional standards.

Other parts of this book examine specific contributions of this approach to police management in some detail. Rather than introduce material that will be examined later in a variety of contexts, let's take two major figures steeped in this tradition and examine them as typical examples of the scientific management approach: O.W. Wilson and William H. Parker.

O.W. Wilson

Orlando Winfield Wilson served as a patrol officer under August Vollmer, chief of the Berkeley, California, Police Department, from 1921 to 1925. His career included being chief of police in Fullerton, California (1925–1928), and Wichita, Kansas (1928–1939); professor of criminology at the University of California at Berkeley (1939–1960); and then dean (1950–1960). In World War II, Colonel Wilson served as chief public safety officer in Italy, England, and Germany (1943–1947). From 1960 to 1967, he was the reform-minded chief of police in the Chicago Police Department. His book, *Police Administration*, first published in 1950, became the most influential management textbook for use by modern police managers and police management faculties in the United States.

Basically, Wilson carried on Vollmer's sound approach to police management under the main principles of encouraging the following:

1. A professional police department divorced from politics
2. Rigorous police personnel selection and training processes
3. Use of the latest technological innovations available for law enforcement (for example, maximum use of patrol cars, radio systems, computerized record keeping).

Interestingly, Wilson was both committed to the professionalization of policing and opposed to civil service. He felt that civil service tests and rules of seniority hampered the police chief in selecting the most qualified personnel for law enforcement and promotion to leadership positions.

Wilson organized his book around three basic administrative processes: (1) planning, (2) activating, and (3) controlling. In 1963, he wrote, "Wisely conceived plans are the keystones of administration; without them the entire venture may fail" (p. 89). He went on to explain the key part planning has in his organizational scheme. Good planning, based on the study of needs and used as a continuing process, serves to bind an organization together, to implement the policy underlying its aims and purposes, to direct its efforts into the proper channels, and to guide in both training and performance. He saw the process of activating as one primarily of organization and leadership. Accordingly (1963: 9), "the essence of leadership is the ability to obtain from each member of the force the highest quality of service that he has the capacity to render." Wilson stressed that this leadership was a positive force and that relying on punishments ultimately means a failure of leadership.

His third process of control related to police organizations was accountability. He opposed the creation of civilian review boards since police leadership should be accountable for all officers' actions. He was concerned with punishing officers who used excessive force. As Gazell states in his excellent biographical article (1974: 373), Chief Wilson was "worried about what is sometimes called lawlessness in law enforcement." He considered this to be a definite police management problem that should be handled internally. Gazell sums up O.W. Wilson's legacy to police management (1974: 375):

> As Vollmer's most renowned pupil and disciple, he refined, extended and synthesized the former's work through multiple roles as practitioner, educator, scholar and consultant. His voluminous writings are divisible into the following basic categories: (1) the internal administrative milieu, especially the salience of organization theory, personnel and technology, and (2) the external environment, particularly the importance of foreign models and . . . police interactions with citizens in such disparate areas as inputs, community relations, civil liberties, accountability and organized crime.

William H. Parker

Between 1927 and 1939, William Henry Parker rose from police officer to captain in the Los Angeles Police Department (LAPD), earned an L.L.B. degree, and uncovered scandal in the police promotion process that resulted in a grand jury investigation and general cleanup of the department. During World War II, working under Colonel O.W. Wilson, Parker developed the police and prison plans for the invasion of Europe and organized democratic police departments in Frankfurt and Munich (Gazell, 1976: 29).

Parker shared many of Wilson's concerns. Basically, Parker's main contribution was in the implementation of scientific management in the LAPD, one of the largest police departments in the country, during his tenure as chief from 1950 to 1968. Parker was known for his strong stand on effective law enforcement,

accountability, technocratic innovations, and commitment to police professionalism. Besides the normal background investigation, Chief Parker also
demanded that recruits have IQs of 110 or above, undertake a closely supervised
one-year probation period, and undergo a thorough psychiatric examination.
He also created an exhaustive **modus operandi** (method of procedure) file made
up of over 2 million cards, one of the finest police laboratories in the world, and a
planning and research division that used and still uses state-of-the-art computer
technology. Gazell sums up Parker's internal changes (1976: 33):

> organizational innovations (such as the establishment of the Internal, Intelli-
> gence, and Planning and Research Divisions, as well as the creation of rehabili-
> tation centers for alcoholics), a procedural revamping (such as one-man patrols,
> intradepartmental repairs of equipment, paperwork reductions and a lower ratio
> of police officers to population), and some widely acclaimed results (such as lower
> incidence of crime, vigorous narcotics control, inroads on organized crime and
> few traffic deaths).

Under Parker's leadership, the LAPD became a model for the country in
terms of standards of excellence for police personnel recruitment and training,
sophisticated planning, and a solid image for professional law enforcement.
His willingness to take on technological and some organizational innovation in
the spirit of scientific management served to encourage other departments
throughout the country to accept these innovations. This became especially
true when the **Law Enforcement Assistance Administration (LEAA)** was
willing to provide startup costs and basic capital throughout the 1970s.

Other Contributors

Other noted works on police organization based on the scientific approach ap-
pearing throughout this period were Elmer D. Graper's *American Police
Administration* (1921), August Vollmer's *The Police and Modern Society* (1936),
Raymond B. Fosdick's *European Police Systems* (1915) and *American Police
Systems* (1920), *Municipal Police Administration* (1943) published by the
International City Managers Association, and Bruce Smith's *Police Systems in
the United States* (1940). What appears in the writings of these early observers
is a skepticism toward municipal police operations and a willingness of police
officials to blame immigrants and other public officials for crime problems.
One theme that is most common, however, is the resistance to change by police
officials. For example, Raymond Fosdick wrote in 1920 that uniformed patrol
in many cities was outdated since patrol zones had not changed over the course
of 20 to 40 years (1920: 306). Bruce Smith, who wrote a comprehensive review
of American policing after World War II, had in 1923 addressed operational
and ethical problems with the New Orleans police. When he returned in 1946,
he found many of the same problems he had encountered in his first study.

Nevertheless, the contributions of these early observers collectively forge the basis for present study and discussion on crime and policing. Wilson's classical approach, which emphasizes the traditional elements of the unity of action, division of labor, and centralization of authority, continues to serve as the benchmark for American police administration.

HUMAN RELATIONS AND PARTICIPATIVE MANAGEMENT, 1925 TO PRESENT

Basically, this model does not exist in any one department. It has some of the personnel thrust of the scientific management model and some of the democratization of the team policing approach and its variations.

The **human relations** approach considers the police executive to be a team leader who creates a cooperative effort among line officers through the use of a management team. In Maslow's terms, the police executive is a self-actualizing individual who helps fulfill the social security, self-esteem, and autonomy needs of the personnel in his or her police organization. As found in McGregor's Theory X and Theory Y approach, the manager is responsible for motivating personnel and developing talent. This is done organizationally by having the manager create opportunities and provide guidance so all members can realize their potential in contributing to the organization. The theme here is that management should be group centered. According to Tannenbaum and Schmidt (1975), the manager would basically operate from two premises:

1. The manager defines limits within which the group makes decisions.
2. The manager and the group jointly make decisions within limits defined by organizational constraints.

The team policing approach, as it existed in 22 departments cited by Gay (1977), relied on the police manager acting as a *primus inter pares* (first among equals) rather than as a traditional autocratic administrator. The human relations approach is especially germane to the participatory management model where full-service and multispecialist teams operate with strong community commitment. In other words, team policing is an adaptation of McGregor's Theory Y to the field.

When we examine the components for the production of stress among police officers, the twin Maslow needs of autonomy and security come into play. Basically, the police officer needs to feel that he or she has the prospect of a promotion along a reasonable career line and that his or her job is relatively stable and free from potentially capricious management. Personnel grievance and promotion matters play as large a role in producing stress on the job as does the work on the streets. With the strong perception of danger and the need for alertness to deal with the unexpected in the field, police officers have a special drive and a need for security on the job. Participatory management, when applied correctly, may solve these problems. Traditional, autocratic, scientific management often fails to deal with these human relations problems in a satisfactory manner.

Departmental participatory management models, in which midlevel and line personnel have an important say on how to address local crime problems, become an essential element of community policing, which is discussed in Chapter 8. What comes into play is the formation of a new working relationship between line officers and police administrators that reduces the traditional concept of centralized authority. Participatory management results in more individualized accountability in discipline and rewards. Closely allied to this is the term **empowerment,** which is commonly found in many police articles on participatory management. By definition, empowerment is a condition whereby employees have the authority to make decisions and to take action in their work areas without prior approval.

In recent years, there have been a number of organizational theory books that are modern versions of the 1930s' human relations school. Based on operations in large Japanese and Scandinavian corporations, many observers discuss the positive aspects of employee-management work teams (see the discussion of Theory Z in Chapter 5). This includes the production of high-quality products and the creation of positive employee relations in a noncollective bargaining atmosphere. Theorists like James March and Karl Weick have concluded that it is the informal structures that generally result in getting things done.

Popular in this vein were a series of "prescriptions" based on work by Tom Peters and coauthors (*In Search of Excellence* [1982] and *A Passion for Excellence: The Leadership Difference* [1985]) that veer away from traditional management models and recommend people-oriented, humanistic systems as the basis for future national and international competition by U.S. businesses. Key terms like "management by wandering around," "entrepreneurship," and "client satisfaction" are related to the traditional concepts of planning, forecasting, and budgeting based on the authors' observations of successful companies.

The successful companies discussed by the Peters group are primarily in the private sector, and some from their first book do not exist today. Among the key concepts that can be applied to police management is the idea of a **common culture,** where the mission of the organization is culturally shared between management and employees. The concept of a corporate culture is much like the concept of the police culture, which has been explored thoroughly by writers on policing.

Nearly 20 years after publishing *In Search of Excellence*, Peters was still fond of customer satisfaction and the need for companies to be conscious of "fashion" in their products in order to compete on a global level. The term *fashion* applies not only to the workability of a product but also to such things as color and attractiveness of design. His case studies of successful companies in *Liberation Management* (1992) deal with the hard realities of reorganization and downsizing, which have occurred in both corporate and public sector organizations that sought to decrease levels of middle management or to combine work sites to reduce operating and personnel costs. In the private sector, many multinational corporations "farmed out" or "outsourced" the production of certain units of work to countries or non-union concerns with lower wage rates. If anything, this trend has resulted in the establishment of smaller business enterprises and the demise of worker loyalty to the norms and values of common culture found in large companies.

Closely allied with the participative management model is the concept of quality teams or project teams created by management to address a certain problem. This forms the basis of total quality management (TQM), which uses the participative approach among employees to improve products or service. These concepts are also discussed in Chapter 5. It is important to note that companies using these approaches retain, for the most part, the traditional hierarchy model.

Both management and employees are brought into this corporate culture through vigorous training, constant employee recognition, and reform of organization processes that have a negative impact on employee performance. As discussed in Chapter 2, the police occupational subculture can be used in a positive manner to achieve organizational goals.

BEHAVIORAL MANAGEMENT, 1945 TO PRESENT, AND SYSTEMS MANAGEMENT, 1960 TO PRESENT

These approaches have had their most significant impact in the areas of fiscal organization, day-to-day budgeting, and short-range and long-range planning. Although often seen as competing with the human relations approach, as both systems have evolved in the 1980s, the systems-behavioral management approach complements much of the human relations approach, having developed mechanisms for accountability as it integrated quantitative measures for both fiscal and human behavior goals.

A behavioral goal has three major components:

1. A goal stated in an empirical manner so that any ordinary person would be able to see, hear, taste, smell, or feel something
2. A criterion of success that is normally less than 100 percent
3. A context in which to measure the goal developed in empirical terms

Here are two examples:

The patrol officer will increase by one hour each shift the time spent on foot patrol from his or her radio car. The location and time is to be based on the crime situation of the community. Time is to be logged as special foot patrol and will be exclusive of routine property and business area checks. (A realistic goal is to attempt an increase in preventive patrol, apprehension, and community relations.)

The investigator shall interview an average of three to five suspects for every 40-hour tour of duty and shall document these interviews in a written report within one 8-hour tour of duty of the documented end of each interview. (This would constitute an increase in the productivity of an officer whose main duties consist of such interviews.)

Where possible, such behavioral objectives can develop into excellent tools of accountability for management. However, there is a risk of creating goals that are too detailed and involve an inordinate amount of paperwork compared with the amount needed to get the job done.

Proponents of the systems-behavioral approach developed a number of systems for accountability, forward planning, and fiscal organization:

1. Management by objectives (MBO)
2. Program evaluation and review techniques (PERT)
3. Programming, planning, and budgeting (PPB)
4. Organizational development (OD)
5. Zero-based budgeting

These various approaches will be reviewed in the appropriate chapters.

PROACTIVE POLICE MANAGEMENT, 1980 TO PRESENT

The **proactive** approach is the focus of this book. Various aspects of this approach are discussed throughout the chapters and reviewed in detail. However, the most significant elements can be outlined here:

1. Objective of policing is crime prevention
2. Strong commitment to community involvement
3. Modern bureaucracy, range of control techniques
4. Full-service department with multispecialist teams
5. Full use of modern communication models (both technological/computer and human relations techniques)
6. Modern budgeting and accounting systems in full use
7. Great emphasis on forward emergency and crisis management planning
8. Consultative management approach (all elements of organization consulted; management team makes final decisions and organizes the implementation of policy decisions)
9. Data-driven department with optimal use of modern technology
10. Emphasis on art of the possible and operational utility of management approaches

Scholars who advocate this approach in their work with community policing include James Q. Wilson, Robert Trojanowicz, George Kelling, and Herman Goldstein. Police managers who serve as recognized leaders in the proactive approach are Lee Brown, former head of the Houston and New York City police departments and former head of the Police Foundation; David Couper, former chief of the Madison, Wisconsin, Police Department; Steven Bishop, former chief of Kansas City; and William Bratton, former New York City police commissioner.

William Bratton

William Bratton started as a patrol officer in the Boston, Massachusetts, Police Department, and attained the rank of superintendent in 1980, the highest ranking position. He was awarded the Boston Police Department's highest medal for valor, which he earned by facing down a bank robber and rescuing a hostage in 1975.

From 1990 to 1992, he served as chief of the New York City Transit Police. He was instrumental in merging the Transit Police and New York City's Housing Police with the New York City Police Department (NYPD). In 1993, he was elected president of the Police Executive Research Forum and was commissioner of the Boston Police (1993–1994). As New York City police commissioner from 1994 to 1996, he was responsible for reengineering the NYPD by decentralizing responsibility to New York City's 76 precinct commanders and institutionalizing Compstat. (See Chapter 7 for a description of Compstat.)

Commissioner Bratton describes his reengineering of the NYPD as follows (Rosen, 1995: 8–10, 8–14):

> Re-engineering is that you take an organization that you think is going one direction and you've made a decision you want it to go into a completely different direction. You then re-engineer the organization to be able to accomplish the new goals in the new direction.

Doing this resulted in crime dropping dramatically in New York City while the quality of life improved. In the past, he indicated, the department was too reactive, too centralized. He discovered that random patrol did not scare criminals. His major goals were to reduce fear in the neighborhoods and to prevent crime from happening. In the previous 20 years, he said, the NYPD had "judged success by numbers of arrest and rapid response." Using reengineering, a corporation model, he created 12 task forces to shake up the department. "My bottom line each day is crime reduction." He considers crime reduction to be the major product of any police department.

He also took the concept of "broken windows" to heart and states how pleased he was with increasing the quality of life and disorder control. He embraced community policing and problem solving as a major efforts in dealing with the community in individual precincts. He sends a clear message for one of the major goals of community policing: "Police can return to the role for which we were invented: preventing crime. . . . Police can control behavior with crime prevention" (Anonymous, 2000: 2). According to Bratton, the NYPD works in partnership with the community through precinct councils and precinct commanders.

The crime-patrol planning model Compstat was his major success when he was commissioner of the NYPD. Compstat is based on four major principles:

1. Timely, accurate intelligence: He emphasized that old information did not work; only up-to-date information worked.

2. Rapid response: He gives an example of target hardening a site to stop terrorists from blowing it up, in other words, crime prevention.
3. Effective tactics: To stop drug dealers, the focus should be on where there has been a great number of shootings, for example.
4. Relentness follow-up: Review programs and strategies and keep them updated.

Under Commissioner Howard Safire, who took over from Bratton, the system that Bratton had put in place has, for the most part, been working very well. From 1996 to 1998, the crime rates continued their dramatic downward trend. Commissioner Bratton deserves the credit for turning around the largest police department in the country and making it work successfully.

Lee P. Brown

Lee Brown began his career in 1960 as a patrol officer in San Jose, California. He was sheriff of Mulnomah County, Oregon; commissioner of public safety in Atlanta; chief of the Houston Police Department, 1982–1990; New York City police commissioner, 1990–1992; and director of national drug policy, 1993–1995. He held a cabinet position in the federal government and became the first African-American mayor of Houston in 1998.

The son of farmworkers, Lee Brown earned a bachelor's degree from Fresno State University, a master's degree from San Jose State University, and a Ph.D. from the University of California at Berkeley in 1970. He was a professor at Texas Southern University and Rice University.

While he was chief of the Houston Police Department, Brown initiated one of the early models of community policing, which he called Neighborhood-Oriented Policing (NOP). He wanted to involve citizens directly with the police. He wanted to change the police officer from an enforcer of neighborhood beats to an officer who would become involved with problem solving with the community (Oettmeier and Brown, 1998: 13): Here is his philosophy:

> The more desired perception is for the officer to be viewed as someone that can provide help and assistance, someone that expresses compassion through emphasizing and sympathizing with victims of crime, and someone that can organize community groups, inspire and motivate groups, and facilitate and coordinate the collective efforts and endeavors of others.

The beats were redesigned to conform to neighborhoods, and beat officers were permanently assigned to specific neighborhoods. Some investigation was decentralized. Police supervisors and managers were encouraged to support beat officers in solving neighborhood problems. The deterrence of crime became the criteria for evaluating the beat officer. This meant that there should be less crime, traffic accidents, and calls for service because the beat officers were solving problems.

In New York City, Commissioner Brown continued with his philosophy of community policing, initiating problem-oriented policing (POP). He claims that his earlier work with community policing with NYPD set the stage for the success of Compstat and the crime-attack planning model.

Female Police Executives

The number of women in policing has risen slowly over the years. According to the FBI's *Uniform Crime Report* (2000), women account for approximately 11 percent of the 650,000 municipal, county, and state police officers in the United States. In 1993, this number was estimated at 9.4 percent.

The number of female executives today is very small. According to Schultz (2002), only 172 police chiefs in the entire country are female, which amounts to about 1 percent of all departments surveyed. Of this number, 40 lead college or university police departments with full-time police officers, and 48 manage municipal departments. Two head state police forces. As in other American industries and professions, the number of female police executives will steadily rise in the next decade as women are promoted and transfer into major command and policy-making levels.

Already, changes are being felt in the national policy-making arena. For example, Chief Mary Ann Viverette of the Gaithersburg, Maryland, police department will assume the presidency of the International Association of Chiefs of Police (IACP) in the next three years. She received degrees from the University of Maryland, graduated from the FBI National Academy, and has served in her department for more than 20 years. Recently, she received national recognition for her work on reducing gun violence and motor vehicle theft. She was also a founding member of the **National Association of Women Law Enforcement Executives (NAWLEE)**.

Like similar associations in other professional occupations, NAWLEE was created primarily as a mentoring organization for rising female executives. The current president, Teresa Chambers, was the former chief of the Durham, North Carolina, Police Department and now heads the U.S. Park Force. In Durham, she was credited with significantly reducing crime and improving employee retention. She also served more than 21 years in the Prince George's County, Maryland, Police Department and retired with the rank of major before moving to Durham. She is a graduate of the University of Maryland, Johns Hopkins University, and the FBI National Academy.

CONCLUSION

The history of police management is an evolving field of study. Every theoretical approach offers something of operational and theoretical use to the modern police executive. The secret of success is to select and synthesize the approaches that will work for a particular department, given its specific problems and political context. The proactive approach is meant to be flexible and utilitarian yet adhere to principles that will give coherence to police management as it responds in the world of the twenty-first century. The proactive model, of course, incorporates many of the previous schools of theory presented, including community-oriented policing (COP), problem-oriented policing (POP), and total quality management (TQM), which are being applied to police operations today.

Police management evolved from the rather rigid (semimilitary) organizational model of the late nineteenth century to a more flexible approach that emphasizes human relations skills. Proactive police managers who have been professionally trained and college educated synthesize contributions from all periods of police management.

From the traditional model, these managers develop a finely honed sense of bureaucratic organization. The organization itself has to be created, and this means the creation of a hierarchical organization. The scientific management period focused on goals and the placing of these goals in organizational context. O.W. Wilson and William H. Parker adapted the basic bureaucratic model from Max Weber to make Weber's model functional in today's communication-sophisticated society. The approach depends on having a central organization along with the ability to respond rapidly to ordinary as well as unusual crises.

Although the human relations approach tended to overemphasize the importance of democratic management, its emphasis on the vital importance of human relations and personnel skills contributed significantly to modern police administration. One finding from this movement is the recognition of the need for training in human relations skills for both middle managers and supervising personnel. Besides having a good sense of leadership and organization, sergeants and lieutenants must be able to persuade police officers to do their jobs with the utmost efficiency. Sergeants especially are important to the morale and the optimal use of personnel.

Our modern manager grounds himself or herself in behavioral reality by utilizing the contribution of the behavioral management movement. After becoming firmly grounded in achievable practical behavioral objectives, the police organization can adopt the proactive police community management model of anticipation and the forward planning needed in all aspects of police management: personnel, fiscal, community, and operations.

QUESTIONS FOR REVIEW

1. Discuss the basic principles of the following managerial models: traditional, scientific, human relations, behavioral, systems, and proactive.
2. Explain the significance of the following individuals to police management: Sir Robert Peel, Frederick Taylor, O.W. Wilson, and William H. Parker.
3. Discuss the contributions of the English police system to the American system of policing.

4. Explain why the American system of policing has evolved into the existing complex structure of overlapping authorities and jurisdictions.

BIBLIOGRAPHY

ANONYMOUS. On Patrol Web site (www.onpatrol.com/brantin/html), January 26, 2000.

BEARD, EUGENE. "The Black Police in Washington, D.C." *Journal of Police Science and Administration*, 5, no. 1 (March 1977), pp. 48–52.

BLAU, PETER M., and MARSHALL W. MEYER. *Bureaucracy in Modern Society* (2nd ed.). New York: Random House, 1971.

BRATTON, WILLIAM, with PETER KNOBLER. *How America's Top Cop Reversed the Crime Epidemic*. New York: Random House, 1998.

BROWN, LEE. *Community Policing: A Practical Guide for Police Officials*. Washington, D.C.: National Institute of Justice, 1989.

BROWN, LEE P., and MARY ANN WYCOFF. "Policing Houston: Recycling Fear and Improving Service." *Crime and Delinquency*, 35 (January 1986), pp. 71–89.

———. "Policing Houston." In Larry Sherman et al., *Preventing Crime*. College Park, Md.: University of Maryland, 1997.

FEDERAL BUREAU OF INVESTIGATION. *Crime in the United States, 2000: Uniform Crime Reports*. Washington, D.C.: U.S. Government Printing Office, 2000.

FOSDICK, RAYMOND B. *European Police Systems*. Montclair, N.J.: Patterson Smith, 1915, reprinted 1969.

———. *American Police Systems*. Montclair, N.J.: Patterson Smith, 1920, reprinted 1969.

GAY, WILLIAM G., T.H. SCHELL, and S. SCHACK. *Improving Patrol Productivity*, Vol. 1: *Routine Patrol*. Washington, D.C.: U.S. Government Printing Office, 1977.

GAZELL, JAMES A. "O.W. Wilson's Essential Legacy for Police Administrators." *Journal of Police Science and Administration*, 2, no. 4 (December 1974), pp. 365–375.

———. "William H. Parker, Police Professionalism and the Public: An Assessment." *Journal of Police Science and Administration*, 4, no. 1 (March 1976), pp. 28–37.

GELLER, WILLIAM A., ed. *Local Government Police Management* (3rd ed.) Washington, D.C.: International City Management Association, 1991.

GRAPER, ELMER D. *American Police Administration*. Montclair, N.J.: Patterson Smith, 1921, reprinted 1969.

HOY, WAYNE K., and CECIL G. MISKEL. *Educational Administration: Theory, Research and Practice*. New York: McGraw-Hill, 1991.

INTERNATIONAL CITY MANAGERS ASSOCIATION. *Municipal Police Administration*. Chicago: International City Managers Association, 1943, reprinted 1969.

NIGRO, FELIX A., and LLOYD G. NIGRO. *Modern Public Administration* (3rd ed.). New York: Harper and Row, 1973.

OETTMEIR, T.N., and L.P. BROWN. "Role Expectations and the Concept of Neighborhood-Oriented Police." In *Development of Neighborhood Oriented Policing*. Arlington, Va.: International Association of Chiefs of Police, 1988.

PETERS, THOMAS J., and NANCY AUSTIN. *A Passion for Excellence: The Leadership Difference*. New York: Random House, 1985.

PETERS, THOMAS J., and ROBERT H. WATERMAN. *In Search of Excellence: Lessons from America's Best Run Companies*. New York: Harper and Row, 1982.

PETERS, TOM. *Liberation Management.* New York: Alfred A. Knopf, 1992.

RIETH, CHARLES. *A New Study of Police History.* Edinburgh: Oliver and Boyd, 1956.

———. *The Blind Eye of History.* Montclair, N.J.: Patterson Smith, 1952, reprinted 1975.

ROSEN, MARIE SIMONETTI. "A LEN Interview with Commissioner Bratton of New York." *Law Enforcement News,* June 30, 1995, pp. 8–10, 8–14.

SCHULTZ, DOROTHY. "Law Enforcement Leaders: A Survey of Women Police Chiefs in the United States." *Police Chief* (March 2002), pp. 25–28.

SHERMAN, LAWRENCE W. "The Sociology and Social Reform of the American Police: 1950–1973," *Journal of Police Science and Administration,* 2, no. 3 (September 1974), pp. 255–262.

SHERMAN, LEWIS J. "An Evaluation of Policewomen on Patrol in a Suburban Police Department," *Journal of Police Science and Administration,* 3, no. 4 (December 1975), pp. 434–438.

SMITH, BRUCE. *Police Systems in the United States.* New York: Harper and Row, 1940, revised 1960.

TANNENBAUM, R., and W.H. SCHMIDT. "How to Choose a Leadership Pattern," *Harvard Business Review* (March/April 1958), p. 36; reprinted in *Business Classics: Fifteen Key Concepts for Managerial Success.* Cambridge, Mass.: Harvard University Press, 1975.

TRAJANOWITZ, ROBERT, ET AL. *Community Policing: A Contemporary Perspective* (2nd ed.). Cincinnati: Anderson, 1998.

VOLLMER, AUGUST. *The Police and Modern Society.* Montclair, N.J.: Patterson Smith, 1936, reprinted 1970.

WILSON, O.W. *Police Administration* (2nd ed.). New York: McGraw Hill, 1963.

POLICE CULTURE

KEY TERMS

argot	peer group
blue minority	rabbi
coop	role entrapment
gemeinschaft	secrecy
gesellschaft	social isolation
Guardians	solidarity
hook	subculture
horse	thin blue line
informal organization	tin
macho	Uncle Tom
main man	

Police management operates within the context of one of the strongest vocational subcultures existing in American society. In this chapter, we have two objectives. First, we are going to look at the police subculture and examine its effect on day-to-day business and on police managers. Then, we will consider the informal organization that exists in all police departments and that all managers must reckon with. The informal organization can be used to increase effectiveness and efficiency, or it can be turned to managerial sabotage.

THE CONCEPT: POLICE SUBCULTURE

According to Edward B. Tylor (1871), with whom many anthropologists seem to agree,

> Culture . . . is that complex whole which includes knowledge, belief, art, morals, law, custom, and any other capabilities and habits acquired by man as a member of a society.

The police, although part of the American culture, form a distinctive **subculture** because of characteristics of their particular vocation: law enforcement.

A subculture is "a group that shares in the overall culture of the society but also has its own distinctive values, norms, and lifestyle" (Robertson, 1987: 76). Police subculture has its own set of cultural norms. Robertson defines *norms* as "shared rules or guidelines that proscribe the behavior appropriate in a given situation" (1987: 62). These norms create a lifestyle for a police officer both on and off the job. The major norms of the police subculture are **secrecy, solidarity,** and **social isolation**. These three *S*'s define the everyday life of every police officer in the nation.

Secrecy

Police deal with people's valuable reputations, which can be destroyed by routine police investigations. A school official might be a target of an investigation in which a young woman was raped in a van. Any public knowledge of the investigation can destroy the official's reputation, even if the investigation is proved to have been unfounded. Many months can go into a drug investigation. Talking about the investigation, even to a spouse, means jeopardizing lives.

Solidarity

The officer is part of a police family. The children are police children. The spouse is a police wife or a police husband. Police officers stick together. They protect the brother and sister officer from a hostile public and from their own brass. The operating norm is "You are never alone."

Social Isolation

The perception of a hostile public is part of what makes police officers feel alone (Shernock, 1988). Officers carry a gun and arrest people. They know they can trust a cop but never an outsider. Every day, officers deal with the underclass in society—people who steal, drunks and drug dealers, people who sell dope to children, and child molesters who prey on the weak and innocent. Police officers are doing "dirty work." This is work that deals with an undesirable population. Officers in the public eye can take on the stigma of that population. As one author stated, "I guess what our job really boils down to is not letting the assholes take over the city. . . . They're the ones that make it tough. You take the majority of what we do and it's nothing more than asshole control" (Van Maanen, 1978: 221). So the officer's friends and family are other cops and people in the "business."

Many police officers are unaware of the cultural norms that affect their daily lives. Still, all officers have to take these norms into account—for example, the role of secrecy, the norms of police unity and loyalty, and the perception of danger and suspicion that pervades this subculture.

CHARACTERISTICS OF THE POLICE SUBCULTURE

A.B. Hollingshead has given us the basic definition of a vocational subculture and its major characteristics (Arnold, 1970: 22): "a group of specialists recognized by society, as well as by themselves, who possess an identifiable complex of common culture, values, communication devices (argot or other symbols), techniques, and appropriate behavior patterns." Two forces in American society have a monopoly on the use of legal force: (1) the armed forces concerning outside threats and (2) the law enforcement community concerning internal social control. The police department is a human service agency that specializes in the use of legitimate force and is recognized as such by law. The police themselves make a great distinction between those who have a "tin" and those who are civilians. Those who have a piece of **tin**—that is, a police badge—are sworn police officers and have the right to carry a gun.

George Kirkham, a professor who became a sworn officer, expresses the feeling of many officers in this vocational subculture when he says, "Every police officer understands that his ability to back up the lawful authority, which he represents, is the only thing which stands between civilization and the jungle of lawlessness" (1974: 19). Although this seems to be a dramatic point of view, it does have meaning for police officers who really do feel that they are the **thin blue line** of legitimate authority protecting civilization. This theme is heard daily in every police department in the country. It is part of the web of common values that ties the subculture together.

Argot

Police officers in every region of the nation have developed an **argot** (specialized vocabulary of a profession) that is generally not shared by outsiders. This stems, in part, from the nature of normal communication between officers. Police officers spend considerable time riding in patrol cars or patrolling on foot with miniaturized portable radios attached to their belts. They are also continually involved with their state's penal law. Much of police argot revolves around (1) citations to the penal law, (2) words and phrases that are coded and phrased so that they can be heard without ambiguity over a radio, and (3) criminal and street jargon laced liberally with obscenities.

Examples of argot from the major police forces have become well known. In the New York City Police Department, officers may have a **rabbi** (a highly placed police official) who can help them out if they get caught cooping (sleeping on duty). In other departments, the rabbi might be called a **hook** or a

horse. Argot from the black community also creeps in, such as when a rabbi becomes a **main man.**

Consider the following radio transmission:

> Car 56, signal 79 possible 80 at intersection of Academy Place and Stacy Place. A 78 and 75 dispatched. Driver may be 1192. You are out at 2330.

This says that police car 56 has been directed to respond to the Academy Place and Stacy Place location to investigate a vehicular accident (signal 79) with the possibility of an injury (signal 80). An ambulance (78) and a tow truck (75) are being sent to the scene. The driver may be intoxicated (1192). The patrol car was dispatched at 11:30 at night (2330 military time). Two police officers who meet in public can communicate openly and yet be incomprehensible to civilians.

Esoteric Knowledge

Hollingshead's second major characteristic of a vocational subculture is an excellent description of what researchers refer to as the transition from the police academy recruit to police officer which he calls: "the acquisition by initiates of the body of esoteric knowledge and appropriate behavior patterns before the novices are accepted by the initiated." (Arnold, 1970: 22) The police academy spends hundreds of hours teaching such subjects as marksmanship and safety around weapons, unarmed combat, preservation of a crime scene, and basic investigation techniques. Today, increasing time is being spent on human relations, family crisis intervention, and other human service subjects, such as child and drug abuse. The objective of the police academy, over and above teaching basic knowledge and skills, is to instill into the recruit an acceptance of the police role model. This means an acceptance of both the formal and informal codes and discipline making up a police officer.

Cynicism

Arthur Niederhoffer, in his classic work *Behind the Shield*, shows the stages of cynicism as the police recruit moves from the idealistic role models of the police academy to the street (1969: 104). The first stage, *pseudo-cynicism*, occurs at the training school/recruit level and is an attitude that "barely conceals the idealism and commitment beneath the surface." The second stage, *romantic cynicism*, comes within the first five years of an officer's career. The third stage, *aggressive cynicism*, is evident at the 10-year mark, when "resentment and hostility become obvious." At this stage, Niederhoffer talks about a subculture of cynicism. The end of the police officer's career is what Niederhoffer calls *resigned cynicism*, when an officer accepts the flaws of the system.

This cynicism has also been called *realism* (Wilt and Bannon, 1976: 43): "The writers are of the opinion that there is a meaningful degree of realism—at least for Detroit officers—reflected in their 'cynical' responses. Objective data cause us to question Niederhoffer's operationalization of cynicism." Whether you wish to call it cynicism or realism, the recruit continues to be socialized into a role model different from that of the academy. The emphasis is on the harsh realities of street violence and internal police organizational politics.

Internal Sanctions

Hollingshead's final point on the characteristics of a vocational subculture focuses on the internal social control that helps describe how a police department's informal structure actually works (Arnold, 1970: 22): "Appropriate sanctions [are] applied by the membership to control members in their relations with one another and with the larger society and to control non-members in their relations with members." **Peer group** pressure concerning loyalty to the police profession is enormous and overwhelming. William Westley, an earlier researcher in the sociology of the police, showed that the police in Gary, Indiana, would even be willing to perjure themselves to protect a brother officer (Westley, 1970). Although the research was done in the 1950s, the conclusions hold for today's police culture.

Westley has given us a list of standard sanctions that are normally applied to officers (1970: 115): "Sanctions that would be applied or that the men thought would be applied, should they break the group rules . . . include a program in which the culprit would be an outcast, isolated from social relationships so that nobody would talk to him, so that he wouldn't know what was going on, so that the other men would go out of their way to get the man in trouble."

As we will see later, these are especially powerful sanctions in a vocational subculture that is isolated from the rest of the community. Police officers depend on one another for both professional and private friendships and social life. These sanctions and this internal loyalty also become powerful tools for the managers of police departments.

Solidarity

As has been shown, there is a great deal of pressure for conformity among police officers. Reiser (1974: 158) considers peer influence to be "one of the most profound pressures operating in police organizations." He shows how it functions: "It bolsters and supports the individual officer's esteem and confidence, which then allows him to tolerate higher levels of anger, hostility and abuse from external sources." Reiser, a department psychologist for the Los Angeles Police Department (LAPD), has pointed out an important factor concerning peer pressure: It can be a positive force in the life of the individual police officer. One of the most profound statements that any police officer can make is that he or she is never alone once having become a sworn officer. On the job, the call for "officer in trouble" will mean that officers in and outside the immediate vicinity will normally drop what they are doing and rush to that officer's aid. Even officers who are off duty will feel compelled to come to that officer's aid, even from a distance. Reiser stresses the cost of this group support (1974: 158): the "loss of autonomy in the areas of values and attitudes." It seems that group values become shared while there is a great deal of rationalization created to support conformity to the police group.

Examples of this type of pressure appears in many of the novels of veteran LAPD officer Joseph Wambaugh (especially in *The Choir Boys*). The following advice is from Wambaugh's first novel, *The New Centurions* (1970: 81):

> "I hope I can do this job," Gus blurted, surprised at the desperate tone in his own voice.
>
> "Police work is seventy percent common sense. That's about what makes a policeman, common sense, and the ability to make a quick decision. . . . You'll learn to appreciate this in your fellow policeman. Pretty soon, you won't be able to feel the same way about your friends in the lodge or church or in your neighborhood because they won't measure up to policemen in these ways."

Joseph Wambaugh himself experienced another kind of pressure once his first novel had been published—jealousy from his peers because of his new fame and earning power. The dedication of his second novel, *The Blue Knight* (1972), reflects how he felt at the time: "I often remember the rookie days and those who had discovered the allure of the beat. Then I thought them just peculiar old men. Now I wish they were all still here and that they might approve this book."

The most frequent example of this feeling of unity, besides the officer-in-trouble call and the need for backup in potentially dangerous situations, is probably seen in the area of professional courtesy. Professional courtesy is normally not discussed in textbooks and articles, but it is practiced every day in police forces. When civilians are stopped for a traffic infraction, they expect a traffic citation. When police officers are stopped, they do not expect a traffic ticket; they expect to be let go because of professional courtesy. When professional courtesy does not occur, it is a story carried from jurisdiction to jurisdiction and can lead to a feud between police officers in two different jurisdictions.

When a police officer has an automobile breakdown, he or she does not necessarily call a garage mechanic but may, in fact, call the nearest police department or highway patrol. Help from the local officers may range from driving the officer to a good garage that will give special service and rates to police to having the police mechanic fix the private auto while the stranded officer has coffee with the other officers.

Social Isolation

Most researchers concerned with police culture agree that police are isolated from the rest of American society (see Banton, 1964; Clark, 1965; Skolnick,

1966; Tauber, 1967; Westley, 1970; Savitz, 1971; Ahern, 1972; Sherman, 1974). A typical response to the question, "What do you do for a living?" in a social gathering often evokes this response from a police officer (Banton, 1964: 198): "If someone asks my wife 'What does your husband do?' I've told her to say, 'He's a clerk,' and that's the way it went because she found that being a policeman's wife—well it wasn't quite a stigma, she didn't feel cut off, but that a sort of invisible wall was up for conversation purposes when a policeman was there." In the United States (the preceding was from a Scottish police officer), we have a similar situation, as reported by Skolnick (1966: 51): "I like the men I work with, but I think it's better that my family doesn't become a police family. I try to put my work into the background, and try not to let people know I'm a policeman. Once you do, you can't have normal relations with them."

These sentiments are repeated time and time again. When asked at a party what he does, the police officer says that he is a government worker. When he is pressed, he walks away. Why does he do this? As many officers have said, "If I tell them that I am a cop, they'll want to give me a hard time about some traffic ticket they got. Next will come some bull concerning police corruption and then they'll hold me personally responsible for some court letting some killer loose on the street. What do you want me to do, spoil all the parties I go to that have civilians there, spoil these parties for myself and my wife? It's really better if you stick to your own." And stick to their own, they do. There are police bars, police picnics, and police poker parties. From these and other social activities dominated by fellow officers and their family, police officers create a feeling that each one of them is part of the **blue minority.** This social isolation has made many police officers consider themselves a persecuted minority. Stan Shernock surveyed 11 police departments and concluded, "As a result of police perception of public hostility toward them, police officers have assumed many of the characteristics of a minority group" (1988, 184). Shernock showed, as Westley did in the 1950s, that police socialize almost exclusively with police. Since Westley did his research there have been no changes in the fundamental police norms of secrecy, solidarity, and social isolation. There have been great communication and technical advances, women and minorities have become part of police culture, and we have educated police officers with advanced degrees throughout the country; but the police are still a blue minority with unchanging subcultural norms.

Perception of Violence and Psychological Distance

However, there is a positive, functional aspect to this social isolation, and that is the need for psychological distance between the police officer and many of his or her clients (Tauber, 1967: 98):

> I will argue that separateness from the public leaves the policeman free to make
> negative moral judgments about a person's character and that without feelings of
> isolation a policeman's job would be untenable.

When a teacher becomes too involved emotionally with students, the job becomes untenable because he or she is not able to make objective judgments. The same thing can happen to a police officer. Police are not always dealing with citizens of goodwill who are unafraid, calm, and friendly. Sometimes they have to deal with drunken drivers who throw up on their uniforms and urinate in the backseat of their patrol car.

Picture yourself going into a low-income neighborhood on what is called "mother's day," the day when welfare checks arrive in the mail. Here is an actual incident.

Two officers answered the call for a domestic dispute. Using good police procedure, they separated the shouting husband and wife, one to the living room and one to the kitchen. The wife was shouting to the officers that her husband tried to beat her up. Her language was obscene, as was her husband's. Both had been drinking alcohol.

The officers returned to the living room and positioned themselves between the husband and wife to try to calm them down. The wife took out a small-caliber handgun and managed to fire a shot at her husband. She was disarmed and taken to police headquarters, but both officers never forgot that incident.

In another case, one of the authors of this book was responding to a domestic dispute call. He approached the front door of the house and promptly encountered a loaded shotgun being thrust into his body. The homeowner explained that he didn't want the officer on his property. After a good deal of talk, the shotgun was withdrawn, and the fight was dealt with. But the author will never forget the incident.

Incidents like these engender statements like George Kirkham's, following his first months as a police officer (1974: 134):

> Some nights I would lie in bed unable to sleep, trying desperately to forget the
> things I had seen during a particular tour of duty: the rat-infested shacks that
> served as homes to those less fortunate than I; a teenage boy dying in my arms
> after being struck by a car; small children clad in rags with stomachs bloated from
> hunger, playing in urine-splattered halls; the victim of a robbery, senselessly
> beaten and murdered.

Officer "Doc" Kirkham concludes: "In my role as a police officer, I found that the victims of crimes ceased to be impersonal statistics."

Stoddard, director of psychological services for the Los Angeles County sheriff's office, shows what happens to officers who are involved in traumatic events, such as killing another human being. Roughly one-third develop major problems that affect their family, and they may leave the profession because of the trauma; about one-third have moderate problems, like waking up scream-ing at night, but they recover; and about one-third have minimal problems (Stoddard, 1984). Stoddard's case notes describe such major trauma for one officer (p. 228):

> Jim S. shot and killed an armed-robbery suspect who was leaving a store. The shooting was necessary and the officer did his job. . . . He told me: "I saw you three years ago after a shooting. . . . I lost 20 pounds. I'm divorced. I've screamed in the middle of the night and have been startled out of nightmares. I don't have the same drive, and my interest in work is lost."

Law enforcement is not just another job. After all, college professors are not expected to shoot people; but police officers do shoot people. Police culture is a total way of life.

A number of police officers have put the situation this way: "You are at the scene of a fatal auto accident on a busy high-speed highway. Spread before you is a young person with a limb cut off, blood flowing across the highway, and guts spilled out. This person is dead, and there is an auto blocking traffic. You don't have time to gag; you have to save lives, you have to make sure there is a call for help, take care of any other injured, and direct traffic so that there are no more bodies spilled out on the highway." This is not a normal experience for a civilian, but it is a normal one for a police officer. You need to have objectivity and distance if you are to be able to go home at night, love your spouse, and hug your children.

When a recruit joins the force, he or she can lose friends. The next per-son you arrest may be an old friend. The question is, "How are you going to keep your professional integrity and live with yourself?" The answer, more of-ten than not, is to have few civilian friends. This is what it means to be a police officer and part of an isolated vocational subculture in America.

INFORMAL GROUP STRUCTURES IN POLICE ORGANIZATIONS

Every organization has a formal and an informal structure. The formal struc-ture involves the organization chart and lines of authority (e.g., police chief, deputy chief, inspectors, captains, lieutenants, sergeants, police officers). Although official business is conducted by the formal organization, the infor-mal structure often determines which decisions will be made and the manner in which these decisions will be carried out.

As Berger and Berger (1972: 202–3) point out, "There is a general notion that every bureaucracy has an informal structure that exists . . . beneath its formal tables of organization. . . . It might serve to maintain the system by smoothing difficult situations, filling in gaps left open by the formal procedures and generally giving staff members feelings of belonging and personal satisfac-tion." Hughes (1971: 12) adds that "an **informal organization** takes on a pat-tern but in a much more individual and personal way."

This is a reality that every manager has to be able to deal with if he or she is going to have a smooth, efficient police organization with high morale. This is the role of the social groups within the informal structure and the effect of these groups on the formal structure and the police manager's ability to manage. Light and Keller give us a widely accepted definition of social group (1975: 184): "A number of people who define themselves as members of a group; who expect certain behavior from members that they do not expect from outsiders; and who others (members and nonmembers) define as belonging to the group." Typical social groups that exist in and influence police in a police department include fraternal orders comprised of officers; officers who play golf, racquetball, or cards together; and ethnic and extended kinship groups.

The Hawthorne Study

In the early 1920s and 1930s, under the leadership of Elton Mayo, the Harvard Business School conducted a series of research projects at the Hawthorne plant of the Western Electric Company (Roethlisberger and Dickson, 1939). Nigro and Nigro, in their standard textbook *Modern Public Administration* (1973: 97–102), also refer to this as the beginning of the human relations approach to management. The key to this approach was the discovery of the informal organization and its communication system.

Management in one part of the Hawthorne plant tried to speed up the production of parts for telephone switches by placing the workers on a piece-rate system. Production did not change, even though the workers could have easily increased production. Researchers discovered informal work norms within the workers' group that placed social penalties on (1) "rate busters" who exceeded the work norm, (2) "chiselers" who did not fulfill the work norm, and (3) "squealers" who might have informed management of this system. This research on the informal structure has been replicated in many organizations both public and private, with much the same results.

The Work Community

We are going to be looking at a variety of groups within the police organization, such as informal cliques, ethnic and racial groups, and fraternal societies. All these make up what Drucker calls the *work community* (1974: 281–84).

According to Drucker, management is interested in making necessary decisions in relation to the mission of its business. He states also that management should not be making incidental decisions related to the work community and that these decisions can clog the organization's decision-making machinery. Decisions on such items as vacation schedule and cafeteria and recreation facilities should be decentralized and left to the work community. Although these decisions may not have a high priority, for the worker they are important and can be a means of fostering leadership opportunities. This is not a participatory democracy, for management organizes the working teams. As Drucker concluded (1974: 228):

> The worker and his group are responsible for their own job and for the relationships between individual jobs. They are responsible for thinking through *how* the work is to be done. They are responsible for meeting performance goals and for quality as well as for quantity. And they are responsible for improving work, job, tools, and processes and their own skills.
>
> These are exacting demands. Yet whenever we have made them, they have been met—providing the planning has been done. Indeed in most cases—IBM is the typical example—workers will set higher performance goals than the industrial engineer and will tend to outdo their goals.

This is an approach that we recommend for modern, reality-based police managers. The officer on the street and his or her immediate supervisor have a great deal of responsibility. Peter Drucker's recommendation enables modern police management to tie this commitment to discretion and responsibility to quality work. As discussed in Chapters 5 and 8, this concept was reinvented in the 1990s for "quality circles" and work teams for community-oriented and problem-oriented policing. However, this takes a precise knowledge of the law enforcement work community and the informal norms and social groups that govern much of this community.

Social scientists, business psychologists, and personnel managers have been studying this informal group structure for many years. A basic concept that they use is that of the primary group as it operates in the secondary or formal organization. This concept must be understood if we are to be able to use it to analyze police organization and how it really operates on a daily basis.

The Effect of the Primary Group on Police Bureaucracy

In the primary group, communication is normally

Deep and extensive
Face-to-face
Intimate
Relaying a sense of belonging
A response to a whole person rather than to a fragmented social role

In addition, the primary group assumes many of the characteristics of what Max Weber calls a **gemeinschaft** group, where there is a high degree of cohesion and the group is often perceived as an enlarged kinship (e.g., when male officers speak of their partners as their wives).

As enlarged on in Chapter 3, which examines bureaucracy, secondary organizations are normally

Impersonal
Formal

Communications are also impersonal and formal, and relations are based on specialized roles. This is what Max Weber calls **gesellschaft,** and that is the modern corporate bureaucracy that is found at the core of many police structures.

Primary groups include the family, personal friends, neighborhood social groups, and people who play friendly card games on a regular basis. Examples of secondary organizations are civil service, organized religion, local government, and military groups.

These secondary organizations normally operate as classical bureaucracies with hierarchical sets of offices and chains of command. As Niederhoffer (1969: 11) states, "Large urban police departments are bureaucracies. Members of the force lose their bearings in the labyrinth of hierarchy, specialization, competitive examinations, red tape, promotions based on seniority and impersonality."

Members of the public discover that they have encountered a bureaucracy in such instances as obtaining an accident report or attempting to find out the status of a case in which they were a witness or the complainant. They are dealt with courteously but impersonally, and the correct form must always be filled out. Although officers in smaller agencies tend to be generalists, offering the entire range of police services, bureaucracy occurs in the smaller setting for the same reason as in the larger urban department.

It is in this impersonal setting that primary groups grow and have a profound influence on organizational life. To feel that he or she is a total human being, the police officer needs roots in the security of a primary group setting within the organization. Primary groups provide the following for individual members:

Personal development

Sense of security

Sense of well-being

Sense of being accepted for one's self

Sense of sustaining one's identity and defining that identity

Primary groups are powerful, supportive mechanisms maintaining a sense of personal identity and security for the individual. They become of major significance for the police manager who recognizes the importance of informal police groups in sustaining morale.

The role of primary groups in the police bureaucracy may be to

Support or undermine the formal police organization

Form a powerful informal police structure

Have a mediating function, binding the individual to the larger police organization

Have a major role in creating social stability in the police organization and in society in general

Generally, these primary groups form around a community of shared experience and proximity. The members of the same police academy class or those who work in the same squad may become members of the same social group. Those who grew up in the same neighborhoods form groups. In larger departments, Irish, Italian, German, Jewish, and African-American social groups may pressure management in many subtle and not-so-subtle ways to have their policies promoted or their group protected or enhanced. The New York City Police Department, for example, has the Emerald Society (Irish), the Columbus Society (Italian), and an influential organization of African-American police officers.

Besides shared experiences, there is often a core of officers who plan group activities and encourage new officers to join. Finally, there are often family ties within and without the group. In relating to the secondary police organization, we must examine the group's informal ties to top management. Is the chief or deputy chief a former member of the group? Does the chief have a relative or close friend in the group? Answers to these kinds of questions often determine who will get an assignment, who will get a promotion, and whose policy will be adopted by the department. This kind of information is simply not available in an organization chart. These organizations may also determine productivity. Officers do not want their colleagues to be rate busters, chiselers, or squealers to management.

In one case, a state trooper assigned to traffic duty on a major superhighway decided to be a rate buster. He issued three times the number of traffic citations that other officers were issuing at that same duty station. Many of the other officers talked to him, but he replied that he would not change and that he thought that his high rate of citations was just part of doing the job. After a few months, most of his fellow officers would not talk to him. His superiors praised him officially for his work but indicated informally that he might have overdone it as a rate buster. Everyone at the station was relieved when he was transferred.

POLICE PEER NORMS

Secrecy, solidarity, and social isolation are the major police norms. They are fiercely strong and have been documented time and again (Niederhoffer, 1969; Westley, 1970; Blumberg, 1985; Balkin, 1988; Shernock, 1988; Peak, 1993). Shernock's report on 11 police departments (1988: 185) showed that secrecy "maintained group identity and supports solidarity." He added a curious footnote: When he asked if the police officers would turn in another officer for illegal behavior, "as many respondents pointed out to the researcher, they possibly 'should' but 'would not' take the aforementioned actions against fellow officers" (1988: 193).

Radano, in discussing internal police norms in his book *Walking the Beat* (1968: 13), gives us a few internal police norms:

A coop is a shelter where cops go to sit down, grab a smoke, escape the weather, or to lie down. . . . Cops move in like the proverbial camel nosing his way into the tent, and soon squatter's rights prevail.

What is obvious from the rest of his discussion is that the **coop** is a resting place for officers shirking their duties and that the officers who know about the coop are under considerable pressure not to inform management of its existence. On coming into the coop, the rookie realizes that he is becoming accepted as a member of the line officer police group. As Radano indicates, the subject of discussion in these coops "is the usual man talk: sex, politics, hemorrhoids, the Sergeant. Not always in that order."

Savitz (1971) documents Westley's finding of strong interpersonal police loyalty in the face of citizen hostility and as a self-protection society of line officers against the brass. Westley documents these internal sanctions, giving them a human dimension (1970: 115):

If I turned a man in everybody would be out to get me. They wouldn't talk to me. They would go out of their way to get me in trouble. When you are on the police force you can't afford to have a man against you. There are too many situations in which you have got to depend on him. . . . If a man would turn you in for one thing he will turn you in for another. This is what I figure.

Interviewer: How serious would a crime have to be before you would turn a fellow officer in?

Answer: I wouldn't turn him in for anything. When you are on the job, police stick together.

Police Corruption and Internal Norms

Another source of information about internal police norms and pressure involves police corruption and police abuses. Some of the better known of these reports and studies are from the Wickersham Commission (National Commission, 1931); Smith's *The Tarnished Badge* (1965); the report on that famous organized crime town in Pennsylvania, Wincanton (Gardiner, 1965), Chevigny's "ride-around" view of police abuses, *Police Power* (1969); Stark's study based on newspaper clippings, *Police Riots* (1972); the well-known Knapp Commission report (1972); and Sherman's study of corruption in four large cities, LEAA report, *Controlling Police Corruption* (1978), and his book *Police Corruption* (1979).

The basic approach of these studies is to examine (1) how police officers corrupt other police officers, (2) the sources of temptation, and (3) whether the payoffs are regular (e.g., the pad) or a one-time affair. The studies include advice to management on how to break up internal cliques and bring about more central control. However, there is very little discussion of the effect of primary group cliques on the formal structure. Sherman focuses on breaking the linkages between local politics and police corruption. He proposes various strategies that police managers can use to control their staff. Sherman's conclusions are (1978: 1)

1. Premonitory strategies (aimed at ongoing corruption) for corruption control can reduce the level of organization of police corruption.
2. Postmonitory strategies (aimed at past corruption) for corruption control do not seem to be as effective as premonitory strategies.
3. The same strategies for corruption control can be employed in a police department of any size, although the tactics may differ.

Corruption cannot exist without the active cooperation of top police officials and major figures in the political hierarchy. As outlined by Dombrink (1991), every major city in the past decade has experienced a corruption scandal, the new variable being narcotics. Still, Sherman's model, with a basis on management control of investigations and employee drug testing, remains a viable strategy.

Corruption, Cliques, Meat Eaters, and Grass Eaters

One of the early research articles on police corruption that investigates primary group cliques in the police structure is that of Stoddard's "The Informal 'Code' of Police Deviance: A Group Approach to 'Blue-Coat Crime' " (1968: 202). Stoddard indicated that it was the cliques dominated by older officers that first corrupted the recruits. The Knapp Commission report (1972: 3–4) revealed widespread corruption:

> The overwhelming majority of those who do take payoffs are "grass eaters," who accept gratuities and solicit five-, ten-, and twenty-dollar payments from contractors, tow truck operators, gamblers, and the like, but do not aggressively pursue corruption payments. "Meat eaters," probably only a small percentage of the force, spend a good deal of their working hours aggressively seeking out situations they can exploit for financial gain, including gambling, narcotics, and other serious offenses which can yield payments of thousands of dollars.

Leonard Savitz (1971: 697) has given management a very good reason why these negative police cliques develop, as he studied a cohort of Philadelphia police recruits over a three-year period:

> With a capricious, uncooperative, and unreliable citizenry, with a bureaucratic structure which does not always properly protect its own, there arises the possibility that latent structures develop which place the highest premium among fellow officers. Secrecy is defined as personal and conscious concealment of information not only from the public but also from supervisory and administrative levels with the organization.

These historical and classic studies will be updated in later chapters.

CASE STUDY

The Wincanton (Reading, PA) Protection System

The following account is taken from the task-force report on organized crime (National Advisory Commission, 1976), which a well-documented government report on how organized crime took over a criminal justice system. Even though the corruption reported here occurred more than 20 years ago, this study is considered to be the classic on corruption and organized crime.

Wincanton, which was a pseudonym for Reading, PA, was an industrial city of about 60,000 population, located in western Pennsylvania. The primary author of the study, John Gardner, describes the relationship between the police, politicians and local gangsters, the most notorious being Irv Stern, who controlled the city's gambling activity after World War II.

Two basic principles were involved in the Wincanton protection system: (1) pay top personnel as much as necessary to keep them happy (and quiet) and (2) pay something to as many others as possible to implicate them in the system and to keep them from talking. The range of payoffs thus went from a weekly salary for some public officials to a Christmas turkey for the patrolman on the beat. Records from the numbers bank listed payment totaling $2,400 each week to some local elected officials, state legislators, the police chief, a captain in charge of detectives, and other people mysteriously labeled "county" and "state." While the list of people to be paid remained fairly constant, the amounts paid varied according to the gambling activities in operation at the time; payoff figures dropped sharply when the FBI put the dice game out of business. When the dice game was running, one official was receiving $750 per week, the chief $100, and a few captains, lieutenants, and detectives lesser amounts.

While the number of officials receiving regular "salary" payoffs was quite restricted (only 15 names were on the payroll found at the number bank), many other officials were paid off in different ways. (Some men were also silenced without charge. Low-ranking policemen, for example, kept quiet after they learned that officers who reported gambling or prostitution were ignored or transferred to the midnight shift; they didn't have to be paid.) Stern was a major (if undisclosed) contributor during political campaigns—sometimes giving money to all candidates, not caring who won, sometimes supporting a "regular" to defeat a possible reformer, sometimes paying a candidate not to oppose a preferred man. Since there were few legitimate sources of large contributions for Democratic candidates, Stern's money was frequently regarded as essential for victory, for the costs of buying radio and television ads and paying poll watchers were high. When popular sentiment was running strongly in favor of reform, however, even Stern's contributions could not guarantee victory. Bob Walasek, later to be as corrupt as any Wincanton mayor, ran as a reform candidate in the Democratic primary and defeated Stern-financed incumbent Gene Donnelly. Never a man to bear grudges, Stern financed Walasek in the general election that year and put him on the "payroll" when he took office.

POLICE TYPOLOGIES

Another approach to the study of internal groups has been the "typology of ideal types" study. The theory of ideal types, introduced into social science by Max Weber, says that models of reality can be created as an extreme form of that reality and used to clarify the relationships embodied in that reality.

Wilson's (1968) styles of policing described as watchman, legalistic and service, is perhaps the most widely known among police administrators. Wilson created these typologies after observing the way law enforcement services were delivered in several American cities, which included Albany, Newburgh, and Nassau County in the Long Island area of New York. Applying these "styles" to a homeless person causing a disturbance, the watchmen officer might take the person into custody or simply warn the person to leave town or else. The legalistic officer, on the other hand, would arrest because the law was broken while the service officer would take the person to a shelter.

Has the legalistic style of policing ever existed in reality? The usual answer is no, not as a style of a police agency or the style of an individual officer. However, some agencies prefer this type of policing, even though the other styles may also exist in a legalistic police agency. The same is true of individual officers. What this and other typologies do is enable the researcher and the student of police management and police culture to use the ideal typology as a tool to analyze police departments and police groups. We will see this tool in use when we look at styles of leadership and management.

Broderick (1987) created a different typology that has been widely used. He has four types. The enforcers "place a relatively high value on social order and keeping society safe and a relatively low value on individual rights and due process of law" (p. 23). The idealists "place a relatively high value on individual rights and due process of law. . . . They also believe that it is their responsibility to keep the peace, to protect citizens from criminals and otherwise preserve social order" (p. 49). Realists "place a relatively low emphasis on both social order and individual rights. . . . Realists seem less frustrated than . . . other officers" (p. 77). These realists are the ultimate cynics and feel that not much can be done about crime and criminals. Optimists "place a relatively high value on individual rights. That is, like the Idealists, they see their jobs as being people-oriented rather than crime-oriented" (p. 99). They do not focus on crime; they like helping people, and they feel police work is rewarding.

This is a typical typology. Broderick then goes on to describe various police behaviors of each type. Police managers need to deal with all kinds of police personalities. They would do well to look over some of these typologies to see if any relationship can be found between these social constructs and police behavior.

Hundreds of typologies have been produced for the study of police management and police culture. There are professional cops, street cops, by-the-book cops, bad cops, good cops, and many others. These studies look at whole departments, styles of leadership and management, and types of police officers. However, these studies rarely take even a brief look at how these models are also characteristic of groups of police officers in an agency.

Consider, for example, a chief with a service orientation who takes over a legalistic-style department. He sends standard operating orders to the officers telling them they should spend time talking to citizens, delivering babies, teaching courses at the local schools, serving as guest speakers, and *also* apprehending criminals. The new chief will find tight-and-fast resistance because the prevailing style gives priority to enforcing the law and apprehending criminals.

Chiefs who do not understand the difference between their style of policing and the one prevailing in the department will fail. Police managers need to understand and consider police styles every day if their orders are to be effective.

MINORITY GROUP STRUCTURES

The research on minority law enforcement officers has generally been directed toward how African-Americans feel about being police officers and what group norms emerge. However, some work has been done on African-American police officers' clubs and social groups and their effect on police administration and management.

African-American Officers

From December 1964 to October 1965, Nicholas Alex interviewed 41 African-American New York City police officers, using a series of open-ended questions. The result was the first book on black police, *Black in Blue* (1969). Alex discovered that black police officers were often accepted as brother police officers but were often excluded from white officers' social activities (p. 87): "It's wonderful in the station house. . . . We are going to do police work together—wonderful. But off duty, that's different. It's funny. When you walk into a room of white cops getting together for a few drinks with their wives, there's a very cold feeling." He quotes another black police officer as belonging to a black officers' social club (p. 97): "Several years ago I belonged to a club. It was a social club of Negro cops and corrections men." However, that is all we find out about this club.

Alex also shows ethnic rivalry in terms of blacks being excluded from the detective division (1969: 111): "The Irish are the bosses. It's an Irish job and they want to keep it. They can't stop you on the promotion jobs, because you take a test and the marks are posted, so everyone knows. But they can stop you from getting into the Detectives, Youth Division, and Plainclothes." There are some data here, but this is basically a descriptive study with little analysis, except in terms of general racial discrimination.

A 1973 article by Bannon and Wilt on black police officers based on a number of interviews with Detroit police of various ranks found that black cops were more often referred to simply as good or bad cops by white police officers. Black police officers did not want to lower the standards to bring more blacks into the police agency since they felt this would lower their own status in the eyes of their fellow police officers. Here you see a closer identification with the prevailing police culture.

However, many of the same problems persisted. Blacks felt that opportunities for promotion had improved over the years. However, they were still disturbed that "assignment to preferred jobs often occurred on a friendship basis, rather than strictly on a qualification basis" (Bannon and Wilt, 1973: 27). The basis of group friendships and its analysis was not carried forward. The social exclusion of black police officers persisted. As one black Detroit police officer stated, "I have observed a certain amount of discrimination in that white officers tend to keep to themselves and exclude blacks from their groups not only socially but even in everyday relations at station houses" (Bannon and Wilt, 1973: 28). No group activities of blacks were documented.

From January 1974 until January 1976, Eugene Beard had 947 (90 percent) of the black officers on the Washington, D.C., police force complete a self-administered questionnaire under orders from the chief of police. The questionnaires were turned in to the officer's desk sergeant. Ten percent were from black female police officers. Nearly 84 percent of the respondents held the rank of private, and more than "65 percent reported that they trusted few or no white officers; black officers rarely socialized with white officers; more than 80 percent believed that blacks were discriminated against in hiring, job assignments, enforcement of rules and regulations and job performance ratings" (1977: 51). Beard also reported that 58 percent felt that "the lack of trust of black police personnel by white police was not a problem" (p. 50).

In a follow-up study to Alex's work, Leinen (1984) discussed racial discrimination in the New York City Police Department from the Civil Rights era to the beginning of the 1980s. Until the 1960s, black officers were assigned only to black neighborhoods and were neither promoted nor assigned to special units. Disciplinary actions against black officers were inequitable when compared to those against white officers. In the last two decades, many improvements have been made in these procedures. Based on a series of interviews with black patrol officers, detectives, and supervisors, Leinen found that institutional discrimination had largely disappeared. He felt this was due to the legal, social, and political events of the civil rights era, along with the efforts of black officer associations like the **Guardians.** Leinen (1984: 255–56) reported that there were some white officers who continued to deny blacks and other nonwhite officers opportunity and mobility in the New York City Police Department. This problem, he maintained, was compounded by the senior positions held by these racist white officers. Although blacks and other minorities have made strides in the department, there was still the obstacle of the racist senior officer to contend with.

A study by McBride (1986) on the recruitment and training process for three medium-sized police departments in New York State found that blacks were generally accepted by their white colleagues based on the black officer's ability to do the job. Based on a series of face-to-face interviews, the study found some instances of discriminatory treatment toward black officers during employment selection and police training.

Black recruits indicated that they had encountered difficulties during field training because of both personality clashes and the treatment of black citizens by their field training officers. The same recruits indicated they had little difficulty in dealing with the areas to which they were assigned after field training, regardless of the racial makeup of the suspects and victims in the area. They felt that the few cries of **"Uncle Tom"** came from citizens who had a bad attitude toward police in general.

The number of African-Americans, Hispanics, and Asians on the force and in officer ranks has continued to grow over the years as a result of affirmative action programs. Even as the research becomes more sophisticated, it is still evident that blacks and other minority officers are generally treated equally on the job by white police officers but continue to be generally isolated from the social activities of white officers.

Female Officers

The first female officer was appointed in the Los Angeles Police Department in 1911 (Sherman, 1973: 383). As Owings pointed out in *Women Police* (1925), the female officer was normally used in three areas: vice, juvenile work, and the handling of female prisoners (police matron). Sherman (1973) indicated that in the early 1970s, women still constituted only 2 to 3 percent of the national police force and that they still held the traditionally female police jobs in the male-dominated departments around the nation.

In 1968, Chief Winston Churchill of the Indianapolis Police Department assigned two women to car 47 to do regular patrol work. He thus earned the distinction of having the first female officers doing "regular" duty. As Sherman points out, "The crew of car 47 has earned open if grudging acceptance from most Indianapolis policemen." "Grudging acceptance" exemplifies the place of women in policing. Police management decides to assign female police officers to regular duty. Over a number of years, these female officers earn the grudging acceptance of the male police officer.

From the many stories that come from jurisdictions around the country, the following trends are well documented.

Catherine Milton (1972) found that female officers were used as secretaries and dispatchers but were infrequently accorded equality with men. By 1974, there were enough female police executives in Pennsylvania that Barbara Price could publish an article entitled "A Study of Leadership Strength of Female Police Executives." Susan Martin, a policewoman in Washington, D.C., interviewed 32 officers on their feelings. She concluded (1979: 322):

> Policewomen as tokens in a male-dominated occupation face a number of dilemmas. . . . They face performance pressures, isolation from co-workers, tests of loyalty and entrapment in stereotypic roles. Expected to outperform others, closely watched for any sign of weakness yet pressured at the same time to

conform to typically feminine behavior and punished with such labels as "bitch" and "lesbian" for failure to act in stereotypic ways, policewomen indeed work under different structural conditions than male officers.

Martin also pointed out a lack of unity among female police officers and noted that they failed to act as a political faction or as a group. Instead, they competed individually and lacked internal political clout.

Let us examine some quotations from female police officers (Dreifus, 1980: 18, 20, 25):

People are always asking me what I'm trying to prove.

Winning acceptance took time. I did it by striking a balance between being tough and funny.

A woman on patrol will never have the equivalent of a wife. No guy wants to be that tolerant.

In 1993, female police officers made up 9.4 percent of sworn police officers and 63.1 percent of civilian employees of police departments in the United States (Macguire and Pastore, 1994: 55).

In 1971, women were only 1.4 percent of sworn police officers (Martin, 1993: 328). In 1990, Martin found that women were 10.5 percent in cities over 50,000 and 11.3 percent in the suburbs. In 1986, nonwhite women were 40 percent of the female officers. Female officers in that year represented 3.3 percent of all supervisors in municipal agencies (Martin, 1993: 328). In 1993, there were four female police chiefs in major cities: Elizabeth Watson of Austin, Texas; Elaine S. Hedtke of Tucson, Arizona; Leslie Martinez of Portsmouth, Virginia; and Mary F. Rabadeau of Elizabeth, New Jersey (Schultz, 1995: 372).

The courts have backed women when they have been discriminated against in hiring and promotion. In *Webb* v. *City of Chester, Ill.*, Webb testified that on the day she got her badge, a member of the Board of Fire and Police Commissioners told her, "I don't want you here, you are a woman and a woman has no business being a police officer." Even though she was at the top of her police academy class, two and one-half weeks after graduation, she was fired. The jury awarded her $20,250 for embarrassment and humiliation and $9,750 as compensation for lost wages. The judgment held on appeal. Webb sued under Section 703(a) of Title VII of the Civil Rights Act of 1964, which states it is illegal to discriminate because of sex.

In *Thomas* v. *City of Evanston* in 1985 and *Baurney* v. *Pawtucket* in 1983, courts decided that a physical agility test discriminated against women. In *Vanguard Justice Society* v. *Hughes* in 1979 and *U.S.* v. *North Carolina* in 1981, courts decided that certain weight requirements also discriminated against women. Hale and Menniti conclude from these and other cases that "where the success rate of a plaintiff class is less than 80 percent, a finding of a disparate impact is appropriate for the courts" (1993: 181–83). This means that if 80 percent of a certain class flunks, then the test or criteria is suspect.

Balkin did an empirical study in 1988 titled "Why Policemen Don't Like Policewomen." He quoted one respondent: "If you are sleeping with someone you are a slut; if not you are a dyke" (Balkin, 1988: 92). The reasons why female police officers have such a hard time being accepted by the male police force are once again the three S's: secrecy, solidarity, and social isolation. Balkin concludes (1988: 35), "This solidarity is in the service of ameliorating the men's sense of isolation from the public and the dangerousness of their work. Women in policing undermine this solidarity. They are not like them and are [therefore] opposed."

Leslie Kay Lord (1986: 89) found that "male officers still harbor grave reservations about women's suitability to be competent police officers." In a study of stress on the female officer, Wexler and Logan indicated that these types of attitudes put a great deal of stress on the female officer. As one officer in their study said, "The academy said they didn't want women. We stuck together and said we were going to make it." One training officer said, "This is my personal opinion. I don't think you should be in this job. You should go home and have babies" (Wexler and Logan, 1983: 50). The researchers concluded, "After 6 years of women on patrol, the men in the department still did not seem to accept them as officers. They were ignored, harassed, watched, gossiped about and viewed as sexual objects. The hostility of the male co-workers has been so substantial that other stressors receded in comparison" (p. 52).

However, another study showed that when the researcher controlled for age, the younger male officers were more accepting of female officers (Wheisheit, 1987). Yet another study found that women reported higher stress than men but that "improvement in status and income associated with entry into male-dominated employment may ameliorate stress consequences for policewomen in comparison to other employed women" (Pendergrass and Ostrove, 1984: 308).

A final issue that has had a negative impact on policewomen and their relationship to their fellow officers and the community is a charge that policewomen are cowardly (Homant, 1983). Some male officers also accuse female officers of being emotionally unstable in the face of violence. However, a 1987 study refutes these stereotypes. Sean A. Grennan (1987: 83) in a study of the New York City Police Department found that there was no gender difference in the number of injuries sustained on patrol. "There is no basic difference between the ways a male or female officer, working in a patrol team, reacts to violent confrontation." He also concluded (1987: 84) that "women police officers, in most cases, are far more emotionally stable than their male counterparts and lack a need to project the **macho** image that seems to be inherent in the personality of most male officers. The female officer, with her less aggressive personality, is more likely to calm a potentially violent situation and avoid injury to all participants." He showed that in a male/female team, the male was more likely to discharge his firearm.

Walking the Thin Blue Line in the Twenty-First Century.   Conditions for women are better now than in the past, but they are far from being fair in the areas of promotions and job selection. Many female authors writing about policewomen have said that the discrimination still exists but that it is more sophisticated.

Teresa Lynn Wertsch interviewed 16 female officers who were "walking the thin blue line." By this she meant that female officers could not be better than male officers, nor could they be worse. They had to walk this thin blue line if they were to avoid being attacked. Wertsch (1998: 31) described the **role entrapment** of female officers. While male officers are dispatched to major criminal and assault calls, females were assigned to family violence, sexual assaults, and rape and traffic accidents/incidents. She blamed sexist police dispatchers.

Role entrapment has been widespread throughout the United States, as numerous studies have shown. One policewoman said that when female officers go to DARE or become a Neighborhood Service Officer, male officers say, "Well, she is only doing this because she can't do *real police work*" (Wertsch, 1998: 35). For these male officers, "real police work" is patrol work and crime fighting.

Gosset and Williams (1998) interviewed 27 female police officers concerning perceived discrimination. Female officers were concerned about the covert discrimination of the 1990s (p. 63). "The officers who perceive discrimination today see it as subtle and inadvertent, 'It is behind the closed door, in one-on-one conversation.'" Another female officer said, "It is not blatant. It is not something that occurs on a daily basis."

What is this covert discrimination? It is the "old boy" system where senior male officers help junior male officers on promotions and job assignments. Male African-American and Hispanic police officers complained about this in the 1980s. That was partially solved when enough Hispanic and African-American officers got promoted and became police chiefs and administrators. Then they could help the junior minority officers in career advancement and job assignment. It happens that it is taking much longer for the female officer to have her "rabbi" or "book" in the upper ranks, compared to minority officers.

Research has shown conclusively in every study that male and female police officers do equally well on the job in all areas. One three-year study of a large police department in the Southeast showed that the female police officers had somewhat fewer citizen complaints (Lersch, 1998). The study also concluded that there were no differences between male and female officers in the type of complaint, including the use of force.

Hale and Wyland (1993: 4) pointed out early in the 1990s that "it is no longer necessary to debate or discuss the effectiveness of women on patrol. It is time however to address the greater issue of how women can unconditionally be accepted by their peers and supervisors." This is a major issue for policing in the twenty-first century.

Female police officers are beginning to emerge as leaders in police departments throughout the United States. Twenty-first-century police departments will have proactive police officers and leaders of both sexes.

Gay and Lesbian Police Officers

Gay and lesbian police officers are starting to "come out of the closet." Police Chief Anthony Ribera of the San Francisco Police Department said in 1993, "In 1979, before the first openly gay police officers entered our department, I had doubts about the propriety of hiring gays as police officers. . . . Today the San Francisco Police Department has 85 openly gay and lesbian police officers. Their performance, professional conduct and loyalty have been exemplary" (Shusta et al., 1995: 54). As in the military, homosexuals in law enforcement are in a period of transition. Some of the same arguments used against hiring women surface in hiring homosexuals. Some police feel that a gay police officer would not be masculine enough to exert authority or to quell a bar fight. Regardless of these attitudes, many states prohibit discrimination in employment based on sexual orientation. A proactive approach, including cultural sensitivity training, can ease the transition to accepting an openly homosexual police officer.

A study of openly gay and lesbian personnel in the San Diego Police Department concluded that "fully integrating gay and lesbian officers has improved the agency's quality and responsiveness to the community." The authors cited San Diego's 10-year history of integration and noted that "diversification and integration were not expensive to implement financially, but they did require some political capital from the police chief." Some officers resented the promotion of openly gay police officers, and some older male officers were unhappy with the program of integration (Belkin and McNichol, 2002).

The report gave three reasons for the success of San Diego's program:

1. Strong support and leadership from three police chiefs
2. A special training program for all new recruits that covered appropriate rules of conduct
3. The use of openly gay and lesbian police officers as special liaisons with the local gay community.

The report also concluded that the acceptance of openly gay and lesbian police officers did not hurt recruitment, and there was no lack of close support for officers in hazardous situations. The police chief marched in gay pride parades in the city, and the department cut off its ties to the Boy Scouts when that organization rejected an openly gay police officer as a teacher in a cadet program.

CASE STUDY

Canal City Police Department

The Canal City Police Department is a traditional, hierarchical department in a small city on the East Coast. The middle-sized department reflects the social and political makeup of the municipality, which is dominated by one ethnic group. The informal relationships that have developed over the years have created a number of strong cliques based on kinship and a variety of interests.

One ethnic group dominates the police hierarchy so much that other officers complain about how these officers stick together. The perception of the other officers is that the officers from this ethnic group do favors for one another, including preferential treatment for promotions, shift assignments, and attendance at special training programs outside the city. This is quite similar to the behavior of the Irish in Boston and the Scandinavians and Germans in parts of the Midwest. Unlike the New York City Police Department, where a number of ethnic groups compete with one another, in Canal City there exists only the one ethnic group and the unorganized others. In Canal City, the "rabbi" who helps officers up the promotion ladder is from this ethnic group. Kinship permeates the ethnic cliques. Favors are performed by uncles, cousins, and godfathers of higher rank for relatives in the lower ranks.

Naturally, in this traditional, autocratic department, the chief and his cronies form the most powerful clique; moreover, the chief retains power and influence, not just through the normal means of command rank, but also through a communication network operated by his clique. Officers who attempt to go against the chief are inevitably discovered by members of this clique, which extends to the lower ranks. When a malcontent officer is identified, the information is conveyed to the chief, and the officer is disciplined.

A unique clause in the union contract allows command officers to participate fully in all union activities. Not surprisingly, the agenda of the Police Benevolent Association's meetings contain few criticisms of the chief or of members of his clique. Thus control is exerted downward through the ever-watchful eyes of the chief's clique, even when he cannot be present.

One shift, shift C, has been a thorn in the side of this autocratic chief. The mainly younger, college-educated officers in this shift have been known to pull pranks that make the chief angry. Once, while the chief was trying to transmit a radio message, members of the shift keyed their microphones in to the chief's frequency, causing considerable interruption. The culprits were invited to report to the chief's office. In the tradition of the fierce loyalty that police officers have for each other, no one reported, and no one told the chief anything. Every man in the shift was ordered to one tour of foot patrol each month, and patrol partners were changed from day to day.

This was a punishment directly attacking the informal organization of the shift. Over the years, partners come together who like and trust each other. In Canal City, partners are often said to be "married" to each other.

Rotating the tours of duty broke up the partnerships and disrupted much of the informal organization of the shift. In sociological terms, this was probably the worst type of punishment the chief could devise in terms of the morale of his young officers.

Within shift C, the following cliques were identified:

The elite clique. Three experienced and powerful men who are close to the chief and enjoy his protection. One is a patrolman, one is a lieutenant, and one is a captain. All have over 20 years of seniority.

The young ambitious. These six with young families are aggressive officers in terms of making arrests and doing "real" police work. They privately voice their opposition to the chief's dictatorial policies and fervently hope that he retires soon. Additionally, they feel that some members of the shift are lazy and corrupt, and they have little use for these officers.

Pistol clubbers. These three married officers belong to the department's pistol club and take part in statewide competitions. The club provides a common meeting place away from the police station for socializing and sharing gossip and criminal information. The pistol club has the blessings of the chief.

Social drinkers. These five officers go drinking together, sharing both police and private gossip. They all have at least seven years of experience and are known to socialize with their families.

The shift also has sportsmen, golfers, and officers attending college. However, these are the main cliques. What makes this shift stand out from the rest is that cliques are formed mainly on the grounds of interests, not ethnic and kinship ties. Every officer knows that when you are dealing with one of these officers, you are also dealing with his clique and the relationship between his clique and your clique.

At times, the entire shift gets together at their favorite police bar to drink and play cards. After the evening shift, 4:00 P.M. to midnight, there are frequent and rather rowdy get-togethers at local bars and in private homes. This has become known in Wambaugh's terminology as "choir practice."

The officers are deeply imbedded in their various social and professional groups, which define power relationships in the department. They also make a fairly large department with strong hierarchical relationships more humane and give the individual officer a sense of personal worth and security.

At present, traditional ethnic cliques dominate the department and support an authoritarian chief. If the young ambitious clique manages to form an alliance with a number of the stronger kinship groups, the chief may have problems, and a new power relationship may be forged in the Canal City Police Department.

This is a real department in which participant observation research has been done. However, considering the explosive nature of the power relationships discussed, the authors have decided not to reveal additional geographic details.

CONCLUSION

This chapter focused on police subculture and informal organizational structure as forces to be dealt with by police managers. We began by defining the concept of subculture and offered examples of how it appears in police argot, esoteric knowledge, internal sanctions, solidarity, social isolation, perception of violence, and psychological distance. The implications for police managers are obvious. Issues and problems based in the notion of subculture have a tendency to become major.

Internal factions based on the primary group organization exist in every police department. It is up to the management to use these groups as positive reinforcement for the basic purpose of the organization. The deep ties of loyalty generated by primary groups operating through the informal social structure can make or break management in any police department. Most books on police management and administration ignore the effect of these groups on the operations of the basic organization and management style.

However, we can no longer afford to ignore the fundamental group dynamics that structure departmental activity on a daily basis. These groups, along with police subculture and unions (described in Chapter 15), operationalize management directives and determine the impact of management decisions on the operation of the organization itself and on the citizens. Primary groups shape and run most organizations in terms of the personal effect on individual officers. No policy can be implemented without taking these groups and their actions into account. The sophisticated police manager knows that there is a long way to go from issuing orders to implementing them in the squad room and on the streets.

QUESTIONS FOR REVIEW

1. List the major characteristics of police departments as vocational subcultures. Give special emphasis to the notions of secrecy, solidarity, and social isolation.
2. Use the concept of police argot to explain some major tenets of the police subculture.
3. How would you, as a police administrator, deal with your department's informal norms and sanctions while trying to introduce a new crime prevention program?
4. Do police really have a daily perception of violence? How does this relate to the perceived need for psychological distance?
5. Explain the differences between the formal organization and the informal organization.
6. Analyze the effect of police primary groups on the police organization.
7. What is the effect of peer group norms on police corruption? As a police administrator, how would you use these norms to deal with the problem of police corruption?
8. Describe, analyze, and apply the different styles of policing—legalistic, watchman, service—to a local police agency.
9. Based on the conclusions of the available research, compare and contrast how Hispanic, African-American, and female police officers fit into both the formal and the informal police organization.
10. Do informal cliques help or hinder good police management? Why?
11. Compare female to minority officers in terms of their acceptance into police culture.

CLASS PROJECT

Compare and contrast the police as a vocational subculture to any other vocational subculture. Interview both a police officer and a member of the other vocation. In your interview, ascertain whether the interviewee feels that his or her occupation is characterized by such things as argot, internal sanctions, solidarity, social isolation, and the like.

BIBLIOGRAPHY

AHERN, JAMES F. *Police in Trouble.* New York: Hawthorne, 1972.

ALEX, NICHOLAS. *Black in Blue.* New York: Appleton-Century-Crofts, 1969.

APPIER, JANIS. *Women in Policing.* Philadelphia: Temple University Press, 1998.

ARNOLD, DAVID O. *The Sociology of Subcultures.* Berkeley, Calif.: Glendessary, 1970.

BALKIN, JOSEPH. "Why Policemen Don't Like Policewomen." *Journal of Police Science and Administration,* 16, no. 1 (March 1988), pp. 29–38.

BANNON, JAMES D., and G. MARIE WILT. "Black Policeman: A Study of Self-Images." *Journal of Police Science and Administration,* 1, no. 1 (March 1973), pp. 21–29.

BANTON, MICHAEL. *The Policeman in the Community.* New York: Basic Books, 1964.

BARKER, THOMAS, and DAVID L. CARTER, eds. *Police Deviance* (3rd ed.). Cincinnati: Anderson, 1994.

BEARD, EUGENE. "The Black Police in Washington, D.C." *Journal of Police Science and Administration,* 5, no. 1 (March 1977), pp. 48–52.

BELKIN, AARON, and JASON MCNICHOL. "Pink and Blue: Outcomes Associated with the Integration of Open Gay and Lesbian Personnel in the San Diego Police Department." *Police Quarterly,* 5, no. 1 (2002), pp. 46–89.

BERGER, PETER L., and BRIGITTE BERGER. *Sociology: A Biographical Approach.* New York: Basic Books, 1972.

BLUMBERG, ABRAHAM, and ELAINE NIEDERHOFFER. *The Ambivalent Force.* Hinsdale, Ill.: Dryden Press, 1985.

BRODERICK, J. *Police in a Time of Change* (2nd ed.). Prospect Heights, Ill.: Waveland Press, 1987.

CARTER, DAVID L., and DARREL W. STEPHENS. "Police Ethics, Integrity and Off-Duty Behavior: Policy Issues on Police Conduct." In Thomas Barker and David L. Carter, eds., *Police Deviance* (2nd ed.). Cincinnati: Anderson, 1994, pp. 29–44.

CHEVIGNY, PAUL. *Police Power: Abuses in New York.* New York: Pantheon, 1969.

CHRISTOPHER COMMISSION. "Report of the Independent Commission of the Los Angeles Police Department." In Thomas Barker and David L. Carter, eds., *Police Deviance* (2nd ed.). Cincinnati: Anderson, 1994, pp. 291–306.

CLARK, JOHN P. "Isolation of the Police: A Comparison of British and American Situations." *Journal of Police Science and Administration,* 56, no. 3 (September 1965), pp. 307–331.

CRANK, JOHN P. *Understanding Police Culture.* Cincinnati: Anderson, 1998.

DIETL, BO, and KEN CROSS. *One Tough Cop.* New York: Pocket Books, 1988.

DREIFUS, CLAUDIA. "Portrait of a Policewoman." *Police Magazine,* 3, no. 2 (March 1980), pp. 18–26.

DRUCKER, PETER F. *Management: Tasks, Responsibilities, Practices.* New York: Harper and Row, 1974.

DUNHAM, ROGER G., and GEOFFREY P. ALPERT. *Critical Issues in Policing.* Prospect Heights, Ill.: Waveland Press, 1997.

GARDINER, JOHN A. "Wincanton: The Politics of Corruption." In President's Commission on Law Enforcement and Administration of Justice, *Task Force Report: Organized Crime.* Washington, D.C.: U.S. Government Printing Office, 1965.

GARNER, J., and E. CLEMMER. *Danger to Police in Domestic Disturbances: A New Look.* Washington, D.C.: U.S. Department of Justice, 1986.

GERTH, H.H., and C. WRIGHT MILLS. *From Max Weber: Essays in Sociology.* New York: Oxford University Press, 1946.

GOLDSTEIN, HERMAN. *Problem Oriented Policing.* New York: McGraw-Hill, 1990.

GOOLKASIAN, GAIL A. *Confronting Domestic Violence: A Guide for Criminal Justice Agencies.* Washington, D.C.: U.S. Department of Justice, 1986.

GOSSETT, JENNIFER LYNN, and JOYCE E. WILLIAMS. "Perceived Discrimination in Law Enforcement." *Women and Criminal Justice*, 10, no. 1 (1998), pp. 23–61.

GRENNAN, SEAN A. "Perspective on Women in Policing." In Roslyn Muraskin and Ted Alleman, eds., *It's a Crime: Women and Justice.* Upper Saddle River, N.J.: Prentice Hall, 1993, pp. 163–176.

———. "Findings on the Role of Officer Gender in Violent Encounters with Citizens." *Journal of Police Science and Administration*, 15, no. 1 (March 1987), pp. 78–85.

HALE, DONNA, and DANIEL J. MENNITI. "Discrimination and Harassment: Litigation by Women in Policing." In Roslyn Muraskin and Ted Alleman, eds., *It's a Crime: Women and Justice.* Upper Saddle River, N.J.: Prentice Hall, 1993, pp. 177–190.

HALE, DONNA, and STACEY WYLAND. "Dragons and Dinosaurs: The Plight of Patrol Women." *Police Forum*, 3 (April 1993), pp. 1–6.

HEIDENSOHEN, F. *Women in Control? The Role of Women in Policing.* New York: Oxford University Press, 1992.

HOMANT, ROBERT J. "The Impact of Policewomen on Community Attitudes Toward the Police." *Journal of Police Science and Administration*, 15, no. 1 (1983), pp. 16–22.

HUGHES, HELEN MACGILL. *Social Organizations.* Boston: Holbrook, 1971.

KELLING, GEORGE L. "Police and Communities: The Quiet Revolution." In Larry J. Siegel, ed., *American Justice: Research of the National Institute of Justice.* St. Paul, Minn.: West, 1991, pp. 121–128.

KIRKHAM, GEORGE L. "From Professor to Policeman: A Fresh Perspective on the Police." *Journal of Police Science and Administration*, 2, no. 2 (June 1974), pp. 127–137.

KNAPP COMMISSION. *Police Corruption in New York.* New York: Whitman Knapp, 1972.

LANIER, MARK M. "An Evolutionary Typology of Women Police Officers." *Women and Criminal Justice*, 8, no. 2 (1996), pp. 35–50.

LEINEN, S. *Black Police, White Society.* New York: Basic Books, 1984.

LIGHT, DONALD, JR., and SUZANNE KELLER. *Sociology.* New York: Alfred A. Knopf, 1975.

LORD, LESLIE KAY. "A Comparison of Male and Female Police Officers' Stereotypic Perception of Women and Women Police Officers." *Journal of Police Science and Administration*, 14, no. 2 (1986), pp. 83–97.

MACGUIRE, KATHLEEN, and TIMOTHY J. FLANAGAN, eds. *Sourcebook of Criminal Justice Statistics, 1994.* Washington, D.C.: U.S. Department of Justice, Bureau of Justice Statistics, 1995.

MACGUIRE, KATHLEEN, TIMOTHY J. FLANAGAN, and ANN L. PASTORE, eds. *Sourcebook of Criminal Justice Statistics, 1995*. Washington, D.C.: U.S. Department of Justice, Bureau of Justice Statistics, 1996.

MARTIN, SUSAN E. "*Police*women and Police *Women:* Occupational Role Dilemmas and Choices of Female Officers." *Journal of Police Science and Administration*, no. 3 (September 1979), pp. 314–323.

———. "Female Officers on the Move." In Roger G. Dunham and Geoffrey P. Alpert, eds., *Critical Issues in Policing* (2nd ed.). Prospect Heights, Ill.: Waveland Press, 1993, pp. 327–347.

MARX, GARY T. *Undercover: Police Surveillance in America*. Berkeley and Los Angeles: University of California Press, 1988.

MCBRIDE, R. BRUCE. "Perceptions of Racial Discrimination within Occupation Socialization Process as Held by Newly Appointed Police Officers in Selected New York State Police Departments." Dissertation, SUNY at Albany, 1986.

MILTON, CATHERINE H. *Women in Policing*. Washington, D.C.: Police Foundation, 1972.

MITTEAGER, JIM. "NYPD's Gay Cops." *National Centurion*, 2, no. 1 (February 1984), pp. 33–36, 71.

MOORE, MARK H., and ROBERT C. TROJANOWICZ. "Policing and Fear of Crime." In Larry J. Siegel, ed., *American Justice: Research of the National Institute of Justice*. St. Paul, Minn.: West, 1991, pp. 129–136.

MORE, HARRY W. *Special Topics in Policing*. Cincinnati: Anderson, 1992.

NATIONAL COMMISSION ON LAW OBSERVANCE AND ENFORCEMENT. George P. Wickersham, chairman, *Wickersham Commission Report 14: Police*. Montclair, N.J.: Patterson Smith, 1931, reprinted 1968.

NIEDERHOFFER, ARTHUR. *Behind the Shield*. Garden City, N.Y.: Doubleday, 1969.

NIEDERHOFFER, ARTHUR, and ABRAHAM BLUMBERG. *The Ambivalent Force*. Hinsdale, Ill.: Dryden Press, 1976.

NIGRO, FELIX A., and LLOYD G. NIGRO. *Modern Public Administration* (3rd ed.). New York: Harper and Row, 1973.

OWINGS, CHLOE. *Women Police*. Montclair, N.J.: Patterson Smith, 1925, reprinted 1969.

PEAK, KENNETH. *Policing America*. Upper Saddle River, N.J.: Prentice Hall, 1993.

PENDERGRASS, VIRGINIA E., and NANCY M. OSTROVE. "A Survey of Stress in Women in Policing." *Journal of Police Science and Administration*, 12, no. 3 (1984), pp. 138–144.

POLICE FOUNDATION. *On the Move: The Status of Women in Policing*. Washington, D.C.: Police Foundation, 1990.

PRICE, BARBARA R. "A Study of Leadership Strength of Female Executives." *Journal of Police Science and Administration*, 2, no. 2 (June 1974), pp. 223–240.

RADANO, GENE. *Walking the Beat*. Cleveland: World, 1968.

REICHER, LISA M., and ROY R. ROBERG. "Community Policing: A Critical Review of Underlying Assumptions." *Journal of Police Science and Administration*, 17, no. 2 (June 1990), pp. 105–114.

REISER, MARTIN. "Some Organization Stresses on Policemen." *Journal of Police Science and Administration*, 2, no. 2 (June 1974), pp. 138–144.

ROBERTSON, IAN. *Sociology* (3rd ed.). New York: Worth, 1987.

ROETHLISBERGER, F.J., and WILLIAM J. DICKSON. *Management and the Worker*. Cambridge, Mass.: Harvard University Press, 1939.

SAVITZ, LEONARD D. *Socialization of the Police.* Final report to the Pennsylvania Criminal Justice Planning Board. Philadelphia: Temple University, 1971.

SCHULTZ, DOROTHY MOSES. *From Social Worker to Crime Fighter: Women in United States Policing.* Westport, Conn.: Praeger, 1995.

SHERMAN, LAWRENCE. *Team Policing: Seven Case Studies.* Washington, D.C.: Police Foundation, 1973b.

SHERMAN, LAWRENCE. "The Sociology and Social Reform of American Police, 1950–1973." *Journal of Police Science and Administration,* 2, no. 3 (September 1974), pp. 255–262.

SHERMAN, LAWRENCE. *Controlling Police Corruption: The Effects of Reform Policies— Summary Report.* Washington, D.C.: U.S. Government Printing Office, 1978.

SHERMAN, LEWIS J. "A Psychological View of Women in Policing." *Journal of Police Science and Administration,* 1, no. 4 (December 1973).

SHERNOCK, STAN. "An Empirical Examination of the Relationship between Police Solidarity and Community Orientation." *Journal of Police Science and Administration,* 16, no. 3 (September 1988), pp. 182–194.

SHUSTA, ROBERT M., et al. *Multicultural Law Enforcement.* Upper Saddle River, N.J.: Prentice Hall, 1995.

SKOLNICK, JEROME H. *Justice without Trial: Law Enforcement in a Democratic Society.* New York: Wiley, 1966.

———. "A Sketch of the Policeman's Working Personality." In Abraham Blumberg and Elaine Niederhoffer, eds., *The Ambivalent Force.* Hinsdale, Ill.: Dryden Press, 1985, pp. 80–90.

SKOLNICK, JEROME H., and THOMAS C. GRAY. *Police in America.* Boston: Little, Brown, 1975.

SMITH, RALPH LEE. *The Tarnished Badge.* New York: Thomas Y. Crowell, 1965.

STANFORD, ROSE MARY, and BONNEY LEE MOWRY. "Domestic Disturbance Danger Rate." *Journal of Police Science and Administration,* 17, no. 4 (December 1990), pp. 244–250.

STARK, RODNEY. *Police Riots.* Belmont, Calif.: Focus, 1972.

STODDARD, ELLWYN R. "The Informal 'Code' of Police Deviance: A Group Approach to 'Blue Coat Crime.'" *Journal of Police Science and Administration,* 59 (June 1968), pp. 201–213.

STODDARD, ELLWYN R. "The Informal 'Code' of Police Deviance: A Group Approach to 'Blue Coat Crime.'" *Journal of Criminal Law, Criminology, and Police Science,* 59 (June 1968), pp. 201–213.

STRATTON, JOHN G. *Police Passages.* Sandusky, Ohio: Glennon, 1984.

TAUBER, RONALD K. "Danger and the Police: A Theoretical Analysis." *Issues in Criminology* (summer 1967), pp. 69–81.

THIBAULT, EDWARD. "The Blue Milieu: Police as a Vocational Subculture." In John W. Bizzack, ed., *Issues in Policing.* Lexington, Ky.: Autumn House, 1993.

THIBAULT, EDWARD, and R. BRUCE MCBRIDE. "Institutionalizing the Community Police Model in Canalville: A Case Study." *Journal of Police Science and Administration,* 9, no. 4 (December 1981), pp. 390–397.

THIBAULT, EDWARD, and NORMAN L. WEINER. "The Anomic Cop." *Humboldt Journal of Social Relations* (fall 1973). Reported in *Human Behavior* (1974).

TYLER, EDWARD B. *Primitive Culture.* London: John Murray, 1871.

VAN MAANEN, JOHN. "The Asshole." In Peter K. Manning and John Van Maanen, eds., *Policing: A View from the Street.* Santa Monica, Calif.: Goodyear, 1978, pp. 221–238.

WALKER, SAMUEL. "Racial Minority and Female Employment in Policing: The Implications of 'Glacial' Change." *Crime and Delinquency,* 31 (October 1985), pp. 355–372.

———. *The Police in America* (3rd ed.). New York: McGraw-Hill, 1999.

WAMBAUGH, JOSEPH. *The New Centurions.* Boston: Little, Brown, 1970.

———. *The Blue Knight.* Boston: Little, Brown, 1972.

WERTSCH, TERESA LYNN. "Walking the Thin Blue Line: Policewomen and Tokenism Today." *Women and Criminal Justice,* 9, no. 3 (1998), pp. 23–61.

WESTLEY, WILLIAM A. *Violence and the Police.* Cambridge: Massachusetts Institute of Technology, 1970.

WEXLER, JUDIE GAFFIN, and DEANA DORMAN LOGAN. "Sources for Stress among Women Police Officers." *Journal of Police Science and Administration,* 11, no. 1 (1983), pp. 46–53.

WHEISHEIT, RALPH A. "Women in the State Police: Concerns of Male and Female Police Officers." *Journal of Police Science and Administration,* 15, no. 2 (1987), pp. 137–144.

WHITE, MERVIN F., TERRY C. COX, and JACK BASEHART. "Theoretical Considerations of Officer Profanity and Obscenity in Formal Contacts with Citizens." In Thomas Barker and David L. Carter, eds., *Police Deviance* (3rd ed.). Cincinnati: Anderson, 1994, pp. 223–246.

WILSON, JAMES Q. *Varieties of Police Behavior.* Cambridge, Mass.: Harvard University Press, 1968.

WILT, G. MARIE, and JAMES D. BANNON. "Cynicism or Realism: A Critique of Niederhoffer's Research into Police Attitudes." *Journal of Police Science and Administration,* 4, no. 1 (March 1976), pp. 38–45.

3

PURPOSES AND PRINCIPLES OF POLICE ORGANIZATIONS

Traditionally, most police agencies tend to be highly reactive **line organizations**; that is, the police wait for citizens to call them and then they react to that phone call for service. Reiss found a solid empirical base for this interpretation in his study of the Boston, Washington, D.C., and Chicago police departments (1971: xii): "Most of the mobilizations, [that is,] 81 percent originated with citizens telephoning the police for service and the department dispatching a one- or two-man beat car to handle the incident." In most departments, officers on patrol generally spend their time in a parked vehicle reading the paper, having coffee, or doing personal errands while waiting for that radio dispatch that sends them roaring to the scene of an incident or crime requiring police intervention. Interspersed are attempts to garner sufficient traffic and parking violations to keep the supervisors off the line officer's back. Very little, if any, time is spent on police patrol.

O.W. Wilson, former superintendent of the Chicago Police Department and author of *Police Administration* (1950), used the term "the **omnipresent** police officer" to characterize the police officer who was everywhere in his random patrol duties, deterring crime by his mere presence. However, a study of the effect of **random patrol** in Kansas City seems to indicate that the mere presence of uniformed police and marked vehicles may not be the deterrent that we once thought (Kelling et al., 1978).

The **Kansas City Experiment** divided that area's 15 precincts into three groups to study three approaches to patrol: (1) respond to calls only, (2) provide normal random patrol, and (3) provide two to three times the normal level of random patrol. This was the conclusion: "The experiment found that the three experimental patrol conditions appeared not to affect crime, service delivery and citizen feelings of security." (Kelling et al., 1978: 164) If this is true, a major activity of line officers has been a waste of time. This kind of research also shows the need for the administrators of an agency to play a more active part in the managing of patrol officers. The nation needs to develop realistic police managers who are able to evaluate critically and implement selected innovations in the area of law enforcement. Proper applications of those appropriate programs should lead to a more proactive police agency.

LAW ENFORCEMENT AS BIG BUSINESS

According to the Federal Bureau of Investigation's *Uniform Crime Reports,* law enforcement agencies across the nation employed an average of 2.5 full-time officers for every 1,000 inhabitants in 2000. When full-time civilian employees were included, the rate was 3.5 per 1,000 inhabitants. The 13,535 city, county, and state police agencies reporting in 2000 collectively employed 654,601 officers and 271,982 civilian employees and provided law enforcement service to approximately 265 million people in the United States (U.S. Department of Justice, 2001: 291). A survey by the Bureau of Justice Statistics (BJS), reported in February 2001, found that federal, state, and local governments across the country spent $147 billion in fiscal year 1999 for criminal and civil justice. Local governments contributed the most (51 percent) to the criminal and civil justice system—almost $75 billion. In 1997, local police departments cost about $67,000 per sworn officer and $150 per resident per year. Sheriffs' offices cost about $73,000 per officer and $49 per resident annually (Bureau of Justice Statistics and Local Law Enforcement Statistics, 2001: 2).

These figures include not only federal, municipal, state, and county departments, but also specialized departments like campus, transit authority, railroad, housing, and environmental conservation units. Exclusive of school boards, the public agencies that make the greatest demands on the tax dollars of most communities are the big three: police, fire, and public works. The police department often leads the field in using up available tax dollars.

The rational citizen, looking at a $40 million business would expect the most administratively competent personnel to be selected to lead this major corporation, the local police agency. Not so. Most police organizations are headed by former line officers who have worked their way up through the hierarchical, civil service organizational structure. While these individuals were generally excellent operating personnel, many lack the skills and knowledge necessary to manage a police organization. Moreover, few have had the opportunity to expand their knowledge of modern management techniques, which is necessary to perform their new responsibilities satisfactorily. Unfortunately, too, some communities even mandate in their municipal charters that the new police chief has to be chosen from existing members of the police force.

If these agencies are to be effective, the traditional concept of police management needs to be changed. However, a number of obstacles must be overcome before a reality-based management approach, using modern business methods, can be incorporated into police agencies.

CIVIL SERVICE AND PROMOTIONS

In many states, the system of civil service, based on examinations, does much to inhibit management success. Consider taking the civil service examination for captain and having to answer the following vehicle and traffic law questions: "How far must a vehicle be parked from the curb?" "How far from a stop sign?" "What is the stopping distance on wet pavement?" This is important information for operating personnel. Any officer taking a captain's examination should know this information. However, wouldn't it be more useful to test the candidate's ability and judgments concerning the administration and management of human and physical resources? Continuing to espouse a line-officer management philosophy in a test for upper-level management positions gives official sanction to a continuation of bad management practices.

In addition, administrators' choices must come from among the top three candidates completing these examinations. In business or industry, on the other hand, we would seek out the best candidate possessing the qualification from within or without the corporation. The lack of lateral entry, the parochialism, and the influence of police associations and unions support the concept that the *best* must come through the ranks.

We are not suggesting that civil service exams be abolished; rather, we would like to see them upgraded and made more relevant to the positions. They should not be used as the sole criterion for promotion. There should be some evaluation of the candidates' past performances—an oral interview and perhaps even a battery of psychological and management tests.

It seems that many agencies, especially in western and southern states, have developed alternative methods of promotion with a more progressive approach to the selection of candidates for the respective positions. Namely, the promotion to sergeant, while being based somewhat on a written examination, is strongly influenced by assessment with established criteria. A promotion from sergeant to lieutenant, while being the prerogative of the chief of police, is often based on an assessment evaluation that includes oral interviews, with the final decision being the chief's. In many instances, promotion to captain or a higher rank rests in the hands of the chief and whatever additional criteria he uses to help in his judgment.

While there is no ideal or foolproof way of getting the best candidates, the above suggests that the progressive administrator has the greatest opportunity of getting the people he feels are the most qualified and/or compatible with his goals and the goals of the community. There is always the problem of favoritism or "political" interference in the system of promotion. However, the professionalism of modern police agencies and the expectations of its leaders make this interference more difficult.

The Use of Civilian Employees

According to the *Uniform Crime Reports*, civilians constituted 29.4 percent of the total law enforcement employee force in the United States in 2000 and represented 22.7 percent of the police employees in cities. Civilian employees comprised 39.4 percent in suburban counties and 38.5 percent in rural counties. Women accounted for 62.7 percent of all civilian employees (U.S. Department of Justice, 2002: 291).

Heininger and Urbanek (1983) surveyed a proportionate stratified random sample of 100 medium-sized and large American cities to determine what effect the use of civilian personnel had on police agencies. Many police managers have been concerned about the replacement of the uniformed police officer by civilians and the hoped-for budget savings. Because of the increasing use of civilians in specialist positions with fairly high salaries, there were few savings in the budget. Here are their conclusions (Heininger and Urbanek, 1983: 205):

> Specifically, the findings suggest that using civilians may not lead to cheaper police protection, that using civilians probably does not "displace" sworn officers, and that there is no apparent relationship between civilians and either the quality of police protection or the risk of danger which must be assumed by sworn officers. These conclusions are more interesting in the light of secondary findings which show that (1) "real" police salaries are down; (2) police departments are commanding a diminishing portion of the municipal budget "pie" while at the same time, (3) both municipal expenditures and personnel levels rose sharply.

Important considerations for the hiring of civilian police personnel are a thorough background check and a psychological assessment. Civilian personnel are now being used in sensitive positions in records, dispatching, computers, and increasingly in making judgment calls that will affect the department and sworn personnel. This should emphasize the need for more attention by management to the proper training necessary to equip these civilians to perform efficiently and effectively.

TRADITIONAL PURPOSES OF POLICE ORGANIZATIONS

The purposes that we have traditionally accepted to be the main thrust of managing a police agency are

1. Protecting life and property
2. Preserving the peace
3. Preventing criminality
4. Apprehending criminals

Although these are still legitimate purposes for policing, they have a major defect: They have become reactive. The activities used to carry out these purposes include routine patrol to discourage wrongdoers, arrest of criminals, recovery of stolen property, monitoring of sporting events, and such additional items as controlling traffic and pedestrian movements. Little encouragement is given to line officers to act proactively.

It has become increasingly apparent today that the concept of policing has embraced a new dimension that encourages us to add a fifth purpose: enhanced community involvement. While police work begins with law enforcement, it does not necessarily end there. Police have always provided services above and beyond what was often described as "police work," and more and more, these services have been refined and identified as "community relations." An excellent article by Solar (2001) discusses the promise of a higher level of effectiveness by giving officers greater autonomy and by encouraging them to become problem solvers and partnership builders under the rubric of community-oriented policing.

TRADITIONAL MEASURES OF POLICE EFFECTIVENESS

Look at the annual report of almost any police department in the country. First, you will see a cover letter from the administrator to his sponsoring institution. This is followed by a brief description of the department, usually accompanied by a standard organization chart. Then comes the bulk of the report, page after page of tabulated statistics—for example, on crimes in the community, cases cleared by arrest, traffic and parking tickets issued, percentage of stolen property recovered, accident rates, and so on.

These tabulations are supposed to show the efficiency of the agency. However, these are indexes of efficiency *after the fact*. At the time of reading, some citizens may have just been killed, injured, robbed, or arrested. The increase or decrease in crime as released to the media through the *Uniform Crime Reports* are taken as an indication of the effectiveness of the police agency. Unfortunately, such reactive measures tend to promote poor management, leading to the issuance of more traffic tickets, the growth of an unofficial quota system, and the "fudging" of crime statistics. For example, it may be that the officer who stops citizens in traffic and advises them concerning their poor driving habits may be more effective than the officer who simply issues tickets. It takes a realistic, superior manager to recognize the difference.

As noted in Chapter 1, the Metropolitan Police Act of 1829 created the first modern police force in London, England. In the force's first duty manual, Sir Charles Rowan stated the primary purpose for having a law enforcement agency (Reith, 1956: 135–36): "It should be understood at the outset, that the principal object to be obtained is the Prevention of Crime." Officers were specifically evaluated and rewarded for the attainment of this goal. This proactive, preventive approach led to better police-community relations.

Citizens are never happy about being the victim of a crime, even if the crime is solved and the goods are returned. From 1829 to the present, this citizen attitude has not changed. In a study of victims of crimes in inner cities outside the South, Block (1970) confirmed this point of view. He found that follow-up and even arrest of criminals who attacked victims had only a slight effect on the victims in terms of their support for police. Victimization itself brought about a significant decrease in support for police. His conclusion backs up the basic insight of the 1829 manual that "the best way for the police to gain support is to strengthen their efforts in crime prevention" (Block, 1970: 12). O.W. Wilson, in *Police Administration* (1950), agreed with this statement on how the police carry out their primary purpose in serving the citizens: "The police do this by preserving the peace and protecting life and property against attacks by criminals and from injury by the careless and inadvertent offender." A proactive department is more concerned with protecting the citizens from harm than with tallying up some kind of score of arrests after the citizen has been victimized.

Another principle, one presented in the nineteenth century by Robert Peel, concerned the efficiency of police. Peel felt that the best test of this efficiency was the absence of crime in society. Citizens should feel that they and their property are safe. This is a positive standard. The traditional standards all take a negative attitude. We should adopt Peel's progressive approach in evaluating officers and promoting good management.

POLICE RESULTS AND PERFORMANCE MEASURES

Police department–funding bodies, such as legislatures, are concerned with what works in policing. They want specific data and performance measures to justify the funding of specific police services. Police researchers and managers have had to develop models that speak to these issues.

One of these performance models has been called a "change agent" model. This model measures inputs and outputs created by police departments for the community. It recommends that police results and performance measures be based on the following four points:

Quantitative Measures

Input:	1. How many services were delivered?
Output:	2. How much did we produce?

Qualitative Measures

Input:	1. How well did we deliver the services?
Output:	2. How good were our products?

The inputs are police services. The outputs are positive changes in the quality of life in the community. For example, a police service input might be burglary investigations. The output might be a drop in the number of burglaries as a quantitative measure. A qualitative measure might be a follow-up questionnaire asking burglary victims for their evaluation of police services, including police officer courtesy and how the victim values the results of the investigation.

This is a proactive budgeting model because when the department needs more resources for a specialized burglary investigation unit, it can use these results as the basis for budgeting the burglary unit. The legislature could take a look at the police department's performance on burglary investigations and see whether the results warrant funding the chief's budget request.

These result measures give citizens specific data so they can see how well their police department is doing. They also provide a clear rationale for the local legislative funding of specific services. In the past, a data-driven department used mostly quantitative measures, such as the rate of homicides or burglaries occurring in a community. The qualitative measure of how well police services were delivered and how good the police services were gives an additional, human dimension to evaluating police performance. Qualitative measures can be done through community leadership meetings and discussions with a questionnaire, focus groups from the community where the services were delivered, and community attitude surveys. Questions about the courtesy of officers, police brutality, how fearful citizens feel, and general questions on how well the police are doing in their community would be effective.

REALITY–BASED, PROACTIVE PURPOSES OF POLICE ORGANIZATIONS

Modern society calls on all police managers to provide satisfaction for the citizens of the community in fulfilling the traditional purposes of policing. However, police managers also need to go beyond the traditional purposes of policing to the following areas of responsibility: (1) performance, (2) preparedness, and (3) progressiveness.

Performance

Specific role definitions of police **performance** and productivity measures need to be created in terms of the daily activity of both the line officer and the police manager. Criteria need to be developed to evaluate effectively and to reward positive, proactive police activity. For example, how do you measure performance in terms of patrol activity? How do you evaluate the effectiveness of response to human service calls and calls that entail referrals to other government and community agencies? Feedback mechanisms must be developed to monitor the performance of line officers and police managers and to evaluate their activities so as to reward appropriate delivery of police services to the community. The focus is on measures of individuals in official positions and measures of organizational effectiveness.

Preparedness

Preparedness speaks to the needs of short-range as well as long-range planning and entails the relation of the police agency to other community and government organizations, such as social welfare and health agencies. Police organizations have normally planned only in terms of police rather than the whole human service group of agencies. Today, all personnel should be trained to handle future problems. Preparedness entails the need for better communication among all agencies. Time and resources need to be developed so that this type of thinking permeates the entire police organization.

Progressiveness

Progressiveness is a basic management-for-change concept in which leaders are flexible and tolerant of ambiguity and are willing to institute new ideas because they may work. Such leaders do not feel threatened by such changes. The opposite of this type is the hierarchically oriented administrator who seeks closure and places limitations on his staff's ideas.

MANAGEMENT PRINCIPLES

To accomplish these purposes, management guidelines are needed. The following six principles allow for both the traditional reactive approach and the aggressive proactive approach: (1) **respond,** (2) **regulate,** (3) **restrain,** (4) **recover,** (5) **repress,** and (6) **reinforce.**

Respond

Most police activities are reactions to calls for service (Cumming, Cumming, and Edell, 1965; Bayley and Mendelsohn, 1969; Webster, 1970; Reiss, 1971). Even in large cities, the calls are largely service oriented. For example, of the

1,027,000 calls received by the Detroit police in 1968, only 16 percent were related to crime (Bercal, 1970: 683). Contrary to the television dramas, calls for crimes in progress are few. Police must also deal with on-scene confrontations, hostage situations, battered children, family crises, and the mentally ill, all of which call for a reaction response by the officers. Many of these situations are highly dangerous and call for split-second response by a highly trained professional police officer.

Traditionally, police respond after a crime has occurred, and there is a victim. As has been noted, victims are more hostile to the police after having been the target of a crime, even if the criminal is apprehended.

There is also a strong controversy in the field over response time. Most departments are told to aim at two minutes or less when responding to a call. This early response time is significant only in cases of crimes in progress or calls of an emergency nature. Response time becomes important in the securing of crime scenes and the immediate apprehension of criminals. It is irrelevant to the majority of service calls. Too much management and training time is spent on this issue of response time.

Regulate

Consider a long line of cars wending its way through the city streets with a funeral hearse in the front and a police vehicle escort. Consider, too, events such as field days, ice cream socials, and ball games that require the police for traffic and crowd control. Police are also used as bodyguards and chauffeurs for visiting dignitaries and even some mayors. These are traditionally noncriminal police activities, and regulations are necessary to prevent crises in our communities. This area of policing provides an excellent opportunity to improve relations with community members, countering the police image as a repressive, restrictive force demanding compliance with rules, ordinances, and so on.

Restrain

This represents one of the traditional purposes for police: the apprehension of criminals. It should also include restraint of mentally ill people and the prevention of one citizen from annoying or doing damage to another. For example, a woman who mows her lawn at midnight just to annoy a neighbor with whom she is feuding might have to be restrained by police.

On a more serious level, we find that many police departments today are beginning to use less-than-lethal techniques to apprehend individuals threatening the safety of citizens or arresting officers. New pepper-ball launchers, beanbag shotguns (Moreland, 2000a, b), foam, and M-26 **Tasers** are among the many devices being used to temporarily immobilize combative or violent subjects. ("Use of M-26 Advanced Taser," 2001: 1–5)

With the increased demand on calls for police services today, we find that many agencies prioritize their calls. The San Diego County Sheriff's Department, for example, prioritizes its calls into four categories. Priority 1 and 2 calls get immediate attention as emergency calls. A priority 1 call might be a serious accident, an officer needing help, an airplane crash, a SWAT alert, a fire, or a natural disaster. Priority 2 calls are mainly crimes against people, arson, weapons, explosions, pursuits, and so on. Priority 3 and 4 calls, such as a burglary not in progress, a damaged mailbox, a minor property damage auto accident, do not demand an immediate response. However, the department takes great pride in responding to every complaint and request for service—something not all law enforcement agencies still do (Moreland, 2000a, b).

Recover

A major effort by police is the recovery of stolen property and its return to the citizens. **Sting operations,** in which a police agency sets up a phony fencing business to entice criminals to sell them stolen goods, result in the arrest of the criminals and some of their fences (those who deal in stolen goods). Millions of dollars in stolen goods are given back to the citizens in the course of such operations. This is one area in which the police provide a very useful service to the community and do recover considerable property of value, reducing insurance and personal losses.

Repress

There are two important elements necessary for a crime to take place. First, the individual must have the desire to commit the crime; second, the opportunity must present itself for the satisfaction of this desire. Police have traditionally attempted to prevent crime by reducing the opportunity of the individual to commit the crime. The random patrol concept is justified by many police managers as a means of reaching this end.

In recent years, drug-control strategies have included targeting "hot spots," such as street areas and crack houses. Green (1995), for example, reviewed a drug-control program in Oakland, California, that relied on police coordination against certain areas to decrease the number of drug sales. This could be termed a repressive technique, in that city resources were targeted against a crime problem. The basic philosophy here is that it is very hard to buy and sell with increased police presence, which included raids, checks for violations of city housing codes, and legal actions against slum landlords.

Although actions such as these result in crime displacement, the study found that drug problems were decreased at target sites and that there was less displacement of narcotics activity in other neighborhood areas.

Reinforce

This activity is designed to reinforce good citizenship and respect for the law and to encourage citizens to aid and assist officers and the agency. Examples of this type of activity are talking to citizen's groups and instituting traffic and bicycle safety programs. Operation **Neighborhood Watch** of the National Sheriff's Association teaches business owners and citizens to burglarproof their premises and to watch their neighbor's property when the neighbor is on vacation. School programs are also used, such as the School Liaison program in elementary schools and the teaching of criminal justice topics by community relations officers in high schools.

In responding to this traditional purpose, police agencies have tended to create special units and to focus on response activities to the detriment of effective service to the public. Although these are legitimate purposes, these purposes are not broad enough to contain the range of legitimate police activity. Each officer should consider himself or herself a community relations specialist.

Defining the Organization

To carry out these six principles, it is necessary to come to an understanding of what the organization itself is all about. Here, we are looking for a definition of *organization* that will fit the requirements of both management and operations. This definition has to be broad enough to encompass the many tasks concerned with the creation of operational policy as well as the duties of administration.

Although a clear understanding of basic relationships specified by modern organizational structures is necessary, we must never forget that the tasks are carried out by real people with human concerns, needs, and emotions. Thus, any concept of organization from the perspective of current practices and theory is basically people oriented. The reason is that if any police organization is to operate efficiently, people have to be motivated to carry out tasks on the job and to put out that little extra effort that makes organizations work. A good argument has been made (Solar, 2001) that the most desirable learning organization is one that includes rules and procedures, covering a variety of low- and high-level tasks, that are continually reviewed for content and practicality. Such an organization is efficient and effective in both routine and non-routine tasks, with an emphasis on cooperation and innovation guided by broad policies and reinforced through training.

THE CONCEPT OF ORGANIZATION

In a staff paper that has been widely used at both the college level and for police executive training sessions, the Northwestern University Traffic Institute (1964: 6) has stressed two aspects of organization as part of the basic definition: the mechanical/structural approach and the humanist approach.

Mechanical

One group says, in effect, "Organization is the thorough arrangement and subdivision of activities to secure economy of effort through specialization and coordination of work, thereby leading to unity of 'action.' " The key parts of this definition are "subdivision to *secure economy of effort*" and "specialization and *coordination leading to unity*." This definition emphasizes the mechanics, or the physical aspects, of organization.

The **mechanical approach** uses bodies to fill boxes in an organization chart. Examples are assembly-line tasks and many military jobs. Police managers have been hiring and promoting to fill slots, without concern for the personal qualifications of the individual.

Humanist

The other group of definitions can be summarized as "dividing and grouping the work that should be done into individual jobs, and defining the established relationships between individuals filling these jobs." This definition emphasizes the people who make up an organization and through whom all work is done.

The **humanist approach** is used in most professional organizations, where a particular skill must be developed at a particular level with the exact knowledge needed to fill a position. Imagine a law firm, for example, that needs a new associate partner in corporate law. The firm's management interviews individuals, looking for specific knowledge, skills, and professional relationships that have developed over the candidate's career. In the same way, modern police organizations should not be limited by a mechanical promotion exam. They should look for talent and professional skills. Just because an officer has been promoted to lieutenant does not make her an expert in personnel, even though the personnel department needs a lieutenant to manage the department.

THE TRADITIONAL CONCEPT OF BUREAUCRACY FROM MAX WEBER

Basic to any modern organization is the concept of bureaucracy. Police organizations, for example, are bureaucracies. Although the term *bureaucracy* has acquired negative overtones, it is the basis for modern civil service and a rational approach to administration and organization. The German sociologist Max Weber (1889–1920) provided the formulation that has become the basis for all modern bureaucracies, including police organization (Gerth and Mills, 1946: 196–244).

A modern bureaucracy depends on having a money economy to pay salaries. The society also must subscribe to the view that success and rewards should be based on merit and hard work rather than on the condition of birth. Moreover, there should be a belief in treating each person equally and providing true equality of opportunity.

The following are, in shortened form, the general rules that Weber felt should govern and define a modern bureaucracy (Gerth and Mills, 1946: 196–204):

1. Regular activities are distributed in a fixed way as official duties.
2. Authority to give commands is distributed in a stable way, and coercive means of sanction are defined by rules in a consistent manner.
3. Only those who have generally regulated qualifications to serve are employed.
4. Fixed jurisdictions are ordered by administrative regulations.
5. An official hierarchical system of superiors and subordinates, monocratically organized, exists.
6. Management is based on written documents, normally called "the files."
7. Specialized officer of management requires thorough, technical, and expert training and knowledge.
8. Generalized rules are
   a. Stable
   b. Exhaustive
   c. Learnable
9. Knowledge of the rules represents special technical knowledge that officials possess (in modern society, accountants and lawyers are special officials who are rule experts).
10. Office holding is a vocation and a career.
11. Officials have more status than the governed: Insulting officials is proscribed by law with appropriate sanctions.
12. Bureaucratic officials are appointed by a superior authority (civil examination), not elected.
13. Tenure in the job is for life.
14. Employees receive regular pecuniary compensation (a regular and fixed salary).
15. Officials have a career in the hierarchy.

This is the ideal by which many modern public organizations are measured. When first developed and applied, it made capitalism work by providing a structural context for capitalists. Bureaucracy provides stability in the delivery of governmental services, even though the political machinery may be in turmoil. Politicians can fight all they wish, but while a modern bureaucracy exists in public service, citizens will receive their police and fire protection, have their mail delivered, and have their sewers fixed. This organizational concept will become more important as we examine how to carry out specific police management tasks in the modern police organization.

CONCLUSION

Managing a police department effectively requires considerable organization. Although humanist concepts and democratic principles are useful in enhancing morale and producing evenhanded personnel policies, they have to be dealt with in the context of a traditional bureaucratic structure.

A police department is a big business with a budget of hundreds of thousands or, in some cases, millions of dollars. The traditions of a nineteenth-century civil service are part and parcel of the organizational style of most police agencies. Part of the reality of modern police administration is the traditional civil service/Weberian bureaucratic structure. To perform the police function, orders have to be written and carried out. Over the years, it has been shown that a traditional hierarchical organization can be an effective medium for fulfilling the major purposes of the police function.

The reality-based, proactive approach adds another dimension to the traditional bureaucratic structure: forward planning. The central core of the proactive approach is the need for police management to have the necessary planning skills to anticipate events. This is in good part what is meant by the three P's:

1. Performance
2. Preparedness
3. Progressiveness

A reality-based, progressive department is flexible enough to adapt to changing events and a changing society. It is prepared with adequate resources to deal effectively with future events and crises. The performance of this department speaks for itself by any reasonable measure of police effectiveness.

Although it is necessary to use the principles of the traditional bureaucratic structure to administer the modern, proactive police department, these principles are applied in a flexible manner. One of the problems with reactive police departments is that they become so bound by rigid, bureaucratic procedures that they lose sight of the real purpose of policing: providing a service to the community. The flexibility instilled in the traditional police structure allows for the anticipation of events and the ability to deal with an ever-changing society. The ideal police structure is the synthesis of proactive, traditional, democratic, and authoritarian styles. This department may be viewed by the citizens as an effective force in achieving a stable community—a good place in which to live and raise children.

QUESTIONS FOR REVIEW

1. Do you agree with the traditional purposes of the police organization? Has the modern police organization fulfilled these purposes? Should it?

2. Distinguish between a proactive and reactive police agency. What major characteristics identify the proactive police agency?

3. Describe the role of planning in terms of (1) performance, (2) preparedness, and (3) progressiveness.

4. Place the following six management principles in order of priority: (a) respond, (b) regulate, (c) restrain, (d) recover, (e) repress, and (f) reinforce. Justify your order.

5. If you were going to create your own police organization, what type of management would you prefer: mechanical or humanist? Explain why. If you have trouble subscribing completely to either view, specify what mix of mechanical and humanist concepts of police organization would perhaps work best.

6. Apply Max Weber's concept of bureaucracy to a local police agency, and contrast Weber's model to what is actually going on in the local bureaucracy.

CLASS PROJECT

Select a local law enforcement agency and observe or review its manner of operations in an attempt to determine whether or not it is a proactive or reactive type of agency. Give your reasons for your determination and your suggestions as to how you might change or improve its mode of providing service to the community.

BIBLIOGRAPHY

ALPERT, GEOFFREY. "Measuring Police Performance in the New Paradigm of Policing." In Roger G. Dunham and Geoffrey P. Alpert, eds., *Critical Issues in Policing* (3rd ed.). Prospect Heights, Ill.: Waveland Press, 1997.

BAYLEY, DAVID H., and HAROLD MENDELSOHN. *Minorities and the Police.* New York: Free Press, 1969.

BERCAL, THOMAS E. "Calls for Police Assistance: Consumer Demands for Public Service." *American Behavioral Scientist*, 13, no. 5/6 (May/August 1970), pp. 681–691.

BLOCK, RICHARD L. "Support for Civil Liberties and Support for the Police." *American Behavioral Scientist*, 13, no. 5/6 (May/June 1970), pp. 10–16.

BRODEUR, JEAN-PAUL, ed. *How to Recognize Good Policing.* Thousand Oaks, Calif.: Sage Publications and Police Executive Research Forum, 1998.

BUREAU OF JUSTICE STATISTICS. *Local Police Departments, 1993.* Washington, D.C.: U.S. Department of Justice, 1996.

BUREAU OF JUSTICE STATISTICS AND LOCAL LAW ENFORCEMENT STATISTICS. *Local Police Departments, 1999.* Washington, D.C.: U.S. Government Printing Office, 2001.

BUTTERFIELD, RONALD W. "Deming's 14 Points Applied to Service." *Training*, 28, no. 3 (March 1991), pp. 50–59.

CLAUSER, FREDERICK J., and GEORGE E. CARPENTER. "Law Enforcement Accreditation: Getting It Done." *Police Chief*, 55, no. 1 (January 1988), pp. 60–63.

COMMISSION ON ACCREDITATION FOR LAW ENFORCEMENT AGENCIES. *Standards for Law Enforcement Agencies.* Fairfax, Va.: Commission on Accreditation for Law Enforcement Agencies, 1984.

CUMMING, ELAINE, IAN CUMMING, and LAURA EDELL. "Policeman as Philosopher, Guide and Friend." *Social Problems*, 12 (winter 1965), pp. 276–286.

GARY, EILEEN M. *Performance Measures: What Works.* Washington, D.C.: National Institute of Justice, 1997.

GERTH, H.H., and C. WRIGHT MILLS. *From Max Weber: Essays in Sociology.* New York: Oxford University Press, 1946.

GREEN, LORRAINE. "Cleaning Up Drug Hot Spots in Oakland, California: The Displacement and Diffusion Effects." *Justice Quarterly*, 12, no. 4 (December 1995), pp. 737–754.

A Guide to Developing Performance Measures in Result-Based Budgeting. Washington, D.C.: Finance Project, 1997.

HALBERSTAM, DAVID. *The Reckoning.* New York: William Morrow, 1986.

HEININGER, BRUCE L., and JANINE URBANEK. "Civilianization of the American Police: 1970–1980." *Journal of Police Science and Administration*, 11, no. 2 (1983), pp. 200–205.

HOLPP, LAWRENCE. "Making Choices: Self-Directed Teams or Total Quality Management?" *Training*, 29, no. 5 (May 1992), pp. 69–76.

HOOVER, LARRY T. *Police Program Evaluation.* Washington, D.C.: Police Executive Research Forum, 1998.

KELLING, GEORGE L., ET AL. *Patrol Experiment: A Summary Report and a Technical Report.* Washington, D.C.: Police Foundation, 1978.

MORELAND, JO. "Changes Might Affect Deputy Response Time." *North County Times*, July 22, 2000a, p. B-2.

———. "Sheriff's Department Shifts Its Crime-Fighting Focus as It Updates." *North County Times*, July 22, 2000b, p. B-2.

NATIONAL ADVISORY COMMISSION ON CRIMINAL JUSTICE STANDARDS AND GOALS. *Police.* Washington, D.C.: U.S. Government Printing Office, 1973.

NEW YORK CITY POLICE DEPARTMENT. *Operation 25.* New York: New York City Police Department, 1955.

NORTHWESTERN UNIVERSITY TRAFFIC INSTITUTE. *Improving Police Effectiveness through Organization.* Evanston, Ill.: Northwestern University Press, 1964.

REISS, ALBERT J. JR. *The Police and the Public.* New Haven, Conn.: Yale University Press, 1971.

REITH, CHARLES. *A New Study of Police History.* Edinburgh: Oliver and Boyd, 1956.

SOLAR, PATRICK J. "The Organizational Context of Effective Policing." *Police Chief* (February 2001), pp. 39–47.

U.S. DEPARTMENT OF JUSTICE. *Crime in the United States: Uniform Crime Reports, 1986.* Washington, D.C.: U.S. Government Printing Office, 1986.

———. *Crime in the United States: Uniform Crime Reports, 2000.* Washington, D.C.: U.S. Government Printing Office, 2002.

Use of M-26 Advanced Taser. Escondido, Calif.: Escondido Police Department, August 2, 2001, pp. 1–5.

WEBSTER, JOHN A. "Police Task and Time Study." *Journal of Criminal Law, Criminology and Police Service*, 61 (1970), pp. 94–100.

WHITAKER, GORDON, ET AL. *Basic Issues in Police Performance*. Washington, D.C.: U.S. Department of Justice, 1980.

WILSON, JAMES Q. *Explaining Crime*. New York: McGraw-Hill, 1975.

———. *Thinking about Crime*. New York: Basic Books, 1975.

WILSON, O.W. *Police Administration*. New York: McGraw-Hill, 1950.

4

OPERATING PRINCIPLES

KEY TERMS

auxiliary/service function	organizing
budgeting	planning
control	policy
coordinating	reporting
directing	staff/administrative function
ethics	staffing
line function	victimless crime
operations	

In every organization, there are three major areas of work:

1. Administration
2. Supervision
3. Operations

Administrative functions are performed by top management and the immediate subordinates of the top-management team. They create and set **policy** (a course of action), providing guidance for the organization. *Supervision* is normally performed by the immediate supervisors of line personnel. They help set the tone of the organization and ensure that the policies created by top management are actually carried out by the line personnel. *Operations* are performed by line personnel who normally have direct contact with the public and who carry out the daily police activities.

ADMINISTRATION

POSDCORB is a classic theoretical model that describes the major functions of an organization and how these functions are carried out. The acronym *POSDCORB* stands for planning, organizing, staffing, directing, coordinating, reporting, and budgeting (Gulick and Urwick, 1937: 1–45).

Planning

This activity includes short-range and long-range **planning** that specifies goals and objectives in cooperation with other public agencies. Cooperating with other public agencies is a requisite. More and more, urban police departments are seeing that they have to involve themselves with the long-range planning of urban renewal, social service, health, and other agencies. Even smaller departments and those in rural areas are beginning to see how long-range planning can help them deal with the increasing complexity of the police role and rural crime on the urban fringe.

Organizing

Organizing deals with the creation of the formal structure of the police organization, the work of the enterprise. The goal is to coordinate all the organizational units to perform most efficiently to meet the purposes of the organization.

The organization itself becomes the total responsibility of the manager and reflects the organizational ability of the top-management team. Modern business principles are combined with a knowledge of public administration and modern police activities. The key to success is to create an organizational structure in which the right person is doing the right job at the highest efficiency with the correct level of personal and organizational morale.

Staffing

This function of management covers such aspects of the organization as hiring, firing, and training, as well as assigning personnel to specific tasks and roles. There is also a concern with establishing satisfactory working conditions, including safe and appropriate physical facilities. For example, patrol cars should operate so as not to endanger the life of an officer. Included also is the need to provide the tools officers need to carry out the job and to keep those tools in functioning order.

In theory, **staffing** includes developing job descriptions. Each job should be clearly defined and filled by a qualified employee. *Qualified* means that the employee has the necessary skills, background, and training to accomplish the tasks that the job description calls for.

Job satisfaction should also be considered. Every attempt should be made to match each employee to a job where he or she is

Satisfied
Qualified
Gratified

Directing

In **directing,** the manager needs to (1) act as the overall leader of the organization and (2) direct the day-to-day activities of the enterprise. As leader of the police organization, the manager has to make decisions and issue orders. Using modern management principles, this is normally a team process in which the leader receives information and advice from the top-management team. The information that is obtained through this consultative process should lead to a firm decision.

A police manager using this approach should seek advice from local community leaders as well as from top-management staff and experts in law enforcement. Then, once a decision has been made, the team is expected to carry out daily the specified directions and procedures.

Coordinating

The two major activities in this category are (1) **coordinating** police agencies with other private and public agencies in the community and (2) coordinating activities within the police department itself. Coordination is designed to bring about agreement on specific courses of action to solve specific problems.

Typical problems that involve the coordination functions include legal ramifications of policy decisions and deciding who is going to be in charge in cases involving overlapping jurisdictions. For example, a visit from a foreign dignitary might entail coordination among civic organizations and local, state, or federal authorities; it could require long-range planning to prepare for problems or situations that might occur. Coordination is an often-overlooked but essential part of police management.

Reporting

Reporting entails keeping the flow of information going up, down, and across the organization. It also includes reporting to the police organization's political superiors: mayors, county executives, and the like. The annual report to the public and legislature has become a major means of communicating organizational goals and accomplishments.

Communication cannot be just one-way if it is to be effective. Communication flows in an organized manner through a three-dimensional matrix to all superiors and subordinates. Increasingly important for modern management is lateral flow to specialists and staff.

Budgeting

Budgeting includes preparing an annual financial plan and operating within the confines of the plan. Budgeting is a form of fiscal planning and requires knowledge of the kinds of budget models available. Typical examples are (1) planned program budgeting system (PPBS), (2) line-item budgeting, and (3) zero-based budgeting. There is increasing pressure on police departments for fiscal accountability and expertise in the realm of financial stability, analysis, and reporting.

Running any law enforcement agency is like running a corporation but expending many public, not private, dollars. Most private corporations have appropriate numbers of experienced executive managers, financial experts, and qualified staff. But there is little of this expertise for such positions in the public corporation we call a *police agency*. There is little doubt that police administrators need more training in financial matters.

SUPERVISION

The supervisor's position in the organization is a vital link between line employees and management. A major problem is that line officers promoted to supervisory positions often do not make the transition to thinking as supervisors. The primary reasons for this are (1) promotion by civil service examinations that often do not test for police management skills and (2) lack of timely in-service training and resocialization into the supervisory role. Officers are often appointed to open supervisory positions without any consideration of their past training, needed training, or knowledge. With these handicaps, it is hard for that newly appointed supervisor to perform well in charge of other officers.

As a supervisor, the newly promoted sergeant will have to modify actions that he or she may have condoned as a line officer. As a newly promoted officer told one of the authors, "The hardest thing about this job is disciplining personal friends, fellow officers with whom I went to the academy." With the correct resocialization into the management role, that line officer will make an excellent supervisor. This takes planning, time, and money. Because the supervisor is a key member of the total management team, the effort is well worth it.

In a small police department of less than 10 officers, the supervisor's role is closer to that of the line officer, with the supervisor often sharing many of the duties of the line officer. Because the role is less narrowly focused than in a large department, the role of the supervisor of the small department deserves special consideration.

Current research in policing focuses mainly on big-city police departments. But training and education have to be concerned with the broad-based, generalist, smaller law enforcement agency supervisors as well. The most common problem for supervisors and chiefs in small agencies is that they may have established personal relationships that make it difficult to delegate or assign tasks in a fair and impartial manner. Invariably, any promotion from within causes hard feelings because someone is always mad at being passed over.

Police administrators and supervisors in small departments readily admit that they are forced to be generalists simply because they are the only person on duty during certain shifts. Thus the chief may perform the daily routine of the street officer as well as deal with administrative tasks. On the other hand, there are very tangible benefits in the absence of a complex chain of command, especially in the areas of direct supervision and communication.

Regardless of size, the top administrator requires conceptual skills, the ability to develop long-range goals, and the ability to communicate with all segments of the community. If anything, by the very nature of their presence in the community, the members of a small department indeed practice community policing by knowing virtually everyone in the community and by providing a wide range of services.

The RESPECT Approach to Supervision

POSDCORB has been a useful approach to organizing basic management functions. What is proposed here is a similar approach to the functions of a supervisor with the rank of sergeant or lieutenant. The acronym *RESPECT* stands for

Reporting and communicating

Evaluation and inspection

Services and community relations

Planning and implementation

Ethics and morale

Control and resource utilization

Teaching and directing

Because the supervisor is the vital organizational link between the street officer and management, the duties and functions of the supervisor must be systematically analyzed. The following functions can be applied by both the small department and the large urban police department. While the applications will differ, the principles remain the same.

Reporting and Communicating.   A police organization, among other things, is a communication network. The police chief receives reports and reviews them for information, clarity, and accuracy. This is a vital responsibility since future actions involving citizens are based on these reports.

In the important area of internal communications, management needs to know what the officers are thinking and how they are acting. The line supervisor and the internal department supervisor are in a position to perform this vital communication function by reviewing reports and recording observations.

Orders must be communicated to staff, and it is the supervisor who converts orders to operational activities. Communication is a vital two-way flow for every police organization.

Supervisors need a basic knowledge of communication skills and communication links if they are to perform effectively. They must distinguish between statements and feelings. Techniques for achieving effective communication are fully developed in Chapters 10 and 12.

Accurate, brief reports are necessary if a department is to operate effectively. Reports have to convey the maximum amount of information in a minimum of space. Time is valuable, and the reading of reports is an expensive way in which to spend time in any organization.

Evaluation and Inspection.   The supervisor's basic responsibility is to evaluate the officers in terms of their appearance, use of equipment, habits, and performance. *Habits* refers to behavior, mannerisms, use of language, and professional attitude; *performance* refers to the knowledge of the job and the ability to do the job in terms of professional qualifications. Dress and demeanor are also part of this evaluation and inspection process.

Even "unmeasurables," such as empathy and the ability to deal with people, have to be a solid part of the evaluation and inspection process. The supervisor becomes the enforcer of professional standards while helping the officers conform to these standards through a solid management support system.

Services and Community Relations.   Since the police department is a public service organization, one of the supervisor's first responsibilities is to maintain the quality of the delivery of services to the citizens. This is done by making community relations activities part of the evaluation of each officer. The supervisor helps the officer understand that he or she represents law enforcement in the community. With support from supervisors, community policing is not just relegated to a public relations department in the police agency but becomes the responsibility of each officer.

The officer needs training to deal with emergencies and the myriad of other services that constitute police work. Although arrest and apprehension of criminals is the most visible part of the business of law enforcement, the human service function is just as vital. Top management must thus constantly reward its supervisors for the effective delivery of human service. Thus an effective law enforcement support team can create a department that is deeply concerned with helping each citizen of the community.

Planning and Implementation.   This function refers to both long-range and short-range planning and implementation. Supervisors are normally involved with daily planning activities like scheduling the roster and reviewing patrol and detective assignments. Management must involve these supervisors in longer-range planning, specifying the needs of the unit(s) for the next month, year, or even decade.

Supervisors are close to the information needed for planning. They generally know the conditions in the street. A major rule in management communication is that the closer you are to your data, the more accurate your knowledge of the data is. As the first line of management, supervisors are vitally needed if planning is to be implemented.

Much of what top management has intended in terms of long-range planning has failed because the supervisors closest to essential planning data were neglected. It is the supervisory managers who will be in charge of actually carrying out the detailed implementation of long-range planning. Supervision and planning need to come together before implementation can be accomplished.

Supervisors have to understand the plans and intent of management and have some general agreement as to the implementation of policy. If supervisors adopt a hostile attitude, the line officers will not readily implement the policy. There are many obvious and subtle ways of not implementing policy. The line officer in the street has a great deal of discretion and can use this discretion to support or harass management. Policy can be implemented so slowly, for example, that the impact of the policy decision is diffused and wasted, or it can be implemented so rapidly that there is no thought of the side effects of implementation. The voluntary cooperation of supervisory personnel is necessary in any implementation of policy. Policy will work in the field only with the active understanding and cooperation of supervisory personnel.

Ethics and Morale.   Professional organizations, including police organizations, have a code of **ethics** (standards of conduct and moral judgment). Implementation of the profession's code of ethics is dependent on the individual supervisor and is strongly related to the morale of personnel. A management guided by ethical principles with a reputation for integrity is more apt to have an organization with high morale.

Morale is also determined by a management that has sympathetic knowledge of the problems of line personnel. As stated previously, an effective communication system will bring management the necessary knowledge of line operating conditions and problems. Problems arise because of lack of communication and inaction. Finally, management's own code of ethics must be operational since each supervisor becomes an ethical role model for personnel in the organization.

Control and Resource Utilization.   Effective management must **control** both personnel and matériel, providing guidance and instilling a sense of responsibility. With increasingly scarce resources available for public agencies, their efficient use will be a paramount measure of management success in the future.

Knowledge of and effective use of personnel is critical because 70 to 90 percent of the average police budget is devoted to personnel. Personnel hours are money. Reactive management wastes human resources by failing to plan aggressively. Allowing officers to read the newspaper in the patrol car while on duty is basically a waste of personnel resources. Management today is being held accountable for employing human resources wisely and efficiently. An aggressive, proactive, reality-based management will develop an efficient and accountable police force.

Teaching and Directing.   The supervisor is concerned with personnel reaching their highest potential. By constantly training personnel in the use of proper procedures for obtaining the objectives of the police organization, supervisors become teachers. The supervisor selects specific individuals for in-service training and evaluates the training in terms of the enhanced worth of personnel to the organization. As corporate management has learned, regular in-service training is needed to run an efficient organization. Training is needed to develop leadership as well as skills. Included in this function is the need to direct personnel, which is also a teaching skill.

The acronym *RESPECT* then symbolizes the need for management to show *respect* for the basic integrity of the individual and to treat each employee in a professional manner. In the absence of this approach, the organization will be inefficient and autocratic and will experience many morale problems. A positive climate conducive to cooperation is created when basic respect is shown by management for all personnel and by all personnel for management. It is always a two-way street—a two-way street that pays big dividends for the modern, reality-based police department.

OPERATIONS

Operations is defined as all the activities necessary to carry out the basic goals of the organization. Controlling crime and providing service are the major goals for law enforcement agencies. Good management carries out these goals without wasting resources on irrelevant activities. Operations include (1) line functions, (2) staff or administrative functions, and (3) auxiliary or service functions. This is the basic way the police organization is structured.

Line Functions

For close to a century, full-service enforcement agencies have organized **line functions** into the following categories: (1) patrol, (2) traffic, (3) investigation (detectives), (4) vice, and (5) juvenile. Recently, some agencies have had to change, consolidate, and even eliminate some of these functions. This will be discussed in Chapters 8 and 9.

Patrol.   When modern communities feel a need for a new police organization, the first function they think of is patrol. This function provides a public manifestation of the police through uniformed personnel being visible in marked patrol vehicles.

This leads to home rule pride and the creation of many new, small police departments. A major concern for modern police management is the consolidation of police forces to eliminate overlapping police jurisdictions and to provide more efficient delivery of services. Thus the patrol function, although central and essential to law enforcement, also creates its own variety of problems that need to be resolved. As we shall see later, the random patrol controversy has become a central management problem in an era of scarce resources.

The patrol function, as used in many departments, treats the patrol officer as a generalist—a professional who can handle anything happening in the streets of the jurisdiction. It also requires the patrol officer to hand over certain activities to police specialists after the immediate street action has been handled. Thus when treating the patrol function in terms of management, we must always be aware of the generalist-specialist concerns and must target specific solutions for this continuing problem area.

Over the past decade police departments in large cities or metropolitan areas created special units to address crime problems related to their jurisdiction. As reported by the Bureau of Justice Statistics (2002), three-fourths of these departments had full-time special units or part-time personnel assigned to various assignments involving general crime prevention, impaired driving enforcement, drug education in schools, missing children, and gang interdiction.

There is an increasing awareness today of the need of smaller agencies to form alliances with neighboring departments to address mutual problems. Examples of this are task forces devoted to regional auto theft, narcotics, and gangs; rapid response teams; and major felony squads. There is also evidence that agencies across local, state, and federal governments are experiencing closer working relationships, especially since the terrorist attacks of September 11, 2001.

Traffic.   This function deals with both the motoring public and pedestrians. Police agencies spend a considerable time on accident investigations and traffic enforcement. When an ever-increasing traffic problem takes too much of an officer's time from normal service and patrol functions, an independent traffic unit may be justified.

Investigation.   Investigation is a function of a nonuniformed follow-up force of detectives. Basically, this specialized unit is established when patrol officers do not have time to do investigations and when a certain level of expertise and experience is needed to deal with crime cases. A vital function of this unit is the preparation of cases for prosecution after arrest.

Vice.   The members of this nonuniformed, investigative unit focus on specific crimes, such as prostitution, gambling, and narcotics. Many of these crimes have been called **victimless crimes,** although many law enforcement managers consider this designation to be quite controversial. Vice units also handle organized crime, such as receiving and transporting stolen goods, extortion, and other continuing criminal conspiracies.

Juvenile.   It is estimated that roughly 80 percent of street crimes are committed by youths between the ages of 8 and 18. The crime statistics are showing increasingly younger offenders, however.

Juvenile laws and due process for juveniles differ from adult penal and criminal process statutes. Officers assigned to this function require specialized training so they can work closely with juveniles, parents, and various juvenile authorities.

Staff/Administrative Functions

The administrative staff directly assists top management. They have no command or patrol duties but are responsible for the everyday activities that concern the management team.

Staff/Administrative Units

Personnel	Inspections office
Training	Intelligence office
Legal advisers	Research and planning office
Public relations	Budget office
Community relations	Crime prevention

The **staff/administrative functions** are necessary to support the line functions, which are directly related to the output services of the agency. Auxiliary functions are important, but the management team normally does not need daily input from these units. In a normal staffing chart, they are delegated down the line from management.

Auxiliary/Service Functions

Auxiliary/service functions are the support and maintenance jobs that need to be performed by every organization. All patrol and investigation units make use of these functions at some time or other. The following services might be included in the police organization:

Auxiliary/Service Units

Records	License section
Data processing	Maintenance section
Identification bureau	Communications
Jail	Crime laboratory
Transport sections	Animal complaints
Property clerk's office	

Over the years, police departments have inherited functions that would normally be serviced by other units of the government. Many of the licensing functions have been relegated to police agencies based on past practice. Some of these functions could be better handled by other governmental agencies. This management problem will be discussed in Chapter 11.

CONCLUSION

The functions discussed in this chapter are the normal functions that exist in every full-service police agency. Students of management must be aware of how these functions are carried out. They also need to be aware of the kinds of criteria that can be applied to determine the success or failure of police agencies in carrying out these functions.

To do this type of examination, we look at how specific departments are organized and how these structures successfully implement or fail to implement these functions. Of course, in the specific application of these functions, we must also judge the worth of the function to departmental goals and general law enforcement goals. In later chapters, this analysis will be done with case histories. At this point, the student needs an understanding of these functions and how they interrelate before undertaking a more elaborate analysis and application. However, the practical application of principles is vital if management is going to be proactive and reality based.

QUESTIONS FOR REVIEW

1. Rank the following in terms of importance: (a) administration, (b) supervision, and (c) operations. Justify your answer.
2. POSDCORB has been a useful theoretical model since 1937. Why is it so useful? Relate the planning function to the other functions of POSDCORB.
3. Explain the difference between administering a small-town police department and a large-city police department.
4. Rank in order of importance the functions of the supervisor as listed in the RESPECT approach to supervision. Justify your answer.
5. How does the operational job of supervision differ from the overall tasks of management?
6. What management and personnel skills does a supervisor need? Why?
7. What are the major distinctions separating staff/administrative functions from auxiliary/service functions? Explain.

CLASS PROJECT

On a sheet of paper list either POSDCORB or RESPECT and give a brief definition for each letter in these terms. Schedule an interview with a police supervisor or administrator and ask the official to rank those items that he or she performs on a daily basis. From this ranking, report on what each model looks like in terms of importance. From POSDCORB you might end up with something that looks like CODPOOB!

If it is impractical to conduct an interview then obtain a job description for police chief from a local governmental entity and cite those duties that would relate to POSDCORB or RESPECT. Use the appropriate letter for each duty for citation purposes.

BIBLIOGRAPHY

BUREAU OF JUSTICE STATISTICS, *Police Departments in Large Cities, 1990–2000*, May 2002. Washington, D.C.

ETZIONI, AMITAI. *Modern Organizations.* Upper Saddle River, N.J.: Prentice Hall, 1964.

GULICK, LUTHER, and L. URWICK, eds. *Papers on the Science of Administration.* New York: Institute of Public Administration, Columbia University, 1937.

HOLDEN, RICHARD N. *Law Enforcement.* Upper Saddle River, N.J.: Prentice Hall, 1992.

IANNONE, N.F. *Supervision of Police Personnel* (4th ed.). Upper Saddle River, N.J.: Prentice Hall, 1980.

LAGRANGE, RANDY L. *Policing American Society.* Chicago: Nelson-Hall, 1997.

STAHL, O. GLENN, and RICHARD A. STAUFENBERGER, eds. *Police Personnel Administration.* Washington, D.C.: Police Foundation, 1974.

SUNHAM, ROGER G., and GEOFFREY P. ALPERT. *Critical Issues in Policing.* Prospect Heights, Ill.: Waverly Press, 1997.

WALKER, SAMUEL. *The Police in America.* New York: McGraw-Hill, 1999.

WHISENSAND, PAUL M., and GEORGE E. RUSH. *Supervising Police Personnel.* Upper Saddle River, N.J.: Prentice Hall, 1993.

WILSON, O.W., and ROY CLINTON MCLAREN. *Police Administration* (4th ed.). New York: McGraw-Hill, 1977.

5

THE ART AND STYLE
OF PROACTIVE POLICE LEADERSHIP

One of the critical management issues of today is leadership. Too often in these past years, the public media have discussed the so-called crisis in leadership or why leaders cannot and do not lead. Ethics also remains a major issue. At a recent leadership conference, we rhetorically asked, Who are the most prominent police leaders in the United States today? The class cited prominent police figures, but they had a hard time naming police leaders whom they would want as models for their own careers.

The irony here is that many of the police leaders whom we cite in Chapter 1 were not held in high esteem by their subordinates during their tenure in office. Others were respected by the troops but not by the public. Former Los Angeles Chief of Police Darryl Gates, for example, was damned by the public for insensitivity and errors of judgment for the department's handling of the Rodney King incident.

Reflecting on leadership as described by Amitai Etzioni, Richard Hall (1996: 139–40) points out that leadership is a special form of power closely related to the ability of the leader to elicit the followers' voluntary compliance in a broad range of matters. Leadership is distinguished from the concept of power in that a leader has influence over subjects, while power implies that subjects' preferences are held in abeyance.

Perusing our personal libraries, we came up with over 30 different definitions of leadership. Simply summarized, **leadership** is the ability to get things done under the right circumstances. So much for definitions. The real challenge is to examine and understand the problems and theoretical parameters involved with the characteristics of leadership in American policing. We decided to mix some of the classical leadership theories required of all graduate students for comprehensive exams with those of some current theories being discussed in the business world.

PROACTIVE LEADERSHIP

Proactive leaders anticipate day-to-day events. They do not wait for events to reach them; they plan for events. They form a team that is flexible enough to seek a wide variety of solutions to the everyday problems of police management. This entails a deep commitment to contingency planning so that the eventual crises that do reach their desks do not overwhelm them. Crises, for a proactive police management team, are something to be dealt with and learned from, not simply reacted to.

To exercise this proactive leadership, three essential areas of competence are needed:

Talent
Experience
Ethics
Training and education

While a whole range of competencies is needed for the exercise of leadership, these three areas are significant enough to become prerequisites for other competencies.

Talent

Authority in an organization can be exercised in two ways: through the person of the officeholder or through the office itself. Of course, the reality is that authority is exercised in a synthesis combining both ways. However, the emphasis can go either way.

Max Weber's concept of **charismatic authority** is one of the earliest and clearest conceptions of authority being exercised through the person rather than the office (Weber, 1961: 628). Weber describes the three major bases for legitimate authority:

1. *Rational grounds,* which rest on a belief in the "legality" of patterns of normative rules and the right of those elevated to authority under such rules to issue commands (legal authority)
2. *Traditional grounds,* which rest on an established belief in the sanctity of immemorial traditions and the legitimacy of the status of those exercising authority under them (traditional authority)
3. *Charismatic grounds,* which rest on devotion to the specific and exceptional sanctity, heroism, or exemplary character of an individual person (charismatic authority)

In its purest form, charismatic authority creates the authority of the office in terms of the person holding the office. Modern figures who are supposed to have exercised a great deal of their authority through the charisma of their person include Mahatma Gandhi, John Kennedy, and Eleanor Roosevelt.

Many police chiefs and sheriffs often depend on the strength of their personalities in exercising public office. However, such authority is short-lived. According to Weber (1961: 697), "In its pure form, charismatic authority has a character specifically foreign to everyday routine structures. The social relationships directly involved are strictly personal." To create stability in the organization, charismatic authority needs to be channeled into the mechanics of a routine bureaucracy, thus taking on all the trappings of legitimate authority based on legal and rational grounds. Charismatic authority, with its reliance on personal relationships, creates inconsistent policies based on personal whims and often breaks down.

Over time, the charismatic figure institutes the normal legalistic aspects of a rational bureaucracy, namely (1) a set of written rules that persist over time and that are adhered to, (2) a clearly identified set of administrative officials with their authority specifically defined and limited, and (3) a hierarchical organization with publicly known operational lines of authority.

A chief who has a strong personality and good rapport with the public may be able to operate for a time, depending on charismatic authority, by ignoring the rules of rational bureaucracy. Modern, organized society, however, is basically a bureaucratic society based on rational **legal authority.** Some charismatic sheriffs who are inconsistent administrators are kept in power by political party officials because of their vote-getting power. However, the rational rules of the organization take over the day-to-day business of the police department and even the most powerful sheriffs have to recognize this, especially when they see their power curbed by police union contracts and the courts. However, a certain amount of charismatic authority is valuable and useful in exercising the duties of police leadership.

A talented police leader is one who also has a high degree of intelligence. He or she must be able to understand theoretical concepts as they relate to the job and be able to create abstract plans and operationalize these plans. This involves a high degree of abstract manipulation of data and the ability to comprehend and make the most use of the computer age.

Talented police leaders must also have what has been called a certain native shrewdness; that is, they have to have a grasp of politics and be pragmatic problem solvers. They must also be goal oriented—that is, individuals who truly want to get the job done. Police leaders have to balance many demands on their time along with conflicting demands that bear on their decisions. Special-interest groups, politicians, fellow police leaders, and their own officers, including the diverse groups within the official police community, all create pressures on their decisions. A leader must have a sense of fair play and balance to get the job done amid conflicting pressures.

Our police leaders must also be excellent communicators. They need to be clear and forceful yet be able to listen and understand other points of view. Their ideas of leadership need to be marketed just as business and industry market ideas. Police leaders have many publics, including their own officers, various community groups, and governmental and criminal justice leaders. Communication ability is crucial. Former New York City Police Commissioner William Bratton was a master at this by appearing at important police events and communicating with the print and electronic media on the progress the department was making in the "crime war." Unfortunately, his media fame and public stature came into conflict with Mayor Rudolf Guiliani's, and Bratton retired in 1996.

After reading these few paragraphs on talent, the reader might begin to wonder if every police leader has to be a comic book superhero. The answer is, not quite. Too often, we have been satisfied in police management with mediocre leadership. The demands of the twenty-first century on police management will no longer allow us this luxury. Today's police leader may not have to be a superhero, but he or she does have to be a supremely talented human being who can bring that talent to bear on the exercise of office.

Experience

There is experience, and there is experience. A police leader does not need 20 years of experience, one year at a time, where nothing is learned about the exercise of leadership talents.

He or she does not need simply operational experience. The chief really does not need to know how to fix a patrol car, how to write a parking ticket, or even how to drive a motorcycle. Management skills are developed through the exercise of management and administrative experience. They may seem obvious, but many departments operate when choosing their leaders as if this fact did not exist. If there were advertisements in the local newspapers for police chiefs, in terms of the history of electing and appointing police leaders, most of them would read like this:

JOB VACANCY FOR POLICE CHIEF
NO MANAGEMENT EXPERIENCE NECESSARY

Experience is necessary, but it has to be experience of a certain kind and quality. Technically trained, operational administrators need experience in making decisions based on complex, often incomplete facts and the human situation.

Experience in the day-to-day activities of police work is valuable and contributes to being a good police administrator. The operational and technical skills needed for administrators must be superseded by the necessary human relations and conceptual skills needed to manage a police department.

Some of this lack of experience can be made up with a good management training program. Police leaders can be trained in how to draw up and present a budget, in what is necessary in exercising leadership skills in relation to personnel, and in what goes into such items as contingency planning and communication networks. Thus, what is necessary in the exercise of proactive police leadership is a careful blend of ability, experience, ethics, and finally, training and education.

Ethics

The downfall of major corporations like Enron, WorldCom, Tyco, and Adelphia, during the past few years was based on executive greed, criminal behavior, and corporate board laissez-faire attitudes. Quite simply, the executives under investigation or in prison were accused of issuing false earnings reports or taking the corporation's money for their personal use. It is no surprise that the issue of ethics is being reviewed in business and management courses around the country.

Police executives face a number of ethical dilemmas every day when striving to make the right choice from the competing choices. Needless to say, outright criminal behavior, violating department policies and regulations, and engaging in conduct unbecoming a police officer does not reflect well in one's ability to lead the organization and to exhort line and staff officers to behave in an ethical manner.

Training and Education

Police leaders are promoted, appointed, and elected, in most cases, without any further training in management skills. In the mid-1970s, the **International Association of Chiefs of Police (IACP)** surveyed the heads of the 49 state police and highway patrol agencies, all the chiefs and sheriffs who headed agencies of 100 or more sworn personnel, and 20 percent of those chiefs with fewer than 100 sworn personnel. The IACP concluded (National Advisory Commission, 1976: 31),

> A majority of the police chiefs surveyed indicated that some law enforcement and management training should be required for future police chief executives. Training tends to refine executive capabilities derived from innate leadership ability and meaningful work experience. . . . For the two-thirds of the police chief executives who advanced from within their organization, training is especially important to prevent agencies from becoming ingrown.

In terms of selecting a police chief, "Ninety-seven percent of police chief executives and 96 percent of their superiors believe that law enforcement training is an important or very important factor." The superiors surveyed were those government officials who supervise police chief executives (mayor, city manager, legislative group).

THE IMPORTANCE OF MANAGEMENT SKILLS

Over the years, a number of private and public agencies have developed courses for police officers and managers. Police academies in the largest agencies routinely offer some management courses, as does the Federal Bureau of Investigation and the International Association of Chiefs of Police. Although both organizations perform an important function in updating the police chief executive and future police executives in current issues, there remains the lack of a systematic approach to basic training for all police managers.

The IACP survey, although dated, identified 14 significant police **management skills** (Table 5–1) and asked the surveyed police executives to rate the importance of each skill on a scale of 0 to 10, with 10 being the most important (National Advisory Commission, 1976: 25).

This list, indeed, makes a fine curriculum for a modern police management academy. When we analyze this list, some skill patterns emerge: organization and administration skills; technical skills, such as fiscal management and knowledge of advanced technology; and, overwhelmingly, communication skills on all levels.

Major metropolitan areas normally maintain their own police academies and offer some management training programs. However, the medium and smaller departments do not have the economies of scale of the larger municipalities and thus have neither the budget nor the continuing demand for such large-scale training. There is a need for systematic leadership/management courses for newly promoted police executives. These should be readily available on a systematic, recurring, and regional basis. Upon promotion, new administrators should have the opportunity to attend a regionally based training academy.

TABLE 5–1   *Importance of Management Skills for Police Chief Executives*

Skill Area	Rating by Police Chief Executives[a]
1. Motivating personnel and maintaining high morale	8.7
2. Developing subordinates into an effective team	8.6
3. Relating to the community	8.4
4. Organizing agency personnel and functions	8.0
5. Administering internal discipline	7.9
6. Maintaining internal review and control	7.9
7. Communicating with all levels within the agency	7.9
8. Establishing and communicating objectives and priorities	7.8
9. Forecasting, planning, and implementing agency activities	7.8
10. Resolving employee relations problems	7.7
11. Budgeting and fiscal management	7.7
12. Utilizing advanced technology	7.2
13. Coordinating agency activity with other organizations	7.2
14. Securing and managing grant-funded projects	6.2

[a]0 = lowest score; 10 = highest score.

Source: National Advisory Commission on Criminal Justice Standards and Goals (1976).

Today, the criteria for police executive selection in progressive departments is like selecting a business executive. Community search committees look for candidates who have a combination of education, training, and field experience. In addition to the management skills presented in Table 5–1, police chief candidates must also be able to define what is the department's organizational vision of the future. As Garner (1993: 3–4) discusses, this vision includes communicating a clear mission statement that is derived from discussion with employees and community leaders. While there is no formal data available, the number of chief executives with bachelor's and master's degrees in fields ranging from criminal justice to law and public administration is growing.

MANAGEMENT STYLES

Over the years, numerous management profiles have been taken from the areas of public and business administration and applied to police management. There is a great deal of overlap in this area with communication models, since the style of police leadership is directly linked to the communication process within the agency. When communication goes from the top to the bottom, with no feedback system, for example, the management style tends toward the hierarchical and autocratic. When communication is two-way, ongoing, and considered to be effective in deciding policy between equals in an organizational structure, the management style tends toward the democratic team approach.

The following approaches will be examined in terms of their applicability to the art and style of proactive police leadership:

1. Managing in chaos
2. Digital nervous system
3. Emotional intelligence
4. Total quality management (TQM)
5. Reengineering
6. Herzberg's eternal triangle
7. Katz's three skills approach
8. Maslow's hierarchy of needs
9. Herzberg's hygiene/motivators approach to job satisfaction
10. McGregor's Theory X and Theory Y
11. Theory Z
12. Blake and Mouton's managerial grid

Managing in Chaos

At a recent seminar on strategic planning, the presenter used the following excerpt from the *New York Times*, which described the leadership challenges facing several executives in charge of offices in the World Trade Center on September 11, 2001 (Wayne and Kaufman, 2001):

> There is no Harvard MBA course, no corporate strategy session, no business celebrity memoir that can prepare a chief executive to lead a corporation, and thousands of employees, when 110 floors fall out from under them. And in the hours that have passed since the collapse of the World Trade Center (WTC), many of the nation's chief executives registered the strange sensation of living in a world that they, always so capable, always so sure, had never encountered.

Responding police and fire unit supervisors and commanders experienced the same feeling. They faced a terrible situation involving the tallest buildings in the world whose upper floors were engulfed in flames because of two kamikaze crashed airliners. They witnessed people jumping out of the buildings rather than face being burned to death. Forget about fire suppression—their first order of business was to get people evacuated. Within 45 minutes, the buildings collapsed, sending a debris surge of cement, paper, dust, and chemical particles throughout Lower Manhattan. Added to this **chaos,** the city's high-tech emergency command center was located in Tower 2 of the WTC and was evacuated minutes before the building was destroyed.

At the Pentagon site, the first responding units saw smoke and fire and, eventually, airplane parts scattered about. The first supervisor assessed the overall situation and began charting on a notepad where to put equipment and personnel in what would become the incident command center for the duration of recovery and cleanup. She then started to issue orders and called for additional assistance according to an emergency plan that the Arlington

County Police Department had practiced several times before September 11 (Farr, 2002).

The following recommendations for addressing disasters of such outrageous proportions are based on our own experiences and from various police and private-sector after-action reviews of September 11:

1. *Be calm*. In one account after another, the emergency responders and the people in charge of businesses and operations at the World Trade Center assessed the situation and began making decisions and issuing orders to subordinates based on the information that each had. There were few reports of people in leadership positions going berserk or abandoning their posts unless ordered to do so. Call it leadership under fire, the leaders that day did not lose their cool in front of their subordinates—at least not in public.

2. *Communicate*. One of the things that the public admired about Mayor Rudolph Guiliani in the days that followed the attacks was his sincere, calm, and matter-of-fact public reviews of the situation and of the actions that he and other city leaders were taking to deal with the massive problems caused by the destruction of the World Trade Center and the surrounding neighborhood. Information was reported and clarified in a professional manner each day for the media. The former mayor recently wrote that he immediately began speaking to reporters on the street as he and his staff were retreating to establish a new command post. "I had to communicate with the public, to do whatever I could to calm people down and contribute to an orderly and safe evacuation," he stated (Guiliani, 2002, p. 36).

3. *Take care of your people*. Firefighters and police officers share an unwritten axiom that you never leave your colleagues behind when retreating from an impossible situation. Many police officers and firefighters were probably lost trying to rescue or locate their comrades. In the chaos that followed, police and fire commanders began to take head counts to determine if their people made it out of the WTC. This was further complicated by the number of off-duty emergency police and fire personnel who went to the scene directly from their homes. With the assistance of New York's construction industry, a massive undertaking was begun to locate survivors who could be trapped under the rubble at Ground Zero. Field managers also had to deal with basic life and operational functions, which included food, equipment replacement, leave arrangements, and rest breaks, which in this case, spanned for months after the event.

    For the police and fire departments, preparations were enacted to deal with survivors of those killed in action or presumed dead. While these procedures are often standard operating procedure (SOP) for police and fire departments, it was a massive, grueling undertaking because of the high number of casualties that occurred on September 11. As discussed in Chapter 12, factors that have to be considered include burial arrangements, return of personal property, and review of insurance and other death benefits with the next of kin. Private-sector managers also had to deal with the same factors for employees killed that day. In New York

State, special legislation was enacted to allow affected families to submit insurance claims without obtaining the traditional death notice, which is based on recovery of the actual body.

4. *Get back to business as soon as possible.* In the days that followed, the city of New York cordoned off the WTC and affected areas and began resuming regular city services. Thanks to around-the-clock efforts by communications workers, the cable networks that run the New York Stock Exchange were repaired, and trading was resumed that following Monday. Subway service was restored, with the exceptions of those stations directly under the World Trade Center. The mayor urged people to get back to work and to return to New York. In Washington, the Pentagon resumed business shortly after the destroyed sections had been cordoned off.

   For psychological and operational reasons, businesses have to return to some sense of normalcy. After the World Trade Center bombing of 1993, most WTC tenants had prepared emergency and business-interruption plans. They had already set up satellite locations in New Jersey and upstate New York and simply moved surviving personnel so they could return to general business operations.

5. *Maintain critical communications.* We have been in a number of critical situations, and in each and every case, command communications during the situation were always a problem. A case in point are the separate radio channels that often exist in a region or a county for the police and fire departments. Field units cannot communicate with each other. Although all reviews are not yet completed of the aftermath of the WTC attack, it appears that the fire department lost most of its communications with field units involved in evacuation efforts.

6. *Have an incident command plan.* This is a plan in which various agencies come together and address a situation at a central location. To be candid, turf battles are common between the police, fire department, and emergency services units in terms of who is in charge and who makes the critical decisions. They often do not practice the plan together, and the chain of command is not defined. The aftermath studies conducted of the rescue efforts of September 11 in New York noted the absence of an incident command plan and found that the fire and police departments did not work with each other during the initial response.

7. *Be prepared to retreat.* Although no one likes to admit it, there are times when it is advisable to retreat to limit casualties and equipment losses and to protect agency heads during a critical incident. As the New York City emergency-management center was destroyed, Mayor Guiliani and his staff moved to several locations until they decided to take up command quarters in the police academy.

8. *Deal with postevent stress and physical conditions.* A number of colleagues we know in the police and emergency services areas have nightmares, drink too much, and fight with their friends and family over minor things weeks and months after dealing with a critical incident. Many rescue workers still complain of having the "WTC cough" from breathing in various particles at the site. Agencies have to be prepared to deal not only with the psychological

needs that occur after such an incident, but also requests for early retirement, claims for worker's compensation, and voluntary resignations. This is why the police department and the people in charge of human resources must have a close working relationship and the expertise to deal with such individual situations.

The Digital Nervous System

The most influential leader in the technological revolution is Bill Gates, CEO of Microsoft, the company that developed the Windows software system. Although the company has been embroiled in a legal dispute with the federal government on its monopolistic practices, the Microsoft Windows operating system is used by most computers in the world. In his book *Business at the Speed of Thought* (1999), Gates reviews the operational and organizational changes taking place through "digitizing" in operational practices ranging from paper reports to organizational design. He presents the following 12 business practices that organizational leaders should consider based on computer operations:

1. Use e-mail for communications so that senders and responders can interact with "reflexlike" speed.
2. Study sales data on-line to find patterns and to share insights.
3. Use PCs for business analysis, and shift knowledge workers into high-level thinking about products, services, and profitability.
4. Use digital tools to create cross-department virtual teams that can share knowledge and build on each other's ideas in real time.
5. Convert every paper process to a digital process to eliminate bottlenecks.
6. For business operations, use digital tools to eliminate single-task jobs or change them into value-added jobs.
7. Create digital feedback loops to improve the efficiency of physical processes and to improve the quality of procedures and services.
8. Use digital systems to route customer complaints immediately.
9. In commerce, use digital communication to redefine the nature of business and boundaries between the organization and the customer.
10. Trade information for time by using digital transactions with suppliers and partners; transform every business process into just-in-time delivery.
11. Use digital delivery of sales and service to eliminate the middleman from customer transactions.
12. Use digital tools to help customers solve problems for themselves and to reserve personal contact (telephone calls, visits, and meetings) to respond to complex, high-value customer needs.

In summary, the personal computer defines how organizational decisions and interactions with customers are created and executed. Gates views this entire enterprise as a "digital nervous system" involving rapid activity and responses both within and outside the organization.

The leadership factor for managing the digital enterprise is important to determine how informational technology can best be obtained, applied, and managed for organizational processes and relations with customers. The most basic tenet here is that the leadership structure must comprehend and understand the technological revolution that is going on and be able to forecast potential applications. There must be a commitment to expend budgetary resources to obtain equipment and training. Even Gates declares that information technology is terribly expensive and that too much money goes for administration rather than applications. Then, too, there has to be a review of the organizational structure and a commitment to creating digital teams to share information and to address issues and problems. This sharing of information, according to Gates, is the development of institutional intelligence, or corporate IQ (1999: 239). Companies with high IQ tend to collaborate effectively so that key people on a given project are well informed. Company leaders must also "lead by example" by sharing both good and bad news with all segments of the organization. In summary, leadership becomes defined by knowledge management, or the extent to which a company and its employees are capable of using information for planning, customer relations, training, and project coordination.

The impact of all this on police organizations is both immediate and abstract. Most police departments remain based in the traditional organizational structure and often have limited resources for acquiring information technology. The application of the digital revolution around the United States creates a sense of both reality and irony for many police departments.

1. Computer crime complaints are increasing, but many smaller police departments still do not have the most basic application of computer technology.
2. Collaboration is often difficult between intradepartment units because of power and turf wars.
3. There appears to be increased sharing of information between departments and districts by the development of localized mobile radio district and crime/suspect networks.
4. The patrol car is slowly becoming the digital office; the patrol officer can run data checks, match suspect information, complete reports in final form, and process a prisoner, all in the front seat of a patrol car.
5. Through Compstat and other forms of crime and police-service analysis, police managers are being held accountable for crime trends and service calls in their area.

Emotional Intelligence

We all are emotional human beings. Psychologist Daniel Goleman points out that leaders need to understand both their own emotions and those of others. When leaders make judgments, they need to have categories that will help them analyze their own emotional judgments. Leaders also have to know how emotions affect police personnel.

Emotional intelligence is a concept that is being embraced by corporate management today. It is an approach that works well with today's community policing and personnel policies. Goleman recommends organizing groups, negotiating solutions, personal connections, and social analysis. Social analysis includes "being able to detect and have insight about people's feeling, motives and concerns" (Goleman, 1995: 118). Emotions are more immediate, intense, and different than conceptual and rational decision making. Successful proactive police management has to anticipate and deal with this aspect of human behavior.

Goleman gave these valuable insights for an emotional competence framework and analytic categories:

Self-Awareness	Emotional awareness, accurate self-assessment, self-confidence
Self-Regulation	Self-control, trustworthiness, conscientiousness, adaptability, innovation
Motivation	Achievement, commitment, initiative, optimism
Empathy	Understanding others, developing others, service orientation, leveraging diversity, political awareness
Social Skills	Influence, communication, conflict management, leadership, change catalyst, building bonds, collaboration and cooperation, team capabilities

Too many of the "old guard" of police leaders feel that they are always making rational decisions. They think that public personnel and the public will judge them rationally and logically. This has never been true. Instant communication and community policing demand more emotional intelligence skills on the part of our police leaders.

Emotional intelligence is being adopted by corporate leadership because of the challenges of global business and e-business. Dealing with worldwide cultures means that corporate leaders must adapt, innovate, and have personal initiative based on emotional intelligence. This is also true of our law enforcement leadership.

Modern police managing requires people skills and team building. Our new police leaders need to encourage field supervisors to grow in their job, take credit for success, and become part of the police leadership team. All police leaders, from the chief's office through supervisory field personnel, must be politically aware and work in the community. Community leadership, like democracy, is always a political process. Creating a positive community leadership–police team is a political process.

Our cities, with new immigrants becoming American citizens from diverse backgrounds, means that diverse cultures must be dealt with by police supervisors and administrators. Besides building bonds with their own department through the norms of police culture, police leaders must make it possible to build bonds with widely diverse community leaders from many cultures in Africa, Asia, and Eastern Europe. This takes empathy, the ability to put yourself emotionally in another person's place.

In a typical arrest or scene of family violence, police officers may need to see how a Russian, Ukrainian, Bosnian, Korean, Vietnamese, or Orthodox Jew would handle these situations. All of these diverse groups are adapting to American culture and American police. Some come from cultures where the police beat and torture people. These people will avoid police and be terrified of them. Some come from cultures where the government raises the children and parents have little or no responsibility. These people come into conflict with the United States child-neglect laws, not knowing that they have done anything wrong.

The police are called in to deal with everyday crises involving diverse groups. Police need training in the various cultures and cultural norms of the groups that they deal with each day in their community. If police officers, supervisors, and administrators can understand points of view from diverse cultural norms, small problems will be solved rather than becoming large disasters. Empathy may be the most crucial human relations skill in twenty-first-century law enforcement.

The Futurist, a publication of the World Future Society, gives a further list of analytic concepts from Goleman's 1998 book. These concepts can help police officers apply emotional intelligence to their jobs ("Emotionally Intelligent Worker," 1999: 14):

Emotional awareness	the ability to know which emotions you are feeling and realizing the link between your feelings and what you think, do and say
Self-control	managing your impulsive feelings, staying composed, thinking clearly and staying focused
Understanding others	sensing their feelings and perspectives and taking an active interest in their concerns
Developing others	sensing other people's developmental needs and bolstering their abilities
Trustworthiness and conscientiousness	maintaining integrity and taking responsibility for personal performance

Self-control has always been a major emotional skill for police officers and police leadership because the job demands major crisis-management skills. Self-control is at the top of the list of emotional skills.

Police leaders need to take more responsibility for their departments. They need to admit when things do not work and then fix them. Defending police brutality and deviance shows no understanding of American values or of others. The blue wall of noncommunication must be destroyed. Emotional intelligence provides a variety of emotional skills that show how this can be done.

Before police leaders can understand the emotions of others, they have to be honest and try to understand their own emotions. Emotions are part of the human condition. Realizing the link between a police leader's own emotions and behavior will mature our police leadership around the country.

The emotional category of developing others is crucially important in all police organizations so that able police leaders can be developed within the organization. Proactive management needs to have specific career ladders for officers as well as leadership training, workshops, and career opportunities. As more police leaders adapt and change, it is crucial to have a formal process to develop and sustain new leadership. Potential police leaders are leaving the public forces and becoming leaders in private security. We must stop this epidemic loss of police leadership to the private sector. Emotional intelligence's major point about developing others will give the current leadership a change in perspective that is needed to develop and reward our new police leaders in training.

As the information revolution proceeds in law enforcement, the ability to communicate and have empathy will become more important. These abilities give police management and supervisors the ability to build teams within a police department and interagency teams. The proactive police leadership that succeeds in the twenty-first century will need emotional intelligence.

Total Quality Management

Total quality management (TQM) was a standard agenda item at police management conferences in the early 1990s. While some of the luster has worn off, the tenets for TQM still remain important for customer relations and modern management practices in terms of product quality. The foundations for TQM were written and discussed before and after World War II by W. Edwards Deming, who served as the leading organizational consultant during the rebuilding of Japanese industry. According to Halberstam (1986: 380), Deming is held with the same regard as General MacArthur by the Japanese with regard to his contributions to postwar economic development. In the United States, however, Deming's ideas were never seriously discussed by organizational theorists until serious inquiry was made into Japanese management practices in the 1980s. In fact, the authors of this book came across Deming's theories as an aside during leisure reading on a comparison of auto industries of the United States and Japan.

By itself, TQM is defined as a strategic, integrated management system for achieving customer satisfaction. TQM involves all managers and employees and uses human resources and managerial and quantitative methods to continually improve organizational processes. According to TQM proponents, it provides attentive leaders, trained workers, data and measurement, a guiding vision, and operating values for any organization.

For example, the Xerox Corporation, which adopted TQM in the early 1980s, made the following statement in a recent company brochure:

> Xerox is a quality company. Quality is the basic business principle for Xerox. Quality means providing our internal and external customers with innovative products and services that satisfy their requirements. Quality improvement is the job of every Xerox employee.

This statement becomes the cornerstone for employee training, assessment of customer satisfaction, creation of management teams, and the corporation's recognition and reward system. An important component in TQM is **benchmarking,** which is defined as "the continuous process of measuring our products, services, and practices against our toughest competitor, or those recognized as world leaders and to identify areas that need improvement" (Xerox, 1991).

The basic components of TQM are summarized according to the 14-point philosophy presented by Deming. As discussed by Butterfield (1991: 50–59) on their application to the service industry, the **14 points** are as follows:

1. A consistency of purpose toward improvement of product and service
2. The adoption of the quality philosophy by management, which must begin with the corporate leaders
3. An emphasis on improving work processes rather than relying on mass inspections
4. The awarding of contracts and business on the basis of quality rather than price tag
5. Constant improvement in production and service
6. Much attention to training
7. Uncovering barriers to workmanship
8. Driving out fear, such as the fear of asking questions or expressing ideas
9. Breaking down communication barriers between departments
10. Eliminating slogans and targets for zero defects and new levels of productivity. Instead, management concentrates on showing people how to do their work more accurately and efficiently.
11. Eliminating work standards that dwell on numerical quotas. Instead, use leadership to look for differences in performance.
12. Remove barriers that rob hourly workers of their pride in workmanship. This is often created by communication barriers between management and employees related to job performance or ways to improve services.
13. Instituting a vigorous program of education and self-improvement for workers for new or improved skills
14. Having everyone in the organization working toward the objective of quality

It is important to stress that TQM does not mean any change in the traditional organizational structure postulated by Weber. There is still the hierarchy, and management is still in control. Quality teams, with the approval of management, are brought together to define and solve problems related to their sphere of influence, but they may have little impact on overall company strategy. Comparing TQM to directed teams, Holpp (1992: 72–73) shows that the main difference is that directed teams in theory are given all kinds of flexibility for production and problem solving.

At the time of this writing, TQM remains an important concept in organizational theory. It should be noted that in the 1950s, Deming used royalties from his books to create the Deming prize for Japanese companies and their quality control initiatives. Ironically, in the United States today, there is a Deming prize and a Baldridge award, which are both awarded to companies that have outstanding quality-control mechanisms.

As discussed in Chapter 1, an important component of TQM is leadership. For Deming, leadership is important insofar as managers must remove barriers to producing quality goods and services. Organizations committed to TQM are committed to quality. If some process does not work or produce the right result, then the components that lead to the output are analyzed by a work team to find solutions. A midsize police department could use TQM to facilitate the return of recovered stolen property to the rightful owners. A team would be formed to look at the problems inherent with the current system. The team might include an evidence technician, a patrol supervisor, a patrol officer, and a representative from the district attorney's office interested in evidence for criminal cases. The team would then ask some basic questions, such as, Why do we have to keep certain items? Could some items be immediately returned? How long after a court disposition do we keep items? How are the items properly tagged and inventoried? What do we do with unclaimed items, and how do we destroy contraband, such as drugs? Each question would be broken down to various distinct components, and the team would try to provide new thinking and processes to answer these questions. This is not a one-shot deal. The team would look at how other organizations deal with the problem of overloaded evidence supply systems. New ideas would be tried, and victims (the customers) would be asked by phone or by mail to evaluate the method used to return their property. The idea is to get the property back to their rightful owners as soon as legally possible and to keep the evidence rooms free of junk. The leadership role in this enterprise is for management to permit formation of the team and to allow it to constructively attack the problem without cumbersome red tape or meddling supervision.

Obviously, this quest for quality must begin at the top and filter down to all layers of the organization. Quality controls and innovations are tied to promotions and rewards. For TQM proponents, there must be true commitment and not lip service; otherwise, the program becomes another fad. According to Halberstam (1986: 313), Deming had little use for managers who had not graduated from the factory floor. At that time, the science of management was exerting itself in many organizations, and many managers dealt with abstractions rather than practical experience.

Reengineering

As businesses were adopting TQM as a way to improve the quality of their goods and services, a concept called **reengineering** was being developed by certain companies as a way to review how tasks were being performed. The term was coined by MIT professor Michael Hammer in 1980 as he observed radical reorganizations undertaken by many major companies. In their book *Reengineering the Corporation*, Hammer and coauthor James Champy wrote that reengineering is the fundamental rethinking and basic redesign of business processes to achieve dramatic improvement in critical contemporary measures of performance, such as cost, quality, service, and speed (1993: 4). In comparison to TQM, reengineering involves a radical review of the entire organizational structure, while TQM programs exist within the framework of existing organizational structure.

Hammer and Champy (1993: 32–36) present the following questions when a company or an organizational unit is considering reengineering:

1. Why do we do what we do?
2. Can we disregard all existing structure and procedures and invent new ways of accomplishing work?
3. Do we need dramatic improvement? Should we blow up the old and replace it with something new?
4. What is the range of activities that creates output that is of value to the customer?

This concept came about because of competition, cost, and the drive for quality facing American companies from Asia and Europe. According to the authors, companies that have undertaken reengineering have ranged from those that were in deep trouble, such as auto manufacturing, to those that were having no discernible difficulties but were not satisfied with current performance. Walmart, Hallmark, Kodak, and others are cited as examples of successful companies that used reengineering as a method to keep an upper hand in their markets.

Companies that have undertaken reengineering are not tied to the idea of centralized control. The development of informational technology, which resulted in information being shared throughout the organization, contributes to this concept by tearing down distance. Units that are miles apart can now teleconference, e-mail, fax, video sell, digitize, use the Internet, and so on.

For his work, *Time* magazine hailed Hammer as one of the 25 most influential people in the United States in 1996. Many observers, however, have used the term *reengineering* in connection to "downsizing," "flattening," or "right-sizing" the organization, which in basic terms means reducing the size of the organization, producing less, and creating more profits for shareholders and executives. In most cases, reengineering means that the company will produce more with fewer departments and levels of control, which indeed results in reduced organizational structures.

In a more recent work, Hammer wrote that reengineering had not just modified ways of working, it had transformed many organizations into structures that could not be recognizable. He states, "The radical character of reengineering, however important and exciting, is not its most significant aspect. The key word in the definition of reengineering is 'process': a complete end-to-end set of activities that together create value for a customer" (1996: xii).

Reengineering operational concepts appear somewhat similar to TQM guidelines. Problem-solving teams are formed to develop new products or processes to achieve results. Managers have to be retrained to think as coaches rather than traditional supervisors. Workers and managers, who share joint responsibilities, are rewarded according to results, not activity. Returning to our TQM discussion on ways of returning property to their rightful owners, a review team undertaking a reengineering of the recovery of stolen property would ask certain questions relating the process to the entire property operation: Why do we have to keep the property in an evidence room? Do we have to have an evidence room? Why can't the district attorney keep the evidence since they deal with the evidence at trial? Okay, let's say that we keep the evidence room, but what if the property is videotaped and returned to the owner immediately?

In this process, the role of the leader is critical. The leader must have a vision and persuade others that reengineering is important. For policing, the chief must be able to delegate responsibility to the review team to come up with ideas and to make them occur. Depending on the size of the organization, the chief or assigned deputy must run interference for the review team and give active support to team members. He or she must keep those with vested interests at bay and allow the team to have an open discussion. Once a new process is achieved and tested, the management team must make sure that it goes into operation (Hammer and Champy, 1993: 104–105).

The above discussion understates the complexity of reengineering planning and decisions undertaken by major corporations with multinational sites. So far, we have seen few examples of reengineering case studies applied to the public sector, mainly because most public organizations are still the sole providers of services in a given geographic area and work rules are tied to union contracts and civil service procedures. Reengineering for police organizations may become part of the lexicon for managers because many large departments are being decentralized through modern technology and community policing, which together place command, information, and responsibility on local units. Traditional departments are being challenged by community and political groups as expensive, not responsive, and at times not necessary in view of the overlap of competing jurisdictions that occurs in many areas. There is also increasing competition for support and resources between certain public departments and private security organizations. Reengineering as a concept provides a method to review the organizational structure in order to improve police services.

Commissioner William Bratton used reengineering to reorganize the New York City Police Department (NYPD). The hierarchy was flattened. Police focus groups created a better information flow. Decision-making authority was brought down to the precinct commander's level. Precinct commanders were rewarded and punished based on the reduction of crime in their precincts. Crime-mapping techniques (Crimetac) were made available to all levels of the police bureaucracy. Detectives, special street crime units, federal and NYPD drug-enforcing units all shared information with precinct commanders. Quality-of-life neighborhood issues were attacked with city civil lawyers assigned to police precincts using nuisance laws to eliminate centers of illegal drugs and prostitution in specific neighborhoods. Public housing projects were successfully targeted as hot spots of crime and drug dealing with massive and swift police responses. Reengineering, which led to the Compstat approach to management, has been continued. The most important lesson learned is that the reduction of crime is dependent on good information flow throughout the police department, but especially to middle management (Silverman, 1999).

Herzberg's Eternal Triangle

Herzberg's **eternal triangle** consists of the following three elements:

1. Organizational theory (work flow)
2. Industrial engineering (jobs)
3. Behavioral science (attitudes) (Herzberg, 1975: 18)

According to Herzberg, the organizational theorist says, "If jobs are organized in a proper manner, the result will be the most efficient job structure, and the most favorable job attitudes will flow as a matter of course." The industrial engineer, on the other hand, tries to create "the most appropriate incentive system and to design the specific working conditions in a way that facilitates the most efficient use of the human machine." Naturally, optimal organizational design is expected to produce positive work attitudes. The behavioral scientist "emphasizes some form of human relations education, in the hope of instilling healthy employee attitudes and an organizational climate that he or she considers to be felicitous to human values." Naturally, this approach is expected to lead to "efficient job and organizational structure."

What needs to be emphasized here is that, if the leadership style is to be effective, it must include all parts of the eternal triangle. Most police department managers are limited to the organizational theory approach to management.

They feel that if there is a proper organizational chart and if the officers understand their job description and operate in terms of the boundaries of this job description while obeying the traditional authority structure, the organization will have high morale and will perform optimally. In many cases, this has degenerated into "management by memorandum," in which additions to the rules and clarifications of the organizational structure are seen as sufficient incentive to motivate personnel to do an efficient job. However, this is not sufficient to provide high morale because of a lack of understanding on management's part as to what motivates people to want to perform in an optimal fashion. As we examine the differing approaches to management style, what does work, in terms of a synthesis of approaches, will become clearer.

Katz's Three Skills Approach

Robert Katz (1975: 23) attempts to answer the question, "What observable skills does an effective administrator demonstrate?" He states (1975: 24):

> It is assumed here that an administrator is one who (a) directs the activities of other persons and (b) undertakes the responsibility for achieving certain objectives through these efforts. Within this definition, successful administration appears to rest on three basic skills, which we will call *technical*, *human*, and *conceptual*.

According to Katz, **technical skill** "involves specialized knowledge, analytical ability within that speciality, and facility in the use of the tools and techniques of the specific discipline." This is the skill most easily trained for. It is more operational than managerial. More complex is **human skill,** which Katz describes as "the executive's ability to work effectively as a group member and to build cooperative effort within the team he leads." Human skill means that the police executive is sensitive to other people's feelings and is aware of his or her own feelings.

This human relations skill involves (1) tolerance of ambiguity and (2) empathy. Tolerance of ambiguity means that the manager is able to handle problems for which insufficient information precludes making a totally informed decision. The effective manager must also have a keen sense of appreciation and understanding of widely different viewpoints and cultures and be able to approach problems and people with no preconceptions.

Empathy is the ability to put oneself in another's place. A good police manager is able to put himself or herself in the place of the patrol officers emotionally and intellectually and thus understand the effect of any issued orders on these officers. The manager must be able to look at a situation from the viewpoint of the minority groups in the community and from that of the superior officer. The effective manager must also be willing to act in terms of these perceptions.

Katz's approach to **conceptual skill** is in terms of an organizing and integrating function (1975: 27), "coordinating and integrating all the activities and interests of the organization toward a common objective." This is not meant to be simply an intellectual process, as Katz considers such skills to include "an ability to translate knowledge into action." Police managers with conceptual skills are able to see their relationship to the rest of the organization of the department and understand how their orders and policy will affect the various structural relationships within the department. For example, an order concerning the use of evidence needs to be examined in terms of how it affects detectives, court cases and evidence flow, the laboratory, the property room, and the work of the line officer. Besides these internal relations, good conceptual managers are also able to understand and operationalize in their daily behavior the relationship their policies have to the place of the police department in the local government, community, and, when necessary, state and nation.

As Katz points out, these skills are divided for analytic reasons. However, in the day-to-day activities of the police manager, all these skills are brought into play with the emphasis changing depending on the problems and the organizational context of the department. Katz also emphasizes that these skills can be taught to current and future executives just as any other skill can. Thus, good administrators are not simply born but can be trained in the classroom and by practicing the skill in the field. His conclusion should be printed in capital letters and placed in the office of anyone who has a hand in choosing and/or training police executives (1975: 33):

> The administrator needs: (a) sufficient technical skill to accomplish the mechanics of the particular job for which he is responsible; (b) sufficient human skill in working with others to be an effective group member and to be able to build cooperative effort within the team he leads; (c) sufficient conceptual skill to recognize the interrelationships of the various factors involved in his situation, which will lead him to take that action which is likely to achieve the maximum good for the total organization.

Maslow's Hierarchy of Needs

Maslow attempted to understand what motivates human beings. If police managers understand this, they should be able to motivate their personnel and understand their own needs and satisfactions so that they can become more effective. According to Maslow, first there is a basic need to feel secure and to have one's physical needs taken care of. Next is the need to have good social relations. The third need is that of feeling worthwhile in terms of one's work and place in the organization. Many police administrators call this need a need to be respected by one's fellow officers and superiors. Fourth, there is a need to feel that one has enough authority where one's opinions are listened to and that the individual is actually participating in making policy in the organization. Finally, there is the ultimate need that some people will never have satisfied, what

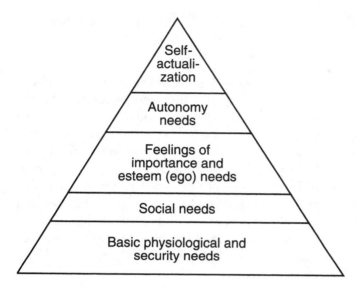

FIGURE 5—1   Maslow's hierarchy of needs.

Maslow call the need for self-actualization or self-fulfillment. This combines a feeling of wanting personal growth along with such factors as being a creative self-starter who will be able to grow to his or her potential as a human being in this job. This **hierarchy of needs** is often diagrammed as a triangle going from basic needs of security to self-actualization at the top (see Figure 5–1).

1. Security needs
   a. The feeling of security in the position
2. Social needs
   a. The opportunity to give help to other people
   b. The opportunity to develop close friendships
3. Importance, self-esteem needs
   a. The feeling of importance from being in the position
   b. The importance of the position inside the agency (i.e., the regard received from others in the police agency)
   c. The importance of the position outside the agency (i.e., the regard and esteem received from others who are not members of the police agency)
4. Autonomy needs
   a. The authority connected with the position
   b. The opportunity for independent thought and action
   c. The opportunity for participation in the meeting of agency goals
   d. The opportunity for participation in the determination of methods and procedures
5. Self-actualization needs
   a. The opportunity for personal growth and development in the police management position

      b. The feeling of self-fulfillment (i.e., the feeling of being able to use one's own unique capabilities, realizing one's potentialities)

      c. The feeling of worthwhile accomplishment

To obtain a full range of answers concerning the police executive's feelings about his or her position in terms of fulfilling his or her needs, three rating questions are recommended: (1) How much of the characteristic was connected with your police management position? (2) How much of the characteristic do you think should be connected with your police management position? and (3) How important is this characteristic to you? It is obvious that if the manager is to operate successfully, this hierarchy of needs must be satisfied. Maslow warns us that executives vary in terms of how much of each need has to be fulfilled and which needs have priority; however, some attention in any organization has to be given to these needs if managers are going to feel that they are being rewarded for their efforts. Herzberg has tried to operationalize a similar scheme.

Herzberg's Hygiene/Motivators Approach to Job Satisfaction

Frederick Herzberg feels that the externally generated, traditional kick-in-the-pants approach, which he calls **KITA,** has not worked (1975: 13):

> KITA—the externally imposed attempt by management to "install a generator" in the employee—has been demonstrated to be a total failure. . . . The absence of such "hygiene" factors as good supervisor-employee relations and liberal fringe benefits can make a worker unhappy, but their presence will not make him want to work harder. Essentially meaningless changes in the tasks that workers are assigned to do have not accomplished the desired objective either. The only way to motivate the employee is to give him challenging work in which he can assume responsibility.

Herzberg looked at what he called **hygiene factors** contributing to job dissatisfaction and found in a sample of 1,685 employees that these factors contributed 69 percent to job dissatisfaction and only 19 percent to job satisfaction, whereas what he calls **motivators** contributed 81 percent to job satisfaction and 31 percent to job dissatisfaction. Police managers who wish to be effective in motivating their employees and even themselves need to be aware of these dimensions of job satisfaction. Herzberg's chart (Figure 5–2), outlines his findings. As can be seen, Herzberg's positive motivators are similar to those of Maslow. However, Herzberg also gives specific recommendations concerning how, for example, a police manager might apply these motivators to members of his or her management team (1975: 19).

Herzberg's approach is to apply what he calls motivators to management personnel. He does this by relating certain principles to the motivators involved. By removing a certain number of controls but still keeping the principle of accountability, he feels that personnel will retain a sense of responsibility and

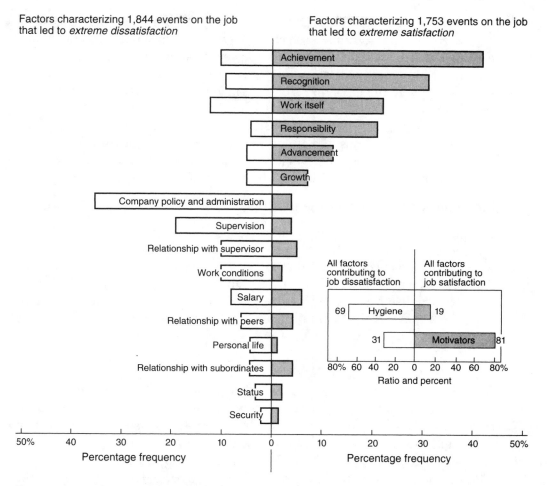

Factors characterizing 1,844 events on the job that led to *extreme dissatisfaction*

Factors characterizing 1,753 events on the job that led to *extreme satisfaction*

Achievement
Recognition
Work itself
Responsiblity
Advancement
Growth
Company policy and administration
Supervision
Relationship with supervisor
Work conditions
Salary
Relationship with peers
Personal life
Relationship with subordinates
Status
Security

All factors contributing to job dissatisfaction

All factors contributing to job satisfaction

| 69 | Hygiene | 19 |
| 31 | Motivators | 81 |

80% 60 40 20   0   20 40 60 80%
Ratio and percent

50% 40 30 20 10   0   10 20 30 40 50%
Percentage frequency   Percentage frequency

FIGURE 5–2 Herzberg's factors affecting job attitudes.
(*Source:* Reprinted by permission of *Harvard Business Review*. An exhibit from "One More Time: How Do You Motivate Employees," by Frederick Herzberg [January/February 1968]. Copyright © 1968 by the Harvard Business School Publishing Corporation; all rights reserved.)

personal achievement. He emphasizes that by holding individuals increasingly accountable for their work, a sense of responsibility and personal recognition will be achieved. Along this same line, he recommends giving personnel an area of work for which they are responsible, which will result in a sense of achievement, responsibility, and recognition. Decentralizing authority and thus allowing more job freedom should also bring about an increase in these three areas. Internal recognition is obtained by sharing periodic reports with personnel as well as supervisors. Personnel are seen to achieve growth and learning through the handling of new and more difficult tasks. Finally, growth, achievement, and responsibility are increased by allowing personnel to become experts through the handling of specialized tasks.

The whole idea of motivating employees is an important concept begun by Herzberg that continues today through the concept of empowerment. *Empowerment* is defined as allowing employees to actively participate in setting and achieving department or unit objectives. This results in a sense of ownership and pride in the tasks that are performed (Garner, 1993: 4). In the police case studies in which empowerment as a concept was presented, the main motivators were those described by Herzberg that lead to extreme satisfaction. Police managers also must pay attention to hygiene factors because officers and staff may leave for better-paying organizations. As with any participative management scheme, the chief must be able to share and delegate power.

McGregor's Theory X and Theory Y

Douglas Murray McGregor's approach to management is similar to Herzberg's insofar as McGregor's advocates an industrial humanism that would provide a check against the autocracy created by stifling hierarchical discipline (McGregor, 1978: 188–92). See Table 5–2.

Most police organizations currently operate according to **Theory X.** It will take a great deal of commitment for departments to develop the more modern approach of **Theory Y.**

Theory Z

McGregor's management approach talked about a humanistic approach to management. However, we have a corporate culture that involves both **high touch,** that is, the humanistic approach for terms of personnel management skills, and the use of high technolgy for day-to-day business. John Naisbitt, author of *Megatrends,* in his book *Re-inventing the Corporation,* states that "the old bureaucratic layers are giving way to the more natural arrangements of the new information society" (Naisbitt and Aburdene, 1985: 36). This is also true of police managers, who have to learn new ways of processing information. However, as Naisbitt and Aburdene state, "Information is no substitute for thinking and thinking is no substitute for information" (1985: 149).

It is not simply information or using a new technology. As Peter F. Drucker states, "The 'new technology' is entrepreneurial management." It is a management that knows how to use the new technology in a context of being able to motivate the workers to be efficient and loyal to the organization (Drucker, 1986: 11). The latter is actually a reformulation of McGregor's humanist approach but in the context of the new technology.

One approach to the use of both high touch and high technology is **Theory Z,** as characterized by the following (Ouchi, 1981: 60–79):

1. There is a guarantee of lifetime career and employment in the agency.
2. One's career develops with different jobs throughout the agency rather than being limited to one specialization.

TABLE 5–2 *McGregor's Theory X and Theory Y*

THEORY X (TRADITIONAL, HIERARCHICAL MANAGEMENT)	THEORY Y (HUMANIST, PARTICIPATORY MANAGEMENT)
1. Management is responsible for organizing the elements of productive enterprise—money, materials, equipment, and people—in the interests of economic ends.	1. Management is responsible for organizing the elements of productive enterprise—money, materials, equipment, and people—in the interests of economic ends.
2. With respect to people, this is a process of directing their efforts, motivating them, controlling their actions, and modifying their behavior to fit the needs of the organization.	2. People are not by nature passive or resistant to organizational needs. They have become so as a result of experience and organization.
3. Without this active intervention by management, people would be passive, even resistant, to organizational needs. They must therefore be persuaded, rewarded, punished, and controlled. Their activities must be directed. Management consists of getting things done through other people.	3. The motivation, the potential for development, the capacity for assuming responsibility, and the readiness to direct behavior toward organizational goals are all present in people. Management does not put them there. It is a responsibility of management to make it possible for people to recognize and develop these human characteristics for themselves.
4. The average person is by nature indolent—he works as little as possible. He lacks ambition, dislikes responsibility, and prefers to be led. He is inherently self-centered, indifferent to organizational needs. He is by nature resistant to change. He is gullible, not very bright, and the ready dupe of the charlatan and the demagogue.	4. The essential task of management is to arrange organizational conditions and methods of operation so that people can achieve their own goals best by directing their own efforts toward organizational objectives. This is a process of creating opportunities, releasing potential, removing obstacles, encouraging growth, and providing guidance.
5. Management is by control.	5. Management is by objectives.

Source: McGregor (1978).

3. Decisions are developed relying on a high-technology total information system.
4. Management is characterized by the use of modern information and accounting systems, formal planning, management by objectives, and formal means of control of the system by management.
5. Decision making is initially consensual and democratic, where employees take a great deal of time agreeing to changes and talking about it. When a decision is made by top management, everyone is expected to go along with it and carry out the new decision.

The Japanese style of consensus building is foreign to American management philosophy as well as police management, which tends to be autocratic in dealing with individuals. However, some of the principles of the Type Z approach are already characteristic of many police organizations, including a lifelong career and both a formal and an emotional support system for the individual officer. Police management is used to giving orders from the top, and the Japanese group culture may not work in America. On the other hand, American police managers dealing with the new information society may want to look at ways of building a consensus before major decisions are made in a police agency. Some of the mechanisms of decision making and placing of responsibility and authority lower down the chain of command might work for some departments. Access to new technology and information processing all the way down to the line officer may mean that the police management of the twenty-first century may have to look at new ways of making decisions and become more flexible in the granting of authority to first-line supervisors and line officers.

Blake and Mouton's Managerial Grid

The **managerial grid,** another approach that focuses on management style, relates it to the two orientations of (1) a concern for people by management and (2) a major concern for production. In this case, Blake and Mouton are concerned with large-scale organization development and executive development in relation to five theories of managerial behavior (Blake 1975: 162). See Figure 5–3.

This is a program based on behavioral science concepts drawn primarily from the organizational development approach to management. The author's objective, through various training programs, is to bring the organization around to the 9,9 part of the grid with a maximum concern for both people and production using a team concept. Some of the training approaches include the following (Blake, et al. 1975: 163–64):

1. *Laboratory-seminar training.* Twelve to 48 individuals are assigned to be members of problem-solving teams with face-to-face feedback. The focus is on managerial styles rather than personal behavior characteristics.
2. *Team development.* The focus is on the operating practices of the agency once the ground rules and relationships have been established.
3. *Intergroup development.* Group-to-group working relationships within the organization are established on an operational level.
4. *Organizational goal setting.* The groups work on specific problems (e.g., union-management relations, promotional policies). "The goals prove to be 'practical' when managers who must implement them also establish responsibilities for implementation."

Finally, using a case method similar to the Harvard Business School approach, specific problems are worked out by the management-organizational development teams, and the approach is stabilized as a permanent working relationship for the organization. The authors, working with Barnes and Greiner, implemented their approach in one industry and came to these

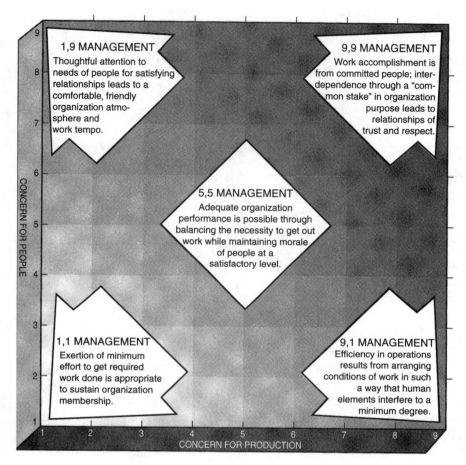

FIGURE 5–3   Blake and Mouton's managerial grid.
(*Source:* Reprinted by permission of *Harvard Business Review*. An exhibit from "Breakthrough in Organization Development," by Robert R. Blake, Jane S. Mouton, Louis B. Barnes, and Larry E. Greiner [November/December 1964]. Copyright © 1964 by the Harvard Business School Publishing Corporation; all rights reserved.)

conclusions concerning the type of organization that can successfully implement their approach (Blake, et al. 1975: 181):

> Demanding but tolerant headquarters
>
> An enthusiastic and involved top manager and senior management group
>
> Educational strategy that effectively and continuously builds team problem solving and mutual support into work-related issues
>
> An organization whose work requires some interdependent effort and common values

Most police agencies have the potential to implement this approach for a good deal of the organizational procedure in the department. However, many have a long way to go to meet the conditions necessary to implement this organizational development strategy. Because this strategy can give members of the management team an insight into their individual working philosophies and how these philosophies affect their superiors, peers, and subordinates, this approach to managerial leadership operates best where there is no pressure to make immediate decisions.

CONCLUSION

The art and style of proactive leadership is based on talent, experience, and training and formal education. Proactive leaders are goal oriented and have the ability to communicate their vision and the agency's mission to all members of the department and to the community. They have had a variety of learning and leadership experiences on their way to the top of the organization hierarchy. They look on critical situations not as problems but rather as leadership opportunities.

The greatest dilemma facing police managers once they have achieved higher-ranking positions is in the area of continuing training and education. The focus of police training courses today remains directed to line and supervisory personnel on operational skills and not to executive development. Many large departments and state training agencies are just beginning to fill this void with management courses for chiefs and their deputies and higher-education degrees in criminal justice management as a formal or informal norm for promotion. To this day, we begin our own management seminars with the question, What is the latest book or article you have read regarding police management? Unfortunately, the question draws much nervous laughter, which forces us to conclude that greater attention must be directed to management training.

The chapter also introduced the leading organizational theories related to proactive police leadership. These range from the traditional concepts found in every management course (Maslow's hierarchy of needs, Theory X and Theory Y) to newer concepts (chaos, TQM, reengineering). Each concept has an application to a wide variety of department and management problems in police organizations. However, no single concept represents a quick fix for departments with serious problems.

QUESTIONS FOR REVIEW

1. Make a chart comparing styles of leadership along a continuum, from totally democratic leadership to totally authoritarian leadership.
2. Create your own theory of leadership, and defend this theory in terms of maximizing employee morale.
3. Defend or attack Herzberg's eternal triangle as it applies to a local police agency.

4. Is Maslow's hierarchy of needs relevant to police work? Why or why not?

5. Explain why McGregor's Theory X and Theory Y is so popular among textbook writers concerned with police leadership. Would this theory be useful in a local police department? Why or why not? Would it make sense in terms of a police department of 10 professionals or fewer? Explain.

6. Analyze and apply the managerial grid to a large metropolitan police department that has a corruption problem.

7. Review the theories concerning leadership, and choose the one that you consider best suited for a midsize police department. Defend your choice.

CLASS PROJECT

The challenges and dilemmas of leadership are often portrayed in the popular media. Take a visit to your local video/DVD store and select a work that deals with the leadership issues and theories presented in this chapter. Focus also on the issues confronting subordinates who must deal with their supervisors. Some of our favorites include *Band of Brothers, Full Metal Jacket, K19: The Widowmaker, Training Day, Copland, Sum of all Fears, Green Mile,* and *Schindler's List.*

BIBLIOGRAPHY

BLAKE, ROBERT R., ET AL. "Break-through in Organization Development." In *Business Classics: Fifteen Key Concepts for Managerial Success.* Cambridge, Mass.: Harvard University Press, 1975, pp. 159–181.

BUTTERFIELD, RONALD W. "Deming's 14 Points Applied to Service." *Training,* 28, no. 3 (March 1991), pp. 50–59.

"The Emotionally Intelligent Worker." *Futurist,* March 1999, p. 14.

DRUCKER, PETER F. *Innovation and Entrepreneurship.* New York: Harper and Row, 1986.

FARR, JAY. "Review of the Pentagon Attack—9.11." Presentation to WMD Training Workgroup for State and Local Police Academies and Campus Law Enforcement, Louisiana State University, Baton Rouge, La., March 26, 2002.

GARNER, RONNIE. "Leadership in the Nineties." *FBI Law Enforcement Bulletin,* 62, no. 12 (December 1993), p. 4.

GATES, BILL. *Business at the Speed of Thought.* New York: Warner, 1999.

GOLEMAN, DANIEL. *Emotional Intelligence.* New York: Bantam, 1995.

———. *Working with Emotional Intelligence.* New York: Bantam, 1998.

GUILIANI, RUDOLPH. *Leadership.* New York: Hyperiors, 2002.

HALBERSTAM, DAVID. *The Reckoning.* New York: William Morrow, 1986.

HALL, RICHARD H. *Organizations: Structures, Processes and Outcomes.* Upper Saddle River, N.J.: Prentice Hall, 1996.

HAMMER, MICHAEL. *Beyond Reengineering.* New York: Harper Business, 1996.

HAMMER, MICHAEL, and JAMES CHAMPY. *Reengineering the Corporation*. New York: Harper Business, 1993.

HERZBERG, FREDERICK. "One More Time: How Do You Motivate Employees?" In *Business Classics: Fifteen Key Concepts for Managerial Success*. Cambridge, Mass.: Harvard University Press, 1975, pp. 13–22.

HOLPP, LAWRENCE. "Making Choices: Self-Directed Teams or Total Quality Management?" *Training*, 29, no. 5 (May 1992), pp. 69–76.

KATZ, DANIEL, and ROBERT L. KAHN. *The Social Psychology of Organizations*. New York: Wiley, 1966.

KATZ, ROBERT L. "Skills of an Effective Administrator." In *Business Classics: Fifteen Key Concepts for Managerial Success*. Cambridge, Mass.: Harvard University Press, 1975, pp. 23–35.

LIKERT, RENSIS. *New Patterns of Management*. New York: McGraw-Hill, 1961.

———. *The Human Organization*. New York: McGraw-Hill, 1967.

———. "Profile of Organizational Characteristics." In John P. Robinson, Robert Athanasiou, and Kendra B. Head, eds., *Measures of Occupational Attitudes and Occupational Characteristics*. Ann Arbor: Institute for Social Research, University of Michigan, 1969, pp. 276–280.

MCGREGOR, DOUGLAS MURRAY. "The Human Side of Enterprise." In *Classics of Public Administration*. Oak Park, Ill.: Moore, 1978, pp. 187–193.

NAISBITT, JOHN, and PATRICIA ABURDENE. *Re-inventing the Corporation*. New York: Warner, 1985.

NATIONAL ADVISORY COMMISSION ON CRIMINAL JUSTICE STANDARDS AND GOALS. *Police Chief Executive*. Washington, D.C.: U.S. Government Printing Office, 1976.

NATIONAL COMMISSION ON LAW OBSERVANCE AND ENFORCEMENT. *Wickersham Report 14, Police*. Montclair, N.J.: Patterson Smith, 1931, reprinted 1968.

OUCHI, WILLIAM G. *Theory Z*. New York: Avon, 1981.

PORTER, LYMAN W. *Job Attitudes in Management: Perceived Satisfaction and Importance of Needs*. Berkeley: Institute of Industrial Relations, University of California, 1964.

———. "Need Fulfillment Questionnaire for Management." In John P. Robinson, Robert Athanasiou, and Kendra B. Head, eds., *Measures of Occupational Attitudes and Occupational Characteristics*. Ann Arbor: Institute for Social Research, University of Michigan, 1969, pp. 148–150.

PRESIDENT'S COMMISSION ON LAW ENFORCEMENT AND THE ADMINISTRATION OF JUSTICE. *The Police*. Washington, D.C.: U.S. Government Printing Office, 1967.

SILVERMAN, ELI B. *NYPD Battles Crime*. Boston: Northeastern University Press, 1999.

WAYNE, LESLIE, and LESLIE KAUFMAN. "Leading in Turbulent Times." *New York Times*, September 16, 2001.

WEBER, MAX. "Power and Bureaucracy." In Kenneth Thompson and Jeremy Tunstal, eds., *Sociological Perspectives*. Middlesex, England: Penguin, 1961.

XEROX. "The Xerox Quest for Quality." Rochester, N.Y.: Xerox, 1991.

6

PROACTIVE COMMUNICATION AND INFORMATION MANAGEMENT

KEY TERMS

all-channel communication

assumption

bypassing

chain of command

decoding

directive

duty manual

feedback

GO

inference

Johari window

medium

MEMO

network

overgeneralization

SO

SOP

subscript

symbol

TOP

"Y" communication

Laptop computers, palm computers, cell phones, e-mail, and the need for encryption have moved communication beyond standing orders and paper forms. The twenty-first-century police department is quickly moving to electronic forms of communication while still depending on paper orders, radio communication, and the telephone. However, human-to-human communication still needs organization, good grammar, and clarity. Policing is still largely a human enterprise delivering human services to citizens.

This chapter will look at the analysis, organization, and conceptualization of police communication. A persistent issue among all police organizations involves communication between all members of the department and between department members with the external environment. This simple premise has been made more complex with innovations in e-mail, faxing, and video communication. The communication system in an organizational setting is based on the human element and design. As Whisenand and Rush discuss in their textbook on supervision (1993), information, statements, views, instructions, and policies are transmitted through various kinds of messages that can often vary in length, form, and content. The purpose of this chapter is to discuss communications theory and the basic forms by which managers operationalize communications.

COMMUNICATION DEFINED

According to Richard A. McDonnel in his chapter on information management for *Local Government Police Management* (1977: 406), "Communication is essentially a social affair involving the sharing of information." He goes on to add, "The ultimate conclusion was that the most valuable tool that could be made available to the police officer, on whatever specific assignment, was *information*." This broad-based approach to communication encompasses the essentially two-way street of basic human interaction as well as the more narrow approach of technological communication. The emphasis is always on the sharing of information between two communicators. Communication should never be one-way. The more sharing that is involved, the clearer the message.

In most police departments, communication has traditionally included dispatching, radio communication, and records. These essentials of good policing must be part of any well-ordered management plan for communication. However, police information management entails more than these technological aspects. Information management also includes, as McDonnel emphasized, communication as a social affair, involving the sharing of information between two or more human beings. The emphasis for proactive management is on the sharing aspect of communication.

In one-way communication, the chief gives orders to his or her subordinates. The subordinates then give orders to the line officers, and some action is expected to take place. Conversely, the social sharing of information is essentially a two-way process. When we talk to anyone, we expect **feedback.** This feedback could be as varied as a nod, a stance, an answer to a question, an agreement to orders, or a recommendation to modify orders. The recognition and feedback that we continually receive keep the communication process clear. Feedback enables the sender to know that the message was sent, received, and understood in some manner by the receiver.

Thomas C. Neil has summarized the typical model of communications that is in most general use (1980: 17):

> A typical model . . . contains the following parts: the *sender* of the original message; the *receiver* of this message; *encoding*, which is the translation of personal meaning into symbols; *decoding*, which is the reverse of encoding; and *channel*, which is the means by which stimuli are sent and received [author's emphasis].

The sender could be a police chief, and the receiver could be a line officer. The encoding is normally in the form of an order in writing, such as a standard operating procedure (SOP). **Decoding** takes place when the line officer reads the order and attempts to place it in behavioral terms. The channel in this procedure is the written order that is transmitted through a standard communication process.

The chief might, for example, be worried about the line officers wasting time talking to each other on duty. Let us also assume that the chief happens to be authoritarian. The following is a paraphrase of an actual order in an actual department:

Standard Operating Procedure, Order 538.71

No sworn officer shall converse with another sworn officer while on duty for more than two minutes, unless the conversation shall consist of information concerning official duties.

The chief has encoded his concern into an order. The receiver, the line officer, decodes the message: "I'd better watch the time I spend socializing and having coffee with the other officers. I might have to justify that time in terms of some departmental business. That two-minute limit really doesn't make much sense given the nature of our patrol duties. So I'll ignore the two-minute part of the message, but I'll watch the time I spend socializing." The line officer also took a look at the **medium** of the message: an official order. The officer will take this message more seriously than if the officer had heard a rumor that the chief was worried about officers' socializing too much.

The channel has also been called the "medium by which the message is sent." It can be the difference between a rumor and a written memorandum. Teletype messages are expected to be short, fact-filled pieces of information. An incident described in a teletype message would have different details and content than the same incident reported in a newspaper story. An officer telling a fellow officer at a social affair about the incident might fill out the story with details and colorful words that would never appear in an official report. The incident may be the same, but the messages are decidedly different. The media used to convey the messages—teletype, official report, newspaper story, casual conversation at a social affair—change the messages.

Although we do not agree with McDonnel that the medium is the message, since there is content to every message, we do agree that every police manager has to be aware of how different communication media can affect the interpretation of the content of messages. Thus police managers have to use both the formal and the informal communication system to send different kinds of messages. By using both media effectively, chiefs will find that they can communicate effectively and receive both informal and formal feedback to their messages. In the two-minute talking-limit example, it is hoped that this chief will receive feedback through informal channels that the memorandum is unrealistic. Then, if the chief has developed any good communication skills, he or she will modify the message to meet the needs of the line officer.

ENCODING AND DECODING: THE MEANING OF MEANING

Whenever we use language, we are taking an incident and encoding it into a prestructured formula. General semantics indicates that the symbol is not the thing and the map is not the terrain. **Symbols,** which include all words, stand for something else. When we pull down a map of the ocean, we do not get wet because the map is a symbol for the wet ocean—the map is not the ocean itself. Therefore, the map, and words, are something less than an immediate apprehension of the ocean. In short, a map of the ocean is less than the experience we would have standing on a sandy or rocky beach, listening to ocean sounds, smelling the ocean smells, and gazing at the endless horizon. What does this mean when we try to communicate?

We all talk in **subscripts.** Subscript 1 might be what the sender means by a word. The various receivers might be receiving subscripts 2 and 3 and so on. Let's try an illustration.

Officer Smith tells Officers Jones and Brown that he arrested a juvenile in a tough section of town on his duty shift, late at night. Officer Smith is thinking of a blond-haired, middle-class boy who had run away from home and found himself in a tough neighborhood. Smith's juvenile is $JUVENILE_1$. Officer Jones, who knows that neighborhood, might be thinking of a young tough who smokes marijuana, has black hair, and runs with a gang. Jones's juvenile is $JUVENILE_2$. Officer Brown might be thinking of a young girl he had picked up recently in that neighborhood for prostitution. She is a crack user. Brown's juvenile is $JUVENILE_3$. Unless there is some kind of feedback to Smith's message and a clarification from Officer Smith, the symbol *JUVENILE* might lead to some real problems in this communication.

Very simple words—for example, *desk, car,* or *juvenile*, can refer to a number of different actual things or types. Language is actually a form of shorthand. It is hard for every communicator and receiver to have experienced everything that they may want to discuss. The shorthand of language is used where general descriptions of the symbols are accepted until specifics are added. However, in the case of symbols, people normally add their own subscript, thereby shaping the reality of the spoken word into a picture that may or may not be meant by various communicators. It is necessary to add subscripts to the word symbol since the word symbol can never encompass all the empirical referents. The symbol is often used to describe a particular sensory experience, for example, that middle-class juvenile boy with blond hair that Officer Smith picked up while on duty last night.

A perfect process would occur when the encoder and the decoder know exactly what each symbol means and what the relationship of each symbol is to every other symbol. This happens in simple mechanical means of encoding the decoding, such as Morse code. You have a symbol chart, and you simply relate the dots and dashes to the symbol chart and come out with letters. However, encoding and decoding language and orders entails a more complex process prone to error. Continual feedback to the encoder, explaining what the symbols means to the decoder, keeps messages clear.

FEEDBACK

Two-way communication is always clearer than one-way communication. One-way, hierarchical communication lacks the essential feedback that tells the encoder that his or her message has been decoded in the manner he or she desired. With no feedback mechanism, the encoder/sender will not know if the decoder/receiver will receive the message in terms of (1) JUVENILE$_1$, or (2) JUVENILE$_2$, or (3) JUVENILE$_3$.

To have consistency in message communication, the decoder must have the same basic understanding of the encoding language that the transmitter has. The receiver must decode the message and fulfill the intentions of the person doing the transmitting. That is one reason why law enforcement officers often use codes and other shorthand devices. They know that the receiver—that is, another police officer—will understand the message since the decoding content of the message has already been agreed on. Thus, when an officer hears the code for an officer in trouble, he or she knows that this message (1) demands immediate action and (2) has top priority.

Feedback is what makes management aware of problems in the communication process. Orders sent down the line may get lost if there is no feedback. For example, there could be a fairly general order issued concerning checking certain businesses at night. Sergeants would then detail this duty to specific officers in the area during the times specified. However, the police administrator may have no idea that action is taking place unless there is feedback. The administrator needs to know at a minimum (1) if the message was clear and specific enough, (2) what kind of action took place as a result of the message (order), and (3) what modifications should be made to the message as a result of the actions taken or not taken.

Who Communicates to Whom, and How?

When we consider communication in context, we are looking at a situation. Is the situation an emergency, or is it routine? What are the ranks of the message sender and the message receiver? Will citizens be receiving the message? Who communicates with whom, and how are the elements to be considered in communication? Let's look at some examples.

A judge tells a citizen that he is convicted of a crime and will be sent to prison. The context is the court setting. The result is a change of status of the individual from civilian to prisoner. The context is charged with authority, and there is a powerful difference in the status of the judge and the citizen who is about to be sentenced.

It is of vital importance that top police management understand the effects of their communication within the context of authority relations. We also have to consider what audience hears the message (e.g., civilians or uniformed officers). The chief can take an officer aside and reprimand him or her for wearing a sloppy uniform. Or the chief can communicate this at lineup in front of fellow officers. Or the chief can give the officer the same message while the officer is engaged in an investigation in the presence of news reporters. It is the same message but different audiences. It also makes a difference whether it is the chief of the department or some fellow officer making the same statements. In this case, it is the same statement, different message. It is obvious from these examples that managers who wish to communicate clearly have to understand

1. The authority context of any message, giving the relative status of the sender and receiver of messages
2. the audience receiving the message
3. the effect of the message on both the person receiving the message and the audience that may also be hearing the message

The style of delivering messages deserves consideration, too. Messages from police commanders and other management personnel in law enforcement tend to be brusque, unfeeling, and in the form of orders. In a tense street confrontation with immediate potential violence, for example, this might be the correct approach. However, in many situations, this brusque approach will only tend to alienate line officers and citizens.

A commander could tell a line officer, "You are ordered to change your vacation time because the department needs more personnel at that time." Or the commander might say, "I know that you planned this vacation time and that it is important to your family. However, we have a special event and we really need the extra coverage. I would appreciate it if you would change your vacation time, or maybe you could trade with another officer who has that time off. Try to work something out. You know if we can't work something out, I'm simply going to have to draft an order. I would rather not do that. Could you see me in a couple of days concerning this matter? I really appreciate your help here. Thanks." What did we accomplish with the second version of the message? The commander told the officer that he knew and felt sorry about inconveniencing the officer's family. He also told the officer that no matter what, the department was going to need the extra officers. He also gave the officer some flexibility in fulfilling the departmental need. Yes, it would have been easier to have simply written the order. However, the second message would make for a department with much higher morale than a department that simply writes orders.

In the second message, the police commander was also telling the officer to use his support **network.** In every police department, over the years, everybody owes somebody for something. It could be simply a cup of coffee after a bad moment. It could be some help with a family affair or backup in a difficult situation. That is the nature of the police business: A supportive network of fellow officers is built up over the years.

What is important for an officer to learn—from the first day on the job—is that one of the officer's strongest psychological and emotional support resources is the existing network of fellow police officers. This means that when messages go out, even though they are hierarchical in form, they are actually going to a network. The network exchanges messages continually with everyone. Given all the messages a police officer receives and sends from his or her fellow officers in one 24-hour day, each officer would be surrounded by so many lines that it would be hard to see the officer in the midst of this concentration of messages. This networking approach to communications is often called **all-channel communication.** All-channel communication is a participatory management style with communication channels open between all parties.

Most departments, although deeply imbedded in the police network style of communication, have an official departmental style of formal communication called *chain communication.* Chain communication is the chain-of-command style where person 1 does not communicate with person 4 except through persons 2 and 3. This means if a line officer wants a message to reach the chief, he or she has to give that message to the sergeant, who gives it to the lieutenant, who gives it to the captain, who gives it to the chief or even the deputy chief. It also means that if the chief wants to communicate with that line officer, he or she has to go through the **chain of command.** The communication process is most rigid going from the bottom to the top. A top officer may bypass part of the chain of command.

However, while this formal process is going on, at least two interesting phenomena are occurring. First, the networking effect takes over, and all kinds of people in the uniformed department have either part of the message or one of various versions of the message. The informal communication network in policing is very strong.

Second are the friendships that have been formed that skip a rank. For example, sergeants do not normally become great friends with lieutenants; captains and sergeants are more likely to become friends, as are lieutenants and line officers. This means that the message may, in fact, informally skip some of the chain of command while formally going up or down the chain of command. Except for routine communications that are noncontroversial, the chain of command is a cumbersome communication process. The chain of command becomes especially costly in two important areas: distortion of messages and the time it takes a message to reach the bottom and have the feedback reach the top.

Another style is **"Y" communication,** in which two superiors communicate to the same subordinate. The subsequent communications may go from subordinate to subordinate. An example of this is one secretary with two bosses. Pity the poor secretary when she receives priorities or contradicting messages from each boss. If this style is to work at all, there must be a key communicator at the junction of the "Y." Then two bosses give messages to the key communicator, who sorts out priorities and eliminates contradictions and sends the messages to the subordinates. In general, "Y" communication systems fail because of the built-in conflicts.

OBSTACLES TO COMMUNICATION

People fail to communicate with each other even when they truly want to reach out and communicate. A major problem is that we communicate through symbols. As mentioned earlier, what one officer means by *juvenile* may incorporate violent actions, whereas another officer may consider a juvenile to be a smart kid who talks back. Police officers rely on penal law definitions, in part, for the official purpose of arresting offenders.

Another problem is **inference,** as when we attach meanings to a message that the message giver never intended to be part of the communication. For example, Officer Brown says, "We need to roust that kid." Officer Smith says, "Yeah, I know. I'll go over to his house tonight, stand him up against the wall, threaten to arrest him, and see if he will agree to let me take a look at his room." Officer Brown says, "No, I didn't mean for you to do that. I think we could just stop by and question him concerning the crime. He has helped us in the past, and there is no reason why he wouldn't help us again." The key is "I didn't mean for you to do that." Officer Smith created a message by inference. He thought that the original message included content that was not actually in the message—by inference.

Officers make **assumptions** about messages that become part of the message but were not meant to be part of the message originally. Assumptions exist when you think that there are specific grounds for the content of a message, but these grounds may not exist. Assumptions may be warranted or unwarranted. For example, Officer Brown may feel that a juvenile who has a record of violent crime and with whom he has dealt personally in violent situations may, in fact, be responsible for a violent crime. Now, if there is evidence that matches the youth's profile, Officer Brown may be correct. He has a warranted assumption concerning the potentiality of that particular youth's behavior. His assumption is based on reasonable evidence.

On the other hand, Officer Brown may have known that another youth comes from a bad family. He may have arrested that particular youth's brother for burglary and known that the youth's sister was a drug addict. Therefore, when there is a burglary in the vicinity and that youth is seen around the burglarized premises, Officer Brown may assume that the youth from the bad family is a likely suspect. Unknown to Officer Brown, this particular youth is an honor student at school and has just been awarded an athletic scholarship to a good college. Officer Brown's assumption is unwarranted because it is not based on good evidence. In fact, by saying that all members of the family are most likely bad, he has unfairly labeled every child in that family.

Bypassing, another obstacle to communication, occurs when two people talk to each other and miss each other with their meanings; that is, the same words can mean different things to different people. Bypassing is a common occurrence in the ordinary life of a line officer. For example, a sergeant asks a line officer to finish up a sick officer's reports. The line officer then stays overtime to finish the reports. The next day, the sergeant tells the line officer that he meant for him to finish the reports during normal duty hours. The line officer says, "I thought you meant immediately!" Another obstacle to communication, **overgeneralization,** is basically a variation using unwarranted assumptions. A common example is when a police officer refers to someone as "a good guy." The general meaning of a "good guy" is someone who is helpful and will assist anyone recommended by the officer simply by dropping a name; for example, "Hello, Dr. Forest. This is Sergeant Francis over at Riverview Station. I spoke to Detective Williams, and she said you're someone who could assist me on a case I'm working on."

The "good guy" is simply a generalization that is used for network referencing and assists in daily communication within and between complex organizations. However, in situations involving misconduct or corruption, a "good guy" is someone who may assist in a coverup or turn the other way "to see nothing." A "good guy" can also be one to bend the rules; for example, "Lou, be a good guy and don't report that dent I put in the fender of car 203 last night."

Proactive police managers need to have a basic awareness of these problems and prepare strategies that provide for better communications before miscommunications occur.

THE JOHARI WINDOW

The **Johari window** is a basic exercise in communication flow that monitors how information is passed from the police manager to others and back again according to interpersonal style. It is a basic two-by-two table based on (1) information known and not known to yourself about yourself and (2) information known and not known to others about you (see Figure 6–1).

When you and others share information, this occurs in region I, the *arena*. Mutually held information becomes the most valuable approach to communication. If others know information and you do not know the information, you may suffer a *blind spot*, region II. It is a personal handicap for the manager since he or she cannot understand the behavior of others if he or she lacks essential

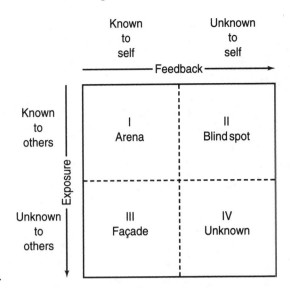

FIGURE 6-1   Johari window.

information concerning why they behave the way they do. This was involved in the example of Officer Brown thinking that a youth from a bad family was a likely crime suspect. Brown lacked information that the youth was an honor student with a good career ahead of him. This was Officer Brown's Johari window blind spot.

When you have information that is unknown to others, it is called region III, the *façade*. The façade is a protective front where information is withheld from others to protect the self. The question is how much defensiveness should be tolerated before the withholding of information interferes with good management communication.

When information is unknown by self and others, it is considered an area of potential creativity, region IV, *unknown*. As management communication becomes more effective, the unknown becomes known, and region IV diminishes in size.

The two basic processes for the creation of information are exposure of self in terms of giving information, including information about emotions and attitudes, and the feedback process, where others expose themselves and give information to self. The model calls for a climate of mutual exposure to achieve maximum communication and thus calls for an open, democratic management model. This would normally be in direct contradiction to the strict hierarchical chain of communication model.

The model calls for four types of communication in relation to the two processes of exposure and feedback. Type A is an impersonal style characterized by minimal exposure and feedback: the traditional police chief–dominated department. Type B minimizes exposure of self but attempts to maximize feedback. Management distrusts others but wishes emotional and general information from others. This normally results in a basic management model based on mutual distrust, often reverting back to type A.

Type C is an overuse of exposure to self and a minimal use of feedback from others, a giant ego ride. This is the "cult of personality" police chief with idiosyncratic policies. You generally know what the chief is thinking, and the chief does not care what you think or feel. This style triggers feelings of hostility and resentment from the general officer population, especially the line officer population. The preferred style according to this model of communication is type D, open and frank communication—that is, a mutuality of maximum exposure and feedback. It is hoped that over time a context of trust and creativity will be created in the police department. Given the various demands of police departments, especially for emergency procedures, this is difficult to achieve. Type D communication is most often found in a police department dedicated to a democratic management style. It is often tied in with some variation of team and community policing styles.

The basic exercise is for individuals to answer a number of questions concerning their exposure/feedback styles and then, using standard scores for the model, see where they stand in terms of the four regions. You then examine various strategies that would bring the maximum number of members of the police management team into the open communication model designated as the arena. According to the model, the larger the size of the arena in relation to the other three regions, the more effective will be the management communication model used by the police organization. The secret seems to be to bring employees, colleagues, and supervisors into a feedback/exposure position that will maximize their communication with one another in the arena.

This type of model can be useful—up to a point. Everyone in the department is expected to spend some time communicating his or her emotions to everyone else in the department to gain maximum feedback, but there probably is not enough time to fulfill this requirement completely. Also, normal psychological health demands a certain amount of private space for individuals. Exposure and feedback in terms of producing some basic honesty in human relations can be useful for getting the job done, but spending too much time discussing emotional relationships can become counterproductive. After all, the department still has to arrest criminals and deal with myriad social problems.

As with other theoretical models drawn from the social sciences, business, and public administration, the Johari window communication model also needs to be tempered by the reality of managing real police departments with real problems. For too long, police organizations have been closed and rigid in their authoritarian management style. Conversely, however, reliance on feelings and democratic ideals will not work for police organizations either. The proactive approach is a tempered approach: consultative with enough exposure and feedback to do the job with sensitivity and efficiency. It is a forward-looking communication model where feedback becomes part of the planning process, and the planning process is a consultative process for all members of the police agency. This is an effective use of the Johari window as another analytic tool used to bring about consultative, effective communication.

OPERATIONAL COMMUNICATIONS

This type of communication normally takes the form of writing. Written documents have one advantage in that they can be referred to with ease. They are normally more precise than informal and verbal communication. They provide a certain consistency of standards, along with rules and norms for the police organization.

Certain objectives need to be established and met if the organizational goals of the police agency are to be accomplished. These goals are achieved through the six objectives of written communication:

1. To make plans operational
2. To carry on day-to-day operations
3. To relay and interpret policies
4. To provide details for activity completion
5. To complete assignments satisfactorily
6. To provide for evaluation and feedback

Types of Orders

Specific assignments are needed to give managers and line officers direction concerning how to carry out the vital activities of the police agency. Traditionally, these written activities have taken the following forms:

SOP	Standard operating procedure
TOP	Temporary operating procedure
GO	General order
SO	Special order
MEMO	Memorandum

First, there are the written **directives,** which are necessary for the daily operations of every police agency. They may be gathered into a volume called the **duty manual.** These directives are expected to operate consistently over time. While duty manuals should be kept up to date, they generally change in only minor ways from year to year and from one police administration to the next.

SOPs: Standard Operating Procedures.   These are the procedures that will affect the total department on an ongoing basis over time. They have a specific starting date but no ending date. They are changed by the creation of a new **SOP** that says the old SOP is no longer in effect. They are numbered and dated for filing purposes.

Basically, all new SOPs should be incorporated into an annually revised duty manual. This way, all the officers in the department will have access to an organized set of rules. When this does not occur, the duty manual becomes dated, and new officers have to resort to file cabinets of SOPs to learn the basic rules of the department. Even experienced officers can become confused when the duty manual consists of hundreds of files.

SOPs include what is and is not acceptable communication under a wide variety of circumstances and authority relationships as they are met in the normal course of police business. The duty manual is simply an organized way of having all of the SOPs in one place.

TOPs: Temporary Operating Procedures.   These have all the characteristics of SOPs with one exception: They have a termination date. That means that on the termination date, the **TOP** is no longer in effect. Of course, they are dated and numbered. Events that are handled by TOPs would be one-time events, such as sporting events, parades, and visits from dignitaries.

GOs: General Orders.   Like SOPs, these are numbered and dated and distributed to all personnel. The **GO** is created for informational purposes, whereas the SOP and the TOP are operational orders. Legal changes, such as those created by search and seizure cases, would be GOs. New procedures for handling drunken persons according to new state directives would go out as GOs. Relations with mental health or probation agencies might go to all personnel in the form of GOs.

SOs: Special Orders.   **SOs** are numbered and dated and refer only to personnel matters. They are very specific and refer to such items as transfers, job assignments, promotions, and disciplinary actions.

MEMOs: Memorandums.   **MEMOs** are written to communicate information or orders of short duration. These are dated but not numbered. They are generally for very limited distribution. MEMOs are used when a verbal order is adequate but putting the order in writing will eliminate all possible misunderstandings. (They might apply in such mundane matters as having a patrol car fixed by the police mechanic.) MEMOs are especially useful in maintaining continuity of information to a staff that is operating on various shifts over a 24-hour period and a seven-day week.

Basically, these directives are of vital importance for the maintenance of communication in a department. All should be written with care. There should also be a time period when these various types of communications are either destroyed—all copies—or codified in some manner. Operational orders that last over time should be incorporated in the duty manual. Personnel matters become part of permanent personnel files when they are significant enough to affect an officer's performance appraisal. Occasionally, the department may wish to resort to microfilm or microfiche for the storage of some of these materials. However, at the end of a specified period, most of this paperwork should be destroyed. This normally entails a change in some state laws concerning document retention.

The Effectively Organized Directive

Directives can be effective, or they can be jumbled and vague. They should be both precise and concise. Police departments tend to drown in a sea of ill-conceived, badly worded phrases. If the department is to be effective, these general rules for writing directives should be followed:

1. The contents of the directive must be achievable and reasonable. To carry out the order, the recipient must have the means and the ability to act effectively.
2. The instructions concerning the directive should be sufficiently detailed to ensure the completion of the task. An example might be a directive concerning the disassembly of weapons. A directive that simply says that the officer must be able to assemble and disassemble his or her weapon does not contain enough information. Detailed information is needed concerning the variety of weapons at an officer's disposal. The directive might also include specific training procedures for officers needing additional information and skills to disassemble specific weapons.
3. Directives should use normal English language that would be understandable at the tenth-grade reading level. Although all police officers are high school graduates, they may not be able to read at a twelfth-grade level. Many college texts at the freshman level are being written with a tenth-grade vocabulary. It is vital that technical terms be clarified in simple English.
4. Orders that need explanation should be given some justification concerning why the order has been issued. This enhances morale, compliance, understanding, and two-way communication.
5. Orders should be edited. First drafts should be examined for clarity by a close colleague of the originator. If possible, the directive should be edited by a member of the management team other than the author. After editing for clarity and use of language, you can then decide whether the order actually means what you meant.
6. The directive should be of sufficient importance to the management of the department to justify its being written. Given today's proliferation of paperwork, directives should not be written unless there is a proven need. In general, a directive should
   a. be an order of some complexity,
   b. extend over a fairly long period of time,
   c. go to more than one officer, and
   d. affect a fairly large number of personnel.

Basically, the more personnel affected by an order, the greater the justification for putting the order in the form of a written directive.

7. A feedback mechanism should be part of every order. Some directives may be followed up automatically, but this does not always happen. A police management team is only as good as the information at its disposal. Management needs to know if the directive (1) was carried out, (2) in what manner, and (3) with what effect.

THE DUTY MANUAL

The codification of the written rules of the police agency is variously called the *operations manual*, the *procedures manual, rules and regulations*, and even *standard operating procedures*. The usual title is *duty manual*.

The duty manual governs many aspects of an officer's private life as well as his or her behavior during a tour of active duty. Most duty manuals are very specific. For example, concerning a part-time job, a duty manual may specify that the officer needs the permission of the department. It may also specify the length of hair, the length of sideburns, and the width of mustaches. Officers are expected to be fit and ready for duty at all times. They are often expected to carry their badges and even their guns while off duty.

The duty manual of the London Metropolitan Police in 1829 specifies how the duty manual was expected to be used (Reith, 1956: 135):

> The following General Instructions . . . are not to be understood as containing rules of conduct applicable to every variety of circumstance that may occur in the performance . . . of duty; something must necessarily be left to the intelligence and discretion of individuals; and according to the degree in which they show themselves possessed of these qualities and to their zeal, activity and judgment on all occasions will be their claims to future promotion and reward.

Duty manuals were rightly expected to contain some flexibility in terms of interpreting the general rules of the department. A professional police agency must leave a great deal to the intelligence and discretion of the individual police officers.

O.W. Wilson ably stated what is now considered the normal definition of the duty manual (1963: 33):

> DUTY MANUAL: Describes procedures and defines the duties of officers assigned to specific posts or positions. . . . Duty manuals and changes in them should be made effective by general order; the changes should be incorporated into the first revision of the duty manual.

The duty manual usually has a chart of the organization and some job descriptions. This is to fulfill the need for consistency and fairness in normal departmental regulations.

A typical duty manual might describe the general duties of a sergeant as follows:

> A sergeant of police will be responsible for the enforcement of all laws and ordinances, department rules and regulations, orders, procedures, discipline, punctuality and attendance, appearance, good order, and efficiency of members of the police agency within assigned jurisdictions.

Besides this general job description, a good duty manual would also outline some of the specifics of the job of sergeant:

1. Train, direct, supervise, and evaluate members in their assigned duties. Recommend remedial or disciplinary action for inefficient, incompetent, and unsuitable members.
2. Inform his or her relief of all necessary police matters.
3. Report to his or her commanding officer absentees and any deficiencies in personnel and equipment.
4. Ensure that recovered property is handled in accordance with department orders.
5. Without unnecessary delay, visit all officers of the force on duty in the territory subject to supervision. Advise them of all important information or details relating to the efficient operation of the department functions and inquire as to the conditions of the member's post. Report all matters requiring police action to the desk officer.
6. Visit at least twice during each tour of duty the patrol officer(s) assigned to special posts, hospitals, or other details located within the territory subject to supervision.

Of course, many other duties, both general and specific, could be spelled out. However, this gives some idea of how the duty manual is organized and how specific it should be. The duty manual must provide enough detailed information so that the job can be accomplished with the maximum amount of efficiency and yet not be so detailed as to abolish that necessary use of intelligence and discretion that makes for good police work.

The duty manual is a clear, concise, and logical way in which to order procedure in a police department. It also helps to order normal business by describing the duties of each rank of officer and the way in which the ranks relate to one another. It can and does succinctly incorporate procedures to be used for such emergencies as natural disasters. The general rule is that the operations mandated by the duty manual, along with personnel procedures, must be of a recurrent nature. This is something that the department will have to deal with on an ongoing basis.

Some duty manuals become very specific. This happens when one-time incidents are used to create a general rule. Often, these rules become unrealistic, and good management must always be on the lookout to make sure that the duty manual specifies rules and regulations that are efficient, humane, and, above all, reasonable.

Examples of some very specific rules from an actual duty manual follow:

No smoking on the job. No member of the department shall smoke on post or beat while in uniform or while conducting an investigation of any nature.

No entering places where intoxicants are sold. No member of the department, while on duty, shall enter any place in which intoxicating liquors are sold except in the immediate performance of his or her duties.

No inebriation off duty. No member of the department shall drink intoxicants at any time off duty to the extent that he or she becomes unfit for duty.

Two-minute limit for talking on duty. Conversations of more than two minutes between members of the force on patrol, unless concerned with their immediate performance of duty, are prohibited.

Many regulations are either too specific or too general to be obeyed. Their purpose often derives from the chief's need to exert internal control over his or her officers. With modern civil service legislation, it is difficult to fire a police officer. Therefore, the chief may write down a number of rules simply to pinpoint an officer who is violating the rules. This is not a good way to handle internal police discipline since many of the rules are unfair and cannot be enforced in a just manner.

CASE STUDY

Rules and Regulations

Are trivial rules enforced so that autocratic and often unprofessional police leadership can exert control and harass professional police officers? The following is adapted from a newspaper account of an actual incident.

A man ran into the station house with a loaded shotgun. After the man was disarmed, the officers saw that he was cut with a knife, and the man was taken to a hospital. Meanwhile, a television camera crew interviewed an officer who had handled the incident. The officer appeared on television . . . hatless! The commissioner gave the officer an official reprimand for appearing hatless on television. The officer said, "In the confusion, I inadvertently left my hat in the station house."

The commissioner decided not to take disciplinary action against the officer but gave out a strongly worded memorandum the next day concerning proper dress. The commissioner stated in his memorandum, "Any violations of the procedures and regulations concerning the wearing of proper and mandated articles of uniform will be dealt with severely. Disciplinary action, which could result in charges against a violator, will positively be taken. The most flagrant violation of the regulations concerning the wearing of uniform relates to not wearing the police cap."

This is a good example of the misuse of the duty manual. A normal regulation referring to the wearing of a uniform, neatly, has been used to harass police officers in the performance of their duty. Adverse publicity was generated, and the chief looked like an incompetent and a petty tyrant.

If the rules of the duty manual are seen as being unreasonable and used to "set up" officers, the agency will have a growing morale problem. The duty manual will not be seen as an effective instrument for the implementation of policy. When the rules are clear and reasonable, the duty manual can legitimately be used for official reprimands and even the firing of an officer. In general, the rules contained in the duty manual should

1. Be kept short so that everyone can read and understand the total manual in a relatively short time
2. Be consistent
3. Be reasonable
4. Conform to principles of good management
5. Be humane
6. Be enforceable
7. Be stated in an unambiguous manner
8. Be related to the actual operations of police procedures
9. Not deal with the trivial
10. Be written in a good English format with a professional tone to the choice of words

It is especially important (see principle 10) that any words that denote an autocratic, arbitrary manner should be deleted.

An effective and fair duty manual is an essential tool for the efficient operation of a police agency. If an officer is reprimanded or fired because of failure to comply with the rules and regulations of the duty manual, he or she must be able to see some essential honesty and fairness involved in this procedure. At that point, the duty manual becomes an effective management communication tool and legitimately produces general rules for the social control of the civil service police force by the police management team.

PROACTIVE ORGANIZATIONAL COMMUNICATION MODEL

A proactive communication model must include the following elements:

Planning
Organizing
Operationalizing
Evaluating

All these elements have to be related to an ongoing feedback system if this communication model is to operate effectively. These elements are naturally related on an ongoing basis to actual operational procedures and the objectives of the police organization.

The proactive communication grid in Figure 6–2 shows how these elements are interrelated. The double-headed arrows show that each element has to be related to every other element of communication and that all the elements need to be related to an effective feedback system.

FIGURE 6–2   The proactive communication grid.

Planning

1. Identifying needs
2. Forecasting
3. Researching and developing
4. Ensuring conformity to goals and objectives
5. Using staff in developing the planning process
6. Getting input from police personnel
7. Consulting and coordinating with outside sources
8. Making decisions

Organizing

1. Hiring personnel
2. Training
3. Creating rules of procedure and directives
4. Developing auxiliary services and infrastructure of support
5. Servicing, capitalizing, and maintaining physical plant and equipment
6. Drawing up implementation orders

Operationalizing

1. Supervising implementation procedures
2. Providing continuing direction and control
3. Coordinating various parts and segments of the police agency
4. Coordinating with outside agencies

Evaluating

1. Developing standards that lead to operationalized evaluations
2. Listing criteria of success
3. Developing evaluation procedures and relating them to empirical standards of success

4. Creating a centralized data file
5. Creating a centralized staff of research analysts
6. Outlining inspection procedures
7. Obtaining feedback with recommendations for planning

CONCLUSION

The central concern of police communication is mutual, unambiguous under-standing among all communicators. Communication can and does shape the nature of the police organization. If it is all one-way, from the top to the bot-tom, and with little or no feedback, the department will be organized in an au-tocratic manner. The autocratic style, although effective in terms of rapid response, actually fosters inefficiency. Management needs to know which or-ders are effective in operation and which are not, and this is determined through a solid feedback system. With such a system, ineffective orders can be eliminated or modified until they become effective.

For communication to be understood by all parties involved, orders should be written in a consistent and organized manner. Unambiguous com-munication is especially important in police work, where the professional officer has to respond time and again to citizens in crisis. The line officer has to be an effective communicator, but this can be achieved only when the officer is supported by an orderly process of departmental communication. With so much time spent on paperwork, as well as on giving and receiving orders, all police organizations should develop an ongoing, proactive com-munication system.

QUESTIONS FOR REVIEW

1. Interview a police supervisor about one-way and two-way communi-cations. How do the supervisor's answers compare with the recom-mendations of this chapter? How do you account for similarities and differences?
2. Imagine you are a patrol officer on the radio discussing a tense hostage situation with a commanding officer. Identify (1) the sender, (2) the receiver, (3) the encoding, (4) the decoding, and (5) the channel.
3. If you were a supervising officer of a patrol operation, describe the feedback system you would institute. Defend the efficiency of the system in terms of its information-flow patterns.
4. One of the major problems in communications is misunderstanding and misinformation. Explain how you would deal with these two problems if you supervised a small, rural police agency. Also identify how you would deal with these problems in terms of communica-tions with other police agencies in nearby jurisdictions.

5. List the major obstacles to communications in the day-to-day work of a police agency, and detail the major strategies you would use to overcome these obstacles.

6. If you were a police commander, in what part of the Johari window would you locate yourself, and why? Choose another student in class, and state where you would locate him or her in the Johari window. Justify your answer.

7. Imagine that you are a supervising officer. You have noticed that many of your patrol officers are wasting too much time in stores. It is not just a question of gaining information and community support but an inefficient use of the officers' time. Specify the type of order (SOP, TOP, GO, SO, MEMO) you would issue, and justify your choice in the face of a grievance from one of your officers concerning your order.

8. Define *reasonable* in police management terms, and apply this definition to what you would consider a reasonable duty manual.

9. Apply the proactive communication approach to a local police department. How would this communication model work in the field in the midst of the usual practical difficulties?

CLASS PROJECT

The best illustration that shows the complexities of communication is giving directions to another person. Select a location that is not too well known near your classroom which requires a classmate to make three to four different moves over a period of about five minutes. Go to the location and leave "markers," which for this exercise can be notes, envelopes, or some piece of paper that you tape to the wall or leave with another person.

Present the directions to your classmate and have them go to the location, take one marker and then bring the marker back to you. If they are successful, then have the classmate do the same thing with another person and continue. If they are not successful, then select another person and see what happens.

During this time, apply the main concepts of communication theory to your instructions and reactions with your fellow classmate.

BIBLIOGRAPHY

BLANCHARD, WESLEY. "Digital Dictation a Boon for Warwick." *Police Chief*, 57, no. 3 (March 1989), p. 53.

COLTON, KENT W., MARGARET L. BRANDEAU, and JAMES M. TIEN. *A National Assessment of Police Command, Control, and Communication Systems*. Washington, D.C.: National Institute of Justice, 1983.

CORDNER, GARY W., and ROBERT SHEEHAN. *Police Administration*. Cincinnati: Anderson, 1999.

MCDONNEL, RICHARD A. "Information Management." In Bernard L. Garmie, ed., *Local Government Police Management*. Washington, D.C.: International City Management Association, 1977.

NEIL, THOMAS C. *Interpersonal Communications for Criminal Justice Personnel*. Boston:Allyn and Bacon, 1980.

REITH, CHARLES A. *A New Study of Police History*. Edinburgh: Oliver and Boyd, 1956.

REYNOLDS, JEAN, and MARY MARIANI. *Police Talk*. Upper Saddle River, N.J.: Prentice Hall, 2002.

SCHROEDER, DONALD J., FRANK LOMBARDO, and JERRY STROLLO. *Management and Supervision of Law Enforcement Personnel*. Binghamton, N.Y.: Gould, 1995.

WHISENAND, PAUL M., and GEORGE E. RUSH. *Supervising Police Personnel*. Upper Saddle River, N.J.: Prentice Hall, 1993.

WILSON, O.W. *Police Administration* (2nd ed.). New York: McGraw-Hill, 1963.

PROACTIVE POLICE TECHNOLOGY FOR THE TWENTY-FIRST CENTURY

KEY TERMS

automatic vehicle monitoring (AVM)

Compstat

computer-aided dispatch (CAD)

crime mapping

electronic form

laptop

mobile digital communications (MDC)

mobile digital terminal (MDT)

modus operandi

National Crime Information System (NCIC)

911 system

regional communication system (RCS)

World Wide Web

Welcome to the mid-twenty-first century. The paperless police department has become a reality as all police forms have been digitalized and can be accessed from every police car. Instant communication includes encrypted messages through laptop computers and special police palm computers for individual officers. Each police car and officer can be located through global positioning. Global communications provide individual officers with criminal information locally, nationally, and cross-nationally. Officers can access information on international drug smuggling as easily as they can obtain a report of a stolen car.

Officer Rauke spots a car with an erratic driver. She types in the license plate and is given a stolen car identification. The data screen indicates that the car may contain a dangerous felon. She calls for backup. Officer Rauke accesses the computer chip in the fleeing car, which immobilizes the car. Backup arrives and the driver steps out of the car. With backup standing by, the officer scans the back of the suspects hand for DNA identification. A warrant for felony drug dealing with positive identification comes up on the officer's handheld computer screen. A secure arrest is made.

Science fiction or reality? Only two pieces of technology cited here are not available at this moment. The electronic auto-stopping chip is on its way. DNA identification needs some work on field sampling devices and a larger data bank. If the problem is a burglary, a computer map would give all incidences of burglary in the last two months in the immediate area, along with a list of suspects who are not in custody and the suspects' addresses. A suspect-sorting program could then be used to create a short list for investigation. Witness descriptions could provide sorts based on gender, race, height, and so on.

A major problem for police managers in the next decades will be controlling and organizing technology. Technology must not drive police decisions. Police decisions need to be controlled by human police managers. A major problem with **World Wide Web** information is that there is simply too much information for any human being to comprehend. Another problem is identifying information sources that can be trusted. Today, rather than adding features, program developers are learning how to simplify programs to a more useful, human scale. Technology that makes life easier on police managers has to be on a human scale.

When police went from walking a beat to patrolling in cars, the technology drove policy. Police rode around in their patrol cars and were insulated from the public. It took a proactive use of community policing to move beyond the isolated officer in the patrol car. The 911 universal emergency phone number has once again resulted in technology controlling management policy. The enormous growth of service calls from 911 created a reaction-driven department overwhelmed by these service calls, from critical emergency calls through trivial calls. The proactive police manager institutes a split force, prioritizes the responses to calls, and takes control of this unique communication system (see Chapter 8 on patrol).

As all institutions become more information driven, linking information access to policy making through computers becomes vital. This information has to be managed through proactive planning, packaging, and accessing. Computer mapping makes good use of crime data and 911 information to pinpoint hot spots and to help decide different levels of service in different neighborhoods at specific times during a day. Linking information from radio, 911, and computer communication to policy decisions concerning deployment and even personnel decisions is a smart use of information.

Laptop computers become useful only when there is a management system in place to take advantage of them. Secure information channels and organized reporting systems have to be in place before any computer is turned on. This means that the computer is only as good as the information put into the system and the intelligent use of the computer information system by human beings. If you put bad information into your computer system, a bad decision will come out of that system. The bottom line is that police managers need to make sure they are in charge of the system. If that is accomplished, the system becomes a valuable tool for every police manager, from a village police chief to the police commissioner of a major city.

COMPUTER APPLICATIONS FOR INFORMATION MANAGEMENT

Before computerization, paper records got lost, created storage problems in terms of bulk, and were hard to handle. In order not to lose information, great redundancy was built into all police information systems. It took considerable time just to find things. Files would occasionally get misfiled or lost, with disastrous results. Accessibility and security were in constant conflict. How could police management provide instant access to all records for appropriate police personnel while keeping the access limited in terms of security considerations? There was no solution until the computer. Now information can be processed in a rapid manner, while access is limited by use of security codes.

However, the computer is simply a tool, a machine, to process information. The computer does not create solutions, manage problems, or become a panacea for all solutions. Police managers manage and solve problems using the computer. Given this warning concerning the overreliance on computer technology, we also have the opposite end of the spectrum—that is, fear of computers. There are still police managers who cannot operate without hard copy (a piece of paper) and who are fearful concerning the use of computers. These managers need to be retooled or retired. This may sound harsh, but the realities of the information age in terms of an efficient means of organizing so much information are overwhelming.

When mainframe computers first came into existence, data were generated with huge amounts of output overwhelming police managers and administrators. When one of the authors first did a survey run of police attitudes on an old IBM 360, he ran hundreds of tables, creating a paper pile over three feet high. The second thing he did was throw away this three-foot-high stack of tables. The police managers, with their mainframes, also threw out hundreds of feet of output. Why? What happened?

It was so easy to get the data and the data output that police managers asked for everything without thinking through what they wanted. Managers need to use computers as tools and ask for only the output they need to get their jobs done in the most efficient manner. The ability to ask the right question is the basic talent needed for police administration.

Police managers need to free up their time in terms of detail while having access to essential information. The areas that lend themselves to the optimum use of data processing for the police manager are as follows:

1. *Payroll:* periodic payroll records, actual paying of personnel, and analysis of payroll records in relation to time sheets, court time, sick time, and so on, with enhanced fiscal planning ability.
2. *Budget:* fiscal control of the existing budget with up-to-date record of expenditures; fiscal impact of any emergency/overtime procedures; planning capability in terms of generating future budgets; the manipulation of fiscal data for mayors, city managers, legislators, police management, and so on.
3. *Purchasing* of uniforms, supplies, equipment, and so on. Data processing provides controls for purchasing, especially when correlated with maintenance and depletion schedules, for example. The cost of uniforms provided for personnel by contract in many departments can be a large expenditure that benefits from good control. Also, there is a need for controls in terms of bulk versus retail purchases with the use of a cost/benefit subroutine.
4. *Vehicle maintenance,* including patrol cars, boats, bicycles, and so on. Detailed records are needed to get comparative cost per mile and such information as the optimum trade-in mileage.
5. *Annual report:* gathering the necessary data to justify department operations to the legislature, administrative officials like mayors and county executives, and the general public.
6. *Inventory:* providing adequate control of department assets along with replacement schedules and similar details.
7. *Personnel:* maintaining current personnel records, allowing convenience of updating with a subroutine that permits selective information to be readily available to the police manager.
8. *Training records:* maintaining information related to the past, ongoing, and future training of the members of the department. This has become increasingly important in today's litigious society, where training is an issue in relation to liability.
9. *Scheduling of personnel.* One of the most difficult tasks is to schedule 24-hour, seven-day coverage for patrol officers patrolling a community. The police manager needs to consider a number of variables, such as shift changes, vacation time, rest days, and training time. There is also a need to have enough personnel to cover effectively the different numbers of calls for service at different times. Computer software programs have come a long way in making such scheduling easier.
10. *Community relations:* maintaining records on the speaker's bureau, tours of the department, press and media relations, and so on, including the use of desktop publishing for newsletters and news releases.

Productivity can be increased throughout the department by using data processing, at least in the following areas:

Crime reports	Found property
Evidence control	Warrant files
Modi operandi	Court appearances
Traffic tickets	Burglar alarms
Vacant house checks	Daily bulletins
Hazardous conditions	Computer mapping

The use of microcomputers, which allow data input into systems, enhances the ability of administrators and officers to have instant and adequate input and output of essential information. Security codes and encryption can protect files while providing access to authorized personnel.

Computer-Aided Dispatch

Computer-aided dispatch (CAD) enhances calls for service from the public and the dispatching of police cars and personnel. The CAD system verifies addresses, determines the beat of incidents, and gives a case number and priority number to each call. Some systems even report "dangerous histories." The computer automatically records all calls and can recommend to the dispatcher a choice of units to dispatch to the call. The time of dispatch is recorded as well as time on the scene and time the unit is free. Thus, CAD provides real-time monitoring of vehicle status and a continuously updated incident file, allows supervisors to monitor the incident status, and provides telephone, radio, and digital activity statistics. The system can also generate crime statistics reports, flag deviations and trends, automatically generate required data for resource allocation models, and provide on-line information for line supervisors, administrators, and officers. The system's features are summarized in Table 7–1.

CAD, combined with information laptop technology and computer mapping, can supply a great deal of data and services to officers in their patrol cars. Its uses in technologically smart departments include the following:

1. Allocation of resources
2. Patrol planning
3. Hotspot identification
4. Analysis of service calls for proactive planning
5. Notification to emergency fire and medical services
6. Improved officer safety through driver and vehicle identification
7. Crime mapping for service call responses
8. Accessing multiple data resources, including stolen cars, outstanding warrants, and other calls to same location
9. Verification of all data
10. Improved service through the use of information technology

Mobile Digital Communications

Mobile digital communications (MDC) provides a nonverbal means of transmitting dispatch and status messages between a law enforcement communications center and patrol units as well as accessing data files by both the communications center and the patrol units. A **mobile digital terminal (MDT)** is the basic element of the system, along with an encoder and decoder

TABLE 7–1   *Features of Computer-Aided Dispatch Systems*

FUNCTION	CAD-RELATED FEATURES
Needs identification	Complaint clerk enters incident-related information into the computer
	CAD adds routine data (incident number, date, time, etc.)
	Computer checks data validity (address verification, etc.)
	Computer assigns a call priority
	Computer assigns a beat number
	Computer checks for previous incidents at this address or related data (e.g., hazardous materials information)
	Computer estimates length of time until a unit can respond to the call
	Backup operator handles lengthy calls
Status monitoring	CAD provides real-time monitoring of vehicle status (and vehicle location, if tied to automatic vehicle monitoring)
	CAD maintains a continuously updated incident file (assigned, unassigned, cases cleared, etc.)
	Supervisor can monitor unit and incident status by calling up complaint clerk and dispatcher displays
Response/adjustment	Operator has computerized files of frequently used telephone numbers (ambulance, tow, etc.)
	CAD routes incident information to appropriate dispatcher
	Computer provides a summary list of incidents in the system
	Computer recommends which unit(s) to select (based on estimated unit location)
	Computer automatically times calls and raises a "flag" if a call takes longer than a specified time
	Computer provides telephone, radio, and digital activity statistics
	Unit status can be updated automatically (with mobile digital communications) or through an operator (using CAD or a separate system)
	Personnel can automatically sign in as "available" at shift change using remote terminals
	Database queries can be handled automatically (via mobile digital communications) or through an operator (using CAD or a separate system)
	Dispatcher can have one, two, or more video monitors
	Computer maintains temporary situation files (e.g., traffic and street repairs)
	CAD supports coordination of multiple unit (and/or agency) assignments to one incident
	CAD provides a basis for officers' daily incident reports
	Computer handles routine log-off operations (e.g., adds time and date, and stores in closed incident file)

Function	CAD-Related Features
Resource management	Computer periodically generates crime statistics reports for state and federal use
	Computer reports can be generated off-line
	Computer provides statistics by any desired set of categories (type of crime, area, time of day, etc.)
	Computer generates management reports from CAD for departmental use (e.g., incident logs, officer activity logs)
	Computer can automatically flag deviations or trends
	One-time, special reports (e.g., particular crime activity patterns) can be generated
	Computer can automatically generate required data for resource allocation models
	On-line information is available via remote terminals for patrol personnel, sergeants, etc.

Source: Colton et al. (1983: 23–24).

with message switching and display of messages controlled by a microcomputer. The goals of MDC are as follows (Colton et al., 1983: 43):

To reduce voice congestion and expand the communications capability of existing radio channels using digital signals that have a higher transmission rate than voice signals

To increase officer effectiveness through easier access to remote data files, which could potentially result in more "hits" (apprehensions and recoveries)

To increase dispatcher effectiveness by relieving the dispatcher of routine data inquiries, patrol status updates, message repetitions, and dispatches of some (noncritical) calls for service

To increase officer safety through easier database access, increased communications capability, and an emergency button on MDT units

To improve message security using digital signals, which are more difficult to decipher than voice messages

To improve accuracy and decrease message repetition using mobile digital terminals that can provide hard copies

To allow selective routing of messages using terminals that can be addressed either collectively or individually, on a "need to know" basis

To allow unattended message reception using terminals that can record messages while an officer is out of a vehicle

Various departments have used MDC with widely varying levels of sophistication.

Automatic Vehicle Monitoring

Automatic vehicle monitoring (AVM) provides the location and status of the vehicle, such as in pursuit, en route to scene, door open, and so on. It is more inclusive than an automatic vehicle location (AVL) system, which simply provides a vehicle's location. Location is provided by four devices: (1) a navigation (hyperbolic) system that uses a radio location technique called Loran C, a system used by ships at sea; (2) a trilateration system that uses radio location from three or more fixed sites; (3) a signpost/proximity system that locates a vehicle through the use of fixed electronic signposts located throughout an area; and (4) a dead-reckoning system that uses computer-assisted instruments to track vehicles on a city map (e.g., utilizing an advanced geocoding system).

The first AVM program, a signpost transmitter system, was installed in Monterey, California, in the early 1970s. Both the St. Louis and the Dallas police departments have installed AVM systems. The stated objectives of the AVM systems are as follows (Colton et al., 1983: 52):

> To reduce response time through reductions in dispatch and travel times
>
> To increase apprehension rates through reduced response time
>
> To improve officer safety by continually monitoring the status and location of police vehicles
>
> To improve dispatch efficiency and coordination by providing the dispatcher with precise data on unit status and location
>
> To improve tactical command and control through on-line direction of such special tactical events as high-speed chases, bank robberies, emergency deployment, and support for covert operations
>
> To improve patrol efficiency and effectiveness through the availability of *direct* information regarding the location and allocation of the patrol force and through the *indirect* realization of patrol officers that they are being monitored
>
> To improve supervision of the patrol force through better on-line supervision of officers in the field and through the use of the management information generated by the AVM system
>
> To reduce voice-band congestion when linked with some type of mobile digital communications

The AVM systems are not without their critics. One reason for the controversy becomes very obvious to both management and line officers: There is greater control and supervision of the patrol force. It stands to reason that if supervisors know the condition of all patrol cars and where the cars are at all times, they also have a pretty good idea of where the patrol officers are and what the status of the patrol officer is. This has great potential for increasing police productivity in terms of service to the public.

911

The **911 system** provides one phone number for calling all police agencies in a geographic area with one central dispatch system. The 911 system has achieved a high degree of acceptance from the police and the public. Generally, when this system is not in existence, it is due to interference by local politics rather than technical difficulties, which have been and can be overcome. A basic 911 system also provides a number of useful features: (1) automatic identification and display of the calling number and address of the caller; (2) jurisdiction selective routing, which allows routing of the 911 call to the appropriate jurisdiction; (3) supplementary dispatch/support data, which give the police beat, fire alarm area, and ambulance zone of the location of the call; (4) internal selective routing, which allows routing of calls to the appropriate operator in large law enforcement jurisdictions; and (5) automatic registered name identification, which automatically displays the name of the person who owns the phone used for the call. Although the 911 system should be adopted by every jurisdiction, there are two major problems that need to be dealt with: (1) duplication of street names and (2) mobile phones that move through too many locations.

Linked to 911 is the **regional communication system (RCS),** whereby a number of law enforcement agencies cooperate in the creation of a common communication network. RCS decreases operating costs, especially personnel and total equipment and installation costs. Jurisdictions are able to afford computer-assisted communication systems that would otherwise be out of reach of their budgets. This approach can also overcome channel congestion problems, coordinate police actions during emergencies, and provide a regional base for attracting outside funding. As with 911, many efforts at establishing a regional communication system have been blocked by petty politics.

A major reason for adopting an RCS is cost savings: Through consolidation, a regional communication system may decrease operating costs (especially personnel-related costs) and total equipment and installation costs. Furthermore, by creating an RCS, cities may be able to afford technologies—such as CAD—that they could not afford on their own.

Ideally, all these systems would be in place, and then, of course, they would be integrated with regional, statewide, national, and international networks. Every police agency in the United States should be able to access information on criminals from all resources.

National Crime Information Center

The **National Crime Information Center (NCIC)** maintains a computerized filing system, including such information as wanted persons, stolen property, criminal history, and information on identifiable persons in relation to investigations of reported crimes. The NCIC system is supported by the federal government and has a national advisory board made up of police administrators from all over the United States. This advisory board makes recommendations to the director of the Federal Bureau of Investigation (FBI) in terms of NCIC policy. Since its creation in 1967, the NCIC has accomplished the following goals (U.S. Department of Justice, 1985: Intro-1):

1. Enhancing the development of state, county, and metropolitan computerized criminal justice information systems, thereby making NCIC information more readily available to the officer on the street
2. Establishing uniformity of coding standards for the exchange of criminal justice information
3. Increasing the probability of criminal detection by providing law enforcement with the timely and accurate information necessary to combat today's highly mobile criminal
4. Improving the overall crime solution rate

With the number of mobile data terminals and agency users currently at 110,000, the system is currently involved in an upgrading program entitled NCIC 2000. The purposes of the enhancements are the following:

1. Establish national distribution system for data sets stored by states instead of keeping a central database
2. Establish the National Fingerprint File, which will allow for electronic transmittal and identification of fingerprints
3. Establish the Alcohol, Tobacco, and Firearms Violent Felon File, which will create files of people who are terrorist suspects or of interest to law enforcement officials

Automated Regional Justice Information System

The Automated Regional Justice Information System (ARJIS) operates in California and is similar to other state data networks, such as the Criminal History and Information Recovery System network in New York State. ARJIS consists of nine components:

1. Arrests and juvenile contacts
2. Automated worthless document index
3. Citations (misdemeanor citations, traffic citations, traffic warnings, traffic accidents)
4. Crime analysis
5. Crime cases
6. Field interviews
7. Master operations index
8. Personnel
9. Property (pawned/wanted property)

Each police agency has one or more terminals that allow on-line access for either inquiry or update activity. For example, the worthless document index deals with forgeries, while crime analysis allows searches by name, partial name, or nickname; date; pawned, stolen, lost, or found property; addresses; and so on. Crime cases allow for searches by **modus operandi,** or method of procedure. It is obvious that when these systems are in place, a great deal of sophisticated information sifting can take place. In California, as in most states, additional information is accessible from standardized files, called the Criminal Justice Information System, which contains six systems:

1. Stolen vehicle system
2. Automated boat system
3. Wanted persons system
4. Criminal history system
5. Automated firearms system
6. Automated property system

The Paperless Police Department

Related to the new changes in computer technology is the transformation that has occurred in report writing and record keeping. Every police activity or crime incident demands a report on some kind of form. The majority of police patrol reports written before 1975 were handwritten; typewriters were reserved for detectives who needed four carbon copies for depositions and court papers. Standardized forms were introduced at this time to assist in data processing for mainframe crime analysis and to reduce the narrative portion of the report. Writing reports and completing forms takes time. Booking processes for the average misdemeanor take about two hours. Police administrators continue to look for ways to reduce the paperwork associated with arrests and investigations.

Today, officers can write reports on small notebook computers located in the front seat of the patrol units. Spell-check functions in these report programs are useful timesaving features.

Laptop computers with forms-based software and smart keys that conform to the police forms can make police more efficient. The paperwork done on an arrest, for example, can be spell-checked and ready for downloading for access by administrators, prosecutors, and defense lawyers. With proper encryption programs and security codes, information can be obtained from data systems throughout the world.

E-mail can be distributed to administrators and can bring experts on-line during an ongoing investigation. Legal statutes, community and human service addresses, and personnel can be directly accessed during routine calls. Information and forms can be printed and handed to administrators and citizens as needed. Everything, from warrant checks and stolen vehicles to mug shots and detailed maps, is immediately accessible.

Record keeping is another problem that is being addressed through imaging technology. The Syracuse Police Department in New York reported that it was making 26 copies of every record or about four million copies a year (*Proceedings*, 1993: 136). To reduce the "paper monster," the department invested in computerized imaging, which scans the record and then stores it on a 12-inch optical disk. One disk can store 35,000 pages. Although paper records have not entirely disappeared, the amount of time and the number of employees devoted to copying and retrieval has been reduced.

New Technologies for Police Managers

What is possible today? Each officer can have a personal locator transmitter that keeps track of the officer and offers hands-free communication. The Remote Control Information System (RCIS) is portable and has full-color video, two-way audio, and officer location and monitors and transmits vital signs. A smart card with storage capacity that turns itself off with tampering will provide secure identification in the size of a credit card. People can be identified with computerized signatures provided by fingerprints, DNA, and voiceprint.

The Advanced Regional Justice Information System, a user-friendly, client-based, PC system, provides information for an investigation or just for a beat officer. Graphics such as computer mapping and photo lineups will be available in the field, along with form-based software for field reports via the laptop.

Each officer will have access to an immense amount of data, including graphic and photographic interfaces for identification of suspects. Officers can interview a victim while calling up an identity kit program to focus on victim image and then compare this to suspect profiles and modis operandi. Eastman Kodak has a writable CD that provides 20 file cabinets full of storage, combining image-processing technology with case-management functions for the detective on the street or in the courtroom. Voice-recognition technology is now available, enabling officers to speak their reports into the system.

The World Wide Web provides incredible services but needs organizing. The International Association of Chiefs of Police has its own Web page, as do agencies such as the Drug Enforcement Administration, FBI, Federal Bureau of Prisons, National Institute of Justice, Supreme Court Decisions, ERIC gopher on juvenile delinquency, Bureau of Justice Statistics, RAND, National Criminal Justice Links, and U.S. Department of Justice. There is also a Criminal Justice e-mail listserv. On-line newsletters are available, such as *American Police Beat*, *Justice Information Distributions List*, *Journal of CJ*, and *Popular Culture*.

The United Nations Criminal Justice Information Network provides a worldwide automated system used for communicating and exchanging criminal justice information, including a gopher-based electronic discussion forum. The United Nations Online Justice Clearinghouse will provide access to criminal justice member holdings all over the world, including an e-mail service.

There are sites called Cops, Help Locate a Fugitive, Internet Crime Writing Network, and many others. For example, Justice Technology Information Network (JUSTNET) "provides information on new technologies, equipment and other products and services available to the law enforcement, corrections and criminal justice communities." JUSTNET provides news and information services, a chat line, a topic board, and data and publication services. For registered law enforcement and correction users, there are data links to agencies that have used the products.

One of the major issues is security, including encryption protocols and privacy for address linkages and chat groups. What if you are tracking a serial killer and want to set up a law enforcement board, data link, and some kind of round-table discussion group? It would be important to *not* transmit this information to the criminal community. Personal encryption, which allows only the receiver to decrypt the message, offers a solution.

Computer-assisted dispatch is being teamed up with record-management systems (RMS) to look at CAD patterns and past patterns—crime locations, vehicle locations, officer response, and so on—to make policy. It acts as a paper for every single incident, with appropriate linkages to police investigation, court, and human service data banks, dispositions, and feedback. There are over 200 RMS companies in the United States that are eager to provide these services to police management. Once the programs are in place, information needs to be entered only once into the system, and then it is on its way to data bank linkages and a proactive management-based information system (PMBIS).

Proactive Management-Based Information System

A PMBIS combines a CAD system and an RMS with linkages to other systems. The innovation here is the use of installed management-based software configured for your police department with this combined system.

One of the best reviews in the field concerning this high technology is found in an article in *The Police Chief*, "High Technology Solutions" (Pilant, 1996). Pilant gives us an example of this type of system: "Dispatch Automation . . . has a Records Information Management System (RIMS) that not only does computer-aided dispatching, records management and mapping but acts as an interface for state and NCIC information for mobile computers; CLUES (Comprehensive Law Enforcement Systems, Inc.), which offers CAD/RMS and acts as a common database so agencies can share information" (pp. 45–46).

Communication between cars and dispatch will also include conferencing, monitoring vehicle location, and in-vehicle information. The chief will know where the vehicle has been on a computer map (and be able to trace a route with time and date), when the door was opened and closed, how long the motor ran, and what its gas mileage is. This makes for close monitoring and data messaging by anyone who has access to the system. Open architecture allows the department to add on system modules from a variety of sources. The RMS capability, along with management software, makes this enormous amount of data usable for policy making.

These systems work best when management can fully utilize them. For example, distributed collaborative planning (DCP) systems that link commands at multiple locations are useful for large departments, regional police problem solving, and interagency collaboration. DCP provides real-time software decision-making models, shared information retrieval, digital video teleconferences, and shared computer desktops, including textual, verbal, digital, and pictorial information. Current and archival data can be shared for homicide investigations and, for example, for crowd control during riots, with each unit providing and sharing information (Rome Laboratory Law Enforcement Technology Team, 1996).

Crime Mapping

Crime mapping superimposes computer-generated data on a city street grid or other map. Data sets are taken from various public agencies, such as:

Demographic data from the Census Bureau

Property tax agencies for location, condition, and paid or unpaid property taxes

Traffic corridor maps, with number of cars using these corridors

Local police statistics and *Uniform Crime Reports*

Local crime and victimization surveys

Court and community corrections files supplying residence and work addresses of parolees, probationers, and court-processed criminals

Licensing units and public health data

This is just a sampling. Information detailing the number and location of various crimes, such as rapes, burglaries, family violence, and robberies, has proved useful.

Some data that can be added to a map include location of offenders, police cars, and medical emergency vehicles using the global positioning system; convicted offenders being tracked by electronic monitoring systems; and hot-spot identification based on police calls to specific locations. Maps also can indicate where schools, fire stations, hospitals, drug markets, major shopping malls, and bars are located.

Hypothesis-generation data with a spatial dimension, such as "broken windows," includes such items as abandoned cars, vacant buildings, litter, graffiti, and houses with a three-year nonpayment of property taxes. These variables are useful for arson investigations when an arson incident map is superimposed over "broken windows" variables.

Relationship data can be graphed to show the following (Rich, 1999):

Distance from an offender's residence to the location of the offender's crime

Relationship between crime and bars and liquor stores

Police interventions and spillover to crime in other areas

Easy access to getaway routes

Property crimes and muggings

Powerful software helps the viewer make sense of disparate data through the use of symbols and color. The New York City Police Department's Crimetac system has a program that summarizes data on a map by shading in such dimensions as number of burglaries, robberies, or muggings. The higher the number of crimes, the darker the shading. This is done also by graphing—by time, hour, day, week, or month—whatever time dimension is most useful.

Chicago's Information Collection for Automated Mapping program lets the police officer or manager zoom in on a particular area and add data to a map of crime incidents, such as elevated rail stops, vacant buildings, schools, or liquor licenses. The system can also create a map that lists all offenses within a specified beat, sector, or district and then display it in a table, such as a bar graph (Rich, 1996). Researchers at the Illinois Criminal Justice Information Authority use the Spatial and Temporal Analysis of Crime program to construct ellipses around dense concentrations of crime. This information is distributed to 200 agencies (Rich, 1999: 7).

Compstat

> Compstat has become synonymous with a proactive style of policing that allows an agency to critically analyze crime data, predict and/or quickly discover 'spikes' and react effectively. (O'Connell and Straub, 1999: 8)

Many police administrators and scholars have asked about the origin of Compstat, and now it can be told. **Compstat** was originally a computer file called Compare Stats for the New York City annual report of crime statistics. It became a management program committed to management accountability at the precinct level and to the lowering of real crime rates. Weekly Compstat meetings have become a basis for planning, coordination, and evaluating crime fighting at the precinct level.

In New York City, from 1994 to 1997, the rates of various serious crimes dropped significantly (Silverman, 1996: 10):

Homicide dropped 50 percent
Rape, over 8 percent
Robbery, over 40 percent
Felonious assault, over 25 percent
Burglary, 37 percent
Grand larceny, over 31 percent
Grand larceny autos, over 45 percent

This real decrease in crime was due to new policies and actions by the New York City Police Department and Commissioner William Bratton. The general contextual and demographic data for New York City changed very little during that time. Hence, the police department can take credit for the successful drop in crime rates.

During Commissioner Bratton's first year in office, two-thirds of the 76 precinct commanders were replaced. Some of the centralized responsibilities for drug enforcement, public morals, and auto theft were transferred to the borough and precinct commands. There was an attempt to integrate detective squads with precinct commands.

Responsibility and decision making were decentralized down to the precinct level, and the precinct commander was held responsible for the level of crime in the precinct. The geography of the precincts was the unit of analysis and control rather than citywide functional units. Specialized domestic violence officers, appointed in each precinct, used a specialized family database to facilitate precinct planning. In the past, centralized databases were difficult or impossible to access. Databases like the Narcotic Investigation Tracking of Recidivist Offenders (NITR), which tracked career felony drug offenders, were made accessible to precinct-level officers and members of the detective and drug units. Access to various intelligence and databases at the precinct level was crucial to the success of the Compstat approach.

At the start of this process, statistical crime data were available only on a six-month basis. Pins pushed into a map with acetate overlays were the main graphic device. At the end of this process, data were available on laptop and other computers on a weekly basis with overlays, computer-generated maps, and graphs. Computer mapping became the basis of the weekly Compstat meetings at police headquarters.

At a 7:00 A.M. Compstat meeting, precinct commanders appear before the police brass to view two huge screens showing the latest crime statistics in the precinct. The meeting is devoted to strategies for fighting crime. Precinct commanders have more authority than they have had in years, but they also have more accountability. The key elements are timely and accurate intelligence, rapid deployment of resources, and relentless follow-up and assessment. Precinct commanders are summoned to the meeting randomly.

If the top managers of NYPD do not like the results, the commanders can be transferred immediately. This has resulted in the loss of experienced precinct commanders. After he retired in 1999, after 20 years on the job, Captain John Munro, commander of the 114th Precinct in Queens, said, "It is much more difficult to be a precinct commander today than it was years ago. You are held accountable for everything, and the hours that the process stole from my family absolutely impacted on my decision" (Flynn, 2000: 29).

In 1999, 66 officers who held the rank of captain or higher retired; in 1996, 65 retired. The pressure was noted by union officials, who said the retirements were greatly influenced by "frustration with a constant pressure to produce, a burden that . . . has fallen particularly hard on precinct commanders as they struggle to secure continuing drops in crime" (Flynn, 2000: 29). It is revealing that in 1995, "more than 70 percent of officers who held the rank of captain had more than 20 years on the job. Today less than 50 percent do" (Flynn, 2000: 34).

When Bratton came in, there was a massive change of precinct commanders, which was well thought of by competent commanders, but the process is continuing, as capable, aggressive precinct commanders leave. As one recently retired middle-management police officer said, "First we got rid of commanders who were not competent but now, we are eating our own." What he meant was that now the competent commanders are leaving because of the Compstat pressure.

According to Eli B. Silverman (1996: 12), this information revolution to "retrieve, organize, disseminate and act on information" has resulted in

> the large increase in quality of life and drug-crime enforcement in all precincts and the flexibility, anticipation and rapid response to problems through attention to gangs, social clubs, crime hot-spots and seasonal fluctuations like summer and Christmas holiday crime.

Compstat pressures and accountability have resulted in flexibility and creative problem solving for crimes that affect the quality of life in a neighborhood. The following case history shows how the process encourages creative solutions to preventing crime. Compstat maps charted a large number of daylight burglaries within a few blocks of schools. After discussing this problem with school authorities, neighbors, and line patrol officers, the precinct commander came up with a unique solution. A bus went around the precinct during school hours. When teenagers were found to be on the street, they were asked why they were not in school. The police then put these students who were playing hooky on the bus and brought them back to their schools. Daylight burglaries went down dramatically. A simple but brilliant solution.

A balanced look at Compstat starts with the judgment that it really does work as a crime-fighting strategy. However, as time passes and it becomes more difficult to bring down crime, it might not work as well, as it places too much stress on precinct commanders. The heart of any police organization is its middle management: sergeants, lieutenants, and captains. It is imperative to keep experienced middle management on the job and to keep what has worked with Compstat and to improve on it.

Compstat Lessons Learned: What Worked

1. Instantly accessible information in an easy-to-understand format
2. Accountability and decision making at the level of unit commanders
3. Wide sharing of information
4. Flexibility and creativity in crime fighting
5. Policy decisions based on hard data
6. Quality-of-life enforcement

Compstat Lessons Learned: How to Make It Better

1. Eliminate unreasonable pressure and stress on street-level unit commanders and their line officers.
2. Once Compstat has brought down crime, do not create unreasonable demands to bring crime down even more when it is not possible. Unreasonable demands on street units can produce police brutality. This political interference in police management creates failure out of success.
3. Integrate computer mapping crime fighting with community policing by sharing information and decision making with community groups.

Compstat is being tried in other communities, including New Orleans, Louisiana; Montgomery County, Maryland; Birmingham, Alabama; and Memphis, Tennessee. Here, there has been investment in hardware and software, a willingness to bring decision making down to street-level units and a major commitment of both resources and management changes.

When Memphis was considering how to use Compstat, William Bratton's consulting firm issued a report stating that Birmingham "lacked a coherent crime fighting strategy, inadequate technological resources, low pay and inadequate promotional opportunities that have led to poor morale in the ranks." The report continued by stating that Birmingham would adopt

> the implementation of a computer-driven crime analysis program to more effectively deploy personnel, conduct weekly meetings at the precinct level, decentralize command structure, and put more responsibility for crime control on commanders in the city's four precincts and upgrade technology including the installation of mobile data terminals in patrol cars. ("Birmingham Looks to Bratton," 1997: 13)

As Compstat and other computer-mapping crime-fighting strategies become more widely used, they will have to be combined with community policing and manage the stress of street-level middle-management officers and line officers.

Compstat has become a planning tool for the twenty-first century by combining extensive crime-mapping data accumulation and reengineering. Vincent Henry, in his *Compstat Paradigm* (2002), sees Compstat as a tool that will be used to involve middle management in the proactive crime-control process. William Bratton, a Compstat pioneer, has been selected to lead the Los Angeles Police Department. Los Angeles is one of the most understaffed departments in the United States with one of the most diverse and multicultural urban communities in the world. LAPD will be a challenge for Chief Bratton's proactive approach.

Defending against Cyberterror and Cyberattacks

Going beyond virus detectors and firewalls, police agencies have to use proactive attacks and defenses to protect the nation's cyberstructure. Cyberattacks and cyberterror come in the following main forms (Ballard et al., 2002):

1. Altering and destroying the contents of electronic files and computer systems.
2. Destroying and disrupting hardware, operating platforms, and programs.
3. Using encrypted messages and steganographic encapsulation in a graphic file or in an audio file to transmit plans for terrorist attacks, incite attacks, and facilitate traditional terrorism. With the present technology these cyberfiles can be either impossible or nearly impossible to find and decode.
4. Using the Internet to raise funds for and promote hate groups, violent political terrorism, and violent terrorist action.

The FBI and the 2001 USA PATRIOT Act have promoted a proactive approach through the use of the Carnivore and Magic Lantern programs, while international surveillance is promoted by Echelon. The FBI's Carnivore is described by the FBI administrator as follows (Levin, 2002: 985):

> It works by "sniffing" the proper portions of network packets and copying and storing only those packets which match a finely defined filter set programmed in conformity with the court order. This filter can be extremely complex and this provides the FBI with an ability to collect transmissions which comply with pen register court orders, trap and trace court orders, Title III interception orders, etc.

Magic Lantern, delivered by e-mail, "records every keystroke used by a suspect for its use by authorities. It is particularly useful for finding passwords and keys to encrypted messages." Australia, New Zealand, the United Kingdom, Canada, and the U.S. National Security Agency use Echelon for "intercepting land and cellular phone communications, e-mails, fax transmissions, web browsing, browsing histories and satellite signals." Of course, there are many programs that can simply take over computer screens through simple e-mail worms. Proactive intelligence-gathering capacity is available now and being used but will invade all privacy all the time. We need to develop sharing protocols with different police agencies, privacy ground rules, free-speech protocols, and really good filters to test the significance of the data. Human intelligence analysis is the most needed police talent in this war on domestic and international terrorists and hate groups. It seems that the USA PATRIOT Act of 2001 has opened many doors for intelligence gathering.

Cross-Jurisdictional High-Speed Notification

The Bowling Green, Kentucky, Police Department has gone from a neighborhood watch phone tree in 1976 to a 2002 high-speed notification that operates in minutes in both secure and nonsecure modes. When a tornado touched down with softball-sized hail that damaged 11,000 roofs, the system notified other police agencies, hospitals, schools, daycare centers, the media, and so on, in minutes. The advance notice to citizens and emergency personnel minimized personal injuries. When a woman tried to pass a suspicious check at one bank, notification went out, and she was arrested within minutes at another bank.

Over 100 scenarios have been tested. The emergency medical service (EMS) system and a multijurisdictional Drug Interdiction Task Force along miles of a major highway have been connected. The department is working with a U.S. Attorney's office to set up an antiterrorist task force notification system. "During a test in March, 2002, more than 90 taskforce members were contacted within six minutes" (Rayner, 2002: 38–39).

There are a number of high-speed notification systems available on the market, and each has to be evaluated to see if it suits the needs of a specific police department. The cross-jurisdictional use of this technology is absolutely vital if local police departments are to be proactively involved in coping with terrorism and regional emergencies.

Law Enforcement at the Speed of Thought

In *Business at the Speed of Thought* (1999), Bill Gates talks about organizations with "digital nervous systems" that include internal and interagency e-mail, public Web sites accessed by the public for government services, electronic forms for all major applications in an organization, and all routine information being handled by computer with a customer service value-added orientation. The last point is the major function of community policing, in which the customers are the citizens.

Gates quotes the ancient Chinese military strategist Sun-Tzu: "Intelligence is of the essence in warfare—it is what the armies depend in their every move" (p. 382). This idea is applicable to police departments as well as businesses, as Compstat has shown us. A police department is as good as its intelligence. Reliable and immediately accessible information equals good management. Bad intelligence makes for bad management decisions.

Gates recommends laptop computers for all knowledge workers. Police officers and their supervisors are both knowledge workers and service providers to citizens.

Kenneth B. Marshall, supervisor of the Ohio State Police, believes in the benefits of mobile data access using laptop computers and wireless network technology brought into a single data system (1996: 9):

> According to a report issued by the Ohio Law Enforcement Automated Data System (LEADS) enforcement officers with in-car data access technology make more than eight times as many inquiries on driving records, vehicle registrations, and wanted persons/property per eight hour shift than do officers without in-car computers.

The officers made more arrests, issued more citations, and felt that, with the increased information, they made better-quality arrests.

The following example helps make the case for law enforcement use of mobile data access. An officer was running random vehicle inquires at a local restaurant and received an alert on the system. A vehicle's owner had both a record of a previous homicide and two current warrants for domestic violence. Backup was called, and the suspect was taken into custody without incident. A passenger with active warrants was also arrested.

Gates (1999: 339–44) gives an example of an ambulance and air medical service in rural Lousiana that uses information technology in depth. It is the largest ambulance company in the United States. The company has 1,200 employees and serves 26 parishes across 17,000 square miles of rough country, including bayous. It handles 500 to 600 calls a day and has $90 million in revenues. Its use of PC-based software reduces the length of all 911 calls by 60 to 90 lifesaving seconds.

Here is how Gates's example might be adapted to a police department: After a police car has been dispatched to the scene of a crime or emergency, software walks the dispatcher through a series of questions to ask the caller. The dispatcher asks about any hazards at the scene, such as a person with a gun, for example. The dispatcher downloads the information to the police car immediately. Police supervisors at the computer-assisted dispatch center consider needed action and then order backup, fire or medical emergency vehicles, and additional personnel.

A search is done for any previous calls made from the address and any criminal record of the names given by the caller. This information is downloaded. A computer map shows recent calls for service made in the area.

A pen chart laptop system on electronic report forms is filled in by the officers in the car to give immediate information to the supervisor concerning the call for service. Once the forms are completed, they are uploaded via remote access to the police information system. All data are automatically encrypted to protect the citizen's privacy and police confidentiality.

Any report that is not filed by the end of a shift is tagged by a supervising police officer and is followed up on. This information will be merged with the police database, and pertinent information will be sent to the courts or jail, when appropriate.

Vehicle maintenance information will also be automatically uploaded and sent to the police fleet supervisor's database. The pertinent parts of the electronic report will be downloaded to booking, if needed.

With these daily reports automatically logged electronically, police managers and supervisors can identify any anomalies and can determine the need to adjust the number of personnel in relation to the number of calls, the time spent on each call, and the identification of hot spots. All police desks will have computer stations, so all this information will be available all the time.

CONCLUSION

In this chapter, we reviewed available information systems and previewed the more sophisticated systems of the future. However, all these systems are limited by the programs that sort and label information and by the human be-ings who use them. Police managers must understand the potential of these systems and be able to use them if they want to manage modern police depart-ments successfully.

Technology must be controlled and understood by human management. Police technology must be human friendly and easily accessible in emergency situations. Training time is expensive and should be kept to a minimum. Police managers need to have technology that enhances clarity of communication rather than causing information overload. Prioritization must be in place along with an information flow system of command capability.

Digitizing standard forms makes for ease of transmission throughout the criminal justice system. The human element is designing forms for clarity and speed of information flow and deciding who needs the information on the forms. This is good management and where today's management needs educa-tion and training. The best technology will not save a badly designed informa-tion flow form such as an arrest form that may be needed by supervisors, investigators, and the courts.

When buying a system and software, police management should select a company that has a good track record, has been in business for a number of years, offers good service support, and can change with new technology. Managers need a system that will work for their department today and for the next few years rather than a complex Star Wars system that few understand. "Keep It Simple!" is a motto that should hang in big letters in every police communication center.

Buy the latest technology that works for your line officers and for your management team. Technology has been improving, and prices have been dropping, but it is still a huge capital investment. Make sure that the system is affordable and that training is available. Place a high priority on reliable, affordable technical assistance from human beings who talk in plain English rather than some obscure technical language.

Most importantly, listen to your top management, middle management, and line officers, and survey their opinions and needs. A system is only as good as its users. Surveys should be done before and after new technology is in-stalled. NYPD management worked closely with line officers and middle man-agement in reengineering the department and gaining feedback before Compstat went into operation. Police management needs feedback in terms of ease of use, problems encountered, and changes needed. In larger departments, focus groups have worked.

Think proactively, and deal with problems before they grow. With this positive attitude, police managers will have better human- and police-oriented technology that really works for them. Changes and new technology will only be put in place when there is a need and it is shown to be a good decision for the department.

QUESTIONS FOR REVIEW

1. Which three areas listed in "Computer Applications to Information Management" would you optimize with handheld wireless technology, and which three areas would not be enhanced by this technology? Why?
2. How does "Computer-Aided Dispatch" contribute to general public safety and the safety of patrol and investigative officers?
3. What problems occur with 911 in terms of misuse by the public?
4. Show how crime mapping can reduce crime in your community. Include an interview with a local police manager in your answer.
5. Present five strong points and three criticisms of Compstat.
6. Define cyberterror and show how it could affect services at your school.
7. Visit a local police department, and compare its operations to the ideal of the paperless police department.

CLASS PROJECT

Take three of the technological developments presented in this chapter and compare them with the technology that is used by an area police department. To what extent is the department using or planning to acquire the technology described in this section?

BIBLIOGRAPHY

BALLARD, JAMES DAVID, JOSEPH G. HORNICK, and DOUGLAS MCKENZIE. "Technological Facilitation of Terrorism." In Harvey W. Kushner, ed., *Cyberterrorism in the Twenty-First Century*. Thousand Oaks, Calif.: Sage, 2002.

"Birmingham Looks to Bratton for PD Help." *Law Enforcement News*, 1997, p. 13.

BOLZ, FRANK, JR., KENNETH J. DUDONIS, and DAVID P. SCHULZ. *The Counterterrorism Book*. Boca Raton, Fla: CRC Press, 2002.

BOWKER, ARTHUR L. "Downloading Computer Information." *Law Enforcement Bulletin* (June 1996), pp. 1–10.

BRATTON, WILLIAM, with PETER KNOBLER. *Turnaround: How America's Top Cop Reversed the Criminal Epidemic*. New York: Random House, 1998.

COLTON, KENT W., MARGARET L. BRANDEAU, and JAMES M. TIEN. *A National Assessment of Police Command, Control, and Communication Systems*. Washington, D.C.: National Institute of Justice, 1983.

CURTI, KEITH J. "Laptop Computers." *Law Enforcement Bulletin* (February 1996), pp. 1–9.

DOERING, R.D. *Vehicle Location Feasibility Study: Final Report*. Orlando, Florida: Technological University, 1974.

FLYNN, KEVIN. "Ranking Officers Retire as Opportunities Call and Pressures Mount." *New York Times*, January 16, 2000, pp. 29–34.

GATES, WILLIAM. *Business at the Speed of Thought: Using a Digital Nervous System*. New York: Time-Warner, 1999.

GOLDSMITH, VICTOR, ET AL. *Analyzing Crime Patterns*. Thousand Oaks, Calif.: Sage, 2000.

GREEK, CECIL, and DEBORAH B. HENRY. "Criminal Justice Resources on the Internet." *Journal of Criminal Justice Education*, 8, no. 1 (spring 1997), pp. 91–100.

HENRY, VINCENT. *The Compstat Paradigm*. Flushing, N.Y.: Looseleaf Publications, 2002.

HOGE, JAMES F., JR., and GIDEON ROSE. *How Did This Happen?* New York: Public Affairs, 2002.

JULIAN, JAY. "Fourth Generation Languages: The New Law Enforcement Combat Masterpiece." *Police Chief*, 56, no. 6 (June 1989), pp. 41–43.

KARMEN, ANDREW. *New York Mystery*. New York: New York University Press, 2000.

KASHEY, DANIEL R. "Mobile Digital Terminals: Police Communicators of the Future." *Law and Order* (February 1978), pp. 26–38.

KUSHNER, HARVEY W., ed. *Cyberterrorism in the Twenty-First Century*. Thousand Oaks, Calif.: Sage, 2002.

LARSON, G.C. *Evaluation of an AVM System Implemented City-Wide in St. Louis: A Summary Report*. Cambridge, Mass.: Public Systems Evaluation, 1978.

LA VIGNE, NANCY, and JULIE WARTELL, eds. *Crime Mapping Case Studies: Success in the Field*. Washington, D.C.: Police Executive Forum, 1998.

LEVIN, BRIAN. "Cyberhate." In HARVEY W. KUSHNER, ed., *Cyberterrorism in the Twenty-First Century*. Thousand Oaks, Calif.: Sage, 2002.

LUTZ, WILLIAM E. "Computer Mapping Helps Identify Arson Targets." In *The Police Chief*. Gaithersburg, Md.: International Association of Chiefs of Police, 1998.

MAMALIAN, CYNTHIA A., ET AL. *The Use of Computerized Crime Mapping by Law Enforcement: Survey Results*. Washington, D.C.: National Institute of Justice, 1999.

MAPLE, JACK, with CHRIS MITCHELL. *The Crime Fighter*. New York: Doubleday, 1999.

MARSHALL, KENNETH B. *The Many Benefits of Mobile Data Access*. Washington, D.C.: National Institute of Justice, 1996.

McDONNEL, RICHARD A. "Information Management." In Bernard L. Garmie, ed., *Local Government Police Management*. Washington, D.C.: International City Management Association, 1977.

"NYS Office Takes the Point against Terror." *Law Enforcement News*, February 14, 2002, p. 11.

OFFICE OF TELECOMMUNICATIONS POLICY. *Nine-One-One: The Emergency Telephone Number—A Handbook for Community Planning*. Washington, D.C.: U.S. Department of Commerce, 1973.

PILANT, LOIS. "High Technology." *Police Chief* (May 1996), pp. 38–51.

Proceedings: Criminal Justice System and Technology Conference. Albany, N.Y.: Department of Criminal Justice Services, 1993.

RASHBAUM, WILLIAM. "A Map Goes beyond Crime to City Quirks." *New York Times*, March 24, 2002, pp. 43–44.

RAYNER, GENE. "Obtaining and Using High-Speed Notification Technology in a Cross-Jurisdictional Setting." *Police Chief* (June 2002), pp. 38–39.

REITH, CHARLES. *A New Study of Police History*. Edinburgh: Oliver and Boyd, 1956.

RICH, THOMAS F. "The Use of Computerized Mapping in Crime Control and Prevention Programs." Washington, D.C.: National Institute of Justice, 1995.

———. *The Chicago Police Department Information Collection for Automated Mapping (ICAM)*. Washington, D.C.: National Institute of Justice, 1996.

———. *Law Enforcement News*, June 30, 1997, pp. 8, 10.

———. "Mapping the Path to Problem Solving." *National Institute of Justice Journal* (October 1999), pp. 2–9.

ROME LABORATORY LAW ENFORCEMENT TECHNOLOGY TEAM. "The New Horizon: Transferring Defense Technology to Law Enforcement." *Law Enforcement Bulletin* (April 1966), pp. 10–20.

RUSSEL, MICHEL J. *Toward the Paperless Police Department: The Use of Laptop Computers.* Washington, D.C.: National Institute of Justice, 1993, pp. 2–9.

SHERMAN, LAWRENCE. *Evidence Based Policing.* Washington, D.C.: Police Foundation, 1998a.

———. *Preventing Crime: What Works, What Doesn't, What's Promising.* Washington, D.C.: National Institute of Justice, 1998b.

SILVERMAN, ELI B. "Mapping Change." *Law Enforcement News,* 1996, pp. 10–12.

———. *NYPD Battles Crime: Innovative Strategies in Policing.* Boston: Northeastern University Press, 1999.

SILVERMAN, IRA. *NYPD Battles Crime.* Boston: Northeastern University Press, 1999.

SOHN, R.L. *Application of Computer-Aided Dispatch in Law Enforcement: An Introductory Planning Guide.* Pasadena, Calif.: Jet Propulsion Laboratory, 1975.

U.S. DEPARTMENT OF JUSTICE. *NCIC Operating Manual.* Washington, D.C.: U.S. Government Printing Office, 1985.

WEST, WILLIAM L., JR. "Automated Dispatching for Small Town Communications." *Communications* (February 1979), pp. 20–25.

PATROL OPERATIONS AND COMMUNITY POLICING

The increased use of technology and research has changed the face of patrol operations. Today's police supervisors can keep in constant communication with patrol cars and officers. Reports can be dictated into a computer, and police can have access to nationwide information while working the streets. The advent of the 911 systems has drastically changed citizen's access to law enforcement services. A 911-driven department is a totally reactive department that has no time for special programs and citizen-interaction approaches, such as community policing.

The nation's police forces have moved beyond random patrol. This began with the conclusions from two Kansas City, Missouri, studies that showed the ineffectiveness of random patrol and rapid response. "The study concluded that preventive patrol did not necessarily prevent crime or reassure citizens. Similar experiments with similar results were subsequently conducted in St. Louis, Missouri and Minneapolis, Minnesota." The study on rapid response concluded that "police response time was unrelated to the probability of making an arrest or locating a witness and that neither dispatch nor travel time was associated with citizen satisfactions" (National Institute of Justice, 1994: 12).

A majority of a police officer's time is still spent on patrol and responding to calls for assistance. Police managers are increasingly looking for alternative ways of providing services. A major question in police management is how to control certain calls so that they do not overwhelm scarce police resources. The Police Executive Research Forum developed a Differential Police Response System in which trained dispatchers coded all police calls as "critical" or "noncritical." Noncritical calls were "stacked" by order of importance or threat to personal safety and citizens were asked to file reports, and critical calls were answered immediately. Many police departments have adopted these procedures along with other systems of prioritizing police calls.

Police managers want to be able to choose from various approaches beyond police response to 911. Some approaches are community policing, neighborhood policing, fear-reduction policing, problem-solving and task force approaches, and hot-spot targeting. Of note, the Bureau of Justice Statistics (2003) reported that 66 percent of local police departments surveyed in 2000 were engaging in community-policing activities. As federal funding for these programs is directed to homeland security and other programs, it is difficult to predict whether these efforts will continue.

In this chapter, we will discuss new programs that have emerged as a result of study and discussion of this issue. We will also review the current managerial issues related to patrol and offer suggestions for improvement.

THE TRADITIONAL MODEL

Until recently, administrative attitudes and practices toward police patrol had changed little since the London Metropolitan Police duty manual, written in 1829. The first police constables assigned to patrol had to walk designated beats within a given time span. Although the automobile replaced many foot patrols in the twentieth century, patrol beats were assigned on the basis of the needs of the community, geographic limitations, and available personnel.

Police patrol continues to consist of the following activities: calls for assistance, patrol officer–initiated activity, preventive patrol, and administrative activities. The jurisdiction of the department is divided into various zones, and one vehicle is assigned to each zone each shift. Certain highly populated zones, such as shopping malls, business districts, and apartment complexes, may be assigned a foot-patrol officer.

In the public's mind, and perhaps reinforced by television, the patrol officer and his or her partner cruise an area, answer a few calls, and occasionally spot a suspicious person or vehicle, leading to a spectacular arrest. The practice of cruising is **preventive patrol.** The rationale behind this is that the deployment of various foot and patrol units can prevent and deter criminal activity. While many officers would like to roam an area in the manner just described, actual preventive patrol depends on numerous variables, such as the number of crimes in a reported area, potential or consistent trouble spots, heavy traffic patterns at certain times, and the whimsy of the officer and his or her supervisor. In large departments, assigned sectors are strictly maintained or jealously guarded by officers and supervisors. Patrol units are not allowed to go beyond their designated sectors except when dispatched or in "hot" pursuit. Preventive patrol time is also spent goofing off, going on personal errands, having coffee, or meeting other patrol units to share gossip. In smaller departments, the same runs true. The great difference is that the patrol unit(s) on duty are supposed to stay within the jurisdiction and not venture outside village or town limits.

Preventive patrol is interrupted by calls for assistance that may be of a criminal or a service nature. On receiving a call, the patrol unit is supposed to suspend preventive patrol and respond to a location. Calls for both criminal and noncriminal matters account for 25 to 40 percent of all patrol time, which, of course, depends on the size of the sector, economic conditions (e.g., inner-city versus suburban middle-class neighborhood), and number of units available for the entire jurisdiction during that shift.

Incorporated with preventive patrol are officer-initiated activities. These include questioning suspicious individuals, stopping vehicles, operating radar, or conducting informal community-service activities (e.g., talking to business-people or schoolchildren or making unassigned business checks). Officer-initiated activities account for only 14 percent of patrol time, although this figure may be higher during early morning tours of duty when there are few calls.

The rest of patrol time is designated as administrative. Tasks of this nature include prisoner transport, writing reports, appearance in court, and vehicle maintenance. Administrative tasks consume large blocks of time during all shifts, but especially during the normal working hours of 9:00 A.M. to 5:00 P.M.

THE KANSAS CITY STUDIES

While many departments continue with traditional patrol in the manner just described, a few major urban departments began experimenting with new patrol tactics around the beginning of 1970. One often-cited study is the so-called **Kansas City Study** conducted by the Kansas City, Missouri, Police Department and the Police Foundation. The general hypotheses of preventive patrol were tested by dividing the southern portion of the city into 15 police beats. These 15 beats were then divided into five groups, each group having three matched beats. For these matched groups, there was one in which patrol was greatly increased, a second beat in which patrol was eliminated altogether except for calls for service, and a control beat, in which patrol continued at the same pace as before the experiment. As Wilson (1975b: 109) reports,

After a year, no substantial differences among the three areas were observed in criminal activity, amount of reported crime, rate of victimization as revealed in the followup survey, level of citizen fear, or degree of citizen satisfaction with the police.

In addition, citizen satisfaction was found to have increased in the second and the control beats, whereas it decreased somewhat in the beat where patrol was greatly increased. Today, many researchers and police administrators continue to discuss these conclusions. There have been many criticisms of this experiment because of faulty experimental design and methodology. Nevertheless, this experiment opened the door for further discussion of the benefits of preventive patrol and the hypothesis that random patrol may be a waste of time.

Further issues were raised by a second experiment conducted in Kansas City in 1977 to study the relationship between response time and crime. The orthodox notion of police patrol maintains that crime will decrease if the police are quick to arrive on the scene. The study found that since citizens generally take too long to report crime, response time has nothing to do with the number of arrests and the rate of crime. Moreover, for nonemergency calls, there were few citizen complaints of the police taking their time to respond to calls as long as the dispatchers advised the complainant of what to expect in terms of estimated time of arrival for the patrol.

RETHINKING THE TRADITIONAL MODEL

Although this model was developed in the 1970s, Table 8–1 conceptualizes some of the current problems that police administrators must deal with when they attempt to improve patrol operations. The general goal for improvement is to (1) reduce administration, preventive patrol, and calls for assistance and (2) add to

TABLE 8-1   *Patrol Allocation/Improvement*

PATROL ACTIVITY	TIME USED (PERCENTAGE PER SHIFT HOUR)	GENERAL PLAN FOR IMPROVEMENT
Administration	23	Reduce the amount of time such tasks detract from patrol
Calls for assistance	23	Manage calls better, especially those of noncriminal nature; create priority system of call returns
Preventive patrol	40	Incorporate specific objectives during this time period; reduce to less than 10 minutes per shift hour
Directed patrol	14	Based on time reduction of other tasks, more time will be available for this activity

Source: W.G. Gay et al. (1977b: 3).

time spent on directed patrol and crime analysis related to directed patrol. Since 85 percent of all police interactions with citizens come from calls for assistance (Reiss, 1971), this category will remain the same or will expand by a few minutes. The major modification will be that all calls for assistance do not have to have a police car within two minutes. The phone operators, who will be trained for this task and have guidance sheets created by department administrative staff, will judge priorities of the call. Each call will have a priority code assigned to it, and the call will go out to the patrol cars coded in terms of high, medium, or low priority.

Preventive Patrol

Although preventive patrol takes 40 percent of an officer's time, it is the crux on which modern police practice rests. There are several reasons why patrol units are mobile and do not stay in a garage and respond as needed in fire-department fashion. These are the objectives of preventive patrol:

Detecting crime
Apprehending criminal offenders
Recovering stolen property
Maintaining a sense of public security and confidence in the police for the community
Satisfying public demands for noncriminal services

These objectives raise many questions. For example, preventive patrol may really have nothing to do with detecting crime and apprehending criminal offenders. In reality, most arrests that occur "in progress" within a few minutes after the commission of a crime stem from the police having been at the right place at the right time.

The same may be true on the issue of deterrence. While many administrators assume that the police presence suggests a higher probability that criminals will not commit crimes, there is little evidence to suggest that traditional patrol practice leads to this objective. The basis for this objective rests with the assumption that the criminals are always on the lookout for police patrols and view these patrols as a serious hindrance to the commission of a crime. In reality, many crimes are spontaneous enterprises that lack long-term planning. In other cases, criminal activity occurs under the eyes of the police in certain areas that are high-crime districts. For example, drug sales on the street in large metropolitan areas may go on uninterrupted even as a police cruiser passes by.

Arrest data are often used to back up this assumption by way of crime clearance rates. Patrol is then deemed effective or ineffective on the basis of apprehensions in a certain area. However, even the freshman criminal justice student knows that crime rates are affected by a number of factors that have nothing to do with the police presence (e.g., family situation, economics, immigration). In short, we do not have satisfactory means for evaluating the effect of patrol tactics.

While recovery of stolen property is cited as an objective of patrol, the fact is that stolen property is usually recovered by investigators following up on a case rather than by the uniformed patrol presence. The only exception to this might be stolen automobiles. But even with a stolen auto, the recovery most often occurs because of the careless driving habits of the offender. It is rare for an officer to recover a stolen vehicle as a result of spotting the license plates or vehicle description. Many experienced officers know of vehicles that were parked for weeks in shopping malls, airports, or apartment complexes before being discovered as stolen because of an abandoned-vehicle complaint filed by the owner of the property or a security guard.

If anything, patrol may be the best public relations exercise utilized by the police in the United States. In essence, the citizen sees the patrol vehicle cruise by and may therefore perceive that the police are "out there" doing their jobs. Research, however, has shown that other factors have to be taken into consideration before one can conclude that the public is satisfied with the police. Such factors are overall crime rates, officer treatment of the public, the level of police corruption, and other community issues.

If anything, traditional police patrol does indeed provide a number of services to the community that are dependent on community norms. Historically, all police agencies respond to domestic disputes, lost-person reports, traffic accidents, loud-party complaints, and so on. In many areas, the community dictates what services the police provide above and beyond the traditional crime-related tasks (e.g., escorting funeral processions, directing traffic near churches on Sunday, providing oxygen to individuals having difficulty breathing, transporting blood from a blood bank to a hospital). Yet, as Schell and his associates (1973) point out, these services may contribute nothing to public satisfaction with the police simply because the amount of time spent on these activities cannot be measured in terms of citizen satisfaction. Still, as one administrator remarked, "I agree with you, but you should hear the complaints that come in once it is found that we are not providing funeral escorts, blood runs, or other such goodies!"

Calls for Service

A common assumption made by the American public is that when you call the police, they will immediately respond—no matter how serious the incident may be. Many observers of patrol believe that there may be a need to dispel the tradition that all calls merit immediate response. In fact, perhaps 40 percent of all calls could be handled by communications personnel. This would save a great deal of time from dispatch to completion of a written report.

Many departments are starting to use various methodologies to handle complaints other than sending a patrol unit to the scene. Some departments are experimenting with mailed-out forms to collect information on traffic accidents of a minor nature and petty larcenies. Other agencies advise the complainant to come down to the station at his or her convenience to complete a report. Additionally, many agencies are developing community-referral systems to refer complaints to other public or private agencies that might be of greater assistance in handling certain problems.

One immediate benefit of utilizing these methods involves improving officer morale. It is no secret that many officers dislike wasting time on so-called junk calls in which there are no suspects and the complainant really wants the police investigation report for insurance purposes. Nevertheless, when compared with procedures of policing, these are radical changes, especially for citizens who may feel that they are being given the runaround. Any new method for reducing patrol responses requires a period of public education by way of media campaigns, civic meetings, and coffee hours. It will also require the dispatcher or a supervisor of the officer on the street to explain the new procedures to citizens and callers.

Another controversial method for reducing the time spent on nonessential calls for assistance by patrol units is called *stacking*. Stacking simply involves classifying calls in terms of priority, thereby increasing the amount of time that can be allocated for uninterrupted patrol for certain units.

Another method to reduce time on minor calls for service involves the use of nonsworn personnel or parapolice officers, such as community-service officers. In many departments, these nonsworn personnel are assigned to a variety of duties, including desk duty, writing parking tickets, directing traffic, conducting crime-prevention campaigns, and other similar assignments.

Administrative Tasks

In this age of high technology, many police departments are experimenting with new devices and procedures to cut down on the amount of time uniformed and plainclothes officers spend on administrative tasks. With regard to police procedures ranging from arrests to prisoner transports, many departments are asking the question, How can we improve the amount of time an officer can spend on crucial tasks? In many cases, the answer requires a revision of existing laws, such as those mandating that the arresting officer must appear at arraignment with a defendant in court the next day. In other instances, the duty manual is subject to review and update to cut out unnecessary tasks.

While these issues are often resolved by in-house review, a basic problem that continues to plague all police officers is paperwork. On average, police agencies use over 50 different forms, ranging from arrest reports to motor vehicle accident reports. In fact, the average arrest requires that more than 10 different forms be completed. While many of these forms can be eliminated or combined, the problem of writing reports remains.

Some agencies are adopting programs and procedures taken for granted in private business by having patrol officers tape-record reports for future transcription or use laptop computers. Some agencies have gone so far as to have the officer call in the report by telephone immediately after the investigation. At any rate, once these skills are mastered, administrative time is reduced.

Directed Patrol

When administrative tasks, calls for service, and preventive patrol are reanalyzed, the final objective will be the allocation of greater time for directed patrol. For our purposes, **directed patrol** can be defined as the allocation of patrol services in a planned and rational manner. Departments have applied directed patrol in a variety of ways that will be discussed. In addition, directed patrol depends on two other variables: crime analysis and shift design.

Crime Analysis.   Too frequently, patrol deployment is made without referral to when and where the crimes are occurring. Many police personnel prefer to operate by tradition or rule-of-thumb methods rather than rely on **crime analysis.** A minority of police departments in the United States, however, delve into crime analysis with the assistance of federal grants. At present, crime analysis in the United States ranges from sophisticated computer programming to pin mapping.

After pertinent data have been obtained from field reports, arrest sheets, or dispatch logs, the information is collated, analyzed, and then communicated to line supervisors and field personnel. With this information, the patrol supervisor can make rational decisions for deploying staff or devising specialized patrol techniques. Crime mapping has a solid future in crime analysis.

Shift Design.   Crime analysis can be very useful in analyzing workloads by shift or season. At present, most police departments allocate an equal number of officers to each shift, usually three shifts in a 24-hour period. Despite this allocation, all departments realize that criminal activity increases between the hours of 4 P.M. and 2 A.M., which can present some problems with regard to police operations since officers are unable to perform directed patrol when they have to rush from call to call. In recognition of this dilemma, many departments have redeployed their patrol personnel based on need rather than on equalization. For example, many agencies have designed the following programs:

9–40   In this program, the officer works nine hours a day, four days a week, for a total of 36 hours; another four hours are taken up with physical fitness, in-service training, and roll call.

4–10   In this very common program, the workweek consists of 10 hours a day, four days a week.

In addition to these and other proposed designs, deployment extends beyond the traditional equal shift allocation in that the shifts are redesigned to provide increased coverage between the hours of 7 P.M. and 1 A.M. Agencies on a five-day 40-hour workweek would be able to do the same thing, provided that there were permanent shifts with more personnel being assigned to high-crime hours. The main problem with shift redesign in traditional agencies stems from union or personnel opposition since most officers prefer the day shifts with as many weekends off as possible. Proponents of 9–40 and 4–10 point out that accommodations can be made with weekends off by way of rotation.

Specialized Patrol.   In some departments, directed patrol comes under the heading of specialized patrol, where specific units are assigned to a special area (e.g., burglary squad, sneaker squad for inner-city street crime). The following tactics are commonly employed by these units:

1. *Decoys*. In **decoy squads,** an officer disguised as a "victim" is assisted by several backup officers. This tactic is used for such crimes as muggings, purse snatchings, and assaults.
2. *Stakeouts*. In **stakeouts,** officers—either physically or by use of electronic equipment—are assigned to a likely target area. Crimes in progress are frequently interrupted.
3. *Suspect surveillance*. In suspect **surveillance,** police personnel watch and follow individuals who are suspected of committing offenses with frequency (e.g., burglary, robbery, drugs, organized crime).
4. *General area surveillance*. As with stakeouts, general area surveillance is used against either specific criminals or in a wide area with a variety of targets. Some jurisdictions even go so far as to station video cameras on certain high-crime street corners.

The assignment of a specialized patrol unit to a problem is based on the analysis of crime data. Specialized patrol is an example of a proactive system that operates according to a rational plan of crime detection rather than randomly stumbling about waiting for something to happen.

Some of the advantages of specialized patrol are as follows:

1. Specific units are assigned to a specific problem so that management knows exactly who is responsible for solving that crime problem.
2. The unit normally exhibits a high degree of teamwork and high morale.
3. There is improved skill development in the specialized area over a period of time, with officers being called on by all members of the department in their area of expertise.
4. A great deal of positive public interest might be generated by media attention.

On the other hand, there are problems with specialized units that affect the whole department. There is always the problem of communication (e.g., deciding who is responsible for what problems, like having a burglary unit that may not respond to other street crimes). Officers in regular squads resent the "hot shot" specialists who attain glory and prestige while regular patrol has to take care of more mundane matters. This is especially acute in departments where factions operate in a negative fashion. Departmental morale can be destroyed by resentment over specialized units.

The use of aggressive enforcement tactics also produces negative public attention. People get upset when stakeout squads use heavy-caliber weapons to kill robbers. Citizens also complain about area surveillance, particularly the use of video cameras in high-crime areas. While the outlook toward professional law enforcement services is generally positive, serious questions are raised on the use of heavy-handed tactics and technology.

Foot Patrol

Some police managers feel that automobile patrolling has led to a police alienation from neighborhoods and loss of a feeling of security that was generated by **foot patrol.** Foot patrol can have a positive benefit in high-density neighborhoods. When Newark, New Jersey, and Flint, Michigan, reinstituted foot patrol, these were the results (Kelling, 1987):

1. When foot patrol is added in neighborhoods, levels of fear decrease significantly.
2. When foot patrol is withdrawn from neighborhoods, levels of fear increase significantly.
3. Citizen satisfaction with police increases when foot patrol is added in neighborhoods.
4. Police who patrol on foot have a greater appreciation for the values of the neighborhood residents than do police who patrol the same area in automobiles.
5. Police who patrol on foot have greater job satisfaction, less fear, and higher morale than officers who patrol in automobiles.

Personal-contact patrol also brought about fear reduction in Houston. The police started "to drive through the neighborhoods, knock on doors and chat with pedestrians, thus creating a visible presence" (Sherman, 1987). The major object of these programs is not crime reduction, although this has happened in some cases. Foot patrol and personal-contact patrol do increase a feeling of security by citizens and lower the fear of crime.

Bicycle Patrol

Police officers around the world have used bicycles for patrol purposes since the nineteenth century. With the advent of modern mountain bikes, police bike patrols have been established. The Seattle Police Department and other West Coast departments in the United States use bikes for patrol operations all year. The idea has become popular with university and college police departments. Other applications are found in airport parking lots, resort and recreation areas, and locations that impede motorized patrol units. In these locations, bike patrol personnel can respond quicker than vehicles to emergencies.

As with any other function, bike patrols require a great deal of planning with regard to equipment, training, personnel needs, and supervision. Equipment includes mountain bikes, seasonal uniforms, helmets, and foul-weather gear. Equipment or contract services have to be purchased for parts and repairs. Personnel selected for this assignment have to be physically fit. Training programs, such as the one used by the University Police Department at the State University of New York at Albany, include such topics as bike nomenclature, proper riding and equipment, emergency response, tactical pursuit, and safety in such areas as woods, stairways, and shopping malls.

The bicycle patrols used by public safety agencies today provide the following benefits:

1. Increased interaction between officers and the community
2. Access to remote or vehicle-inaccessible locations
3. Improved physical fitness for participants

Bicycle patrols should not be viewed as a specialized function but rather as a part of normal assignment.

CASE STUDY

Bicycle Maneuvers

The Power Slide

With the power slide, officers direct their bikes to slide to a particular location. When using the power slide, officers approach a subject at a high rate of speed. On reaching the suspect, they plant either their left or right foot on the ground with the knees slightly bent to make the bike lean away from the suspect. The officers then apply the rear brake with enough pressure to lock up the rear tire, causing the bike to spin around. Power slides can be performed to the right or left side, depending on which is the officer's stronger side.

The Panic Stop

To stop the bike at any given moment, officers use the panic stop. In this case, they apply the rear brake to lock up the rear tire and move their center of gravity (torso) to the rear of the seat, causing a controllable skid and stop.

The Rolling Dismount

The rolling dismount is a technique used by officers to get off their bicycle quickly. Officers slow the bicycle down to a controllable speed with one foot on the pedal, while engaging the kickstand with the other foot. The rolling dismount is performed in a quick, fluid motion, ending with the bike in the standby/ready position.

Source: FBI Law Enforcement Bulletin, September 1993.

TEAM POLICING

In the 1960s, the concept of team policing received considerable attention by criminal justice educators, planners, and practitioners. It was seen as a possible solution to the major problems faced by many American police departments: (1) poor police-community relations, (2) duplication of effort, (3) the rise of crime, and (4) the increasing costs of police budgets. **Team policing** involves decentralizing the existing police organizational structure and reorganizing services into specific subunits. These subunits are usually based on geographic, ethnic, and other socioeconomic boundaries found in particular communities. In each subunit, the team is charged with the allocation of patrol, investigation, and other police services and programs, according to the needs of the community.

History of Team Policing

The concept of team policing originated in Aberdeen, Scotland, in the late 1940s as an experiment to counteract low morale and boredom experienced by single officers patrolling quiet areas. A change was made from the one-unit, one-beat method of patrol to teams of 5 or 10 patrolling an area divided according to the concentration of crime and calls for service (Sherman, 1976: xiii). In 1966, because of a personnel shortage, the Coventry constabulary in England began a form of team policing called unit beat policing, whereby constables were formed into teams, and each team was assigned to a specific area. Information from the team was fed to a central collator who passed on the information to other teams. Although the Aberdeen patrol method was abandoned in 1963, other British constabularies and a few American police forces have adopted similar plans.

In the United States, the urban and campus unrest of the 1960s brought forth renewed interest in police patrol tactics and police-community relations. It was generally concluded that a gap had developed between the police and the public. This was due to the decline of the neighborhood foot-patrol officer and the abandonment of many precinct stations in favor of centralization. The 1967 Presidential Commission on Law Enforcement and the Administration of Justice recommended that agencies introduce team policing as a means to lessen this gap. Team policing was also expected to increase community involvement with crime prevention and detection.

Positive Aspects of Team Policing

The positive aspects of team policing are as follows:

1. The police services rendered by the team become more personal to the community, and in return the relations between the police and the community are improved.

2. Team policing provides a flexible structure for its members in that innovation is made possible and professionalism is increased through the development of shared knowledge and peer review.
3. Patrol and investigatory functions are merged into one task, thus eliminating the social barriers of communication and status conflict between uniformed and plainclothes personnel.
4. A reduction is attained in the chain of command in that decision making is done by supervisors and operating personnel.
5. Each member of the team is given a chance to utilize discretion and enhance personal skills. As a result, greater work satisfaction is expected.

Team Policing and Tactical Patrol

Team policing is often confused with **tactical patrol** techniques. Tactical patrol deals with selective law enforcement for a specific problem in the area. Examples of this type of enforcement are robberies, murders, muggings, and purse snatchings occurring in a routine manner, in a specific geographic area. With team policing, emphasis is placed on territorial exclusivity, maintaining stable and close ties with the citizens of the neighborhood, participation in planning and management, and an orientation toward results in presenting the police mission (Edgar et al., 1976: v).

Between 1970 and 1974, a number of municipalities introduced team policing into their areas, with and without assistance from federal and private funding sources. Evaluation of these programs brought mixed reviews. The Rochester, New York, investigative-team program was deemed successful for improving clearance rates and reducing crime. The community investigative-team programs in New York City and Albuquerque, New Mexico, were assessed as failures, generally because of overall departmental problems. In New York City, the teams failed to change the role of the patrol officer or to increase his or her job satisfaction. In Albuquerque, the teams were unable to deliver a higher level of community service. San Diego, California, had greater success with its program. The officers adapted to their new role, delivered community services, and improved their attitudes toward the community. The full-service teams in Albany (Arbor Hill), Cincinnati, and Los Angeles were extensively evaluated, and the results were somewhat mixed (Gay et al., 1977b: 41):

> While indicators of workload management, investigative effectiveness and police attitudes towards the community have improved, there has been no change in officer job satisfaction and community attitudes.

PROBLEM-ORIENTED POLICING

In 1979, Herman Goldstein proposed what he described as a problem-oriented approach to law enforcement (Goldstein, 1979). In the late 1970s and throughout the 1980s, police managers, faced with more and more personnel with college degrees, attempted a number of approaches at improving job satisfactions, task forces, quality circles, and management by objectives. **Problem-oriented policing (POP)** is another one of these approaches that utilizes the educated police force in a more proactive manner. According to the authors, traditional police patrol is a reactive system where police departments deliver services by "reacting to individual events reported by citizens' gathering information from victims, witnesses and offenders; involving the criminal justice process and using aggregate crime statistics to evaluate performance" (Spelman and Eck, 1987: 3).

In Newport News, Virginia, police were trained in a four-stage approach:

1. *Scanning*. Identify major problems (e.g., burglaries in an apartment complex, thefts from autos downtown, and prostitution-related robberies).
2. *Analysis*. Collect and analyze information from a variety of public and private resources, not just from police data.
3. *Response*. Work with other agencies and the public to tailor actions suitable to the problem.
4. *Assessment*. Evaluate the effectiveness of the actions to see whether the problem was alleviated or solved.

As a result of this approach, downtown robberies were reduced by 39 percent, burglaries in that apartment complex were reduced by 35 percent, and thefts from parked vehicles outside a manufacturing plant dropped by 53 percent. Table 8–2 shows the problem analysis model, which worked well for the Newport News police agency's problem-oriented policing.

TABLE 8–2   *Problem Analysis Model*

ACTORS	INCIDENTS	RESPONSES
Victims	Sequence of events	Community
Lifestyle	Events preceding	Neighborhood affected
Security measures taken	criminal act	by problem
Victimization history	Event itself	City as a whole
	Events following act	People outside the city
Offenders	Physical contact	
Identity and physical	Time	Institutional
description	Location	Criminal justice agencies
Lifestyle, education,	Access control and	Other public agencies
employment history	surveillance	Mass media
Criminal history		Business sector
	Social context	
Third parties	Likelihood and probable	
Personal data	actions of witnesses	
Connection to	Apparent attitude of residents	
victimization	toward neighborhood	

Source: Spelman and Eck (1987a: 6).

FIGURE 8-1   The problem-oriented policing system flowchart.
(*Source:* New York Bureau for Municipal Police, Albany, New York, 1990.)

To find out what were important problems for the citizens, a number of citywide and neighborhood surveys were conducted. Citywide problems included domestic homicides, gas station drive-offs, assaults on police officers, runaway youths, drunk driving, and disturbances at convenience stores. Specific neighborhood problems included drug dealing, robberies, vacant buildings, burglaries, larcenies, thefts from autos, and rowdy youths. In one apartment complex, the police successfully organized a building association and had the city intervene in the maintenance of the complex, which resulted in better living conditions and a 35-percent drop in the burglary rate.

The problem-oriented process is summarized in a flowchart from the New York Bureau for Municipal Police (Figure 8–1). What is important is that the community is involved in solving problems, whether these are drug deals, stolen bicycles, or loud-noise complaints. The basic tenets of Goldstein's article were later incorporated into full discussion in his book *Problem-Oriented Policing* (1990). The term is often used interchangeably with **community-oriented policing (COP),** but there are some basic theoretical differences between the two. What problem-oriented policing does is provide a planning model for dealing with specific issues in the wider view of community policing.

Model Program and Examples of Excellence

The Police Executive Research Forum's 2001 Herman Goldstein Awards for Excellence in Problem-Solving Policing were based on the Newport News, Virginia, SARA model (Police Executive Research Forum, 2001: 2). The SARA model includes

Scanning	Identify recurring problems of concern to the public and the police.
	Prioritize problems.
	Develop broad goals.
	Confirm that the problems exist.
	Select one problem for examination.
Analysis	Try to identify and understand the events and conditions that precede and accompany the problem.
	Identify the consequence of the problem for the community.
	Determine how frequently the problem occurs and how long it has been taking place.
	Identify the conditions that give rise to the problem.
	Narrow the scope of the problem as specifically as possible.
	Identify a variety of resources that may be of assistance in developing a deeper understanding of the problem.
Response	Search for what other communities with similar problems have done.
	Brainstorm interventions.
	Choose among the alternative solutions.
	Outline a response plan and identify responsible parties.
	State the specific goals for the response plan.
	Carry out the planned activities.
Assessment	Determine whether the plan was implemented.
	Determine whether the goals were obtained, and collect pre- and post-response qualitative and quantitative data.
	Identify any new strategies needed to augment the original plan.
	Conduct ongoing assessment to ensure continued effectiveness.

The winner was the Corridor Safety Plan of the California Highway Patrol, which reduced fatalities and injuries along a busy highway corridor that had had 48 fatalities in the previous three years. The response plan included enhanced enforcement of traffic laws, increased fines, no-passing zones, shoulder and signage improvements, installation of roadside call boxes to facilitate emergency assistance, and increased public awareness. The decreased rate of collision in the first year saved 21 lives.

The other award finalists were

Buffalo, New York. Police targeted "johns" and decreased prostitution calls in the downtown Allentown area. The plan included alternate sentencing, outreach programs for prostitutes, and environmental changes.

Chula Vista, California. An estimated 100 burglaries were prevented annually in new housing construction. Police interviewed victims and burglars, conducted environmental assessment, and analyzed incident reports to develop a plan for new security improvements.

Rogers County, Oklahoma. The sheriff's office virtually eliminated stolen general livestock, horse, and flatbed trailers by installing microchips for tracking and by working with the media and regional associations.

Salt Lake City, Utah. Police implemented a verified-response strategy for false alarms, which shifted false-alarm problems to private security by dispatching officers to calls only after eyewitness verification.

South Euclid, Ohio. Police reduced bullying in public schools and helped at-risk students by targeting hot-spot bullying and increasing the awareness of the problem by students, parents, and teachers.

COMMUNITY POLICING

In 1982, George L. Kelling and James Q. Wilson published an article titled "Broken Windows," which captured the attention of police administrators. They described how Philip Zimbardo, a noted sociologist at Stanford University, placed an abandoned car in a tough Bronx neighborhood and another abandoned vehicle in a wealthy area in Palo Alto, California. The vehicle in the Bronx was immediately vandalized and became a stripped hulk within a week. The car in Palo Alto remained untouched until Professor Zimbardo intentionally broke its window. The vehicle was then stripped of usable parts by vandals. Kelling and Wilson used this field experiment to present the idea that run-down neighborhoods attract crime and fear.

They recommended foot patrol in tough neighborhoods. The idea was not to simply reduce crime but to have a police presence to make people feel safer. Technology had allowed the police to abandon the streets of the city. Police officers, with their fancy computers and communication systems, rode around in police cars and simply did not communicate with citizens. Foot patrol, with the goal of giving citizens a feeling of safety, was tried around the United States, beginning with Newark, New Jersey, in 1981. Other sites followed: Oakland in 1984, a second Newark program in 1985, Houston in 1987, and Boston in 1986. Although the crime rate usually did not go down, the general conclusion was that the citizens "felt safer and less worried about personal property victimization" (Greene, 1989: 361). This evolved over a number of years into fear-reduction programs and finally into **community policing**—all of which have their original roots in the team policing of the 1970s.

One of the major differences between the reactive patrolling of the 911 police force and community-oriented policing is that community-oriented policing can become proactive. By working closely with citizens, police can anticipate and prevent crime. Community policing, when done right, is one of the most proactive programs that a professional police department can adopt.

Traditional and Community Policing Compared

One of the questions asked time and time again is, What makes community-oriented policing so different from traditional policing? In the past, when an officer walked a beat visiting neighbors and businesses daily, we had a form of community policing. Now that police are barricaded inside their police vehicles, reacting to citizen calls only after a crime has taken place, we have the opposite of community policing.

Giving out traffic tickets is also reactive since it takes place after the fact. Police do not station themselves outside of bars where citizens are known to get drunk and then drive. Instead, police wait for those drunk drivers to drive many miles, possibly injuring or killing someone, before they give out their tickets—much, much too late. Working with the community outside such bars to stop drunken people from driving would be both community-oriented policing and proactive policing.

The comparison of traditional policing with community-oriented policing in Table 8–3 was published by the National Institute of Justice (Sparrow, 1988: 8–9). To summarize Table 8–3, community police consider themselves part of the public they serve. They work proactively by taking steps to eliminate crime and disorder. Community policing focuses on the citizens' problems and concerns.

The Implementation of Community Policing

According to *Implementing Community Policing: The Administrative Problem* by Kelling and Bratton (1993: 4), the police reformers who are carrying out community policing are using middle managers, such as the leadership of line operating units and staff units (e.g., planning and training):

> Thus, the solution to the administrative problem in police departments was the establishment of a powerful mid-management group that: 1) extended the reach of chiefs throughout police departments and 2) became the locus of the practice and skill base of the occupation. As such, mid-managers became the leading edge in the establishment of centralized control over police departments' internal environment and organizational operations.

To establish useful and sustained change in any police department, police managers must overcome the overwhelming resistance of the established police culture. This is especially true in the case of community policing, which attempts to reach outside the police department to involve civilians in police matters. The research on police culture, from Westley's (1970) dissertation on the Gary, Indiana, Police Department in 1950 to Thibault's article "The Blue Milieu," indicates that police have been socially isolated from the public

TABLE 8-3   *Traditional versus Community Policing: Questions and Answers*

	Answers	
Question	**Traditional**	**Community Policing**
Who are the police?	A government agency principally responsible for law enforcement	Police are the public, and the public are the police. Police officers are those who are paid to give full-time attention to the duties of every citizen.
What is the relationship of the police force to other public service departments?	Priorities often conflict	The police are one department among many responsible for improving the quality of life.
What is the role of the police?	Focusing on solving crimes	A broader problem-solving approach
How is police efficiency measured?	By detection and arrest rates	By the absence of crime and disorder
What are the highest priorities?	Crimes that are high value (e.g., bank robberies) and those involving violence	Whatever problems disturb the community most
What, specifically, do police deal with?	Incidents	Citizens' problems and concerns
What determines the effectiveness of police?	Response times	Public cooperation
What view do police take of service calls?	Deal with them only if there is no real police work to do	Vital function and great opportunity
What is police professionalism?	Swift, effective response to serious crime	Keeping close to the community
What kind of intelligence is most important?	Crime intelligence (study of particular crimes or series of crimes)	Criminal intelligence (information about the activities of individuals or groups)
What is the essential nature of police accountability?	Highly centralized; governed by rules, regulations, and policy directives; accountable to the law	Emphasis on local accountability to community needs
What is the role of headquarters?	To provide the necessary rules and policy directives	To preach organizational values
What is the role of the press liaison department?	To keep the "heat" off operational officers so they can get on with the job	To coordinate an essential channel of communication with the community
How do the police regard prosecutions?	As an important goal	As one tool among many

(minority groups in particular), hostile to the public, threatened by any type of change, and very secretive (Thibault, 1992).

The only way a police chief can implement community policing is to have middle management convince the patrol officer that community policing

Does not threaten his or her sense of identity as a police officer

Does not lower the professional status or authority of a police officer

Rewards police officers in terms of postings and promotions for implementing community policing

Will remain a permanent part of departmental police procedures

The old-timers will say, "I remember that team policing crap. We worked with the community and formed what they would call today quality teams. Well, the chief felt that his power was threatened, and *boom!* That was the end of team policing." Only middle management has the staying power to convince these officers, who have heard it all, that community policing is a permanent part of law enforcement.

In Dallas, the lieutenants (middle management) opposed community policing. As Kelling and Bratton report (1993: 5), "Before a single operational element of the strategy was in place [the police chief] was fired . . . and the planning unit . . . was renounced and liquidated." That was the end of community policing for Dallas.

In Cincinnati in the 1970s, decentralized team policing was instituted by the chief and his managers without involving middle management. They jazzed it up with the behavioral jargon of management by objectives, further alienating the middle managers. The result was predictable (Kelling and Bratton, 1993: 6): "By the end of 1975, . . . while some forms of team policing still existed, little of substance remained."

Kansas City, which has one of the most progressive police departments in the nation, used outside money to create problem-centered policing task forces.

Recommendations for Implementation

How can a police manager decide if community policing is really taking place? The following seven criteria have to be in place:

1. *The agenda for police activities must be set by citizens*, not by the police administrators. This means there must be formal ways of finding out what the citizens want, such as surveys and the formal involvement of citizen associations.
2. *Middle management must be trained and directly involved in the implementation of community policing*, from inception to final performance. This includes captains, lieutenants, and sergeants.
3. *There must be a split force.* Community policing has to be protected from 911 service calls so officers have time to interact with citizen associations and to plan mutual problem solving with these citizens.

4. *Community policing must be a permanent policy of the department*, not dependent on grant money, which comes and goes. The policies and philosophy of community policing must be part of standard operating procedures. There must be a permanent reward structure for the implementation of community policing by line officers.

5. *Community problem solving groups* are created to identify problems and explore solutions with police managers.

6. *The prevention of crime must be the major police goal.* This policy is intended to stop crime before it happens rather than arrest criminals after citizens have been victimized.

7. *Officers must strive to improve the quality of life in a community*. This is accomplished by preventing crime, fixing broken windows, repairing or tearing down empty buildings, reducing fear in the community, and cleaning up vacant lots.

If police programs measure up to these seven criteria, they will be judged community-policing programs. If the policing programs are missing one or more of the seven criteria, they will be considered public relations programs or something other than community policing.

St. Petersburg: 911 Incident-Driven Service Police Officers Compared to Community-Service Police Officers

St. Petersburg, Florida, is building community policing among a group of officers while the rest of the department is made up of incident-driven 911 patrol officers. Each group has a different philosophy of policing. A survey of all of the officers in the department found (National Institute of Justice, 1998b: 21–22):

> More than two-thirds of the interviewed officers identified handling calls for service as one of the top two goals. That view reflects a traditional incident-driven focus, as does the importance attributed to making arrests, issuing citations and seizing guns and drugs.

Comparing the two groups of officers, the community-service officers' philosophy comes from the seven criteria for community policing:

> Compared with 911 officers, community police officers express as a group, the following:
>
> • Stronger agreement that assisting citizens is as important as enforcing the law.
> • Stronger support for seeking out the views of neighborhood residents.
> • Stronger disagreement that police have reason to be distrustful of citizens.

Two-thirds of the community police officers considered reducing the number of repeat calls as an important goal. This is a community-policing crime-prevention goal. Sixty percent wanted to involve the public in improving neighborhoods. This includes the two community policing goals of improving the quality of life in neighborhoods and increasing citizen involvement.

One-third of the officers of the whole St. Petersburg department accepted problem solving as an approach to policing. The report concludes, "In general, 911 officers spent more time dealing with traditional police work, while community police officers spent more time on activities that community policing advocates have identified."

Middle managers were involved, for example, testing preventive patrol as a strategy and working on juvenile problems around the schools. The projects were successfully implemented; however, when the money ran out, the police went back to business as usual. This happened to team policing and directed-patrol strategies throughout the United States. In almost all cases, the departments went back to business as usual when the outside money ran out (Kelling and Bratton, 1992).

Seattle: Successful Implementation of Community Policing

In Seattle, a citizens' group, the South Seattle Crime Prevention Council, worked closely with the police department to target certain activities that the community wanted the police to deal with:

Narcotic activity reports. 1,219 citizen complaints of drug activity were actively followed up in the streets by teams of detectives.

Criminal trespass program. More than 100 businesses signed up to give permission to police to enter their properties, which were posted No Trespassing, in order to cite or arrest individuals loitering to do drug transactions. Citations for cooperation were given to 1,044 citizens.

Pay telephone program. Pay phones were programmed for outgoing calls only so drug dealers could not receive incoming calls.

Owner notification of drug trafficking. Property owners were given notice that their tenants faced legal action for dealing drugs on their property.

Over time, other areas of the city were involved. A downtown business organization asked for strict enforcement of liquor laws and for foot and bicycle patrol where young people congregated. A crime-prevention division in the city police department, staffed by civilians, created a Block Watch program with organizers assigned to permanent stations in neighborhoods. Other city agencies, including the Seattle Housing Authority, were involved.

Seattle's Public Action Plan.   The voters approved an increase in resources for the police department, including an addition of 147 sworn and civilian positions. Crime-prevention councils and police department advisory councils were created to advise police in precincts throughout the city.

Community-policing teams of five officers and a sergeant were created. Members of the teams were considered full-time community police officers and did not answer 911 service calls. That Seattle was willing to devote part of its force exclusively to community policing marked a significant shift in departmental policy.

The Parks Department joined with police officer volunteers to work with youth in an evening recreational program. The schools and the Department of Social Services were planning to work with police to actively intervene with youth in gangs and youth at high risk to join gangs.

Lessons Learned from Seattle's Community Policing

1. There is a need for police training in human relations skills.
2. Community-policing efforts must focus on problems that the community has identified.
3. The impact of community policing is positive on both the police and the citizens.
4. Police get the benefit of civilian support in neighborhoods and businesses and support for the police budget.
5. The citizens get to know the police as human beings and as professionals.
6. The citizens see police in a positive light because the police are helping to solve the problems in their neighborhoods (Fleissner and others, 1992).

Chicago: Community Policing

In April 1993, **Chicago's Alternate Policing Strategy (CAPS)** was implemented in five districts. The burden of answering 911 calls was shifted to rapid-response teams. Recruits, officers, and supervisors went through several training sessions. Advisory committees at the district level were formed, made up of police and citizens to support local problem-solving efforts. District advisory committees, with strong leadership that focused on specific short-term issues, were more successful than committees that focused on broad social issues. Beat meetings were divisive because citizens focused on community organizing and action while beat officers focused on police action. Locally oriented volunteer groups with a crime prevention and local development agenda were the most successful groups.

There was a decrease in perceived crime problems and perceived physical decay. This included gang violence, drug dealing, building abandonment, and littered streets and sidewalks. Three districts experienced a decline in robbery and auto theft. Police supervisors involved in the CAPS program were more optimistic than supervisors who were not involved. Chicago is currently implementing the CAPS program throughout the city. By reaching out to citizens, community policing produced a positive response to police efforts by the citizens of Chicago (National Institute of Justice, 1995a).

By 1999, CAPS was part of a total departmental approach to policing Chicago. "Both police and citizens play major roles in identifying and prioritizing problems, formulating ways of addressing them, and helping bring community resources to bear in solving them" (Hartnett and Skogan, 1999: 5).

Physical decay had gone down in the original five experimental districts. There was a decline in gang and drug problems in two districts and a decline in major crime in two districts.

In citywide surveys, the views of citizens became more positive. One citizen said, "You have a sense of camaraderie and cooperation between officers and beat officers and community residents. You lose that sense of fear" (Hartnett and Skogan, 1999: 5). CAPS citizen meetings were advertised on television and radio (including Spanish-speaking stations), fliers were sent home with schoolchildren, and meetings were announced in churches. A new program for citizen involvement was initiated, targeting community leaders, especially among the Latino population.

The major elements of community policing in Chicago include the following (Hartnett and Skogan, 1999: 8):

Police

- The entire patrol division is involved
- The program is fully staffed with permanent officers on a regular shift
- Extensive training is given to both officers and supervisors
- All districts and all units are involved
- Program activities are supervised through the regular chain of command and through standard patrol operations

Residents

- Residents are expected to take an active role in solving problems
- Residents are encouraged to meet with police regularly to exchange information and report on actions taken
- Public priorities play an important part in setting beat team priorities
- Residents receive training in Chicago's problem solving model

Municipal Services

- Management systems are in place to trigger a rapid response to service requests
- Agencies are held accountable by the mayor for the effectiveness of their response
- Community policing is the entire city's program, not the police department program.

Chicago hired 1,000 new police officers so the department would have the resources to institute community policing, with its many meetings with citizen groups. All the uniformed officers were trained in problem solving, and supervisors received additional management training, including how to conduct meetings. Traditional 911-oriented officers were more concerned with arresting criminals than listening to citizens. Gradually, a preventive community-policing approach began to work. The officers are pleased with the new technology, especially being able to access offender information and mug shots while on the beat. Officers have become more optimistic about CAPS, and organizing officers into fixed problem-solving beat teams has been significant in helping them accept CAPS. The full support of the mayor has been a great help.

Priority was given to police requests to municipal services related to crime and public safety. A former commander of one of the experimental districts and now an assistant deputy superintendent stated, "By getting the streetlight fixed, it ups the police credibility that they can get things done" (Hartnett and Skogan, 1999: 10).

Community policing is no longer an alternative program in Chicago. It is becoming part of the everyday life of the citizens and is more integrated into the life of the city.

Conclusion: Community Policing

Individual citizen involvement is not enough if true community policing is to be implemented. As Skogan points out, community involvement must be sustained (1996: 32): "One of the conclusions of the Chicago evaluation is that it is difficult to sustain autonomous citizen action, even with the support of the police. Organizations develop agendas that keep their energies focused, even when key leaders tire or turn to other affairs. They provide a focus for identification and commitment and they provide important social benefits to participants."

Community policing cannot be implemented overnight. It takes time, training, a restructuring of departmental resources, and daily work with community groups, but it can be done successfully, as the Seattle experience has demonstrated. Middle management must become involved if the social isolation of the established police culture and the cynicism of the public are to be overcome. Line officers and middle managers must be able to see the benefits of community policing, or it will not work. We recommend that any agency that truly wants to implement community policing ask middle managers from a successful program to work with their middle managers.

Without some additional resources in terms of new civilian and sworn-officer positions, it is very difficult for a reactive police department to implement community-oriented policing. But if you start small, say in one or two neighborhoods, and the people and politicians see that it is actually working, new positions and resources may become available. In the fight for additional resources in these tight-budget times, the best allies of the police are involved citizens who have seen community police programs work. It is not easy, but the benefits to both the police and the community are worth the effort. The federal funding of community policing has made community-policing efforts successful as permanent institutions in major police departments.

The big question is, To what extent will community policing continue if federal funding support ends completely? While we do not claim to have a crystal ball on this, we feel that since this program has made great inroads in American policing, certain community-specific programs will continue for some time. Overall, it has had a positive impact on police-community relations, which will be important for antiterrorism investigations and community-security enhancement in the next few years.

WEED AND SEED

In response to a rise in drug trafficking and the decline of certain inner-city neighborhoods, the Department of Justice initiated a program in 1991 called **Weed and Seed.** The goals of the program are to address violent crime and problems associated with drug sales in high-risk neighborhoods and to provide a safe environment for residents. According to the U.S. Department of Justice (n.d.), the key to Weed and Seed is bringing together a host of law enforcement and community agencies to "weed out" criminals in the neighborhood and to bring revitalization services (seeding) to the area.

The program uses a problem-solving collaborative strategy in forming alliances between law enforcement and social-service groups. The key element is obtaining resident support and participation in program follow-through. As with other aspects of community policing, a primary goal is to improve the quality of life for neighborhood residents. In addition to addressing the crime problem, residents and officials strive to work together to deal with such issues as graffiti and abandoned buildings. At present, approximately 160 weed-and-seed programs are functioning throughout the United States.

The overall organization of this program is fairly straightforward. Communities with a serious crime problem in a specific neighborhood file an application through the U.S. Attorney's office. If the application is approved, funding is then given to the city or town executive that filed for the grant. The daily operations of the program are directed by local authorities, who then create and work with a neighborhood steering committee. The steering group consists of local stakeholders, including state and federal law enforcement, social services, city services, housing authority personnel, neighborhood block associations, and so on. Also important is the collection of data and an audit of neighborhood problems and the resources available to deal with those problems. Federal funds are then used for additional equipment and resources.

Examples of weed-and-seed operations are varied (U.S. Department of Justice, 2001):

Saturation patrols in high-crime neighborhoods

Saturation patrols coupled with an anti–gun violence educational program to deal with firearms on school grounds

Hiring additional off-duty police officers to run athletic programs

Increasing treatment services for neighborhood drug addicts

Community beautification programs, including the removal of graffiti and vacant buildings in rundown areas

The key to the success or failure of a weed-and-seed program is the extent to which the steering committee is able to function and achieve measurable results over time. An evaluation of eight urban sites (Dunsworth and Mills, 1999) showed that serious Part I offenses declined (weeding), especially in those areas where neighborhoods were targeted. The evaluation found that it was too soon to measure the efforts on community development and relationship building (seeding).

HOT SPOTS

All the various proactive patrol strategies, as well as community policing, work only when a police department has a split force. Patrol forces are split into a number of forces. The parts of the patrol force that are held back from servicing the reactive 911 calls are used for other purposes.

Larry Sherman found something very special while analyzing domestic violence calls to the police. He found that "chronically violent couples can be identified and predicted [and] chronic locations of domestic calls can be predicted" (Sherman, 1992: 214). He found that "over half (53%) of all domestic calls in Minneapolis occurred at buildings with four or more calls in 1986" (1992: 227). A few years after this research, Sherman cites a case in the same city where 13 patrol cars responded to seven domestic calls in 48 hours for the same apartment. In Milwaukee, he found that two-thirds of domestic calls "involved couples with two or more incidents in a 33-month period" (1992: 214).

This analysis can be applied to street crimes. In "Repeat Calls for Service: Policing Hot Spots," Sherman noted, "Three percent of the 115,000 addresses and intersections in Minneapolis were the subject of 50 percent of the 321,174 calls to police" (1989: 150). He noted under what he calls "dial-a-cop," his name for the 911 reactive system of policing: "The chronic locations are not given extra attention to try to reduce their heavy demands on police."

With a good data-analysis management system tied into the 911 system, a proactive plan for policing **hot spots** can be created. There are a number of issues:

1. *Specific names are needed for specific locations.* For example, a bar can be known as Teddy's Twilight Bar at 110 Main Street. It can be known as (1) Twilight, (2) Teddy's, (3) 110 Main Street, (4) Twilight Bar, and so on. You might need a computer program to sort this out so that management knows that all calls came from one location.
2. *A criterion must be created for the definition of a "chronic location."* Some examples would be top 50, 100, or 250 called in terms of calls per year,

minimum of 100 calls, 50 calls, and so on. The size of the population
would determine the criterion.

3. *The calls have to be categorized.* False alarm calls and lockouts would have
   policy implications in some jurisdictions, while domestic violence and burglary would be important in other jurisdictions. Discount stores, 24-hour
   convenience stores, various public and private apartments, and medium-
   and low-priced hotels and bars are common hot spots.

4. *An action plan must be formulated and implemented* to reduce the number
   of calls while dealing with the crime and problems generating the calls.

5. *An evaluation must be implemented.* A useful evaluation combines statistics
   related to charges in the number of calls per location and a questionnaire
   given to people at the hot spots. The evaluation should also take into
   account any new hot spots created by the displacement of crimes.

Can focusing on hot spots work? Yes, if there is good analysis with a good
police team involved in the planning and implementation efforts. It is better to
focus on a few hot spots with an experienced team than to spread the police resources too thin. It will also work with the help of other public and private
agencies, including liquor licensing authorities, the telephone company, department of health, and public housing agencies.

POLICE PURSUIT POLICIES

Current data and written policies on **police pursuits** are needed. In a national
sample of pursuit policies in police agencies conducted in 1994 and 1995, 737
agencies were contacted. Thirty-eight percent could not supply usable data,
and 17 agencies refused to supply data. Ninety-one percent of the responding
agencies had written policies, and 48 percent had modified their policies in the
last two years, with 87 percent making them more restrictive (Alpert, 1997b: 2).
This was a survey of 436 agencies of various sizes throughout the nation.

The pursuit data of three agencies were analyzed in depth. The results are
shown in Table 8–4.

TABLE 8–4 *Police Pursuit Data Table*

Agency	Number of Pursuits	Pursuit for Property Damage	Pursuit for Personal Injuries	Pursuit for Traffic Violations
Miami-Dade, Florida	1,000	41% (428)	20% (213)	45%
Omaha, Nebraska	229	40% (91)	14% (31)	51%

Aiken County, South Carolina, reported only 18 pursuits and is omitted from the table because of
the small numbers.
Source: Alpert, 1997b: 3.

The most likely location for personal injury and property damages was on urban and suburban streets rather than on limited-access highways. The higher the number of pursuing vehicles, the more police agencies involved, and the higher the speed, the greater the likelihood of an accident.

It was also clear that the more permissive the police management pursuit policy, the larger the number of pursuits and resulting pursuit accidents. In Miami-Dade, when more restrictive policies were put in place, pursuits went from 279 to 51. In Omaha, when more permissive policies were put in place, pursuits rose from 17 to 122.

On May 26, 1998, the U.S. Supreme Court, in *County of Sacramento* v. *Lewis*, ruled,

> Accordingly, we hold that high-speed chases with no intent to harm suspects physically or to worsen their legal plight do not give rise to liability under the Fourteenth Amendment redressible by an action under § 1983.

As Alpert and Clarke (1998: 2) report, "The Court closed the door on the constitutional liability for officers involved in pursuits that do not 'shock the conscience.'" In the *Lewis* case, the police officer was pursuing two boys who were on a motorcycle for a refusal to halt and a possible traffic violation of speeding. The officer's vehicle skidded into one of the teenagers at 40 miles an hour and killed him. Speeds during the pursuit reached 100 miles an hour. What will "shock the conscience" is a high barrier, indeed.

The Court did not specifically rule on municipal liability in the case and said so. However, in *City of Canton* v. *Harris* (1989), the Supreme Court earlier ruled that the lack of training created municipal liability (Alpert and Clarke, 1998: 3):

> We hold today that the inadequacy of police training may serve as the basis for a § 1983 liability only where the failure to train amounts to deliberate indifference to the rights of persons with whom the police come into contact.

Let us now look at proactive police management policies that will protect citizens and municipal liability while balancing the need to arrest high-risk and dangerous offenders who can harm the public. Given the high property and personal damages in pursuit driving, proactive police managers should create the most restrictive written pursuit policies. Alpert and Clarke (1998: 8) recommend a policy like the one instituted by Chief Wall of Virginia Beach, Virginia, on May 28, 1998, in General Order 8.04:

> Vehicle pursuit shall only be initiated when an officer can articulate a reasonable belief that the occupant(s) of the fleeing vehicle have committed or attempted to commit a violent felony or offense involving the unlawful use, discharge,

threatened use, display or possession of a firearm or destructive/explosive device or bomb. All other pursuits are prohibited.

If officers' and citizens' lives and property are put at risk, the pursuit reason should be more serious than a routine traffic violation.

The Pursuit Management Task Force (National Institute of Justice, 1998a: 1) recommended the development of "vehicle-stopping technologies currently available, under development, and potentially available." The vehicle-stopping device that is available now is an inflatable device that is placed in front of fleeing vehicles to pierce their tires. In development are devices to shut down a vehicle's electrical system.

Helicopters allow for safer pursuits. Police vehicles can slow down and still know where the pursued vehicle is by talking to the helicopter crew. Helicopters can also illuminate the fleeing vehicle and surroundings. As Alpert (1998: 2) states, "The helicopter can assist ground units as a platform from which to observe, track and illuminate people or places on the ground. . . . Flight crews . . . can provide information to direct towards an intended position or away from a dangerous one."

With the advent of computer-controlled vehicle systems, an electronic solution to vehicle pursuit should be in our immediate future and would change vehicle-pursuit policies to vehicle-stopping policies. Vehicle-stopping policies are preferable to the present pursuit policies with their high risk for personal injury and property damage.

Pursuit Policy Recommendations

1. The most restrictive written pursuit policy should be in place as a general order.
2. Police pursuit training needs to be universal and continual for all patrol officers.
3. Police pursuit training needs to include the discussion of the criteria used by a police officer to pursue a fleeing vehicle and how to operationalize these criteria.
4. Low-risk, low-speed pursuits are preferable to high-risk, high-speed pursuits.
5. Alternative vehicle-stopping devices are preferable to police pursuit.
6. Vehicle-stopping policies should eventually be substituted for the present high-risk pursuit policies.

CONCLUSION

Patrol is the most visible function in police operations. The concept of preventive patrol has come under great scrutiny based on the cost of vehicles and personnel and the seeming noneffect it has on crime incidents. Various studies and experimental programs have concluded that patrol should be directed to certain areas based on criminal activity and that all citizen calls do not merit a two-minute response time. The strategy is to cut down on patrol costs and to create the optimum use of a professional police officer's time. However, political policy for many communities dictates the need for a police presence to reduce fear despite these fiscal and operational considerations.

The need for increased police presence and for new ways to address fundamental crime problems forms the basis for community and problem-oriented policing. In this chapter, we examined the theoretical differences between these two concepts, which are often used interchangeably. Some writers on community policing refer to community policing as the philosophy and to problem-oriented policing as an analytic tool for dealing with the causes of crime.

Community policing continues to attract much attention at professional conferences and seminars—especially as it relates to homeland security. The concept, however, cannot be perceived as a panacea for a community's crime problem, and it involves a long-term political and fiscal commitment. Recall that team police programs were shelved once federal or state grant support ended. The key players for any change are line and middle-management personnel in the department, which can be a difficult process in view of our discussion on police subculture.

QUESTIONS FOR REVIEW

1. What is meant by traditional police patrol? What activities are the usual components of traditional police patrol?
2. What is the significance of the Kansas City Studies?
3. What variables might lead one to conclude that traditional police patrol is a waste of time?
4. How are many agencies rethinking traditional police patrol in terms of administrative tasks and nonessential calls?
5. Why is crime analysis an important component of directed patrol?
6. What is the track record of cities that have experimented with directed patrol? With team policing? With POP and COP?
7. How does directed patrol differ from specialized patrol? What are some examples of specialized patrol?
8. Why might proactive patrol be an important police methodology in the future?
9. Discuss the positive and negative attributes of community policing.
10. Explain the differences between tactical patrol and team policing.
11. Present the various components needed for community policing implementation.

12. Outline the major management styles and leadership styles that would (1) be useful for implementing community policing and (2) be detrimental to the implementation of community policing. Explain.

CLASS PROJECT

Select three major police departments in three different states and locate them on the World Wide Web. From their homepage, go to those sites that publicize community-policing programs. Write a brief description of each program and compare them with your selections and those of your classmates. See if any of the programs are related to homeland security concerns.

From the information gathered, analyze whether the programs fit the formal definition of community policing or community relations. A note of caution—pay attention to when the Web site was updated. You may find that many sites are out of date!

BIBLIOGRAPHY

ALPERT, GEOFFREY P. *Police Pursuit: Policies and Training*. Washington, D.C.: National Institute of Justice, 1997a.

———. "Pursuit Driving: Planning Policies and Action from Agency, Offer and Public Information." *Police Forum* (January 1997b), pp. 1–12.

———. *Helicopter in Pursuit Operations*. Washington, D.C.: National Institute of Justice, 1998.

ALPERT, GEOFFREY P., and ANDREW CLARKE. "*County of Sacramento* v. *Lewis:* Its Impact and Unresolved Issues." *Police Forum* (October 1998), pp. 1–9.

ALPERT, GEOFFREY P., ET AL. *Police Pursuits and the Use of Force: A Final Report to the National Institute of Justice*. Washington, DC.: National Institute of Justice, 1996.

AUTEN, JAMES. *An Analysis of Police Pursuit Driving Operations*. Vols. 1 and 2. Champaign, Ill.: Police Training Institute, 1994.

BARBER, ROBERT R. "Neighborhood Service Team." *Law Enforcement Bulletin* (January 1996), pp. 17–22.

BLOCH, PETER B., and DAVID SPECHT. *Neighborhood Team Policing*. Washington, D.C.: U.S. Government Printing Office, 1973.

BLUMBERG, ABRAHAM, and ELAINE NIEDERHOFFER. *The Ambivalent Force*. Hinsdale, Ill.: Dryden Press, 1985.

BROWN, LEE. *Community Policing: A Practical Guide for Police Officials*. Washington, D.C.: National Institute of Justice, 1989.

BUREAU OF JUSTICE STATISTICS. "Law Enforcement Management and Administrative Statistics—Local Police Departments 2000." Washington, D.C.: United States Department of Justice—Office of Justice Program, January 2003. Web posted at www.ojp.usdoj.gov/bjs/pu. Accessed March 15, 2003.

BUREAU FOR MUNICIPAL POLICE, STATE OF NEW YORK. Seminar on Community Policing. New York: John Jay College, April 9, 1990.

CHAIKEN, J.M. *Patrol Allocation Methodology for Police Departments*. Santa Monica, Calif.: RAND, 1975.

COMMUNITY POLICING EXCHANGE. Washington, D.C.: Community Policing Consortium, 1995–1998.

DART, R., V. LUBANS, and R. SHOWALTER. *Plan to Increase Police Productivity: A Report on the Reorganization of the East Hartford Police Department*. Bethesda, Md.: Social Development Corporation, 1974.

DUNHAM, ROGER G., and GEOFFREY P. ALPERT. *Critical Issues in Policing*. Prospect Heights, Ill.: Waveland Press, 1997.

DUNSORTH, TERRENCE, and GREGORY MILLS. *National Evaluation of Weed and Seed*. Washington, D.C.: U.S. Department of Justice, 1999.

ECK, JOHN E., and WILLIAM SPELMAN. "Problem-Oriented Policing in Newport News." In Roger G. Dunham and Geoffrey P. Alpert, eds., *Critical Issues in Policing*. Prospect Heights, Ill.: Waveland Press, 1993.

EDGAR, JAMES M., ET AL. *Team Policing: A Selected Bibliography*. Washington, D.C.: U.S. Government Printing Office, 1976.

ELLIOTT, J.F. *Interception Patrol: An Examination of the Theory of Random Patrol as a Municipal Police Tactic*. Springfield, Ill.: Charles C Thomas, 1973a.

———. *New Police: A Description of a Possible Form of What the Municipal Police Will Evolve Into, Why They Must Change, and How Evolution May Be Accomplished*. Springfield, Ill.: Charles C Thomas, 1973b.

FLEISSNER, DAN, ET AL. *Community Policing in Seattle: A Model Partnership between Citizens and Police*. Washington, D.C.: U.S. Department of Justice, 1992.

GARNER J., and E. CLEMMER. *Danger to Police in Domestic Disturbances—A New Look*. Washington, D.C.: U.S. Department of Justice, 1986.

GAY, W.G., H. TALMADGE DAY, and JANE P. WOODWARD. *Phase I Summary Report: Neighborhood Team Policing*. Washington, D.C.: U.S. Government Printing Office, 1977a.

GAY, W.G., T.H. SCHELL, and S. SCHACK. *Improving Patrol Productivity*, Vol. 1: *Routine Patrol*. Washington, D.C.: U.S. Government Printing Office, 1977b.

GOLDSTEIN, HERMAN. "Improving Policing: A Problem-Oriented Approach." *Crime and Delinquency*, 25 (1979), pp. 236–58.

———. *Problem-Oriented Policing*. New York: McGraw-Hill, 1990.

GRABIN, SCOTT D. "Bike Patrol Policing Public Housing Developments." *FBI Law Enforcement Bulletin* (September 1993). Web posted at www.fbi.gov/publications/leb/1989–1995. Accessed March 10, 2003.

GREENE, JACK R. "Police and Community Relations: Where Have We Been and Where Are We Going?" In *Critical Issues in Policing*. Prospect Heights, Ill.: Waveland Press, 1989, pp. 349–368.

HARTNETT, SUSAN M., and WESLEY G. SKOGAN. "Community Policing: Chicago's Experience." *National Institute of Justice Journal* (April 1999), pp. 13–17.

KELLING, GEORGE. *Foot Patrol*. Washington, D.C.: National Institute of Justice, 1987.

———. "Police and Communities: The Quiet Revolution." In Larry J. Siegel, ed., *American Justice: Research of the National Institute of Justice*. St. Paul, Minn.: West, 1991, pp. 121–128.

KELLING, GEORGE, and WILLIAM J. BRATTON. *Implementing Community Policing: The Administrative Problem.* Washington, D.C.: U.S. Department of Justice, 1993.

KELLING, GEORGE, ET AL. *Patrol Experiment: A Summary Report and a Technical Report.* Washington, D.C.: Police Foundation, 1974.

LARSON, RICHARD C., and MICHAEL F. CAHN. *Synthesizing and Extending the Results of Police Patrol Studies.* Washington, D.C.: National Institute of Justice, 1985.

LEVINE, MARGARET J., and J. THOMAS MCEWEN. *Patrol Deployment.* Washington, D.C.: National Institute of Justice, 1985.

MOORE, MARK H., and ROBERT C. TROJANOWICZ. "Policing and Fear of Crime." In Larry J. Siegel, ed., *American Justice: Research of the National Institute of Justice.* St. Paul, Minn.: West, 1991, pp. 129–136.

MUSTOFSKI, S., R.B. PARKS, and R.E. WORDEN. *Community Policing in Action: Lessons from an Observational Study.* Washington, D.C.: National Institute of Justice, 1998.

NATIONAL ADVISORY COMMISSION ON CRIMINAL JUSTICE STANDARDS AND GOALS. *Police.* Washington, D.C.: U.S. Government Printing Office, 1973.

NATIONAL COMMISSION ON THE CAUSES AND PREVENTION OF VIOLENCE. *Rights in Conflict* (Walker Report). New York: New American Library, 1968.

———. *To Establish Justice to Insure Domestic Tranquility.* Final Report. Washington, D.C.: U.S. Government Printing Office, December 1969a.

———. *Staff Reports.* Vols. 1–15. Washington, D.C.: U.S. Government Printing Office, 1969b.

———. *Twenty-Five Years of Criminal Justice Research.* Washington, D.C.: National Institute of Justice, December 1994.

NATIONAL INSTITUTE OF JUSTICE. *Community Policing in Chicago: Year Two.* Washington, D.C.: National Institute of Justice, 1995a.

———. *Policing Drug Hot Spots.* Washington, D.C.: U.S. Department of Justice, 1996.

———. *Pursuit Management Task Force.* Washington, D.C.: Department of Justice, 1998a.

———. *Year in Review, 1997.* Washington, D.C.: Department of Justice, 1998b.

———. *Public Involvement: Community Policing in Chicago.* Washington, D.C.: National Institute of Justice, 2000.

O'CONNER, TARA, and ANN C. GRANT. *Problem Oriented Policing.* Washington, D.C.: Police Executive Research Forum, 1998.

O'KEEFE, GARRETT, ET AL. *"Taking a Bite Out of Crime": The Impact of a Mass Media Crime Prevention Campaign.* Washington, D.C.: National Institute of Justice, 1984.

OLIVER, WILLARD M. *Community Policing.* Upper Saddle River, N.J.: Prentice Hall, 2000.

PALMIOTT, MICHAEL. *Community Policing.* Gaithersburg, Md.: Aspen, 2000.

PATE, ANTONY MICHAEL. "Community-Oriented Policing in Baltimore." In Dennis Jay Kenny, ed., *Police and Policing: Contemporary Issues.* New York: Praeger, 1989.

POLICE EXECUTIVE RESEARCH FORUM. *Excellence in Problem-Oriented Policing: The 2001 Herman Goldstein Award Winners.* Washington, D.C.: Police Executive Research Forum, 2001.

PRESIDENT'S COMMISSION ON LAW ENFORCEMENT AND THE ADMINISTRATION OF JUSTICE. *The Police.* Washington, D.C.: U.S. Government Printing Office, 1967.

QUINT, THURMAN, and EDMUND E. MCGARRELL. *Community Policing in a Rural Setting.* Cincinnati: Anderson, 1997.

QUINT, THURMAN, JIHONG ZHAO, and ANDREW L. GIACOMAZZI. *Community Policing in a Community Era*. Los Angeles: Roxbury, 2001.

REICHER, LISA M., and ROY R. ROBERT. "Community Policing: A Critical Review of Underlying Assumptions." *Journal of Police Science and Administration*, 17, no. 2 (June 1990), pp. 105–114.

REINER, HOBART G. *Crime Analysis in Support of Patrol*. Washington, D.C.: National Institute of Law Enforcement and Criminal Justice, 1977.

REISS, ALBERT J., JR. *The Police and the Public*. New Haven, Conn.: Yale University Press, 1971.

RICHARDSON, J.F. *Urban Police in the United States*. Port Washington, N.Y.: Kennikat, 1974.

SCHACK, S., and W.G. GAY. *Improving Patrol Productivity*, Vol. 2: *Specialized Patrol*. Washington, D.C.: University City Science Center, 1977.

SCHELL, T.H., ET AL. *Traditional Preventive Patrol—Summary Report—National Evaluation Program—Phase I Report*. Washington, D.C.: University City Science Center, 1973.

SHELLY, TARA O'CONNOR, and ANNE C. GRANT, eds. *Problem Oriented Policing: Crime-Specific Problems, Critical Issues and Making POP Work*. Washington, D.C.: Police Executive Research Forum, 1998.

SHERMAN, LAWRENCE. *Team Policing: Seven Case Studies*. Washington, D.C.: University City Science Center, 1976.

SHERMAN, LAWRENCE W., ed. *Police Corruption: A Sociological Perspective*. Garden City, N.Y: Doubleday/Anchor, 1974.

SILVER, ISIDORE. *Neighborhood Safety*. Washington, D.C.: National Institute of Justice, 1987.

———. "Repeat Calls for Service: Policing Hot Spots." In Dennis Jay Kenney, ed., *Police and Policing*. New York: Praeger, 1989.

———. *Police Civil Liability*. New York: Matthew Bender, 1992a.

———. *Policing Domestic Violence*. New York: Free Press, 1992b.

SKOGAN, WESLEY G. "The Community Role in Community Policing." *National Institute of Justice Journal* (August 1996), pp. 31–32.

SKOGAN, WESLEY G., and S.M. HARTNETT. *Community Policing Chicago Style*. New York: Oxford University Press, 1997.

SPARROW, MALCOLM K. *Implementing Community Policing*. Washington, D.C: National Institute of Justice, 1988.

SPELMAN, WILLIAM, and JOHN E. ECK. "Newport News Tests Problem-Oriented Policing." *National Institute of Justice Reports* (January/February 1987a), pp. 2–8.

———. *Problem-Oriented Policing*. Washington, D.C.: National Institute of Justice, 1987b.

THIBAULT, EDWARD. "The Blue Milieu: Police as a Vocational Subculture." In John W. Bizzack, ed., *New Perspectives: Issues in Policing*. Lexington, Ky.: Autumn House, 1992.

THURMAN, QUINT C., and EDMUND F. MCGARRELL. *Community Policing in Rural America*. Cincinnati: Anderson, 1997.

TROJANOWICZ, ROBERT, and BONNIE BUSQUEROUX. *Community Policing*. Cincinnati: Anderson, 1990.

TROJANOWICZ, ROBERT, ET AL. *Community Policing: A Contemporary Perspective* (2nd ed.). Cincinnati: Anderson, 1998.

U.S. DEPARTMENT OF JUSTICE. *Executive Office for Weed and Seed: Implementation Manual.* Washington, D.C.: Office of Justice Programs, n.d.

———. *Weed and Seed In-Sites Magazine,* 9, no. 5 (November/December 2001).

WESTLEY, WILLIAM. *Violence and the Police.* Cambridge, Mass.: MIT Press, 1970.

WILSON, JAMES Q. *Thinking About Crime.* New York: Basic Books, 1975.

9

BASIC LINE FUNCTIONS

KEY TERMS

Amber Alert

Boston Gun Project

career criminal

case screening

doli incapax

Drug Abuse Resistance
  Education (DARE)

informant

In re Gault

Managing Criminal
  Investigations (MCI)

neutral zone

parens patriae

PRELIMINARY

racial profiling

ride-along program

school violence

station-house probation

status offense

stranger-danger program

vice

Although patrol is the major line function, policing encompasses a variety of other functions designed to provide an entire range of law enforcement services to the community. These services can be classified as

Traffic

Vice

Juvenile

Investigations

Other specialized line functions include hostage and negotiating teams, arson and narcotics task forces, and emergency services.

In larger departments, these functions—as well as patrol—are organized as separate entities and are assigned specific responsibilities; in smaller departments, each officer may provide the entire range of services. During one tour of duty, it would not be unusual for a village police officer to investigate a car accident, follow through on a continuing burglary investigation, and arrest a juvenile suspect. In larger departments, these tasks would be handled separately by the traffic division, the investigation unit, and the juvenile unit.

The number of divisions that exist in a department depends on the size and history of both the community and the law enforcement agency. Specific problems may warrant the creation of new organizational units. A city with a large banking community may have a computer/financial fraud unit. In one department of 140 sworn officers, the traffic division handled all matters related to traffic enforcement: accident investigations, issuing parking tickets, processing drunk-driving arrests, and even supervising the installation of traffic signs. In another department of similar size, these tasks were delegated as general patrol work.

In discussing this matter of police line functions, it must be stressed that although similar tasks need to be carried out and thus the general descriptions are useful, specific organizational structures will vary. The variables of agency size, community need, and history are of great importance when making realistic comparisons of police organizational structure.

GENERALIST–SPECIALIST CONTROVERSY

A question that normally arises at this point is, Why not simply have the patrol officer handle every type of complaint and situation? This is the standard generalist-versus-specialist argument that police have been engaged in for decades. Realizing that all police officers have to be generalists to some extent, there are good arguments for specialization and the organization of departments into specific divisions.

The first major argument is that of control. Especially in larger departments with hundreds of personnel, organization into divisions is a mechanism with which to direct the overall activities of the agency. Thus, personnel are allocated according to bureau or division to address specifics in a certain category of police problems.

Second, priorities have to be set, and work has to get done in an organized manner. Given the wide range of tasks that police agencies confront, the commander of a division and the chief in charge of all divisions can set up priorities. The delegation of duties by division or squad is traditionally taken to remedy the delivery of specific police services. For example, there may be an outcry in the community concerning juvenile crime. The resources of the juvenile division can be expanded, and the commander in charge of that division can set priorities, depending on community demand.

Finally, there is the traditional argument—namely, that specialization leads to expertise and that the police agency receives the benefit of efficient, knowledgeable experts by organizing according to divisions. Over time, the delegation of the same type of responsibilities to the same officers means that these officers are continually gathering current information concerning these specialized problems. It means that the department can allocate its in-service training resources to send a few specialists to high-powered training sessions in their fields of expertise. These expert professional law enforcement officers can then apply this specialized knowledge in their divisions. As a consequence, the department does not need to send every officer to every specialized training session to have their offices informed and up to date.

An example might help to clarify this issue. An officer assigned to the traffic division dealing with traffic and accident investigation will expect to be familiar with a wide variety of traffic topics. Subspecialties might be developed in traffic-flow planning, community education, accident investigation, vehicle and traffic law, and drunk driving. Another officer might develop expertise in disaster planning (for example, blizzards, hurricanes, and floods and their relationship to traffic flow and accidents).

Looking at the other side of the generalist-specialist controversy, what occurs when specialization goes too far? The answer is often that communication breaks down among divisions and individual commanders begin to build bureaucratic empires, wherein one bureau tries to outdo another in competition for perceived glory and resources.

This happens too often in the competition between the patrol and detective divisions. Patrol officers are tightly supervised and are expected to control the crime scene and to report the crime to the detective division. Detectives are expected to give the reporting officers credit for their work and to follow up the crime with analysis and investigation. Patrol officers are often jealous of the status that an officer in the detective division enjoys. They also feel that patrol officers may be the first on the scene but the last to receive credit and praise. Often, detectives do feel they are superior and neglect the patrol officers. Over time this can result in patrol officers rationalizing, "Why go out of our way for those guys?" or "Let the detectives do it; it's not our job." Sloppy jobs are done on crime scenes, and detectives end up *not* utilizing the talents of the patrol officers. Management has to be aware of these tendencies in all divisions and take steps to improve communication continually.

In discussing the duties and responsibilities of line functions, we will also be looking at certain general principles that can lead to managerial improvements:

1. Assignments for all personnel should be based on the assumption that the job should present new challenges and lead to the acquisition and development of professional skills.
2. The best person should be selected for the job based on ability, credentials, and track record.
3. Police agencies should accept that there is a need for certain specialists but should keep the number of specialists and their areas of specialization within reason.
4. Periodically, each agency should review the number of subgroups that exist in the formal organization and the need for their existence. This evaluation

should take place in terms of each bureau's contribution to the police mission and whether its functions should be merged or returned to another bureau or division (e.g., patrol).

In agencies where the patrol officer is a generalist, performance improvement is best reviewed by tasks rather than by bureaucratic function. This topic is discussed in Chapter 8.

TRAFFIC

As the United States continues to rely on automobile transportation, traffic patterns and enforcement remain very important. Throughout the country, suburbs continue to proliferate outside central cities, resulting in traffic congestion and flow problems. The new problems faced by highway police units include major traffic tie-ups from even the most minor accidents, aggressive driving on freeways, and assaults with vehicles and weapons between drivers engaged in aggressive traffic behaviors, often referred to as *road rage*. In many states, there has been an increase in new traffic safety laws, such as mandatory seat-belt and child-restraint use, and an aggressive stance toward driving while under the influence of alcohol or drugs. Traffic enforcement can often yield other benefits, such as the solving of major cases. Recall that a traffic stop for a minor violation resulted in the arrest of Oklahoma City bomber Timothy McVeigh.

Against this background, the role of the police in this function is varied, involving the following:

Elimination of accident causes and congestion

Identification of potential traffic problems and hazards

Regulation of parking on the street and at municipal facilities

Investigation of property damage and personal-injury automobile accidents

Direction of public awareness toward the proper use of motor vehicles and bicycles

Arrest of offenders

Effective Management in Traffic Matters

The amount of resources and the number of personnel devoted to traffic enforcement depend, of course, on the needs of the community. We do, however, offer the following guidelines:

1. Parking enforcement should be the responsibility of civilians or traffic wardens. There is little need for trained police officers to be solely involved with issuing parking tickets or directing traffic. These functions are, for the most part, mechanical and do not require a high level of expertise.

2. Patrol officers should be trained in all areas of traffic enforcement, including preliminary accident investigations, use of speed- and alcohol-detection devices, and knowledge of vehicle and traffic laws. This aspect of police training is especially important because of the high number of traffic cases that make their way into civil and criminal courts and require review of the actions of the investigating officers and the policies of the department.

3. Certain officers, according to their interests, should be trained in specialized topics, such as traffic planning, fatality investigation, and community-awareness programs. A number of excellent programs, funded by state and federal highway safety grants, are available for such training. One example is the course offered by the Traffic Institute sponsored by Northwestern University.

Highways remain the primary means of inter- and intrastate commerce for goods and services. As a result, many state police agencies have highway units devoted to the enforcement of commercial trucking and bus regulations related to trailer weight, hazardous cargo, and driver records.

The use of vehicles as the primary means of drug transportation results in aggressive enforcement of state drug statutes based on traffic enforcement stops. This has resulted in increased high-speed chases and high-risk traffic stops between officers and narcotics traffickers. It has also raised the issue of allegedly biased traffic stops by police in which African-American or Hispanic drivers are stopped with greater frequency than white drivers.

Technology continues to change the face of traffic enforcement. While pull-overs by a single patrol unit remain the mainstay of enforcement, new strategies involve targeting traffic problem areas with multijurisdictional units. In certain municipalities, digital cameras mounted on light poles activate when a driver goes through a red light. The summons is then mailed to the owner of the vehicle. In one state, state patrol officers use cameras mounted in a van to capture speeders on major expressways, eliminating pull-overs in densely driven areas.

Racial Profiling

Major incidents in New Jersey, Maryland, and Colorado have made **racial profiling** a police management problem. By September 2002, 21 states had adopted legislation or policies to prevent racial profiling. In many departments, traffic officers are expected to check off the race of the citizen involved in a traffic stop on a traffic form. The St. Paul Police Department has agreed to the following "racial profile Miranda warning" in a consent decree with the National Association for the Advancement of Colored People (Buerger and Farrell, 2002: 406):

I would like to search you or your vehicle.

You should know you have a right to refuse to allow me to search you or your vehicle.

If you do grant me permission, you may stop the search at any time.

If I find anything, you will likely be arrested and prosecuted.

May I search you? May I search your vehicle?

How have we come to this? In 1999, 19.3 million drivers were pulled over in traffic stops; they included over 14 million whites, 2.2 million blacks, and 1.6 million Hispanics. White officers ticketed 52.1 percent of white drivers and 60.6 percent of black drivers. Black officers ticketed 58.3 percent of white drivers and 65.9 percent of black drivers. White officers arrested 2.6 percent of white drivers and 5.3 percent of black drivers. Black officers arrested 1.3 percent of white drivers and 4.6 percent of black drivers (Langan et al., 2001: 14, 19). Looking at these overall numbers, black officers issued as many tickets on black drivers. This gives a reasonable perspective on racial profiling as a nationwide problem.

The U.S. General Accounting Office defined *racial profiling* in 2000 as "using race as a key factor in deciding to make a traffic stop." Chapter 228 of the Massachusetts Law of 2000 defines profiling as "the suspicion of an entire class of people without any individualized suspicion of the particular person being stopped." (This definition would fit any type of profiling, including gender, religion, and nationality.)

Racial profiling in traffic enforcement can be traced to 1984 with the Drug Enforcement Administration's (DEA) Operation Pipeline. For this program, the DEA created a profile of major drug "mule" drivers in Florida driving north: two black or Hispanic males in a fast rented car or a junker, one ignition key, driving above the posted speed limit in shifts with fast-food wrappers in the car, pillows and blankets for sleeping, and air fresheners to conceal the smell of drugs. This became the rationale for racial profiling and the basis for a number of major law suits, which include the following:

State of New Jersey v. *Pedro et al.* (1996). Seventeen drug charges based on vehicle stops made by the southern New Jersey drug intervention unit were rejected because of racial profiling. While 15 percent of motorists violating traffic laws were black, as determined by a rolling survey by John Lambreth of Temple University, 46 percent of violators pulled over in a 40-month period on the New Jersey Turnpike were black. Lamreth said black drivers were pulled over 4.85 times more often than white drivers. The court concluded that the "de facto policy of targeting Blacks for investigation and arrest" violated equal protection and due process. The evidence was dismissed (Buerger and Farrell, 2002: 277–79).

Wilkins v. *Maryland State Police* (1992). Police patrols stopped Robert Wilkins and his family and made them stand by the side of the road in the dark and the rain while a drug-sniffing dog was brought to the scene. No drugs were found, and the driver was issued a ticket and let go. Professor Lambreth did another rolling survey. Of the 823 searches done by Maryland State Troopers on the I-95 corridor, 661 were of minority motorists. Contraband was found in 29.9

percent of the stops, which was comparable to statewide stops. The case was settled and sealed before trial.

Whitefield v. *Board of Commissioners of Eagle County, Colorado* (1993). The High County Drug Task Force used the Operation Pipeline profile to stop cars. The court ruled that the profile did not constitute probable cause for stopping cars and suppressed 23 pounds of cocaine as evidence. The court stated, "An equation of race with suspicious criminal activity would be nothing more than a racist assumption." It was unconstitutional to stop cars based solely on "race, ethnicity or state of residence" (Buerger and Farrell, 2002: 283–84).

The major case that attracted national attention occurred on the New Jersey Turnpike. On April 23, 1998, at 11:00 P.M., two New Jersey state troopers stopped three Hispanic males and one black male. Their Dodge Caravan rolled slowly backward at one point, and the troopers fired 11 shots into the vehicle, wounding three occupants. A search found no drugs or contraband. A reenactment a year later by a team of experts showed that the whole incident took 10 seconds. Lawyers asserted a pattern of discriminatory stops by troopers. A grand jury indicted the officers for attempted murder.

The Department of Justice threatened to file a suit based on a pattern and practice of racial discrimination on traffic stops by the New Jersey State Police. In 2000, the state of New Jersey settled the civil lawsuit for $12.95 million. The two troopers pleaded guilty to obstructing the investigation by lying about the race of the drivers they had stopped on other occasions to conceal that they were singling out blacks and Hispanics, and they paid a fine of $280 each. Based on 91,000 pages of documents, the New Jersey Attorney General said that eight out of 10 automobile searches by state troopers were done on vehicles driven by Hispanics or blacks. A consent decree signed with the Justice Department "included a prohibition against relying on race or national or ethnic origin of motorist in selecting vehicles for stops and . . . post-stop actions" (Buerger and Farrell, 2002: 280–91).

Racial profiling is also an issue in the fight against terrorism. However, specific information on members of a group or organization wanted for crimes or acts of terror that includes race as a descriptor may be used as a probable cause for stopping a citizen. Rabbi David Lapin, a member of California's Diversity Advisory Council for Police Officers, states (2002: 9), "In the fight against terrorism, law enforcement is seeking members of known groups with declared intent to harm, kill and commit crimes. Using any descriptive profile to identify possible members of these groups within the bound of the law is ethical." He stresses that this profiling is based on intelligence rather than mere suspicion.

False positives are a major problem of using race or ethnicity to stop citizens, whether they are driving cars or not. Too many innocent citizens are stopped, and it is a huge waste of a police officer's time. Stopping citizens because of their race is unethical and should be treated with zero tolerance.

Profiling has been used successfully in tracking down serial killers, however. Patterns of criminal behavior, or modi operandi, are a type of profiling based on specific data. For example, serial killers are mostly white males in their twenties who plan their crimes very carefully and are motivated by power and sadism (Fox and Levin, 2001: 102–108).

VICE

Vice is generally considered to be crimes against public morals. Examples of vice offenses are

> Pornography
> Prostitution
> Gambling
> Illegal drugs (controlled substances)
> Illegal sale and manufacture of alcohol

These have historically been the province of the police because of public clamor for enforcement of laws created to eliminate these activities.

In theory, these offenses are considered victimless, or nonpredatory, crimes. The offender is normally offering a service or buying a service. If there were no customers for vice crimes, there would be no vice. In the area of drug addiction, however, there are secondary victims, as the drug addict attempts to "feed his habit" through street crimes. Also, there are cases of pimps placing young women on habit-forming drugs to enslave them in a life of prostitution. However, because these crimes are perceived as victimless by much of the public, vice laws are especially hard to enforce. In some communities, there is political pressure not to enforce certain vice laws. In other locales, what is a crime in one community may be legal a few feet across the county or state line. This is especially true in states that have legalized gambling.

The term *organized crime* often comes up when discussing organizational dimensions of vice activity. Based on our experience, organized crime occurs when you have a continuing criminal economic enterprise with a succession of leadership. From a media perspective, there is the Italian mafia, the Russian mafia, the Colombian mafia, and so on. However, organized criminal enterprises and groups have to be studied from local, regional, national, and international perspectives in terms of activities, leadership succession, and their involvement in legal and illegal activities.

Drugs

In 1986, James Inciardi concluded in *The War on Drugs* that "drug related crime is out of control" (1986: 131–32). In 1992, he reported a decline in drug use but noted, "The drug trafficking/terrorism connection is important primarily because one tends to facilitate the other" (1991: 227). Drugs, although a major vice problem, had moved beyond the streets to fund terrorism. In 1995, in *The American Drug Scene*, Inciardi says, "If anything has been learned about drug use in the United States, it is an awareness that the problem is dynamic and continuous" (1995: ix).

Drug epidemics come and go. Heroin was popular for a few years, then crack/cocaine raged across the nation, and at the beginning of the twenty-first century, designer drugs and ecstasy became popular. Marijuana is always popular, and cross-addicted alcoholics are common at "hot spot" bars. Meanwhile, we constantly hear from prison authorities that well over 80 percent of incarcerated felons are in prison because of crimes related to drugs and alcohol abuse. The felons are feeding their drug habits, selling and using drugs, and are usually high while they commit property and violent crimes.

In *Criminology Today*, Schmalleger concludes, "Drug abuse has a long and varied history in American society. . . . Although recent statistics show some declines, a hard-core population of illicit drug users remains" (2002: 412). Larry Siegel summarizes the current situation in *Criminology* (2003: 432):

> The problem of drug abuse stretches across the United States. Large urban areas are beset by drug-dealing gangs, drug users who engage in crime to support their habits and alcohol related violence. Rural areas are important staging centers for the shipment of drugs across the country and are often the production sites for synthetic drugs and marijuana farming.

Some are advocating the legalization of drugs out of frustration, while others want to turn the interdiction of drugs into the country over to the military. The "war on drugs" has largely failed, and most therapeutic intervention programs also have overwhelming failure rates. Police efforts have had some limited success in displacing drugs from one neighborhood to another, with some suppression of drug use and drug-related crime. At the same time, rogue countries like Jamaica, Mexico, and the Dominican Republic protect illicit trade traffickers who flood the United States with a wide variety of illegal drugs.

Suppressing the drug trade comes at enormous costs to local police departments. The federal law agencies have been largely ineffective. Regional police efforts combined with government support of drug intervention therapy have shown some promise, but current local approaches are largely futile. The problem is not going away, and there is a great need for proactive regional and federal cooperation.

Prostitution

Prostitution continues to flourish in most heavily populated metropolitan areas (Lyman and Potter, 2000). The red-light district and brothels, which operated under the protection of gangsters, politicians, and the police, have been replaced by streetwalkers, massage parlors, dating services, and "weekend warriors." The range of organization and the need for protection vary based on the number of employees and the need for payoffs to local officials.

Regardless of any controversy over the organizational structure of syndicated crime, vice street offenses present police agencies with an immediate host of problems, especially if they cluster in a specific area. Beyond the commission of the offense, a variety of secondary effects can occur: Customers may be "rolled," other crimes may be committed, and the area may undergo an economic decline. Vice activity that operates without interference by the police, either in a concentrated or a nonconcentrated area (citywide), is perceived by the public to mean that the police are being paid to look the other way.

The enforcement of vice laws is equally frustrating to police officers. The dictum that "the offender goes back on the street before the arresting officer completes the paperwork" is true! This is due to the relative ease with which offenders raise bail or pay the fines that are meted out by the courts. Police officers often agree with a common public attitude that vice offenses are less harmful than violent crimes. This view can be reflected in organizational policy in terms of low priority for vice enforcement. Gambling enforcement is generally viewed by police officers as a source of frustration and is an unpopular assignment.

Vice Units

While some personnel should be given a long-term assignment to vice investigation to establish continuity, vice assignments should generally be of short duration. Continuity is needed to understand the scope of the problem and the nature of investigation methodology, to establish solid interjurisdictional working arrangements, and to train new officers. Short duration is needed for most vice assignments because faces soon become known, especially in undercover work, and officers lose much of their investigative value. Vice investigation is demoralizing, frustrating, and dangerous and often without the kind of backup officers would like to have. It takes a special kind of individual to work undercover, and vice assignments create definite morale and personnel problems for police management.

Units to investigate organized crime are usually found in federal law enforcement agencies and in large city and state police departments because of the multijurisdictional and international nature of cases. Investigations are very expensive in terms of personnel and equipment requirements. Organized crime units investigate the following activities (Albanese et al., 2003):

1. The distribution and manufacturing of narcotics
2. Unlawful gambling enterprises
3. Professional theft and fencing networks
4. The lending of money at high rates of interest to be collected by force or financial takeover

5. Bribery, extortion, embezzlement, and fraud in unions and businesses
6. Corruption of public officials
7. Economic crimes involving financial offenses against businesses, investors, and consumers
8. Money laundering
9. Alien smuggling
10. Technology theft
11. Internet crimes, such as child pornography and identity theft

Since prosecution is so important in ongoing organized-crime investigations, the most effective units are those that include representatives from county or federal district attorney's offices who can construct and manage cases involving economic criminal conspiracies, such as Racketeering Influenced Criminal Organizations (RICO). They often involve grand jury investigations and the need for subpeona powers. There is also a need for additional funding for informants, equipment, and overtime for physical and electronic surveillance.

The organized-crime unit needs state and federal and, at times, local representatives along with intelligence analysts and other experts. Areas of expertise include those that involve technical skills in the areas of photography, electronic surveillance, polished detective skills, and content expertise in the various areas of organized crime, such as narcotics and fraud. There is a need to include special security controls, including location and protection for informants and witnesses. Since much of this type of investigation, along with a spillover into white-collar crime investigation, means having to follow a line of money to discover the criminals and to convict them, an investigative accountant is essential to the work.

To be successful, there must be a major investment in skilled personnel and equipment accompanied by a great deal of multijurisdictional cooperation. With ongoing investigations, a screened representative from the local vice squad may prove useful. (*Screened* means that the individual has been carefully investigated in terms of the need for security for the total investigation.)

Added to this area of crime investigation is computer crime. Computer crimes include a number of offenses, such as invading systems to scan information, change data, transfer funds and steal money, or place a "bomb" in a program that will "zap" data. This category also includes the commission of crimes with the aid of the computer, such as financial fraud. Because of increased reliance on computers for daily transactions in all areas of life, individual consumers and computer systems are subject to criminal use and invasion and destruction. Examples of computer crime in the daily news are common. However, computer crime investigation units on the state and local level are a rarity. Obviously, personnel involved in computer crime units must have advanced training in computer science and programming and Internet applications. Computer cases are difficult to investigate and to prosecute, mainly because most judges and juries have a difficult time understanding case evidence.

YOUTH SERVICES AND JUVENILE AID UNITS

The police are the main component in the criminal justice system with whom juvenile offenders come into contact, and the police confrontation is highly significant in determining the number and types of cases that eventually proceed to juvenile court. Many jurisdictions agree with the *least coercive* recommendation of the task force report *Juvenile Justice and Delinquency Prevention* (National Advisory Commission, 1976: 186): "To respect family autonomy and minimize coercive State intervention, law enforcement officers dealing with juveniles should be authorized and encouraged to use the least coercive among reasonable alternatives, consistent with preserving public safety, order and individual liberty."

Thus, in most jurisdictions, almost all police-juvenile interactions and confrontations result in informal action or are settled with warnings of future severe action. Most jurisdictions follow the task force recommendations on when counseling and releasing should take place rather than court action. They instruct police officers to consider (1976: 210):

1. *The nature of the alleged delinquent act.* In cases of minor delinquent acts, such as disorderly conduct where there are no other serious negative factors, police should consider releasing the youth.
2. *The juvenile's previous behavioral history.* The presence or absence of a prior history of serious law violations should be given substantial weight in making a release decision.
3. *Circumstances possibly contributing to the alleged delinquent act.* Investigation may turn up important information about the youth's neighborhood or associates, which may be influencing negative behavior.
4. *The juvenile's willingness to reform.* The juvenile should demonstrate a cooperative attitude; assurance of good conduct is an important factor.
5. *Parental supervision.* The interest and attitude of the parents or guardians toward the juvenile and the alleged law violation, as well as their ability to provide the necessary supervision and guidance, are important considerations.

The task force also recommended interviewing the parents at home. Judgments can be best made by the police officer concerning the youth's living conditions and the ability of the parents to supervise the youth in the youth's home environment.

In cases that are more serious or that involve repeat offenders or suspects who have attitude problems, the result may be official action followed by an appearance in family court. This also happens when the complainant presses for some official action. In large departments, this action might take place at a juvenile bureau that is part of the investigation division; in medium-size departments, this action might take place in a juvenile unit that is part of the patrol division; in smaller departments, most likely a juvenile officer who reports directly to the chief would handle this matter.

Background

Juvenile aid divisions were formed in the early part of the twentieth century in response to urban crime and related social problems involving children, many of whom were newly arrived immigrants. The legal and social reforms that gave certain protections and services to children were based, in part, on two theories developed in the common law: (1) **doli incapax** (a child under a certain age is incapable of wrongdoing) and (2) **parens patriae** (the state must assume the role of the parents if the parents cannot live up to their responsibilities in the care of the child). In all states, children under a certain age, usually 16, are accorded the title of *juvenile* for criminal and civil matters.

Until the 1960s, the rules of criminal prosecution for children regarding their legal rights under due process were ill defined. In 1967, in a case titled ***In re Gault,*** the U.S. Supreme Court ruled that children must be afforded the same legal protections as adults. In many localities, the investigation and prosecution of juvenile cases is strictly defined by state statute and is reinforced by rules and procedures of juvenile court. In most states, a juvenile suspect cannot be questioned unless accompanied by a parent. The place where the interrogation occurs has to have a nonpolice atmosphere, which is defined as being a room or office away from the mainstream of police activity. Juveniles cannot be confined in adult jail lockups but must be transported and held in special juvenile facilities.

The range of juvenile offenses, however, also incorporates offenses that would not be considered offenses if the act or activity were committed by an adult. We are referring here to **status offenses.** These include running away from home, truancy, and not behaving according to parental rules in the home.

Many officials and the general public remain concerned about the rise of juvenile crime versus the "revolving door" system of justice that appears to let juvenile suspects go free with no punishment. Charles E. Silberman, in his review of the criminal justice system (1980: 355), found that most juveniles do not receive any type of sentence in juvenile court until they have been before a judge four or five times. He concludes,

> If "nothing happens" until the fourth or fifth offense (or, in some instances, the ninth or tenth), young offenders are persuaded that they have an implicit contract with the juvenile court permitting them to break the law. Therefore, when something does happen—when a severe sanction is imposed at an earlier point—delinquents feel that their contract has been violated unilaterally and their sense of justice is outraged. "I was sent here on a bum rap," a youngster in a California training school told me, in tones of great moral indignation. What he meant, I discovered, was not that he was innocent of the robbery charge on which he had been convicted, but that "the judge sent me here on the third offense, instead of waiting until the fifth."

As a result, many states are lowering the age at which the juvenile is treated as an adult if he or she commits a felony, which means criminal court and adult arrest procedures and incarceration. Thus, rape, robbery, arson, and murder become adult offenses if they occur within a certain age bracket and under certain circumstances. The trend is to "get tough," a posture that will have a significant effect on how police behave with juvenile offenders.

The Role of Juvenile Aid

The police juvenile aid operation or division performs a variety of activities. First, it acts as a protector of children's rights, seeing that the rules of criminal prosecution for criminal and status offenses are maintained. Then, it sees that the security of the community is maintained: The public has the right to be safe from youth crimes. Third, it must deal with children who are victims of parental abuse or neglect.

In summary, the juvenile aid division has the following responsibilities:

1. *Investigation of juvenile cases.* This involves not only criminal cases where the suspects may be juveniles, but also cases where juveniles are victims. Generally, cases involving adult crimes committed by juveniles are handled by regular investigative and patrol personnel. When an arrest is made or a suspect is brought in for questioning, juvenile aid personnel should be notified. Those cases involving status offenses or child victims should be handled by the juvenile aid personnel. In many situations, cases of this nature do not involve a typical police response but demand patience, knowledge of referral agencies, family crisis intervention skills, and counseling techniques. The officer may need to handle child abuse. Or there may be cases of simple neglect. In one case, an officer walked into a home and saw a child being bathed in a tub with feces. It takes a strong stomach to handle these cases. Normally, social agencies are available to work with these parents, but in the long night hours, immediate police action may be necessary.

2. *Screening of cases.* Cases forwarded to the juvenile aid division must be screened for a future course of action. The recommendations of the investigator or the patrol officer should be taken into consideration in view of their familiarity with the circumstances surrounding the case. It is at this stage that the juvenile aid officer may wish to divert the case from the normal progression found in the criminal justice system to either a formal or an informal mode of treatment. Such options include referral to a community agency, police counseling, or **station-house probation,** where the offender reports to the juvenile aid division on a regular basis to account for his or her actions during the week. The case may be disposed of if the situation warrants restitution and it is made, or if there are no grounds for future action.

3. *Preparation of cases for juvenile court.* The necessary paperwork and evidence must be gathered by the officer if the case is forwarded to the juvenile court. The experienced juvenile aid officer knows how to present the documentation needed for the court and is able to keep track of when the case will be called. The officer should follow the ultimate disposition of the case and advise the arresting officers of the results.

4. *Community liaison.* This is an important aspect of the juvenile aid function. The police should be viewed as the experts in all areas of crime in the community, especially that related to youth. This is important for the planning and funding of special programs undertaken by community groups for juveniles. At the same time, the police should maintain an active liaison with community groups that are involved with problems with juveniles, such as the YMCA/YWCA, Catholic Charities, and the school district.

   Another aspect of community liaison involves keeping abreast of community programs where children may be referred if special treatment is needed. These might include programs involving youth employment, professional counseling, vocational training, and recreational activities.

5. *Grant preparation.* Since the 1960s, the federal government has offered special funding to police and social service agencies and community consortiums for programs that address youth crime. Such programs might offer drug education, involve gang interdiction, or deal with at-risk youths. Thus, the juvenile aid division becomes an active stakeholder in these grant programs, either as a prime sponsor or as a source of data for the grant application.

6. *Dealing with missing children.* In response to a number of well-publicized child abductions, Congress is currently debating a funding bill that would give states and various communities assistance in setting up an **Amber Alert** system. Named after Amber Hagerman, a nine-year-old girl kidnapped and murdered in Arlington, Texas, in 1996, the Amber Alert would go into effect when a child is reported abducted and in grave danger. Information on the victim, the suspect, and his or her vehicle and direction of travel would be distributed to area police departments, public broadcasts would be made by television and radio stations, and a message would be posted on reader boards at toll booths and along major highways. The concept here is to employ a major public alert to find the victim and suspect before too much time passes. At this time, the merits of this program are being debated; many child abductions are custodial situations in which one parent has taken the child from the other. Supporters of the program refer to various success stories in which abductions were thwarted, and the victims were rescued. Similar alert programs are already in use across the country. To prevent these programs from becoming overused and ineffective, many police departments have strict guidelines before an alert can be activated.

Juvenile Record Keeping

Information regarding youth crime must be stored in an area that is maintained separately from adult files. In most cases, the case folder is confidential and not subject to any review except by youth-division personnel. At the same time, information on youth crime, projected trends, and gang activity that must be available and disseminated to the department and, at times, to the community.

While all officers should have the training to deal in all aspects of juvenile crime, specialization in this area is needed because of the ever-changing rules and statutes on juvenile prosecution as well as the development of new skills and knowledge. In short, personnel assigned to juvenile duties should be trained for and considered experts on all matters of juvenile crime and procedure. They should be consulted by members of the department for their expertise and continually called on for juvenile interactions, especially by the patrol section.

Personnel Selection for Juvenile Aid

In the past, the juvenile aid units were staffed by female officers and older male "father figure" officers. This was unfair to these officers since it stereotyped their professional roles. Personnel in juvenile departments should be highly trained individuals who are picked or volunteer because they have some talent in working with the juvenile offender. The task force report *Juvenile Justice and Delinquency Prevention* was very clear about this (National Advisory Commission, 1976: 256):

> Police juvenile officers should be assigned by chief executives on the basis of departmental written and oral examination rather than being appointed by a civil service or merit commission. Juvenile officers should, if possible, be selected from among the department's experienced line officers. Selection boards established to interview candidates for the position of police juvenile officer should include police department command officers and selected individuals from the juvenile justice system and public youth agencies.

In addition, it is recommended that qualified officers be able to pursue a career as police juvenile specialists and have the same opportunities for advancement and promotion as other officers in the department. Very little has changed in personnel selection since 1976.

Organization of Juvenile Aid Operations

As discussed before, depending on the department, a specialized juvenile unit should be organized. In the smaller departments, at least one officer should have the specialized knowledge needed to deal with juvenile offenders.

A juvenile specialist provides the department with expertise in juvenile court procedures and juvenile offenses, which are normally handled differently from adult offenses. This officer can also develop useful ongoing relationships with whatever youth-service agencies exist in the area. He or she can even provide useful information to help the detective division solve cases. Many a case has been solved through information that juvenile offenders have mentioned casually to the juvenile police specialist.

Some departments have initiated a family-service bureau. Most problems with juvenile offenders start and end in the home. Police officers have found time and time again that the troubled youth of the community come from a disrupted family. To deal with this situation, some departments have combined juvenile services and domestic crisis intervention so that a total approach to potential offenders can be developed. Also, with the family-service bureau approach, it may be more likely that the agency can provide proper referral service for the whole family. For example, the father might be an alcoholic, the mother might be out working, and there is no adult babysitter in the home. The older boy becomes a juvenile delinquent, while the younger children wander the streets. This family needs help, but it might not be provided if only one family member at a time is seen by police officers.

Officers in this juvenile unit could also specialize. One officer might learn the juvenile law and keep abreast of late-breaking legal developments. Another might specialize as a liaison officer with various juvenile agencies in the community. Another might develop relationships with local merchants to help solve and prevent juvenile crime against businesses and commercial establishments (shoplifting, burglary).

However the unit is organized, it can be of great value to the total department. The department will have its own team of experts on juvenile offenders to call on for their knowledge and training.

Related to traditional juvenile aid responsibilities are gang monitoring and suppression. Juvenile gangs are defined as groups composed of youths between the ages of 11 and 18 who commit crimes over a long period of time. These groups have a succession of leadership, are clearly identifiable by various types of dress, and are held together by race, ethnicity, or common geographic area.

Dealing with youth gangs involves monitoring members, training parents and groups dealing with juveniles on gang trends, intercepting and investigating criminal activities, and counseling members when they decide to leave the gang. The activities of gang-intervention personnel also become pivotal when city or area resources are directed to gang suppression, whereby leading members are arrested and prosecuted.

Other gang and juvenile crime-suppression tactics used nationwide involve the following:

1. Active enforcement of school truancy statutes during school hours that could result in fines for students and parents
2. Use of police patrol officers to conduct "spot checks" to review family court mandates involving curfews and association with gang members
3. Use of court-mandated injunctions against juveniles or rowdy college students gathering in certain areas
4. Active enforcement of state alcohol regulations that might result in revocation of driving privileges

Model Youth Programs

The following descriptions are taken from a variety of police youth programs found in a variety of police agencies throughout the United States. Not every agency may wish to promote every item in this program. This model can, however, serve as a source of ideas when youth programs are developed for specific agencies. Let us examine some general guidelines for these programs:

1. The program should be open to all youths in the community regardless of gender or background. Although delinquent youths may be the target population, it would be unfortunate to have all program participants labeled "bad." This outcome will most likely further rather than prevent delinquency.
2. The program should not be expensive to join. Unless they steal or burglarize, most delinquent youths cannot afford expensive equipment. Thus, most programs have to be subsidized or not need expensive equipment. Once again, the program must be open to all the youths in the community.
3. The objectives of the program are to prevent delinquency and to enhance the image of police officers among youth of the community. Another objective is to develop informants and information concerning juvenile activity. Thus, many programs that may seem, on the surface, unrelated to police activities, such as baseball games or canoe trips, become valuable as part of the work of a police juvenile specialist.

Following is a discussion of a variety of programs that have been tried—some with more success than others. All programs must, of course, be adapted to local conditions.

Mobile Neighborhood Watch.   This program is patterned after traditional neighborhood watch programs. Participants use their own vehicles and are equipped with mobile phones to call in for police assistance with juvenile gang activity. Other activities may include graffiti removal, cleanup programs, and youth athletic programs.

Neutral Zones.   Activities for area youth are provided in a designated area, known as a **neutral zone,** during high-crime hours or weekends. In Mountlake Terrace, Washington, the police department and volunteers run such a program in the local high school and provide meals, athletic opportunities, tutoring, and a food and clothing bank. According to the Crime Prevention Coalition (1996) a key concern is safety for the participants; thus, gang affiliation clothing is prohibited, and a pat-down search is required for entry into the area.

Parent Networks.   Through this program, parents are urged to get to know their children's friends and to share ideas and concerns about behavior and activities. Juvenile units provide brochures and speakers to talk about networking and responsible hosting of parties and sleepovers.

Explorer Posts.   Many departments have established police explorer posts to work with youths who have indicated an interest in law enforcement. The Boy Scout model of exploring involves the formation of a post, sponsored by a host agency, that will involve youths between the ages of 14 and 21 in a vocational or educational field. Some larger police departments, such as that in Suffolk County, New York, are able to sponsor as many as seven different explorer posts in their jurisdiction.

The explorer concept is designed to allow youths to gain firsthand information on law enforcement operations and career possibilities. Explorers are assigned various station-house tasks in addition to formal classroom learning. Many agencies even allow their explorers to ride along with regular officers on patrol. Explorer post members can also be of great assistance at parades, field days, and other large public gatherings requiring personnel for traffic and crowd control. Many departments issue their explorers a distinctive uniform for this purpose.

While the explorer concept offers unending possibilities for police-youth interaction, some drawbacks must be pointed out. Agencies that invest their total youth resources on exploring soon learn that not all youths are attracted to this type of program, especially those who would be termed "delinquent." On the other hand, some youths are attracted to police explorer or other volunteer groups since they provide an opportunity to act out authoritarian tendencies or to capture the excitement of police work. Members of explorer posts can be subject to ridicule and abuse in the school setting, since peers view them as police informants. Therefore, the continuance of such a program by the police agency can, at times, be a trying experience. The role of the police adviser will vary from personnel and recruitment manager to counselor and general troubleshooter.

School Liaison Programs.   In many communities, the presence of police patrol cars in the school parking lot signifies that there is trouble of one form or another since school officials generally call for the police only as a last resort. In reality, the police presence at school has become commonplace in many cities and communities because of the rise in assaults, drug use, and property crime occurring during regular school hours. In many cities, police units patrol the school grounds and buildings as a normal assignment.

Recent shootings and murders of school pupils and teachers at Columbine, Colorado; Jonesville, Arkansas; and Edenboro, Pennsylvania, have prompted a national debate on school violence. Not surprisingly, a program on school violence at a national police conference resulted in a standing-room crowd of police executives. As a result, many schools and police agencies have initiated formal and informal relationships in dealing with school crime. Sitting down and discussing mutual concerns can be an important first step for many communities whose citizens may perceive the school and immediate grounds as "out of bounds" for regular police operations. An important part of this relationship is an agreement as to how and when police officers will be summoned for school-related situations, including arrests on campus or during school hours, the types of incidents that result in immediate dispatch of officers, the interception of non-student trespassers on school property, and crowd control at school events.

Other operational issues include random searches of lockers, patrol activity in parking lots, and training for administrators and teachers on crisis management (Dorn, 1998). As one solution, the school liaison officer program, a police officer is assigned to a school on a continuous basis. The officer's presence in the school is not so much for law enforcement or intelligence purposes as it is a learning and community resource for school administrators, teachers, and students. Here the officer might teach a course on crime problems or police operations, assist teachers in the preparation of course materials related to law enforcement and criminal justice, or meet informally with students to discuss issues that are of concern to them.

Emergency-Response Plans.   In addition to these programs, elementary, middle, and high schools have by state laws been required to develop emergency-response plans to deal with varied issues such as bomb threats (a favorite during exams), armed intruders, evacuation protocols, and serious situations involving weather and hazardous materials. The school plan also includes a first-response protocol with the local police department for dealing with critical events. A first-response protocol may include communication between responding officers and school officials, staging areas, and most importantly, guidelines on when police are to be summoned to school grounds by school administrators or staff.

If anything, events involving armed student intruders have forced schools to engage in planning activities with local and regional police departments. Many school districts have encouraged departments to assign patrol officers to spend time in parking lots, cafeterias, and athletic fields as a means of increasing police presence.

Police departments have been forced to review patrol and operations tactics involving schools. Situations involving armed intruders are a case in point. Before 2000, most tactical responses called for the creation of a perimeter to contain the shooter and having a tactical team enter the building to stop the intruder. The main problem with this is that most areas do not have emergency-response teams. What is usual is that police officers from a number of agencies respond to the scene. The police response at Columbine, Colorado, was particularly criticized because the two shooters continued to kill and terrorize students and staff while police waited for a tactical team to assemble. The new model involves the creation of quick-response groups of three to four officers to immediately enter the building and neutralize the shooter. This, of course, requires both training and practice between area police departments and school district officials.

School Violence and the Police

April 20, 1999: Eric Harris, 18 and Dylan Klebod, 17, entered Columbine High School in Littleton, Colorado, carrying a handgun, a rifle, two shotguns, and various explosives. One teacher and 12 students were killed and 23 others wounded.

Both students committed suicide after the attack. The two, dressed in black trench coats and wearing masks, had planned their acts well. They made copies of the school keys, constructed and planted numerous bombs and kept a detailed diary. (Crews and Montgomery, 2000: 19)

School violence is terrifying. However, school violence and juvenile violence have been decreasing, and most schools in the nation are safe. In 1997, juvenile homicides reached the lowest rate in a decade. Nationally, there are between 1,400 and 1,700 juvenile murders each year (Snyder and Sickmund, 1999: 57). The rise and fall of juvenile murder is directly linked to firearms. An exhaustive study published by the American Medical Association came up with a total of 65 school murders for the combined 1992–1993 and 1993–1994 school years. Theft is the most common school crime. "Juveniles are at the highest risk of being victims of violence at the end of the school day" (Snyder and Sickmund, 1999: 31–32). Almost 90 percent of the school districts report no school murders. More than one in four murders occurs in eight of the nation's 3,000 cities: Chicago, Los Angeles, Houston, New York, Baltimore, Detroit, Philadelphia, and Dallas (p. 57).

A 1996 national survey of male youths found that 25 percent of respondents had a friend who had been the victim of a firearm-related crime, and 14 percent said one of their friends carried a weapon. Most "violence among students stems from unprovoked and offensive touches, interference with 'personal space,' perceived slights, insults, accusations and so forth" (Kellam, Prinz, and Sheley, 2000: 41).

In a 1996 national random sample of school administrators, with 48 schools responding, only 19 percent believed violence on campus was serious, and 94 percent said it was not at all likely that students would carry a gun on campus. However, in the preceding three years, 68 percent recalled at least one gun incident on campus, 83 percent one knife incident, and 45 percent a student shot on campus (Kellam, Prinz, and Sheley, 2000: 45–46).

Because of multiple killings in schools around the country and the massive publicity about these incidents, there is great public concern with violence in schools. From 1991 to 1997, 33 people fell victim to mass murder by students on school grounds. The dramatic media publicity created great fear among parents, teachers, school officials, and students. Crews and Montgomery (2000: 4) also report that by 1999, 94 percent of schools across the country had developed zero-tolerance policies, 84 percent had developed low-level security programs, and 78 percent had in place formal school violence programs. Many schools with a history of school and gang violence have stationed police officers at the schools.

In some cases, school violence has been linked to violent youth gangs in inner cities, violent heavy metal lyrics, hate groups like the neo-Nazi skinheads and the Aryan Nation, satanic groups, gothic youth subculture, bullying, alcohol and drug use, and easy access to guns. Most programs developed to combat these negative influences have been school, parent, and community based without the direct involvement of law enforcement. Teachers in troubled urban schools have been equipped with personal security alarms, and there have been numerous teacher-training programs for spotting and defusing potential student violence. While the student use of drugs has gone down over the last 20 years, school drug testing is rising rapidly. There is increased use of surveillance cameras and metal detectors.

The 1996 survey of administrators reported the following measures:

Police on campus	40%
Extra police patrols around school property	27%
Police in school hallways	15%

One-third of the administrators surveyed had instituted photo IDs for students and staff, which should be helpful to police, and had created a gun-free school zone. The higher the dropout rate, the more likely police and ID programs were put in place (Kellam, Prinz, and Sheley, 2000: 48–49).

Police departments can help by training school personnel and students in disaster training for extreme violence. They can train in specific techniques in bringing in professional help, protecting the student body and protecting themselves. Cell phones are everywhere. Both staff and students can call for help but they have to know what to do and a simple 911 call may not be enough. Meanwhile, many experts in dealing with violence recommend bringing in professionals to teach the students and staff in conflict resolution and mediation.

Drug Abuse Resistance Education (DARE)

Drug Abuse Resistance Education (DARE) is presented by specially trained officers to reduce drug, alcohol, and tobacco use by children. Instead of using scare tactics, the program teaches life skills, such as making choices and dealing with peer pressure. Program topics include drug information, assertiveness, stress, personal safety, and the consequences of behavior. The 17-week elementary school curriculum for fifth and sixth graders is taught in classrooms during the regular school day. Many states have adopted this program for implementation in all schools. Posters, T-shirts, DARE patrol vehicles, and other visual aids are provided through private contributions.

DARE is the most popular school-based police program in America, with about 10,000 courses offered in the 1990s. Sherman (1998: 8) has stated that DARE "fails to reduce drug abuse when the original DARE curriculum is used (pre-1993)." Because of the criticism of criminal justice scholars, DARE administrators have made some cosmetic changes. As it stands today, DARE seems to be a fine public-relations program for both police and schools, but it has little or no effect on changing behavior.

DARE was created in the early 1980s by Daryl Gates, chief of the Los Angeles Police Department from 1979 to 1992. He had a son who was addicted to drugs. There has been a great deal of controversy about the changes in DARE. Here are both the old and new curriculums so readers can judge the changes for themselves (Lundman, 2001: 71, 91):

Old DARE Course	*New DARE Course*
1. Personal safety practices	1. Introducing DARE
2. Drug use and misuse	2. Understanding the effects of mind-altering drugs
3. Consequences of using and not using drugs	3. Considering consequences
4. Resisting pressure to use drugs	4. Changing beliefs about drug use
5. Resistance techniques—ways to say no	5. Learning resistance techniques—ways to say no
6. Building self-esteem	6. Building self-esteem
7. Assertiveness	7. Learning assertiveness—a response style
8. Managing stress without using drugs	8. Managing stress without using drugs
9. Media influences on drug use	9. Reducing violence
10. Decision making and risk taking	10. Combating media influence on drug use and violence
11. Alternatives to drug use	11. Making decisions about risky behavior
12. Other activities	12. Saying yes to positive alternatives
13. Officer-planned lesson	13. Having positive role models
14. Role modeling	14. Resisting gang and group violence
15. Project DARE summary	15. Summarizing DARE lessons
16. Taking a stand when pressured to use drugs	16. Taking a stand
17. Assembly graduation	17. DARE culmination

Lundman (2001: 68–94) reports on evaluations of DARE. The old DARE curriculum was taught by a Long Beach police officer in 50-minute lessons once a week for seventeen weeks in fifth grade in 1989. The 3,000 students were arbitrarily split into DARE classes and a control group with no DARE classes. There was almost no difference between the two groups on alcohol use and cigarettes. No drug use was reported. In 1989–1990, Charleston, South Carolina, replicated the Long Beach study and found no significant positive changes in reported behavior by the DARE group.

In 1990, a Kokomo, Indiana, study also reported poor results:

	Control Group	**DARE Group**
Cigarette use	36%	54%
Alcohol use	52%	50%
Marijuana use	24%	31%

Police departments can use DARE as a public-relations program but may be hurt if there is any program evaluation. These studies didn't test actual behavior by examining juvenile court records; they simply relied on what the students told them.

Research shows that education and media campaigns don't work. One of the problems with these programs is lack of facts. The empirical data show that drugs in general do not lead to violence, most soft drug users do not graduate to harder drugs, and 90 percent of the people who drink alcoholic beverages do not become alcoholics. Even with the 10,000 DARE programs, the perceived risk of marijuana use dropped from 32 percent among tenth graders to 19 percent from 1992 to 1997, and well over 90 percent of high school students saw little risk in trying one or two alcoholic beverages. (See Peter Venturelli's excellent article, "Drugs in Schools: Myths and Realities," 2000.) The federal government spent $566 million in 1999 on safe and drug-free schools but doesn't seem to be getting much in terms of behavioral change for its money.

Current Police Youth Programs

Police use a great deal of discretion in handling juveniles. Siegel, in his major text on juvenile delinquency, gives the following juvenile dispositions by police (2000: 491):

Referred to other police agencies	1%
Handled within the department and released	28%
Referred to criminal court	5%
Referred to juvenile court	64%
Referred to welfare agency	2%

In the Teens on Patrol program in Rochester, New York, about 100 teenagers are hired by the police department to work in city parks and to keep them orderly. The New Haven, Connecticut, Police Department and Yale University Child Center provide a 24-hour crisis-intervention program for children who witness violence. The program provided services to 600 children in five years.

Dallas has a curfew that data indicate may be responsible for a 17.7 percent drop in juvenile victimization and a 14 percent drop in juvenile arrests. In Chicago, a curfew titled Time Out showed a 20 percent decrease in juvenile crime in a high-crime district. New Orleans saw a 27 percent decrease in youth crime in an aggressively enforced juvenile curfew (Siegel, 2000: 500–501). Curfew programs are becoming increasingly popular in high-crime neighborhoods around the country.

In 1997, police departments began trying the DARE approach to decrease adolescent involvement in gangs. They call this program Gang Resistance and Education Training (GREAT). Uniformed police officers teach a nine-week course, covering drug resistance; crime's impact on the school, the neighborhood, and victims; cultural sensitivity; conflict resolution; goal setting; and how to fulfill personal needs without joining a gang. In one study, students who completed the program were compared to a nonstandardized group that did not complete the program. The study authors say the program was successful based on self-reports, but they give no data. For example, they claim that the GREAT students "reported lower levels of gang affiliation and self reported delinquency" than the control group (Howell and Hawkins, 1998: 296–97). The program had an after-school component.

Police liaison officers stationed inside schools counsel students, teach drug and alcohol classes, train school personnel and students in security precautions and crime-prevention techniques, and work to improve the safety of the school (Lawrence, 1998: 175). Small police departments also have special youth officers who work with individual youth as well as school administrators. Juvenile units in larger departments perform all of these tasks and become familiar with juvenile court and probation personnel and procedures. Gang units also include units that specialize in adolescent gang activity.

The Hollywood, Florida, Police Department in Broward County has 50 employees who mentor students. Ever since Big Brother and Big Sister programs, youth mentoring has been extremely popular throughout the United States. The federal government has spent millions of dollars on mentoring, with little or no scientific evaluation. However, mentoring programs do report positive results: Mentored youth are less likely to drop out of school, start using drugs, and engage in violent behavior. According to Lieutenant Tom Sanchez (2002: 60) of the Hollywood Police Department, mentoring entails "screening, orientation and training, support and supervision."

Athletic Programs.   In the early part of the twentieth century, many urban police departments formed athletic programs to offer underprivileged youths a chance to participate in organized sports. Today, these Police Athletic Leagues still exist, but in name only. Private charities have taken over the entire responsibility for the programs. The police connection exists only for fund-raising purposes.

Sports and athletic programs provide a good environment and opportunity for police-youth interaction. In most communities, officer volunteers provide the staffing support. Frequently, the department or the police union may sponsor a team in an organized athletic program like Little League or youth hockey, with police officers acting as coaches or trainers.

Outdoor Adventure Programs.   These programs, variations of Outward Bound, offer youths a series of wilderness challenges. Programs of this nature cannot always be operated within a traditional shift and may run into political and union opposition, as the following case study illustrates.

In the absence of opposition, many programs operate successfully for many years. It is hard to feel hostile toward the police officer who guided you on an overnight camping trip, as many a potential delinquent and many an officer have found out to their mutual satisfaction.

Police Youth Program Potpourri

Ride-along programs. Youths ride along with officers in their patrol cars and observe police in action.

Drug-testing programs. Police agencies identify any suspicious materials found in the home.

Speakers' bureaus. Officers are available to speak to youth groups. Speakers may be generalists or specialists.

Columns in youth-oriented publications. Question-and-answer columns for youths on police matters are written for teenage publications; the format can also be used as a weekly radio program on a youth-oriented music station.

Stranger-danger program. Officers work closely with elementary school-children to warn them of the dangers of going with strangers and to identify various abduction techniques.

Station-house probation. In this community restitution program, juveniles are sentenced to work at the police station.

Police probation counseling center. In this center, jointly administered by probation and police agencies, police officers bring youths in trouble and juvenile offenders for counseling and referral to youth-service agencies.

CASE STUDY

One summer, the Oakdale Police Department embarked on an ambitious program for youths in the community: a 10-day canoe trip to the nearby Allegheny Mountains. Youths who had been in trouble with the police during the year were selected as participants. The objective was to give these youngsters a chance to spend time in the outdoors, learn camping skills, and meet the police in a nonconfrontational atmosphere.

One of the two officers assigned to the group was a state-certified guide. Various civilian volunteers also accompanied the group. The officers were paid their normal salaries.

The trip was successful, and plans were made for another trip the following year. Opposition to the idea arose from certain members of the city council, however, who argued that police officers should be paid to patrol city streets, not to conduct camping expeditions. As the controversy mounted, the officers argued that they could only accompany the group if they were paid overtime along with their normal salary, which, since they were away from home for 10 days, amounted to some 200 hours per officer.

Opposition to the program was stifled when community leaders and the newspaper came out in total support of the program.

In the final compromise, it was decided that only youths who lived in the municipality and one police officer would be allowed to go. The trip, moreover, was reduced from 10 days to seven days.

CASE STUDY

Deterring Youth Homicide: The Boston Gun Project

Cesare Beccaria (1738–1794) said that if deterrence is to work, justice must be swift and sure and that an increase in the severity of the punishment alone would not work. For more than 200 years, criminologists and criminal justice researchers have agreed with Beccaria's conclusion. In the ordinary workings of our justice system, with plea bargainings, lenient probation sentences for violent young offenders, and months and months of court delay, justice is not swift, certain, or even severe. For example, in Massachusetts, "the average number of days between arrest and conviction for felony cases disposed by state courts was 173" in 1992 (Kennedy, 1998: 4). That's almost six months! The **Boston Gun Project** aimed to turn this dismal state of affairs around, and it worked.

The Boston statistics were horrifying; 155 youthful victims had been killed by a gun or knife over a five-year period, and there were 125 youthful killers. The target group of teenage killers and victims were chronic offenders who had intense involvement with the criminal justice system with little or no effect on their behavior. The statistics showed the ineffectiveness of the case system to do anything about these homicides. Victims and killers averaged more than nine arraignments per youth, with 41 percent having more than 10 arraignments. There was a total of 1,009 arraignments for the 125 youthful killers. Twenty-six percent of the killers were on probation when they killed, with 54 percent having served time in a facility. The secret of success in Boston was immediate and massive action on the target group, using an interagency task force.

The Boston police targeted the illicit firearms market, while the interagency group targeted violent gang members using all the legal weapons available. They called it "pulling levers." They used federal prosecution rather than state prosecution because of the more severe punishment of a 10-year minimum sentence. There was also less delay in prosecution. The traditional "clunky" approach of the normal case process was rejected because there was no clear-cut message to the violent youth concerning swift and sure punishment.

The Ceasefire Working Group in Boston included the following:

Boston police
School police
Parole officers
Federal prosecutors
Local prosecutors
Clergy
Youth connections
Gang outreach workers
Probation officers
Neighborhood groups
U.S. Drug Enforcement Agency
U.S. Bureau of Alcohol, Tobacco and Firearms
U.S. Immigration and Naturalization Service

This group met every two weeks in addition to informal meetings.

The police met with violent gang members and told them they would use every legal tool they had to stop youth violence in Boston. They sent fliers to people involved in the drug and illicit gun markets. They made sure their target group knew exactly what was happening and repeatedly raided the violent gangs, with swift prosecution. When violent youth were on parole or probation, the police and the community correction professionals used close supervision and scrutiny. They made it clear to the gangs that violence would draw their attention and that this attention meant immediate action.

The cost of a gang homicide to the gang was immediate:

[C]ash-flow problems caused by street drug market disruption, arrests for outstanding warrants, the humiliation of strict probation enforcement, even the possibility of severe sanctions brought by Federal involvement. Those costs were borne by the whole gang, not just the shooter. (Kennedy, 1998: 5–6)

The working group talked to the gangs continually and told them that violence would bring an immediate and strong response. They said to the gangs, "We're ready, we're watching. Who wants to be next?" (Kennedy, 1998: 6).

The Boston Gun Project worked. Boston's Ceasefire Working Group brought the city's youth homicide figures down by two-thirds.

This approach was also tried in Lowell, Massachusetts, and Minneapolis, Minnesota. In 1997, in Lowell, representatives from seven city and state agencies met 20 chronic offenders, 35 less chronic offenders, and 16 members of a street gang. Their message was as follows (Kennedy, 1998: 3):

"We just wanted to tell you that we know who you are," says assistant district attorney Michael Oritz. "If you continue to get into trouble you're going to end up in jail, or hurt, or even dead. But if you want to get out of a gang or back into school, or you want a job or counseling we're here to help."

Youth assaults declined, and there was an immediate quieting effect on a troubled school.

In Minneapolis, the police department arrested 12 members of a violent street gang, the Bogus Boyz, on federal weapons charges. Police and probation officers immediately visited 250 members of the most chronic gang offenders. Once again, the message was made clear to the target group (Kennedy, 1998: 3):

The Bogus Boyz's arrests were no accident. The Bogus Boyz were violent and their violence won them this treatment. This is how the city is doing things from now on. We've got a dozen agencies from probation to the Feds, meeting regularly and focusing on gang violence. When we find it we're going to act.

"Patrol and gang unit police officers, together with ATF agents, also conducted saturation patrols 2 nights per week in targeted areas" (Office of Juvenile Justice and Delinquency Prevention [OJJDP], 1999: 59). This rapid response immediately reacted to shootings that might provoke gang revenge based on Boston's Operation.

They visited injured gang members in the hospitals and gave them a message: "Retaliation will not be tolerated. Remember the Bogus Boyz." Police and probation officers made unannounced visits to gang members' homes. The Law Enforcement Task Force met continually with neighborhood groups.

Homicides fell by 30 percent from 1996 to 1997. From 1997 to 1998, gang-related homicides as a percentage of all homicides fell from 52 to 23 percent (OJJDP, 1999: 60). A commu-

(continued)

nity survey showed a favorable response to safer neighborhoods. Crime was deterred, and crime rates came down.

This proactive approach worked because of immediate action that was swift and sure and because of intense interagency cooperation. One of the secrets of success was clear communication to the target group. The message was that the city would not put up with this violence and that all the authorities would act immediately. Credibility was created by continual and direct action.

INVESTIGATION

Investigation is the police activity concerned with (1) the apprehension of criminals by the gathering of evidence leading to their arrest and (2) the collection and presentation of evidence and testimony for the purpose of obtaining convictions. Investigation is normally divided into two major areas of activity: (1) the preliminary investigation normally carried out by officers in the uniform patrol division and (2) the follow-up investigation normally carried out by officers formally trained in investigative techniques and often part of a detective bureau.

In larger departments, a division or bureau is responsible for follow-up investigations; special investigations are assigned by the chief of police. Additionally, this function also covers the recovery of stolen property, the gathering of criminal intelligence, and the preparation of cases for trial. Organizationally, this division may be called the *Detective, Central Investigation,* or *Criminal Investigation Division.* For our purposes, we will use the simple title of *Investigations.*

The role of the investigator is probably the most glamorous one in the police department. This modern Sherlock Holmes is portrayed in movies, television, and novels as a meticulous and tireless gatherer of evidence that miraculously leads to the arrest and conviction of criminals. As shown on the television series *N.Y.P.D. Blue,* this super police officer is a bit unorthodox, normally at odds with his superiors, and normally willing to bend the rules, especially if this involves a deliberate violation of departmental directives. Embedded in a web of unsavory informers, the heroic investigator maintains his integrity in his unrelenting pursuit of crime and the master criminal.

The public, and to some extent the patrol officer, maintains this glorified notion of what an investigator is all about. Reality, as usual, is a mixture of fact and fiction. In some cases, detective work is all that the media says it is, but in most investigative jobs, it is a series of monotonous tasks that may or may not lead to a break in the case. Long, hard hours are put in interviewing neighbors after a major crime has taken place.

The use of forensic specialists at crime scenes and in laboratories is another recent theme on television and in movies. The reality is that many departments do not have access to this technology unless state or federal police agencies are summoned. Forensic personnel are not deployed except for major felony cases. All police investigators must be trained in the general scope of forensic science to understand the capabilities and limitations of such specialties as DNA testing, ballistics, microscopy, glass and paint analysis, and arson and explosives testing.

Many investigations are solved step by laborious step. Unlike the outcomes on television and in the movies, clearance on crimes investigated against property is less than 20 percent. This means that more than 80 percent of these types of crimes are never solved.

Preliminary Investigation

Cases would not be solved and offenders would not be arrested unless patrol officers were willing and able to use some preliminary investigation skills. The patrol officer's tasks in crime incidents normally entail both investigative and noninvestigative action. O.W. Wilson (1963: 282) gives us an excellent listing of these duties, under the heading **PRELIMINARY:**

P	Proceed to the scene with safety and dispatch.
R	Render assistance to the injured.
E	Effect arrest of perpetrator.
L	Locate and identify witnesses.
I	Interview complainant and witnesses.
M	Maintain scene and protect evidence.
I	Interrogate suspects.
N	Note all conditions, events, and remarks.
A	Arrange for collection of evidence.
R	Report incident fully and accurately.
Y	Yield responsibility to detectives.

One of the most important duties of the police officer responding to a crime call is to secure the crime scene. Cases are often lost because reporters, higher administrative officials, and various other personnel were allowed to indiscriminately contaminate a scene by handling evidence or walking through the area. There have even been cases of patrol officers taking weapons from a crime scene and turning them in two or three days later.

To win a case, there must be continuity of the evidence from the scene of the crime, to the vaults of the police laboratory or property room, to the hands of the prosecuting district attorney. Documentation must be made of any person who handled any piece of evidence and the circumstances under which the evidence was handled. Otherwise, alert defense lawyers can point to the discrepancies and win cases on technicalities.

It is a cardinal rule in most agencies that there should be only one person in charge at any crime scene. Once the scene is secured by the first officer at the scene, those assigned to evidence collection should be in charge. In some instances, this is the responding officer who is also a trained evidence technician, or it may necessitate summoning others with the necessary expertise and equipment. In any event, no one else—victims, witnesses, higher police officials, other police officers not assigned to the case, reporters, TV crews—should be permitted access to the crime scene area until a thorough examination has been completed and all photographs taken and evidence collected.

Evidence should be photographed in place, marked properly by the person discovering it, placed in a sealed or appropriate container to prevent contamination, and prepared for transportation in a manner designed to maintain continuity.

The use of patrol officers for preliminary investigations, as O.W. Wilson points out, helps to relieve the detective force of many time-consuming tasks. This practice enables the detectives to concentrate their specialized skills on the tasks for which they have been trained. This use of the patrol officer is also important for the morale of the total agency.

Since the vast majority of positions in a police agency are for uniformed officers, the average officer will never have an opportunity to become an investigator. Expanding the uniformed officer's role, however, helps (1) make the officer more aware of his or her basic responsibilities in protecting the scene, (2) promote the feeling of belonging to a team rather than being only a reporter called to contain the scene until the specialists arrive, and (3) the officer and the department evaluate future assignments in the investigative areas.

Management should publicly acknowledge the positive contributions of the uniformed police officer as well as his or her detective counterpart in the successful conclusion of cases. When an officer can see that a positive contribution has been made and that he or she will receive recognition for that contribution, the officer will become a more positive and effective employee.

However, patrol officers have limited training in investigative skills and have little time to give to any investigation if the municipality is to have effective police coverage. As a result, the time-consuming process of follow-up investigation is often assigned to specialists.

Follow-up Investigation

The follow-up investigation of a criminal case involves a number of steps:

1. Reviewing all reports relative to the offense and relating physical evidence gathered at the crime scene
2. If necessary, re-interviewing everyone identified by preliminary investigators as having information
3. Communicating necessary crime information to local and national crime-information networks

In most criminal cases, follow-up investigation involves looking for new witnesses with information related to the crime and targeting potential suspects. This often occurs as a result of step 2 or canvassing the neighborhood for information. In major felony cases, investigators may reach out to the general public for information or the location of possible suspects through local and national crime programs like Crimestoppers.

For successful criminal investigations, a suspect is identified and questioned for a confession. Obtaining a confession from a suspect is an art in which the investigator must play a variety of human roles without having the suspect invoke his or her Fifth Amendment rights to counsel, at which time all questioning must cease. There are a number of criminal investigation courses sponsored by agencies and private concerns that focus on this one aspect. Then again, in some cases, the suspect voluntarily surrenders to clear his or her conscience or to "get it over with" in dealing with the criminal justice system.

An important and often overlooked part of the criminal investigation process involves filing appropriate criminal charges against the suspect, locating additional evidence, and obtaining information for later testimony. For major cases, this step involves working with county or state prosecutorial offices and provides the structure for future testimony in hearings and at trial.

As discussed in Chapter 7, one cannot underestimate the use of technology for evidence gathering, processing, and recording. Police investigators today have the luxury of comparing their information with various databases for suspects and modi operandi. At present, it is possible to do a computer search by alias, modus operandi, and thousands of other set sorts. Currently, systems are being interlocked so that a search can take in a local area, a county, a state, and in some instances the entire nation. However, no matter how good the tools, cases are ultimately solved by a well-trained investigator with an instinct for human folly.

Traditional Structure

Historically, the investigations divisions of large urban police departments have been removed from the mainstream of police operations in the station houses. In general, a person enters a detective or investigative squad room by invitation only.

In the early days of policing in the United States, it was the prime task of the police investigator to cultivate informers. This was relatively easy at the time, as both the criminals and the police often grew up in the same neighborhoods. Related to the cultivation of informers was another task: the regulation of vice activity. The combination of these two tasks, with few records being made of payoffs for information and the considerable amounts of unrecorded money surrounding vice activity, led to police corruption, a problem that has persisted to the present.

However, as any competent detective today will tell you, informers are stock-in-trade. Detectives could not stay in business without their informers. In one crucial area, drug investigation, it has been well documented that these investigators could not operate without informants.

In police departments that have a traditional organizational structure, the detective or investigative division still retains an elite position. According to Niederhoffer (1969: 82), many patrol officers aspired to be detectives or investigators in the late 1960s—not only for new challenges, but also to be able to wear street clothes and enjoy relative freedom from constant supervision. Given the present conservative structure of most police departments, this holds true today.

In many cases, appointment to investigator does not entail an increase in rank or pay. What does occur is a raise in status as defined by the police subculture. A major way to gain status in the uniformed culture of the police agency is to get out of uniform. This signifies that the officer is reaching a more professional, executive status where he or she is able to take command of important departmental matters.

The Rand Study

The value of the traditional investigative division in terms of crime solving and contributions to the overall role of the police agency was questioned in a study conducted by Rand Corporation in the mid-1970s (Greenwood and others, 1976). In reviewing the operations of 23 police departments, the researchers found the following:

1. Clearance rates by investigation divisions are unreliable. Most crimes are cleared (an arrest made) during the initial investigation by patrol officers.
2. Many reported felonies receive no more than superficial attention. In reality, minor property crimes are not even investigated.
3. Too much physical evidence is collected. Most items of evidentiary nature cannot be processed in the crime laboratory.
4. For many cases, there is a serious gap between the prosecutor and the investigator. Key evidentiary facts that could help the prosecutor obtain a conviction are not documented by the investigator.
5. Too much time is spent locating witnesses and reviewing reports on cases that will never be solved. There is also considerable time that cannot be accounted for in the daily tour of duty, which leads to suspicion that too much time is spent on personal errands.

The conclusions raised by this study point out that perhaps investigators, in the traditional sense, may not really be all that effective in solving crimes. Is this to say that all investigation units should be disbanded? Not really, but the Rand study shows the need for reappraising the tasks performed by investigative divisions.

Managing Criminal Investigations

The Rand study spurred the federal government, in particular the Law Enforcement Assistance Administration, to review and recommend changes in the investigations function in American policing. Through funding for initial research, a prescriptive package entitled **Managing Criminal Investigations (MCI)** was prepared in 1978 for local law enforcement agencies under the auspices of the University Research Corporation of Washington, D.C. The objective of the MCI program was to improve on police investigative performance by increasing the number of arrests and convictions.

Based on this initial study, discussions and reviews on criminal investigation management by the Police Foundation, the American Management Association, and others concluded the following:

1. *The investigative role of police patrol officers must be enhanced.* As stated before, in many departments, the patrol officer is merely a reporter of crimes that come to the attention of the police; the important follow-up work is conducted by investigators. In many cases, when the investigation division is called to the crime scene, the same questions are asked over and over again to witnesses and victims. For minor felony property crimes, there is often a time lag of hours and perhaps days before the investigator actually arrives at the scene to ask questions, process the crime scene for fingerprints and photographs, and do neighborhood canvassing. At a minimum, patrol officers should be trained and equipped to lift prints, take photographs, conduct neighborhood canvasses, and interrogate suspects. Accordingly, patrol-deployment plans must include ways to allow officers the time and latitude to follow up on their own cases.

2. *Case Screening.* How does one decide to continue further investigation of an incident? Typically, there is no set answer. By rule of thumb, a seasoned officer working a case can predict whether the incident has any chance of being solved based on the variety and amount of information gathered within a given period of time. One might ask, What types of information, what variety, and how much time? Experience might be the only answer. In an effort to quantify this process, researchers at Stanford University developed a screening instrument to predict the chance for future success of any given criminal investigation.

   An important aspect of **case screening,** and overall investigative processes, is the advisement of witnesses and crime victims on case progress. Too often, the victim who made a complaint to the police is kept in the dark as to what efforts were made to solve the case. With case screening, the person making the complaint is advised when the case is suspended based on lack of leads, or variables, related to the case.

3. *The overall caseload must be managed.* Very often, the follow-up portion of an investigation lacks any sense of management. Investigative management programs developed in the 1980s address the following factors in deter-

mining what resources ought to be given to follow-up: the seriousness of the act, its solvability, and the availability of personnel. In reality, public outrage is another factor that comes into play. A basic investigative management plan includes the following:

a. *Centralized filing of all investigative folders.* This ends a tradition of officers keeping their own case folders in their desks and allows all investigative personnel and supervisors to review the folders and obtain information when necessary.

b. *Allocation of review dates by a supervisor.* Here, a date is assigned for all paperwork on the case to be brought up to date.

c. *Use of investigative checklists of standard operating procedures.* The officer investigator can present the steps he or she took in the investigation in checklist form, with further explanation, if needed, recorded in the narrative summary. The following is a listing of items to include on the checklist:

Investigators' checklist

Victim interviewed in person
Victim interviewed by phone
Victim interviewed at home (if not, explain)
Witnesses interviewed in person
Witnesses interviewed by phone
Residential/commercial neighbors interviewed in person
Residential/commercial neighbors interviewed by phone
Officer on scene interviewed in person
Crime scene visited
Crime scene searched
Area of crime canvassed
Fingerprint search conducted
Photos taken at scene
Other forensic support provided
Physical evidence search that produced leads
Modus operandi files searched
Photos of known criminals viewed by victim
Major offenders' files accessed
Local hospital record search (if appropriate)
Prison records on recent releases checked
Parole file checked
Local police departments checked
Checked recent aliases
Informant file checked
Unit members checked for information sources

Administrative attention must also focus on assigning cases, according to the resources of the department or the nature of the case at hand.

4. *Police/prosecutor relations must be improved.* The police investigator and the person who will ultimately prosecute the case, the district attorney

or the public prosecutor, often act in isolation with regard to the tasks that each performs. Seasoned investigators often look on prosecutors as people who do not understand the reality of the case, which results in plea bargaining (referred to as "Let's Make a Deal") or an inept presentation of the case in the courtroom. The prosecutor, on the other hand, often has to deal with a staggering caseload (as does the investigator). Except in sensational cases, the prosecutor does not have the opportunity or the time to analyze every aspect of a criminal investigation. Moreover, the first thing that the prosecutor may observe when presented with the investigation case folder is poor grammar, spelling errors, and the lack of concise information needed to plug legal and criminal procedural gaps related to the case. While investigators are appalled when their hard work results in a dismissal or a reduced charge, prosecutors often wonder why the police even made the arrest. Neither side goes to the other and asks, "What is wrong here?"

Police training courses and various textbooks on criminal investigations recommend that prosecutors and investigators start communicating more frequently before the disposition of the case. This communication can be formal or informal. Participants often have initiated weekly meetings, with representatives of both sides talking about issues or procedures related to criminal investigation and prosecution. The MCI program advocates delegating one officer as liaison between the police and the prosecutor's office. The liaison officer's duties include mediating investigator and prosecutor grievances, providing advice on legal procedures and changes, and communicating day-to-day problems that arise between agencies. In Washington, D.C., the office of the general counsel plays an important role as liaison between the police and the prosecutor. This office reviews all cases that may be disposed of by plea bargaining or trial.

Investigative Issues and Concerns

The following issues and concerns regarding investigations confront police managers today.

Career Criminals.   **Career criminals** are offenders who actively pursue a life of crime. With help from the funding programs of the 1980s, many state and major municipal police agencies established programs to deal with these offenders. After identifying someone as a career criminal, police investigators use such methods as aggressive warrant enforcement, "most-wanted" fugitive advertisements in traditional and electronic media, prearrest surveillance, and working with the state's attorney for timely prosecution and maximum jail sentences. In other words, the offender becomes "targeted," and the objective is to prevent him or her from committing future offenses (Gay and Bowers, 1985).

Informants.   **Informants** are usually divided into three categories: (1) of-fenders who have agreed to work with the state's attorney and investigators to prosecute associates or higher-level criminals in a crime organization; (2) offenders who have been let off from prosecution or given cash by an investigator in exchange for information; (3) citizens in a variety of occupations and situations who like working with the police and are willing to give information.

Informants in the first category are usually under some negotiated plea agreement arranged between their attorney and the state's attorney. The major issue always at hand is the extent to which the informant is given immunity for past offenses. Category 2 offenders—often called confidential informants (CIs)—present a special challenge in that the department or agency may have formal rules for the informants in terms of cash allocations and immunity from prosecution. Many seasoned investigators, however, like to have these people under their own control. This comes at a great risk when questions arise regarding who is working for whom. Typifying this dilemma is the case of an FBI agent who, while working with his informants, allegedly gave information to gangsters that abetted criminal activities (*New York Times*, 2002).

Terrorism.   Since September 11, many federal and state agencies have been reviewing the concept of domestic intelligence gathering. Intelligence is the gathering of various kinds of information to make strategic and tactical decisions in dealing with crime problems. Strategic intelligence is directed to long-term crime issues and planning, while tactical intelligence is directed toward immediate criminal investigations (Lyman, 2002: 148–51). Information for these purposes includes the following data: (1) law enforcement and official sources (federal, state, and local police, immigration and naturalization, county records, national antiterrorist updates); (2) information from non–law enforcement sources (the media, credit reports, insurance reports, school applications); (3) covert information obtained from informants, suspects requesting immunity from prosecution, criminal reports obtained from witnesses, sources or eavesdropping efforts in other investigations.

Obviously, the focus of national and state intelligence gathering is on Middle Eastern communities, groups, and people identified as being possible terrorists or members of "sleeper cells" awaiting orders to attack. Additional attention is being directed at individuals who may have provided aid and assistance to perpetrators of the September 11 attacks.

In addition to the usual methods of obtaining information, ethical and procedural discussions regarding post–September 11 intelligence gathering include the use of undercover operatives who speak Arabic languages and can blend into the community to work the streets. There are also discussions on the use of buy money for information and extraordinary procedures related to giving informants immunity from prosecution or deportation. The work of federal and state antiterrorism efforts, then, is to "connect the dots" to identify potential suspects and to prevent future attacks.

CONCLUSION

Line functions are complementary to the patrol function and form the core of the time spent on activities in the department. However, a major distinction needs to be made between the traffic function covered in this chapter and the other line functions: vice, youth services, and investigations. Officers assigned to the traffic function must receive specialized accident-investigation training. Well-developed human relations skills are important for these officers because they provide direct service to the public. For many small departments and for some state police forces, much of the uniformed officer's time is spent on traffic. Traffic management should combine the knowledge and skills of a good traffic-flow engineer with computer skills that can be used to pinpoint crucial accident areas.

Vice, youth services, and investigations often involve considerable plain-clothes work along with a somewhat different set of skills compared with those used by the uniformed traffic officer. The youth service bureau operates in two major areas: prevention and ongoing investigations. The prevention programs are important to the department both in terms of public relations and in having youth and police on good terms with each other. As most officers who deal with youth have discovered, youths are some of the best informants available. They are everywhere in the community, and they are often willing to volunteer information to police officers they trust. The bulk of the nation's street crime is still committed by youths between the ages of 17 and 25. Thus, it is mandatory that every police department, no matter how large or small, have police officers who specialize in youth work.

Vice and organized crime units are areas of police work that demand special knowledge and skills. It is well known that the only real way to control this type of crime is to be able to deal with the organizers near the top of the crime hierarchy. This means that the department will be involved in lengthy investigations, often with no immediate payoffs. Vice and organized crime are multijurisdictional and international in scope. This means that a department needs experienced officers and the commitment of specialized resources.

Investigations have come a long way since the days of Sherlock Holmes and Dr. Watson. They are no longer the purview of one person; today they have to be managed in terms of a reasonable return on the commitment of professional personnel. This is the major contribution of the MCI system for managing criminal investigations, a cost-effective method of justifying when to commit and not commit personnel to investigations. The system is also useful in providing a communication framework beginning with the patrol officer who might initiate an investigation and ending with the prosecution of the arrested felon in the district attorney's office.

A theme throughout this chapter is the generalist-specialist controversy. The answer to this controversy is related to the line function, the community that the department is policing, and the size of the department. The entire focus of community policing is to provide a wide array of services. In cities, a specific geographic area becomes defined as the community, and line officers are charged to deal with community expectations and needs. A suburban department of 10 sworn officers really needs officers who can perform a wide variety of tasks, from traffic through drug and vice investigations. For the smaller departments, the answer might be having a generalist-specialist community service officer. This means that each officer is expected to do a variety of generalist functions while certain individual officers also have specialties. One officer may be good at giving speeches, another a forensic expert, while another has a special knowledge of the youth community. The way you organize will depend on your department. What is important is that a major focus of police management skills be devoted to the effective administration of the basic line functions.

QUESTIONS FOR REVIEW

1. How are the main line functions classified? Explain how an agency's size affects the organization of these functions.
2. What is the controversy surrounding the generalist versus the specialist with regard to delivering basic line functions to the community?
3. What are the main objectives of traffic enforcement?
4. How might management improve traffic enforcement?
5. How does racial profiling relate to traffic enforcement issues?
6. Why is vice enforcement truly a managerial dilemma?
7. Should vice enforcement be taken over by state and federal agencies? Why or why not?
8. Explain the historical development of juvenile aid divisions.
9. List the main objectives of juvenile aid divisions.
10. How do the following programs assist in the juvenile aid function: explorer posts, school liaison programs, outdoor adventures, stranger-danger programs?
11. Evaluate the role of DARE at a local school.
12. What is the main role of police investigators?

13. What has been the historical basis of detective divisions? How does this affect the investigative function today?

14. Explain the significance of the Rand study and traditional investigations.

15. List and briefly discuss the main components of the MCI program.

16. List and discuss three major issues related to police investigations.

CLASS PROJECT

You have been appointed chief of police in Wilkenson, Wyoming. Until last year, Wilkenson was a travelers' stop for the railroad and Interstate 89. Then oil was discovered. Within one year, the town has grown from 5,000 to 25,000 in population.

Policing before the oil rush was done by the county sheriff's department assisted by the highway patrol. With the rapid population increase, the town now needs a municipal police department. The town council has told you to create a police force regardless of cost.

Your first task is to create an organizational chart showing the police functions. Your instructor will show you how to prepare a basic chart. Include in your chart all those functions that will need to be staffed in the next three years. Write a brief rationale for each position you have created in your organization.

BIBLIOGRAPHY

ALBANESE, JAY S., DILIP K. DAS, and ARVIND VERMA. *Organized Crime: World Perspectives.* Upper Saddle River, N.J.: Prentice Hall, 2003.

BEARD, DARRIN. "Turning Bad Apples Around." *Lowell Sun,* November 16, 1997.

BLAKELY, G. ROBERT, RONALD GOLDSTOCK, and CHARLES H. ROGOVIN. *Rackets Bureaus: Investigations and Prosecution of Organized Crime.* Washington, D.C.: U.S. Government Printing Office, 1978.

BLOCH, P.B., and D.R. WEIDMAN. *Managing Criminal Investigations.* Washington, D.C.: U.S. Government Printing Office, 1975.

BUERGER, MICHAEL. "Supervisory Challenges Arising from Racial Profiling Legislation." *Police Quarterly,* 5, no. 3 (September 2002), pp. 380–408.

BUERGER, MICHAEL E., and AMY FARRELL. "The Evidence of Racial Profiling: Interpreting Documented and Unofficial Resources." *Police Quarterly,* 5, no. 3 (September 2002), pp. 272–305.

BUREAU OF JUSTICE STATISTICS. *Report to the Nation on Crime and Justice.* Washington, D.C.: U.S. Government Printing Office, 1983.

CALDWELL, HARRY. *Basic Law Enforcement.* Pacific Palisades, Calif.: Goodyear, 1972.

CAWLEY, D.F., ET AL. *Managing Criminal Investigations Manual.* Washington, D.C.: University Research Corporation, 1977.

CHAIKEN, JAN M., and MARCIA R. CHAIKEN. *Varieties of Criminal Behavior.* Santa Monica, Calif.: Rand Corporation, 1982.

CLARK, WARREN. *Traffic Management and Collision Investigation.* Upper Saddle River, N.J.: Prentice Hall, 1982.

COOK, P.J., and J. LUDWIG. *Guns in America: Results of a Comprehensive National Survey of Firearms Ownership and Use.* Washington, D.C.: Police Foundation, 1997.

CREWS, GORDON, and REID MONTGOMERY JR. *Chasing Shadows: Confronting Juvenile Violence in America.* Upper Saddle River, N.J.: Prentice Hall, 2000.

CRIME PREVENTION COALITION. *Safer Communities, Brighter Futures.* Washington, D.C.: National Crime Prevention Council, 1996.

DORN, MICHAEL. "Preventing School Weapons Incidents." *Police Chief,* 55, no. 8 (August 1998), pp. 28–36.

FOWLER, FLOYD J., THOMAS W. MANGIONE, and FREDERICK PRATTER. *Gambling Law Enforcement in Major American Cities.* Washington, D.C.: U.S. Government Printing Office, 1978.

FOX, JAMES A., and JACK LEVIN. *The Will to Kill.* Boston: Allyn and Bacon, 2001.

GARMIRE, BERNARD L., ed. *Local Government Police Management.* Washington, D.C.: International City Management Association, 1977.

GAY, WILLIAM G., and ROBERT A. BOWERS. *Targeting Law Enforcement Resources: The Career Criminal Focus.* Washington, D.C.: National Institute of Justice, 1985.

GREENBERG, ELLEN, and ROBERT WASSERMAN. *Managing Criminal Investigations.* Washington, D.C.: National Institute of Law Enforcement and Criminal Justice, 1979.

GREENWOOD, PETER, ET AL. *The Criminal Investigation.* Santa Monica, Calif.: Rand Corporation, 1976.

HASTINGS, THOMAS F. "Criminal Investigation." In Bernard Garmire, ed., *Local Government Police Management.* Washington, D.C.: International City Management Association, 1977.

HOWELL, JAMES C., and J. DAVID HAWKINS. "Prevention of Youth Violence." In Michael Tonry and Mark H. Moore, eds., *Youth Violence.* Chicago: University of Chicago Press, 1998, pp. 263–316.

IANNI, FRANCIS A.J. *Black Mafia: Ethnic Succession in Organized Crime.* New York: Simon and Schuster, 1974.

INCIARDI, JAMES A. *The War on Drugs.* Palo Alto, Calif.: Mayfield, 1986.

INCIARDI, JAMES A. *War on Drugs II.* Mountain View, Calif.: Mayfield, 1991.

INCIARDI, JAMES A., and KAREN McELRATH. *The American Drug Scene.* Los Angeles, Calif.: Roxbury, 1995.

KELLAM, SHEPPARD, ROY PRINZ, and JOSEPH SHELEY. *Preventing School Violence.* Washington, D.C.: National Institute of Justice, 2000.

KENNEDY, DAVID. "Pulling Levers: Getting Deterrence Right." *National Institute of Justice Journal* (July 1998), pp. 5–8.

LANGAN, PATRICK A., ET AL. *Contacts between Police and the Public.* Washington, D.C.: National Institute of Justice, 2001.

LAPIN, DAVID. "Racial Profiling in Anti-terrorism Strategies." *Law Enforcement News,* April 30, 2002, pp. 8–9.

LAWRENCE, RICHARD. *School Crime and Juvenile Justice.* New York: Oxford University Press, 1998.

LUNDMAN, RICHARD. *Prevention and Control of Juvenile Delinquency* (3rd ed.). New York: Oxford University Press, 2001.

LYMAN, MICHAEL D., and GARY POTTER. *Organized Crime* (2nd ed.). Upper Saddle River, N.J.: Prentice Hall, 2000.

MEEHAN, ALBERT, and MICHAEL C. PONDER. "Race and Place: The Ecology of Racial Profiling African American Motorists." *Justice Quarterly,* 19, no. 3 (September 2002), pp. 306–333.

NATIONAL ADVISORY COMMISSION ON CRIMINAL JUSTICE STANDARDS AND GOALS. *Juvenile Justice and Delinquency Prevention.* Washington, D.C.: U.S. Government Printing Office, 1976.

NIEDERHOFFER, ARTHUR. *Behind the Shield: The Police in Urban Society.* Garden City, N.Y.: Doubleday, 1969.

OFFICE OF JUVENILE JUSTICE AND DELINQUENCY PREVENTION. *Promising Strategies to Reduce Gun Violence.* Washington, D.C.: Office of Juvenile Justice and Delinquency Prevention, 1999.

ROWAN, ROY. "The 50 Biggest Mafia Bosses." *Fortune,* 114, no. 11 (November 1986), pp. 24–38.

RUBINSTEIN, JONATHAN. *City Police.* New York: Farrar, Strauss and Giroux, 1973.

SANCHEZ, TOM. "Cops Mentoring Kids." *Police Chief* (June 2002), p. 60.

SCHMALLEGER, FRANK. *Criminology Today* (7th ed.). Upper Saddle River, N.J.: Prentice Hall, 2002.

SEEDMAN, ALBERT A., and PETER HELLMAN. *Chief.* New York: Avon, 1974.

SIEGEL, LARRY J. *Criminology.* Belmont, Calif.: Wadsworth, 2003.

SIEGEL, LARRY J., and JOSEPH SENNA. *Juvenile Delinquency.* Belmont, Calif.: Wadsworth, 2000.

SHERMAN, LAWRENCE, ET AL. *Preventing Crime: What Works, What Doesn't, What's Promising.* Washington, D.C.: National Institute of Justice, 1998.

SILBERMAN, CHARLES E. *Criminal Violence, Criminal Justice.* New York: Vintage, 1980.

SKOLNICK, JEROME H. *Justice without Trial.* New York: Wiley, 1975.

SNYDER, HOWARD, and MELISSA SICKMUND. *Juvenile Offenders and Victims: 1999 National Report.* Washington, D.C.: Office of Juvenile Justice and Delinquency Prevention, 1999.

State of New Jersey v. *Pedro et al.,* 324 Super. 66, 734, A. 2d 350 (1996).

STEFFENSMEIER, DARRELL J. *The Fence: In the Shadow of Two Worlds.* Totowa, N.J.: Rowman and Littlefield, 1986.

TRACY, PAUL E., MARVIN E. WOLFGANG, and ROBERT M. FIGLIO. *Delinquency in Two Birth Cohorts.* Washington, D.C.: U.S. Department of Justice, 1985.

U.S. v. *New Jersey and Division of State Police Department of Law and Public Safety,* Civil No. 99-5970 (MIC), December 31, 1999, consent decree.

VENTURELLI, PETER J. "Drugs in Schools: Myths and Realities." In William Hinkle and Stuart Henry, eds., *School Violence: The Annals.* 2000, pp. 72–87.

Whitefield v. *Board of Commissioners of Eagle County, Colorado,* 837 F. Supp. 338 (1D. Colo. 1993).

Wilkins v. *Maryland State Police,* C.A. No. MJG-93-468 (D. Md. 1992).

WILLIAMS, JAY R., and LAWRENCE J. REDLINGER. "The Role of the Informant in Narcotics Enforcement." Paper presented at the Academy of Criminal Justice Sciences, Cincinnati, Ohio, March 1979.

WILSON, O.W. *Police Administration* (2nd ed.) New York: McGraw-Hill, 1963.

WOLFGANG, MARVIN E., ROBERT M. FIGLIO, and THORSTEIN SELLIN. *Delinquency in a Birth Cohort.* Chicago: University of Chicago Press, 1972.

WRIGHT, RICHARD, and SCOTT DECKER. *Burglars on the Job.* Boston: Northeastern University Press, 1994.

10

ADMINISTRATIVE/STAFF FUNCTIONS

The term *administrative/staff functions* is used in the title of this chapter because many departments use either *administrative function* or *staff function* to describe the same set of services. We will use the term *staff functions* for the purpose of simplicity and clarity.

The police administrator must seek advice and counsel from people who have various areas of expertise. The chief of police, while directing the overall police organization, cannot manage the daily operations of all units or functions as they do their daily tasks. Those areas of the police organization that assist in performing the advisory role are commonly termed *administrative* or *staff services*. In American policing, many of the following functions or divisions are usually included under this title: personnel and training, planning and research, legal adviser, public relations, inspections and internal affairs, and budget and community relations.

In reality, staff personnel actually command directly or indirectly, in that "advice" often constitutes a decision that is binding on the chief administrator. For example, in personnel selection, the personnel supervisor presents a list of candidates who have successfully completed all requirements—civil service, state or county, and departmental—for the position of police officer. Much time and energy on the part of the personnel staff has gone into the preparation of this final list. With all these variables in mind, it would be difficult for the chief administrator to oppose these candidates. A tacit agreement or realization exists in organizational thinking, in which the chief acknowledges that the personnel supervisor is an expert in his or her field, having mastered all affirmative action and civil service regulations affecting this group of police recruits. The chief will review the list of candidates with the personnel supervisor.

The personnel supervisor will have to answer any questions if problems arise in the future; for example, a lawsuit based on alleged discrimination or an action grant being delayed because the department did not conform to civil service guidelines.

LINE/STAFF CONFLICT AND COOPERATION

In the police subculture, individuals assigned to staff services are often looked on with disdain simply because they are considered to be "desk jockeys" engaged in "Monday morning quarterbacking" far removed from the everyday realities of police work being done on the street. The cause for this **line/staff conflict** is that, as Nigro and Nigro (1977: 165) point out, "The line frequently resents the controls exercised by staff officials." The reason for this is that the staff officers, no matter how tactful they are, "exercise a veto over the line." Resentment can build up as the experts on the staff use their best judgment concerning line officers' activities. This judgment should and will entail denying line officers' requests. Although this conflict normally occurs between the line and staff officers, regardless of rank, the situation may be intensified when staff functions are operated and supervised by civilians.

Modern management principles applied to police functions normally result in a general recommendation for the hiring of civilians for many staff functions. The major reason given is that civilians may be less costly to hire than sworn personnel for some functions, and they can also be hired with prior training/education for specialized staff functions. The role of the manager is to be aware of the potential conflict between staff and line personnel and to create a system that can accommodate these potential problems. One recommendation is to make sure that the civilian personnel on staff have enough authority in the department to carry out their functions. At the same time, there should be a process for line officers and staff personnel to appeal to upper management for conflict resolution.

This authority has to be clearly defined. Authority in the department goes from top management to middle management and then to the line officers and sergeants operating in the field. The staff officer and staff civilian personnel have authority concerning their internal functions and units. However, their authority does not extend to issuing orders to managers or line officers. Lines of authority need to be clear in any department if the department is to operate efficiently with a minimum of conflict. In this case, staff may recommend to management and line officers, but staff is not in the line of authority in operating the department.

On the other hand, as Nigro and Nigro relate (1977: 166), staff officers and civilians frequently look down on line officers. Such terms as *medieval, slow to change*, and *ignorant* are frequently heard in discussions on this topic. It is easy to see how this attitude develops, for in reality, the staff personnel do have a major influence in the long-range and short-range policy making for the police organization, regardless of what the line officers feel. A good example of this type of situation is shown in the following case study.

In this incident, management has obviously missed the mark in the positive utilization of staff officer Clement. It has missed the mark, also, in the effective utilization of staff information and recommendations by line officers. However, these problems can be dealt with in a positive manner.

CASE STUDY

Ron Clement

Although Ron Clement deeply enjoyed police work, he felt that something was lacking in his life, and so he decided to go to college. He left police work as a patrol officer and applied his veterans' benefits toward a bachelor's degree and majored in criminal justice planning. Four years later, he walked through the front door of his old police station, only this time as a criminal justice planner.

Ron's responsibilities included preparing a daily summary of crime trends and analyzing different pieces of information that were gleaned from police reports. These daily summaries were copied and presented to patrol officers at the beginning of their shifts. He also assisted the chief of police and his deputies in overall departmental planning and soon became a part of the regular Monday morning administrative conferences.

"I didn't realize that there would be jealousy or animosity toward me. I mean, it was not too long ago that I was a patrol officer. But I suddenly realized that I had lost my connection with the street cops when I began to see my summaries in the roll-call-room wastepaper basket. I actually had to do a sales job with the cops, showing them how the crime summaries would be useful to their patrol work. The younger guys cooperated, but some of the veterans still shrugged me off.

"It really hurt me when I overheard a conversation in the patrol locker room about me. One guy said, 'Clement has become a real jerk. He works inside and now he thinks he knows everything there is to know about running patrol. Why is it when a good cop, a brother patrol officer, goes inside, he becomes an arrogant jerk?'"

This type of conflict is generally dysfunctional for the police organization and its personnel. Recommendations for counteracting this state of affairs include the following:

1. *Get out of the office.* A common complaint is that staff personnel always stay in their office or the station house, thereby having little idea about what is going on outside. It is healthy for staff personnel, sworn and civilian, to ride along on patrol or be temporarily assigned to a line function, so as to keep in touch with the concerns of the line personnel.

2. *Rotate assignments.* Sworn personnel should occasionally be assigned to staff functions. Sworn police officers should be doing police work in the field. On the other hand, assigning line personnel to staff units from time to time can enlarge the former's perspective on the overall nature of police administration so that they can better utilize staff work when they go back out on the streets. It also allows police administrators to review those individuals who have useful technical expertise or who are aspiring to become police administrators. Basically, this can be an excellent training ground for future executives.

3. *Implement line/staff intervention.* In addition to ride-along or staff assignments, further interaction should be encouraged through meetings and seminars. For example, staff research on the right type of vehicle to be used for patrol should include patrol officers since they will eventually be affected by the decision. This is an often-overlooked area of expertise. There are many personnel in agencies who, by virtue of their time on the job and experience, can contribute to the body of knowledge being gathered by staff as input to management decisions.

Although a great variety of staff functions exists, certain staff functions are either used in most police departments or considered more vital to effective administration than others. In a text on police management like this one, which is also concerned with certain aspects of police operations as they affect the management of the department, only a limited number of specific operational functions and units can be examined.

COMMUNITY RELATIONS

Many police agencies have established public relations, or **community relations,** units as a formal means of recapturing or establishing rapport with certain segments of the community. Program objectives of such units are aimed at target populations who either are prone to have violent confrontations with the police or have questions about police activities. The concept of community relations grew from the tensions of the 1960s, when many police and public officials realized that there was a gap in communication between the enforcers of the law and those they policed.

However, community relations are not just the responsibility of an organization unit in a police department; they must also become the personal responsibility of each and every professional police officer. Each officer presents the image of policing and his or her police department to the citizens. How each officer deals with citizens in his or her daily work reflects on the department as a whole. Thus, you cannot have officers who shrug their shoulders and respond to a request by a citizen, "Oh, that's the responsibility of a public relations unit. The officers out on patrol do not have anything to do with that community relations stuff." Instead, the officer should consider him- or herself a mini-community relations unit.

This communications gap has derived from a number of factors. At an earlier time, police patrol officers generally had an intimate knowledge of the neighborhoods they patrolled. Even in immigrant neighborhoods, foot-patrol officers were accessible and generally visible as they made their rounds through the area. The decline of police-citizen contact occurred for a number of reasons. By the end of World War II, police patrol work was done by car, placing glass and steel barriers between officers and the public. Neighborhood precinct houses, which were community centers of information and problem solving, eventually were closed down and centralized into a few station houses or a centralized police station, thereby becoming more inaccessible for the general public. Furthermore, traditional urban boundaries, shaped by ethnicity and geography, were broken down by politics and urban renewal. In many cities, these "old" neighborhoods were eventually populated by black, Hispanic, and other new immigrants, generally poor and unemployed, who sometimes looked on the police as an army of occupation.

This situation is not found only in the inner city. In many suburban areas, whose municipal boundaries are geographically far-flung, citizens may have difficulty identifying the community police since there are often too few officers to serve the population effectively. Or policing may also be carried out by a number of competing agencies that together may have conflict in providing the entire range of police services.

In discussing some popular programs and services that are offered by community affairs units, it will become apparent that each officer should in actuality be a community affairs specialist. In the end, the daily actions of the community police are the only one true variable that increases or decreases tensions within the community. Community relations, whether done by one division or by a single officer, provides a conduit for individuals and community groups to talk to the police. It also provides the department with a mechanism to undo or address perceived or real wrongs committed by officers in the course of their duties.

Public-relations units are often responsible for providing the media with information concerning the department and official police activity. Officers who have been involved in a newsworthy story often do not recognize the incident when it is later written up in the newspaper. Newspaper stories are written to sell newspapers. If the department wants accurate reporting, it must have personnel who deal with the media and are familiar with journalism. These individuals have to establish a rapport with the media so that the latter are treated with respect and are given accurate information concerning police activity. Press police officers need to establish good relationships with professionals in journalism in order to correct any misinformation that may have been published. The key word here is *credibility*. If the department is to have a positive relationship with the press, it must have a credible relationship. This kind of relationship takes time to develop and maintain, but it is vital to the image of the police department in any community.

Personnel for Community Relations

Ideally, we see the specialized community relations assignment as short term and assigned to all officers. Realistically, this is not possible since the very nature of the community relations assignment requires the officer to develop good relationships over a period of time. Moreover, some departments have a few officers that the police managers would prefer "kept under wraps" since their actions and attitudes would do nothing to improve police-community relations. Community relations should not be a "dropping ground" for officers who, for some reason or another, are not able to perform street duties or have been placed inside for disciplinary reasons.

Functions of the Community Relations Unit

The community relations unit functions in two major areas: crime prevention and public relations. However, it must again be stressed that the successful, effective police department is one that is closely identified with the community and one in which the officers do not leave community involvement to a unit of the department. Actually, even though it is not tradition, a better name for this unit would be the community involvement unit, thus showing the close ties of the professional officer to the community. Following are some of the major functions of the community relations unit.

Public Speakers' Bureaus.   Through public speakers' bureaus, officers or administrators make presentations on various aspects of police operations to community and school groups. As a rule, engagements should be planned days in advance and should employ the use of modern audiovisual techniques. The officer in charge of the community relations unit should review any topic that is to be presented with the department speaker so that there is a consistent departmental policy running through all presentations. The community relations department head should actively seek out those officers in the department who have an interesting topic to present and who have some public-speaking talent, experience, or training. A list of these officers and their topics should be on hand when any community group requests a speaker. In the area of race relations, special care should be taken to assign only those individuals who are knowledgeable and able to keep their heads in the midst of often heated and sometimes rather "sharp" discussions.

Tours and Demonstrations.   These programs provide an excellent opportunity to educate the public by reviewing specific police techniques and operations in a realistic setting. Tours should be scheduled in advance, and care and consideration should be given to the nature of the audience so that the operations can be shown and explained in the proper perspective. Care should be exercised so that the tour group does not interfere with police operations going on at the time. Demonstrations in and outside the police station that have sparked community interest include radar use, dusting for fingerprints, use of police dogs, alcohol and drug detection, and computer capabilities.

Department Homepages and Electronic Newsletters.   The Internet has allowed citizens access to the so-called information superhighway, which allows users to communicate, browse, and obtain information from millions of sites around the world. Proactive departments have created Web sites that allow users to obtain general information about the departments, crime prevention tips, and up-to-date information on crime incidents.

Beyond homepages, many departments are now offering **electronic newsletters** to inform residents about crime trends, serious incidents, and department activities. A spin-off to these are e-mail or fax alerts to businesses, neighborhoods, and government units regarding criminal or emergency incidents.

Ride-Alongs.   Scheduled in advance by the community relations unit, a **ride-along** program provides members of the public with a chance to see their community from inside a police car. Departments with such programs have formulated strict procedures on the issues of liability and safety. Basically, we recommend that these programs take place only with officers who volunteer, without coercion, official or otherwise, to have ride-alongs in their patrol cars during their regular shifts.

One problem concerns the selection of these ride-along citizens. In the case of criminal justice students, it is usually clear that these are people with a career orientation seeking knowledge. This may also be true of the ordinary citizen. The patrol officer has to do his or her job, and those who participate in the ride-along program should have some special training in how to handle citizens when tense situations develop. Rules and regulations governing these programs should be clear and in writing. Officers should be able to explain to the citizen the role of patrol in the total functioning of the department.

Civilians need to be instructed in terms of what not to do. At a minimum, the following need to be stated:

1. Civilians should never be armed, even if they have a gun permit.
2. In case of a violent incident, civilians should not leave the patrol car and should leave any confrontation to the professionally trained police officer.
3. Civilians are not allowed to bring tape recorders or cameras.
4. Civilians should be aware that this is a working police officer who has a duty to perform and that they should not, in any way, interfere with the carrying out of that duty.

Some officers do not work well with civilian observers. An officer with personal problems does not need civilians in the patrol car to add to the stress of the job. Thus, for these and a variety of other reasons, officers need to be screened before they can participate in the program. If the department management wishes a ride-along program as a public relations tool, controls must be placed on it in order for it to be a positive force in the community and the department.

College Internships.   Many colleges offering criminal justice degrees have established **student intern** programs in which students are allowed to study the activities of a criminal justice agency for a certain period of time. Mutually agreed-to guidelines should be drawn up between the institution and the police agency regarding the number of hours and the activities that the student will be assigned (Gordon and McBride, 2001). One officer should be assigned to be a mentor for the student. While the student is able to combine theory and practice in a criminal justice setting, agency personnel act in the capacity of field teachers by showing the student how police operations are carried out. In many cases, former interns are later appointed as police officers since the internship has given the agency and the student the opportunity to decide whether policing is a suitable career for the student.

Crime-Prevention Programs.   Many larger departments have separate units that deal with the issue of crime prevention. As noted previously, one major role of the police lies in the prevention of crime. To further this objective, many departments instituted crime-prevention programs in the 1970s as a means to reduce crime. The target populations for these programs were community and special-interest groups that wanted to know how they could help in the fight against crime and at the same time reduce the likelihood that they would be crime victims. Here are three examples of crime-prevention programs:

Operation Identification. In this program, the police department allows citizens to borrow an engraver and etch an identification number on certain valuable items. The item of property and its identification number are then recorded in a police log. This process is useful if the engraved item is stolen and later recovered.

Neighborhood Watch. The **Neighborhood Watch** program, devised by the National Sheriffs Association, incorporates the ancient notion of frankpledge. Each person on a street block is responsible for watching out for suspicious individuals and incidents, especially those related to burglaries. The role of the community relations unit for this program is to foster the need for collective security in the neighborhood and to instruct citizens under what circumstances to call for the police. Residents are issued decals that are posted in windows and doors indicating that the residence participates in the program, thereby attempting to foster some sort of deterrence.

McGruff: Take a Bite Out of Crime. The **McGruff** national media campaign has had a positive impact on law enforcement. It has four major objectives (O'Keefe and others, 1984: 5): "(1) to change unwarranted feelings about crime and the criminal justice system, particularly those feelings of frustration and hopelessness; (2) to generate an individual sense of responsibility among citizens; (3) to encourage citizens, working within their communities and with local law enforcement, to take collective crime prevention actions; and (4) to enhance existing crime prevention programs at local, state and national levels. [The] campaign uses a cartoon dog character 'McGruff,' arrayed in a trenchcoat and admonishing citizens to follow the example of 'real people' prototypes who through various means helped to 'take a bite out of crime.'" Twenty-two percent of a nationwide sample responded "yes" when asked if the campaign affected their behavior; of those who answered affirmatively, 34 percent got new locks for their homes and used them, 21 percent were keeping watch on their neighbors and reporting suspicious activity, and 24 percent said that they were "thinking about doing something in the future that was suggested by the ads that we have been talking about" (O'Keefe and others, 1984: Table 4).

Many crime-prevention programs have been half-hearted attempts to improve police community relations. Often a program is conceived and massive media publicity is generated, but after a few months the program dies. The main problem is that most crime-prevention programs are never evaluated in terms of one question: Does the program have any impact on crime? After instituting the program, the police agency must encourage continuing citizen participation in the program. The truth is that most equipment for Neighborhood Watch, Operation ID, and other similar ventures eventually does nothing but collect dust in police property areas. Thus, each program needs to be evaluated in terms of its permanent value to citizens and to the department.

Citizen Volunteer Programs.   Citizens can participate in a variety of volunteer programs for crime prevention and emergency response:

Community emergency-response teams (CERT)
Neighborhood Watch
Volunteer in Police Service (VIPS)

Terrorism Information and Prevention System (TIPS)

Medical Reserve Corps

These popular programs involve citizen volunteers in auxiliary police activities, but there is no research indicating that any actually prevent crime. These programs, which are sponsored by the federal government, involve citizens with their local police in a variety of positive ways and are currently being brought into many homeland security efforts. Further information can be obtained from the FEMA Web site (www.fema.gov). Descriptive and training materials as well as videotapes are available through this Web site.

The Community Relations Officer

The community relations officer (CRO) acts as a liaison between the department, the media, and public-interest groups. In many departments, this specialist might be assigned to a community relations unit or, in some cases, report directly to the police administrator. In smaller departments, the chief of police often acts as his or her own community relations officer.

In addition to acting as a liaison with the media, the role of the community relations officer is the following:

1. Preparing releases on police-related news. Such news includes a daily police log, the status of investigations, crime trends, and other information deemed necessary for public knowledge.
2. Coordinating the scheduling of press conferences.
3. Preparing or coordinating special audiovisual materials or pamphlets, such as slide shows, handouts, or videotape presentations that portray department operations.
4. Coordinating the creation of homepages or electronic newsletters.

In this role, the CRO must have access to all divisions and personnel in the department. Importantly, his or her viewpoint must relate to the policies of the police administrator and the department.

As has been mentioned, the press officer needs some journalistic training and the ability to have a credible relationship with the press. One problem often encountered is the reporter with a "police blotter" mentality—that is, a reporter, looking for copy for the next day's paper, who simply wants to know what dramatic event happened that evening. The press officer should be trained to handle this kind of mentality and, maybe, guide it to a more positive attitude for the good of both the media and the department.

The press officer should also be trained to speak effectively before the cameras. He or she needs to dress the part of a professional police officer and be articulate. With the new technology of the news (instant replay, portable TV cameras, and mobile units), an incident could happen and an on-the-scene report could be broadcast within minutes. A well-trained, responsible press officer who can handle tough questions in tense situations is needed for the job. This person should be recognized as a high-priority factor in any police budget and should have higher status and rank than he or she does in most departments. We have to get beyond taking press officers from the ranks and placing them before the camera with no special training. This position is vital for the creation of a positive image for the professional police department.

One last note on the press officer's training and rank. The press officer must command enough rank so that he or she has the respect of fellow officers and enough authority to be seen to speak for the department. These officers should have enough time on the road and in rank so that they can be respected for their past police experience and knowledge of the department. Finally, they should have solid training in criminalistics and crime-scene control so that they can educate the public and the press yet protect the confidentiality of an investigation. They must be able to relate to investigators and know what can be said and what should not be said. They are also, on that television set, the department, and their demeanor, training, and knowledge should reflect their professionalism. Since the press officer represents the department to the public, the officer's behavior and language must at all times be professional.

THE LEGAL ADVISER

The daily actions of any police officer are subject to legal review according to the parameters set forth by the courts; so too are the operations of the police organization. Traditionally on criminal matters, police may consult with the local district attorney for advice and assistance in the coordination of criminal procedures and investigations. While this criminal aspect remains important, the police organization and its personnel have recently been the targets of civil suits from individuals or organizations. At one time, the police, as agents of the state, could not be subject to civil suit. Citizens can now sue public officials through various civil rights acts, particularly in the areas of false arrest, employment discrimination, and brutality. The rise of civil suits for money damages necessitates the use of attorneys who specialize in these matters. The role of the police **legal adviser,** then, is to oversee the disposition of civil cases against the department. In addition, his or her duties include keeping the organization updated on changes in criminal and civil laws and procedures as well as advising the chief and staff administrators on methods to decrease the likelihood of successful civil suits against the department. The legal adviser would also be a good resource for the continual problem of search-and-seizure procedures.

The role of the police legal adviser in the future appears most likely to increase with stature in that a civil suit, whether successful or unsuccessful, incorporates procedures that are expensive in terms of legal costs. In many situations, the department or its counsel settles out of court for a lesser sum demanded by the plaintiff simply because of these costs. Successful suits, however, have an effect on the financial and policy operations of the department.

In the 1970s, civil suits against individual police officers became an increasingly important factor when deciding certain departmental policy and individual police behavior (President's Commission, 1967: 30–35; see also Broadway, 1974). Police benevolent associations also became concerned with the threats of such civil action and were involved, through their counsel, in a number of such suits.

Police departments in small municipalities and counties rely on private attorneys or corporation counsels for legal assistance. However, a part-time counsel on retainer with the local department, however small, would be of more benefit since such legal help would be experienced and knowledgeable concerning the special problems of police departments.

Another useful function for counsel hired by police departments is that of the screening of arrest charges. Because of the use of plea bargaining in reducing charges, police officers may tend to overcharge or undercharge in making an arrest. A good police department counsel or, in larger departments, legal staff would make for better arrest charges and create better cooperation with a district attorney staff. The prosecutors would know that there was a screened legal basis for the charges that are handed to the district attorney's office. Fewer errors and fewer citizens awaiting trial for charges that are going to be reduced or dropped also makes for good management, along with positive community relations. In the long run, there should be more and cleaner convictions for crimes committed.

Police attorneys may also find patterns of errors that officers are making. Over time, through internal training sessions and memorandums to management and staff, such errors can be eliminated. Over the long run, again, we should have a better conviction rate.

In terms of good management, of course, the problems become more complicated as we look at the police arrest-and-charging function in the context of policy concerning the total court system. In the decision to charge (Jacoby, 1977: 7):

the prosecutor must make his decision based on the belief that

the individual is guilty;

the prosecution of the case will result in a conviction equal to the effort expended;

the influence of public opinion will be in the prosecutor's favor;

the resulting sentence will match the crime; and

the jurors are not loathe to convict.

Jacoby also spells out the choices available to the prosecutor:

> to charge
> not to charge
> defer prosecution
> divert; or
> return the case to the source of information for further investigation.

Police departments who are using the broken windows/quality-of-life approach make extensive use of civil lawyers working for urban governments to enforce zoning, property, and municipal rental laws. Local and overseas criminal gangs operating in major U.S. cities are laundering their money through real estate investments. Rental places and local food stores have become centers for drug distribution, sometimes with the owner's full knowledge. New York City has a civil nuisance law where a building can be closed down if three felonies take place there during a specific time period. It also includes other provisions which are useful for enforcement. Police working closely with these government civil lawyers are closing down rental and other properties that have become centers for drugs, criminal activity, and prostitution in public housing and single-family neighborhoods. The neighbors cooperate with the police and city officials and are pleased with their safer neighborhoods.

Police legal advisers can be the interface between the police department and the courts. They can deal with the courts and bring policies and opinions back into the department so that arrests are consistent with the prosecutor's policies. They can also explain to the prosecutor's office how difficult it may be for officers in the street to carry out these policies. In the long run, this individual or office can bring about consistent policies in a police/court system, even when the chief administrators for police and prosecutor's offices change. Thus, they are a help in transition periods as well as in the day-to-day work of the department, the courts, and the arresting discretion of the individual police officer in the street.

PROFESSIONAL STANDARDS

From colonial times, officials who enforced the law always had a great deal of latitude in committing crimes during the course of their duties. The histories of many major police departments are replete with accounts of brutality, nonfeasance, bribery, and abetting the activities of gangsters. Although there were periods of reform, corruption generally returned after the ruckus died down (Smith, 1965).

After World War II, many citizens, state and local governments, and interest groups addressed the issue of police corruption in their communities. Spurred by the media, many major police departments in the United States between 1950 and 1974 (and many smaller agencies as well) experienced corruption scandals (Sherman, 1974). This raised issues that still remain un-solved: Who polices the police? How do we stamp out corruption or deal with misconduct?

One rather spectacular failure involved the advent of civilian review boards, which caused what many police administrators of the time (1960s) felt was trial by newspaper, thereby destroying police morale (Richardson, 1974). This was also felt by most police benevolent associations of the time. In New York City, the action involved line officers in a political campaign to abolish the civilian review board, resulting in a resounding victory for the line officers' associations.

One solution to the dilemma of corruption was the formation of a special unit, termed the **internal affairs** unit, that would keep watch on the activities of departmental personnel and investigate alleged acts of corruption or mis-conduct. The title **professional standards** is currently being used in most po-lice agencies. This reflects new thinking on the part of college-educated police administrators and officers. It represents more than just a label change. It re-flects how professional police administrators view their ethical and moral responsibility to the public and their wish to be self-governing, using their own professional standards. The professional-standards unit is expected to enforce a model code of professional standards that would apply to all members of the department. As Fogelson points out (1977: 179), after the Los Angeles Police Department started an Internal Inspections Division for this purpose, virtually every major city adopted a similar model. Today, every police department, large and small, has either a division or a person who handles the internal af-fairs functions, which in addition to corruption, include investigating offenses defined by police duty manuals as "misconduct."

Departments that have professional internal affairs operations are often hampered in their effectiveness by opposition from the rank and file, which is then formally expressed in the union contract. Union rules may include the following for the investigation of police officers:

1. A ban against the use of polygraphs or alcohol-detection devices.
2. Defined hours when an interrogation may occur between a suspected officer and investigators.
3. Advance notice advising an officer that he or she is subject to an investiga-tion. Such notice may include the name and address of the complainant and the alleged act.
4. Complex procedures that make it virtually impossible to dismiss or disci-pline an officer.
5. The right of an officer to pick certain members of the review panel that will hear his or her case.

While such tactics may appear to be self-defeating for addressing the is-sue of police misconduct and corruption, it must be pointed out that these "safeguards" emerged to combat certain investigatory techniques, including interrogation during the early morning hours, not being informed of the nature of the complaint before being questioned by internal affairs, the use of decoys and entrapment tactics, and disciplinary action being taken against officers without due process. A review of an agency's union contract on this issue often reveals either real or perceived abuses of the internal affairs function on the part of the rank and file.

It is valuable to review the training function in terms of anticorruption programs. Recruit training should emphasize departmental policies, procedures, and ethical standards and should be followed up with practical role-playing exercises based on common incidents related to corruption problems on the street. In-service training should also be provided, perhaps in the form of roll-call training to keep these policies constantly in front of all personnel in the agency. We recognize that it is difficult to change attitudes and practices of veteran police officers; however, it is the responsibility of management to correct these problems.

The key to deterring corruption rests with each supervisor's interpretation and enforcement of consistent policies from management. A close liaison and understanding of departmental policy is a must for successful operation.

Managing the Professional Standards/Internal Affairs Unit

Internal affairs is that section of the police agency that handles citizen complaints or initiates investigations of officers committing crimes or misusing their authority. In larger departments, internal affairs is a separate division that receives complaints and conducts investigations. In smaller departments, the chief of police or a delegate may comprise the entire internal affairs unit. It is important to note that internal affairs is not the only section that handles complaints against police. Petty transgressions are handled on an informal basis by midline supervisors or the peer group. Serious complaints, or those initiated by a citizen directly to the police department, usually become the province of internal affairs.

Internal affairs is viewed with suspicion from two fronts. For citizens, suspicions are often raised as to whether making complaints will make any difference since they believe that the police will "whitewash" the incident. For police officers, internal affairs poses a threat in that it abrogates the entire notion of fraternity found in the police subculture—the inconceivable idea that fellow officers will prosecute another, resulting in fines, suspension, forced retirement, or jail.

Outside input deals with most of these misgivings. In many cities, citizens have been added to committees to review police misconduct. A nice balance is shown when police management has a major role is choosing the citizens to be added to these committees, thus protecting internal morale while having an outside check on police misconduct.

Essentially, all complaints should be reviewed and investigated, no matter how minor or serious. It is the responsibility of the police agency to publicize the procedure for filing a complaint against a member of the police force. To prevent false reporting, it should also be publicized that a false complaint may result in prosecution. To prevent charges of "whitewashing," the internal affairs unit should notify the complainant of the results of the investigation and the disciplinary actions taken against the alleged offender. For complaints found to be "unsubstantiated" or when no action is taken, the complainant should still be notified and told the reasons why. If he or she is not satisfied, the complainant should be directed to the district attorney or the U.S. Justice Department, especially in instances of alleged civil rights violations.

Disciplinary Actions

A number of disciplinary actions can be taken against a police officer who has been found to have committed crimes or to have abused his or her authority. If the officer is accused of having committed a crime, the district attorney's office would naturally prosecute. However, while that prosecution takes place, possibly over a period of months, the officer may be kept on the force (presumed innocent until convicted) or may be suspended with or without pay. If the officer is not convicted and has been suspended without pay, he or she is normally reinstated and given back pay. In some cases, the officer may have to bring civil suit to obtain that back pay.

Disciplinary actions can be brought against an officer for a violation of department rules that legally may not be defined as a criminal offense. Examples of such violations include failure to wear proper uniform or use proper equipment, having long hair or dirty shoes, failure to make proper entries in log books, and being late for duty. More serious departmental offenses that would still not be considered criminal offenses might include discourtesy to a citizen during the performance of a duty, an accident with a patrol vehicle, or drinking on duty.

In these cases, there are a range of sanctions that can normally be employed:

1. Field counseling or verbal reprimand
2. Written reprimand/formal counseling
3. Loss of vacation days or fine
4. Suspension with or without pay
5. Reduction in rank or change of assignment
6. Dismissal
7. Criminal prosecution

In cases involving minor deviation from department rules, supervisors usually resort to verbal reprimands. However, when the deviation becomes consistent behavior, such as being late for work, more formal means of discipline are employed.

The philosophy of discipline that we advocate is termed *progressive discipline*. The elements of progressive discipline are as follows:

Documentation. It is the duty of the supervisor to document infractions and bring them to the attention of the officer. In the case of tardiness, some kind of official action must take place the first time the officer is late.

Sanctions. The sanction to be imposed, again ranging from verbal reprimand to a more serious punishment, must be related to the seriousness of the offense. For example, termination from the job is not a proper sanction for an officer who is late for duty for the first time. Termination, however, may be appropriate if the officer has been documented late on 30 occasions over a two-month period.

Administration. The sanctions must be equally administered to all portions of the department. It is not correct practice if discipline is meted out to one shift or sector but not to another. There must be consistency—which is difficult because of the range of situations and personalities involved in supervision.

Department Rules and Collective Bargaining Agreements

Department rules or collective bargaining agreements related to disciplinary actions must be strictly followed. In collective bargaining agreements, disciplinary procedures follow a grievance-like procedure in terms of a written notice to the offender and in some cases stepwise review by a state labor relations board.

For example, for the officer who is tardy, the supervisor may wish to have a formal counseling session. A counseling session should be done in private and on a one-on-one basis between the officer and the supervisor. A written memorandum should follow, outlining the basis for the problem, the reason the problem occurred, and the actions that will be taken to correct the problem. The written memorandum should be signed by both the officer and the supervisor.

Department review boards and state arbitrators become very concerned if the procedure is not followed in disciplinary matters, no matter how slight the occurrence may seem. For example, in one case a labor relations arbitrator dismissed the department's request for loss of six days' pay for an officer who was consistently tardy because supervisors had not formally counseled the officer in ten previous but similar situations over the year. The rule in disciplinary matters is that if the allegation is not in writing and in the officer's personnel file, then it never officially happened!

In cases involving a serious complaint or a criminal allegation, more formal measures are employed. As Weston and Fraley (1980: 153) discuss, the rights of a police officer suspected of wrongdoing involve the following:

1. Notice of the nature of the investigation and the name of the complainant, if known

2. Time and place of interrogation or hearing
3. Right to legal counsel at interrogation or hearing
4. The recording of interrogations and hearings
5. Written notification of determination and disposition of the complaint, with reasons presented for the disposition

Immediate suspension with or without pay before the commencement of a criminal proceeding or departmental review process occurs only if the officer is deemed to be a threat to the public and co-workers or has committed a crime. Consider the following examples based on rulings by state arbitrators and police department review boards:

- Suspension without pay was an appropriate measure when an officer was caught shoplifting in uniform during an unauthorized meal break.
- Request for termination for an officer arrested off duty in early morning hours wearing only sneakers was inappropriate since the employee was not officially on duty.
- An officer was terminated after having consensual sex with a woman in a patrol vehicle while on duty. Before entering into a final hearing, the officer agreed to resign in lieu of losing six months' back pay. The attorney for the department agreed to this plea based on the poor investigation that went into the incident, which could have resulted in a not-guilty verdict and reinstatement of this officer.
- Although criminal charges were dismissed based on lack of probable cause, the termination of a police lieutenant was upheld based on the defendant's service record and complaints involving sexual harassment and the seriousness of the disciplinary complaint—striking a female officer.

If there are three recommendations that can be provided police management in terms of dealing with equity and protecting departmental morale, they would be

Consistency
Consistency
Consistency

This means that written procedures must be followed and that punishment must fit the offense.

PROACTIVE CONTROL OF POLICE VIOLENCE AND DEVIANCE

Police violence is usually dealt with reactively. For example, a citizen is beat up, killed, or ends up in the hospital, and there is a police investigation and sometimes a political investigation. After the investigation, a politically inspired committee devises some remedies that might or might not work, then tells the media. This is not a good way to do business.

In a proactive approach to police violence, a system of prevention is in place before violence happens. Police violence can be prevented, but when it occurs it can be dealt with immediately only if programs are in place. Violence by police officers takes place within the norms of secrecy, solidarity, and social isolation of police culture. To understand police violence requires understanding how these police norms have encouraged police violence and cover-ups. Prevention strategies, investigation techniques, and specific intervention approaches will be examined. Well-thought-out professional intervention approaches can protect the rights of both civilians and police officers while ensuring that cover-ups do not take place.

Obstacles to Decreasing Police Deviance and Violence

Secrecy, solidarity, and social isolation were described in Chapter 2 as the basic norms of police culture. They are neither good nor bad in terms of how police operate. Applying these norms to police deviance and brutality can create great harm for both the public and the police organization.

The Norm of Secrecy.   Police deal with the reputations of people, which can be destroyed through routine investigations. For example, a school official may be the target of an investigation where young women were raped in a van. Any public knowledge of the investigation can destroy the official's reputation, even if the investigation is proved to be unfounded. A drug investigation may take many months to complete. Talking about the investigation, even to a spouse, means that lives can be jeopardized. On the other hand, this norm of secrecy is also used to protect deviant and violent police officers by creating a "blue curtain" between the police and the public.

The Norm of Solidarity.   The officer is part of a police family. His or her children are police children. The spouse is a police wife or a police husband. Police officers stick together. They protect their brother and sister officers from a hostile public and their own brass. The operating norm is "You are never alone."

This solidarity can go too far in treating all nonpolice, including ordinary citizens, as the enemy. Solidarity strengthens the blue curtain that covers up deviant and violent acts by police officers. Solidarity allows each police officer, administrator, and manager to protect violent and deviant cops in order to make the police department look good.

The Norm of Social Isolation.   The perception of a hostile public creates a police attitude that is hostile to the community. Officers carry a gun, do traffic stops, and arrest people, and this isolates them from the community. Police officers know that they can trust a cop but never an outsider. Every day, officers deal with the underclass in society: people who steal, drunks, drug dealers who sell dope to children, and child molesters who prey on the weak and innocent.

Police officers are doing dirty work. This is work that deals with an undesirable population. Officers, in the public eye, can take on the stigma of that population. Under the socially isolated military model, the public becomes the enemy. As Van Maanen (1978: 221) stated, "I guess what our job really boils down to is not letting the assholes take over the city. . . . They're the ones that make it tough. You take the majority of what we do and it's nothing more than asshole control." Police officers' friends become limited to other cops and people in the criminal justice "business." Police protect their own, including dirty cops.

Turning People into Things.   This is especially damaging to the police officers since it turns citizens into things. It starts with using obscenities aimed at citizens and criminals. If a citizen is an "asshole," a thing, that citizen is not a human being. By being a thing, the citizen cannot have any feelings or any humanity and is simply the enemy. Once a person becomes a thing, you can do anything. Things do not feel, do not have families, and do not have children. Things can be hurt without guilt. This can lead to violent behavior by the police against individuals.

The Military Model.   A professional police department has a civilian atmosphere rather than an aggressive military atmosphere. The military mission is different than the police mission. The military's mission is to use the violence necessary to complete the mission. The police mission is to limit violence and to protect citizens from violence. The use of military training and tactics changes the mission of the police and separates the police from the public. Without the military agenda, the members of the community become valuable allies in the fight against criminal activity. Military personnel do a fine professional job fighting a war, but they are not police, nor does the military have a civilian police agenda. In emergencies, the use of military tactics is, of course, justified and necessary.

Internal Affairs.   Secret hearings and investigations by an internal affairs structure create suspicion among the public and the press. Due process police proceedings need to be public affairs that are transparent to citizens and to the press and need to bring serious penalties for police violence and deviance and serious penalties for citizens who bring false charges. Internal affairs, as it works today, can be unfair and dysfunctional for both the individual police officer and the public.

Strategic Interventions for Police Deviance.   The best source of professional readings on police **deviance** is Barker and Carter's *Police Deviance* (3rd ed., 1994). Barker and Carter cite the need for clear, specific directives in a department to control deviance. The directives would include expected standards of behavior to inform both the officer and the community. There would be grounds for discipline and counseling for individual officers, guidelines for officer supervision, and directions for training.

These directives have to be very specific, for example, "Acceptance of any gratuity will be subject to disciplinary action. This includes services, restaurant and fast food meals, and presents of all kinds, including bottles of alcoholic beverages given during holidays. Minimum punishment is suspension without pay for two days."

Police Use of Obscenity.   The use of obscenity on citizens can be considered psychological and emotional violence because it demeans citizens, treats them with no respect, and dehumanizes encounters with the public. White, Cox, and Basehart (1994) give four situational reasons why police officers use obscenity in interactions with citizens:

To gain the attention of the citizen
To establish social distance
To label and degrade citizens
To dominate and control citizens

Once again we have the "asshole" syndrome. Citizens are stigmatized and treated as things. Once the social distance and stigma are established, further acceptance of these slurs establishes the citizen as a nonperson.

White and colleagues also noted that the use of obscenity can lead to aggression. When a police officer labels a citizen an obscene thing, then these citizens are no longer human beings. Once the citizen is socially constructed as a thing, the police officer can do anything he or she wants without guilt or thought. There need to be strong, enforced departmental policies concerning the use of obscenity because obscenity against citizens can lead to police violence against citizens.

Police Use of Deadly Force.   Since the U.S. Supreme Court case of *Tennessee v. Garner* (1985), it has been illegal to use deadly physical force to apprehend nondangerous fleeing felon suspects. With appropriate departmental policies installed, the shooting of fleeing suspects has been reduced (Blumberg, 1994: 518).

As a result of this case and the appropriate departmental regulations, Blumberg also noted that the police use of guns often changed from aggressive use to defensive use. One problem is the lack of accurate data. Nobody knows how many times police have shot at citizens, justifiably or unjustifiably. From the available research, the evidence is overwhelming that a restrictive firearms policy that is tightly enforced can be effective in reducing the number of police shootings.

Police Use of Excessive Force.   The use of excessive force by police officers is a major problem, and it seems that a small minority of officers have the most complaints. For example, of the 3,440 complaints against police officers in Boston in the 1980s, 61.5 percent were lodged against 11 percent of the officers (Barker and Carter, 1994: 267). The Report of the Independent Commission of the Los Angeles Police Department (Christopher Commission, 1994: 291–306) on why the beating of Rodney King took place showed some major problems. The commission found that there was a group of police officers who repeatedly used excessive force, that they were known to police supervisors, and that no action was taken. From January 1987 to March 1991, of the 6,000 officers who were implicated in use-of-force reports, 4,000 had one report, 63 had 20 or more reports, which accounted for 20 percent of all the reports.

The commission found that performance evaluations of officers who used excessive force were generally positive. Analyses of tape-recorded messages from patrol cars showed that officers had admitted to beatings. The tapes were not audited by any supervisor. The commission also found that the complaint system was skewed against the complainant and that internal affairs investigated only a few complaints. It was also documented that the department treated excessive-force offenses more leniently than other types of misconduct.

The blue curtain of police secrecy, solidarity, and social isolation needs to be raised so that the brutal police officer is forced from the department. The Los Angeles Police Department (LAPD) was described as "an aggressive police organization that had rapidly distanced itself from the public. While developing as many specialized units as possible and securing as many military gadgets and tactics as the city would allow, Gates instilled a sense of division between police and the public" (Kappler et al., 1994: 135).

Racism, mixed with violence and aggression, also created social isolation of the officers in the LAPD. As LAPD police officers have stated, "I would love to drive down Slausen [an African American neighborhood] with a flame thrower. . . . We would have a barbecue. I almost got me a Mexican last night but he dropped the gun too quick" (Kappler et al., 1994: 140).

Early-Warning Systems to Identify Problem Officers

It is possible to manage the risk of police officers being involved in **corruption** or brutalizing behavior by developing an **early-warning (EW) system** to identify officers who are at risk. This early-warning system works best in departments that are committed to uncovering and working with problem officers. It stops hidden problems from growing and becoming major police scandals, and it makes it hard for the department to ignore and cover up the behavior of problem officers.

The Miami Police Department uses the following criteria to identify problem officers (Walker and Alpert, 2001):

1. Complaints—officers with five or more complaints with a finding of sustained or inclusive during the past two years
2. Control of persons (use of force)—officers involved as principals in five or more use-of-force incidents during the past two years
3. Reprimands—employees with five or more reprimands during the past five years
4. Discharge of firearms—officers who discharged their firearms on three or more occasions during the past five years

The supervisors notify officers who meet any of these criteria that they are being placed in the early-warning system and will be investigated. In Miami, the system affects very few officers, but it is nevertheless a good, proactive management tool.

Also needed are programs to work with problem officers. Miami has six different ways to handle these officers (Walker and Alpert, 2002):

Reassignment

Retraining

Transfer

Referral to an employee-assistance program

Fitness-for-duty evaluation

Dismissal pursuant to civil rules and regulations

Intervention efforts must involve more than the immediate supervisor. There is hope that the early-warning system will deter problem officers and that intervention will help problem officers become good police officers. This system might also be used to identify problem supervisors.

THE POLICE MISCONDUCT MODEL

Police **misconduct** has been a persistent problem for police administrators, civilian policy makers, and citizen groups. It remains an important public policy issue because police officers have a wide range of powers affecting liberty and life. They also can take actions under the color of law that would be designated as crimes for ordinary citizens, such as the use of deadly physical force.

Exactly what constitutes misconduct and the reasons for this problem remain a continuing topic of academic debate. Before 1990, most inquiries and studies into police wrongdoing focused on corruption, which took the form of bribes and payoffs from gangsters, protection schemes promoted by officers, and a variety of felony crimes committed by officers while on duty. The most famous study was the Knapp Commission inquiry into police corruption (1972), which among other ideas, presented the concept of "meat eaters" and "grass eaters." A meat eater was defined as an officer who actively sought out graft and money, while a grass eater was one who participated in lesser forms of corruption, such as accepting free meals, discounts on services, and gifts and money that fell their way. The "rotten apple theory" was also presented by administrators to explain that corruption was just limited to a few officers and did not involve the entire department. In some cases, academic studies, grand juries, or official commissions found that the entire barrel, the whole community criminal justice system, was indeed corrupt.

After a number of cases involving the use of deadly force, including the Rodney King beating in Los Angeles, academic and professional police inquiry expanded into other areas of police deviance and misconduct. Most administrators use the term *police misconduct* when a supervisor or an officer is in violation of the state or federal law, department policies, or administrative rules. These violations might range from the most mundane—failing to gas up the patrol vehicle at the end of a shift—to the more serious, such as executing a drug dealer. As will be discussed, the current inquiry into police misconduct focuses on serious behaviors that can be criminal or civilly liable.

From the police misconduct model, a departmental systems approach was also being reviewed as a way to explain and control police misconduct. The Mollen investigation in New York City (1994) and the Ramparts investigation in Los Angeles (2000) found, in those precincts, serious problems based on officer quality, lack of supervision, lack of management audit and oversight, and poor working conditions. In both cases, most of the issues were tied to drug enforcement and related schemes to sell evidence and to punish drug dealers who did not pay for protection (Lersch, 2002).

Based on recent works by Barker and Carter (1994) and Lersch (2002), police misconduct activities can be said to include the following:

- Felony and misdemeanor crimes committed by officers on and off duty
- Payoffs for not performing a duty
- Nonfeasance (failure to perform an official duty) or performing a duty incorrectly
- Gratuities
- Sexual abuse and sexual favors
- Free services and goods
- Abuse of deadly and physical force
- "Noble-cause reasons," which deal with by-passing department procedures, lying under oath, or violating a suspect's constitutional rights to enforce the law

Under the heading of "noble cause" are a range of activities that are related to drug offenses. These include planting evidence, lying under oath, stealing money and drugs from raids or evidence lockers, supplying informants with drugs, and killing suspects.

Sexual abuse has received attention recently; media-publicized incidents have involved rape, sexual harassment, and stalking. In one case, an officer ordered female traffic violators suspected of driving while intoxicated to undress or face arrest and immediate imprisonment. These incidents have prompted a number of academic studies, such as McGurrin and Kappler's (2002) review of media accounts of police sexual violence.

THE INTERNAL AUDIT

Police departments should routinely conduct internal **audits** of their operations to ascertain whether they meet department and applicable state standards and expectations. An audit for this purpose is simply a test or review of a department practice or policy as it relates to the delivery of a specific police service. Unlike accreditation, where the department presents its written policies and operations for external review, the internal audit deals with how well the policy or practice is working. The audit can serve as an important planning tool for improving services and identifying potential problems.

The audit is closely related to what is often called *inspections*. In large departments, the inspections unit is often related to internal affairs. Inspectors deal with citizen complaints and audit typical criminal investigation functions, such as evidence processing, case disposition, and personnel complaints.

The audit concept can apply to a number of operational areas that include not only basic line operations, but also training, records, communications, recruitment and selection, promotions, equipment, crime prevention, and community relations. The auditor, who should be a command-level person, prepares questions to "test" the operational item or practice in terms of overall benefit to the department or any administrative concerns and issues. For example, an audit of the police vehicle fleet would include a review of the number of vehicles, their age and condition, the cost for gas and maintenance, accident records, and "likes and dislikes" of drivers. While such an exercise would be important for budgetary reasons, the audit should review not only overall vehicle cost, but also the use of vehicles as they relate to services. In one case, an audit found the possibility that gasoline was being stolen. Further review found that certain investigators were not filling out gas tickets when taking assigned vehicles home.

Another audit might involve the use of police overtime. Again, while most departments have overall budget numbers, they may not keep records as to the allocation of overtime for each department member, shift, and intended purpose. An audit test in a suburban department found that most overtime costs were driven by external requests for security at professional sports and social events and that the sponsors were not compensating the department.

Audits of citizens can also be undertaken. For quality assurance, one police department polls a sample of crime and accident victims to see if the responding officers were courteous and knowledgeable in dealing with their cases. They also want to know if the officers returned phone calls to address victim concerns.

The Misconduct Review

Police administrators have to sit down and seriously review the department or divisional areas that are prone to misconduct (McCarthy, 2000; Close, 2001). This misconduct risk assessment is a review of behavior in operational areas that could result in criminal prosecution, civil legal action, internal discipline, or media attention. Misconduct assessment is based on three major premises:

1. Prohibited conduct is defined in the department rules manual, and the department manual is a "living" document that is kept updated and is constantly used for reference.
2. Citizens can make a complaint in person, by letter, by phone, or anonymously. Complaint procedures are well publicized.
3. The steps for complaint investigation, follow-up, and resolution are known not only to department members, but to the community at large. This includes officer protections provided in state civil service rules or the collective bargaining agreement.

When conducting a misconduct assessment, the first step is the internal review. The following questions should be asked during an annual review:

1. How many civil lawsuits are we facing? How much have we paid in legal fees and judgments?
2. How many civilian complaints did we receive? What was the breakdown of these complaints: discourteous behavior, poor driving habits, use of force, drug use, spousal abuse, and so on? How were these complaints resolved? Were they found to be justified? If so, what discipline was taken?
3. How many disciplinary actions were initiated by the department based on supervisory referrals? What were the categories? How were they resolved? How many officers were punished?
4. How many use-of-force actions were taken by department members? Were they justified, based on internal or external (e.g., grand jury) review?
5. Do the civilian or departmental disciplinary actions seem to be directed toward a certain group of officers?
6. What is the relationship between performance evaluations and disciplinary actions for officers and supervisors?
7. Based on after-action reports, polls, and media articles, how does the public perceive us?
8. To what extent is ethics training conducted at all department levels?
9. How are department policies and regulations updated to reflect legal changes or new case law?
10. What new training programs may be needed to address specific legal issues?

When the information is being gathered, certain key operational areas always seem to emerge as problem areas. These include evidence room procedures and review for money and narcotics cases, selection and training of personnel assigned to special vice and narcotics units, and the overall conduct of narcotics investigations, including the use of informants.

Once these and other questions have been answered, the department can prioritize the areas that need attention. Basic to this would be a standard operations policy that deals with the steps to address complaints. As prepared by the International Association of Chiefs of Police (2000), a policy of this nature addresses the following:

1. Procedures that are taken for discipline based on violations of law, agency policy, rules, or regulations
2. The acceptance and filing of complaints. This addresses the forms that are used and what office or supervisor receives the complaint.
3. Investigation procedures by either the supervisor or another administrator
4. Interview procedures of employees and witnesses
5. Rules for drug or blood tests of employees
6. The right of employees to have union representation or counsel
7. The filing of charges if necessary
8. The resolution of the charges

Many misconduct policies also have language regarding the confidentiality of records and the prevention of employee misconduct. The former means that the department, as a general rule, is guided by the values of fairness, justice, and accountability to agency standards.

Using Proactive Community Policing to Decrease Police Deviance

An alternative to the military model, with its adversarial aggressive stance, is the community policing model, by which the community sets the police agenda. Police middle management and line officers become empowered by working closely with community groups on the community's agenda.

For example, police management might be concerned with a rise in burglaries, while the community might be concerned with the growing power of drug dealers. In a world of scarce police resources, choices must be made. With the military command structure model, the pursuit of burglaries would be the police policy agenda. With the proactive community policing model, efforts would be made, with interagency cooperation, to curb the use of illegal drugs in the community and to arrest as many drug dealers as possible. This would be combined with drug education in the schools, preaching against drugs in local churches, using government agencies to condemn crack houses, and providing reports to community groups on the success of these efforts.

This approach also curbs the effects of the police norms of solidarity, secrecy, and social isolation. The military model encourages secret decisions made by police management in the interest of security and isolates the police from the community by creating a feeling of police being different and superior to the public. It encourages many of the bad aspects of solidarity by using such terms as "unity of command" and creating a warrior mystique (Jetmore, 1997). The proactive community model encourages more transparency for decision making by helping the community understand decision making as it exists in the police organization and having the community help set police policy concerning the goals of law enforcement in their community. It is much harder to have an aggressive, unchecked violent police effort when officers work closely with the community to lower crime. Without a military agenda, the members of the community become valuable allies in the fight against criminal activity.

Police culture is a given for police organizations, but it can be modified if the police managers want to do so and if they involve police middle management and the community in the effort. Keeping the best aspects of police cultural norms while curbing their negative aspects is a constant struggle for proactive police management, but it is worth the effort.

Due Process for the Police and the Public.   Police managers need to establish a procedure that treats officers accused of misconduct with respect; otherwise, the internal process of justice within the department begins to degrade officers and treat them as things. Officers need to have self-respect if they are to respect citizens. Managers need to establish "self-respect criteria" in all police hearings to protect both the public and the police officer.

Due process rights for police officers during a police hearing were established in *Morrisey* v. *Brewer* in 1972 by the U.S. Supreme Court (More, 1998). These procedural due process rights are as follows:

1. Written notice of the claimed violation
2. Disclosure of evidence
3. Opportunity to be heard in person and to present witnesses and documentary evidence
4. Right to confront and cross-examine witnesses
5. Neutral and detached hearing body
6. Written statement by the fact finders as to the evidence relied on and the reasons for the actions taken

A basically honest due process along with a sense of fair play for all parties concerned may seem to be an unrealizable and idealistic set of goals. However, without the implementation of these goals, the police officers and the public can be brutalized. Civic standards must be enforced daily.

Police departments experiencing problems, including both excessive force and other police deviance cases, need to institute new policies. Some combination of the following intervention policies needs to be analyzed in relation to the specific problems and the size and nature of the police department.

Intervention Policies

1. Identification of officers who consistently use excessive force or other police deviance with active intervention through a combination of counseling, sanctions, and removal from the police force if necessary. The use of

excessive force and obscenities should be reflected in the officer's performance evaluations.

2. Analysis and random monitoring of tape-recorded patrol car messages,
with special emphasis on officers who are part of a targeted excessive-force
group or who use a consistent pattern of obscenities and racist remarks.
This policy may be thwarted by the use of cell phones.

3. Special investigation and intervention by a team of departmental investigators, lawyers, and counselors. This office needs resources and support by
the chief of police.

4. Written procedures for all investigations of police misconduct, including
rules for witnesses and other rules of evidence, to be published and made
available to all police officers and the public. Resources and policies are
needed to resolve these complaints, including the use of mediators and the
availability of a legal staff. This will protect the rights of both police
officers and the public.

5. Specific departmental rules outlining the limits of force used by police
officers, to be published and made available to both police officers and
the public. This should include both legal guidelines and departmental
rules.

6. Ongoing analysis of excessive use of force as part of the schedule of analysis
and written reports by departmental research staff or, if the department
lacks expertise and staff time, outside consultants.

7. Swift prosecution of any illegal acts by police officers and any false accusations by citizens.

8. Ongoing training for dealing with stress and anger control. Officers should
have access to counseling for these and other problems.

9. Procedures for informing citizens and officers of the outcome of any complaint, in writing, with documentation, and in a timely manner.

10. Transparent internal affairs proceedings that include the public and the
press in the process. Secret internal affairs proceedings create distrust.
Police officers who feel that internal affairs treated them unfairly in secret
proceedings support public proceedings.

11. Appeal for unsatisfied complaints by both the officers and citizens to an
authority outside the department. Possibilities include a civil service board,
an ombudsman, a judicial panel, binding arbitration, and the use of courts
and torts.

The secret of success is to deal with every problem in a swift and fair manner without any cover-up. This means that all written rules and procedures
should be written in clear English and should be short and to the point. They
should be made available in sufficient quantity for everyone. The rules then
need to be followed in a fair and consistent manner for both the police officers
and any complaining civilians. Once a reputation for fairness is established,
both officer morale and citizen respect will increase.

James J. Fyfe, writing about the "split-second syndrome" of police violence,
states, "The urgent, involuntary and public relationship between police and

client creates a high potential for violence. To avert it, police must apply considerable diagnostic skills" (1997: 539). A proactive police department will have these skills:

1. Strict and enforced departmental rules in place concerning the use of police violence
2. A stress-management and anger-control system that actively engages officers on an ongoing basis
3. A fair and public due process system for both the police and the public
4. A civilian rather than a military police management subculture
5. A professional follow-up team that deals with the use of all police violence—reasonable, excessive, justifiable, and unjustifiable

Proactive management teams and professional police officers plan ahead by creating and following programs and policies that are in place and part of the everyday life of every officer in the department.

CONCLUSION

Central administrative functions structure the day-to-day activities of the police agency. These functions are part of management prerogatives and are central to the major administrative authority in the department. When management talks about the internal staff of the agency, it is referring to the support personnel that administer to the needs of the line operations.

There is a natural antipathy between line officers and the administrative staff. The administrative staff structures and carries out the basic policies of the department and delivers these policies to the management. Supervisory staff are expected to exercise authority over the line officers in carrying out these tasks. Full communication between line and staff is essential if the cooperation that is needed to have a well-run department is to be achieved.

Three major staff functions are community relations, legal advice, and internal affairs. Community relations can be as simple as an individual officer in the small department or as complicated as a separate unit in the larger department. Traditionally, community relations officers have given speeches and have participated in a wide range of community programs. However, the proactive management approach advocates a more active role for the police officers in the community. This means that all officers are trained in community relations and are expected to make community relations a part of their duties as police officers, taking part, for example, in such activities as teaching a minicourse in criminal justice at the local high school and organizing sports teams for teenagers.

The legal adviser, something of an innovation over the last 10 years, is usually a full-time attorney employed by the department who can provide up-to-date training in changes in the law and screen cases so that the department has a better conviction record. This is a cost-efficient position.

Professional standards/internal affairs is one of the most difficult units to organize. To be effective, it must be even-handed and represent the rights of both the citizens who are being policed and the officers who are doing the policing. It must be proactive in the sense of having an ongoing anticorruption program. This means that the rules and regulations concerning discipline and corruption are in place and operational before there is any hint of a problem. Too many times, these internal rules and regulations are written and organized in reaction to specific instances of discipline problems and corruption. These reactive rules are often inconsistent since they relate to specific instances rather than to general behavior. Consistency and fairness have to be the major goal of any internal affairs unit.

These administrative functions, although closely tied to management, are essential to the operation of the total department. They affect all the personnel and, in the instances of community relations and internal affairs, can have a major impact on the department's image in the community. If the department is to be considered a professional police agency by the citizens of the community, these administrative functions have to be managed with a great deal of skill, knowledge, and consistency.

Police deviance and use of excessive force have become major concerns for police management in the United States today. Immediate and systematic attention has to be paid to these issues. Some departments are taking a proactive and honest approach, while other departments are still in the cover-up and making-excuses stages. Police management in the twenty-first century of global information, Web sites, and press and citizen scrutiny has to have policies and an openness that makes sense under existing conditions. The proactive approach to controlling police deviance and violence can and will work, but it will take a great deal of change and personal courage.

QUESTIONS FOR REVIEW

1. In your community, what recourse is available to a person who complains of police misconduct or corruption? To what agencies may he or she submit the complaint?

2. What are the causes of line/staff tension in police organizations? How can these problems be addressed?

3. It would appear that every police officer is a community relations person. Why, then, is it necessary to have specific personnel assigned to this task?

4. Explain the strengths and weaknesses of the following community relations programs: tours and demonstrations, ride-alongs, college internships, and crime-prevention programs.

5. In general, what are the duties of a community relations officer?

6. List the main points of the anticorruption program presented in this chapter.
7. Why has police corruption and misconduct been a persistent problem in the United States?

CLASS PROJECT

Select a police department in your community and call the police dispatcher (use the administrative number, do not use 911 or some other emergency number). Ask if the department has a reporting form that citizens may use to report an incident of police misconduct. If the person reports that they do not, ask how citizens can make complaints. Also see if there are forms available on the World Wide Web.

BIBLIOGRAPHY

BALKIN, JOSEPH. "Why Policemen Don't Like Policewomen." *Journal of Police Science and Administration* (March 1988), pp. 29–38.

BARKER, THOMAS, and DAVID L. CARTER. "A Typology of Police Deviance." In Thomas Barker and David L. Carter, eds., *Police Deviance* (2nd ed.). Cincinnati: Anderson, 1994, pp. 3–30.

———. *Police Deviance* (2nd ed.). Cincinnati: Anderson, 1994.

BLUMBERG, MARK. "Controlling Police Use of Deadly Force: Assessing Two Decades of Progress." In Roger G. Dunham and Godfrey P. Alpert, eds., *Critical Issues in Policing*. Prospect Heights, Ill.: Waveland Press, 1997, pp. 507–530.

BROADWAY, FRED. "Police Misconduct: Positive Alternatives." *Journal of Police Science and Administration*, 2, no. 2 (1974), pp. 224–232.

CARTER, DAVID L., and DARREL W. STEPHENS. "Police Ethics, Integrity and Off-Duty Behavior: Policy Issues on Police Conduct." In Thomas Barker and David L. Carter, eds., *Police Deviance* (3rd ed.). Cincinnati: Anderson, 1994, pp. 29–44.

CHRISTOPHER COMMISSION. "Report of the Independent Commission of the Los Angeles Police Department." In Thomas Barker and David L. Carter, eds., *Police Deviance* (2nd ed.). Cincinnati: Anderson, 1994, pp. 291–306.

CLOSE, DALE H. "How Chiefs Should Prepare for Nine Liability Risks." *Police Chief* (June 2001), pp. 16–27.

FOGELSON, ROBERT M. *Big City Police*. Cambridge, Mass.: Harvard University Press, 1977.

FYFE, JAMES J. "The Split Second Syndrome and Other Determinates of Police Violence." In Roger G. Dunham and Godfrey P. Alpert, eds., *Critical Issues in Policing*. Prospect Heights, Ill.: Waveland Press, 1997, pp. 531–546.

GOLDSTEIN, HERMAN. *Problem Oriented Policing*. New York: McGraw-Hill, 1990.

GORDON, GARY, and BRUCE McBRIDE. *Criminal Justice Internships: Theory into Practice* (4th ed.). Cincinnati: Anderson, 2001.

GRENNAN, SEAN. "A Perspective on Women in Policing." In Roslyn Muraskin and Ted Alleman, eds., *It's a Crime: Women and Justice*. Englewood Cliffs, N.J.: Regents/Prentice Hall, 1993, pp. 163–176.

HALE, DONNA, and DANIEL J. MENNITI. "Discrimination and Harassment: Litigation by Women in Policing." In Roslyn Muraskin and Ted Alleman, eds., *It's a Crime: Women and Justice.* Englewood Cliffs, N.J.: Regents/Prentice Hall, 1993, pp. 177–190.

INTERNATIONAL ASSOCIATION OF CHIEFS OF POLICE. "Model Policy Offers Guidance on Investigating Officer Misconduct." *Police Chief* (October 2000), pp. 44–47.

JACOBY, JOAN E. *The Prosecutor's Charging Decision.* Washington, D.C.: U.S. Government Printing Office, 1977.

JETMORE, LARRY F. *The Path of the Warrior.* Flushing, N.Y.: Looseleaf Law Publications, 1997.

KAPPLER, VICTOR E., RICHARD D. SLUDER, and GEOFFREY P. ALPERT. *Forces of Deviance: Understanding the Dark Side of Policing* (2nd ed.). Prospect Heights, Ill.: Waveland Press, 1994.

KNAPP COMMISSION. *Police Corruption in New York.* New York: Whitman Knapp, 1972.

KRAJACK, KEVIN. "Internal Affairs." *Police Magazine* (1979), pp. 9–16.

LERSCH, KIM M. *Policing and Misconduct.* Upper Saddle River, N.J.: Prentice Hall, 2002.

MACQUIRE, KATHLEEN, and TIMOTHY J. FLANAGAN, eds. *Sourcebook of Criminal Justice Statistics, 1994.* Washington, D.C.: Bureau of Justice Statistics, 1995.

MARX, GARY T. *Undercover: Police Surveillance in America.* Berkeley and Los Angeles: University of California Press, 1988.

MCCARTHY, ROBERT. "Steps Chiefs Can Take to Prevent Unethical Behavior." *Police Chief* (October 2000), pp. 36–40.

MCGURRIN, DANIELLE, and KAPPLER, VICTOR. "Media Accounts of Police Sexual Violence: Rotten Apples or State-Supported Violence." In Kim M. Lersch, ed., *Policing and Misconduct.* Upper Saddle River, N.J.: Prentice Hall, 2002.

MORE, H.W. *Special Topics in Policing* (2nd ed.). Cincinnati: Anderson, 1998.

NATIONAL INSTITUTE OF JUSTICE. *Community Policing in Chicago: Year Two.* Washington, D.C.: National Institute of Justice, 1995.

———. *25 Years of Criminal Justice Research.* Washington, D.C.: National Institute of Justice, 1995.

NIGRO, FELIX A., and LLOYD G. NIGRO. *Modern Public Administration* (4th ed.). New York: Harper and Row, 1977.

O'KEEFE, GARRET, ET AL. "Taking a Bite Out of Crime: The Impact of a Mass Media Crime Prevention Campaign. Washington, D.C., National Institute of Justice, 1984.

PEAK, KENNETH. *Policing America.* Englewood Cliffs, N.J.: Regents/Prentice Hall, 1993.

PRESIDENT'S COMMISSION ON LAW ENFORCEMENT AND THE ADMINISTRATION OF JUSTICE. *The Police.* Washington, D.C.: U.S. Government Printing Office, 1967.

RICHARDSON, J.E. *Urban Police in the United States.* Port Washington, NY: Kennikat, 1974.

SHERMAN, LAWRENCE. "The Sociology and Social Reform of American Police, 1950–1973." *Journal of Police Science and Administration* (September 1974), pp. 255–262.

SKOGAN, WESLEY G. "The Community Role in Community Policing." *National Institute of Justice Journal* (August 1996), pp. 31–32.

SMITH, RALPH LEE. *The Tarnished Badge.* New York: Crowley Press, 1965.

STARK, RODNEY. *Police Riots.* Belmont, Calif.: Focus, 1972.

STRATTON, JOHN G. *Police Passages*. Sandusky, Ohio: Glennon, 1984.

STODDARD, ELLWYN R. "The Informal Code of Police Deviance: A Group Approach to Blue Coat Crime." *Journal of Police Science and Administration* (June 1968), pp. 201–213.

THIBAULT, EDWARD. "The Blue Milieu: Police as a Vocational Subculture." In John W. Bizzack, ed., *Issues in Policing*. Lexington, Ky.: Autumn House, 1993.

VAN MAANEN, JOHN. "The Asshole." In Peter K. Manning and John Van Maanen, eds., *Policing: A View from the Street*. Santa Monica, Calif.: Goodyear, 1978, pp. 221–238.

WALKER, SAMUEL, GEOFFREY P. ALPERT, and DENNIS J. KENNY. "Early Warning System: Responding to the Problem Police Officer." Washington, D.C.: National Institute of Justice, 2001.

WESTLEY, WILLIAM A. *Violence and the Police*. Cambridge, Mass.: MIT Press, 1970.

WESTON, PAUL B., and PHILIP K. FRALEY. *Police Personnel Management*. Englewood Cliffs, N.J.: Prentice Hall, 1980.

WHITE, MERVIN F., TERRY C. COX, and JACK BASEHART. "Theoretical Considerations of Officer Profanity and Obscenity in Formal Contacts with Citizens." In Thomas Barker and David L. Carter, eds., *Police Deviance* (2nd ed.). Cincinnati: Anderson, 1994, pp. 223–246.

11

AUXILIARY FUNCTIONS

KEY TERMS

Automatic Fingerprint Identifications System (AFIS)	mobile radio district (MRD)
	PCP
criminalistics	purging
deoxyribonucleic acid (DNA)	records
emergency plan	sealing
forensic science	temporary detention facility
Freedom of Information Act	computer crime

Police organizations, no matter what the size, need personnel to direct and supply resources to those units or individuals who provide police services to the community. Portions of the organization that fulfill this function are called *auxiliary services*. Auxiliary services provide the "behind-the-scenes" support for the police organization. They could also be titled *supporting services* since these services are necessary, normally, to support the daily business of the police agency.

The discussion in this chapter concerns the major auxiliary functions that appear in most departments. Depending on local conditions, other supporting services may be necessary. The auxiliary functions used by most police agencies include (1) communications, encompassing case records, criminal records, and identification officers; (2) records; (3) property control; (4) vehicle maintenance; (5) building maintenance; (6) licensing; (7) the crime laboratory, including photographic, chemistry, and physical evidence laboratories; and (8) ancillary public safety services, including emergency mobilization, animal control, and emergency medical services.

COMMUNICATIONS

Some agencies assign communications to the patrol division since a great deal of communications is related to the patrol function. However, communications serves the whole department. Traffic officers, detectives, laboratory specialists, and experts from other special units all need access to communications. In a modern department, a centralized communications and records unit is considered the most efficient way to organize this major auxiliary section.

The efficiency and effectiveness of daily police operations depend on the nature of the communications unit maintained by the department. This unit must be able to provide the following:

1. Telephone reception for emergency, nonemergency, and inquiry calls
2. Base-to-field communications and return by wireless radio
3. Retrieval of police information related to wanted individuals, lost property, vehicle ownership, and motorist information (commonly referred to as the DATA function)
4. Interface with or scanning of area and statewide police agencies
5. Interface with or scanning of area fire and ambulance services.

The degree to which these services are provided depends not only on the size and jurisdiction of the police agency, but also on the degree of economic investment that the municipality wishes to make for computerized communications equipment. At present, the advances made in communications and computer technology provide the opportunity for every police department in the United States to offer these services to personnel and the community.

CASE STUDY

Communications

On April 12, 2002, Mrs. Stephen Jones telephoned the Riverside Police Department, stating that her husband was threatening to kill her and that she had locked herself in a bedroom. Her call was recorded on a telephone tape unit. Units 303 and 410 were dispatched to the residence. While en route, the communicator replayed the conversation to the officers on channel 1 of their multichannel mobile radio. The officers responding to the scene therefore had a general picture of the situation as related by Mrs. Jones. At the conclusion of the playback, Unit 303 "punched" the husband's name into the mobile data terminal and found that a man of the same name and address had been arrested by the department four years ago for assault with a deadly weapon. On arrival at the scene, one officer noted that a black BMW sports car was parked in the driveway.

Using the mobile data terminal, the officer looked up the license plate and found that it belonged to a subject by the name of Stephen Jones, who had three outstanding warrants for burglary and assault. A detective unit also arrived at the scene. Using a cellular telephone, the detective called the residence and asked for Mr. Jones. Using his powers of persuasion, the detective asked Mr. Jones to come outside to talk to him about the outstanding parking tickets issued to his valuable sports car.

This incident illustrates some of the capabilities of modern communications systems. The nearest cars from the jurisdiction were dispatched since this was a regional communications system. Also the system had a tape-recording capability, which had not existed a few years previously. In addition, the dispatched officers had instant access to all records—local, state, and national. In terms of providing the maximum amount of information in a very short time, the system had lived up to expectations.

Consolidation

In an effort to solve communications inferiority, some police agencies have pooled their resources and have formed a **mobile radio district (MRD),** making a centralized communications center the main reception center for telephone calls for police assistance. Member agencies in the MRD are dispatched according to their jurisdiction. If an officer is in trouble or if a serious emergency occurs requiring the presence of many patrol units from the member agencies, the communications center will be able to act as the focal point for activity coordination. Computers for local and national police information are maintained and operated at the center, and member agencies are provided with a terminal to be used in their own station houses. Mobile, portable, and base-station radio equipment is procured and maintained under the coordination of the MRD. To address issues that arise on procedures or other situations, the MRD has a representative committee of member agencies that meets frequently to iron out any problems.

Consolidated communications centers using the MRD model have been established all over the United States in heavily populated metropolitan areas. One problem that arises in MRD formation is the influence that the political faction or agency that controls the communications center may have on all police operations for that area. This is a common problem when an agency, such as the state police, the sheriff's department, or a town police department, has concurrent jurisdiction with city, village, or town agencies. The question that always comes up is, Who will receive the "glory" calls? This is usually solved by de facto arrangements and formal guidelines ensuring that city units will respond to calls in their jurisdiction and that other units will respond only in emergencies or at the request of the agency. The solution of this problem has been crucial in the formation of consolidated police communications networks.

Communications Personnel

The police subculture may view those personnel who work inside the station house as second-class citizens since they are not out on the streets doing "real" police work. As a result, officers assigned to communications are looked on with some measure of disdain. In some agencies, the communications assignment is viewed as being for those who have physical ailments or have "screwed up" in some way; yet there is nothing second-class about police communications.

These attitudes are in the process of change because of the importance of the communications function and the amount of technological expertise needed. It is not uncommon for police communications supervisors in large agencies to have formal degrees in electronics, computers, or communications and to be able to write grants and computer programs for elaborate police information-communications systems. Because personnel with this type of background are difficult to recruit for general police work, many agencies have relied on civilians with relevant work and educational backgrounds to manage their communications systems.

The communications person is the "ambassador" of the department to the outside world. His or her tone and manner of dealing with questions and situations has immediate impact for many clients, ranging from first responders to community leaders. Communications personnel have to think like police officers when they speak to callers. They often have to go beyond the simple question-and-answer scenarios. For example, a woman calling about being locked out of her car was asked, "Is there anyone locked inside your car?" As it turned out, her five-month-old son was in his carseat, and the temperature was 92 degrees. Her simple request now required an emergency response.

Some departments have begun to use civilians as communicators. In addition to classroom training, the civilian communicator should be assigned to observe patrol operations so as to get a feel for the geography and personalities of the sworn officers with whom he or she will be working. In the same vein, rookie police officers should be assigned to the communications sector for the same reasons. Supervision of a shift in the communications section should be by an experienced sworn officer who, in addition to normal administrative tasks, will act as commander for emergency situations.

In small police departments, the communications function is handled by one person who, in addition to police responsibilities, also has to act as desk clerk and fire dispatcher. Again, there is no clear-cut formula for the number of people assigned to this function. It depends on the size of the agency and jurisdiction as well as on the amount of police activity that the agency has to handle.

Personal Attributes

Police communicators should be familiar with all aspects of police operations and agency procedures. A good communicator, in practice, will have the ability to screen calls and solve those situations on the phone that do not require the police presence at the scene. As most police communications personnel relate, working on the police telephones and radios is a stressful job. It requires a number of personal qualities—tact, politeness, coolness, rational decision making—and the ability to perform seven different tasks at once. For the police subculture, the chief client of the communicator is the officer on the street, as he or she is responsible for the safety and informational updating of each and every one of the officers. Experienced communicators know when an officer is in trouble simply by a nuance or failure to call back while doing a task (e.g., a vehicle and traffic stop) in a reasonable length of time. Officers assigned to street duty realize this. One of the first inquiries made at the beginning of the shift is "Who's on the radio?"

Today in police training, communications procedures are a standard part of the basic police curriculum. Academies with a good physical plant may have a mock communications area where recruits respond to mock telephone calls and requests for information, dispatch patrols, and calm irate citizens—all at the same time! Civilian personnel must be trained according to the same procedures and methods as regular police officers. For example, many states requires that all dispatchers complete a one-week training program in police communications. In addition to mock calls, dispatchers learn basic first aid, crisis management, and communications theory.

RECORDS

As in all bureaucracies and complex organizations, the efficient recording and flow of paperwork are essential to the successful operation of the police agency. The records division is often considered part of the communications division or at least it works closely with the communications division.

Although often downgraded in terms of funding and personnel, the records division is an important tool for management. To allocate resources, personnel, and budgeted funds, an accessible information system is needed. This means that the information has to be available in more than raw form. Thus, the chief task of **records** personnel involves classifying, filing, and indexing police paperwork by numerical, alphabetical, and numerous other classification systems, so that this information is accessible for later convenient retrieval. Information is also needed for informing the public and other private and public agencies, such as defense attorneys, prosecutors, and insurance companies.

For police operations, records may be divided into the following categories:

Category	Tasks/Operations
People	Arrestees, complainants, victims, missing persons, wanted persons (for questioning or by warrant), and fingerprints
Motor vehicles	Accidents, inquiries, fatalities, moving violations, and parking tickets

Administration	Personnel, payroll, scheduling, budget, purchases, inventories, and fleet and building maintenance
Crime statistics	Arrests and crime reports by legal statute, area, age, race, and so on
Property	Lost, found, stolen
Other	Jail, operations, court dispositions, bail monies, and referral services

These six categories may or may not be centralized, depending on the management philosophy or operational history of the department. Each line, staff, or auxiliary division might maintain its own records system in addition to a centralized system. Investigative divisions, for example, often maintain a file of suspicious people or incidents via modus operandi. Be it a centralized or a decentralized records system, the overall records function is a mainstay of police operations—providing data for investigative leads, allocating resources for certain types of cases, or preparing state or national crime reports.

One of the main goals of the records section is to present a total reporting picture that is critical for management decision making in such areas as workload, types of incidents, and assessment of hazards. The types of crimes encountered or reported are important for participation in the *Uniform Crime Reports* program. Disposition information is also critical, as indicated by the following disposition descriptors:

1. Arrest made (refer to original offense report)
2. Assistance rendered
3. Canceled by radio
4. Citation issued
5. Civil matter
6. False alarm
7. Follow-up (supplemental report made)
8. No police action possible/necessary
9. Peace restored without incident
10. Referred to agency other than police department
11. Referred to other police department division

Computerization

Police organizations began to use computers in the early 1960s. Not only was the computer, by this time, an important tool for information transmission and storage, but it was also beginning to be used for managerial decision making. As shown in other chapters, computers have been experimented with in determining patrol allocation and operations in many American cities. Plentiful funding for computer acquisition was available throughout the 1960s and early 1970s, which made it possible for many police departments in large metropolitan areas to establish computerized data and communications systems.

At present, computer utilization has been expanded for the records function. The positive attributes of computer utilization for data retrieval are as follows (Bureau of Justice Statistics, 1993):

1. Lower routine operating costs of data processing
2. Faster availability of information
3. Possibility of an audit of the system
4. Generation of new information that has never before been recorded
5. Greater consistency of reporting data
6. Reduced data distortion as the data move from line operations to staff
7. Development of a giant data inventory to be used for testing the environment
8. Greater freedom from mundane, routine record keeping

Computer and Communications Administrator

A new job title that has emerged in this new millennium is that of technical director to administer a department's communications and computer system. Technology has become very important in daily operations. However, there needs to be personnel who are educated and trained to administer this phase of the operation. Administrative tasks overseen by such a person or unit include the following:

Planning and design

Purchasing

Installation

Troubleshooting

Evaluation

Renovation

Staff training

The importance of this function was underscored in Y2K preparations and review. One of the main reasons why there were so few technical problems with computers and communications around the world is that the systems were subjected to repeated testing by in-house and external technical experts.

With the expansion of technology in policing, the most somber task facing many police executives is information systems procurement. As anyone who has attended the annual conference of the International Association of Chiefs of Police can attest, the available equipment and software is endless. It seems that information technology equipment changes almost overnight. The most important issue is the expected life cycle and life cycle cost for the system.

The key to this, according to Begert (1999), lies in carefully planning and presenting a procurement proposal to various vendors. The core question involves having an expert on your staff who can devote him- or herself to this task and analyze department needs and available equipment. What often happens is that department heads use certain vendors to act as their information technology staff. For small departments, obtaining the services of a consultant is advisable.

Storage of Records

Historians bemoan the loss or damage of the nineteenth- and twentieth-century records of many American police departments, especially by fire or paper decomposition. This continues to be a special problem since paper processing requires the use of acids that break down the paper. Also, it is not uncommon to see stacks of police files stored in cardboard boxes gathering dust and moisture in the dark recesses of the station house. This situation has been caused by the lack of storage space for the tons of paperwork created annually and is an unprofessional approach to storage and record retention.

Except for those records that, by law, need to be kept in the original, all storage should be microprocessed. This means that all records are reduced by the various processes available to modern library systems: microfilm, microfiche, or electronic retention in computer-generated files. There also needs to be a specific retention period for all records. There are problems with this cost-efficient approach to record retention and retrieval: (1) the laws need to be changed, (2) the expense of processing records into microform has to be reduced, and (3) the cost of a retrieval system, including readers and machines to produce hard copy from microcopy, has to come down. The costs of such a system are declining as more and more research libraries create systems using microprocessing of research materials. The U.S. government has encouraged and sponsored numerous research projects to bring down the cost of processing and using micromaterials.

Imaging technology, which copies records onto a computer disk, shows great promise in reducing the amount of paper that police departments store.

Security, Sealing, Purging, and Public Access to Records

Police departments generally desire that police records be kept confidential to maintain the effectiveness of law enforcement operations. This is especially important since a large percentage of police information involves the criminal history of suspects and arrestees. It is therefore imperative that the police agency ensures the confidentiality and integrity of criminal history information through administrative, computer, and physical security requirements. Based on Department of Justice regulations with regard to security of federally funded information systems, the following guidelines apply to all police agencies:

1. Access to criminal history information—namely, records, computer files, or the operating environments where police information is stored—should be restricted to authorized personnel.

2. Police personnel that have access to criminal history information are responsible for protecting this information from unauthorized access, disclosure, or dissemination.

3. The supervisors assigned to oversee the records function are ultimately responsible for all records.

4. Through written directives, standard operating procedures, and updated procedures, each member of the police organization should be familiar with the substance and intent of record security regulations (New York State Department of Criminal Justice Services, 1990).

While police organizations are intent on protecting the confidentiality of their records, there has been a nationwide trend for allowing citizens to have access to police information, especially when that information is related to the individual. In the 1970s, a number of acts were passed by Congress as reforms to the abuses of federal and state domestic spying and increased classification of government operations. The **Freedom of Information Act** of 1974 allowed citizens to request public records and to attend meetings of a nonconfidential nature. The Privacy Act, passed in the same year, gave individuals access to personal records and restricted the collection, maintenance, and distribution of personal information in both private and public agencies. In general, an individual requesting a federal document must go through a formalized process to obtain a copy of the record.

Federal and state regulations give every person who is the subject of a criminal history record the right to do the following:

- Request to be shown a copy of the record at a reasonably convenient location and time
- Review the record (with assistance of a reader/translator, if needed)
- Receive a copy of the record for purpose of challenge
- Request that a record be corrected on a showing of inaccuracy or incompleteness
- Obtain administrative review of record-correction denial
- Request, for purpose of correction, a list of noncriminal-justice recipients of inaccurate information (criminal justice recipients to be notified directly by criminal justice agency)

The regulations do not provide a right to review the following:

- Any information other than "criminal history information"
- Any information contained in intelligence or investigatory files

State and/or local criminal justice agencies are required to establish procedures for

- Review of criminal history information by the record subject
- Challenge by the record subject of information that is believed to be inaccurate or incomplete

- Review of source documents by the criminal justice agency to detemine accuracy/completeness of challenged information
- Administrative appeal by the record subject of an agency's refusal to correct a record
- Correction of information that has been disseminated that is shown to be incorrect

Citizens may or may not be allowed access to their own criminal files, depending on the state. In the case of the FBI record, on payment of a fee or proof of indigency, a citizen may receive a copy of his or her record. However, the FBI will accept corrections to the record only from the agency that sent the FBI the original data.

For police operations, the right to privacy may come into conflict with the need for accurate data on criminal suspects. Yet much police data contain information of little value or outdated relevancy. For example, many people are arrested whose cases result in dismissal or acquittal. When police information systems keep a record of wanted or arrested individuals by street address, it is often the case that the information is outdated. The suggestion that a suspect may still be living on the premises indeed affects the officer's perceptions as he or she responds to a call to the location in question. Both hand-recorded and computerized police information systems, therefore, should have policies that allow the removal of outdated or incorrect information. Two methods that apply to this procedure are (1) **purging,** as when the record is either destroyed or returned to the individual (this often occurs for the arrest records and fingerprint cards of individuals who have been acquitted or found not guilty), and (2) **sealing,** as when general access to the information is strictly limited except for certain instances or individuals. Sealing is generally done for juvenile offenders; only youth officers or officials of the juvenile court can officially have access to the information.

Purging and sealing are used for outdated or declassified information or when legal changes are made, for example, the decriminalization of alcohol or drug offenses.

PROPERTY CONTROL

The property clerk, who may be a sworn officer or a civilian, is the person in charge of the property section. Property is divided into (1) inventory control of physical property, (2) evidence control for court cases, and (3) found property, such as bicycles that have been abandoned in the street. Some police agencies that provide uniforms also have the property clerk serve as quartermaster, issuing and taking care of uniforms.

Inventory Control

Inventory control of physical property can have a major impact on the budget in that this property is being used 24 hours a day, as opposed to the more normal eight-hour or 12-hour day. Thus, planning—including regular maintenance and replacement control—becomes significant to day-to-day operations. Thus, to control inventory, the property clerk has to be on top of what is happening to the physical property. Examples of physical property are desks, chairs, file cabinets, the buildings themselves, heating and cooling units, and so on. Desktop computers may cost over a thousand dollars each and have to be maintained and replaced regularly so the department will be able to recoup residual values by selling these items as secondhand equipment. All this takes strict auditing as well as inventory control. Businesslike procedures created by a full-time property clerk are necessary if the department is to justify this part of the budget to legislative authorities. Estimates must be made of the life use of each item in a police setting, and periodic physical inspections must be conducted to confirm this life use.

In some cases, inventory purchases may be out of the jurisdiction of the property section because of a state or county purchase plan. However, the same principles apply. Also, any civilian agency has to be made aware of the special problems of servicing a 24-hour police department.

Evidence Control

Evidence control will be treated more fully when we examine the basic management of the police laboratory. However, two major principles apply here: continuity and security. A record must be kept of anyone handling any police evidence, and detailed records must be maintained concerning what happens to a piece of evidence whenever it leaves the property room. The second principle of security is paramount in any police agency. However, in the use of civilian personnel, special background checks should be made, and in-and-out security measures need to be strictly observed. One of the major problems relates to keeping drugs in the property room. Small amounts of certain drugs are worth so much money in the street that the temptation of civilians and officers to make a quick dollar is always there. Professional security measures using current technology should solve most of these problems.

Continuity of Evidence. Continuity of evidence means that there is a clearly documented record of where a piece of evidence has been, along with a record of who handled the evidence and why, from the time the evidence is picked up at the crime scene until it appears in a court case. Any break in the continuity of evidence is an opportunity for a sharp defense lawyer to break a case. The property clerk maintains the security of evidence as it is delivered from the crime scene and documents continuity in the following way:

1. Evidence is collected by evidence technicians at the crime scene and is sealed in plastic bags or appropriate containers to prevent contamination. It is also marked for future identification, giving date and circumstance of

obtaining the evidence on the package or article. On this container or article will be a form that everyone who handles the evidence will sign and date; they will also give a reason for handling the evidence.

2. Evidence goes to the lab if necessary or to the property clerk. Any detective or police officer who handles any evidence during investigation signs in and out for the evidence. All evidence is to be returned to the property clerk for safeguarding when not needed.

3. At the end of the investigation, evidence normally is transferred to the district attorney's office, where continuity of evidence must be maintained in case of appeal. The evidence is considered to be the prosecutor's responsibility until he or she returns it to the property clerk.

4. In addition, there must be security and oversight measures for high-risk evidence (narcotics, money, jewels, and firearms). These items must be inventoried on a routine basis, and only certain personnel may have clearance to enter the evidence area. There also must be a process by which old evidence is either returned to owners, auctioned off, or destroyed. It is no secret that many property rooms are full of items gathering dust.

Found Property

Found property is something of a nuisance for the department to handle, but it can be a real service to the citizen who is able to recover a $450 bicycle that went missing one day. At periodic intervals, after the property has been kept for a reasonable period of time, a public auction is held to sell remaining property. The money from the auction goes into the general coffers.

VEHICLE MAINTENANCE

Next to personnel, police vehicle acquisition, operation, and maintenance represent a major portion of budgetary expenditures whether the department has a fleet numbering three or 300 vehicles. A fully equipped police vehicle (lights, siren, radio, security devices) may well average over $40,000 per unit. And with today's gasoline prices, many police departments are seeking ways to reduce vehicle operating costs by redefining patrol objectives, increasing foot patrols, redesigning patrol sectors, or experimenting with smaller, more fuel-efficient vehicles. Departments are also using bicycle patrols in certain areas.

Police vehicles are on the road a good part of the 24-hour day. They normally clock between 80,000 and 100,000 miles before they are retired, depending on increased maintenance costs and downtime records. A car used by police is normally an adapted stock vehicle. Adaptation normally includes special lights, communication insertions, heavy-duty shocks, alternators, and roll bars. Thus, we have vehicles that are purchased in large quantities, often with a state or municipal contract, but have added features that result in added costs and lower gas mileage.

With these variables in mind, patrol vehicle selection is an important decision. The chief criterion is the environment. Rural and suburban departments generally need vehicles that have space for equipment as well as passengers since the patrol car serves as an office. Municipal departments that operate comparatively close to the police station can be best served by fuel-efficient vehicles. Terrain and weather are also important considerations for the selection of four-wheel-drive vehicles that can operate in the snow, on hillsides, or in beach areas.

One problem affecting many departments is that exact specifications need to be drawn for specific job requirements. However, if the police vehicle cannot accelerate or corner better than the normal stock vehicle, then, especially on highway patrol jobs, the police job simply cannot be done.

Each department should have a preventive maintenance program to detect problems before actual breakdowns occur. With the exception of patrol operations on interstate highways and rural areas, most patrol cars operate on "idle" or stop-and-start situations and then suddenly must increase speed from 0 to 60 miles per hour in emergency situations. Considering the potholed streets, bumpy parking lots, and fields they travel, it is no wonder that most patrol vehicles are functionally dead by 100,000 miles. Moreover, because of the lack of spare vehicles, many departments actually keep their cars running 24 hours a day with "time off" only for maintenance or shift changes.

Preventive and actual maintenance for vehicles is handled by police or municipally operated central garages or, in smaller communities, by private contractors. In any case, each administrator will have to decide which method is desirable based on cost effectiveness and availability of service and facilities offered by the municipal government. Mechanics who work on the police vehicles and maintenance records should be considered important resources for data on vehicle effectiveness, operating costs, and systems that are prone to break down (e.g., electrical system, cooling system, tires).

Preventive maintenance is also important because of the variety of drivers for each vehicle, the heavy use, and the use of the vehicles in life-and-death situations. Management needs to be aware of the driving habits of its personnel, including the need for review classes on driving habits and continual testing. Part of this process is the creation of an accident review board where all accidents are strictly analyzed. The result of such a review may mean disciplinary action against sworn personnel and vehicle maintenance staff. It can also mean that management will have to review when a vehicle should no longer be in use. Some models of cars last longer than others, and safety can be maintained only through the use of continual review. Many departments prefer to purchase half their fleet every year, whereas smaller departments may wait for two or perhaps three years to update. Many factors enter into this decision, including the rotation of vehicles into other units of the agency requiring less demanding vehicle usage.

The most important aspect of this discussion lies with the individual officer assigned to the vehicle. He or she is responsible not only for operating the vehicle in a safe manner, but also for reporting all minor and major defects that come to his or her attention. Preventive maintenance includes checking oil levels, tire pressure, and emergency equipment before each shift. Cleanliness of interiors is important for public appearance and morale. Some officers would agree that their patrol units look like the devil because of exterior dirt, ashtrays filled to the brim with cigarette butts and waste paper, and candy wrappers and dirt strewn about the interior.

Personal Patrol Car

The use of the personal patrol car has been a controversial topic. In the most common program model, the officer is assigned a marked patrol unit and drives it home at the conclusion of the shift. Variations of the program include one vehicle being assigned to a group of officers who live near one another. Proponents view the program as a way of increasing police presence in neighborhoods and improving emergency response time to critical situations. In theory, the officer assigned to a car would take better care of it and would make sure that scheduled routine maintenance is completed.

A study of personal patrol vehicles for a sheriff's department in a rural area by Fitzgerald (2002) found that the capital costs in purchasing vehicles and equipment was substantially higher when compared to purchasing a centralized fleet of vehicles. However, the operating costs were lower, and the vehicles were able to stay in service years beyond the normal range for fleet vehicles.

There are a number of management issues with personal patrol vehicles. Although changing shifts in the field may save some time and gas in going to a central office, management loses control over the officer and direct communication. Supervisory problems are created in that traditionally an officer would be subject to inspection of his or her person and equipment at a station roll call. Lack of regular inspections can lead to potential abuses of personal hygiene or equipment violations. Also, the lines of communication become more critical, and careful checks must be maintained to avoid miscommunicating the routine daily orders and directives.

In a few cases, there may be some justification for this approach, as when (1) the canine corps needs special vehicles, (2) undercover cars are needed for surveillance, and (3) large rural areas are involved. In the case of rural areas, regional garages may help to modify the distance problems.

One last problem of personal-use police cars is that police officers, while off duty, may involve civilian friends and their families in police business where there is potential violence. This means increased insurance concerning potential harm of these civilians. It also could mean an increase in damage suits by civilians against the police agency. When the officer is off duty and wearing old clothes (e.g., cleaning out a basement and then going to a hardware store), he or she does not evoke a professional image in a personal patrol car. Although the increased presence of police cars has had an effect, there is a question whether this is a positive or a negative effect. In summary, departments embarking on this program must have very direct guidelines on when the vehicle may be used and under what conditions.

BUILDING MAINTENANCE

Police stations in many cities in the United States are outdated facilities that retain most of the attributes of nineteenth-century architecture. In some cities, the police station was built like a medieval castle to protect the police from mob attacks. In smaller cities, towns, and villages, police facilities are tucked away in some remote recesses of the municipal building or fire station, generally as an afterthought to the original plans. Overall, it appears that all police stations, whether old or modern, share a common problem of maintenance and upkeep since they are 24-hour operations.

As the police station is a place where men and women must work and citizens must visit, we feel that it should be properly maintained and provide a sense of pride for the community. Sometimes officers loathe having tour groups come through their station houses because of the deplorable conditions.

With many departments contemplating new police stations, a number of architectural designs exist that can be adapted to fit the community environment. We offer the following planning suggestions:

1. *Security.* Most police stations in the United States are easy targets for terrorist attacks. Although we do not advocate that police station architecture return to medieval design, public access to the various areas of operations should be strictly controlled. While a main desk should be available for the public for information and complaints, the rest of the police operations should be sealed off by remote-controlled or keyed doors. Further security should be incorporated for communications centers, power plants, and lockup areas. Distinctive identification cards should be worn by personnel and visitors, and anyone who does not display such a card should be immediately stopped and questioned as a matter of course by any in-house personnel. Security considerations must also be extended to parking facilities and grounds near the police station. Ironically, many property crimes occur adjacent to police facilities, especially to patrol and privately owned vehicles.

2. *Personnel facilities.* The police station should have separate locker rooms and shower and bathroom facilities for male and female personnel. A trend is occurring in some departments where a country club atmosphere prevails in terms of a television room being located within the confines of the police locker room. Although additions of this nature are paid for by

volunteer contributions or funds from the police union, a negative image can result in that certain segments of the public may feel that such equipment was purchased with public monies. If any "fringes" are to be included in the police personnel facilities, we would advocate adding wellness equipment.

3. *Location to public.* The community police station should be accessible to the general public; this means building in a populated, central area of the community with ample parking facilities and measures to accommodate the disabled. In many suburban areas, state and other municipal police departments have been experimenting with ministations or substations in areas of high public or business traffic, such as in shopping malls, on a full- or part-time basis, to provide this aspect of accessibility. Some college campuses are placing stations in the student unions.

4. *Backup power system.* We know of many cases of chaos that occurred once electricity was disrupted by weather or unexpected emergencies. Each police administrator should ask this question: Can my station function if regular electric power is withdrawn? The solution to this dilemma, of course, lies with backup power generators or battery systems.

5. *Compliance with state and local codes.* Like any other public facility, police stations must be in compliance with a host of rules, laws, and regulations that include building codes, fire codes, state regulations regarding access for the disabled, regulations for interviewing juvenile suspects, and state regulations for temporary holding facilities.

Temporary Detention Facility

Certain states allow municipal and police agencies to maintain a **temporary detention facility**—often called a *lockup*—for prisoners awaiting arraignment, release on bail, or transport. It is here, however, where many serious problems occur. Jail suicide is a common occurrence in temporary detention areas since it is here that the offender finally realizes the various effects that arrest will have on his or her personal life. In other cases, prisoners begin to plot an escape while they wait for the next stage of processing. In still other instances, prisoners have died because of complications arising from being intoxicated, drugged, or beaten by police or other suspects during and after the course of arrest.

It is important that detention facilities in the police station be tightly supervised, that rigorous procedures be maintained for searching inmates, and that careful inventory of property and contraband be maintained. We suggest that whenever possible, audiovisual recording units be used to monitor prisoners in the booking area. This protects the agency from civil suits arising from charges of brutality, theft of prisoner property, and negligence.

It cannot be stressed too highly that, for the purposes of police management, this is a temporary holding facility (jail) and is not meant to be a permanent correctional setting. This is basically a lockup pending court appearance for those awaiting bail or for those unable to make bail. For stays of more than a few days, prisoners should be transferred to a permanent correctional facility.

There are also the normal problems of state and federal regulations concerning the separation of adults from juveniles and females from males, plus the security problem of smuggling in and using drugs. This is a crisis period for many detainees, and there is a strong potential toward self-destruction. Thus, constant and professional security must be maintained in the cell area. In the case of separation of adults and juveniles, this may not always be possible in smaller facilities. When it comes to these standard issues of corrections, including that of contact visits, there is a need, at that point, to transfer prisoners to a more permanent location where correctional professionals are in charge.

LICENSING

Based on historical precedent, many police departments serve as the licensing bureau for various public-related activities. These may include issuing permits for parades, use of municipally owned facilities, bike registrations, and business licenses for bars and related entertainment activities.

There is some feeling among professional law enforcement managers that licensing should be placed in the hands of civilians and possibly another government agency. However, there is also some disagreement because of the historical context of the licensing function. Licensing traditionally grew around three police problems:

1. *Vice control:* licensing of taverns, taxies, and bingo games
2. *Crowd control:* parade permits, sports events, and rallies
3. *Organized crime:* with an overlap on vice and such things as the licensing of jukeboxes

Although it may not be necessary for the police department to have direct control over the licensing functions of municipal government, some control and good communication are needed. Police agencies need to be informed concerning activities taking place in the community so that they may take the necessary steps to provide the services needed to control the situation.

THE CRIME LABORATORY

Every police department needs access to a laboratory. There are three main ways of identifying criminals:

1. Eyewitness testimony, which is generally unreliable
2. Confessions, the use of which has been severely curtailed by the courts
3. Circumstantial evidence

Criminal justice officials have been relying more and more on circumstantial evidence in helping to convict criminals. Circumstantial evidence is developed by good laboratory techniques, both at the regional laboratory and in the field with good preliminary work by evidence technicians.

Crime laboratories are found in large municipal and state police agencies in the United States. The main operations of the crime laboratory involve the following:

1. Chemical analysis or evaluation of inorganic materials
2. Biological analysis or examination of physiological fluids and organic materials, such as blood, human tissue, and hair, and DNA analysis
3. Firearms examinations and tool marks
4. Document examination for items involving forgeries, primarily checks, and handwriting and typewriting comparisons
5. Processing crime-scene photos
6. Latent fingerprint identification
7. Photographic examples for court presentation
8. Micro- and macrophotography

Smaller agencies, which are generally limited in equipment and personnel by budgetary restraints, cannot afford to have the specialists who are needed for good laboratory work. Also, they cannot afford to have their top command personnel tied up in laboratory work. Major forensic work, for these agencies, is sent to a state regional laboratory or to the Federal Bureau of Investigation. To provide for the rapid deployment and acquisition of physical evidence at crime scenes, many departments assign officers as evidence technicians, training them to gather evidence, take photographs, dust and lift latent fingerprints, and make measurements of crime and accident scenes. This makes more sense than dispatching a criminalist from the laboratory or, when he or she is off duty, from his or her residence. The necessary equipment for processing crime scenes is kept in the patrol car and is available at all times.

First, however, we ought to define the difference between the terms *criminalistics* and *forensic science*. **Forensic science** applies scientific or medical knowledge to legal matters. **Criminalistics** is one form of forensic science; it is concerned with the examination of blood, hair, glass, bullets, and other evidence found at crime scenes. Other forensic sciences include forensic toxicology (poisons and toxic substances), forensic pathology (examination of people who have died under questionable circumstances), forensic anthropology (skeletal remains), forensic odontology (teeth), forensic psychiatry, and document identification.

A crime laboratory must serve either a large jurisdiction or multiple jurisdictions to justify the costs of the needed specialists. In most cases, civilian experts are needed, rather than uniformed officers who may be assigned but who possess little or no technical skill.

Crime laboratories need full-time directors who work closely with detectives, evidence technicians, the courts, and the training unit. The following are typical functional subdivisions of a normal laboratory (Sullivan and O'Brien, 1980: 277):

Arson
Chemistry
Documents
Firearms
Hairs and fibers
Serology
Criminalistics
Field teams

Sullivan and O'Brien show the flow of evidence in an investigation (Figure 11–1). The laboratory supervisor would be in charge of quality control, distribution of cases, and coordination of laboratory services. The civilian manager in charge of this evidence flow, the director of the crime laboratory, should report directly to top command personnel when the laboratory is located in one police department. The crime laboratory should be equipped with sufficient technology and qualified personnel to do both dry and wet chemistry and micro- and macroexaminations with crime scene reproduction capabilities. Most laboratories located in police agencies consist of photography laboratories along with physical evidence examination capability and field narcotics testing. Any operations more complicated that will stand up to courtroom cross-examination entail a major capital and personnel investment.

Eighty percent of the more than 300 forensic laboratories in the United States are located in police agencies. Most crime laboratories represent less than 0.05 percent of a police budget. A nationwide survey has indicated that 60 to 80 percent of a crime laboratory's caseload consists of fingerprinting and drugs, with the next most frequent use being firearms, blood and bloodstains, and semen (Peterson, 1987: 3). The study also found that "cases where scientific evidence is analyzed are cleared at significantly higher rates" and that drug and alcohol cases, which represent more than 50 percent of a laboratory's caseload, were displacing other cases, such as burglary and robbery. Police managers need to be aware of these trends and look closely at the relationship between funding and caseload of the laboratories. One recommendation of the study will become increasingly imporant in the future: "Increased funding

FIGURE 11–1   Flow of evidence in a police investigation.

should be used primarily to broaden and intensify the caseloads of crime labs beyond predominant analysis of drug and alcohol analysis" (Peterson, 1987: 5).

The current trend is toward the use of independent regional laboratories funded by a fee system, even though most forensic laboratories are still located in police agencies. The necessary distribution of costs would help to increase this trend. Services and expert testimony would be readily available to local agencies with this limited decentralization of regional facilities. It is expected that if this trend continues, most police agencies will be expanding their use of evidence technicians rather than maintaining local laboratory facilities.

Perhaps the most innovative and controversial innovation in forensic science is DNA testing. **Deoxyribonucleic acid (DNA)** is a molecule that is found in all life forms and defines their genetically inherited characteristics. According to Bashinski and Peterson (1991: 512), the genetic code found in a specimen is unique for every individual. Thus, the genetic code found in a specimen of blood, semen, or hair can be directed to one individual. In the early 1990s, DNA testing was done only in a handful of private laboratories and by the Federal Bureau of Investigation. Today, it has been expanded to regional and state police laboratories and to private laboratories under state contract. Concurrently, many states have created DNA databases of individuals convicted of violent felony offenses. These databases have been used to clear previously unsolved cases or to exonerate people in jail. DNA was also an invaluable tool in identifying those who died at the World Trade Center on September 11, 2001.

The successful prosecution of a criminal for physical and sexual assaults receives much media attention. For example, in Buffalo, New York, the "University Heights rapist" eluded police capture for over two years despite his repeated attacks. He was eventually prosecuted after his identity was learned and his DNA was matched with the semen found at crime scenes. The advantages of DNA testing include the usability of small samples, the possibility of testing one lab sample against another lab sample, and the computerization of results. The main drawback of DNA testing is its expense for equipment and the experience and training required for serologists to achieve technical expertise.

If police management is to have the maximum use of the technical expertise of a regional laboratory, low-priority work needs to be screened out of the system. This means that police officers need basic crime scene training. Sullivan and O'Brien eliminated some low-priority work by training local police officers in the techniques needed to identify marijuana and provided them with enough technical expertise that they could be court witnesses and survive cross-examination. We would also suggest that middle management be trained to recognize evidence. Thus, investigators have to stay away from the shotgun approach, where, for example, they might ask the laboratory to test for seminal stains where there is no suspect identified, analyze narcotics found on property where there are no suspects, or examine tool marks without submission of the suspected evidence (Sullivan and O'Brien, 1980: 232).

Evidence technicians are sworn police officers who have been specially trained in the handling and gathering of evidence. Evidence technicians are normally not responsible for protecting the crime scene. Instead, they photograph and diagram the crime scene; identify, collect, and transport evidence; complete reports; and give testimony. The list of activities includes these (Lyman 2002):

1. Determining items of evidentiary value
2. Being proficient in the use of several pieces of camera equipment, including close-up equipment; using various collection techniques for blood and fluids; and using silicone or plaster techniques on tire and shoe impressions
3. Collecting minute items of trace evidence, such as hair, fiber, and thread
4. Marking and recovering various types of firearm evidence
5. Collecting and packaging evidence to protect it from contamination
6. Lifting latent fingerprints
7. Examining deceased individuals, charting and photographing wounds, and lifting fingerprints from partially decomposed or mutilated bodies
8. Examining bodies of living people to collect foreign material, fingernail scrapings, and so on
9. Preparing a crime-scene sketch
10. Preparing detailed reports to maintain a chain of custody
11. Giving expert court testimony

In deciding how to screen cases for processing as evidence, a time-management system needs to be created for laboratory personnel. Sullivan and O'Brien suggest an ordering of priorities that should prove useful (1980: 237):

Priority 1	Police emergency case
Priority 2	Death investigation, in-jail narcotic case (no bail), narcotic case (buy-sale-burst)
Priority 3	Crime against people, possession (any drug other than marijuana)
Priority 4	Crimes against property, in-jail case (with additional charges)
Priority 5	Prints only, marijuana only, controlled bugs, other low-priority cases

Priority 5 would have 10 days as a target date and 30 days as a deadline for chemistry work; all other units would have 30 days as a target date and 45 days as a deadline date.

Every police agency should have at least one well-trained evidence technician available for every shift of patrol duty. Larger departments should have a team of evidence technicians. This is an efficient use of personnel and saves the use of expensive laboratory time while winning cases because of good evidence and good continuity. With a modest but realistic investment in training and additional equipment, police managers can gain a great deal of respect from the legislature and community because of their efficient use of evidence technicians.

Computers and Fingerprints

Computerized fingerprint identification systems such as the **Automatic Fingerprint Identification System (AFIS)** have made it possible for latent fingerprints to be matched with a suspect's prints in minutes. Until this development, a latent fingerprint (a print lifted from a person or object at a crime scene) had to be matched visually with a 10-print set of prints taken from the suspect. This old process often took days. Identification officers are playing a greater role in investigations because of this. Before, detectives needed a suspect, which is now being done on cold searches.

Many states, such as Virginia and New York, have begun statewide programs, and this has created management issues such as coordination of equipment procurement, procedures for data entry, and operation protocols. The FBI is in the early stages of implementing a new image-based identification system that can meet projected increases.

As presented by the Bureau of Justice Statistics (1993), computer equipment can scan impressions and automatically extract and digitize identifying characteristics in detail, enabling the computer to distinguish a single fingerprint from millions of file prints that have been similarly scanned and stored.

Even the taking of fingerprints is changing. "Live scan" is a new technology that eliminates the need for rolling ink onto a pad. Instead, the subject's uninked fingers are rolled onto a scanning pad attached to a live scan device that captures an image of the prints. If the quality of the prints is good, then copies can be electronically transmitted to state repositories and other agencies for storage or analysis via "card scan" technology. AFIS is expensive. The cost can run in the millions of dollars, depending on the agencies participating and the complexity of the system. In all, AFIS programs have led to the greater use of prints and increasing identification of suspects. As the technology improves, there will be a great decline in the use of standard fingerprint cards for analysis and transmission to other agencies.

Computer Crime Investigation Unit

Computer crime is becoming a major problem in the United States, but most police departments lack the resources for the investigation and preparation of cases that can be prosecuted. Some of the major problems are a lack of case law, specific laws for computer crimes, current computer hardware resources, training, and specific investigative software. When investigating private-business computer crime, if business files are altered or destroyed during the investigation, the investigators may be liable for thousands of dollars in damages. Current laws are based on trespassing felonies and larceny and are simply inadequate for good prosecution. There are also jurisdictional problems. To do an investigation in Michigan concerning e-mail, for example, it may be necessary to secure a search warrant in Virginia, where America Online has its corporate headquarters. Computer crime can quickly assume national and global dimensions at a furious pace.

Computer Crime Categories

Theft of money	Thieves can steal pennies from bank or credit card accounts. With a million or more accounts, petty theft quickly becomes millions of dollars. This would include embezzlement, such as altering welfare, pension, bank, and business records. Paying checks to fictional people over fairly long periods of time is very lucrative.
Theft of services	Long-distance phone calls are just the most obvious example. It gets expensive when a thief sells stolen long-distance service, which can easily run into hundreds of thousands of dollars.
Theft of goods	This goes all the way from commercial software to whole warehouses full of goods. One of the original computer thieves was rerouting goods to warehouses in California over 30 years ago and selling the goods. He was turned in by one of his disgruntled employees but was never caught in the act. He was subsequently hired for a highly placed security position and had a fine career.
Theft of identity	With information such as name and date of birth, other information on individuals can easily be obtained. Knowing Social Security numbers helps with this theft. Businesses, colleges, and medical facilities keep all this information around in unsecured databases, making it easy to steal. Then comes the credit report, which is easily obtainable, and the thieves are in business. Once an identity is stolen, credit cards are created and billed to the person, creating a financial and personal nightmare for the victim.

Destruction of data	Intruders place many types of destructive viruses in machines worldwide, with billions of dollars lost. Software is altered and destroyed. Thousands of personal computers and whole computer systems crash.
Child pornography	This has mostly been done by amateurs who do not disguise a path to their home computer and are easily caught. However, there are services that will disguise the origin of e-mail, and most investigations of such e-mail fail.
Selling illegal goods	This is a multi-million-dollar business and includes drugs, medicines, untaxed goods like cigarettes, and alcoholic beverages to minors. Some states interested in protecting tax revenues have set up investigation units, but these efforts may be challenged in court. One problem is whether an untaxed item is an illegal good.
Invasion of privacy	This is generally legal at this time. E-businesses are collecting vast databases full of information on customers and are using this data to market goods. States have also sold private information to market vendors. There is a lack of good privacy laws. When better laws are passed, they will create the computer crime of invasion of privacy.

As this partial list suggests, computer crime is a billion-dollar worldwide problem. Theft of just high-tech components has been estimated to be a $5 billion industry (Eyres, 1999: 25). This is just the tip of the iceberg for known computer thefts. Much theft is employee theft, but attacks and thefts can come from anywhere in the world.

Laws written specifically for all aspects of computer crime are sorely needed. Such crime will not go away. Trespass, fraud, and larceny laws are not specific enough for investigators and prosecutors.

Police departments need to create teams made up of private security investigators and police investigators with help from local, state, and federal experts, investigators, and specialized prosecutors. There has been some success in the field involving interagency teams. Operation Westchips set up a storefront operation to buy stolen electronic components in San Jose, California. More than 120 people were prosecuted. Operation Bytes Dust investigated drugs and high-tech armed robberies, making 40 arrests across the country.

Industry, police, and prosecutors formed the Sacramento Valley High-Tech Crime Task Force as a long-range approach to investigate and prosecute computer crime (Eyres, 1999: 25).

A survey was made of police agencies with 100 or more sworn officers. There was a 31 percent response rate (165 agencies) (Meyer and Joyce, 1998: 28). The authors noted that "criminals are more computer literate than the investigators who track them." The most productive computer investigation units formed alliances with local business for training, hardware, and software. Only half the police agencies responding said that they provided any training for their computer investigators. Keeping current is a major problem. IACP and SEARCH in California provide training. Tracing computer crime also takes a great deal of professional time.

First Response training is needed for all officers, not just computer crime investigators. This training tells officers who respond to a call related to computers how to secure a computer without losing data or damaging its files. Inexperienced officers without this specialized training can destroy evidence easily (Meyer and Joyce, 1998). After the initial response, a specialized computer investigation unit will have to continue the investigation.

Meyer and Joyce (1998: 35) describe the ideal computer crime investigator:

> The officer chosen to investigate computer crime should be an experienced, competent investigator with the ability to think analytically. He should have a complete understanding of computer fraud related laws as well as their application. He should receive advanced training in the investigation of computer crime as well as being familiar with the major operating systems. This investigator should develop professional contacts that would assist in conducting investigations.

In the national survey, 50 percent of the departments provided no computer investigation training. Computer crime will not go away. Payroll accounts are in the computer, as are the major accounts for most businesses. When fraud is committed in both large and small businesses, it is often computer based. The United States needs a massive effort to combat computer crime in the twenty-first century.

ANCILLARY PUBLIC SAFETY SERVICES

Many services provided by American police departments fall under the heading of public safety. These include the following:

1. *Emergency mobilization.* A response plan is required in times of natural disaster or special community needs. These situations can range from a parade that shuts down traffic for five hours to a riot or earthquake that immobilizes the community for days. An **emergency plan** includes

resources that can be used for events, as well as procedures that define chain-of-command and coordination responsibilities. The critical piece of this plan for police operations is calling in internal personnel and acquiring radios, vehicles, and other equipment. A police department's emergency mobilization plan may be just one part of a countywide or statewide emergency action plan. Many plans include the use of civilians or auxiliary police who can do the following:

    a. Assist regular forces at crowd-control scenes (sports events, parades, concerts, fires)

    b. Assume routine or inside jobs to free up regular officers for street duty for riot control, concentrated investigation activities, or hostage situations needing additional personnel

    c. Augment the regular forces by supplying a second person in a car on patrol or working with the Neighborhood Watch programs

The importance of emergency mobilizations has intensified since September 11, and further discussion of these plans is presented in Chapter 14.

2. *Animal control.* A Bureau of Justice Statistics survey on local police departments (1996) found that almost one-half of the departments in its sample were responsible for animal control. This includes enforcing local ordinances related to pets and capturing or destroying wild animals that are a nuisance.

3. *Emergency medical services.* The same survey reported that 20 percent of local police departments in the sample were the primary provider of emergency medical services. This means that officers are trained and equipped not only for police situations but also for emergency first-response procedures, such as heart attacks, accidents, and broken limbs.

CONCLUSION

The major auxiliary functions of police organizations were analyzed in this chapter. As we noted, auxiliary services direct and supply resources to those units or individuals who provide police services to the community. Central to auxiliary services is communications, insofar as all units or divisions of the police organization must have access to this service. Reviewing main needs and capabilities, we pointed out that technology is rapidly advancing in this area. Many departments, however, have difficulty purchasing updated equipment simply because of their limited size and resources. We emphasized the pooling of resources through the formation of a mobile radio district. Interagency competition and political considerations, however, are main stumbling blocks in adopting such a program. Our discussion in the communications area also included personnel. Of all the services provided by the police organization, communications is one in which personnel competence is a crucial factor.

Police organizations, like many others, seem to operate by paper; therefore, the efficient recording and flow of paperwork is essential. As with communications, computerized technology for record keeping and word processing continues to advance. The silicon-chip revolution is bringing down the cost of small computer systems, making these advances accessible to all departments.

In this chapter, we included a discussion on security, sealing, purging, and public access to police records. Current procedures related to the Freedom of Information Act (1974) and updated regulations pertaining to records were presented. An issue that will continue to be addressed in the future is the citizen's right to privacy and access to personal information versus the police's need for accurate data on criminal suspects.

Although often overlooked, the property section has responsibilities involving inventory control of physical property, evidence, and found property. Maintaining the security of evidence as it is delivered from the crime scene may appear to be a mundane task, but it is of crucial importance to the investigative process.

The acquisition and equipping of patrol vehicles remains an important administrative task for all police departments. The type and size of patrol vehicle is dependent on the environment where patrol is conducted. As patrol vehicles are used virtually 24 hours a day and driven by varied types of driving styles, routine vehicle maintenance is a must.

Physical plant considerations were also presented in this chapter. Our discussion included issues related to security, facilities, morale, location, and emergency power needs. The temporary detention facility, or lockup, was discussed in some detail because of general concern over jail suicides and other incidents.

We briefly touched on the licensing section, which may or may not be under the control of the municipal police in many communities.

As with other technology, smaller agencies have difficulty both in procuring and in fiscally defending the need for a crime laboratory of any meaningful size. Crime laboratories are, therefore, found mostly in larger municipal and state police agencies and serve many departments on a regional basis. The main operations of a crime laboratory include chemical and biological analysis of evidence, firearms, tool marks and document examinations, latent fingerprint identification, and the collection and processing of crime-scene photography. In our general discussion of laboratory operations, we noted that there is a definite need for procedures for screening cases for processing. The capabilities of laboratory personnel were also discussed in terms of applying scientific know-how to law enforcement operations.

Computerization has streamlined crime-laboratory services, ranging from routine record keeping to management systems for death cases, accident reconstruction, criminal profiling, and photography reconstruction and storage. The new challenge for the twenty-first century is computer crime. New laws are needed along with specialized computer systems and procedures training.

We concluded the chapter with a review of various ancillary services that relate to the public safety function.

QUESTIONS FOR REVIEW

1. What functions usually come under the organizational heading of auxiliary services?
2. What capabilities must communications units provide? What limitations are placed on many agencies in obtaining updated technology for communications?
3. The authors proposed consolidation as a means of solving police communications inferiority. What are some hindrances to this solution?
4. Why are communications personnel often referred to as "key people" in police operations?
5. List the main categories of police records. How is the computer proving to be a useful tool for record-keeping tasks?
6. Name some general guidelines related to public access of police records. What types of records are not governed by public access regulations (e.g., the Freedom of Information Act)?
7. What kinds of data may be released about an individual who was not convicted of a crime?
8. What are the main duties of the property section? How does this section assist in the continuity of evidence?
9. Why is it said that police vehicles are exposed to the worst road and driving conditions? Why is preventive maintenance important?
10. What general items must be considered in designing or maintaining a police station?
11. List the main functions of a crime laboratory.
12. Outline the flow of evidence from crime scene to crime laboratory. Why is case screening an important procedure?
13. What are five duties of crime-scene technicians?
14. How would you investigate theft of identity?
15. How would you set up a computer crime unit and procedures?

BIBLIOGRAPHY

BASHINSKI, JAN S., and JOSEPH L. PETERSON. "Forensic Science." In *Local Government Police Management* (3rd ed.). Washington, D.C.: International Management Association, 1991.

BEGERT, MATT. "Spotlight on Information Systems Procurement." *Police Chief*, 6 (June 1999), pp. 40–45.

BUREAU OF JUSTICE STATISTICS. *Use and Management of Criminal History Record Information*. Washington, D.C.: U.S. Department of Justice, 1993.

————. *Local Police Departments, 1993.* Washington, D.C.: U.S. Department of Justice, 1996.

CARTER, DAVID L., and ANDRA J. KATZ. "Computer Crime." *Law Enforcement Bulletin,* 65, no. 12 (December 1996), pp. 1–9.

COLTON, KENT W. *Police Computer Technology.* Lexington, Mass.: Lexington Books, 1978.

EYRES, WILLIAM E. "Putting the Brakes on Information Age Crime." *Police Chief,* 16, no. 6 (June 1999), pp. 22–32.

FITZGERALD, CHRIS. "Take Home Patrol Cars for Police Officers." Utica College of Syracuse University: unpublished paper, 2002.

FOX, RICHARD H. "Criminalistics." In Bernard L. Garmire, ed., *Local Government Police Management.* Washington, D.C.: International City Management Association, 1977, pp. 457–474.

HAYDEN, TRUDY, and JACK NOVIK. *Your Rights to Privacy.* New York: Avon Books/American Civil Liberties Union, 1980.

LYMAN, MICHAEL D. *Criminal Investigation: The Art and the Science.* Upper Saddle River, N.J.: Prentice Hall, 2002.

MEYER, JON'A F., and MATT JOYCE. "Investigating Computer Crime." *Police Chief,* 15, no. 5 (May 1998), pp. 28–35.

NATIONAL ADVISORY COMMISSION ON CRIMINAL JUSTICE STANDARDS AND GOALS. *Police.* Washington, D.C.: U.S. Government Printing Office, 1973.

NEW YORK STATE DEPARTMENT OF CRIMINAL JUSTICE SERVICES. *Regulations for Criminal Justice Data.* Albany, 1990.

PETERSON, JOSEPH L. *Use of Forensic Evidence by the Police and Courts.* Washington, D.C.: National Institute of Justice, 1987.

PLIANT, LOIS. "Spotlight on . . . Equipping a Forensics Lab." *Police Chief,* 59, no. 9 (September 1992), pp. 36–47.

RUEGG, ROSALIE. "Life-Cycle Cost Evaluation of the Personal Patrol Car Program." *Journal of Police Science and Administration,* 3, no. 3 (September 1975), pp. 290–298.

SMITH, KIMBERLY. "Integrated Automated Fingerprint Identification System: Twenty-First Century Technology for Law Enforcement." *Police Chief,* 15, no. 8 (May 1998), p. 14.

SULLIVAN, ROBERT C., and KEVIN O'BRIEN. "A Systems Approach to Crime Laboratory Management." *Public Management,* 8, no. 2 (June 1980), pp. 225–238.

UNITED NATIONS COMMISSION ON CRIME AND CRIMINAL JUSTICE. *United Nations Manual on the Prevention and Control of Computer Related Crime.* New York: United Nations, 1995.

12

HUMAN RESOURCE MANAGEMENT

KEY TERMS

affirmative action

Americans with Disabilities
   Act (ADA)

assessment center

dipping

disparate impact theory

drug testing

Equal Employment Opportunity
   Commission (EEOC)

Fat Albert

Fatigue

hostile work environment

lateral entry

overtime

Pendleton Act

polygraph

private police

rule of three

sexual harassment

spoils system

stress

Title VII

The objective of police recruitment and selection is to find qualified candidates for law enforcement positions in terms of their talents, ethics, drive, and emotional stability. In the modern police department, computer and human relations skills and the ability to deal with diverse cultures and perhaps speak a foreign language have become important. Additionally, "with the advent of community and problem-oriented policing, personnel management issues have become increasingly complex as earlier homogeneous departments have given way to more modern departments reflective of the community population" (Kenny, 1996: v).

There is also the need to have officers and managers who possess emotional intelligence and stability to perform a variety of often difficult and taxing duties. The challenge to recruitment is to keep the highest standards in order to recruit a talented professional police officer while bringing in the skills and backgrounds that are needed in the twenty-first-century police department. Matching police personnel with the appropriate jobs will be discussed throughout this chapter.

PERSONNEL: THE MAJOR COST

Law enforcement is a labor-intensive service industry; 80 to 90 percent of police agency budgets are devoted to personnel costs. Paradoxically, most managers do not realize the investment they have in terms of their human capital: police officers. Just a few of the expenses involve testing, oral interviews, background checks, uniforms and equipment, and the police academy program. As a rule, it takes about a year and a half before the police recruit becomes a police officer, who then makes a working contribution to the agency and community.

POLICE CIVIL SERVICE SELECTION: HISTORICAL BACKGROUND

Figure 12–1 illustrates the police personnel selection process used in many states. The chief criteria in this selection process are the portions overseen by state civil service or the individual department—written test, physical agility examinations, and physical requirements. Candidates who complete a written examination and physical agility test and measure up to the physical requirements are then placed in either a pool or a rank-order certification list prepared by the civil service commission. Many states with a rank-order process continue to follow the **rule of three,** whereby one of the first three candidates on the list is chosen while the other two candidates are returned to the pool for the next ranking of three. This method of selection may seem outmoded, but it is still viewed by many as a reform measure when compared with practices that existed in the nineteenth century.

PUBLIC SERVICE EMPLOYMENT

In the early days of the republic, government service was looked on as a duty reserved for those of aristocratic background. The change of presidential administrations, however, heralded a new break from tradition in that all presidential appointees were replaced by those of the new victor. This was the beginning of the **spoils system** (doling out positions for political support), which became firmly entrenched by 1830. The practice soon spread to all municipalities on the state and local levels. This process affected early police organizations, which often underwent a complete personnel turnover after the victory of the out-of-office party.

In the early days of American policing, there were no requirements for becoming a police officer except having the right connections and being willing to fight to protect yourself. Sadly enough, most police officers were no more than political hacks who received their positions in exchange for a payment

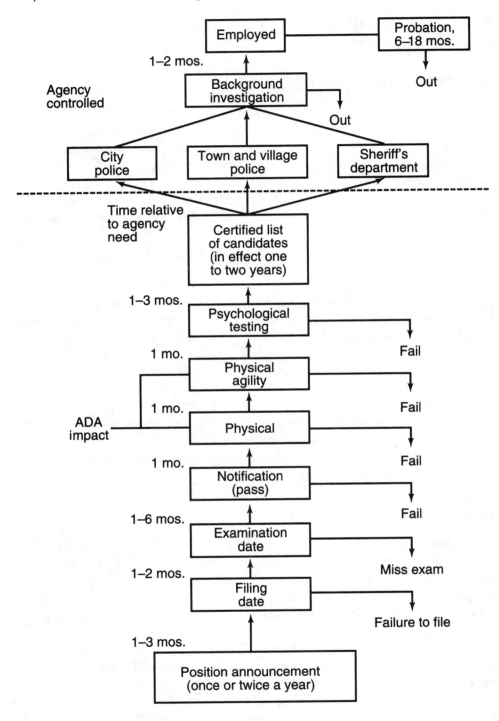

FIGURE 12-1   Personnel selection process.

to a public official. Many times in urban areas, a local gangster chieftain might have some say as to who would enforce the law in the community. A career in policing, moreover, was seen as an avenue of economic improvement by each wave of immigrants to the United States in the early nineteenth century. Police jobs, which were not often sought after by the native middle-class population, were readily dispensed by the political machine to immigrants in return for votes and support.

Because of the negative effects of the spoils system, such as mismanagement and bribery, a reform movement for personnel selection was under way by the beginning of the 1880s. In 1883, Congress passed the **Pendleton Act,** which covered a majority of federal positions. This law sought to ban political patronage as the sole criterion for personnel selection, replacing it with a system whereby employees would be selected and retained on the basis of open competition according to experience and ability. Moreover, the new law sought to protect employees against arbitrary discharge or discrimination, especially discrimination based on political influences. In that same year, New York and other states enacted similar laws. The assassination of President Garfield in 1881 by a disgruntled office seeker had focused public attention on problems with the spoils system and had helped to speed up enactment of Pendleton-style legislation in other states.

The passage of civil service statutes did not result in overnight reform. In his history of American policing, Robert Fogelson (1977) showed that civil service reform was stymied by the political machines that existed in most urban communities. He states, "The machine politicians proved to be formidable opponents. When they dominated city hall, which was most of the time, they could usually prevail on the authorities to sidetrack, postpone, or vote down the reform schemes. Even when the reformers took over, the politicians generally counted on their cronies in the police forces, prosecutor's offices, local courts and other agencies to undo any inopportune changes" (p. 110).

From the nineteenth century to today, political interference in American policing has not disappeared, even in states that have civil service requirements. Moreover, many municipalities and states still do not provide civil service protection to police officers. For example, county sheriff's departments in many states are often not regulated by any civil service guidelines; often, police selection is strictly a matter of political patronage.

Police employment in civil service–regulated states does not necessarily bring great monetary benefits, but it does provide (1) job security, (2) a pension, and (3) a generous number of vacation and personal days. The Great Depression from 1929 through the 1930s underscored the security of public employment as millions of workers were laid off by private industry. As the range of government services has grown since World War II, the number of workers has likewise risen, making government on the federal, state, and local levels this nation's number one employer.

However, some new factors have altered the traditional notion of government service:

1. In many states and on the federal level, wages and benefits have matched those provided by private industry. This has made government service even more attractive when coupled with pensions, retirements, and time off.
2. As the number and range of government services has increased, taxes have also risen. The taxpayer revolts in the 1990s may have affected the number of workers in public service.
3. Researchers are undecided as to whether this will affect the number of government services since budget surpluses were obtained in previous years, thus stalling layoffs. The notion of government employment being secure has been altered by the financial dilemmas faced by many municipalities. This has forced the laying off of police, firefighters, and other public service workers.

While these general trends have all affected police administration, one other movement has had a striking effect on selection and promotion: Equal Employment Opportunity legislation.

EQUAL EMPLOYMENT OPPORTUNITY

Although the Fifth, Thirteenth, and Fourteenth Amendments to the U.S. Constitution provide the basis for due process, government was slow to adopt a strict interpretation of these amendments, especially with regard to employment of blacks, Hispanics, and women. Both the Thirteenth and the Fourteenth Amendments gave Congress the right to enact legislation to enforce the provision of law, which resulted in civil rights legislation in 1866 and 1871 on the issue of employment discrimination. Presidents Franklin D. Roosevelt (1941) and John F. Kennedy (1961) issued presidential executive orders for fair employment of minority groups, which have had an impact in industries on government-related contracts. The 1961 order by Kennedy was significant in that it imposed the first requirement for affirmative action in government employment—mainly that each agency had to plan and implement a program to ensure that employment practices were nondiscriminatory in application and had to set out methods by which the effects of past discriminatory employment practices could be corrected. This executive order was updated by Presidents Lyndon B. Johnson (1965) and Richard M. Nixon (1971), who made affirmative action an important area for all government service (Territo and others, 1977: 21–22).

But the real boon to affirmative action resided not with executive orders, but with the passage of the Civil Rights Act of 1964, which had a number of titles dealing with various facets of discrimination. The significant legislation for personnel practices was found in **Title VII,** which provided the following (Public Law 92-261, Section 703[a]):

It shall be unlawful employment practice for an employer (1) to fail or refuse to hire, or discharge any individual or otherwise to discriminate against any individual with respect to his compensation, terms, conditions, or privileges of employment, because of such individual's race, color, religion, sex, or national origin; (2) to limit, segregate, or classify his employees or applicants for employment in any way which would deprive or tend to deprive any individual of employment opportunity or otherwise adversely affect his status as an employee because of such individual's race, color, religion, sex, or national origin.

Title VII was directed at employers with more than 25 employees, labor organizations with more than 25 members, and private employment agencies. Title VII was further upgraded two years later to include coverage of both private and public employment agencies, including those on the state and local levels employing 15 or more people. The amendment to Title VII also established the **Equal Employment Opportunity Commission (EEOC)** as a regulatory agency to oversee compliance with Title VII. It is the EEOC to which many complaints on police hiring practices are directed. Complaints handled by the EEOC or, in some cases, in the federal court system under Title VII include discrimination in hiring or promotions and a "hostile work environment." Title VII forms the basis for complaints of sexual harassment, which will be discussed later in this chapter. On the state level, there are various corresponding agencies that also deal with complaints of employment discrimination.

AFFIRMATIVE ACTION

Affirmative action is a concept applied to personnel administration in which an employer takes positive steps to expand employment opportunities for nonwhite people and women. These steps include addressing and abolishing past discriminatory employment practices, soliciting more minority and female applicants from different hiring pools, and setting goals for the hiring or promotion of underrepresented minorities and women in the organization.

The statutory language and political intent of initial Title VII legislation did not include preferential treatment for nonwhites and women for employment and promotion considerations over white candidates (Glazer, 1975; Territo and others, 1977; Fallon and Weiler, 1985). Starting in 1964, however, federal and state case law, EEOC administrative rulings, and police agency employment practices determined that the statistical imbalances between the number of nonwhites represented in an organization and the determined labor pool constitute a *prima facie* case for discrimination. Remedies to address imbalances included quota systems and preferential treatment for nonwhites and women in employee selection.

Despite strong political and legal opposition by private- and public-sector labor unions and aggrieved individuals, these remedies were constitutionally upheld. The Supreme Court in 1979 upheld the use of a voluntary quota system for selecting black candidates for a training program over the objections of an unsuccessful white applicant who claimed that he had been the victim of discrimination (*United Steel Workers* v. *Weber*, 1979). In his majority opinion, Justice Brennan wrote that the intent of Title VII was to improve the economic plight of nonwhites through the use of preferred selection systems.

Before the *Weber* case, the use of quotas and preferential treatment had received judicial approval through a number of Supreme Court cases and EEOC rulings under the **disparate impact theory.** In the 1971 case *Griggs* v. *Duke Power Company*, the Court ruled that employment tests and practices that exclude a disproportionate number of nonwhites and women may be discriminatory regardless of whether there was intent by an employer to discriminate. If a situation of disparate impact exists, the employer must demonstrate that such tests and practices relate to a business necessity and the demands of the position. Disparate impact is any case where a civil service test, for example, admits more white male employees to the occupation than minorities or women, even if the white applicants have higher civil service scores on the test than those of the minority or female candidates. This legal reasoning raises complaints about reverse discrimination and the use of quotas when using civil service tests for the admission of new candidates for employment.

Disparate impact was applied to police departments because of their failure to recruit nonwhites and women in comparison to a statistical representation of these minorities in a designated community. Disparate impact formed the basis for court orders and consent decrees by which police agencies had to remedy the historical effects of discrimination through quotas. Agencies, under court orders, were forced to review their hiring and testing procedures in light of the principle of disparate impact. In the case of consent decrees between police agency employers and federal or state courts, there was no admission of intentional discrimination on the part of the employing agency.

When representation in a police agency matches minority representation in a defined community labor pool, affirmative action was said to be successful (Hochstedler, 1984). Quotas and preferred hiring have had a blacklash effect because many qualified whites have complained that they were not considered for employment simply because of race. In police circles, this practice is known as **dipping,** charges of reverse discrimination have been made in the following situations:

1. The use of racial preferences to prescribe the selection of candidates who otherwise appear less qualified than rival candidates
2. The use of preferences for candidates who have not proved that they were the victims of past discrimination
3. The use of targets and goals to determine the number of nonwhite candidates to be hired on the basis of race

Reverse discrimination related to employment was the basis of many lawsuits and public policy debates with regard to voluntary and court-mandated affirmative action plans and consent decrees. Since 1978, the federal government has altered considerably its policy on racial imbalances. The Reagan and Bush administrations, for example, did not seem to feel that affirmative action should be used to remedy racial imbalances.

Disparate impact theory was challenged in the 1989 Supreme Court ruling in *Ward's Cove Packing* v. *Atonio*. Filipino and native Alaskan cannery workers employed at several companies charged discrimination on the basis of statistics because the majority of skilled jobs were filled by whites. Because of the unique seasonal nature of the work and the makeup of both the skilled and unskilled workforce, the court ruled that statistical imbalances alone could not be used to prove disparate impact discrimination. Instead, it had to be shown that the imbalance occurred because of the application of a particular employment practice. The court also added that it was the plaintiff's responsibility to prove discrimination instead of the company's having to defend its practices. This ruling led to others in a similar vein that appeared to halt statistical imbalance lawsuits. However, the 1991 Civil Rights Act restored disparate impact premises so that "neutral employment practices" that resulted in discrimination could continue to be challenged. Since 1990, federal and state court rulings regarding affirmative action discrimination cases have been very specifically applied to the employment practices and existing affirmative action plans of an agency or municipality.

Dramatic changes in affirmative action as a public policy occurred in 1995. The landmark case involving affirmative action was *Adarand Constructors* v. *Pena*, which involved a lawsuit filed by a construction company. The company was the low bidder for a public works project and contested the work being awarded to a Hispanic-owned company. The main contractor for the project, in turn, received a monetary award by the federal government for furthering an affirmative action plan. The Supreme Court struck down the awarding of the contract, ruling that affirmative action plans that created racial discrimination must meet a strict scrutiny test according to the following guidelines:

1. There must be a compelling reason why a program was put in place.
2. The plan must be temporary, with a definite end in sight.

The End of Affirmative Action?

At the same time that the *Adarand* case was being argued, the California Board of Regents in 1995 dismantled its affirmative action–based programs, arguing that the set-aside programs in college admissions are discriminatory. In another closely watched higher-education case, the U.S. Court of Appeals for the Fifth Circuit (Texas, Louisiana, and Mississippi) in 1994 found that admissions procedures at the University of Texas that promoted racial and ethnic diversity were improper (*Hopwood* v. *Texas*, 1994). In 1996, the Supreme Court announced that it would not review the decision. Although the ruling applies only to institutions of higher education in these states, it has prompted many colleges and universities to review their admissions standards and procedures.

As for policing, many agencies have ended their quota programs for recruitment and promotion, pointing out that the workforce was representative of the resident population. McWhirter (1996) argued that most state and federal government affirmative action programs created in the 1970s and 1980s that create quotas or set-aside programs will not stand this strict scrutiny test. Affirmative action as a governmental policy is not going to dissolve completely, however. Many police agencies have readjusted their programs to consider affirmative action as a way to conduct proactive recruitment for underrepresented populations in the workforce and to review employment hiring practices that may be discriminatory.

Current affirmative action issues have arisen over promotions, especially when a department opts to use a quota system or some other initiative to achieve racial and ethnic diversity when statistical and historical evidence shows past discrimination. For example, in *McNamera* v. *City of Chicago* (1998), a special civil service list category was upheld by a federal appeals court so that African-American and Hispanic firefighters could achieve representation in the position of captain.

As a social policy, affirmative action continues to have a profound impact in many areas of human resource management, college admissions, and the awarding of contracts. Based on our experiences and observations in classroom discussions and agency personnel hirings over the last two decades, we can say the following about affirmative action:

- It created deep divisions in American society in that many whites could not understand why preferential treatment and quota programs were fair.
- It allowed women and people of various races access to police organizations that hitherto were not representative of their communities. As Bergmann (1996: 19) states, the job market in many occupations remains stacked against African-Americans and women.
- It challenged formal and informal methods of discrimination that had prevented women, African-Americans, Hispanics, Asians, and members of other groups from becoming police officers.

THE ROLE OF THE POLICE HUMAN RESOURCE ADMINISTRATOR

The director of human resources and his or her staff hold key positions in determining employment practices and promotion qualifications. Although their judgments are based, in part, on myriad court cases, legislative acts, and administrative law rulings, their decisions will have a profound effect on the level of quality personnel in a department.

In the small agency, the chief police administrator, normally the police chief working with a human resource office, performs most of the tasks of a personnel department in a larger agency. In some small agencies, the political unit, be it county, town, or village, has a personnel office that handles staffing for all municipal offices.

More than 70 percent of a police administrator's time is spent on human resource issues, such as recruitment, selection and training, promotions, evaluations, discipline, and quality-of-life issues. Because of the procedural and legal concerns that can arise, it is critical that the police chief have either a staff member or a key liaison at the municipal department of personnel with the expertise to assist in policy development and issue resolution. This expertise should include agency policies, the collective bargaining agreement (if applicable), and the wide scope of federal and state public employment law.

PERSONNEL SELECTION: ISSUES AND CONCERNS

Before 1965, the police personnel selection process generally consisted of a written examination, a physical agility test, a physical, and perhaps an oral interview. Based on these criteria, a list was established of successful candidates, and the police administrator picked new officers from this list. Various aspects of this process are continually under attack and revision because of the emergence of affirmative action. We will now review the police personnel selection process, especially those areas affected by Title VII.

Written Tests

The civil service procedures of the nineteenth century incorporated the extensive use of written tests as a chief criterion of selection. These tests were usually composed of multiple-choice questions related to the position being sought. But according to Schachter (1979: 86), "Traditional written examinations do not measure many of the skills and competencies which effective police work requires. In fact, a written test of this nature cannot really assess the entire range of skills and situations that are related to job competency." On this issue, she comments further:

> Generic traits are necessary for effective performance in almost any professional or managerial position and include the ability to communicate orally with sensitivity and a sense of authority, to make decisions, to work with many different types of others, and to solve problems under stress and within severe constraints of time and resources.

The affirmative action movement of the 1970s resulted in legal attacks on written civil service testing for a wide variety of reasons. The major arguments center on the following issues:

1. The relationship between the test and the job (often called the *attitude/behavior relationship* in research literature on testing)
2. Content validity of the testing instrument
3. Reliability of test items

Age

The normal age for application ranges from 21 to 29, although some agencies will accept recruits as young as 18. This lower age has been the subject of much controversy since many police administrators feel that this lower age limit will recruit police officers who lack mature judgment. At this time, no research data are generally available to document anything concerning this controversy. Although age requirements are published and adhered to in most cases, there are an increasing number of age exceptions.

Exceptions to the higher age limit are given to wartime veterans. The intent is to be able to recruit qualified future officers from the military without penalizing them for their years of military service. For example, if the veteran is age 32 and has 10 years' service in the military, he is qualified to enter a department with a maximum age limit for recruitment of 29 years of age. State civil service limits the number of veteran years that can be subtracted. In the past, especially during the early part of the twentieth century, former military men were considered prime candidates for the police department. At present, veterans' preference and exceptions are resented by many younger recruits who lack military service.

Why are there age limits? One reason is related to the physical requirements that are supposed to be justified in terms of the rigors of the job.

Another major reason for the age requirement is the lifetime of work of the police officer compared with retirement and training costs. This is an especially crucial point when considering the 20- and 25-year retirement programs. This means that the best and most experienced officers are often lost at the peak of their use to the department and only to receive half-pay for not working. Surprisingly, police agencies with these policies allow their best people to go at a time when private business would consider them to be in their prime productive years.

The Age Discrimination in Employment Act of 1974 extended coverage of age discrimination to state and local police agencies, and many state constitutions have developed antidiscrimination policies concerning age. There have been a number of cases throughout the nation concerning age discrimination by police departments, and these police agencies have had mixed results in defending their policies. At the moment, the trend seems to be a breakdown of the upper age requirement unless there is specific state legislation empowering the civil service department to set an upper age limit.

Physical Fitness

Physical fitness concerns the health of the individual officer and is a measure of his or her physiological readiness to perform critical physical tasks when required. Physical fitness has been demonstrated to be a bona fide occupational qualification.

Historically, police officers have been expected to be physically fit. Pre-service selection and training academy programs generally have some component for physical training and testing. The type of agility tests and courses vary from department to department. The types of tests commonly employed include running, an obstacle course, climbing ropes, barbell push-ups, chin-ups, scaling walls, and climbing through tubes. What is lacking in these tests, however, is applicability to the job of police officer.

To address job relatedness, the Cooper Institute for Aerobics Research of Dallas, Texas, developed a testing regimen that is being adopted by many departments. Based on national scores and a review of physical agility needs for the police officer, the Cooper Method tests for the following competencies (Cooper Institute for Aerobics Research, 2003):

1. *Aerobic power.* A 1.5-mile run is scored to measure cardiovascular endurance or aerobic power. The run can be conducted on a treadmill or correlated to a 12-minute distance run.
2. *Flexibility.* A sit-and-reach test serves as an important measure of hip and back flexibility. *Flexibility* is defined as the range of possible movements in a joint or group of joints. These joints can be tested to determine their functional ability through a full range of motion indicated by the sit-and-reach test.
3. *Maximum strength.* This is defined as the amount of tension a muscle can exhibit in one maximum contraction. The one-repetition maximum bench press correlates well with total body strength.
4. *Muscular endurance.* The sit-up (with knees bent) is used to determine a person's endurance effort.

Because of the Americans with Disabilities Act (ADA), physical tests have come under greater scrutiny. Departments are required to address the following questions regarding their standards:

1. The relationship between the standard and the job performed by officers
2. The relationship between the standard and the training required for the basic academy and advanced schools
3. The applicability of standards to all members of the department

Another method to address physical fitness policy is the creation of a job-task simulation. In this scenario, the actual parts of a police officer's job are broken down to ascertain whether the candidate can perform various tasks within a specific amount of time. Such tasks might include running for several yards after alighting from a parked patrol vehicle, climbing a fence, climbing through a window, and moving a 150-pound dummy from one position to another. As Weidner (1996) discusses, a job-task simulation does not measure physical fitness but only a small percentage of the range of physical tasks performed by law enforcement officers.

Related to this issue is the reality that most departments do not enforce any physical standards on their officers once the officer has passed recruit training. By the end of a five-year period, many officers have exceeded recruit weight requirements, and many must wear glasses. Sadly, many seasoned officers cannot run a mile. Should all officers who do not meet the rigid physical entering requirements be fired? Do you disqualify an officer because he or she becomes obese, develops flat feet or poor vision, or has heart problems?

Because of the protection afforded by civil service and union contracts, physically unqualified officers are able to retain their police jobs. Others go on permanent disability because of injuries that might have been avoided if the officer had been in top physical shape. As a result, many departments are initiating formal programs involving physical reconditioning and mandatory medical checkups. Some have gone so far as to issue **Fat Albert** letters to officers with unchecked obesity problems. Utilizing informal group relationships, other departments use peer pressure as an incentive for the officer to keep in physical shape.

Eyesight Standards. Traditional physical fitness standards related to vision are also being contested. Until this decade, most departments required police recruits to have vision corrected to 20/20 and be free of color blindness. The theory behind these standards is that officers must be able to identify suspects, vehicles, and other items at a reasonable distance, to function without glasses in serious situations, and to correctly identify the color of objects like vehicles. A review of vision standards by Holden (1993) shows that these reasons cannot be supported by agency data or empirical research. A national review of vision standards by the author shows a wide range of variance, ranging from the traditional 20/20 corrected standard to no standards. He concludes that most standards are merely supported by what-if scenarios.

There is still another aspect to this issue. In the future, we may see different physical requirements being specified for different categories of police jobs. It may be that officers on patrol must meet one standard and that older officers assigned to administrative tasks must meet a different standard. There may come a time when all officers will be physically certified in terms of the jobs they will be allowed to do within the department.

Americans with Disabilities Act. The **Americans with Disabilities Act (ADA)**, which became fully effective in July 1992, prohibits discrimination against disabled people in employment, public services, transportation, public accommodations, and telecommunications. The law (PL 101-336) very broadly interprets *disability* as any impairment limiting a major life activity. Disability thus includes sight, hearing, suffering with a disease like AIDS (acquired immunodeficiency syndrome), and disfigurement that does not result in an actual impairment. Those who feel that they have been discriminated against on the basis of a disability may file complaints with the EEOC. Preceding the ADA was the Federal Rehabilitation Act of 1974, which prohibited discrimination by the federal government and its contractors against federal benefit recipients.

Title I of the ADA applies to all areas of police employment, such as testing, hiring, assignments, evaluations and disciplinary actions, training, promotions, sick leave, and termination. The immediate impact of ADA on police already has been felt in preemployment processes like physical medical tests. A department that disqualifies a person because of a disability must show why the rejection is job related and consistent with business necessity. Furthermore, the agency must be able to demonstrate that it cannot make a reasonable accommodation to enable the individual to perform the essential job functions or that the accommodation would impose an undue hardship. The concept of reasonable accommodation is quite broad. It ranges from making physical adaptations to the work environment to changing policies and work practices.

Returning to our civil service selection chart in Figure 12–1, it is important to note that qualified candidates cannot be screened out because of their disability before their actual ability to do the job is evaluated. Thus, police employers have to make a tentative job offer before medical testing is undertaken.

The ADA has prompted a review of preemployment medical and physical agility standards in terms of those factors necessary for performing the essential elements of police work. Each department or state regulatory agency, such as civil service, must define the minimum physical agility requirements that are needed. A person who is disqualified on the basis of a disability, such as impaired hearing or loss of a limb, can seek a challenge to see whether a reasonable accommodation can be made.

Alcoholics and recovered drug abusers are also considered to be disabled under this act. Certain cynics have charged that the ADA could force a department to hire a recovered drug abuser. Other observers point out that the ADA has no impact on character investigations or on physical agility tests. Thus, a substance abuser could be disqualified because he or she disobeyed the law in conducting his or her drug use.

Thus, the ADA has resulted in large numbers of unsuccessful candidates filing lawsuits addressing normally held medical and agility standards related to police employment. For example, in *Joyce* v. *Suffolk County* the court rejected a candidate's contention that he was a disabled person within the definition of ADA because he failed eyesight and blood pressure requirements for the position of police officer. These conditions, the court ruled, might render him unfit for the position, but they in no way constitute a major impairment limiting major life activity. In 1999, this concept was further upheld in a number of cases reviewed by the Supreme Court. For example, in *Sutton and Hinton* v. *United Airlines* (1999), the Supreme Court ruled that correctable eyesight problems did not constitute a disability or a major impairment within the scope of the ADA.

This case and others demonstrate that the police department must be able to define the essential functions of the job and, on a case-by-case basis, determine whether the person's condition constitutes a disability within the legal definition of the ADA. It should be noted that assignment and staffing practices will be taken into consideration to ascertain whether reasonable accommodation can be made.

The main intent of the ADA is to combat discrimination against the disabled by attacking commonly held notions related to the disability and matching the disability with the essential functions of the job. ADA cases involving law enforcement operations have been involved mainly with disabilities like back disorders and job-related injuries.

In some cases, civil service and the collective bargaining agreement may have an impact on the following questions:

1. Does the physical or mental injury or impairment affect a major life function, as defined under the ADA?
2. To what extent does the injury affect the essential functions of the position?
3. Can the department provide reasonable accommodation, such as a light-duty assignment?
4. To what extent is the accommodation reasonable and effective?

This does not mean that local remedies have to be exhausted before an ADA tort action. In *Wright* v. *Universal Maritime Service Corp.* (1998), the Supreme Court held that an employee could sue under the ADA without first using the grievance procedure contained in the collective bargaining agreement.

The following are some sample law enforcement cases (Webster, 1996; Deskbook, 1999):

> *Santos* v. *Port Authority of New York and New Jersey* (1995). After an officer injured his foot, he sought permanent administrative duty assignment. Even though the plaintiff had been placed on light duty, the court ruled in favor of the police department, stating that the officer could no longer perform the essential functions of the position of police officer.
>
> *Williams* v. *City of Charlotte, North Carolina* (1995). A sergeant suffering from a sleep disorder sued after the city failed to honor her request for a shift assignment. The court found that her condition did not qualify as a disability and that the officer had reasonable access to thousands of jobs in her geographic area.
>
> *Krocka* v. *Reigler* (1997). After a police department found that an officer was being treated with Prozac for depression, he was assigned to a personal concerns program for disciplinary problem officers. He complained that he was

subject to harassment and intensive supervision. As his depression was classified as a "disability," the district court ruled in his favor, citing that a disabled person cannot be segregated or classified in a way that adversely affects job opportunities or status.

Spades v. City of Walnut Ridge (1999). A police officer who shot himself after failing to take his antidepression medication sued the city for unlawful termination under the ADA. The court ruled that the officer did not have an ADA-protected disability as his medication controlled the depression and that the termination reduced the possibility for further liability against the city.

The Background Investigation

After a candidate has passed the written and physical portions of the selection process, a background investigation is conducted by the agency. The objective is to obtain information relating to the candidate's suitability (or nonsuitability) for police employment. Because of the mobility of today's population, the background investigation is an expensive long-term process that may cover a variety of locations in many states. Informal relationships among police agencies are tapped for this facet of police personnel selection since it is economically impossible for investigators to check every location.

ESSENTIAL FUNCTIONS

What are the essential functions of a police officer position? Based on a job analysis, essential functions include arrest and detention of suspects, controlling civil disorder, collecting and preserving evidence, conducting a crime scene search, operating a motor vehicle, and using physical force. Under these general headings, there are a number of essential tasks that must be performed. For example, under the heading of "Using Physical Force," we have the following essential tasks:

1. Break up a fight between two or more people
2. Carry by yourself an immobile child
3. Pull a person out of a vehicle to effect rescue
4. Subdue an attacker
5. Use weaponless defense tactics
6. Subdue a person resisting arrest
7. Disarm violent armed suspect
8. Pull person out of vehicle who is resisting arrest
9. Search for a person in a darkened building or environment
10. Strike a person with a baton

Equipment that a police officer must use to perform these essential tasks are baton, flashlight, flexicuffs, and handcuffs.

The thoroughness of the background investigation varies from agency to agency. In some cases, it is perfunctory; in other cases, it is meticulous. Based on the candidate's application, each place of residence (usually within a 10-year period) and the immediate neighborhood are checked. Neighbors and landlords are asked questions related to the candidate's character that cover a wide range of topics (e.g., the number of parties held while the candidate lived in the premises; drinking habits; driving habits; relations with spouse, girlfriend or boyfriend, and so on). Former and present employers are also questioned about the candidate's honesty and work habits. Other areas that are reviewed are educational and military history.

But the most important information that investigators wish to learn is the candidate's criminal history, especially incidents that were not included on the employment application. As a routine practice, information as to a possible criminal record is obtained from criminal computer banks maintained by federal, state, and local law enforcement agencies. A copy of the candidate's fingerprints is also sent to the Federal Bureau of Investigation and state criminal justice records divisions. During the background investigation, police investigators also wish to know of offenses for which the candidate was arrested that may not be classified as crimes, such as public intoxication, disorderly conduct, harassment, and various violations of local municipal ordinances.

Related to the check for criminal history is the driving record. Most police agencies have access to data on all aspects of motor vehicle operation and registration in just about every state through a computer terminal in the police station. Hence, this information is readily obtained. An important issue that comes to light with regard to background checks is the use of these investigations to "weed out" undesirable candidates. Having excessive traffic tickets is a common reason for rejection, as is falsification of any information.

Residency

Many departments give preference to applicants who live within the boundaries of the local police jurisdiction. This is handled in a number of ways. In one approach, only citizens with prior residency in the local agency jurisdiction are eligible for police employment. Prior residency varies from a few weeks to many months. In other jurisdictions, residency is required only after employment. Others give a preference to prior residents on the hiring list; this means that local residents will be hired before the residents of any other jurisdiction will be considered. One of the authors' students who placed fourth on a local civil service police examination discovered that he had been placed 64th on the list when the examiners found out that he lived about a mile outside the city limits. He had not been aware of these residency preferences when he took the examination, but he was certainly aware of them after the civil service lists were published.

Residency areas vary widely. They can be limited to the municipality in question or extended to contiguous counties or throughout the state. In one city, officers had to live no farther than "five air miles" from the police station in order to respond to emergencies. Some departments, such as those in Houston and Los Angeles, have nationwide recruitment programs with no prior residency requirements. They are looking for the best talent, nationwide, for their departments.

The issue of residency is related to the questions of (1) merit and talent versus the need for local knowledge and adherence to local customs that local citizens would have and (2) the wish to give preference in the spending of tax dollars to those who provide those tax dollars. Reform-minded police managers, especially those in the larger departments, prefer talented and meritorious candidates regardless of place of residence. Local conservative politicians appeal to home rule and local pride in establishing rigid residency requirements. If police departments are to upgrade their personnel, rigid residency requirements will have to be abolished since these requirements limit the talent pool from which potential officers can be drawn.

Psychological Testing

Personnel managers who use psychometric testing and clinical evaluation in assessing police recruits are looking for a stable personality that is flexible enough to adjust to the stress of police work along with the complex peer relations. Police managers are especially concerned with having some idea as to whether that particular recruit is apt to "break" in a stressful situation in the future. If that is, in fact, a major concern, then the authors would recommend that personnel managers in police departments create a series of stress interviews to use in selecting recruits. One problem with this type of testing is that researchers have barely scratched the surface in testing the predictability of these tests in police performance. However, we do have an extensive research literature on industrial and business personality profile testing and have excellent empirical evidence in terms of predictability of performance and standardized group scores.

Psychological testing is useful in weeding out psychotic and potentially dangerous human beings. However, most professionals agree that psychological testing is useful only for rejecting the truly abnormal. In that gray area encompassing normal-neurotic-deviant, different kinds of judgments need to be made to be fair to the recruits.

What is rather scary is that some smaller police departments use no psychological screening for recruits. If, say, even 10 percent can be rejected for potentially psychotic behavior, then what we have created by not using this technique is a group of unguided missiles with great potential for harm. Industry and businesses have found these techniques to be useful and spend millions of dollars a year to employ them. Businesses would not go to this expense unless there was clear-cut evidence that these tests are useful in judging future performance. It is now time for law enforcement to catch up with the private sector by using personnel-evaluation techniques of proven value.

Lateral Entry

Lateral entry allows recruitment for various levels in a police agency. It allows for mobility in that an officer can transfer at a rank above recruit and below such elected or politically appointed positions as chief, sheriff, and deputy chief. This means that a sergeant in one agency may be able to transfer laterally to another police agency, keeping his or her rank.

Of course, lateral entry is almost nonexistent. Mobility comes only to the lowest and highest levels of policing. In relation to the entry-level positions, it is normally a termination of one job and an entry into another job. Lateral entry at the bottom is difficult to distinguish from simple job mobility. This may mean an upgrading of the officer from a local police job to a more prestigious county, state, or federal law enforcement occupation. This is a simple case of upward mobility rather than lateral entry.

At the top level, we see chiefs easily moving from jurisdiction to jurisdiction. We see William Bratton moving from Boston to lead the New York City Police Department. Willy Brown moved from Philadelphia to Los Angeles just after the riots caused by the Rodney King incident. Chiefs and top administrators move all over the country without a problem.

In smaller communities, state civil service commissions have created the civil service position of chief. The net result is normally freezing the chief in his position and reducing mobility. In fact, some small communities require through their police charter that the chief must come from the ranks regardless of qualifications. This indeed reduces mobility.

There are a number of real restrictions on the creation of a lateral entry system: (1) nonuniform retirement systems, (2) differences in pay scales for the same positions, (3) residency requirements, (4) nonuniform training for different levels of staffing, and (5) differences in civil service requirements for the same management level. Generally, in many of these cases, it would take a major adjustment by local management and the police benevolent association's personnel policies and in some cases change in local and state laws to implement a lateral entry personnel system.

Polygraph Testing

A **polygraph** is an instrument that is used to measure physiological responses to questions. Three variables—breathing, blood pressure, and amount of perspiration—are monitored as the subject is introduced to stimuli by way of specific questions, such as, "Have you smoked marijuana in the last five years?"

Today, the polygraph is increasingly being used by law enforcement agencies as a preemployment screening device as well as an investigatory tool. The objective in utilizing the polygraph for police personnel selection is to uncover those aspects of a person's character that would be deemed undesirable for a career in law enforcement. These include excessive drinking, gambling, immoral sexual conduct, and criminal behavior that might not be uncovered during a background investigation. Police agencies that use the polygraph for their personnel selection point to the high number of applicants who are disqualified based on information obtained during the course of the polygraph test. Also, by publicizing the use of the polygraph for police selection, many agencies feel that this tends to deter candidates who would ultimately be found unsuitable.

Many important questions emerge on the use of the polygraph for selection purposes. First, the polygraphist must be well trained. This involves a rigorous course of some 600 hours, followed by refresher seminars to keep him or her abreast of new trends. Then the department has to establish criteria that would disqualify a candidate, that is, to determine what past or present behavior is unsuitable for police work. For example, should candidate Jones be disqualified because he smoked marijuana five years ago while in college? If Jones admits to stealing while he was a juvenile, what type of stolen property would result in his disqualification? A car? A fountain pen?

In essence, the use of the polygraph is based on the subjective judgments of the polygraphist and the overall policies of the department. There is increasing criticism of the usefulness and accuracy of polygraph testing today.

The Interview

Traditionally, the candidate is either required or invited to have an interview with the chief of police regarding his or her candidacy for employment. In states where civil service prevails, this interview may be perfunctory or an important portion of the process if the department is able to select from a pool or a certified list of candidates. The purpose of the interview is for the administrator to meet the candidate and ask questions to determine whether he or she would be a good police officer and an asset to the department.

Many departments have turned the interview into a stressful group process whereby the candidate meets with three to six interviewers from the department, the community, or both. Difficult questions are asked, ranging from personal philosophy to judgment in police situations, and the candidate's responses are measured accordingly. This process gives the department something that no multiple-choice tests can ever give—the ability to examine the potential officer in a stressful situation; in the interview room, the candidate is required to make immediate judgments on the questions presented.

A review of group interview questions from a variety of sources yields the following examples:

1. What unique skills, strengths, and abilities will you bring to the department?
2. What do you expect from a supervisor?
3. What kind of call would be distasteful (or most stressful) to you?
4. Suppose that while you are on patrol, you receive a call to go to a residence where a baby is crying. There is a babysitter inside the residence, but no one comes to the door. What do you do?

The candidate is judged not only on his or her responses, but also on his or her ability to communicate and to make judgments. Interviews range from structured questions that require the demonstration of specific types of knowledge to interviews that include a few structured questions but the interviewers are allowed to free-associate and probe the candidate's replies.

College Education Requirements

Of the many programs created by the Law Enforcement Assistance Administration, some that will endure are the college criminal justice programs that were created in response to the mandate of the President's Commission on Law Enforcement and Administration of Justice that all police officers must possess college degrees. In the 1970s, a trend began for police departments and civil service commissions to raise educational requirements from the traditional high school diploma to two or four years of college study with a major in criminal justice or a related field.

While this would appear to be a step toward creating a professional police force and attracting candidates who are able to think, write, and speak well about the social problems affecting the community, many police administrators and college educators question the value of a college education as it relates to police work. Detractors or those neutral to the idea point out that the realities of the police role (making arrests, seeing people at their worst) may nullify the value of classroom study (Weiner, 1976). Furthering this controversy, the National Advisory Commission on Higher Education for Police Officers (1979) concluded that many criminal justice college programs were no more than extensions of the police training academy, staffed by former police officers, that offered "how-to" courses (scoffed at as "Handcuffs 101") rather than courses related to important social and police managerial issues. Others have contended that college cannot teach common sense and that many college graduates do not know how to read and write well. Some college educators have replied that common sense is simply the sum total of the prejudices that one has developed over a lifetime. They also have argued that much of this "common sense" is not 20 years of professional growth but that same rookie year repeated 20 times with all the mistakes integrated into a rigid approach to law enforcement.

Stepping back from this argument, many criminal justice educators and police professionals recommend that learning be a combination of knowledge and experience. Those college and training programs that synthesize the two are generally lauded by police administrators. It makes no sense to reinvent the wheel each year because the recruit was never given the knowledge of how wheels operate.

In a textbook on the role of the police, Radalet and Carter (1993: 152) cite research that suggests that higher education provides a number of benefits for law enforcement personnel. In addition to learning more about history, law, and ethics, which contributes to an officer's information base, higher education benefits may include the following:

1. Developing greater empathy and tolerance for people with different lifestyles and ideologies, which in turn helps with communication skills
2. Helping officers make decisions and use discretion while handling individual cases without direct supervision
3. Permitting officers to be innovative and flexible while dealing with complex policing strategies, such as problem-oriented or community policing
4. Enabling officers to cope better with stress, resulting in more stable and reliable employees
5. Helping officers communicate and respond to situations and to the service needs of the public in a civil manner

The Assessment Center

While most agencies have continued to utilize the various traditional steps just discussed for police personnel selection and wrestle with affirmative action complaints, others have adopted selection models from private industry. One that shows promise is the **assessment center,** a concept first used by the German and British military in World War II for selecting servicepeople qualified to perform special missions. After the war, the idea caught on in private industry in the United States. Some federal and municipal law enforcement agencies are experimenting with or are using the assessment center concept.

At the assessment center, the candidate participates in a number of activities, ranging from a structured interview to group simulation exercises. In the group exercise, the candidate must confront a problem that might be encountered on the job, such as intervening in a family fight. Trained assessors rate the candidate on how well he or she performs the assigned tasks.

As Gavin and Hamilton (1975) conclude, these exercises simulate on-the-job behavior in a way that traditional pen-and-paper tests cannot. Moreover, a large amount of information can be obtained in a relatively short period of time. Although various methods are used, the exercises are constant for all candidates undergoing the process.

An assessment process, first cited by Gavin and Hamilton in 1975 and now used by the University of Wisconsin Police Department, might include the following steps:

Phase I

1. Written examination
2. Verbal screening
3. Psychological testing

Phase II

1. Oral board interview, composed of a senior police officer, a psychologist, and a community representative, in which questions are asked concerning the candidate's background and motivations for entering police work
2. Situational testing, in which the candidate is confronted with typical police situations (assessors watch the exercise behind a one-way mirror)
3. Leaderless group discussions, at which time the applicants are presented with a police-related topic. At the end of the discussion, the candidates present their conclusions. The assessors watch the discussions and rate the candidates on their participation.
4. Individual psychological interview
5. Combining the data gathered from phases I and II and ranking the candidates.

Phase III

Based on successful completion of phases I and II, the candidates then undergo a polygraph examination, background check, physical examinations, and police/staff interviews.

The assessment center can be expensive or even inaccessible for smaller departments because of geographic considerations.

RECRUITMENT TECHNIQUES

The basic considerations in recruiting are who you want to reach and the cost per sworn-in recruit. The department needs to provide funds for travel for the recruitment team as well as funds for printed materials. Any media messages should be produced by professionals for maximum impact. Professional organizations will be able to provide cost figures in terms of populations reached and numbers in those populations. The department needs to quiz new recruits in terms of how they found out about the available positions and use this information in charting recruitment costs.

The first step in any recruitment campaign is to make potential applicants identify with the organization. There are a number of ways that this can be achieved. Recruitment brochures and Web sites should reflect the existing diversity of the department in terms of pictures and programs. In some cases, personal vignettes can be presented. As discussed by Milgram (2002), many potential candidates use the Internet to review job openings and position requirements. Thus, it is important that the official Web site also reflect the diversity of the department. Similarly, the recruiters who are assigned to job fairs and recruitment details at high schools and colleges should recruit women and minorities. Smaller departments could combine with other police departments to make a regional effort to recruit, printing common brochures and hiring full-time regional recruiters.

Toward a Rational Model of Police Selection

The authors feel that the multistep traditional model of police selection has served its usefulness—in essence, the dictates of the 1883 Pendleton Act are still being employed as the chief criteria for selection. What we propose is a new model that attempts to include methodologies used for personnel selection both in private industry and by some law enforcement agencies in the United States.

In reviewing this chapter, it becomes obvious that the traditional civil service selection process is outmoded on two bases. First, we are no farther ahead than we ever were in abolishing certain personnel abuses that existed before 1870, especially those related to the influence on the police by the community political establishment. Although the wholesale firing of police officers after election day has ended, the outright spoils system that existed in the nineteenth century has been replaced by a system that we call *sophisticated patronage*, in which party affiliation becomes a factor in who gets selected in a rule-of-three situation. Moreover, not all police departments use civil service. In many states, and even in those states that have civil service, some departments still use a selection process based on political influence and informal community relations (e.g., "I am a friend of the chief, and I have lived here all my life").

Many police administrators, moreover, are fed up with civil service. Although there are many qualified candidates who wish to become police officers, these individuals are forced to put off career plans simply because they must take a pencil-and-paper test that may be scheduled only once a year. Frequently, too, the results of the test are not made known until months after the examination. When coupled with the other factors related to the selection process—interviews, background checks, polygraph examinations, and so on—it may take a year and a half from the time of the examination to eventual employment. Many departments have solved this dilemma by doing most of the process, excluding the background examination, within a specific time frame of a week or days.

Police administrators who desire a specific candidate are still able to find loopholes to further the cause of sophisticated patronage. One department studied conducted its own selection process and hired a number of officers under the statute terms of provisional appointment. When the civil service test was held, the new officers, who had been on the job for a year, had to take the examination with other candidates. The results showed that some of the year-old appointees did not rank very high on the list. The administrator solved the dilemma by importing a residency requirement (again within the terms of the state law) that eventually eliminated all the applicants who had taken the examination except for the officers previously hired.

Another aspect of civil service is the problem of terminating incompetent officers who are under the protection of civil service. The termination of police employees according to civil service procedures is a long and drawn-out process. In many cases, informal methods, such as forced resignation and managerial harassment, are used instead.

Many police administrators and reformers are unhappy with civil service, and the rise of affirmative action in the 1970s has prompted the move for reform and a review of traditional civil service requirements. As a result, many departments have been forced by the courts and by federal agencies to introduce reforms or quota systems. The use of a federally induced quota, while seen as an immediate solution, is an ineffective long-term remedy in terms of employee and agency dissatisfaction, charges of lower entry standards, "dipping," countersuits, and on-the-job harassment. Against this background, many researchers employed by police departments, colleges, or research institutions are attempting to upgrade the existing process by answering diverse legal and methodological questions related to job performance and specific portions of the process. To date, this has resulted only in the allocation of time and monetary resources to upgrade the status quo.

New Police Recruitment Selection Model

To address the issues presented, we propose a model for police recruit selection. This rational model for police selection is based on three premises:

1. There is a need for better designed entry-level, pencil-and-paper tests. Current tests often fail to predict on-the-job performance or the potential of the candidate.
2. The responsibility for police personnel selection rests with each state in terms of allocating financial and human resources for this objective. Since 90 percent of the police departments in the United States are small agencies composed of 15 officers or fewer, it is obvious that most agencies cannot afford to maintain an ongoing professional selection process. At the same time, each police agency must abide by state requirements for the position of police officer.
3. Civil service personnel in existing departments need to be retooled to perform ably in this proposed model. The present personnel must be retrained, acquiring (1) new skills and (2) new attitudes toward their role as police officer. This entails the various tasks police officers perform.

To be considered for the position of police officer, based on this proposed model, a candidate should be able to fulfill the following requirements:

1. *Age.* A minimum age of 21 years is recommended. It is at age 22 that most people in the United States embark on careers. There is no set maximum age to give each department the flexibility to decide on what kinds of experience and skills potential employees need. At the same time, those departments with 20-year retirement systems will have to adjust their pension systems for the older worker. This would be a proportionate pension system based on years of service to the retirement age.

2. *Education.* Under this new model, each candidate would have to possess a bachelor's degree from an accredited college or university. The bachelor's degree is the accepted norm for most professional careers. It is assumed that routine and clerical tasks would be performed by civilian employees and that police officers would serve as professional law enforcement officers. Thus, the kind of education that allows one to deal with a large range of cultures and roles and that teaches one to write well would be of value. District attorneys have known for years that cases written up by college-educated police officers are better than those written by officers without a college education. A college-educated police force of professionals whose job description is related to professional skills and knowledge will be a superior police force.

3. *Physical requirements.* Each candidate must be in good health and physical condition according to a national standard like Cooper. Nevertheless, each department would have physical requirements for selecting officers to special units (e.g., special weapons and tactics (SWAT) teams, hostage-negotiation, bicycle patrol, and emergency services). Candidates must be free of any disease or physical ailments that would keep them disabled for long periods of time or prevent them from performing police duties.

After fulfilling these three basic requirements, the candidate would then report to a regional assessment center. Here the candidate would undergo a variety of tests currently in use by many police agencies. The testing would include a battery of psychological examinations.

On successful completion of the assessment center review, the candidate would then be eligible to attend the regionally operated police academy. The academy curriculum would include the basic tasks related to police work: firearms, crisis intervention, law, introduction to the criminal justice system, and physical conditioning. Candidates who fail tests or firearms requirements would be eliminated.

On completing the assessment center and police academy stages, the candidate would then be issued a certificate making him or her eligible to be a law enforcement officer for state and local agencies. The officer would be notified of available openings in the various departments and would be required to notify the department of his or her interest in working for that agency. From this pool of applicants, the agency would select the police officers for its department. The selection process would be based on the desires of the department and the community.

OTHER PERSONNEL ISSUES

Sexual Harassment

The presidency of William Clinton prompted continued interest in the topic of **sexual harassment,** especially with regard to interpersonal relationships in the workplace. Sexual harassment consists of the following:

1. The supervisor demands sexual consideration in exchange for job benefit.
2. An employee makes unwelcome sexual advances toward another employee in the form of pressure for dates, stalking, love letters, and calls.
3. Activities or behavior by one or more employees creates a hostile work environment for the complainant regardless of the loss of economic or tangible job benefits. These activities might include pranks, jokes, and comments of a sexual nature.

Sexual harassment can include incidents between people of the same gender.

Prohibitions against sexual harassment are not new. In the 1980s, a number of federal and state court cases concluded that sexual harassment activities violated EEOC guidelines and Title VII of the Civil Rights Act of 1964.

The demand for sexual favors in exchange for job benefits is a very understandable concept for most employers and employees because of the quid pro quo that is involved. The **hostile work environment** standard, however, is very complex and often depends on the pattern of behavior in the work environment. Employer liability with regard to fines also depends on the extent to which the employer knew or could have reasonably known and prevented the sexual harassing activity. In a number of noted cases, public and private companies were fined by either state or federal courts for failing to stop the activity.

Today, most police departments have policies prohibiting sexual harassment and have established processes by which employees can make complaints and seek resolution of sexual harassment. Many have conducted training sessions for employees and supervisors to discuss the various aspects of sexual harassment and its negative effect on the mission of the department.

The crux of police department efforts against sexual harassment remain departmental disciplinary processes insofar as investigations, hearings, and sanctions must be meted out according to due process standards. In situations where the department fails to address sexual harassment complaints, the employee may go outside the department and file a complaint through either a state or a federal regulatory agency. Policing remains a male-dominated occupation in many departments throughout the United States. While the number of female officers has increased in many large state and metropolitan departments, there are few or no women in small agencies. Regardless of agency size, sexual harassment and the "hostile work environment" remain a problem for male and female supervisors and agency heads because of the delicate, complex nature of interpersonal relationships. We suggest that sexual harassment is a problem that must be continually addressed through training seminars, roll-call training, departmental advisories, and efficient complaint/resolution procedures.

Drug Testing

Drug testing for police personnel became widely used in the mid-1980s in response to the widespread use of illegal substances by citizens coupled with the dramatic rise of drug-related police corruption cases. Policy makers, legislators, and police administrators reasoned that the so-called war on drugs could not be waged by police officers who use illegal substances. Aside from the negative effects on physiomotor skills, the use of illegal substances by police officers provides a wide range of moral and legal dilemmas regarding drug enforcement. Perhaps the most profound are those life-and-death implications for drug-enforcement officers who are compromised or threatened by fellow officers "bought" by drug dealers. Discussing the extent of police drug testing and citing Bureau of Justice statistics, Mieczkowski (2002) reports that nearly 80 percent of all local police departments have some form of drug testing for either recruit officers or on a random basis for personnel involved in narcotics units.

Despite widespread use, drug testing remains controversial among police officers and police unions because of the invasion of personal privacy and the legal consequences for personnel who test positive. Departments that have drug screening may use one or a combination of the following programs:

1. Random testing for all personnel on a routine basis
2. Mandatory testing for all preemployment applicants
3. Testing for preservice and in-service officers based on reasonable suspicion that the person is using illegal substances. Reasonable suspicion may be based on (1) internal investigation in response to a complaint, (2) observation of behavior at work (e.g., slurred speech, unsteady gait), or (3) long-term work patterns regarding sick time and attendance.
4. Testing of officers being considered for sensitive assignments, such as narcotics enforcement, helicopter operations, explosives, and special weapons and tactics
5. Voluntary testing by officers to show that they are above reproach

Legally, drug screening is based on the Fourth and Fourteenth Amendments regarding searches and procedural due process. By the end of the 1980s, both the U.S. Supreme Court and higher state courts ruled on the legality of certain kinds of searches related to drug testing. The most noted case was *Skinner* v. *Railway Labor Executives Association* (1989), in which the Supreme Court decided that drug testing undertaken for railroad workers after accidents and safety violations constituted a search within the confines of the Fourth Amendment. The Court reasoned that the need to regulate the conduct of employees for safety purposes was far greater than the need for individual privacy. The same logic was applied to drug screening for U.S. Customs officers assigned to law enforcement duties. In *National Treasury Employees Union* v. *VonRaab* (1989), the Court concluded that preventing the entry and promotion of drug users into sensitive positions outweighed privacy interests in view of the physical and ethical demands related to the position. In both cases, the Court also discussed the deterrence value of drug screening; in each situation, employees had fair warning that the tests would be conducted.

The upholding of drug testing in these cases does not mean that testing for all personnel will automatically be upheld. In either a court or an administrative hearing setting, the following key elements will be analyzed: the nature of the testing (random versus postincident), the preliminary notice given to employees who are to be tested, the laboratory procedures used and their validation, and the need for testing based on the particular functions of the job.

In 1988, the Police Executive Research Forum surveyed police chiefs around the country. The following are the policies the chiefs favored:

- Drug testing if reasonable grounds existed to suspect an officer using drugs (87.7 percent)
- Drug screening of police applicants (76.4 percent)
- Regular drug testing of officers during probationary period (66 percent)
- Random drug testing of officers in "sensitive" positions (64.7 percent)

These policies would be subject to legal and union contract considerations. In order to have credibility with the public, it is necessary to have specific alcohol- and drug-abuse policies that are enforced. Police unions favor drug- and alcohol-abuse policies geared toward rehabilitation, with sanctions as a last resort.

Drug Testing in Practice.   The most common screening procedure used at this time is urine testing by way of the Enzyme Multiplied Immunoassay Technique (EMIT). In this procedure, a urine sample is analyzed for the presence of a single substance or a class of drugs or metabolites by separating the various enzymes. The procedure is inexpensive and, thus, widely used. The use of EMIT suggests only the presence of a substance, it does not show quantity and level of impairment. As Connors (1989: 165) suggests, there must be further testing and investigation through gas chromatography and mass spectrometry to address the problem of "false positives." The key elements in screening

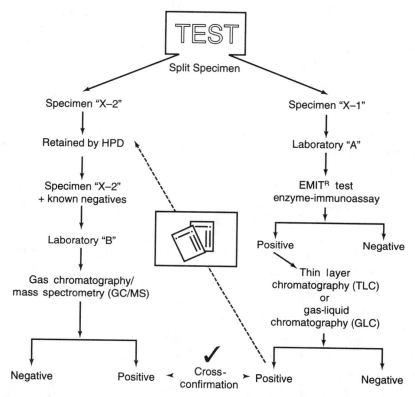

FIGURE 12-2 The Honolulu Police Department's drug-testing methods.

procedures are the safeguards used in this testing, including such variables as the quality of equipment, chain of custody of evidence, training of personnel administering the test, and the test-site procedures. See Figure 12–2.

For in-service personnel who test positive in random or periodic testing programs, the next course of action by management involves interrogation and disciplinary action. Most police unions have at this time negotiated a series of steps to protect the interests of employees in situations when an employee has been ordered to submit to drug testing and related interrogation. These steps—representation by counsel, written notice of charges, reasonable privacy during urination, and second-opinion testing of the suspected employee—are generally in addition to any other rights negotiated by contract. To support administrators in situations in which a complaint about drug use by an officer is based on the testimony of a confidential informant, language of the collective bargaining agreement often states that the employer does not have to reveal the name of the informant.

Police executives generally agree that termination of employment is perhaps the only fitting way to deal with confirmed illegal drug users. Connors

(1989) points to the legal aspects of the situations, including possession of a controlled substance and association with known drug users. Some departments, in concert with their police unions, have started programs of drug-abuse education and professional assistance for personnel who voluntarily declare that they have a substance-abuse problem. The success and employee acceptance of these programs varies because police officers generally stay away from these programs if assistance offices are located in the police station or if confidentiality is not ensured. Some collective bargaining agreements declare that the officer will not be subject to drug screening if he or she voluntarily enters a rehabilitation program. Whether the officer is temporarily suspended or allowed to continue in another assignment varies from program to program.

This trend in drug screening and discipline will not change drastically as long as state court and administrative rulings continue to uphold valid screening programs and disciplinary sanctions for drug abuse committed in both on-duty and off-duty situations. Further, a related federal policy for drug-free workplaces and schools was ensured by the end of the 1980s. In 1988, the Federal Drug Free Workplace Act was signed into law. It requires employers with federal contracts in excess of $25,000 to certify that they will provide a drug-free workplace through the following: (1) providing publications and education about drug awareness, (2) requiring notification to the employer by the employee if he or she is arrested for criminal violations occurring in the workplace, (3) requiring convicted employees to participate in a drug-abuse assistance or rehabilitation program, and (4) notifying employees of possible sanctions that might be taken against them by the company. The language and intent of the 1988 act were also applied in the Drug Free Schools Act, which stipulates that financial aid can be withheld from students convicted of drug violations.

Public Police and Private Security

It is estimated that there are over one million people employed as private security officers by contract agencies, private corporations and transportation firms (Simonsen, 1998: 73). The industry today is estimated to bring in revenues of over $12 billion annually (Hall, 2003). In comparison, there are approximately 441,000 full-time sworn state and local police officers with another 125,000 employed in various civilian capacities (Bureau of Justice Statistics, 2003). Additionally, there are about 62,000 personnel employed as sworn part-time police. It is estimated that there will be sustained continued growth in the private security industry especially after the attacks of September 11, 2000.

Samuel Walker tells us that the existence of this large number of private security personnel has produced a need for private and public police cooperation and for improved standards and training for private police (Walker, 1999: 58). Some standards exist because of government licensing, the professionalization

movement for private security, and the government giving public police powers to private police licensed as special police. Overall government standards
have been weak and are not widely enforced. Until September 11, 2001, there
was a deep separation between the public police and private security that bor-
dered on arrogance. The reality is that public police officers are better trained
and paid than their private counterparts. Despite these differences, there is a
growing acknowledgment that the public sector cannot provide all the necessary services for homeland security. Thus, there is a need for greater communication and joint training. Unfortunately, increasing training for many private
security officers on emergency response procedures and homeland security
topics has been overall negligible.

The International Association of Chiefs of Police and the American
Society for Industrial Security have created the Joint Council of Law
Enforcement and Private Security Associations to encourage public and private police cooperation (Simonsen, 1998: 68). It is hoped that the community
policing model will bring about more cooperation as public police work to involve all of the community resources, including private security, in an effort to
prevent and control crime.

Contract Police Issues

Albert Reiss Jr. (1988: 9) produced three models of secondary employment that
are still useful today.

1. The *officer contract model*, where each officer is a principal who independently contracts with an employer for a particular job. . . .
2. The *union brokerage model*, [where] an officer's union or association brokers
   the employment for its members so that they need not search for their own
   job and negotiate pay. . . .
3. The *department contract model*, where the department is the principal agent
   for officers and contracts their secondary employment.

There are many variations of the officer contract model. For example,
Arlington, Virginia, restricts outside employment to the state of Virginia,
county of Arlington, and the U.S. government. Cincinnati handles the billing
and compensation of officers when the contracting party is the city; otherwise,
it lets its officers contract on their own for employment.

According to Reiss, under the union brokerage model, the union sets conditions and pay for paid details and may bargain with the police department
concerning status and condition of paid details. The Seattle Police Officers'
Guild coordinates requests for off-duty employment, but the officers act as independent contractors. For special events held at the Seattle Center complex,
off-duty officers "are employed by the complex's director of security and compensated by an outside accounting firm" (Reiss, 1988: 11).

Under the department contract model, the police department performs three major functions (Reiss, 1988: 11): It "(1) contracts with employers for paid details; (2) assigns officers to details; and (3) pays the officers from reimbursements by employers." The Metro-Dade Florida Police Department contracts for all police-related work, but "officers are allowed to contract independently for non-police related work on application for a specific job and under permit for that employment." Metro-Dade is unusual in that it subcontracts police services for private security. Boston, Colorado Springs, New Haven, and St. Petersburg operate primarily with the department contract model.

The three major issues that restrict employment of the public police are (1) potential conflict of interest, (2) threat to the dignity of police as an occupation, and (3) "an unacceptable risk of temporary or disabling injury that would limit their [the police officer's] return to regular duty" (Reiss, 1988: 11).

Most departments have rules and regulations and issue work permits for all outside employment. Departments place even more stringent restrictions when the public police officer is employed in uniform. Many departments and police unions also restrict the rate of compensation that can be earned, for example, demanding a minimum rate. They also restrict the type of employment and the amount of time spent on secondary employment, such as a maximum number of hours outside work per week. The exact time of employment—for example, working prior to coming on duty—is also an area of concern. These restrictions are normally enforced by issuing or denying work permits to individual officers. All in all, the relationship between private and public police will continue to be a major concern of police managers in the public sector.

Police Overtime

Millions of dollars are spent on police **overtime,** yet there are practically no published studies on this topic. Since police normally deal with emergencies, disasters, mass demonstrations, murders, and major performances drawing thousands of fans, the public should expect police managers to plan for these events with a minimal use of overtime or with a program to recoup overtime costs from event sponsors. The lack of attention and planning on this issue can result in bloated budgets, an inefficient use of police personnel, police officer exhaustion, and unnecessary tension between line officers and police supervisors.

This is sometimes complicated if the department or unit is not adequately staffed. Many functions operating 24 hours a day require five or six people to carry out the duties of one position. A discussion on staffing planning can be found in Chapter 14.

A nationwide study of overtime involving 2,183 police agencies found that the major reasons for overtime were shift extensions, court appearances, emergency situations, and contract requirements. Other reasons were briefings and roll calls, callbacks to duty, and meetings and training outside of work hours. In some departments, a homicide was treated as an emergency requiring overtime (Bayley and Worden, 1998: 3, 4).

Labor contracts and state and federal laws normally charge overtime at time and a half of an officer's hourly wage rate. These contracts can often create costly, artificial overtime charges. Some examples of excessive labor contract provisions are the following:

- Brief court appearances earning, by contract, three or four hours in overtime
- Standbys earning a minimum of three hours of overtime
- Overtime of 15 to 30 minutes given for roll calls
- Having all meetings outside the department charged to overtime

Removing these provisions from contracts should be a high priority in negotiations with police unions. It may be necessary to make these labor abuses public in order to eliminate them.

The high cost of overtime needs to be controlled through proactive police management, including recording, analyzing, managing, and supervision. The most vital issue is to have basic records of the following:

- Number of overtime minutes
- What the overtime was used for
- Officers and units performing the overtime work
- A daily, computerized usage record in a retrievable form

Only 38 percent of the departments surveyed in the nationwide sample were able to provide the number of overtime hours worked.

Compensatory time is repaying overtime with time off at one and one-half more cost than straight time. This creates more problems when professional personnel are simply not available for normal duties because they are on "comp" time. As Bayley and Worden (1998: 3) stress, "Paid overtime increases policing activity while compensatory time results in less policing because every hour worked must be repaid by the department at time and a half time taken away from other activities."

Bayley and Worden found one department in which all overtime was paid in cash, overtime was tracked by unit and function, and a report was distributed to management every two weeks. Thus, it is possible to create a system that works in controlling overtime. With good records, overtime can be controlled by police management. Overtime cannot be totally eliminated given the nature of police work, but with proactive policies in place, millions of dollars can be saved.

Proactive Policies for Controlling Overtime

1. A program is required that notifies management any time a unit or officer is building up overtime so the reason can be looked into immediately.

2. An agreement should be reached with the courts to limit personnel needed in court, to eliminate the need for supervisory police personnel, and to create a court schedule that conforms to straight time as much as possible. With instant communications and computer scheduling available, police officers should be able to work other duties while awaiting court appearances.

3. Written guidelines are needed instructing supervisors when to approve shift extensions. The overtime should be immediately entered into the overtime computer program, with the reason for the shift extension and the officer names and units granted the extension noted.

4. Good records on overtime are mandatory. When elected officials consider the costs of police personnel, a report should be on their desks giving the reasons for overtime costs in understaffed police departments.

5. Emergency planning must be done with straight-time personnel. Emergencies can also be planned for with a mobilization plan and an interagency agreement with other police departments.

6. Special events, including traffic control, need to be planned well ahead of time, using special police officers on straight time, and should involve other agencies. Event sponsors may need to pay for extra police coverage.

7. Adjustable and flexible work schedules are a first line of defense. The schedules must be available to senior management, planning personnel, and line supervisors.

8. All overtime should be paid for in cash, never in compensatory time.

9. Departments should have adequate staffing to cover line and auxiliary functions and should not depend on overtime for basic coverage.

Proactive control of overtime through data analysis and an instantly available computer-based information system will give proactive police management the following:

- The tools to explain the use of overtime to legislatures
- The ability to eliminate costly labor contract provisions
- The ability to create an efficient system to monitor and control overtime

Stress Management

Police work entails high **stress,** and managing that work can produce a great deal of stress. Stress itself can be good or bad. "Manageable" stress is a positive factor in organizational life if it motivates employees to complete a job and act in a responsible manner. If stress leads to avoidance of work or creates a feeling of being overwhelmed by events, it can become a strong negative force.

More and more studies are being written on the subject of police stress. The major issues relate to stress created by the organization and stress created by the individual. Organizational stress is created by lack of communication or by miscommunication. A lack of consistency may cause the line officer and his or her immediate superiors to think that they lack control over their jobs.

Individual stress is often created by a personality type attracted to police work that has been labeled *type A*. Type A personalities tend to overcommit themselves to a wide variety of tasks and feel that they have to be doing something all the time. They feel that they must be in control of all situations affecting them. They often have insomnia, but they also accomplish a great deal of what they set out to do.

This is in contrast to *type B* personalities, who accomplish what they can, worry a bit about what they have control over, and do not worry about what they cannot control. If the job is not finished on one day, this individual feels that there will be other days to finish it. The type A personality, in contrast, would either finish the job in the time allotted or be overwhelmed by guilt. When stress management consultants do their task well, they are able to apply type A and type B personality profiles to individuals and work out specific exercises that strike a balance between the two personality types. This is a very real challenge that can make or break a police organization. Meditation, posture work, and a variety of exercises are excellent tools that have been used to deal with stress and stressors. Remember that stress, itself, is not bad. It is uncontrolled stress that is destructive.

Stress-reduction techniques should be part of every in-service police training program. However, all the techniques in the world will not change stress-producing situations. By the nature of their work, police officers are often confronted by dangerous situations. However, perceptions of violence and techniques for handling violence can reduce stress on individual officers. An officer must have enough training and experience to handle and control stress-producing situations. That is why, for example, training in domestic crisis intervention is so vital for the patrol officer, as is specific training in riot and crowd control, the handling of juveniles, and so on. The more skills an officer has, the less stress he or she will experience.

Organizational structures can produce or diminish stress. In plain English, this means that police personnel need consistency of command, time to assimilate new orders, and a good feedback system that allows for modification of orders in terms of the needs of the line officer. Officers and managers, especially middle managers, need communication skills so that the line officer will feel that (1) someone up there in management land is listening and that (2) he or she has a real and responsible input into the orders that affect his or her everyday professional life. People need to feel in control of their lives. Capricious orders with no explanation destroy this feeling of control.

When a number of police officers from different departments are drinking coffee at 2:00 A.M. in the middle of a patrol assignment, what is the talk about? Is it about crime, forensics, or how to patrol more effectively? Not usually. The talk is normally about promotions, orders, personalities in the police force, and individual stories about police-related incidents. Good police managers know this and will take steps to assure line officers and supervisors some control over the affairs that dominate their lives.

Stress management is a major concern for police managers. A bibliography published in 1979 by the National Institute of Justice listed 113 published sources and 33 training films on police stress and stress management (Duncan and others, 1979). Police have to make instant life-and-death decisions and face violence, and yet they are also stressed by boredom. Some stress-related factors in police work are the following (Niederhoffer, 1974; Terry, 1983; Stratton, 1984):

- Shift work
- A quasimilitary structure
- The need to repress emotions and keep a psychological distance
- Lack of promotions and very few lateral transfers
- Having to live up to the media image of the supercop
- Police cynicism
- Frustration and lack of input into the police bureaucracy
- Fear and danger (killing a citizen or having a fellow officer killed, especially your partner)
- Social isolation
- Retirement
- Excessive paperwork
- Frustration with the judicial system
- Impact of a profession stressing danger and imposing stress on the spouse and children

Police officers, despite the social solidarity of police, often do not trust one another. Unlike other professions, police officers do not like to show personal weaknesses. There is also a stigma of seeking professional counseling. Until recent years, many departments did not recognize or acknowledge the symptoms brought about by postcritical incident stress.

John Stratton, former director of Psychological Services in the Los Angeles County Sheriff's Department, also gives many practical examples and suggestions in his book *Police Passages* (1984). These include counseling programs for spouses, police widows and widowers, officers approaching retirement, and the availability of a 24-hour crisis hot line for police officers.

Violanti (1983) showed that stress increases in what he calls the first two stages of a police career: 0 through 5 years, the alarm stage, and 6 through 13 years, the disenchantment stage. He recommends that programs on stress management be focused on these years. He concludes with this hopeful note (Violanti, 1983: 216): "Despite strong pressures and the imbalanced nature of the police functions, officers managed in time to reduce stress." He felt that "individual perception is the most important factor in determining stress levels." Thus, stress can be coped with both by the individual and by the police organization through positive intervention strategies.

One approach that large departments can use and smaller departments can create on a regional level is what Robert Loo, the first chief psychologist of the Royal Canadian Mounted Police, calls his proactive approach to psychological services. He recommends the creation of a center that will have a career-cycle perceptive on providing psychological services, including "recruit selection, support of force training programs, the support of members in the workplace and pre-retirement services" (Loo, 1985: 134). In the past, he felt that police agencies simply reacted to such problems as low morale, stress reactions, drug abuse by police personnel, and community/citizen complaints against police officers. He feels that this proactive approach will help police managers deal more adequately with these problems.

Family stress can be decreased by departmental intervention. At the training level, spouses and domestic partners should learn about the job and the stressors in the job, tour the police unit, and take part in a ride-along program. Emergency communication and debriefing procedures for critical incidents, along with counseling for families, need to be available. Counseling and support groups need to be created with the support of the police administration. These can provide stress-management workshops, social affairs, and volunteer opportunities.

Officers need to be physically fit and should have good eating and sleeping habits in order to reduce stress. Departments need to set up nutritional guidelines and physical fitness programs that are related to an officer's age, work, and physical condition. Many departments consider this a frill. However, given the investment in training and work experience in the human capital of police officer and police supervisor, the approach should be considered essential to the job.

In *Stress Management for Law Enforcement Officers* (1995: 283), Anderson, Swenson, and Clay show four major factors that affect officers' negative attitudes toward their work: "(1) the particular stresses they face, (2) the extent to which the legal system backs them and rewards them with convictions for the good arrests, (3) their zone of stability, and (4) their support system."

The zone of a person's stability is "the range of stimulation (excitement, arousal) from the least to the most an individual can handle without signs of distress" (Anderson and others, 1995: 17). People operating below their zone of stability will be bored and uncomfortable; when operating above the zone of stability, they will feel stressed and pressured. Good police managers need to know their own zone of stability and their subordinates' zones of stability so that there is enough good stress to keep people moving without exceeding their comfort zones.

Supervisors, such as sergeants, lieutenants, or captains, who are trained in supervision techniques are less stressed and create less stress for subordinates. This approach improves the morale of the whole police department. As one lieutenant and shift commander stated, "The daily stressors associated with management . . . can produce the same kind of stress reactions among supervisors . . . as a domestic disturbances call might provoke among line officers"

(Standfest, 1996: 10). Training and stress management is just as important for supervisors and managers as for any line officer.

Standfest has a four-stage approach:

1. *Assessment.* Through assessment, police executives learn which stressors are affecting their supervisors.
2. *Planning.* The police executives remove the stressors in a cost-effective manner. Standfest says that fundamental approaches, such as repairing station houses and vehicles, could reduce a great deal of stress at low cost.
3. *Action.* Police executives carry out fully any plans and let the supervisors know what is going on.
4. *Follow-through.* Police executives evaluate the action, making sure that the orders were fully carried out, and assess the outcomes.

Anderson and colleagues (1995: 130) show the nature of police role stressors and role overload. These recommendations can be summarized as follows:

1. Clear and current policies and procedures concerning work tasks reduce police role ambiguity.
2. A consistent expectation by supervisors concerning their subordinates, along with a clear two-way feedback system, is essential.
3. Officers and supervisors need to have a high tolerance of ambiguity.
4. Active participation by all authority levels in decision making provides a system of mutual responsibility that continually relieves stress.

Supervisors can reduce stress by "(1) teaching the officers 'verbal judo'; that is, how to use words to control citizens' behavior; (2) showing the officers the laws that apply and when to use them; and (3) explaining the nature and characteristics of the particular public they serve" (Anderson and others, 1995: 285).

This is exactly what proactive participatory management and proactive community policing do when they are working effectively.

Fatigue Management

Scientists working at Walter Reed Army Institute report the following (Vila, 2000: 26):

> Sleep deprivation degrades the higher, more complex mental processes. Soldiers lose battlefield awareness. . . . They can shoot and shoot accurately but no longer can distinguish friend from foe.

Studies by Vila showed that officers identified as "fatigued" had slow reactions to various kinds of mechanical and speed tests and were high risks for motor vehicle accidents. Unlike truck drivers and railroad engineers, there is no **fatigue** standard for police officers. However, the alertness assurance program is a proactive approach that can help protect departments from lawsuits resulting from mistakes made by tired officers. These are some elements of the program:

- Implementing a consistent and biocompatible work schedule with controls for overtime
- Teaching employees and their families about how to manage shift work
- Not letting employees drive home while fatigued by providing free rides and a place to nap
- Setting up a permanent employee/management task force to manage fatigue

Vila offers other recommendations for fatigue management (2000: 146):

- Minimize shift changes.
- Maximize work hour regularity.
- Never use weekly shift changes.
- Always rotate forward.
- Don't let tired cops hit the streets.
- Minimize mandatory overtime, and develop an overtime policy.
- Provide a bright, stimulating nighttime environment with opportunities to eat healthful food.

The research also found that most officers who took time off—that is, sick days, vacation days, or a regular number of days off between shifts—recovered from fatigue.

Behind some of these recommendations are useful training concepts, such as "alertness switches," which can affect an officer's performance during night-time hours:

1. Spotting a suspect or finding people in crisis heightens alertness.
2. Dawn brings natural alertness and new energy. Midnight to dawn is a down time for the human body.
3. Not having enough sleep over more than a day drains your "sleep bank."
4. Coffee and donuts provide immediate stimulation but cause a crash within the hour.
5. Cold air from a car window brings alertness, whereas hot, humid air brings drowsiness.
6. When the hum of the car tires start to lull you to sleep, stopping and walking around will help.

This is the kind of knowledge supervisors must bring home to police officers. A carefully planned session on managing fatigue is needed both at roll call and during recruit training. Supervisors need to recognize the symptoms of fatigue, and police managers need to use the principles of managing fatigue when creating a work schedule. Controlling and minimizing overtime and off-duty jobs is essential to reducing officer fatigue.

Employee-Assistance Programs

During the past decade, police departments have learned the painful lesson that their employees have personal problems similar to those of the general population. This theme has been picked up by popular television programs that show police at their best and worst. From time to time, police officers have to cope with marital problems, alcohol and drug dependence, children with delinquency and academic problems, job stress, and burnout. The reasons police officers have these problems are the same as for people in any other occupation. What is different is the physically demanding task of adjusting to shift work and the mentally demanding task of seeing people at their worst or dying. One officer has a recurring nightmare about a drowning incident: "He comes to me at night when I sleep. Sometimes once or twice every week. His hand was above the water, but my supervisor held on to me to prevent me from going in after him. The water was electrified—there was not one goddamn thing I could do to help."

Many departments, under their own initiative or through union pressure, have begun employee-assistance programs (EAPs) to deal with these problems. Smaller agencies participate through regional arrangements or with state- or county-sponsored programs. Generally, these programs are staffed by fellow police officers who receive training in counseling and referral. Larger departments have the services of professional counselors and psychologists.

When these programs first began, many officers stayed away for fear of being thought crybabies or cowards or destined for the rubber gun squad. Confidentiality was and remains an issue, and many early programs were doomed to failure when their offices were located in central headquarters. Begrudgingly, police officers have accepted the value of these programs, and the stigma associated with going to EAP has declined somewhat.

The trauma associated with critical incidents like shootings, mass disaster, and gruesome death has received special attention in training and operations policies. In one seminar attended by one of the authors, a panel of veteran police officers recounted the following posttrauma experiences to a class of police recruits:

- Killing a person who was trying to choke an officer
- Responding to a car accident in which the officer's daughter died
- Search-and-recovery operations after a drowning
- Being gunned down by an armed suspect

An officer who takes another human life goes through a number of physical and mental reactions that will never entirely go away (Myles, 1986). He or she will be questioned by investigators, and his or her actions will be reviewed in grand jury proceedings, administrative hearings, and perhaps at trial. There will also be pressure on the officer's family and children. Thus, many departments have posttrauma policies (e.g., supervisory reaction, rules on interrogation) and counseling to deal with these problems.

Many departments have also initiated written line-of-duty death-notification policies to address a number of concerns related to on- and off-duty deaths. Policies of this nature address guidelines for death notification and for working with the family for the wake and funeral ceremonies. Some policies address situations in which the family is taken to the emergency room. The key issues related to situations of this nature include review of insurance and workers' compensation benefits, media relations, assistance to out-of-town family members, and post-funeral assistance for survivors. At all times, the wishes of the family are paramount in terms of the department's involvement in these matters.

CONCLUSION

Personnel is a major expense in law enforcement, and personnel matters take up approximately 80 percent of an administrator's time. Once a recruit has completed probation, he or she stays on the job until retirement. The majority of police departments in the United States continue to have permanent appointment or tenure for officers, which means that the employee cannot be fired without a lengthy hearing unless he or she has been arrested for a crime or has made a series of grave mistakes. It is not surprising that police candidates are carefully evaluated during the probationary period; during this time, the employee serves at the pleasure of the department and often can be terminated without a formal hearing.

The first step in police hiring is the written test, which is administered either by the department or by state or local civil service units. This test measures the candidate's ability to understand written material and gives some indication of situational judgment. Oral interviews are commonly used, and they are very important for assessing interpersonal skills. The assessment center is particularly useful for candidate selection because of cost. Issues related to personnel selection and administration were presented, such as college education requirements, physical agility and medical standards, background checks, age requirements, drug testing, residency requirements, and the use of polygraph testing. In the absence of national or state hiring standards, each issue must be evaluated according to local agency and state personnel practices and procedures.

Drug testing for new candidates has now become routine as a method of deterring drug users from becoming police officers. Recent court cases conclude that there is public support for reducing drug use by police officers. However, drug testing for in-service employees is subject to collective bargaining negotiations, and court cases have ruled that testing cannot be applied to all classes of employees. Commenting on random testing, Webster and Brown (1989: 6) conclude that mandatory testing programs have been upheld when there is evidence of a drug problem in the department.

Since 1970, affirmative action legislation and related court cases and administrative rulings have had the most profound impact on police candidate selection through judicial review of hiring processes and criteria. Police hiring processes underwent critical scrutiny based on the nonrepresentation of women and minorities in the police workforce. Certain agencies were forced to hire and promote under consent decrees or quota systems as a means of creating a diverse workforce, which led to allegations of lowered standards and reverse discrimination by white male candidates and veteran police officers. Nevertheless, the trend now is to end quota programs where statistical representation has been achieved.

The increased number of women in the police workforce has forced all departments to review sexual harassment complaints and referral policies and training on this topic for all line and management personnel. In our experience, the most common complaints by female officers are related to hostile work environments that include pranks, jokes, and offensive comments.

The Americans with Disabilities Act (ADA) has had a profound impact on police hiring. This law has already forced agencies to review medical standards and the actual duties performed by officers. At this time, many departments in the United States have precise medical and physical agility standards for candidates and police academy recruits but not for in-service personnel. Candidates disqualified because of eyesight, weight, or other standards will no doubt challenge their disqualification based on the relationship between the standard and the duties performed by in-service police officers. Court cases and administrative rulings will lead to medical-physical standards, which will apply to all in-service officers, a situation that will require periodic medical and physical agility retesting.

QUESTIONS FOR REVIEW

1. Compare and contrast police hiring practices of the nineteenth century with those of today.
2. What is the controversy surrounding affirmative action programs?
3. What are the benefits of the following personnel selection tools: polygraph test, assessment center, interview, and lateral entry? Also, give criticisms of each.
4. Explain why written tests have generated great controversy in police personnel selection.
5. Explain how the ADA affects assignment decisions.
6. How can management eliminate excessive overtime?
7. Produce a stress-reduction plan for a medium-sized police department.
8. Explain the importance of drug testing for police personnel.

CLASS PROJECTS

1. Role play an interview. There should be no more than three or four interviewers. The interviewers may assume the following roles: a police personnel officer, a detective, a civilian who is head of a local civil rights group, and a patrol officer. One member of the class will portray the police candidate. As the interviewers ask their questions, the rest of the class should rate the responses of the candidate. After the interview, the class members will discuss their reactions to the interview process, their assessment of the candidate, and various issues regarding interviews.

2. Review the recruitment officer hiring standards for a local or state police department. In the standards, list the qualifications for the position which might include a written test, a physical agility test, background check, and so on. What are the physical agility requirements for the position? Are there in-service requirements after you graduate from the academy? Do the standards reflect the Cooper items or job-related tasks?

BIBLIOGRAPHY

Adarand Constructors v. *Federico Pena*, 132 L.Ed.2d 158 (1995).

ANDERSON, WAYNE, DAVID SWENSON, and DANIEL CLAY. *Stress Management for Law Enforcement Officers.* Upper Saddle River, N.J.: Prentice Hall, 1995.

APPLEBAUM, DAVID. "Looking Down the Wrong Side of the Gun: The Problems of the Police Use of Lethal Force. *Police Chief* (May 1993), pp. 55–58.

AYRES, R.M., and G.S. FLANAGAN. *Preventing Law Enforcement Stress: The Organization's Role.* Washington, D.C.: U.S. Department of Justice, 1990.

BAEHR, M., J.E. FURCON, and E.C. FROEMAL. *Psychological Assessment of Patrolman Qualifications in Relation to Field Performance.* Chicago: Industrial Relations Center, University of Chicago, 1968.

BALLES, JOE, ET AL. "City of Madison Police Department Overtime Project." Madison, Wis.: Madison Police Department, 1989.

BAYLEY, DAVID H., and ROBERT E. WORDEN. *Police Overtime: An Examination of Key Issues.* Washington, D.C.: U.S. Department of Justice, 1998.

BERGMANN, BARBARA R. *In Defense of Affirmative Action.* New York: Basic Books, 1996.

BURBECK, ELIZABETH, and ADRIAN FURNHAM. "Police Officer Selection: A Critical Review of the Literature." *Journal of Police Science and Administration*, 13, no. 1 (1985), pp. 58–69.

BUREAU OF JUSTICE STATISTICS. *Local Police Departments.* Washington, D.C.: U.S. Government Printing Office, 1996.

CALDWELL, D.S., and E.W. DORLING. "Preventing Burnout in Police Organizations." *Police Chief* (April 1993), pp. 156–159.

CONNORS, EDWARD F. ET AL. "Employee Drug Testing in Police Departments." In James J. Fyfe, *Police Practice in the '90s.* Washington, D.C.: International City Management Association, 1989, pp. 160–171.

CUNNINGHAM, WILLIAM C., JOHN L. STRAUCHS, and CLIFFORD W. VAN METER. *Private Security Trends, 1970–2000: The Haldcrest Report II.* Boston: Butterworth-Heinemann, 1990.

CUNNINGHAM, WILLIIAM C., and TODD H. TAYLOR. *Private Security and Police in America: The Haldcrest Report*. Boston: Butterworth-Heinemann, 1985.

DESKBOOK ENCYCLOPEDIA OF PUBLIC EMPLOYMENT LAW (9th ed.). Rosemont, Mich.: Oakstone, 2000.

FALLON, R.H. and P.C. WEILER. *Firefighters v. Stotts: Conflicting Models of Racial Justice—Supreme Court Review*. Chicago: University of Chicago Press, 1985.

FOGELSON, ROBERT M. *Big City Police*. Cambridge, Mass.: Harvard University Press, 1977.

GAVIN, JAMES F., and JOHN W. HAMILTON. "Selecting Police Using Assessment Center Methodology." *Journal of Police Science and Administration*, 3, no. 2 (June 1975), pp. 166–176.

GLAZER, N. *Affirmative Discrimination: Ethnic Inequality and Public Policy*. New York: Basic Books, 1975.

GOODMAN, A.M. "A Model for Police Officer Burnout." *Journal of Business and Psychology* (May 1990), pp. 85–99.

Griggs v. *Duke Power Company*, 401 U.S. 424 (1971).

HAMMETT, THEODORE M. *AIDS and the Law Enforcement Officer*. Washington, D.C.: National Institute of Justice, 1987.

HOCHSTEDLER, E. "Impediments to Hiring Minorities in Public Police Agencies." *Journal of Police Science and Administration*, 12, no. 2 (1984), pp. 227–240.

HOLDEN, JAMES, "The Myths of Eyesight Requirements." *FBI Law Enforcement Bulletin*, June 1993. Web posted at www.fbi.gov/leb. Accessed March 15, 2003.

Hopwood v. *Texas*, 861 F. Supp. 551 (1994).

KANNADY, G. "Developing Stress-Resistant Police Families." *Police Chief* (August 1993), pp. 21–26.

KENNEY, DENNIS JAY. "Intelligence and the Selection of Police Recruits." In Dennis J. Kenney and Gary W. Cordner, eds., *Managing Police Personnel*, Cincinnati: Anderson, 1996.

Krocka v. *Reigler*, 958 F. Supp. 1333 (ND. Ill. 1997).

LEMANN, NICHOLAS. "Taking Affirmative Action Apart." *New York Times Magazine*, June 11, 1995, p. 40.

MacKINNON, CATHERINE A. "Sexual Harrassment: Its First Decade in Court." In Barbara Raffel Price and Natalie J. Sokoloff, eds., *The Criminal Justice System and Women* (2nd ed.). New York: McGraw-Hill, 1995, pp. 297–311.

McNamera v. *City of Chicago*, 959 F. Supp. 870 (ND. Ill. 1998).

McWHIRTER, DARIEN A. *The End of Affirmative Action*. New York: Birch Lane, 1996.

MIECZKOWSKI, TOM. "Drug Abuse, Corruption, and Officer Drug Testing: An Overview." In Kim Lersch, ed., *Policing and Misconduct*. Upper Saddle River, N.J.: Prentice Hall, 2002, pp. 157–192.

MILGRAM, DONNA. "Recruiting Women to Policing." *Police Chief* (April 2002), pp. 23–29.

MOORE-EDE, MARTIN. *Working Nights: Health and Safety Guide*. Cambridge, Mass.: Circadian Information, 1997.

MYLES, GREGORY. "Post Incident Trauma Seminar." Albany: New York State Police Academy, summer 1986.

NATIONAL ADVISORY COMMISSION ON HIGHER EDUCATION FOR POLICE OFFICERS. *Proceedings of the National Symposium on Higher Education for Police Officers.* Washington, D.C.: Police Foundation, 1979.

National Treasury Employees Union v. *VonRaab*, 109 S.Ct. 1384 (1989).

O'CONNOR, MARTIN. *Brief Notes Regarding the ADA.* Yapank, N.Y.: Suffolk County Police Department, 1991.

REISS, ALBERT J., JR. *Private Employment of Public Police.* Washington, D.C.: National Institute of Justice, 1988.

ROBINSON, JOHN P., ROBERT ANTHANASIOU, and KENDRA B. HEAD. *Measures of Occupational Attitudes and Occupational Characteristics.* Ann Arbor, Mich.: Institute for Social Research, 1969, pp. 276–280.

Santos v. *Port Authority of New York and New Jersey*, No. 94 Civ. 8427 (1995).

SCHACHTER, HINDY LAUER. "Job Related Examinations for Police: Two Developments." *Journal of Police Science and Administration* (March 1979), pp. 86–89.

SIMONSEN, CLIFFORD E. *Private Security in America.* Upper Saddle River, N.J.: Prentice Hall, 1998.

Skinner v. *Railway Labor Executives Association* 109 S.Ct. 1402 (1989).

Spades v. *City of Walnut Ridge*, 166 F. 3d 897 (6th Cir., 1999).

STAHL, O. GLEN, and RICHARD A. STAUFENBERGER, eds. *Police Personnel Administration.* Washington, D.C.: Police Foundation, 1974.

STANDFEST, STEVEN R. "The Police Supervisors and Stress." *Law Enforcement Bulletin,* 65, no. 5 (May 1996), pp. 7–10.

Sutton and Hinton v. *United Airlines*, 527 U.S. 471 (1999).

SWANSON, CHERYL G., and CHARLES D. HALE. "A Question of Height Revisited: Assaults on Police." *Journal of Police Science and Administration* (June 1975), pp. 183–188.

TERRITO, LEONARD, and JAMES D. SEWELL, eds. *Stress Management in Law Enforcement.* Durham, N.C.: Carolina Academic Press, 1999.

TERRITO, LEONARD, C.R. SWANSON JR., and NEIL C. CHAMELIN. *The Police Personnel Selection Process.* Indianapolis: Bobbs-Merrill, 1977.

THIBAULT, EDWARD A. "The Blue Milieu: Police as a Vocational Subculture." *New Perspective: Issues in Policing* (1992), pp. 53–74.

THOMANN, THOMAS, and TINA M. SERRITELLA. "Preventing Sexual Harrassment in Law Enforcement Agencies." *Police Chief* (September 1994), pp. 31–38.

United States of America v. *State of New York et al.*, 77 C.V. 343 (1979).

United Steel Workers v. *Weber*, 443 U.S. 193 (1979).

Vila, Bryan. *Tired Cops.* Washington, D.C.: Police Executive Research Forum, 2000.

Ward's Cove Packing Co. v. *Atonio*, 49 FEP 1520 (1989).

WALKER, SAMUEL. *The Police in America* (3rd ed.). New York: McGraw-Hill, 1999.

WEBSTER, BARBARA, and JERROLD BROWN. *Mandatory and Random Drug Testing in the Honolulu Police Department.* Washington, D.C.: National Institute of Justice, October 1989.

WEBSTER, STEPHANIE. "The Future of ADA Litigation." *Police Chief,* 53, no. 2 (February 1996), pp. 12–14.

WEINER, NIEL ALAN, MARGARET A. ZAHN, and RITA J. SAGI. *Violence: Patterns, Causes, Public Policy.* Orlando: Harcourt Brace Jovanovich, 1990.

WEINER, NORMAN L. *The Role of the Police in Urban Society: Conflicts and Consequences.* Indianapolis: Bobbs-Merrill, 1976.

WHISENAND, PAUL M., and GEORGE E. RUSH. *Supervising Police Personnel* (4th ed.). Upper Saddle River, N.J.: Prentice Hall, 2001.

Williams v. *City of Charlotte, North Carolina*, 899 F. Supp. 1484 (1995).

Wright v. *Universal Maritime Service Corp.*, 119 S.Ct. 391 (1998).

13

TRAINING POLICIES

KEY TERMS

blood-borne pathogen
civil liability
diversity
domestic violence
field training
field training officer (FTO)
hate crime

phase approach
planning
Project STAR
stalking
virtual reality
weapons of mass destruction
  (WMD)

HISTORICAL PERSPECTIVES

Modern police training has come a long way since the early days when a police officer might have been told the following (Sullivan, 1971: 250) as part of his training by veteran police officers:

- When you hit a suspect, hit him hard.
- When you tell someone something, tell him only once because once is enough.
- Do not trust anyone—not even your wife.

Herbert Jenkins, an Atlanta, Georgia, police chief, described the full range of training when he entered the force in Atlanta (1970: 1):

> When I joined the Atlanta Police Department in the early thirties I was issued a badge, a revolver, blackjack, and Sam Browne belt, and sent out on patrol with a senior police officer. After one week of "training" I was a full fledged policeman on my own.

As late as 1952, Charles Reith, the well-known writer on police history, was able to comment, "Ignorance of police duties is no handicap to a successful

career as a policeman" (1975: 106–107). He went on to point out "in their handling of criminals and armed gangsters, ignorance and a lack of training and
understanding are defined as being the causes of the frequency of police dis-
comfiture." Although this was true of most departments in that era, based on
personal visits to American police departments from 1915 to 1917, Raymond
B. Fosdick related some outstanding examples of police training schools of that
day (1969: 298–99):

> Probably the most ambitious police school at the present time is in Berkeley,
> California. Here the class, which meets one hour a day, takes three years to com-
> plete the courses included in the curriculum. The New York school involves two
> months of full-time instruction; in Chicago, Philadelphia, St. Louis, Detroit and
> Newark, the training period is four weeks; in Cleveland it is three. In Cincinnati
> and Louisville only part of the day is devoted to school work, the remainder being
> spent in the performance of regular duty.

The Berkeley police school had an extensive curriculum, including the
following subjects over a three-year period: physics, chemistry, biology, physiology, anatomy, anthropology, criminal psychology, psychiatry, theoretical
and applied criminology, police organization and administration, police practice
and procedure, microbiology, microanalysis, public health, first aid, and elementary and criminal law. Interestingly, during this same period, in Milwaukee,
police officers went to in-service training one night a week, all year long
(Fosdick, 1969: 299).

In 1970, one of the most extensive surveys on police training was published. It is still the best information available today. It entailed a nationwide
survey in which letters were sent to 360 agencies; 60 usable replies were received. Excluding Boston, which included extensive patrol operations in its
1,600 hours of training with 1,015 hours of its curriculum devoted to patrol and
traffic training, the Chicago Police Department, with 1,085 hours of training,
had the longest training period; Kalamazoo, Michigan—at 120 hours—had the
shortest. In other words, the Chicago police recruit spent 27 40-hour weeks in
training, whereas the Kalamazoo recruit spent three weeks (McManus, 1970:
175, 183).

Based on national survey data gathered by the Bureau of Justice
Statistics in 2000, local police recruits were required to complete an average of about 1,600 hours of academy and field training in departments serving 100,000 or more residents. Officers serving populations less than 2,500
were required to complete about 800 hours. In sheriff's departments, new
deputy recruits serving 100,000 or more residents were required to complete an average of 1,400 hours of training. Sheriff's deputies serving populations less than 10,000 fulfilled 780 hours (Bureau of Justice Statistics,
2003).

GENERAL NEED FOR TRAINING

Lack of morale, surges of unnecessary grievances, and such factors as negative relations with citizen groups and ethnic communities all reflect a need for training. Officers who do not know how to handle situations are criticized by police management, the press, and victims. They become the subject of bad publicity for the department and may even be subject to civil suits by citizens. As will be discussed, if an officer deprives a citizen of his or her legal rights and civil liberties just because the officer has not been trained properly, then the citizen may have legal recourse to ask for compensation for this loss.

Poor judgment may not be the police officer's fault. It could be the fault of the department and the law. Two major causes may be the following:

1. Officers who have been on the force for less than a year may not have received any training, including training in the use of a deadly weapon. Most state laws let departments appoint officers and then give them a period of months for the officer to begin his or her training. Meanwhile, untrained and often dangerous personnel are on the streets wearing badges and carrying guns.
2. Some departments provide no more training than the state's minimum requirements. These programs lack trained instructors and modern curricula. The newly trained officer may not know what to do when a hostage situation develops or a domestic crisis looks like it will become violent. Thus, lives are lost because the department felt that training in domestic crisis intervention and hostage negotiation was a "frill."

These may not be the only reasons that an officer fails to respond in an effective and professional manner to stressful situations, but they are reasons that have been cited too often in the past. Many modern police administrators feel that lack of training should never exist because the department's reputation and citizen's lives are at stake. One mistake made by a poorly trained or untrained officer is one mistake too many.

Most states set minimum training standards. However, these standards normally deal with what has been called "nuts and bolts" training, dealing with a "how-to" approach to essential tasks. Such programs might include weapons training, report writing, basic criminal law, minor criminal investigations techniques, including some crime scene control, and so on. Most states also include training for human relations skills.

Common Deficiencies in Current Training Programs

1. *Program content.* Police training curricula may not cover major areas of human relations and communications, such as diversity, internal communication, victim/witness assistance, basic communication with citizens, and adult and juvenile behavior.
2. *Quality control of instructors.* Instructors may be pulled from the field but not know how to teach. Too often, "instructors" are command and supervisory

officers who relate stories about policing just to impress young recruits with their experience. Some modern police academies go to the opposite extreme, bringing in a professor who talks about research on violence in families, for example, without ever relating this research to practical skills. The goal is to strike a balance between the common practice of using police instructors from the field and basing instruction on the findings of academicians. This is an area in which rank should *not* have its privileges. The best instructors are needed, regardless of rank. The chief of police is not necessarily a good instructor. The major question that must be asked for each instructor is this: Can this instructor communicate effectively and serve as a role model for the recruits?

3. *Training facilities.* In the past, training has taken place in basements of jails, gyms, auditoriums, and so on. Most instruction is lecture style. Multimedia and small-group instruction, including role-playing activities, need to be made available for all instruction sessions. Isolated and secure facilities for weapons training and driving instruction, are needed.

4. *Training equipment.* This is closely tied to the upgrading of facilities. Instructional technology and methodology should include the use of trans-parencies, videotapes and DVD programs, PowerPoint equipment, and so on. Demonstrations and hands-on work have to be an integral part of the instruction. Basically, seven hours of lectures over five days equals 35 hours of boredom.

5. *Part-time training instructors and directors.* Training should be provided by full-time instructors, but experts should be brought in part-time from higher education and the field as part of the overall instructional program taught by the full-time staff.

6. *Full-time attendance.* Recruits should attend the academy full-time and have no other job-related duties. Part-time students and part-time work make for tired officers and half-trained students who fall asleep during instruction.

7. *Training before exercising police power.* All recruits should be made employees of their respective police departments as recruits but should not be permit-ted to use full police powers until they have graduated from the academy. This accomplishes two major goals of professional law enforcement: (1) It takes untrained officers off of the street, and (2) recruits do not have to unlearn any bad habits from the street.

8. *Follow-up training.* Training should take place at planned intervals for two years after the recruit has graduated from the academy.

9. *Field training officers.* Specially trained officers who are experienced should be used to evaluate the recruit's work in the field.

10. *Teaching methods.* Beyond driving, weapons, and defensive tactics, most top-ics are taught in the basic lecture format followed by a quiz or multichoice exam. Students memorize the material and, according to one old adage, forget it once the examination is over. Advanced programs have adopted the "student-centered learning" strategy, whereby students are presented with basic knowledge and then are asked to apply the information to oper-ational problems. Assessment is based on how the student identifies and

then solves the problem. The learning process often involves working with other members of the class. For example, in a burglary investigation class, the student would be introduced to the basic legal and investigative concepts. The instructor would then present a crime scene problem and ask the student group how they would address the situation. The group not only has to recall the information related to the burglary class but also other classes, such as criminal law, report writing, and interviewing techniques. The goal is to present the training information in an applied, realistic manner.

LOCATION AND TIMING OF BASIC TRAINING

When we discuss the police academy, we are talking about the three main types of police academies in this country: agency, regional, and college sponsored. Agency schools are generally found in large municipal areas or are established for the state police or highway patrol. They are staffed and operated by individual police departments and offer recruit training as well as a variety of in-service courses. Regional academies handle the training functions for both large and small departments located in a designated geographic area. Finally, there are training academies operated on the premises of postsecondary institutions, particularly community colleges. These college-sponsored academies allow a person to take police training and earn college credit. As will be discussed, the curriculum for an academy must follow a state mandate for police training that is overseen by a training agency. Regardless of training model, police agencies have two basic objectives:

1. Train the recruit in the skills necessary to perform the functions of a police officer
2. Socialize the recruit into the police profession, the insignias of the office—uniform, handgun, nightstick, shield—and what former New York City Police Inspector Arthur Neiderhoffer calls "the web of protocol and ceremony that characterizes any quasi-military hierarchy" (1969: 43)

The traditional model of recruit training consists of an officer being sent to the academy after appointment. Certain states, such as California and Minnesota, allow nonsworn officers to fulfill basic training as a requirement before appointment at their own time and expense. This training allows the candidate to seek employment in a local department for a specific period of time. On appointment, the candidate must then complete field training and probationary requirements related to the department's rules and practices. Not all agencies in these states embrace this model. For example, all recruits for the Los Angeles Police Department must complete that department's academy regardless of past training and experience.

The obvious advantage to the preemployment training model is that the appointing agency saves time and money for basic recruit training. Opponents of this practice, especially those in large departments, argue that the department would rather "train its own" in order to socialize and teach basic skills according to department dictates. They also argue that police training should only be given to people who have undergone a full background check as part of the police hiring process.

Field Training for Police Officers

Field training involves the evaluation of a recruit officer by a trained **field training officer (FTO)** as the new officer performs various patrol functions. The evaluation involves breaking down police tasks into distinct functions and behaviors.

Until the mid-1970s, the concept of field training was unheard of. Officers who graduated from the training academy were "turned loose" by themselves or perhaps were paired to a senior officer for a period of time without any formal evaluation or feedback. Soon departments developed checklists that listed the various duties that an officer should learn after the academy, but this training too was conducted without formal daily evaluation.

Field training programs that use practical problems to train police officers on the streets have been advocated for a number of years. Michael S. McCampbell (1986) surveyed a random sample of 588 police departments throughout the nation concerning their use of field training. He found that 64 percent (183) of the responding departments used field training. Some major advantages of field training were a decrease in the number of civil liability complaints, the standardization of the training process, and better documentation of recruit performance.

San Jose, California, had one of the first field training programs, which was established in 1972. It continues to serve as a model training program for other departments. In San Jose, "the Patrol Division administers the field training program: six-officer teams consisting entirely of FTOs and their sergeants conduct the training. . . . The recruit normally spends four weeks with three different FTO's" (McCampbell, 1986: 4).

There are three phases to the San Jose training program:

Phase I, for weeks 1 through 16, has 14 weeks of a standardized training academy; if the recruit passes, then there are two weeks of in-house classroom training.

Phase II, for weeks 17 through 30, consists of (1) four weeks with one FTO, a district evaluation, then (2) four more weeks with a different FTO on another shift, another district evaluation, (3) four more weeks with another FTO on yet another shift, a district evaluation, and (4) a final two weeks with the FTO that the recruit started with. There are daily observation reports by FTOs and weekly evaluation reports by supervisors. At the end of this stage, the recruit passes on to phase III, is given remedial training, or is dismissed from the force.

Phase III, for weeks 31 through 52, starts with a solo beat outside the training district and biweekly evaluation reports by the supervisors. At the end of 10 months, there is a review board, and if the recruit is certified, he or she returns to the solo beat outside the training district. Then there are monthly evaluations by the supervisor. At the end of this period, the recruit is either certified as a permanent employee or phase III is extended.

Field training can be a valuable experience for both recruit and trainer. FTOs are encouraged to explore various ways of introducing the police recruit to fieldwork instead of waiting for situations to occur. For example, one of the authors used role playing during quiet times to simulate traffic accidents, robberies in progress, and so on. Gradually, recruits took on performing tasks by themselves after being introduced by the FTO to the specific skill. This was done under the dictum that the FTO would step in at any time if he or she felt that things were not going well.

McCampbell (1986: 6–7) presents a series of recommendations that still work for police managers who wish to use field training:

1. Chief executives should view the field training program as a normal part of the recruit selection process.
2. Administrative control of the field training program in larger agencies should be assigned to the patrol function.
3. All training in the field program should occur in a planned, organized sequence and be identified by clearly written policies.
4. Agencies should perform a task analysis for the job of patrol officer and use the analysis as the basis for evaluating recruits.
5. Agencies should use standardized evaluation guidelines to reduce FTO discretion.
6. FTOs should give recruits a written evaluation every day.
7. Each recruit should be assigned to several FTOs.
8. The FTO's role as trainer and patrol officer should be well defined [to avoid conflict between the two roles].
9. Agencies should conduct a job task analysis for the position of FTO.
10. FTOs should receive at least 40 hours of training before they are allowed to assume their duties.
11. Agencies should consider offering extra compensation to ensure that the most qualified personnel are attracted to and retained in the position of FTO.
12. Field training programs should be evaluated at least annually.

These recommendations have been used by Michael Payne (1999) in the *Police Field Training Officer Course*. Because individuals learn in different ways, there should be opportunities for remedial training. If a recruit officer does not achieve agency standards, then the person should be terminated in a process that is fair and consistent. It is obvious that the daily and weekly evaluation reports will be very important if there is a lawsuit contesting the termination.

Field training, if planned carefully, with special emphasis on having the most qualified officers as field training officers, can be an excellent way to train recruits, increase professionalism, and diminish police cynicism.

The Importance of Training to Police Managers

Police training is of paramount importance to both police supervisors and command personnel. Supervisors need to feel confident that their officers know the fundamentals of the job. They also have to be concerned that their officers develop skills in both the technical aspects of patrol operation and defensive tactics and in the area of human relations. On-the-job training of fundamental skills like these becomes dangerous since police are often dealing with people in tense situations.

If there are too many poorly trained individuals, command personnel cannot rely on the officers to carry out their commands because the officers do not know how to carry them out. Without trained personnel, investigations become error prone, paperwork becomes confused, and morale gets lower and lower as the officers become more frustrated with their own inadequacies.

Modern managers realize that training their forces in modern police methods over a long period of time is a capital investment for a department with high morale. It takes years to train a whole force fully, including in-service training. The investment pays off as morale rises and the officers realize that they can handle situations that were formerly unnerving. Confidence breeds confidence.

Now let's examine the model programs that captured the imagination of professional law enforcement managers in the 1970s.

HISTORICAL RECOMMENDATIONS FOR POLICE TRAINING

In 1973, the National Advisory Commission on Criminal Justice Standards and Goals, Task Force on Police, published a volume of policy recommendations titled *Police*. The recommendations reflected the consensus of professional opinion from the more advanced police departments of the day and national agencies concerned with the training of police. This report sparked a great deal of discussion and some change in police training methods, curricula, and basic organization.

Because of its importance to the police professional, we will examine some highlights from its recommendations. *Preparatory training* is emphasized, and a minimum of 400 hours of basic police training is recommended. Besides police subjects, law, psychology, and sociology as related to police-community relations are to be emphasized. Ongoing in-service training is mandated, as is a minimum of four months of field training. In all, this is a rigorous but effective series of recommendations.

The recommended curriculum based on a variety of experiences from Dayton, Ohio; Oakland, California; Seattle, Washington; Chicago, Illinois; and Los Angeles, California is as follows:

Introduction to criminal justice system	8%
Law	10%
Human values and problems	22%
Patrol and investigation procedures	33%
Police proficiency	18%
Administration	9%

Training before promotion as a policy was likely to produce some self-confidence and better efficiency if an officer knew what to do on the job before promotion. It was also felt that middle-management training programs should be integrated with college and business programs (National Advisory Commission, 1973: 399).

In-service training was a significant part of the report, with a recommendation of a minimum of 40 hours per year up to and including captains. This was considered to be a routine, mandated procedure that would be a normal part of every police budget.

Instruction quality control, with certification for specific training subjects, was mandated to ensure that training performance objectives would be met. This included an annual review of instructional materials along with the use of up-to-date audiovisual and computer-assisted instruction.

Police training academies and criminal justice training centers were mandated, with 1978 being the target date for the availability in every state of such training for every police officer in the state. In terms of quality control, there was state certification of the basic police training along with encouragement of the states for interagency cooperation. The authors feel that regional police academies make major contributions to police professionalism and efficiency of training. They

1. Offer benefits from economies of scale. Classes can be large enough to justify expert instructors along with the use of expensive training equipment.
2. Begin the fight against parochialism and localism in law enforcement. By being trained regionally, officers, at the start, would look at the big picture of crime fighting and act in a more professional manner.
3. Encourage the formation of professional relationships and friendships with officers outside of the local department at the start of an officer's career. This leads to more cooperation, especially on a regional basis, which becomes increasingly important as recruits rise in rank and begin to cooperate on fencing rings, white-collar crime, and regional solutions to crime problems.

Other benefits may exist, but these begin to explain why this is a significant approach for management to use in the creation of a training program.

PROJECT STAR

Originally developed by the California Commission on Peace Officer Standards and Training in 1969, **Project STAR** (System and Training Analysis of Requirements for Criminal Justice Participants) eventually involved four states:

California, Michigan, New Jersey, and Texas. Project STAR, in its 1976 report (Smith and others, 1976), relied on a systems approach emphasizing management by objectives and the breaking down of police behaviors into specific roles and tasks.

Project STAR identified 13 roles that were to be filled by 33 tasks. For example, a role would be "building respect for law and the criminal justice system," whereas related tasks might be "deterring crime," "interacting with other agencies," and "participating in community relations and educational programs." Using the standard behavioral objective format, performance objectives for each task may be stated in behavioral terms with a context and criterion of success.

For example, in the role titled "building respect," a performance objective would be (Smith and others 1976: 103) "avoid making unreasonable demands of citizens and other criminal justice personnel in terms of time and scheduling." The problems with these kind of objectives are the undefined terms—for example, *unreasonable*.

What STAR was trying to do, along with much of the educational community of the day, was to state the tasks that needed to be learned in such a way that they would be easily measured in empirical terms and evaluated. Let's review another example from Smith and others (1976: 107):

> Maintain self-control when interacting with citizens or suspects as you carry out your required duties.
>
> Deter violation of the law and criminal activity through your continual interaction with people in the community.
>
> Maintain appropriate order among people as you discharge the responsibilities of your position.

These performance objectives lack the "punch" of the everyday reality of the street.

STAR recommended a sound liberal arts education along with specific skills and knowledge in criminal justice (Smith and others, 1976: xix): "Further, *public* education recommendations were developed in areas such as law, the criminal justice system, human behavior and social relationships." However, STAR did not wish to recommend a specific set of curricula (Smith and others, 1976: xix): "Finally, due to the independent nature of the educational system in the United States, no recommendations were made for specific curricula organization, prerequisites, detailed course outline, credit hours or credentials." Thus, the STAR approach is basically a humanistic, liberal arts, and behavioristic approach.

STAR Recommendations

Project STAR also found that police officers should have courses in the following topics:

Alternatives to arrest
Constitutional law
Criminal law
Criminal justice
Criminal justice system description
Criminal procedures
Economics
Ethics
General law
Human behavior
Journalism
Law
Organization and management
Philosophy (ethics, logic, aesthetics)
Political science
Public administration
Science (physiology, chemistry, narcotics, research methodology, statistics)
Social relationships
Speech
Techniques of crime control

The recommendations in management were organizational theory, setting of goals and objectives, organizational alternatives, planning and scheduling, systems analysis, resource acquisition and allocation, identifying and overcoming constraints, administrative behavior, information and system development, evaluation of achievement, and general description of alternatives and methods for the criminal justice system to organize, set goals and objectives, plan and schedule, analyze requirements, acquire and allocate resources, manage cases and processes, identify and overcome restraints, provide leadership and supervision, develop and use information systems, and evaluate achievement.

While none of these recommendations were fully adopted, STAR did form the basis for curricula in criminal justice higher education and basic police training courses, including field training.

CHANGES IN THE TRAINING CURRICULUM, 1952 TO PRESENT

In 1952, Thomas Frost did a survey of training curricula in 33 police departments of various sizes around the country. This survey was then replicated by Frost with Magnus Seng in 1982 (Frost and Seng, 1984). They discovered that the entry-level training programs had grown from an average of 342 hours in 1952 to an average of 633 hours in 1982. However, much of the content had not changed. The percentage of time devoted to military drill went down but

TABLE 13-1   *Content and Minimum Hourly Requirements—California, 2002*

DOMAIN NUMBER	DOMAIN DESCRIPTION	MINIMUM HOURS
01	History, professionalism, and ethics	8
02	Criminal justice system	4
03	Community relations	12
04	Victimology/crisis interventions	6
05	Introduction to criminal law	6
06	Crimes against property	10
07	Crimes against persons	10
08	General criminal statutes	4
09	Crimes against children	6
10	Sex crimes	6
11	Juvenile law and procedure	6
12	Controlled substances	12
13	ABC law	4
14	Laws of arrest	12
15	Search and seizure	12
16	Presentation of evidence	8
17	Investigative report writing	40
18	Vehicle operations	24
19	Use of force	12
20	Patrol techniques	12
21	Vehicle pullovers	14
22	Crimes in progress	16
23	Handling disputes/crowd control	12
24	Domestic violence	8
25	Unusual occurrences	4
26	Missing persons	4
27	Traffic enforcement	22
28	Traffic accident investigation	12
29	Preliminary investigation	42
30	Custody	4
31	Physical fitness/officer stress	40
32	Person searches, baton, etc.	60
33	First aid and CPR	21
34	Firearms/chemical agents	72
35	Information systems	4
36	Persons with disabilities	6
37	Gang awareness	8
38	Crimes against the justice system	4
39	Weapons violations	4

DOMAIN NUMBER	DOMAIN DESCRIPTION	MINIMUM HOURS
40	Hazardous materials	4
41	Cultural diversity/discrimination	24
Minimum instructional hours		599

The minimum number of hours allocated to testing in the regular basic courses are shown below.

TEST TYPE	HOURS
Scenario tests	40
POST-constructed knowledge tests	25
Total minimum required hours	664

[a]Time required for exercise testing, learning activities, and physical abilities testing is included in instructional time.

Source: California Commission on Peace Officer Standards and Training, 2002.

was replaced by a rise in the time devoted to general physical fitness, while the time devoted to firearms training remained about the same.

As discussed earlier, the average length for a police recruit training program today is 640 hours. Table 13–1 gives an overview of minimum training requirements for California law enforcement officers, as presented by the Commission on Peace Officer Standards and Training (POST). This curriculum lists classes and the number of hours devoted to each topic.

Nationally, most training programs can be divided into the following areas:

Administrative procedures: quizzes, graduation, and instruction on note taking

Administration of justice: history of law enforcement, police organization, probation, parole, and social services

Basic law: constitutional law, offenses, criminal procedure, vehicle and traffic law, juvenile law and procedures, and civil liability

Police procedures: patrol observation; crimes in progress; field notes; intoxication; mental illness; disorderly conduct; domestic violence; police communication; alcoholic beverage control; civil disorder; crowd and riot control; normal duties related to traffic enforcement, including accidents and emergency vehicle operations; criminal investigation, including interviews and interrogations; control of evidence; and various kinds of cases, such as burglary, robbery, injury, sex crime, drugs, organized crime, arson, and gambling

Police proficiency: normal firearm training, arrest techniques, emergency aid, courtroom testimony and demeanor, and bomb threats and bombs

Community relations: psychology for police, cultural diversity, news media relationships, telephone courtesy, identification of community resources, victim/witness services, crime prevention, officer stress awareness, law enforcement family, and police ethics

TOPICAL ISSUES IN TRAINING

Some of the newer topics that have been covered in police training are discussed briefly in this section.

Terrorism and Emergency Management

A result of the events of September 11, 2001, has been recognition of the need for training in terrorism and emergency management. Executives of U.S. law enforcement agencies have found that they must train their command staff and line officers in the following areas:

- Terrorist group identification
- Intelligence gathering and reporting
- Community threat analysis
- Response to incidents involving possible **weapons of mass destruction (WMD)**
- Security of critical facilities
- Legal issues related to counterterrorism
- Document fraud and identification (motor vehicle and immigration)
- Traumatic stress from WMD incidents
- Ethical issues related to post–September 11 policing

Most counterterrorist activities and investigations involve federal intelligence and military agencies, as most terrorist activity is transnational. However, federal law enforcement and the various border control agencies must be able to identify and deter terrorist suspects from entering the country. Additionally, under new and wide-sweeping surveillance and tracking statutes, such as the so-called USA PATRIOT Act (2001), federal law enforcement must identify the sources of economic and operational support. For instance, certain Muslim social and religious organizations are alleged to serve as recruitment and economic fronts for Al Qaeda. State and local law enforcement will be drawn into these investigations, which brings on a whole host of issues, such as agency cooperation, intelligence gathering and sharing, and the use of local informants. Accordingly, many states have passed legislation which mirrors the USA PATRIOT Act in terms of obtaining roving wiretaps and enacting offense categories for crimes involving terrorism, possession or use of chemical or biological weapons, and committing hate crimes. This, of course, raises all kinds of ethical issues, such as racial profiling, related to the use of these new powers.

An important training agenda for state and local law enforcement has been in the areas of identifying targets and analyzing and responding to potential incidents of weapons of mass destruction. These include nuclear, biological, and chemical agents, as well as incendiary and explosive devices, that are weaponized and used to cause massive personnel casualties and property destruction. Responding to incidents of mass destruction has become very important since the attacks of September 11 and the anthrax-related criminal incidents that followed.

In threat assessment, police officers are trained to identify potential terrorist targets and to use enhanced patrol techniques to deter terrorist acts. Potential targets include transportation facilities, chemical installations, and water resource facilities. While all of this may seem like common sense, a detailed step-by-step analysis in one community found that there were potentially explosive chemical tank cars in a railroad yard adjacent to a major police station and that the local university had a nuclear reactor for academic research—and all of this was unknown to city emergency planners! Enhanced patrol for potential targets can range from prohibiting access to certain areas to having patrol units maintaining higher vigilance while performing routine duties. For example, an unmarked work truck parked under a major bridge or a person walking near a water reservoir requires further investigation.

AIDS and Other Blood-Borne Pathogens

Concern regarding AIDS (acquired immunodeficiency syndrome) and hepatitis B brought about safety regulations and training requirements from the Occupational Safety and Health Administration (OSHA) with regard to **blood-borne pathogens** (any microorganism or virus that can cause disease). Because police and other public safety personnel frequently come in contact with blood and other body fluids, the regulations call for agency control plans to limit direct exposure and to administer a vaccine for hepatitis B to affected employees. The regulations also call for training regarding measures one should take to prevent contamination. Stewart (1993) suggests the following training topics:

- Means of human immunodeficiency virus and hepatitis B virus transmission
- Suggested personal prevention practices
- Universal precaution strategies
- Protective equipment
- Specific workplace prevention practices
- Exposure management and treatment procedures

Domestic Violence

One of the many legacies of the O.J. Simpson trial was renewed public policy discussion on **domestic violence**. Traditionally, domestic violence offenses occurred between married people and involved such crimes as assault and harassment. In the vast majority of cases, the victim is a woman. Murder, which frequently occurs in these situations, was usually not mentioned in earlier discussions of domestic violence.

Previously, law enforcement and prosecution offices did not give these situations high priority or serious attention because they occurred behind closed doors, and the role of the wife was considered to be subservient to the husband. An instructor in one of the authors' basic recruit classes in 1973 called these situations "get in and get out calls" because complainants do not press charges the next day even if you make an arrest.

It was not until the early 1980s that this attitude changed. Research on violent crime and murder concluded that many cases were the result of domestic violence. The women's rights movement paid particular attention to the role of women in society and the "battered wife cycle." Presented in various ways, this cycle consists of stages that start with emotional abuse and then end up with serious physical assault. If, despite police intervention, the abuser and the victim make up, in many cases the cycle begins all over again. In response to this, many communities established 24-hour crisis hot lines and safe houses, where women with children can find refuge and obtain counseling. Police training programs include the topic of domestic violence calls as part of their training, especially because of the potential for serious physical injury against responding officers.

In the 1990s, many states changed their laws and arrest policies regarding domestic violence so that an officer could make an arrest for a petty offense without witnessing the act and without the express consent of the victim. In Florida, for example, a law enforcement officer in domestic violence situations may arrest the suspect and does not need to witness the abuse.

This pro-arrest policy is based on the theory that immediate intervention will stem the cycle of violence. Additionally, the definition of *domestic violence* has been expanded by laws and police agency policies to include offenses in which the people involved have an intimate relationship and police intervention is requested (N.Y. State Office for the Prevention of Domestic Violence, 1995).

In addition to reviewing laws and departmental response policies regarding domestic violence, training programs include such topics as protecting yourself against injury, listening skills, preparation of special reports, investigation of domestic violence complaints, procedures for the arrest and detention of offenders, and victim assistance programs.

Stalking

Closely related to domestic violence incidents are **stalking** crimes. These are crimes in which a person willfully, maliciously, and repeatedly follows or harasses another person and makes a credible threat with the intention of placing that person in reasonable fear of death or serious bodily injury. Examples of high-profile cases include the murder of actress Rebecca Shaffer and the shooting of Robert Hoskins by a security guard as he attempted to break into Madonna's house. Stalkers are profiled as individuals who are obsessed with someone or as erotomaniacs who believe that the target is "really in love" with them and who will do anything to get the attention of the victim. The stalking eventually may result in violent assault and murder against the victim if the stalker believes that he or she has been rejected. Stalkers may be former spouses or partners who have been spurned by the victim and arrested for domestic violence crimes or criminal predators who follow people at random and eventually assault and kill them. Police training for stalking situations includes investigatory skills, such as threat assessment and denying access to the victim. Access denial can result from police interviewing the stalker or having the target change daily lifestyle habits (Williams and others, 1996). Some cases may require 24-hour protection coupled with a manhunt to intercept the stalker.

Tactical Operations

This is usually an in-service training course for veteran officers to review basic academy topics such as use of personal weapons, handcuffing techniques, high-risk vehicle stops, and building-entry techniques. The focus here is not only on review, but also on encouraging a partner-team approach in high-risk situations. Courses of this nature include hands-on exercises, low-light situations, and even the use of blank or paint guns for realism.

Diversity

Cultural **diversity** is defined as having empathy toward other cultures and ways of life in order to explain why people feel the way they do. In the late 1980s, instruction in cultural sensitivity (sometimes called *cross-cultural training*) for officers was initiated to improve community relations and to reduce, in part, citizen or community complaints against police officers for unwarranted use of force or arrest powers on underrepresented members of the community. These issues are not new but a continuation of the historical animosity between the police and minority groups in the community. As discussed by Johnson (1992), the police represent the majority culture in a community and are often viewed as the defenders of the status quo or the ruling elites. Ideas, lifestyles, and people outside the mainstream are often viewed by the police with distrust, and vice versa. What happens, as recounted by Weaver (1992: 3), is a "clash between two icebergs," as typified in the following routine situation:

> A Nigerian cab driver runs a red light. An officer pulls him over in the next block, stopping the patrol car at least three car lengths behind the cab. Before the police officer can exit the patrol car, the cabbie gets out of his vehicle and approaches the officer. Talking rapidly in a high-pitched voice and gesturing wildly, the cab driver appears to be out of control, or so the officer believes.
>
> As the officer steps from his car, he yells for the cab driver to stop, but the cabbie continues to walk toward the officer. When he is about two feet away, the officer orders the cabbie to step back and keep his hands to his sides. But the cab

driver continues to babble and advance toward the officer. He does not make eye contact and appears to be talking to the ground.

Finally, the officer commands the cab driver to place his hands on the patrol vehicle and spread his feet. What began as a routine stop for a traffic violation culminates in charges of disorderly conduct and resisting arrest.

According to Weaver (1992: 4), the situation escalates out of control because of a breakdown in nonverbal communication. While most Americans are socialized into staying in their vehicles, the cab driver felt that it was a sign of respect to exit his vehicle and not trouble the officer to leave his patrol car. As the driver approached the officer, the social safe distance between the two decreased, and the driver ignored the "step back" command. The social distance for conversation in Nigeria is much closer than in the United States. In the mind of the officer, the lack of eye contact and the rapid, high-pitched voice denoted a person who was dangerous to the officer.

Training, according to Shusta and others (1995), prepares officers to deal with the various ethnic groups in their communities and with one another in a professional manner. Knowledge of words, gestures, and communication norms can increase communication and also enhance officer safety. It is important to note that this training must be undertaken before and not after an incident occurs. Too often we have seen training used as an intended panacea to address a community relations problem. Most after-the-event classes don't work because officers view them as disciplinary in nature.

Hate Crime

The Bureau of Justice Assistance (1997: ix) gives the broadest definition of "hate crimes or bias motivated crimes as offenses motivated by hatred against a victim based on his or her race, religion, sexual orientation, handicap or national origin." In 1990, Congress passed the Federal Hate Crime Statistics Act, which helped focus law enforcement on **hate crimes**. In October 1998, the *New York Times* (Lyman, 1998: 6) reported that 41 states had hate crime legislation, including penalty enhancement (hate crimes penalties added to criminal felonies, creating longer sentences). Typical hate crime organizations are the Ku Klux Klan, American Nazi Party, Church of Jesus Christ Christian, Aryan Nations, and White Aryan Resistance (Ridgeway, 1995; Potok, 2000). Their major means of communication is the World Wide Web. There are other American and Arab groups.

Bias crime police units have problems sorting out hate crime from free speech and other types of crimes. Three questions asked by the New York Police Department's Bias Incident Investigating Unit might help (Jacobs, 1998: 155–56):

1. Is the victim the only member or one of a few members of the targeted group in the neighborhood?

2. Are the victims and perpetrator from different racial, religious, ethnic, or sexual orientation groups? . . .
3. Were the real intentions of the responsible person motivated in whole or part by bias against the victim's race, religion, ethnicity or sexual orientation or was the motivation based on something other than bias, (e.g.: a childish prank, unrelated vandalism, etc.)?

Today we need hate crime police training, police bias investigation units for larger departments, and prosecutors who understand hate crime legislation and can sort it out from free speech.

Americans with Disabilities Act

As discussed in Chapter 12, the act requires police departments to provide services to people with disabilities. Department policies and training must address ways for officers to deal with the disabled (e.g., a mugging victim who is blind or an arrestee who requires a wheelchair). Training programs should also include responses to routine and emergency calls for services for the disabled. Sometimes, people with disabilities or illnesses are not properly identified right away—for example, a diabetic suffering a seizure may appear to be a disorderly drunk but is actually in need of insulin.

Computer and Video Simulation

In the past five years, computer-aided training has been applied to police training. Borrowing from earlier technologies for airline pilots and driver education, computer and video instruction was developed for firearms training. Through video, students are presented with various street scenarios for which they must decide whether or not to shoot. The instructor can observe and evaluate the proper draw, stance, and shooting technique of each trainee. The computer evaluates whether the plastic round hitting the video screen hit the suspect or an innocent bystander and whether the officer fired within an appropriate time period. What is impressive about this type of learning is the noise and realism.

New Technologies

Through satellite communications, many colleges, universities, and government agencies are able to sponsor teleconferences where participants can hear a presentation and phone in questions and comments. From the experience of the authors, a great deal of preparation is required, and the audience attention span for a teleconference is about two hours. Teleconferencing is ideal for transmitting information to multiple sites, thus reducing the time and cost for travel and lodging. Courses offered through the Internet are a new and different way to provide police training. Right now, the most practical application is in specialized and in-service course.

Specific training for police departments is offered through the Law Enforcement Television Network (LETN), which offers a TV schedule of training programs and police information updates. The monthly cost for service varies by the number of people in the department. The majority of programs are good and geared to police audiences. Because the program content is directed at a national audience, there may be some differences with state and local laws and departmental policies. Departments that use LETN as a major format for in-serve training also use pretest and posttest exams to gauge the effectiveness of the programs.

There is also more specific training available for specialized units, such as special weapons and tactics (SWAT) teams, major felony squads, regional arson investigation teams, and so on. Instruction includes courses in computer security and electronic surveillance as well as emergency vehicle handling, "routine" traffic stops, and crowd control.

Recently, one of the authors entered an amusement arcade and found customers pumping quarters into machines to play a game of shooting bandits in a Dodge City setting. While commonplace today, games like these will soon be outdated with the release of the next generation of games, which will be based on **virtual reality.** Virtual reality is a computer-generated, three-dimensional environment that engulfs the senses of sight, sound, and touch (Hormann, 1995: 8). For police training, the computer creates environments that are viewed by a trainee in a helmet. The trainee is also connected to the computer by a special glove that manipulates objects and deploys weapons. Unlike current computer-generated training, where one faces a screen and reacts, virtual reality allows the person to turn around, open doors, switch transmission gears, and perform other tasks while feeling the "action" as if it were real.

Hormann (1995) points out that virtual reality is a cost-effective and safe training method for such courses as firearms, pursuit driving, and critical incidents. Law enforcement applications at this time are still in the works, and the technology is far from perfect. It is costly to obtain the equipment and software programs, and the helmet apparatus is somewhat bulky. The computer, moreover, cannot generate images faster than the eye, so a reaction called "simulator sickness" can result from trainee disorientation. However, these shortcomings are being addressed through further research and software design.

Computer Crime Investigation

In many basic training programs, a new course being offered to police recruits is computer crime investigation. A course at this level typically reviews the basics of a computer and certain do's and don'ts for handling software and hardware for evidence collection and forensic analysis. A computer can be an instrument for the commission of crime, such as stealing credit card information, destroying data, embezzling money, and stealing software. In like manner, a computer or a computer system can be the target of a criminal attack by a person or group seeking access to databases. Increasingly, police and prosecutorial agencies are now developing special units and investigations training programs for computer crime cases. The laws and search-and-seizure rules were not written for electronic data. Computer evidence can be easily altered and destroyed unknowingly by an unskilled investigator.

The increased popularity of the Internet has also increased criminal activity. One of the new orientation programs for college students is Internet privacy and security. The increased use of financial transactions over the Internet has also increased the number of crimes. These include the purchase of contraband, such as drugs, liquor, weapons, and child pornography. Some users have developed personal relations and sometimes marriages through introductions over the Internet. Not surprisingly, killers and rapists view the Internet as a medium for making contact with potential victims via chat groups.

THE PHASE APPROACH TO TRAINING*

With the exception of basic recruit training programs, much of law enforcement training is haphazard at best. This is not to say that specific courses, seminars, or workshops lack quality. Indeed, most are very good. The problem is lack of goals, objectives, and coordination for the overall training program. In short, there is not enough planning.

Planning is a basic function of a manager. As the administrator of training, planning is no less important to the training director. Planning answers the questions what, when, where, who, and by whom and allows us to avoid the common mistake of "training for training's sake." During the last decade, the expansion of law enforcement training has been phenomenal. Added to the ever-increasing demands that are placed on police officers are concerns about civil and vicarious liability.

Recognizing these factors, the Greensboro, North Carolina, Police Department began the development of a framework for planning the training program. This led to a concept that was termed the **phase approach** to training. In essence, the department recognized that there are multiple phases in the training and development of police officers, and a standard training program for each of these phases was established. Although developed in the 1980s, this remains a useful approach.

Phase I: Recruit Training

New officers enter the department in trainee status and are given 560 hours of recruit training in the police basic introductory course. On successful completion

*The following discussion presents an advanced model training program from Wood (1980).

of this course, new employees are promoted to sworn status as Police Officer I's. As Police Officer I's, they are assigned to a field training program under the supervision of a police squad leader, who serves as their training coach. When they have successfully completed the field training, the officers receive patrol duty assignments in one of the four field operations divisions.

Phase II: Intermediate Training

On assignment as a patrol officer, a Police Officer I enters the second phase of training and development. During this period of approximately one and a half years, the officer's training will consist primarily of on-the-job training within his or her assigned field division. This is supplemented with quarterly in-service training, consisting of eight-hour sessions based on the training needs of the department. In addition, shorter two-hour sessions are presented monthly during roll-call training sessions.

Phase III: Advanced Training

After two years on the job, an officer is eligible for promotion to Police Officer II. This is accomplished by passing a written competency test consisting of questions concerning knowledge gained by the officer during phases I and II of his or her development.

In phase III, officers continue to receive quarterly in-service and monthly roll-call training. In addition, they receive advanced training through periodic seminars and workshops presented in developmental as well as performance oriented frameworks. The objective is to have as many officers as possible receive this type of training. Accordingly, assignments are made on the basis of seniority and are rotated so that each officer attends one seminar or workshop before a senior officer is assigned to a second one.

Phase IV: Developmental Training

A Police Officer II is eligible to participate in two developmental programs: a career development program and a police squad leader program. Officers participating in the career development program receive a short-term temporary assignment (six to eight months) to one of the investigative or staff divisions. During this assignment, the officer receives approximately 30 days of orientation within his or her selected area, followed by supervised on-the-job training. The officer also attends seminars and workshops related to the specialty area. Both the Builford Technical Institute and the North Carolina Justice Academy offer the desired training in this area at little or no cost to the department.

Officers in the police squad leader program go through an established selection procedure before being promoted. This promotion adds two important dimensions to the officer's responsibilities: He or she periodically serves as training coach for newly assigned officers and, when so designated, acts as the squad supervisor in the absence of the regularly assigned supervisor. These added job dimensions necessitate additional training for the officer, including officer coach training, instructor training, and introduction to supervision.

Participation in the police-squad-leader program is not a prerequisite for promotion to sergeant, and not all officers choose to participate. Many of the officers who do participate choose to withdraw after a period of time to accept assignments in other areas or to participate in the career development program. This is encouraged by both the low pay differential (5 percent) for a police squad leader and the desirability of other assignments. Participation in the program offers the officer an excellent opportunity to develop his or her supervisory skills.

Phase V: Specialist Training

Officers assigned to specialized units, such as criminal investigation, vice/narcotics, youth, traffic, or training, are provided seminars and workshops to develop their expertise in these areas. Primarily, external resources offering the needed training are used for these activities. These resources include the Northwestern University Traffic Institute, Southern Police Institute, FBI National Academy, and others. Refresher or advanced training in these areas may also be provided, depending on the length of the officer's assignment, job performance, new developments in the specialized areas, or other factors. Officers in specialized assignments will also be assigned to quarterly in-service training sessions.

Phase V also encompasses officers who participate as members of special teams, such as a special response team, underwater recovery, or bomb squad. Instructors at the academy also fall within the realm of the specialist training phase and are provided any additional training required for this function.

Phase VI: Supervisory Training

Officers promoted to sergeant enter into the supervisory training phase. As soon as possible, all newly promoted sergeants are scheduled for a practical supervisors' course. In addition, they attend an in-house supervisory orientation program to familiarize themselves with specific departmental policies, programs, and procedures.

Following one year in a probationary status, sergeants are eligible for assignment to a basic administration course. At present, the department uses two primary sources for this training: the Institute of Government in Chapel Hill, North Carolina, and the North Carolina Governor's Highway Safety Program. Both offer a management-administration course consisting of approximately 200 hours of instruction.

In addition to these programs, we recommend the following model for first-line supervisory training. Police first-line supervisors, meaning sergeants and lieutenants, are usually the first managers to arrive at the scene of critical field situations. The first responders, that is, the officers who first respond to service calls, are normally the department's line officers. Routinely, these first-line supervisors also make decisions on a myriad of issues ranging from employee discipline to civil liability. In many departments, peer pressure becomes an important issue since a promotion means that the new supervisor is now directing the activities of fellow officers whom he or she worked and socialized with previously as an equal. It requires special skills and talents to make this transition from a line officer to a management-oriented supervisor. Unfortunately, in some agencies some police officers wearing stripes are not really functioning as supervisors. The paper-and-pencil tests used for promotion in most departments cannot predict command presence or the attainment of communication and decision-making skills under stress.

A first-line supervisory training course must provide the knowledge and skills needed by the supervisor to function effectively, efficiently, and professionally. The course needs to provide a framework to assist the new supervisor in developing strategies aimed at dealing with the supervisor's critical role in the department's operation. The model proposed is a two-week or four-week intensive program. Departments may vary in their requirements and demand a more extensive course of study.

This is seen as an intensive residential program in which the student prepares for each class with out-of-class readings and other homework assignments. The students live and work together and, in addition to daytime classes, have additional evening classes. This training should be given before the officer assumes the duties of a supervisor as part of a one-year civil service probationary period before certification as a supervisor. If the officer fails the training program, he or she will return to line officer status.

A Model First-Line Manager's (Supervisor's) Course.[*]   The following program covers the major things a first-line supervisor needs to know and provides an opportunity for supervisors to practice skills and be critiqued in this new role. The major portion of the program is presented in the classroom with daily quizzes and weekly comprehensive examinations. Students are expected to attend all classes, maintain an academic average of 70 or better for the daily quizzes, and achieve a score of 80 or better on the two comprehensive examinations.

The director of the program welcomes each student during an opening ceremony and informs them that they are supervising a mythical squad of line officers. Throughout the program, the students complete the following in-basket exercises with this mythical squad: (1) conducting briefings, (2) issuing

---

[*]This model supervisory curriculum is adapted from the revised supervisor's curriculum being used in New York State.

orders, (3) planning events, (4) attending to routine administrative matters, and (5) dealing with a variety of personnel problems. The squad exists only on paper; however, it will be as realistic as possible, consisting of a number of police officers who will be described in vivid detail. Assignments will be linked to daily class topics, and the results will be graded on a pass/fail basis. All "fails" have to be repeated until the student passes.

1. *Registration and overview of the program.* This consists of a review of the academic requirements of the program and an introduction to the details of the mythical squad.

2. *Role of supervisor and leadership skills.* This course presents the role of the supervisor in the formal and informal organization. Leadership concepts and styles are defined. Important concepts covered are delegation, command presence, span of control, and formal and informal organization.

3. *Wellness program (every morning).* These morning physical exercises include running, aerobics, and team sports, along with physical examinations and counseling for any personal health problems.

4. *Supervisor communications and media relations.* The purpose of this part of the course is for the student to recognize effective communication channels. Methods for clearing obstacles from existing written and oral channels are discussed. The program uses role playing to demonstrate the effective flow of the communication's grid and then goes on to deal with specific problems related to the print and electronic media, general communications, and the use of computer-assisted communications.

5. *Civil liability.* This part of the course reviews major national and state tort law cases, with an emphasis on the liability of supervisors who fail to supervise or train subordinates properly. Liability issues related to legally high-risk police operations, such as high-speed car chases and the use of deadly physical force, are also reviewed. Included are a review of defenses with regard to negligence, failure to perform, and the purview of indemnification under prevailing public officers' law.

6. *Evaluation, counseling, and discipline.* This part of the course is composed of the following components: (1) review of existing collective bargaining contracts and departmental policies, (2) review of evaluation methods for employees by supervisors, (3) progressive discipline based on departmental policies, (4) state common law, (5) techniques for dealing with problem employees, (6) conducting successful counseling sessions, (7) the role of the supervisor in documenting employee problems, and (8) preparation for administrative hearings. Preclass readings consist of collective bargaining agreements, along with departmental policies relating to discipline and grievances.

7. *Intermediate law.* This portion of the course of study reviews the rights of individuals in relation to (1) victim/witness rights, (2) employee rights, and (3) juvenile rights. The rights of the accused are analyzed through the case study method, along with a review of changes in the penal law, criminal procedure law, and search-and-seizure issues.

8. *Crime prevention and community relations.* The student is expected to develop specific crime-prevention and citizen-cooperation programs. Techniques for improving good cooperation from citizens in all areas are discussed.

9. *Stress management.* Major stressors are identified for supervisors and subordinates. Stress-reduction techniques are practiced.

10. *Incident and critical-incident management.* As frontline administrators, supervisors in their capacity as lieutenants and sergeants must immediately take command of crime scenes. Other incidents, such as demonstrations and parade details, need to be planned. The differences between an *incident* (a parade) and a *critical incident* (a homicide) are discussed, including the issue of the prioritization of incidents.

    In dealing with critical incidents like the use of deadly physical force, physical injury/death, hostage negotiations, and environmental safety accidents, emphasis is placed on protecting the crime scene and protecting personnel. Patrol operations related to the supervision of crimes in progress and sensitive crimes like sexual assault and child abuse are also reviewed.

11. *Personnel issues.* This section of the course develops an awareness and ability to deal effectively with a wide range of employee issues and problems, including sexual harassment, substance abuse, burnout, and prejudice.

12. *Use of deadly physical force.* The first part of this training deals with legal issues, while the second portion presents defense tactics, such as the proper techniques for handcuffing, takedowns, use of the baton, and use of mace.

13. *Report review.* Students are taught how to review reports of crime incidents, legal papers, and summonses. They are also taught corrective techniques.

14. *Supervisor as trainer.* Supervisors train recruits and veteran officers. The focus of this portion of the course is to have the supervisor identify training needs for his or her subordinates through observing firsthand, reviewing reports, and identifying the need for remediation.

Only first-rate instructors drawn from the field and from higher education institutions should be used. Each instructor needs to use a variety of classroom techniques that go beyond the normal lecture and discussion (e.g., role playing). Handheld VCR camcorders provide an opportunity for immediate feedback for many of the exercises in the course of study. Many state police and regional academies have introduced computerized work-board simulations where a miniature town is created and supervisors deploy resources as conditions change.

Phase VII: Management Training

Promotion to lieutenant marks the next phase of an officer's development. At this level, the officer functions primarily in a management capacity, and newly promoted lieutenants are scheduled for training in this area. Their initial training consists of either a three-month police administration course at the University of Louisville Southern Police Institute or the three-month traffic police administration training program offered by Northwestern University

Traffic Institute. After attaining the rank of captain, one is eligible to apply to the FBI National Academy for continued management training.

In addition to these major programs, officers who are lieutenants, captains, or majors may participate in a variety of seminars, workshops, and retraining conferences to stay abreast of changes and new developments in the field of law enforcement.

Using this framework allows the department to anticipate the bulk of its training needs and plan accordingly, yet there is flexibility. Specific programs in any phase can be changed to meet the changing needs of the department. Entire phases can be deleted or others added. The concept is not intended as a rigid structure to be religiously followed; instead, it is a tool to be used in the planning process.

We are aware that police executive courses are needed. Despite the fact that law enforcement is an expensive business in terms of the impact that equipment and personnel costs have on the community, few police command officers have had the benefit and experience of executive police training. Police command officers are personnel in policymaking positions, such as chiefs, deputy chiefs, majors, captains, and directors of public safety. It is difficult to come to closure on the necessary training needed for a good police executive. Certain chiefs would even say that executives have the benefit of both experience as well as graduate education in administration, criminal justice, business, and law.

A number of courses are offered throughout the country on a departmental or regional basis. The National Academy sponsored by the Federal Bureau of Investigation offers advanced-level courses to police executives at Quantico, Virginia. Such topics as public administration, budgeting, forensic management, and critical incident management are covered. To qualify for this course of study, a candidate must apply to the FBI and be sponsored by the employing police agency. This is also a self-selected program, where either the student or his agency must assume the travel and living costs. It is the closest program to the police-college model that exists in many European countries and that offers required programs to command officials. Many departments use attendance at this program as a means of selecting future executives. Smaller departments sponsor the chief or assistant chief as a way to obtain formal management education.

Not all police executives have the opportunity to attend the National Academy. What, then, is the prerequisite formal training one needs in order to be a proactive police executive?

The police executive course, offered by the Southwestern Law Enforcement Institute at the University of Texas, Dallas, offers the following topics for police executives:

> Introduction to public administration, with an emphasis on organizational theory
> Statistics for public policy analysis

An introductory course in the use of computers

Communication skills, with an emphasis on public speaking and organizational writing

Research methods, with an emphasis on those common to police policy analysis

Command-level courses in critical incident management, with an emphasis on planning

An introductory course in accounting and budgeting, followed by an elective in public budgeting

History of American policing through a review of the great books on policing, major police figures, and social trends affecting police administration

Human resource management, including crucial personnel topics like exercising discipline procedures and stress management

Civil law, with an emphasis on liability

Summary

The phase approach to training provides a number of benefits to the department. First, it helps to ensure that officers have the skills and knowledge to perform at each level of their development in the department. Second, the concept ensures that the officers continue career development on a timely basis. Third, officers know what they can expect from the department in the area of training and development. This can be very beneficial to officers' morale. Fourth, it provides for a fair and equitable system in which every officer receives approximately the same level of training. In addition to being a positive morale factor, this is also beneficial in administering the department's affirmative action plan. Fifth, the phase approach to training aids in the coordination and planning of the department's overall training program and helps to avoid many of the common pitfalls in administering the program.

CIVIL LIABILITY AND TRAINING

In the early 1980s, federal courts established that municipalities can be held liable for a police officer's negligence and intentional wrongdoing. During the Reconstruction period of the Civil War, Congress provided citizen access to the federal courts when their constitutional rights under the Thirteenth and Fourteenth Amendments had been infringed on. Before this change, the Sovereign Immunity doctrine stated that governments could not be sued. This was the first step in chipping away at this legal doctrine. Over time, state and local governments became civil defendants when citizens sought monetary awards and injunctive or declaratory relief based on allegations of unconstitutional acts.

These torts defined civil wrongs that resulted in lawsuits by the party being harmed. Currently, a majority of torts against state officials are filed under 42 Section 1983 of the United States Code (USC), which forbids any deprivation of constitutional rights by public officials acting in their official capacity or "under color of state law." In cases involving federal officials, these actions are begun under the Bill of Rights and are known as *Biven's actions* (Silver, 1993).

The landmark decision was a 1978 case involving a requirement for pregnant employees to take unpaid leaves of absence before medically necessary. In *Monell v. Department of Social Services* (1978), the Supreme Court ruled that governments could be sued directly when the government is held responsible for constitutional violations inflicted under the auspices of official policy in violation of Section 1983 USC. Local governments were also held liable for the attorney's fees of a successful complainant. Federal and state courts have ruled that municipalities are liable for action by employees and their supervisors who are directly involved in such incidents. The interpretation of what is official policy has ranged from written standards of a police department all the way to a series of unwritten practices over time.

Training has become an important legal issue in tort actions involving negligence and nonfeasance. Legally, training is an affirmative duty of police administrators. **Civil liability** exists in the failure to train a police officer or in training a police officer in a negligent fashion. In tort actions directly or indirectly related to training, questions will be asked that focus on state minimum standards regarding training and the scope of duties performed by the trained or untrained employee. Certification of instructors and even lesson plans used in training have become legal issues. The following are a few examples of the complex tort issues that have been raised:

Sager v. *City of Woodland Park* (1982). This is an example that is often used in police training liability discussions. A film used in a police academy training session in Colorado showed how not to do something in a felony stop. A police officer who had been to this training academy, while attempting to handcuff a suspect, shot and killed the suspect. The burden of responsibility shifted from the municipality to the regional police academy conducting the training.

Oklahoma City v. *Tuttle* (1985). A single incident of police misconduct did not, in and of itself, prove a policy of inadequate police training or supervision in holding a municipality liable. Where the policy itself is not unconstitutional, there is a need for more proof than a single incident to establish requisite fault and the causal connection between "policy" and constitutional deprivation.

Tennessee v. *Garner* (1985). The U.S. Supreme Court held that the use of deadly force to prevent the escape of a fleeing, unarmed burglary suspect constituted an unreasonable seizure in violation of the Fourth Amendment. Review was conducted of departmental operational training policies related to the use of deadly force in these situations.

Voutour v. *Vitale* (1985). The police department was found liable for a wrongful shooting involving procedures that were supposed to be taught at a six-week training program. A 30-minute training film at roll call was substituted for the regular training.

Kibbe v. *City of Springfield* (1985). Reviewing the actions of officers involved in a high-speed chase that resulted in the death of the fleeing suspect, the Court of Appeals for the First Circuit found that the police officers involved were inadequately trained and that departmental policies on high-speed pursuits and alternatives to pursuits contributed to the death of the suspect. During the course of this event, there were three separate shooting incidents involving 10 officers. A kidnapping victim was also present in the suspect vehicle during the pursuit. The city of Springfield argued that civil rights liability litigation was not appropriate litigation for the actions of the officers. The Supreme Court dismissed the case as being improvidently granted.

City of Canton v. *Harris* (1989). In this landmark decision, the Supreme Court ruled that a failure to train might create municipal liability when there is deliberate indifference to the rights of citizens. In this case, a woman under police custody fell down several times and was incoherent. She could not respond when asked if she needed medical assistance. The police department had a policy whereby the shift supervisor could decide when to summon medical assistance. In this case, medical assistance was not summoned. She was later released and taken to a hospital by her family. After a year or so of hospitalization, the woman sued under Section 1983 USC, and a federal district court awarded monetary damages against the city since the actions taken by the supervisor were "shocking" and training in medical emergency procedures was lacking. The Court of Appeals upheld the decision of the district court but remanded the case for a new trial based on legal questions regarding jury instruction by the court judge.

The case was heard by the Supreme Court, which remanded the case for a new trial based on new standards that were defined in its ruling. The Court ruled that a municipality may be held liable under Section 1983 when constitutional violations result from the failure to train its employees and when such "failure to train" results in a deliberate indifference on the part of the municipality to protecting the constitutional rights of its inhabitants. The concept of deliberate indifference was defined by the Court to mean that the municipality's failure-to-train policy results in intentional recklessness or gross negligence in protecting the constitutional rights of citizens. The municipality, moreover, must have notice of a training deficiency in either of two ways. First, notice may be implied where failure to train officers or employees is very likely to result in a violation of constitutional rights and that the need for training is obvious. The most common example is when a municipality issues firearms to its police officers but fails to train them on the proper use of force. The second example of notice is when a municipality is formally notified of regularly occurring situations that threaten the constitutional rights of citizens and of inadequate training or remediation to deal with the situation. A case in point might be not addressing recurring civil rights violations at the city lockup over a period of time after a series of complaints.

As first stated in *Tuttle*, one single incident does not constitute a policy (see *Garbriel* v. *City of Plano*, 2000). There must be a series of incidents resulting in direct constitutional injuries to citizens. The policy of deliberate indifference must also deal with constitutional issues. In *Collins* v. *City of Harker Heights*

(1992), the Court ruled that the accidental death of a municipal sewer line worker for "failure to train" by the city was not a constitutional due process issue. In an expanded discussion of due process, the Court found that the lack of training was not a deliberate effort to deprive an employee of his civil rights but rather a state safety matter.

Based on the cases presented since *Harris*, there are a number of factors that departments should consider to address failure to train or deliberate indifference issues. The worst-case scenario would be when the police department does not address citizen complaints that deal with civil rights issues over a period of time. Another scenario would be failing to train supervisors and officers on basic police procedures, department operational guidelines, or issued weapons.

Interestingly enough, failure to train in canine use of force or to monitor the use of dogs has resulted in training-related tort actions. In *Kerr* v. *City of West Palm Beach* (1989), the deliberate-indifference standard was used in a complaint against the department for failure to issue operational guidelines and to conduct training for its canine unit.

These are only a small sample of cases that have raised issues regarding training in tort actions. Proactive police managers need to realize that their police agencies, municipalities, and even individual employees may be sued and that issues in relation to training may very well be raised.

Following is a basic checklist that police managers should use to prevent such tort actions:

1. Do not allow untrained officers to perform any field police duties! An untrained officer is any officer who has not successfully completed basic school and field training.
2. Training academies need to keep accurate records, including (1) lesson plans, (2) attendance of all students, (3) instructor qualifications, (4) test scores, (5) all handout materials given to students, and (6) all films and videos shown to students. In addition, it might be a good idea in skill-related courses, such as the use of the baton, to videotape students to document their proficiency in the skill area.
3. Official departmental policies should be reflected in training. For example, the policy on using deadly physical force should be presented within the context of a course of instruction on deadly physical force.
4. Lesson plans, policies, and instructional techniques need to be reviewed and updated. A saying for instructors that is especially true in tort cases is "Do not laminate your lesson plans, for they will probably become obsolete next year!"

CONCLUSION

In the future, training will continue to play a key role in law enforcement. However, as we have seen, the training will become increasingly sophisticated. Law enforcement is attracting more and more college graduates. Human relations skills, including such topics as stress management, will continue to be emphasized and will become a larger part of the curriculum. At the same time, police training officials will attempt to fill in the technological gap with the use of personal computers, which are now part of the everyday life of many departments. Knowledge of communication has always been a significant need in training and will continue to be so.

One of the key innovations that has affected training around the country has been field training. When carefully planned and staffed with adequately trained and well-selected field training officers, field training combines theory and practice and has a significant impact on new police officers.

Civil liability is becoming an increasingly significant issue for both line officers and police managers. Solid, professional, documented training remains one of the best protections for civil liability.

More training is also needed for police executives as well as supervisory personnel. Major corporations provide hundreds of thousands of dollars for training their major executives, while police agencies are just starting to create training programs in this vital area.

It is hoped that we will also see more in-service training for middle management personnel. Newly promoted officers, especially, need to develop new knowledge along with personnel, management, and administrative skills. A curriculum providing the technological and human relations skills to operate in a modern police department will take commitment on the part of a proactive management. Personnel can anticipate events that they have been trained to recognize as familiar situations. A truly proactive department will synthesize planning and training so that line officers and police supervisors will have a positive, plan-ahead perspective on their respective roles in the police organization.

QUESTIONS FOR REVIEW

1. Why must police training be improved?
2. List four common deficiencies in many current training programs.
3. Why is training of crucial importance to police managers?
4. Outline the main recommendations for training offered by the 1973 task force report.
5. Why does the regional-training concept offer many remedies to small police agencies?
6. What are the major components of Project STAR? What are the strengths and weaknesses of this program?
7. Explain the importance of the following training topics: crisis intervention, first aid, firearms training, ethics, domestic violence, stress management, and terrorism.

CLASS PROJECTS

1. Depending on size, the class is divided into a number of task forces. The instructor asks each task force to review the curriculum of a police academy either in the area or in the state. (If possible, the task force should visit the academy.) Compare and contrast the curriculum in terms of recommendations made by this book, the task force report, or Project STAR.
2. Devise your own training curriculum so that (1) everything that you think is relevant for police work is covered and (2) the course can take place in a maximum of 16 weeks. Compare this training curriculum with a local training curriculum, and explain how your plan differs from the local curriculum.

BIBLIOGRAPHY

BUREAU OF JUSTICE ASSISTANCE. *A Policymaker's Guide to Hate Crimes.* Washington, D.C.: U.S. Department of Justice, 1997.

BUREAU OF JUSTICE STATISTICS. "Law Enforcement Management and Administrative Statistics—Local Police Departments 2000." Washington, DC: United States Department of Justice—Office of Justice Program, January 2003. Web posted at www.ojp.usdoj.gov/bjs/pu. Accessed March 15, 2003.

City of Canton v. Harris, 489 U.S. 378 (1989).

Collins v. City of Harker Heights, 503 U.S. 115 (1992).

DUNNETTE, MARVIN D., and STEPHAN J. MOTOWIDLE. *Police Selection and Career Assessment.* Washington, D.C.: U.S. Government Printing Office, 1976.

Dye v. Wargo, 233 F. 3d 296 (2001).

FOSDICK, RAYMOND B. *American Police Systems.* Montclair, N.J.: Patterson Smith, 1920, reprinted 1969.

FROST, THOMAS M., and MAGNUS J. SENG. "Police Entry Level Curriculum: A Thirty Year Perspective." *Journal of Police Science and Administration,* 12, no. 1 (1984), pp. 251–259.

Gabriel v. City of Plano, 202 F. 3d 741 (2000).

HORMANN, JEFFREY S. "Virtual Reality: The Future of Law Enforcement Training." *FBI Law Enforcement Bulletin,* 64, no. 7 (July 1995), pp. 7–9.

JACOBS, JAMES B. "The Emergence and Implication of American Hate Crime Jurisprudence." In Robert J. Kelly and Jess Meghan, eds., *Hate Crimes.* Carbondale, Ill.: Southern Illinois Press, 1998.

JENKINS, HERBERT. *Keeping the Peace: A Police Chief Looks at His Job.* New York: Harper and Row, 1970.

JOHNSON, ROGER. *Cultural Diversity.* Albany, N.Y.: Human Resources Training, 1992.

Kerr v. City of West Palm Beach, 875 F. 2d 1546 (11 Cir. 1989).

Kibbe v. City of Springfield, 777 F. 2d 801 (1985).

LYMAN, RICK. "Hate Laws Don't Matter Except When They Do." *New York Times,* October 18, 1998, section WK, p. 6.

MATTHEWS, ROBERT A., and LLOYD W. ROWLAND. *How to Recognize and Handle Abnormal People: A Manual for Police Officers* (5th ed.). Arlington, Va.: Mental Health Association, 1978.

McCAMPBELL, MICHAEL S. *Field Training for Police Officers: State of the Art.* Washington, D.C.: National Institute of Justice, 1986.

McMANUS, GEORGE P. *Police Training and Performance Study.* Washington, D.C.: U.S. Government Printing Office/Law Enforcement Assistance Administration, 1970.

"Memorandum on Handling Bias Related Incidents." Albany: Office of University Public Safety, State University of New York, 1988.

Monell v. *Department of Social Services,* 436 U.S. 658 (1978).

NATIONAL ADVISORY COMMISSION ON CRIMINAL JUSTICE STANDARDS AND GOALS. *Police.* Washington, D.C.: U.S. Government Printing Office, 1973.

NEIDERHOFFER, ARTHUR. *Behind the Shield: The Police in Urban Society.* Garden City, N.Y.: Doubleday, 1969.

NEW YORK STATE BUREAU FOR MUNICIPAL POLICE. *A Guide to the Police Officers Basic Training Course.* Albany, N.Y.: Division of Criminal Justice Services, Bureau for Municipal Police, Municipal Police Training Council, 1986.

NEW YORK STATE OFFICE FOR THE PREVENTION OF DOMESTIC VIOLENCE. "Domestic Violence Incident Policy: Model Law Enforcement Policy Language." (July 1995).

Oklahoma City v. *Tuttle,* 105 S.Ct. 2427 (1985).

PAYNE, MICHAEL. *Police Field Training Officer Course.* Albany: Division of Criminal Justice Services, Office of Public Safety, 1999.

POTOK, MARK, ed. *The Southern Poverty Law Center's Intelligence Report.* No. 97 (winter 2000).

REITH, CHARLES. *The Blind Eye of History.* Montclair, N.J.: Patterson Smith, 1952, reprinted 1975.

RIDGEWAY, JAMES. *Blood in the Face* (2nd ed.). New York: Thundermouth Press, 1995.

SHUSTA, ROBERT M., ET AL. *Multicultural Law Enforcement: Strategies for Peacekeeping in a Diverse Society.* Upper Saddle River, N.J.: Prentice Hall, 1995.

Sager v. *City of Woodland Park,* 543 F. Supp. 282 (1982).

SILVER, ISIDORE. *Police Civil Liability.* New York: Matthew Bender, 1993.

SMITH, CHARLES P., DONALD E. PEHLKE, and CHARLES D. WELLER. *Project STAR: Police Officer Role Training Program.* Cincinnati: Anderson, 1976.

STEWART, JERRY D. "Bloodborne Diseases: Developing a Training Curriculum." *FBI Law Enforcement Bulletin,* 62, no. 5 (May 1993), pp. 11–15.

SULLIVAN, JOHN L. *Introduction to Police Science.* New York: McGraw-Hill, 1971.

Tennessee v. *Garner,* 105 S.Ct. 1694 (1985).

VanZANDT, CLINTON R. "Stalkers: Their Threat to Our Nation's College Campuses." Paper presented to the International Association of Campus Law Enforcement Administrators, Charleston, S.C., 1996.

Voutour v. *Vitale,* 761 F. 2d 812 (1985).

WEAVER, GARY. "Cultural Diversity." *FBI Law Enforcement Bulletin,* 61, no. 9 (1992), pp. 1–7.

WILLIAMS, WILLIE L., JOHN LANE, and MICHAEL A. ZONA. "Stalking: Successful Intervention Strategies." *Police Chief,* 53, no. 2 (1996), pp. 24–26.

WOOD, DANIEL E. "Phase Approach to Training." *FBI Law Enforcement Bulletin,* 49, no. 5 (May 1980), pp. 13–15.

14

PROACTIVE PLANNING: OPERATIONAL AND FISCAL

KEY TERMS

budget
centralization
Compstat
contingency plan
decentralization
emergency mobilization
evaluation
extrapolation
forecast
forfeiture
infrastructure
instrumental planning

intuitive approach
line-item budgeting
macroforecasting
networking
normative planning
operational planning
patrol allocation plan
planned program budgeting system (PPBS)
planning and evaluation
terrorism
zero-based budgeting (ZBB)

Proactive police management is the result of effective planning. Police management teams need to develop the necessary control to manage future events and to anticipate future action. This control is developed through a planning function that draws on solid, empirical research. Police planners need to develop contingencies based on documented and known facts with conservative extrapolation indexes. **Extrapolation** is the ability to forecast future events based on current trends. The **forecast** is usually stated in terms of probabilities; for example, a 95 percent probability that a burglary will occur in a certain four-block area during the midnight shift. There is also **macroforecasting,** which is the attempt to give probability curves and indexes to large-scale events. One example would be an 80 percent probability that police manpower needs will increase during a major national disaster, therefore demanding an increased manpower budget and certain types of reorganization of the police structure to meet this demand.

PLANNING DEFINED

O.W. Wilson, one of the best-known police administrators to consider planning essential to the police function, gives the following definition of *planning* (1952: 3): "a process of developing a method of procedure or an arrangement of parts intended to facilitate the achievement of a defined objective." Wilson is specific in his view of the planning process in that he is looking at implementing procedures that are aimed at well-defined objectives that are largely operational. This means that planning is not a series of abstract, analytical notions, but rather a blueprint for immediate, practical use.

Hudzik and others, in their overview of personnel planning (1981: 133), reinforce this approach with their three-pronged definition of planning:

> First, there is recognition that planning is future oriented, that it somehow links present actions to future conditions. Second, there is either implicit or explicit mention of a conscious process of gathering information in support of such assertions about cause and effect. And third, there seems to be agreement that planning is action oriented, primarily intended to affect the real world of things rather than simply the world of ideas.

They reinforce this last point by quoting a 1979 report of the National Academy of Public Administration that states that "planning differs from academic analysis, which mainly seeks understanding, in that planning aims toward getting something done." That is what this chapter is all about: the creation of a solid planning base so that there can be a proactive police approach to getting that "something done."

Souryal quotes Yehezkel Dror's succinct definition of planning and then elaborates on it (Souryal, 1977: 280): "The process of preparing a set of decisions for action in the future directed at achieving goals by optimal means." This is an activity-oriented definition with the emphasis on using efficient methods of achieving the goals sought. Planning is seen as a continuing activity concerned with a set of interdependent parts, where a number of alternate choices are developed in relation to future events. Besides the concept of optimization of means to achieve goals, another major contribution of this approach is the concept of developing alternate means of reaching the desired goals. Too often, police planning units tend to look for a single answer to a problem when the good management choice is to decide among an equal number of viable alternative means and be able to switch from one choice to another, depending on events. Here, *flexibility* is a key word, but an organized flexibility with clearly spelled out parameters in terms of real choices.

Another major distinction is that between normative and instrumental planning. **Instrumental planning** occurs when choices are created in terms of the means of obtaining goals that have been stated and given. Normally, the goals, under instrumental planning, are not questioned. **Normative planning** occurs when the goals to be chosen are considered part of the planning process. Thus, planning, under normative planning, is clearly linked to public policy analysis and the creation and implementation of public police policy. Police agencies have no problem, in most cases, with the setting of certain public policy in relation to organizational goals. However, some managers consider this type of broad police-policy goal setting as part of the political process, and many feel that this should be left in the hands of local legislators and political executives. However, if a police manager is to deal with future events and have an understanding and feel for controlling these events, normative planning must be part of his or her particular management style. A forward-planning chief police executive must be able to develop policy alternatives and not feel locked into given policy goals and a constricted set of policy alternatives.

THE SIGNIFICANCE OF PLANNING

People talk about intuitive knowledge and hunches and often use such knowledge to achieve results. In some cases, this approach may seem reasonable, especially when decisions have to be made in the absence of essential data. However, if police management is going to operate at optimal efficiency, something more than hunches is necessary. Good police managers wish to operate in an organized and efficient manner and eliminate as many errors as possible. This does not mean that the **intuitive approach** should be eliminated but, rather, that the intuitive approach needs to be channeled and controlled. One of the major thrusts of proactive police management is to have an alert, rational, and efficient organization with the known purpose of controlling unknown variables and creating a reasonable base for future action.

A major objective of planning is to create consistency over time so that day-to-day police operations are uniform. Policies need to be made known to all the officers in the organization, and thus they need to be written and understood easily. Moreover, these policies must be applied in an even-handed manner to police personnel, citizens, and situations.

Police deal every day with many volatile situations, and officers need a secure base from which to operate if they are to reduce their feelings of stress in relation to the organization. Consistent and forward-looking planning accomplishes reduced organizational stress for individual police officers as well as for managers and administrators and lets individuals in the organization know that policies will not change abruptly. A secure organizational base will provide the stability needed to make wise policy decisions and to ensure fairness and equity.

Planning also helps to define organizational roles for all ranks in the police department and the formal relationships between these roles. Since roles are often considered simply a pattern of expected behaviors, this will also reduce police officer and manager stress by creating a stable base of role expectations. It lets individuals in all ranks and positions know, within reason, what is expected of them in their organizational role. Police administrators often need to have the parameters of their jobs defined. This is done through organizational charts and standard operating procedures.

A well-organized planning staff that works closely with management can help administrators and officers understand the limits of each position in the organization. It will also anticipate the need for advanced training and positive two-way communication whenever there is a need to change the parameters of the various roles in the organizational structure. For example, from time to time, training officers take on additional duties in relation to recruitment, especially in the area of affirmative action. Traditional departments without a planning component simply write an order and assign the additional duties to the head of the training sections. A proactive, planning-oriented department calls the officers in to discuss the additional duties with members of the management team. A plan of action is formulated with the planning unit, and any additional training that is needed begins before the officers have to take on the additional duties.

ACCREDITATION FOR LAW ENFORCEMENT AGENCIES

The International Association of Chiefs of Police, the National Organization of Black Law Enforcement Executives, the National Sheriff's Association, and the Police Executive Research Forum formed the Commission on Accreditation for Law Enforcement Agencies (CALEA). The commission set up 84 management guidelines that each member agency would have to address. These guidelines, which became known in law enforcement circles as *standards*, were divided into the following: (1) responsibilities and relationships, (2) organization and administration, (3) personnel structure, (4) personnel process, (5) law enforcement operations, (6) operations support, (7) traffic operations, (8) prisoner- and court-related activities, and (9) auxiliary and technical services, such as communications, evidence, and property management. For example, one standard related to administration calls for written directives that require the formulation, annual updating, and distribution to all personnel of written goals and objectives for the agency and for each organizational component within the agency (Commission, 1984: 1). Another example would be directive 33.3.2, on training instruction: "A written directive governs the tenure of instructors in all agency-operated training programs" (Commission, 1984: 33).

This has become a controversial program in which the commission uses these standards to evaluate a police agency. The evaluation itself comes at a considerable expense for the department and has to be budgeted for. To meet the standards, there may be additional expenses, and the local elected officials may not wish to spend money on upgrading the police agency. Although the standards are an excellent idea and go into enough detail to be operationalized, not all the standards apply to all departments, especially the smaller police agencies. However, given the increasing concern with civil liability for both individual officers and departments, the meeting of professional standards promulgated by respected professional associations may become more common in the future. The question of standards is often raised in civil suits.

The purposes of accreditation, according to CALEA, are to

1. Increase a department's capabilities to control crime
2. Enhance effectiveness and efficiency of services
3. Improve cooperation with citizens and with other agencies in the criminal justice system
4. Increase citizen and employee confidence in goals, objectives, policies, and practices

The accreditation process follows a similar program used by colleges, universities, and professional groups for regional and professional accreditation, which consists of (1) application and review of materials, (2) agency self-study to meet all standards, (3) site visit by accreditation team to review self-study and to interview officers and community representatives, (4) response by agency to team review, (5) final discussion on points of dispute, and (6) awarding or denial of accreditation. As Behan (1989) points out, the standards are not prescriptive; agency personnel must decide how to deal with such issues as personnel selection, training, and arrest procedures. Adopting state and national practices, however, is not a one-time deal. Within a period of five years, the agency must seek reaccreditation and go through a similar review process. Thus, the agency is responsible for maintaining both accreditation and its operating standards.

An endeavor of this nature involves much time and work, especially in the review of agency practices during the self-assessment period. Some may ask, "Why bother?" Proponents point out that accreditation is an important management tool. It allows the department to formally measure its strengths and weaknesses according to national norms with the goal of self-improvement. Accreditation also carries prestige for department members and the community. It is also reasoned that liability costs can be controlled since all high-risk activities will have operating and training guidelines. Further, it provides an opportunity to modernize certain equipment (provided budget support is available) as well as procedures and practices.

Not everyone is convinced that accreditation is all that it purports to be. It is very expensive and time consuming in terms of staff and department involvement. According to Oettmeier (1993), reports, policies, and directives have to be reviewed and rewritten. This can result in the paper-tiger syndrome, in which the process becomes more important than anything else. Further, the objectives of accreditation may not immediately result in the stated purposes for accreditation. In other words, an accredited department may not be that effective and efficient in controlling crime or in increasing cooperation with other agencies.

Successful agencies, moreover, may not need accreditation since they are being proactive in addressing problems. What is lacking in the accreditation movement, Oettmeier feels, is the attention to the quality of services and other questions, such as employee satisfaction and creativity. More importantly, critics suggest that CALEA and other groups involved in accreditation should explore changes that can be employed in such areas as police training and practices.

CALEA does not hold a monopoly on accreditation. Because of the costs and an argument that CALEA standards cannot apply to all the states and to small departments (10 sworn employees or less), certain states, such as New York, Colorado, and Washington, have begun their own accreditation programs. In New York, the number of standards for the state's accreditation program have been reduced to 400 to comply with existing statutes, statewide practices, and collective bargaining agreements. According to McCarty (1993), New York State provides technical assistance to departments interested in developing policies related to standards.

In summary, accreditation, whether national or state, is a useful managerial process for departments that want to measure their operations according to a set of professional standards. It is probably a necessary tool for departments that are attempting to deal with poor personnel practices, negative community relations, corruption problems, and administrative ineptitude.

THE NEED FOR A PLANNING OFFICER OR A PLANNING UNIT

Whether there is a planning officer or a separate planning unit naturally depends on the size of the department. Whatever the case, every department, regardless of its size, needs a specific location in the organizational chart in which planning activities are carried out. For the sake of brevity, we will speak of the planning unit with the realization that in smaller departments this planning unit will most likely consist of a single officer who does the bulk of the planning and research work of the department.

Basically, the planning unit provides staff services to the proactive police management team in five vital areas:

1. Dissemination of information
2. Preparation of orders
3. Long-range planning of departmental procedures
4. Development of legal and statistical information
5. Provision of specific and general assistance in the decision-making process

These services are performed in terms of the three basic functions of planning and research in any police department:

1. *Records and reports:* maintain statistical records, rules, and regulations of the department; design, formulate, modify, and, when necessary, eliminate departmental forms

2. *Data and fiscal analysis:* assist in budget preparation both internally and for presentation to external funding sources, such as political executives and legislatures; provide trend analysis of crime statistics for both managerial planning and the line officer's daily needs; prepare annual reports; and so on

3. *Legal:* interpret recent court decisions for use by staff and line officers; assist in departmental hearings, provide information and database needed for future criminal justice legislation, provide copies of new laws that affect operations, and prepare explanations and analysis of new laws using ordinary English rather than legal jargon; provide explanations of new technical legal jargon that affects planning and operational activity

With the exception of keeping some records and reporting data to the Uniform Crime Reporting Program, many of these needs are not met in many medium-sized and smaller departments. However, they are vital to both the short-range and long-range health of any police organization. Positive, effective management includes an information machine that digests enormous amounts of data into summarized and analyzed forms. The planning unit provides such uniform and timely information for the proactive management team.

STEPS IN THE PLANNING PROCESS

As in the development of any process, certain factors or conditions need to be determined to follow through logically to a successful conclusion. In the planning process, the following steps have been identified:

1. *Recognize and analyze the problem, specifying the need for a plan.* This is one of the most difficult steps in the planning process. There is a need to make sure that the problem really exists and is one that is relevant to the police organization. Is this a problem that is unique and simply needs to be dealt with on an ad hoc basis, or will there be a continuing need to deal with this problem in terms of future organizational activity? Planning resources should be targeted toward problems that are relevant and significant to the police organization.

   Ultimately, the problem needs to be defined so that it can be resolved through the use of empirical data. General questions of ethics or metaphysical notions cannot be resolved by planning units. Also, the problem needs to be stated in such a way that it can be resolved with the tools and resources that the planning unit has available. Specifics are also needed in terms of the resolution of problems and the creation of specific plans. For example, rather than an increase or decrease in crime rate in general as a problem, planning units should specify a narrower scope—for example, the decrease in burglaries in a specific area of the police jurisdiction.

2. *Formulate a detailed set of objectives.* This goal-setting activity should be formulated in specific empirical terms—that is, be stated so that the data gathered are either directly or potentially verifiable through the five senses: seeing, hearing, feeling (touch), smelling, or tasting. A context for the

verification has to be identified—that is, a laboratory procedure, gathering of statistical data, interviews, and so on. Also, a standard of goal attainment needs to be stated. Rather than simply a reduction in property crime, it would be better to state that there should be a 5 percent reduction in robberies in certain geographic locations within a specified time period. Internally, planning could propose a 10 percent reduction in personnel grievances against middle management. However stated, the goals, or behavioral objectives, must be (1) specific; (2) obtainable, that is, possible; (3) empirical; and (4) related to general goals of the police organization.

3. *Gather data.* Literally anything can be called *data:* gunshots and noises, gossip, scientific experiments, even people crossing the street. The major test of the data gatherer is that of considering what is significant (relevant) in relation to the problem to be solved. If you use too fine a net to gather data, your time is wasted, and your files are filled with irrelevancies. If the mesh of your data-gathering net is too large, then significant facts may slip through and be lost to the investigation.

   Data gathering is not simply looking at random events and choosing facts with little or no judgment. There is a need for a crude but effective cost-benefit flowchart at this stage of the problem-solving planning process. For some data, cost is literally not a factor. In the solution of homicides, for example, both the police and the public are willing to sustain high costs. Data are collected that might be considered irrelevent in less important cases, on the off chance that something might be there that would lead to solving the crime. In a highly publicized multiple murder, for example, the data net is fine indeed, and costs are generally not even considered.

   Increased availability of computer-generated information has stressed a need for personnel trained in analysis and the ability to make sound judgments concerning relevance. A major problem in current practices is not the lack of data but rather existence of too much information. The secret of success is the ability to have enough analytic skills to use the significant data you have to solve the planning problem while discarding or, better yet, not gathering the irrelevant data.

4. *Plan the attack.* This is where highly organized analytic skills come into focus. Technical data, for example, need to be digested, interpreted, and refashioned in such a manner that they become useful to planners and management. This might include the reorganization of statistical and evaluative data in clear English. Thus, conclusions can be drawn that can be used to organize and identify the plan of attack.

   The plan of attack needs to be specific enough that it makes sense to both line officers and supervisors. Orders have to be drawn and definite action commitments have to be made in terms of specific timetables. Definite procedural orders are needed so that line personnel will know what they have to do to implement the attack plan.

CASE STUDY

Orders Implementing Emergency Management Planning by Administrative Assistant to Chief

1.10 General Duties

Assistant, who reports directly to the chief of police, will be responsible for the planning and co-ordination of emergency management planning for this jurisdiction. As commanding officer of the Administrative Staff Unit, the administrative assistant will address the following areas related to emergency planning:

1.20 Research and Planning

1. Research and study recommendations for the coordination of the activities of all units of the department related to an emergency.
2. Review department rules, orders, and procedures and recommend amendments thereto as required.
3. Provide ongoing research on major emergency situations, major events and situations involving terrorism.

1.30 Personnel

1. Provide statistical data concerning staffing as required.

1.40 Training

1. Coordinate recruit and in-service training with Police Academy and other training or academic programs related to emergency management situations.
2. Conduct roll-call training within the department as needed regarding emergency situations.
3. Conduct practice sessions for members on a periodic basis related to emergency situations.

1.50 Data Gathering

1. Review activities and services of organizations that may assist the department in fulfilling its obligation of service to the community.

1.70 Records and Orders

1. Maintain an order system of communication within the department for dealing with emergency situations which would include contact of command personnel and call-up of off-duty and reserve personnel.

This example was taken from a planning study of a police department of around 35 sworn personnel. The plan was designed to develop a unit that would take care of administrative detail and provide planning continuity for the police chief. The unit could have consisted of anywhere from one to three people. The chief would decide which ones would be civilians and which ones would be uniformed.

5. *Get the agreement of those involved in the plan (obtain concurrences).* In the military, *obtaining concurrences* means obtaining the agreement of those who are to be involved with the operationalization of the plan. In some cases, it would be valuable to obtain specific input from line officers. The obtaining of concurrences is an attempt to have the officers and agencies involved agree at an early stage on the details of how the plan is going to be carried out. If this is done, positive cooperation is more likely to occur. The reason for this positive feeling is that officers who are consulted concerning the implementation of plans will feel that they are part of the team and have something personal at stake in the success of the plan. In addition, involved officers are less likely to place obstacles in the way of implementing the plan.

   A further practical reason for obtaining concurrence is the need to receive input from those who are most familiar with the fieldwork necessary to operationalize a plan. Without such input, necessary details may be missed. Concurrence should also mean that those carrying out the plan will have a better understanding of the need of the plan and its success. They will be able to anticipate problems and obstacles to implementation because of prior consultation. Involvement of this kind, in basic management decisions, normally increases morale among all levels of personnel.

6. *Evaluate.* Needless to say, unless the plan is actually made operational and there is a means of evaluating its success, much time and effort will have been wasted. Unfortunately, many good plans fail to reach the operational stage for a variety of reasons (e.g., administrative change, change of priorities, lack of budgetary support, internal conflict).

TYPES OF PLANS

Planning, doing, and controlling are three phases of the management process. Total planning helps to ensure success of both the doing and the controlling. It is essential that planning be well thought out. In that regard, we have divided our discussion into long-range administrative/management plans, fiscal plans, and short-range operational/tactical plans.

Long-Range Administrative/Management Plans

These are plans that concern the basic structure of the police organization. They are the responsibility of the jurisdictional officials who created the agency and of the department head who is charged with its daily operation. It is at this level that the policies governing the departmental activities are formulated.

Policy is defined as a "may do" activity as opposed to lower-level procedures, which usually are detailed and presented as "must do" activities. Special emphasis is placed on interfacing and overlapping areas of authority. Following are central issues to be considered in formulating these types of long-range plans:

1. *Decentralization versus centralization.* One of the most difficult tasks facing the long-range planner is resolving the issue of **decentralization** versus **centralization**—that is, determining at what level in the organizational structure the administrator is willing to allow subordinates to make decisions. This fundamental management decision focuses on how much control there should be for central management versus how much for line supervisors. Although this planning problem has often been considered in terms of internal organizational concerns, there is a wider arena in which this problem should be considered. The major question is, How much does either organizational mode speed up the optimal delivery of services to the citizen? Another is, How much change in terms of authority roles can be sustained by personnel in the organization while keeping morale high? Larger police organizations tend to shift their emphasis in terms of centralized authority in a number of ways and rather sharply in terms of time needed for organizational change. So much time may be spent centralizing or decentralizing authority that the major missions of the police organizations are lost in the organizational shuffle. Although these types of plans should be examined quite carefully and implemented rather infrequently, there are times when these types of plans need to be implemented. The management team should not hesitate to bring about needed organizational change when it is justified in terms of operational efficiency and the goals of the organization.

2. *Changes in basic organization.* This can include the centralization-versus-decentralization issue but is much broader in concept. It could mean, for example, a shift in where the major investigations take place: in the detective division or among a team of field police officers. This includes a basic change in the authority relationships and functions of the different units of the police organization. A hard look at current organizational practices is taken in conjunction with the planning unit. Developing authority relationships are examined in the light of the need for an efficient department. Optimization of general administrative and managerial practices in conjunction with effective leadership styles is also examined. The question to be asked is, Do these relationships optimize the effective administration of the police organization, or is there a more effective mode of organization that should be implemented?

3. *Long-range personnel deployment.* This includes hiring, firing, grievance procedures, fringe-benefits negotiation and implementation, along with effective use and maintenance of the tools of the trade, such as vehicles, armaments, mobile communications, and so on. In a service organization like law enforcement, where up to 90 percent of the budget may be

devoted to personnel and the servicing of personnel, effective planning in this area may have a serious impact on the police organization. Budgets have to be related to the optimizing of individual morale and efficiency, and this has to be related to the overall operations.

4. *Training needs and requirements.* In the budget-cutting process that police budgets experience at the hands of legislators, training is often considered a luxury. Politicians often fail to see the relationship between effective training and effective operations in the field. When training monies are cut and a plan is being implemented, there may not be enough of a budget to train personnel in implementing the plan. Personnel might need new skills, a possible change in attitudes and perceptions, and new knowledge in order to facilitate the implementation of certain plans. When personnel are not able to acquire these effective tools for planning implementation, then plans fail, not because the plan was bad, but because the training budget was cut. Without the implementation of the training function as part of the overall planning process, management may need to implement training in the middle of a plan and with less than adequate training personnel. What happens in such a situation is that the plan limps along at higher cost and with lower morale. The training plan should be implemented prior to and concurrent with the general plan of attack. Police managers have to educate legislators to the notion that effective training is essential to solid management planning. Training is not a luxury but is essential to every budget. Training needs to be written in as essential to any change in organizational structure and in the implementation of new plans.

Fiscal Plans

Fiscal planning, which should be a continuous departmental activity, requires that the department be able to project a number of fiscal futures, pick one of these futures, add on the normal contingency plans, and live within this **budget.** If this is not done, the department will not have resources when it needs them, and politicians and legislatures will end up specifying the needs of the department. Every department develops an annual budget to deal with its specific needs. What is needed is long-range fiscal planning that projects beyond the immediate needs of the annual budget. Solid fiscal planning is always a part of long-range planning.

The fiscal plan is normally prepared from one to three years in advance and often becomes one of the few bridges between old and new police administrations. Although these budgets may be modified and changed within limits by new administrations, most new administrations live with the old budgets until they can prepare a new budget with their own priorities. Good fiscal planning can help to improve police operations and delivery of services to the community in a more effective manner.

Most administrators lack training in fiscal planning. The normal approach of police administrators who lack budgetary skills or access to personnel who do have these skills is simply to add 10 percent to the old budget when they submit their new line budget and hope for the best. When these administrators run out of fiscal resources, they depend on crisis management to deal with the situation, often approaching the local government for more money. This type of approach is no longer feasible in an era of fiscal constraint. Police administrators have to either become more sophisticated about the budget process or be able to hire the experts needed. Of course, the top administrators must be able to understand the fiscal experts that they hire, or they will not understand their own budgets.

Types of Budgets.   Most budgets can be broken down into three types:

1. Line-item budget
2. Planned program budgeting system (PPBS)
3. Zero-based budget (ZBB)

Most other types of budgets that are referred to in public management and police management texts are variations on these three approaches.

The approaches to budgeting under these systems include the following (Lewis, 1978: 229):

1. Open-end budgeting
2. Fixed-ceiling budgeting
3. Work measurement or unit costing
4. Increase-decrease analysis
5. Priority listings
6. Item-by-item control

In an *open-end budget*, the manager submitting the budget attempts to justify the fiscal request in terms of services performed with few or no guidelines. In a *fixed-ceiling budget*, an executive or legislative body gives the police agency a dollar amount that it will fund and then tells the police management team to create a budget and justify it in terms of the given dollar ceiling. *Work measurement* or *unit costing* is more sophisticated and is often used with PPBS or ZBB, where each service performed by a police department is given a dollar value in terms of the cost of that service and then is justified for budgetary purposes.

In *increase-decrease analysis*, the funding body or executive in control asks for justifications in the police budget only where there is an increase or decrease in a budget request compared with the prior year's requests. In *priority listing*, the police management team lists budget items in order from most important to least important. This is especially useful to a local legislature that is interested in cutting the police budget. Finally, in *item-by-item control*, often called *line-item control*, the executive or funding body exercises control in terms of approval of specific fiscal decisions concerning certain line items in the budget during the fiscal year. The funding body actually exercises a veto over certain police management decisions concerning the spending of funds during the fiscal year. This last approach makes it difficult to exercise management control over the fiscal policies of a police department. It should be done only in times of fiscal emergencies or fiscal chaos.

Whatever approach is used for the budgeting process, every police manager must observe certain principles:

1. The focus should be on future as well as on present problems.
2. Budgeting should be considered as one aspect of the overall planning process.
3. Budgets should be created in terms of an overall philosophy of law enforcement, thereby enabling management to set general goals for the law enforcement agency.
4. Specific, attainable, and measurable objectives need to be set if the overall goals are to be met.

Keeping these principles in mind makes it easier to take a look at the different kind of budgets; many different approaches and types of budgets will fulfill these principles, but some types and approaches will work better than others.

Line-Item Budgeting. **Line-item budgeting** is the most widely used approach because (1) it is simplest to construct, and (2) it is easily understandable by people who lack fiscal expertise and training. The line-item budget simply makes a list of all personnel in terms of rank and salary. This personnel list normally makes up 85 to 90 percent of the budget. Equipment, including such items as desks, laboratory equipment, and so on, are listed with their costs. Next, fixed charges—heat, light, gas for buildings, gasoline for vehicles, pensions and other fringe benefits—are listed with their costs. Most of these items are normally given as totals under these or similar categories. A sample line-item budget is shown in Table 14–1.

The line-item budget is normally passed from police administrator to police administrator and fiscal year to fiscal year with additional costs and requests simply added to the appropriate category. Some administrators may simply increase the requests by 10 percent over the last fiscal year when creating a new budget. Thus, this type of incremental budget often

> Lacks details of the specific costs of each operation
> Does not relate costs to general goals and specific objectives
> Lacks fiscal justification

As a result, this is one of the hardest budgets to defend before a legislative body that wants to cut costs. It is also one of the easiest budgets to cut. Because of the broad categories involved, legislative bodies and fiscally hard-pressed executives may simply tell the police manager to cut the budget by an overall percentage

TABLE 14–1 *Basic School Costs*

		00/01 24 STUDENTS	01/02 30 STUDENTS
.01	Director ($900/week)	$13,500	$14,400
.02	Temporary service for administrative assistance	3,000	3,500
.03	Books/equipment	900	900
.04	Recruit lodging	26,520	25,200
.05	Instructors' lodging	3,600	3,800
.06	Food	15,600	19,000
.07	Physical education uniforms	900	900
.08	Physical education instructor	4,000	4,200
.10	Travel for instructors	3,000	3,800
.14	Bus rental for crime-prevention program	400	
.20	Emergency vehicle operations course	400	
.21	Emergency vehicle operations course equipment	400	350
.22	Defensive driving course training	350	345
.23	Psychological testing	1,500	1,200
.30	Classroom rental	3,250	4,825
.31	Honorariums for nonpolice personnel	800	800
.40	Telephone charges	120	300
.45	Miscellaneous	400	400
.50	Awards		500
.60	Composite class picture		500
	Total	$78,640	$84,920

or to eliminate certain categories. Since these budgets generally do not relate budget items to specific services performed for a community, it makes it difficult to justify the costs. Because of the nature of this budget, it is difficult for a police executive to say whether an increase or decrease in categories of the budget will lead to a *significant* increase or decrease in what the police executive considers a needed police service for the local community. Thus, what a police manager gains in the advantage of the ease of preparation of the line-item budget may be lost when it is cost-cutting time for the local legislature.

Planned Program Budgeting System.   The **planned program budgeting system (PPBS)** is a more difficult budget to formulate because it demands an analysis of the organizational structure of the police agency and the individual units of the agency. In social science, this is a structural-functional approach. The planning unit or officer draws up an organizational chart of the agency showing the authority relationships. This is the structure part. Then the function of each unit is described, much in the same manner as the civil service would describe the services to be performed in a standard job description. This is the function part.

Once you know how the units relate to one another and what function each unit is supposed to perform in the law enforcement organization, it is possible to set specific objectives for each unit in light of the overall goals of the organization. These objectives are created in conjunction with middle management and supervisors in charge of each unit. The objectives are expected to be attainable and measurable, and all have to be justified in practical, empirical terms and related to all fiscal requests. The distribution of personnel and materials is identified with each planning unit or subsystem in the organization, and each unit is related to the structure of the total police organization to create the overall fiscal justification for the services that the police organization performs. This is a planning-oriented budget.

This approach, according to Schick, has produced convergence of three developments in public policy analysis (1978: 59):

1. Economic analysis—macro and micro—has had an increasing part in the shaping of fiscal and budgetary policy.
2. The development of new informational and decisional technologies has enlarged the applicability of objective analysis to policy making.
3. There has been a gradual convergence of planning and budgetary processes.

According to our approach to planning, the planning and fiscal analysis functions of management are brought together. In the 1990s, in an era of fiscal constraint, the two processes will be even more closely related as fiscal matters become more important. The successful police manager of the future will be able to relate budgeting and planning on a daily basis as well as for the purposes of overall planning.

PPBS is basically a performance budgeting system in which management examines how the police organization and its different units perform, or function. Catherine Seckler-Hudson feels that all public agency budgets should conform to a central public policy. She has given us a useful checklist of questions that police managers should be able to answer if they are creating an effective performance-based budget (Seckler-Hudson, 1978: 88):

1. Does the budget have well-defined work programs and activities and a careful definition of their costs?
2. Is there a system of work measurement? Are performance standards used?
3. Does administrative reporting include reporting on a functional basis?
4. Are records kept in terms of functional activities that have been accomplished?
5. Are cost accounting and accrual accounting methods used where applicable?
6. Is there provision for continuous management analysis and improvement, including a system of internal auditing?
7. Are expenditures divided into appropriate major categories?
8. Is the appropriation structure presented in terms of programs and activities to be achieved?

If the answers to all these questions are yes, then the police agency has a modern fiscal management structure that should be able to stand up to the scrutiny of any audit or legislative body. It is also obvious from this list of questions that the budget is not simply an annual affair. With the yes answers, budgeting becomes another planning tool for the management team to use to implement proactive planning and management.

Because budgeting is being justified in terms of the programs in the department that are being undertaken, a justification for each program or service that is performed is a normal part of the budgetary process. Management can take a look at this justification and relate it to the costs incurred and monies asked for. Then management decisions are made based on what management feels the service itself and the quality and level of services that are being performed are worth. This makes the ongoing fiscal management of the law enforcement agency part of the evaluative process that should continually be active in any professionally managed police agency.

The review process needed to create and justify a PPBS budget gives the top police administrators a unique opportunity to examine waste and duplication and thus plan for the optimal utilization of resources. This process also allows the police manager to place responsibility on appropriate supervisors and middle managers. Thus, personnel are held accountable for both fiscal and operational matters. This accountability makes personnel and unit leaders sensitive to the optimum use of scarce resources, thus generating an awareness of what fiscal responsibility means operationally. Requisitions have to be justified and justified even more so if they exceed the original requests developed by the PPBS system.

The process of justifying fiscal items in terms of the service performed to the department and the community makes a PPBS budget harder to cut. There are objectives for each budget item, and these objectives lead to the delivery of needed police services. If a legislator wishes to cut this budget, he or she has to justify his or her budget cut in terms of the acceptance of a lower level of police service to the community.

Zero-Based Budgeting.   The **zero-based budgeting (ZBB)** approach creates and justifies an entirely new budget each year; there is no reliance on precedent and incremental planning from previous years. The object is to force agency planners and administrators to create new justifications for every expenditure, thereby providing a comprehensive fiscal analysis of every unit of the agency in relation to (1) a justification for the very existence of the unit and the services it provides and (2) the relationship between the justification of the services provided and the cost of these services. The originators of this approach helped both to encourage comprehensive planning and to eliminate waste and inefficiency. As Wildavsky and Hammond state (1978: 243)

The major purpose of the zero-based budget was to examine all programs at the same time and from the ground up to discover programs continuing through inertia or design that did not warrant being continued at all or at their present level of expenditure.

Monies saved by this analysis would then be used for programs of a higher priority than the ones defined as redundant or would simply be a means of reducing expenditure for the total budget.

Zero-based budgeting is part of a long tradition of comprehensive fiscal planning that fiscal experts have tried to have public agencies adopt for many decades. In 1940, V.O. Key Jr. defined a *completed budget* (1978: 20): "The completed budgetary document (although the budget-maker may be quite unaware of it) represents a judgment upon how scarce means should be allocated to bring a maximum return in social utility." This point needs to be emphasized when looking at any fiscal process. Because there are never enough resources to meet all demands—and is true of all public agencies, including law enforcement—the basic decision to be made is how to allocate these resources. This allocation, after all the fiscal experts have completed their budgets, may, in the end, be a political decision.

However, ZBB has met full force one of the major points that V.O. Key Jr. made in his classic 1940 article (1978: 20):

> Whether a particular agency is utilizing and plans to utilize its resources with the maximum efficiency is of great importance, but this approach leaves untouched a more fundamental problem. If it is assumed that the agency is operating at maximum efficiency, the question remains whether the function is worth carrying out at all, or whether it should be carried out on a reduced or enlarged scale, with resulting transfers of funds to or from other activities of greater or lesser social utility.

This, in fact, is the basis behind ZBB: Whether a function should be carried out at all is the real question. Also, a standard approach of ZBB is to ask the different units what kinds of services they would provide at different funding levels (e.g., a 90 percent funding level or a 70 percent funding level). This allows policy makers to cut their budgets in a logical manner with a reasonable awareness of the specific consequences of the budget cuts in the delivery of services by various units of the police agency.

Criticisms and Contributions of PPBS and ZBB.   The major contribution of PPBS is that the budget became a management tool of analysis for the overall picture and for an analysis of each unit. On the other hand, ZBB asks a fundamental question of each unit: How do you justify your existence in terms of services performed? It also encourages managers to develop a comprehensive picture of their fiscal process rather than rely on the line-item approach of incremental additions to an already existing budget. Both are excellent tools of analysis, and the kinds of reports that are expected of unit managers make these managers more analytic in justifying their existence in terms of performance. Thus, another major contribution of these approaches is to force police managers and administrators from the lowest supervisor to the police chief or commissioner to think in terms of the utility of services performed. Performance-based budgets mean that unit police managers have to be responsible for justifying the use of scarce resources in terms of the performance of the police personnel under their command. As daily fiscal controls are built into department operations through the increased use of computer technology, it will become absolutely vital that professional police managers become aware of these various budgetary approaches.

The criticisms of PPBS and ZBB are basically the same: Both tend to create unneeded paperwork, and both use too much jargon that is often unrelated to the actual job being done. In other words, the implementation of a jargon-laden abstract system may confuse even competent police supervisors, administrators, and managers.

In addition, the definition of *social utility* and the setting of priorities of police services is, more often than not, a political decision. Consider the saying, "People get the level of service they want." Law enforcement is a public service, and the public should have some say in the overall priorities of its public institutions, including police service. In a well-ordered democracy, this often takes place at the budgetary level in terms of appropriations. A professional police department that is run objectively without political interference reflects the needs and values of the community. Therefore, police managers should have to defend their budgets in terms of the definition of social utility that makes sense for their individual communities. Elected officials need to respond to this definition of social utility in a responsible manner so that (1) there is no political interference with professionally managed law enforcement agencies, (2) adequate funding will provide services in the area of public safety and emergency police services, and (3) the public will have a representative to set priorities in terms of services delivered to the public.

Supplementing the Police Budget.   Throughout the country, police budgets are becoming pinched. This section points out some strategies that police managers may use to supplement their police budget while doing a great deal of good for their departments. The most successful strategies for law enforcement agencies to raise money outside the normal budget have been donation programs and forfeiture. Another strategy, the charging of user fees for police services (e.g., special patrols, copying of accident reports) is the least effective way and creates a great deal of resentment among citizens. However, the Miami Police Department was able to raise $3 million in a two-year period by aggressively charging user fees.

Donation drives often generate free positive publicity for police agencies. A private fund drive in Chicago, for example, raised $1.5 million for equipping the patrol force with body armor, with the result that within a few months, four police officers' lives had been saved by their vests. New York City has its New York City Police Foundation, which regularly raises over $1 million each year to be spent on such items as health screening, scholarships, mounted patrol, automation of records, training, and rewards (Stellwagen and Wylie, 1985). These examples illustrate the two major approaches to this type of fund-raising: special-issue campaigns and ongoing foundations.

If the donation approach is going to work, it must be run and controlled by police managers rather than by professional fund-raisers. Professional fund-raisers are very commercial, often taking a large percentage of the gross (up to 90 percent) for overpriced services; in some cases, they have been indicted and convicted of illegal activity in the area of fund-raising. Donation programs can work, but only when they are controlled by police management and are part of a community effort.

Of great interest to police managers around the nation is the **forfeiture** approach, where goods and monies gained illegally are forfeited to the police department. Departments have seized such items as cars, airplanes, and yachts; one department even obtained a computer. The Atlanta, Georgia, Police Department broke up a 10-county high-tech gambling operation. Through the use of forfeiture, they confiscated the gambler's personal computer and now use it to keep track of radio usage, gasoline consumption, and the hourly activities of the officers.

The most successful forfeiture operations involve drug cases on the coast of Florida, in part because Florida, in 1980, enacted one of the broadest state forfeiture laws in the country. The Florida Contraband Forfeiture Act allows for the forfeiture of any "instrumentality" used in the commission of a felony. Under this system, police departments get to keep everything they confiscate and can hire their own lawyers for the civil proceedings. In addition, local governments cannot reduce the police budget because of forfeiture income. The Fort Lauderdale Police Department in a two-year period seized 20 vessels, $1.4 million in cash, 89 vehicles, and two airplanes, with the total forfeiture amounting to over $3.3 million. In a three-year period, the amount rose to $5.5 million. Even the Delray Beach Police Department, a small department, in one year confiscated a $24,000 Formula boat, $240,000 in cash, a Mercedes-Benz, and a Cadillac.

If forfeiture is going to hurt the criminal element while helping the police department, it has to be planned carefully. First, the chief needs to be familiar with forfeiture laws in his or her jurisdiction. Many laws are needlessly complex, limit the monies that can go to the police department, or place all monies in a general fund. Second, the chief needs to protect the detectives from getting involved in entrapment and/or criminal soliciting. Third, there are costs involved: lawyers, storage, upkeep of property, advertising, and the selling of confiscated items. Finally, drug dealers are becoming more sophisticated and are keeping large loans attached to their property to protect themselves from the forfeiture laws. Forfeiture can work and has worked on the coast of Florida, but once again, good police management means proactive planning.

The imposition of fines, which are much like user fees, may prove useful. Many departments, especially those in rich suburbs, have had to impose fines for false alarms coming from burglar alarms. Responding to false alarms is a waste of police time. In Danbury, Connecticut, a survey revealed that 12 percent of the police service calls were due to burglar alarms, but only 0.01 percent of the alarms were due to any criminal activity. Los Angeles did a survey and found that there was a 97.9 percent false alarm rate in 1983, which cost the department nearly $100,000 in police officers' time (Stellwagen and Wylie, 1985: 60). There is also the fable of the boy who cried "wolf" when there was no wolf. With these many false alarms crying "wolf," police officers may be less than alert when the alarms and the burglars actually get together.

Miami, Florida, has a sliding scale with a yearly fee of $25; if there are no false alarms, subsequent yearly renewals are free. Each user is given five free false alarms, and then the following fee system is imposed (Stellwagen and Wylie, 1985: 60–61):

> $25 for false alarms 6 through 8
>
> $50 and a letter from the alarm service saying that the system works for false alarm 9, with number 10 being free
>
> $100 for false alarm 11, with number 12 being free
>
> $250 and police inspection for false alarm 13, with numbers 14 and 15 being free
>
> $350 for false alarm 16, with numbers 17 through 19 being free
>
> $500 for each subsequent false alarm

Miami collected $270,000 in permit charges and false alarm fees for 1983. The object is to reduce the false alarm rate by making those people who create the unnecessary work pay for it.

Finally, the Internal Revenue Service gives a finder's fee to people who turn in tax evaders. The city of Atlanta found that they were able to turn in tax evaders uncovered during the investigation of racketeers. Atlanta has an arrangement whereby the finder fees are paid to the city through the comptroller for Atlanta.

Short-Range Operational/Tactical Plans

Up to this point, we have been examining planning as a long-range endeavor. Of the types discussed, fiscal planning comes closest to short-range planning in that immediate needs in the fiscal year are normally analyzed in terms of function and performance. However, for long-range planning to work, specific objectives and even orders need to be created to carry out the plan. Long-range plans also need feedback-evaluation systems that can be used to modify the plan as it is operationally carried out.

Operational Plan.   Long-range planning, including fiscal planning, sets the basic principles and the context for short-range **operational planning.** To carry out any planning, specific procedures have to be drawn up and implemented. Operational plans control the day-to-day activity of the police organization in a uniform manner. Specific procedures have to be created to carry out police duties in a predictable manner so that there can be accountability and consistency.

1. *The duty manual.* The major example of an operational plan, although many police chief executives do not recognize it as such, is the standard police duty manual. The duty manual creates standard operating procedures for the department, including job descriptions and authority relationships. Specifics, such as procedures concerning the use of deadly force, may be a combination of law and operational procedures created in a standard order by the police agency. However, the list of operational procedures includes virtually every operation of the police agency (patrol procedure, evidence flow, civil emergencies, lineup procedures, and so on). Although often codified in a duty manual, operational procedures are changed according to condition. Thus, the duty manual is supplemented by both temporary operating procedures (TOPs) and standard operating procedures (SOPs). If these two supplementary procedures are in place, they may become part of the duty manual. However, one problem with this type of procedure is in keeping the SOPs and TOPs to a minimum so that the duty manual is a useful document. Another problem is to have the duty manual be comprehensive enough to cover operations but not so bulky that it loses its utility.

2. *Patrol planning.* Another major example of an operational plan and one that dominates a department is a **patrol allocation plan.** The overwhelming majority of resources in a police agency are devoted to patrol. Table 14–2 shows the general trends that have occurred in patrol planning through a comparison of traditional and recent plans. Items in the traditional categories really require no planning; the chief simply divides the patrol force into three shifts and maps out patrol zones based on the geography of the municipality and some personal rule of thumb. Plans reviewed by Levine and McEwen (1985: 9) involve obtaining activity data. Patrol personnel and vehicles are allocated according to calls for service, which include both service and crime incident responses.

Patrol Staffing Model.   There are a number of patrol planning models that are used in the United States. One developed by the International Association of Chiefs of Police involves measuring calls for service to determine the number of patrol posts and staff needed to fill these posts. This is done according to the following steps (McDougall, 1992: 15):

TABLE 14–2   *Trends in Patrol Planning*

TRADITIONAL	RECENT
Equal staffing on three shifts	Staffing proportional to workload
	Overlapping shifts for extra coverage during peak demand periods
Little emphasis on scheduling	Overlapping and delayed shifts implemented
	Development of models to guide scheduling decisions
Enough patrol units available to provide an immediate mobile response to all calls for service	Enough patrol units available to provide an immediate mobile response to emergency calls for service
	Diverting calls for service to telephone reporting units, queuing calls for delayed response, setting appointments for taking reports, referring calls to other agencies
Time not spent on calls for service largely devoted to unstructured, random patrol (preventive patrol)	Time not spent on calls for service devoted to both routine patrol and directed patrol
	Directed patrol assignments planned in response to problems identified through crime analysis
Minimal analysis of patrol operations	Increased use of data processing for analysis
	Routine monitoring of reports generated for management
	Recognition of the integrated relationship of patrol with other police functions and inclusion of representatives from such functions in decisions that affect patrol

Source: Levine and McEwen (1985: 9).

1. The total calls for service for each tour of duty are obtained for one year (12 months).
2. The 12-month total is multiplied by the average time required to respond to a call for service and to complete the preliminary investigation. This provides the number of hours per year spent in handling calls for service. Previous studies show that the average time required to investigate adequately at the preliminary level by members of a patrol force is 45 minutes (.75 hours).
3. The hours per year in calls for service are multiplied by 3. This is a "buffer" factor to account for the time spent on preventive patrol, inspectional services, vehicle servicing, and personal needs. This gives total patrol hours.
4. The total hours are divided by 2,920, the number of hours necessary to staff one post on one eight-hour shift for one year (8 hours × 365 = 2,920). The quotient equals the minimum number of patrol posts needed for the particular tour of duty.

This model was used to review staffing for a small police department located in upstate New York. The first step was to determine the number of patrol posts, which is outlined in Table 14–3.

TABLE 14–3   *Determining Patrol Posts for a Police Department*

SHIFT HOURS	ACTUAL CALLS FOR SERVICE
7 A.M.–3 P.M.	2,781
3 P.M.–11 P.M.	3,810
11 P.M.–7 A.M.	2,336

Next, these numbers were multiplied by .75 to get the average time expended by officers on a call over the year.

SHIFT HOURS	APPROXIMATE TIME EXPENDED
7 A.M.–3 P.M.	2,085.75
3 P.M.–11 P.M.	2,857.5
11 P.M.–7 A.M.	1,752

These figures are converted to include a buffer and time for routine patrol activity ($\times$ 3).

SHIFT HOURS	PROJECTED TIME EXPENDED
7 A.M.–3 P.M.	6,257.25 hours/year
3 P.M.–11 P.M.	8,572.5 hours/year
11 P.M.–7 A.M.	5,256 hours/year

These numbers are then divided by 2,920, or the total hours needed to fill an eight-hour post for one year ($365 \times 8 = 2,920$).

SHIFT HOURS	POST NEEDED
7 A.M.–3 P.M.	2.14
3 P.M.–11 P.M.	2.93
11 P.M.–7 A.M.	1.80

Source: McDougall (1992: 17).

Once posts have been determined, the next step is to obtain the number of personnel to staff these posts. Because of regular days off, sick days, holidays, personal leave, and other factors, an assignment availability factor must be determined. This is obtained by subtracting the number of "average hours off" from 2,920 hours, which is the total number of hours needed to cover a shift. Table 14–4 calculates the assignment/availability factor for this police department.

The figure of 1,432.56 is the number of hours an officer is away from duty each year. This is subtracted from 2,920 hours to produce an hours-available figure of 1,487.44. An assignment/availability factor is obtained by dividing the hours-available figure of 1,487.44 hours into 2,920 hours, which creates a factor of 1.96, the number of personnel needed to fill each post. Table 14–5 applied this factor to determine staffing for this department, which was found to need 14 people.

The Myth of Rapid Response.   Although response time is part of the planning model, a word of caution must be exercised. Police managers have often felt that if their response was two minutes or less to service calls, this was a

TABLE 14–4   *Determining Assignment/Availability Factor*

Factor	Number of Days × 8	=	Hours Off
Regular days off	104.62	=	836.96
Vacation	27.41	=	219.28
Personal leave	4.95	=	39.60
Sick/injury	15.84	=	126.72
Holidays	12.00	=	96.00
Court time	1.60	=	12.80
Training	11.81	=	94.48
Other	0.84	=	6.72
Total	179.07		1,432.56 average hours off

Hours in Staff-Year		Average Hours Off		Hours Available
2,920	−	1,432.56	=	1,487.44

Total Hours in a Staff-Year		Hours Available		Assignment/Availability Factor
2,920	÷	1,487.44	=	1.96

Source: McDougall (1992: 17).

mark of an efficient department. The opposite may well be true. A two-minute response to every service call may mean that the patrol force is not properly distributed. Response is important to emergencies and crimes in progress. For most other service calls, the two-minute response is normally irrelevant.

There were a number of studies critical of response time in the 1970s (Bercal, 1970; Reiss, 1971; Meyer, 1976; Maxfield, 1979). Less than 20 percent of service calls are related to criminal matters, and emergency calls account for less than 15 percent of all service calls. Even in relation to crime, normally too much time elapses from the time the crime is committed and when police are called. Cohen and McEwen (1984: 4) report that "research [Farmer, 1981;

TABLE 14–5   *Recommended Staffing for a Small Police Department*

Post	7 A.M.–3 P.M.	3 P.M.–11 P.M.	11 P.M.–7 A.M.	Raw Score	Staff Needed
Chief[a]	1.00			1.00	1
Lieutenant[a]		1.00	1.00	2.00	2
Post #1	1.96	1.96	1.96	5.88	6
Post #2	1.96	1.96		3.92	4
Secretary	1.00			1.00	1
				Total =	14

[a]Supervisory ranks and administrative personnel are given a value of 1.00.
Source: McDougall (1992: 18).

Spelman and Brown, 1981] showed that police response time had no effect on the chances of on-scene arrest in 70 to 85 percent of serious crime cases." Are citizens dissatisfied with slower response time? The answer is that citizens are dissatisfied only if they expect rapid response time. However, "if callers were told to expect a delay, their satisfaction did not significantly decrease if response time was slower" (Cohen and McEwen, 1984: 4).

Response time may be helpful for emergencies and a few cases of crimes in progress; overall, departments should be careful not to place too much emphasis on providing rapid response for all service calls. Complaint clerks who take calls for service and dispatchers who dispatch the vehicles need specialized training. This includes training in telephone courtesy, screening, and referrals to other agencies. All agencies need to use a priority classification dispatching system.

The operational plans serve as control mechanisms for management by providing guidelines for employees, both civilian and uniformed. Operational plans give supervisors a means of evaluating personnel in relation to specific duties that are clearly defined and in writing. Evaluation and discipline can take place only in the light of written guidelines that both supervisory personnel and line officers understand. They have to be clearly stated, unambiguous in content, and practical enough to be carried out daily. They also have to have internal consistency and be in line with the long-range goals of the department, including the philosophy of social utility and law enforcement that is demanded by the community in which the police agency is located.

Contingency Plans.   **Contingency plans** are made for specific events and occurrences but are not part of the daily duties of police department personnel. This type of planning demands some specific detail in terms of procedures, but because of changing conditions in the field, it often demands more flexibility than do other types of planning. There are two major types of contingency plans:

1. *Tactical plans*, which are plans for major events, such as crowd control at athletic events and VIP escorts
2. *Emergency plans*, which are plans for general situations with the specifics to be inserted when the emergency occurs. When done in conjunction with other agencies, this type of planning is often termed *planning for emergency mobilization.*

Tactical plans are formulated based on what is expected to take place. A recurrent event is one that is expected to happen again; however, the time and place of the event may not be known. Tactical plans are made for mundane events (parades, political rallies) as well as for natural disasters (blizzards, floods).

Emergencies come and go, and no one can predict when they will strike. However, contingency plans offer a general framework for action. Emergency planning has been considered by some police managers as a type of tactical plan for unusual occurrences and crisis situations.

Emergency Mobilizations and the FEMA Model.   Emergency mobilizations are the response by local, state, and federal authorities to natural disasters, riots, civilian disorders, terrorism, and large events that disrupt the normal flow of commerce and life in a community or region. The police department is one important group that has to be organized as part of an overall plan for mobilization. This generally calls for specific contingency planning under the auspices of a governmental entity or a regional emergency authority, such as a state or county emergency planning commission.

To develop a reasonable plan for emergency and crisis management, departments, in concert with other agencies, should focus on overall planning efforts to four specific crisis or emergency levels:

1. *Crisis intervention:* an emergency situation localized to one person or a small group of people
2. *Community emergency:* an emergency affecting a community involving disruption of services caused by fire, large crowds, criminal event, or weather
3. *Regional emergency:* an emergency that is larger in scope and caused by human or environmental factors
4. *Major emergency:* an emergency that affects a state or an entire region, such as storms, nuclear-related accidents, and civil disturbances

A planning model developed by the Federal Emergency Management Agency (FEMA) calls for the following planning strategy for dealing with these emergencies (FEMA, 2003):

Step 1: Establish a planning team
Form the team
Establish authority from the chief executive
Issue a mission statement
Establish a schedule and budget

Step 2: Analyze capabilities and hazards
Where do you stand right now?

Review internal plans and policies
Meet with all "stakeholders" and agencies: fire, EMS, Haz-mat
Identify codes and regulations
Identify critical services and operations
Identify resources and capabilities

Conduct a hazard analysis

List potential emergencies (both natural and man made)
Estimate probability
Assess the potential human impact
Assess the potential property and business impact

Assess the potential business impact
Assess internal and external resources
Address terrorist situations

Step 3: Develop the plan

Plan components
Executive summary
Emergency management team identification
Emergency response assignments and call-up
Functional annexes for operational responses

The development process
Identify challenges, and prioritize activities
Write the plan
Establish a training schedule
Continue to coordinate with outside organizations
Review, conduct training, and test the plan

Step 4: Implement the plan

Integrate the plan into agency operations, and conduct training
Distribute the plan
Conduct training activities
Evaluate and modify the plan

Further information on emergency response planning can be found on the Internet at http://www.fema.gov or at state Web sites under the heading "emergency management."

Police Response to Special Populations: Networking.   Police have been called for assistance with special populations, such as the public inebriate, the mentally ill, and the homeless. However, these are not police problems but problems that really demand a human services solution. Deinstitutionalization of the mentally ill and alcoholics have left many of these people on the street, often without adequate housing. It makes sense for police to use the human service agency network when it is available. However, **networking** cannot be done at random. Police managers need to do the following (Finn and Sullivan, 1987: 6):

1. Develop a formal agreement to collaborate—preferably a written document that commits each group to the partnership.
2. Describe the specific activities in the agreements that each party in the network will undertake.
3. Sooner or later involve every important agency and facility that provides emergency services to the target population.
4. Make sure that the arrangements benefit every participant.

Los Angeles has created a special relationship with the county department of mental health, while the Boston police work with the Pine Street Inn, which serves 3,000 to 4,000 homeless each year, and San Diego has a seven-minute dropoff for public inebriates at an inebriate reception center. The sheriff in Washtenaw County, Michigan, has developed a two-tier approach to assisting the mentally ill. The executive directors of the sheriff's department, community mental health department, community services agency, county planning department, department of social services, public health department, and the United Way formed a policy team. At the same time, midlevel managers from these agencies formed an operational team to oversee day-to-day operations.

These are just a few examples. Police agency networking can range from just one agency to multiple-agency agreements. The benefits of the approach are many, as shown in Table 14–6.

POLICING TERRORISM: PROACTIVE HOMELAND SECURITY

The object of **terrorism** is to disrupt a community and implant fear in order to advance a political, social, or religious agenda. Terrorists are radical ethnic, religious, or political ideologues. Examples are anarchists, Marxists, racist hate groups, anti-Semitic groups, ethnic and tribal groups, extreme nationalists, ecoterrorists, political extremists, and religious fanatics. In 1789, Robespierre used the terror of public executions by "Madame Guillotine" during the French Revolution to instill terror, and in 2001, Osama bin Laden used bombings to attack the United States for political and religious reasons.

Proactive planning is the best way to contain a terrorist agenda. Proactive police managers plan ahead, anticipate events, and act to prevent terror and crime. This approach calms the local community and lets the world know that the elected and appointed representatives of the citizens are in charge.

Proactive police departments need to deal with terrorism in four specific stages:

1. Preventing terrorist acts through proactive planning, investigation, and the gathering and sharing of local, regional, and national intelligence
2. Handling terrorist act through cooperation with and coordination of local, regional, and national agencies with a proactively planned agenda of activity
3. Dealing with the aftermath of a terrorist act, including the coordination of posttrauma human service, physical reconstruction, and the uplifting of the community in an integrated effort
4. Learning from the terrorist act and working with community groups to prevent another—the essence of the proactive approach

TABLE 14–6   *Benefits of Networking*

For Law Enforcement	For the Social Service System
Saves time by reducing or eliminating the need to Stabilize the situation at the scene "Shop" for an available facility Wait at the facility Book the individual Make repeat runs for the same individual Testify in court	*Save time* by reducing or eliminating the need to Evaluate, treat, or transfer inappropriate referrals
Reduces danger because Trained staff take over volatile situations Social workers warn officers about potentially dangerous cases Officers receive training in handling problem individuals	*Reduces danger* because Officers come quickly to help in situations involving violence in the facility or in a home
Increases job satisfaction because Fewer repeat cases are handled Feedback on case results is provided Positive relationships with social service workers develop Homicides involving problem individuals and jail suicides are reduced Municipal police department working relationships improve with jail officials concerned about overcrowding Dispositions are available that are more appropriate than jail or doing nothing	*Improves job performance* because Clients are referred to facilities that have treated them before Trained officers testify at commitment hearings Agency's image in the community improves Positive relationships develop with law enforcement officers Client contact with criminal justice system is reduced

For Local Government Officials

Increases political support because
Constituents are pleased to see a serious community problem addressed
Businesspeople are pleased to have the downtown made more attractive to customers
Embarrassing incidents are less likely to occur
Prevents political crises and unexpected expenses because
Chances of a lawsuit are reduced
Jail overcrowding is alleviated

Source: Finn and Sullivan (1987: 7).

For American law enforcement, terrorist groups fall into two main categories:

1. *Domestic groups.* The American terrorist groups are small in number but occasionally extremely violent in behavior. The 400-pound bomb that destroyed the Murrah Federal Building in Oklahoma City in 1995 was set

off by members of the Michigan Militia. Domestic militia and hate groups have to be monitored by state and local police agencies.

2. *Overseas political/religious groups.* At the moment, the overseas terrorist groups that affect the United States are mainly anti-American Muslim fundamentalists that have support from the Sudan, Iran, Iraq, and Saudi Arabia. The 1993 and September 11, 2001, bombings of the World Trade Center in New York City are the most dramatic examples of their actions.

Criminal Groups versus Terrorist Groups

Terrorists are members of groups who use planned violence for their own ends. Some terrorist networks work with domestic and cross-national organized crime groups and commit crimes for money, but their objectives are ideological rather than motivated by profit. Cross-national organized crime groups launder money and sell arms and other support items to terrorist groups (Grennan and others, 2000; Lyman and Potter, 2000).

The "Black Hand," was a Sicilian immigrant group that terrorized small businesses in the early twentieth century to extort money. They beat people up, torched businesses, and poured acid on cloth and clothes. In the 1990s, the Dominican Republic C&C gang controlled a whole neighborhood in the Mott Haven section of the Bronx in New York City. The gang extorted money from drug dealers by charging them "rent" (Grennan and others, 2000). Asian gangs have traditionally extorted money from small businesses in Chinatowns throughout the United States. This is all done for money. When Willy Sutton was asked why he robbed banks, he explained that that's where the money is. Extortionist's may use terror to obtain money, but they have no ideological agenda.

In contrast, when the Taliban worked its lucrative heroin business, the money was used to buy arms and to support fundamentalist Muslim terrorist groups in the Central Asian states of the former Soviet Union. When Al Qaeda, Hamas, and Hezbollah looted Muslim charities, the money was funneled to terrorist activities (Wechsler, 2002). In the 1980s, a racist, anti-Semitic hate group called the Order, robbed two armored trucks, netting $1.3 million. They used the money to finance various terrorist activities, burning a synagogue, assaulting homosexuals, and killing a Jewish talk show host, Alan Berg. They were hunted down by the FBI, which employed an informant, among other tactics (Zellner, 1995). The group's leader, Jay Matthews, was killed in a shootout. Most of the other members are now in prison. It took good police work to do this, and it was a police job, not a military effort. The groups that made up the membership of this violent little band reads like a who's who of hate groups in the 1980s: Aryan Nation, Aryan Brotherhood, National Alliance, Ku Klux Klan (KKK), and the Covenant, Sword and Arm of the Lord (CSA).

The same tactics of proactive intelligence gathering and use of informants are used for investigating organized criminal groups and terrorist groups. Up to now, the FBI has been a reactive agency that investigates criminal organizations after a terrorist act or crime has been committed. The FBI has been criticized for refusing to share information with local police agencies. Historically, the FBI has done a fine job of intelligence investigation and prosecution of a few major organized crime figures. The bureau is now targeting new cross-national organized crime and terrorist groups that exist in the United States. The Central Intelligence Agency, set up to coordinate foreign intelligence, has never really cooperated with any police agency in the United States, even when the criminal or terrorist activity was of foreign origin.

Hate Groups and Militias in the United States

Hate groups are intensely biased against specific groups of people based on their race, ethnicity, religion, disability, or sexual orientation. They use violent, bigoted language against these groups and have resorted to criminal violence, which includes destroying property and human lives. Immigrants have historically been a focus of domestic hate groups.

According to Klanwatch, there are 474 known hate groups in America, and they run at least 200 Web sites. An unknown number are engaged in what has been called hate group "leaderless resistance." Floyd Cochran, a spokesman, recruiter, and strategist for Aryan Nation, said in 1993 that there are "500 card-holding members, from Ku Klux Klan, Nazi skin heads, 366 hate web sites, 1,200 jailed members, 40,000 active members among all white supremacy groups and 200,000 people that order literature which supports the Aryan Nation" (Cochran, 1993). The same number of Web sites, 366, was identified in 2000 as being sponsored by KKK, neo-Nazi groups, and racist skinheads, the same mix of hate groups as in 1993 (Levin, 2002). Not much has changed. The Southern Poverty Law Center, which sponsors Klanwatch and Hate Watch, has a Web site that provides a map of the location of hate groups throughout the United States.

Proactive police intelligence units in local, state, and federal police agencies can easily access this information, locate and infiltrate local hate groups, and keep track of them. Police agencies that refuse to do this are simply irresponsible. We can no longer afford to ignore the responsibility of national and local police agencies to share intelligence.

Domestic hate groups are always communicating and organizing. Hate groups also join with militia and survivalist groups. The militia and survivalist groups have hundreds, possibly thousands, of hidden weapons and ammunition. Nobody knows their real membership numbers. The worldwide Internet is a major means of recruiting and advertising hate groups in the United States. Lee and Leets (2002) surveyed adolescents on the effect of hate Web sites and concluded that they were effective in getting their hate message across but that the effect was short-lived. The Boston Police Department has a special hate crime unit enforcing Massachusetts's hate crime laws.

Proactive Policies for Combating Terrorism

1. National authorities must share terrorism intelligence with state and local police agencies whenever there is a local credible threat. The Central Intelligence Agency (CIA) was originally created to coordinate and be a central gathering point for all the federal intelligence agencies. It should do what it was created to do. Homeland security needs the funds and authority to coordinate terrorism intelligence. The focus should be on terrorist attacks on America and on American assests at home and abroad. The FBI and the CIA need to give up their decades-long feuding and coordinate their intelligence on terrorism. The FBI also needs to assist and share intelligence with state and local police.

   State offices of anti-terrorism are currently spending millions to establish, among other needs, a counterterrorism network that will transmit intelligence data from the state and federal level to local police departments. In New York State, for example, computers transmit filtered data—from suspect profiles through bioterrorism threats—to each of the state's 543 police agencies. The objective is to involve local police agencies in preventing future terrorism and create a standardized warning system that will work all the way down to the beat cop. Maryland is currently establishing a statewide emergency response communications system to facilitate early warning and integration of police communications ("NYS Office Takes the Point against Terror," 2002: 11).

2. Local police must be given the authority to deal with foreign-based terrorist threats within their jurisdiction. Police outside of Tallahassee, Florida, stopped a rental truck full of 26 men and women who did not speak English and had no documentation. They called federal immigration officials, but none showed up. The illegal immigrants had to be let go. Florida has proposed that 35 local and state police officers who operate on anti-terrorism teams be given federal training by the U.S. Immigration and Naturalization Service and the authority to arrest illegal immigrants. Business and Hispanic interest groups that wish to protect illegal immigration to the United States are opposing this approach ("Give Us Your Tired," 2002: 1, 14).

3. An office of terrorism intelligence must be created in every major police agency. It should also coordinate the protection of major terrorist targets. Local and state police budgets will have to be part of the federal homeland defense funding and federal training resources.

   There also needs to be intense coordination between public and private police. Private police protect major corporate properties and executive personnel, but they have no powers to arrest. Professional standards created by state law and enforced by state agents have to be in place.

Public police will also have to coordinate with the National Guard and the armed forces in protecting national monuments, bridges, reservoirs, nuclear energy units, airports, tunnels, ports, and power grids. This is already being done in every modern industrial country in the world. With overtime and the need for specially trained units and extra personnel, new funding may be required, such as the home security bond California is proposing. The National Conference of Mayors has estimated that additional security will cost municipalities $2.1 billion in 2002 ("From Coast to Coast," 2002: 11).

4. Proactive police defensive and offensive coordination and plans for terrorist attacks have to be in place, and private and public agencies should be at the same or better level as civil defense in time of war. Much of this civil defense, critical incident, and disaster planning is already in place. Now local and regional police agencies and police coordinating bodies will have to look at these plans in the light of a terrorist attack, from blowing up buildings to bioterrorism. The Federal Emergency Management Agency (FEMA) is the lead agency in times of natural disaster and would normally be the federal agency to help coordinate any crisis. The FBI has a Nuclear Incident Contingency Plan and a Chemical/Biological Contingency Plan. These plans need to be shared with other police agencies. The armed forces, including the Reserves and the National Guard, have had contingency plans since 1998 for dealing with weapons of mass destruction and the subsequent cleanup. Biological, radiological, and chemical defense preparedness has been a priority of the armed forces for many years and can be of great help in civilian and police planning and coordination.

Critical Infrastructure Assessment and Protection

Protection of the community **infrastructure** should be part of the planning agenda for every police department. Critical infrastructure includes bridges, power lines, and electric-generation plants, including nuclear plants. Police responsibility extends to the protection of banking, finance, energy, transportation, vital human services, and physical assets.

Police need to train and communicate with civil defense and other emergency services agencies when planning their reaction to chemical and biological attacks. There is a great reliance on national, regional, and local communications systems and their protection in terms of both physical assets and cyberterrorism. The federal government is preparing to spend $3.9 billion on critical infrastructure protection (Marburger, 2002).

James K. Kallstrom (2002), special adviser to a state governor on counterterrorism, recommends a "prevention, detection, response and recovery" approach when considering a terrorist attack. He is especially concerned with a cyberattack and has set up a cybersecurity task force, which includes experts from federal and state governments, universities, and private corporations and businesses. It is establishing a list of private vendors to call on in case of a cyberattack.

Planners are concerned with "catastrophic loss of life, disruption of essential services and incapacitation/destruction of critical infrastructure." The worst-case scenarios being considered are these:

1. The malfunction of air traffic control equipment
2. The circulation of poisonous gas through the heating and air-conditioning systems of a large office complex
3. Interruption in 911 telephone communications
4. Electrical blackouts
5. The destruction of power dams, causing major flooding and endangering thousands
6. The disruption of financial markets

Local police departments, in cooperation with other government agencies, need to do a survey of critical infrastructure within their jurisdiction and consider whether they have the necessary expertise and resources to protect this infrastructure. Law enforcement departments cannot do everything and be everywhere. Risk assessment, the identifying of crucial assets, and priority planning focus scarce resources on the essentials. The questions to be answered in this police emergency planning process are these:

1. What are the major elements of the infrastructure in the local community?
2. What private and public protection is needed for this infrastructure under various levels of threat?
3. What are the most essential and important targets to the community, and how do we prioritize them?
4. What private and public assets are available to protect this infrastructure, and how do we mobilize these assets?

Proactive planning will allow law enforcement to focus its scarce resources to maximize their efficient use for public protection.

Summary: Police Planning for Terrorism

In some ways, it is business as usual in planning for domestic and cross-national organized crime and drug syndicate investigations. Civil defense and natural preparedness planning should be a normal part of police planning. Hate crime laws and hate groups have caught the attention of proactive police management.

In other ways, after September 11, 2001, proactive policing is an Orwellian "brave new world." Militia and hate group members blow up a federal building and go on killing rampages, killing even children. Muslim terrorist groups blow up major New York City buildings and the Pentagon after learning to fly airplanes and living in America. Money to fund terrorism comes from our "allies" in the Middle East and from "charities," some of which are located in the United States. We worry about our privacy and civil liberties in this brave new world, but we don't want our friends and families killed by these fanatics who come to our towns and cities.

To protect both our civil liberties and our nation from terrorism, we must have calm, careful, proactive police planning, the elimination of interagency rivalries, and further integration of services. Coordination and communication will give the American civilian police forces a way of professionally and democratically protecting our local community from future terrorist acts.

COMPSTAT AS A PROACTIVE PLANNING TOOL: A REENGINEERING, DATA–DRIVEN APPROACH

In Chapter 7, **Compstat** is presented as a management tool for reducing crime. Compstat is also a strong technological innovation because of its "on time" data retrieval of crime statistics, its geographic mapping of neighborhood crime data, its use in operational planning, and the results-oriented evaluation of police supervisors. Vincent Henry, who was the major developer and operational planner for Compstat, discusses in his book, *The Compstat Paradigm* (2002), how this planning took place.

In 1994, Compstat and reengineering were used to turn the New York City Police Department around. Focus groups and a general survey of police officers showed what the officers thought important and what they thought the management thought important. The major revolution was creating goals to match what the officers wanted as goals for the department (Henry, 2002: 201).

Goals Officers Considered Most Important to Management	Goals Officers Considered Most Important to Themselves
1. Write tickets	1. Reduce crime, disorder, and fear
2. Hold down overtime	2. Make gun arrests
3. Stay out of trouble	3. Provide police services to those who request them
4. Respond quickly to radio calls	4. Gain public confidence in police integrity
5. Report police corruption	5. Arrest drug dollars
6. Treat supervisors with deference	6. Correct quality-of-life conditions
7. Reduce crime, disorder, and fear	7. Stay out of trouble

Ten crime-control and quality-of-life strategies were developed over the years. The following revisions apply those strategies to a more general audience (2002: 227–29):

1. *Get guns off the streets.* In New York, this included training and resources to investigate and identify gun traffickers.
2. *Curb youth violence in the schools and on the streets.* Included school safety plans, increased number of youth officers, and having patrol officers return truants to school. Planning data showed a significant relationship between truancy and delinquency.

3. *Drive drug dealers out of the city.* Increased patrol officer involvement in narcotic investigations, with the focus of the department on more midlevel and high-level drug deals and increased forfeiture of drug dealers' assets.
4. *Break the cycle of domestic violence.* Used databases to track violence and to intervene proactively, providing a proarrest policy along with cooperation with social services.
5. *Reclaim public spaces.* A "broken windows" quality-of-life approach, using loitering, public nuisance, and noise ordinances. Sound meters were distributed.
6. *Reduce auto-related crime.* Included sting operations of "chop shops" that dismantled autos, identification of license plates of stolen cars, and increased training and intelligence gathering.
7. *Root out corruption and build integrity.* Included the use of local commanders and took internal affairs out of dealing with petty complaints so that its focus would be on major corruption.
8. *Reclaim the roads of the city.* Established a traffic-control unit to plan and analyze reasons for congestion and incidents and increased the response time of personnel.
9. *Heighten courtesy, professionalism, and respect.* Increased training and set performance goals and measures to evaluate how well the principles were practiced.
10. Bring fugitives to justice. Strengthened patrol officers' capacity to track down court absconders and warrant violators.

These goals would be useful for many police departments. Having the whole department involved in planning for these goals is part of the reengineering approach. In New York, the responsibility, authority, and resources for carrying out these policies were brought down to the supervisor's level, and the supervisors were evaluated using data from the Compstat computer program. Organizational lines were flattened, and the command structure was brought down to the borough level. In departments around the country, this would bring the flattened bureaucratic structure down to a multineighborhood and neighborhood level.

Jack Maple (1999: 246–47) shows how Compstat works operationally once the major planning has taken place:

Operations at every level must be guided by the four steps of Compstat:

- accurate and timely intelligence that is clearly communicated to all
- rapid, concentrated and synchronized deployment
- effective tactics and strategies
- relentless follow-up and assessment.

Performance in relation to the four steps must become the subject of regular crime meetings at four different levels—between the executive corps and the field commanders; between the field commanders and their lieutenants; between lieutenants and sergeants; and most significantly, between sergeants and their officers on roll call.

Henry (2002: 235) also describes the basic process of communication, information, accountability, and result. He says it can be used for organizational diagnosis, which we would consider as a planning tool (2002: 229–30):

> assessing the current state of the police agency and its culture, identifying problems and developing solutions—as a basis for redesigning the agency's structures and policies as well as designing new strategies that support the Compstat paradigm.

As a planning tool, computer mapping combined with the principles of reengineering can redesign police departmental structures and operations. Besides crime data, traffic, housing, and demographic variables can be added to the basic Compstat program and be used for advanced forward city, county, and police planning.

CONCLUSION

Planning is an important tool that enables proactive police managers to anticipate events and, in some sense, respond. A number of definitions were offered regarding planning, which, in essence, consists of developing a method for achieving organizational goals.

As we noted, all police agencies, consciously or unconsciously, engage in planning. Planning is useful to the police organization in that it operationalizes rational decision-making procedures for organizational policies. It also assists in defining organizational roles for all members of the agency. Whether there is a formal planning unit or one officer or manager assigned to the planning task, planning involves disseminating information and assisting in the managerial decision-making process.

The planning process for our purposes consists of six functions: (1) recognizing and analyzing the problem; (2) setting objectives; (3) gathering data; (4) making a plan of attack; (5) getting the agreement of those involved in the plan; and (6) conducting an evaluation. Various types of plans were discussed.

Specific attention was devoted to fiscal planning. Three widely used budgets—line-item, PPBS, and zero-based—were presented, and their strengths and weaknesses were analyzed.

The chapter examined some innovations in the planning process: (1) procedures to supplement the police budget, including donation programs, forfeiture, user fees, and fines; (2) a model for patrol planning: automated resource allocation; and (3) responses to special populations, such as the mentally ill, the homeless, and the public inebriate through networking with social service agencies.

We also looked at the myth of rapid response. This example showed the need to plan with specific goals in mind and not waste limited resources on responding to all service calls within two minutes. Rapid response should be limited to crimes in progress and emergencies. While the chapter emphasized long-range planning, we included short-range, contingency, and emergency mobilization planning, as they are also important to all police agencies.

The economic realities of the twenty-first century demand responsible fiscal and contingency planning. Expertise, anticipation of events, evaluation, and the responsible supervision of personnel are the traits that will characterize police managers of the future.

QUESTIONS FOR REVIEW

1. What are the benefits of planning for police organizations?
2. List the duties of a planning officer or a planning unit.
3. What are the main steps of the planning process?
4. Discuss three types of plans.
5. What are the differences between long-range and short-range planning?
6. Why is budgeting an important part of the managerial process?
7. What are the main attributes of emergency mobilizations?
8. How do you plan proactively for terrorism?
9. How can Compstat be used as a planning tool?

CLASS PROJECTS

1. Police budgets are public documents. Obtain from a local agency an operating budget for the past fiscal year, and answer the following questions:
   a. What portion of the budget is devoted to personnel costs (e.g., salaries, benefits, overtime), equipment, training, and miscellaneous items?
   b. What is the fiscal year for this department?
   c. Is this budget document representative of line-item, PPBS, or ZBB fiscal planning?
   d. If possible, try to determine whether this budget represents an increase or decrease in police costs compared with the budget for the year before. If a large increase or decrease is noted, in what areas did it occur? What do you suspect are the reasons for the increase or decrease?
2. Suppose the police department of your community has asked your class to help with the planning of a Fourth of July parade. According to the mayor, this will be the biggest parade ever. Considering the geographic variables in your community, prepare a plan to provide police coverage for this parade. Your instructor will supply the needed additional information (proposed number of marchers, units, general route). Your plan must take into account all factors related to police operations during the event and the costs for this coverage. Follow the guidelines in this chapter.

BIBLIOGRAPHY

ARMSTRONG, KAREN. "Was It Inevitable? Islam through History." In James F. Hoge Jr. and Gideon Rose, *How Did This Happen?* New York: Public Affairs, 2002, pp. 53–70.

BALLARD, JAMES DAVID, JOSEPH G. HORNICK, and DOUGLAS MCKENZIE. "Technological Facilitation of Terrorism." In Harvey W. Kushner, ed., *Cyberterrorism in the Twenty-First Century*. Thousand Oaks, Calif.: Sage, 2002.

BERCAL, THOMAS E. "Calls for Police Assistance: Consumer Demands for Public Service." *American Behavioral Scientist*, 13, no. 5/6 (May/June 1970), pp. 681–691.

BOLZ, FRANK JR., KENNETH J. DUDONIS, and DAVID P. SCHULZ. *The Counterterrorism Book*. Boca Raton, Fla.: CRC Press, 2002.

COHEN, MARCIA, and J. THOMAS MCEWEN. "Handling Calls for Service: Alternatives to Traditional Policing," *NIJ Reports*, no. 187 (1984), pp. 4–8.

COMMISSION ON ACCREDITATION FOR LAW ENFORCEMENT AGENCIES. *Standards for Law Enforcement Agencies*. Fairfax, Va.: Commission, 1984.

FARMER, MICHAEL T., ed. *Differential Police Response Strategies*. Washington, D.C.: Police Executive Research Forum, 1981.

FEDERAL EMERGENCY MANAGEMENT ADMINISTRATION. *State and Local Guide 101: Guide for All Hazard Emergency Operations Planning*. Washington, D.C.: FEMA, 2003. Posted at www.fema.gov/rrr/gaheop.shtm. Accessed March 15, 2003.

FINN, PETER, and MONIQUE SULLIVAN. *Police Response to Special Populations*. Washington, D.C.: National Institute of Justice, 1987.

"From Coast to Coast, Anti-Terror Plans Take Shape." *Law Enforcement News*, February 28, 2002, p. 11.

GAUSE, F. GREGORY, II. "The Kingdom in the Middle." In James F. Hoge Jr. and Gideon Rose, *How Did This Happen?* New York: Public Affairs, 2002, pp. 109–122.

GAZELL, JAMES A. "O.W. Wilson's Essential Legacy for Police Administrators." *Journal of Police Science and Administration*, 2, no. 4 (December 1974), pp. 365–375.

———. "William H. Parker, Police Professionalism and the Public: An Assessment." *Journal of Police Science and Administration*, 4, no. 1 (March 1976), pp. 28–37.

"Give Us Your Tired, Your Poor. . . : Fla. Cops May Get Immigration Enforcement Powers." *Law Enforcement News*, March 15/31, 2002, pp. 1, 14.

GOLDSMITH, VICTOR, ET AL. *Analyzing Crime Patterns*. Thousand Oaks, Calif.: Sage, 2000.

GRENNAN, SEAN, ET AL. *Gangs: An International Approach*. Upper Saddle River, N.J.: Prentice Hall, 2000.

HAMM, MARK S. *Hate Crimes: International Perspectives on Causes and Control*. Cincinnati: Anderson, 1994.

HENRY, VINCENT. *The Compstat Paradigm*. Flushing, N.Y.: Looseleaf Publications, 2002.

HOGE, JAMES F. JR., and GIDEON ROSE. *How Did This Happen?* New York: Public Affairs, 2002.

HUDZIK, JOHN K., ET AL. *Criminal Justice Manpower Planning: An Overview*. Washington, D.C.: U.S. Government Printing Office, 1981.

KALLSTROM, JAMES. Statement to the Committee on Science, U.S. House of Representatives—Homeland Security, Utica, New York, June 24, 2002.

KARMEN, ANDREW. *New York Mystery*. New York: New York University Press, 2000.

KELLY, ROBERT J., and JESSE MAGHAN. *Hate Crime: The Global Politics of Polarization*. Carbondale: Southern Illinois University Press, 1998.

KEY, V.O., JR. "The Lack of Budgetary Theory." In Albert C. Hyde and Jay M. Shafritz, eds., *Government Budgeting: Theory, Process, Politics.* Oak Park, Ill.: Moore, 1978, pp. 35–38.

KUSHNER, HARVEY W., ed., *Cyberterrorism in the Twenty-First Century.* Thousand Oaks, Calif.: Sage, 2002.

LARSON, RICHARD C., and MICHAEL F. CAHN. *Synthesizing and Extending the Results of Police Patrol Studies.* Washington, D.C.: U.S. Department of Justice, 1985.

LEE, ELISSA, and LAURA LEETS. "Persuasive Storytelling by Hate Groups Online." In Harvey W. Kushner, ed., *Cyberterrorism in the Twenty-First Century.* Thousand Oaks, Calif.: Sage, 2002.

LEVIN, BRIAN. "Cyberhate." In Harvey W. Kushner, ed., *Cyberterrorism in the Twenty-First Century.* Thousand Oaks, Calif.: Sage, 2002.

LEVINE, MARGARET J., and J. THOMAS MCEWEN. *Patrol Deployment.* Washington, D.C.: U.S. Department of Justice, 1985.

LEWIS, VERNE B. "Toward a Theory of Budgeting." In Albert C. Hyde and Jay M. Shafritz, eds., *Government Budgeting: Theory, Process, Politics.* Oak Park, Ill.: Moore, 1978, pp. 221–235.

LYMAN, MICHAEL D., and GARY W. POTTER. *Organized Crime* (2nd ed.). Upper Saddle River, N.J.: Prentice Hall, 2000.

LYNCH, LAWRENCE. *Fulton Police Department: A Management Study.* Syracuse, N.Y.: privately printed, 1976.

MAGEE, JOHN F. "Decision Trees for Decision Making." In *Business Classics: Fifteen Key Concepts for Managerial Success.* Cambridge, Mass.: Harvard University Press, 1975, pp. 83–95.

MAPLE, JACK, with CHRIS MITCHELL. *The Crime Fighter.* New York: Doubleday, 1999.

MARBURGER, JOHN. Statement to the Committee on Science, U.S. House of Representatives—Homeland Security, Utica, New York, June 24, 2002.

MAXFIELD, MICHAEL G. *Discretion and the Delivery of Police Services: Demand, Client Characteristics and Street Level Bureaucrats in Two Cities.* Ann Arbor, Mich.: University Microfilms, 1979.

MCDOUGALL, THEODORE E. *A Study of Police Operations at the SUNY Cobleskill Campus.* Albany, N.Y.: Bureau for Municipal Police, 1992.

MEYER, JOHN C. "Empirical Analysis of Police Service Tasks: Antecedent for Management Planning." *Journal of Police Science and Administration,* 4, no. 3 (1976), pp. 264–273.

NIGRO, FELIX A., and LLOYD G. NIGRO. *Modern Public Administration* (4th ed.). New York: Harper and Row, 1977.

"NYS Office Takes the Point against Terror." *Law Enforcement News,* February 14, 2002, p. 11.

OETTMEIER, TIMOTHY. "Can Accreditation Survive the '90s?" In Bizzack, John W., ed., *Issues in Policing: New Perspectives.* Lexington, Ky.: Autumn House, 1993, pp. 96–112.

RASHBAUM, WILLIAM. "A Map Goes beyond Crime to City Quirks." *New York Times,* (March 24, 2002) pp. 43–44.

REISS, ALBERT J., JR. *The Police and the Public.* New Haven, Conn.: Yale University Press, 1971.

RIDGEWAY, JAMES. *Blood in the Face: A History of Racism and Violence* (2nd ed.). New York: Thundermouth Press, 1995.

SCHICK, ALLEN. "The Road to PPB: The Stages of Budget Reform." In Albert C. Hyde and Jay M. Shafritz, eds., *Government Budgeting: Theory, Process, Politics*. Oak Park, Ill.: Moore, 1978, pp. 47–65.

SECKLER-HUDSON, CATHERINE. "Performance Budgeting in Government." In Albert C. Hyde and Jay M. Shafritz, eds., *Government Budgeting: Theory, Process, Politics*. Oak Park, Ill.: Moore, 1978, pp. 80–93.

SILVERMAN, IRA. *NYPD Battles Crime*. Boston: Northeastern University Press, 1999.

SOURYAL, S.S. *Police Administration and Management*. St. Paul, Minn.: West, 1977.

SPELMAN, WILLIAM, and DALE K. BROWN. *Calling the Police: Citizen Reporting of Serious Crime*. Washington, D.C.: Police Executive Research Forum, 1981.

STATE UNIVERSITY OF NEW YORK. *Chancellor's Task Force on Personal Safety*. Albany: State University of New York, 1997.

STELLWAGEN, LINDSEY D., and KIMBERLY A. WYLIE. *Strategies for Supplementing the Police Budget*. Washington, D.C.: National Institute of Justice, 1985.

TAYLOR, GRAEME M. "Introduction to Zero-Based Budgeting." In Albert C. Hyde and Jay M. Shafritz, eds., *Government Budgeting: Theory, Process, Politics*. Oak Park, Ill.: Moore, 1978, pp. 284–292.

WECHSLER, WILLIAM F. "Strangling the Hydra." In James F. Hoge Jr. and Gideon Rose, *How Did This Happen?* New York: Public Affairs, 2002, pp. 129–144.

WHITE, JONATHON R. *Terrorism*. Stamford, Conn.: Wadsworth/Thompson, 2002.

WILDAVSKY, AARON, and ARTHUR HAMMOND. "Comprehensive versus Incremental Budgeting." In Albert C. Hyde and Jay M. Shafritz, eds., *Government Budgeting: Theory, Process, Politics*. Oak Park, Ill.: Moore, 1978, pp. 236–251.

WILSON, O.W. *Police Administration*. New York: McGraw-Hill, 1952.

ZELLNER, WILLIAM W. *Counter Cultures*. New York: St. Martin's Press, 1995.

COLLECTIVE BARGAINING AND POLICE MANAGEMENT

KEY TERMS

agency shop	improper practice
arbitration	injunction
blue flu	lobbying
Boston police strike	mediation
collective bargaining	negotiator
community of interest	seniority
grievance	strike
impasse	

Police unions have a major influence on daily police operations and basic management decisions in those states and municipalities that allow collective bargaining. Unionism has led to the following:

- The use of job actions to attain goals after negotiations have stalemated
- Activism reflected not only at the bargaining table but in outside political lobbying over various issues affecting police services to the community
- The wide variety of items found in labor contracts that were once deemed areas of management decision
- Increased emphasis on contract administration and the use of municipal or state resources to deal with union grievances before arbitrators and labor boards

In this chapter, we examine the development of police unionism and its effect on the police manager. Specific attention is given to collective bargaining, for this is one of the most important managerial processes affecting the police organization today.

COLLECTIVE BARGAINING DEFINED

According to Bowers (1973: 6), **collective bargaining** is the process by which representatives of labor and management negotiate wages and working conditions for a given employment entity. For both the public and the private labor sectors, bargaining is chiefly an economic enterprise in which two sides negotiate over how much money management will give employees for their work. For the private labor sector, collective bargaining is a bilateral process in that management and the union representing the employee unit are the two factions that determine the wages and benefits that union members will receive. While economic issues remain significant, job protection, employee work rules, and benefits like health insurance are important concerns in the current collective bargaining forum.

In the public sector, politics enters the situation as a third force. The addition of this third factor leads to what is termed a *multilateral labor relationship*; that is, more than two parties are involved. For example, in the preparation of a departmental budget, the budget planner must obtain information from a number of sources before presenting the final proposal. Moreover, in government, many people must have their say to protect their own interests. In the case of public labor unions, the chief effect is on the range and cost of services provided to the community. The length of time that public managers remain in their positions is often determined by how effectively and economically these services are provided to the community.

Other interest groups also enter into the collective bargaining relationship. Often labor negotiations are expanded not only to the political administration but also to public pressure. Outside actors include the judiciary, the governor, and the civil service commission. Nevertheless, politics remains an important factor in the multilateral relationship between the police union and municipal or state management.

The strong political influence of collective bargaining on the municipality or state becomes particularly apparent around election time. This was highlighted in a study of a county election in which the candidate for district attorney made a concerted effort to receive endorsements based on his position of law and order from every police benevolent association in the county. The endorsements received were used in public relations and in a media campaign directed at voters.

HISTORY OF POLICE UNIONISM

In 1919, the Boston Police Department went on strike in an attempt to increase officers' wages. Although other police departments had used the strike tactic as a means of protest, the **Boston police strike** gained nationwide attention, in large part because of the looting, robberies, and general disorder that occurred after it was apparent that there were no patrolmen on the streets. Massachusetts governor Calvin Coolidge eventually ordered the state guard into Boston to police the city and replaced the striking officers with auxiliaries.

Observers of the Boston police strike (Gammage and Sachs, 1972; Juris and Feuille, 1973) agree that the actions taken by state authorities in quelling the strike retarded the development of unionism in American police forces for the next 50 years. Prior to 1919, many metropolitan police departments had formed social clubs to serve as liaisons between the officers and the municipality for the purpose of improving wages and conditions of employment. In Boston, an invitation had already been tendered to the Boston Social Club by the American Federation of Labor to join the national organization. This invitation was withdrawn soon after the strike. The wave of public support toward Massachusetts authorities in their blanket dismissal of the strikers signaled to other budding police labor unions that union militancy would not receive support either from the public or from national labor organizations.

Police unionism in the United States remained dormant until the 1960s, although a few police benevolent associations did join national labor groups for public employees. This general trend held not only for police officers, but also for all public employees. That is, in the public sector between 1920 and 1950, unionism was opposed by both public management and public employees. While wage scales for public employees generally lagged those of private workers, significant benefits were earned by government workers in the form of job security via civil service and a generous system of vacation and personal leave.

After World War II, three main developments altered this trend:

1. An expansion of government services coupled by an increase of government employees
2. A continued policy by the federal government that supported the right of public and private workers to unionize and bargain collectively. For the public sector, this culminated in 1962 with President Kennedy's signing of Executive Order 10988, which allowed most federal employees to organize unions and bargain collectively. Further refinements of Executive Order 10988 were signed by Presidents Johnson, Nixon, and Ford.
3. A significant decline of union membership in the private sector. This trend forced many private union organizations to look for new membership, readily available in the public sector.

It became apparent to many public employees that there was no reason why they should not receive salaries and conditions of employment similar to those earned by their private counterparts in an affluent society. Unions, which were at one time spurned by public employees, were now welcomed as a means by which to achieve employee demands. Private and public union organizations welcomed these new members with open arms to boost sagging union membership. Lobbying efforts were initiated to have cities and states enact comprehensive collective bargaining statutes modeled on existing federal statutes. Starting in the late 1950s, such statutes were enacted by New York City (1956), Wisconsin (1959), and New York State (1967).

It is not surprising that the trend to unionize by public employees was readily accepted by many police officers at this time. These officers felt that they were underpaid and the frequent object of public abuse and criticism for a variety of social problems, particularly the rise in crime. While low pay became the chief determinant for the rise of police unions, an equally significant factor arose from the poor personnel practices that were commonplace in many police organizations. According to Juris and Feuille (1973: 21), the following practices were often cited as a source of contention:

> Lack of internal civil and constitutional rights for officers being investigated for misfeasance and malfeasance.
>
> Lack of a functional grievance procedure.
>
> Being called to duty and held on standby or called to court, for no compensation.
>
> Having to lose a day's pay as penalties for rule infractions.
>
> No premium pay for overtime work.
>
> Being transferred from one shift or job to another with little or no advance warning.
>
> Physical and verbal intimidation and degradation by superior officers.

The demand for higher wages and improved working conditions can also be traced to the influx of younger officers, many with college degrees, who balked at a militaristic bureaucracy that demanded blind obedience. Moreover, the militancy that is often attached to police unionism should come as no surprise. This attitude reflected the mood of the 1960s, in which protest and activism were the main tactics of generally all social change groups, ranging from students to minority groups. It is no wonder that many police unions became particularly adept at protest tactics (calling in with **blue flu,** wearing sneakers while in uniform, not shaving, engaging in street protests) by simply borrowing such methods from groups that they had fought against.

POLICE UNIONS TODAY

Most police unions in the United States today are local organizations that may or may not be affiliated with a national parent organization. The reason for this local orientation is that wages, benefits, and conditions of employment, including promotions, are heavily dependent on local economic and political conditions. The police department is the arm of local county or state government. Unlike multinational corporations, those who control the destinies of the nation's police are clearly tied to the local community, and in police matters, their concerns end at the community boundary.

However, police unions affiliated with national groups have received valuable assistance from outside consultants during negotiations and work actions. The national unions have developed strong campaigns to interest local police in national union affiliation. However, the response has been mixed nationally because of the strong community control over law enforcement.

State legislation on public unions has performed a significant role in the type of unions that have developed in law enforcement. The state legislation on collective bargaining can be divided into two major categories:

1. Those states that have comprehensive statutes that allow police officers to bargain collectively in some manner
2. Those states that make it illegal for police to form a union and absolutely forbid union membership to police officers

The rule in both of these cases is that states, in the light of the 1919 Boston strike, generally forbid police to strike.

In place of this no-strike rule is the concept of binding arbitration, in which unresolved issues or contract disputes go to a neutral arbitrator who makes a decision that is binding on both sides. The use of an arbitrator is frequently seen as an attractive mechanism by which unionized police personnel can obtain equal footing with the employer.

States that do not allow bargaining by police usually allow state agencies and municipalities to "meet and confer" with police representatives to discuss employees' issues and grievances. Despite the existence of no-bargaining statutes, many officers have joined national unions in a first step toward organizing.

More and more police officers have formed benevolent organizations for social and athletic purposes. Eventually, the organization takes on many, if not most, of the characteristics of a union, and these no-union state laws are being either tested or ignored. In general, nonunion states provide some form of binding arbitration. One of the major problems with these binding-arbitration clauses is that the final decision on the contract is made by local and state legislatures.

In states that have comprehensive collective bargaining statutes, such as New York, Ohio, California, Wisconsin, Michigan, and New Jersey, the members of each police department are allowed to form a union. The process begins with a large number of employees expressing their interest in forming a union. This generally involves the presentation of a petition or signature cards to the county or state labor board indicating this goal. Often, a state or national police union will provide professional assistance in the hopes of having the employees join the larger organization. This is followed by an election in which the employees formally decide to form a union and select a collective bargaining agent and affiliation. This decision could result in the formation of a local bargaining unit or affiliation with a national police union. After this occurs, the state labor board certifies that the bargaining unit is the exclusive representative for the job titles that created the unit.

The key elements are that the union is the only recognized body to negotiate with the employer and that the union has the right to collect dues. In certain states, such as New York, legislation allows for the **agency shop,** where the union collects dues from all employees, members and nonmembership alike. The rationale is that all employees should share the cost of negotiating contracts with the employer.

During the past decade, courts have consistently ruled that nonunion members must pay that portion of their dues directed to collective bargaining purposes, which might include political lobbying, national conferences, and other activities related to union business. However, in *Lehnert v. Ferris Valley Faculty Association*, the Supreme Court ruled in 1991 that nonunion public employees did not have to pay dues that were directed to ideological causes. An example of an ideological cause would be support for a political candidate or **lobbying** for a certain bill in the state legislature that union members might not support.

Another important element in the establishment of the union is the question of the categories of employees that will be represented, otherwise known as the **community of interest.** For example, in the New York City Police Department, separate union groups represent patrol officers, supervisors, and middle managers. The community-of-interest question was complicated when detectives formed their own organization, breaking away from the police benevolent association. In other cities and states, all members of the department, including the chief of police, are represented by one union. In some cases, especially in smaller departments, this presents problems since the chief and his or her friends may be able to control the union and, of course, control the collective bargaining process.

Although one union is recognized as the sole representative for collective bargaining, state laws allow for a designated time period when a rival organization may solicit petitions and, if receiving a certain percentage of votes, conduct elections to contest representation. This is an important aspect for police unions that wish to become affiliated with national groups when consensus does not exist in the union membership for such a move.

Finally, states with comprehensive statutes provide the following series of mechanisms to deal with disputes that cannot be resolved during the course of collective bargaining or the administration of the contract:

> *Mediation:* a noncoercive process in which a neutral third party studies the issues in dispute between the two parties. This mediator works behind the scenes with the parties and attempts to act as a go-between in settling the dispute.

Fact finding: another noncoercive procedure by which a third party gathers evidence from the two parties and then offers a solution. The recommendations may be publicly released in an effort to have community pressure enter into the settling of the dispute.

Arbitration: a third-party process in which an official body or representative of a state arbitration board studies the issues in dispute and then makes a ruling. This decision may then be binding on both parties, depending on statute.

These three processes are used to settle disputes between labor and management during the course of collective bargaining when an **impasse** occurs. An impasse is generally understood to occur when labor or management or both have determined that no further progress will be made through negotiations at the table.

For police unions, binding arbitration is often used as a method to forestall a strike. Arbitration can also be used to settle grievances that arise during the administration of the union contract. Basically, a **grievance** occurs when either management or the union feels that the contract has been violated in some way. Grievances can also arise from a violation of the rules and regulations involving employee health, safety, physical facilities, materials, or equipment. Consider the following example of a grievance procedure:

1. A time limit of 10 working days is set as a limit in which a grievance may be filed after an officer becomes aware of the event constituting the alleged grievance.
2. Informal discussion usually marks the next step. Here the employee verbally presents his or her claim promptly to the immediate supervisor, and both parties attempt to solve the situation.
3. If the grievance is not resolved in the informal stage and the employee wishes to continue into the grievance process, a written notice is forwarded to a higher command officer. Again, a time limit is set between the final determination made by the supervisor and the filing of written notice.
4. Within a specific period of time, the ranking supervisor must process the grievance and schedule a hearing. At the hearing, the employee presents written and oral statements on his or her position.
5. Within a specific time frame, the command officer answers in writing his or her course of action on the grievance.
6. If the grievance is still not adjusted at the command-officer level, the grievance is filed with the head of the agency. In some departments, the sheriff or the chief of police has the final say as to the determination of the grievance. In states that have comprehensive collective bargaining statutes, the grievance is handled by a public employee-relations board.

A fifth method of conflict resolution is through litigation. Since the courts are the traditional forum for solving disputes between public agencies, many unions, especially those in large metropolitan jurisdictions or affiliated with national organizations, have a battery of attorneys on the payroll. Litigation sponsored by police unions has produced various noteworthy cases involving drug testing, discipline, and off-duty employment.

Major Police Union Organizations

The trend in policing today appears to be increased unionization, especially in those states that as yet do not allow police officers to form unions. Nonunion police departments are the rule rather than the exception in the South and the Midwest, whereas unions are especially strong in the Northeast and on the West Coast, as states in those areas have comprehensive collective bargaining statutes.

There is also the additional trend for many local police unions to affiliate with national groups to strengthen their bargaining position and to increase union benefits to members. The main national union groups are as follows:

International Union of Police Associations (IUPA). Founded in 1953 as the National Conference of Police Associations, this union was originally organized for networking and legislative lobbying purposes among various police organizations in the United States and Canada (Swanson et al., 2001). In 1978, the organization—then known as the International Conference of Police Associations—split apart after a decision was made to affiliate with the American Federation of Labor and Congress of Industrial Organizations (AFL-CIO). Many departments were opposed to the higher dues and the greater percentage of money that went to the national organization. In the following year, the AFL-CIO granted a charter to the IUPA. Today, the group represents approximately 80,000 officers through 480 local organizations.

Communications Workers of America (CWA). Originally founded to represent telephone and communications technology workers, the CWA decided in the 1990s to expand into the public sector to organize workers in various areas, such graduate students, medical workers, and police officers. The National Coalition of Public Safety Officers (NCPSO), the CWA affiliate for police and public safety officers, represents about 35,000 police officers, deputy sheriffs, probation officers, and correctional officers. What is significant about the NCPSO is its statewide organization of public safety workers in the population growth states of Texas, Arizona, and Florida.

Fraternal Order of Police (FOP). This is the oldest police organization in the United States. The FOP is basically a professional organization that emphasizes collective bargaining in some areas and exists mainly as a social organization in others. Each lodge is independent of control from the national organization. There are now over 2,100 lodges and nearly 300,000 members.

International Brotherhood of Teamsters. This private union was quick to see the potential for government workers to increase membership. Estimates of police officer membership range as high as 15,000. Many police union officials (and management as well) distrust the Teamsters because of its long history of organized crime influence and mismanagement of pension funds via low-interest or no-interest loans to gangsters. Nevertheless, the Teamsters are aggressive in seeking public sector membership and are presently conducting recruitment and organization drives in those southern states that forbid police to form unions. Today, the Teamsters represent officers at 297 police departments in 19 states.

International Brotherhood of Police Officers (IBPO). Founded in Rhode Island in the late 1960s, the IBPO was organized to deal with collective bargaining issues among local police unions in New England. In 1970, the IBPO became affiliated with the National Association of Government Employees, which in 1982 became affiliated with Service Employees International Union, a large collective bargaining group of public-sector service employees that is affiliated with the AFL-CIO. Today, the IBPO continues to represent police officers in New England and has expanded to many states in the western United States.

American Federation of State, County, and Municipal Employees. Affiliated with the American Federation of Labor, this union for public employees was founded in 1936. AFSCME was the first organization to make serious attempts to enroll public employees in the decades before the rise of union membership in 1960. Today, AFSCME is perhaps the largest public-sector union, representing over 1.3 million members. Police unions are organized under AFSCME as separate councils for state and local police departments. Approximately 35,000 police officers are represented by this organization. There are also thousands of federal workers who are in staff and clerical positions in various federal law enforcement agencies. Federal law enforcement officers, such as Secret Service, Federal Bureau of Investigation, Drug Enforcement Administration, and others do not have union representation but have job-related due process rights and salary benefits enacted by Congress. Exceptions to this are the U.S. Marshals, the Border Patrol, and various federal security personnel who are represented by the American Federation of Government Employees, an AFSCME affiliate.

Black Officer Associations. These have been formed in police departments that have a high percentage of minority officers as well as a record of prejudice and discrimination against these officers in terms of recruitment, promotions, or job assignments. Examples of these associations are the Guardians in New York City and Hartford, Connecticut; the Afro-American Patrolmen's League of Chicago; and the Oakland, California, Black Officer's Association. These associations usually remain apart from the union structure of their departments and attempt to settle differences between their members and management by direct negotiations and political lobbying.

The long-term organizational goal for many of these groups is the creation of a national police union. This appeared to be a real possibility in the 1970s with the large increases in membership and activism associated with police unions. The decentralization of American police, the state of the economy, and the changing nature of American unionism makes a national union less likely today and in the future. However, various local unions do join formal and informal state and national networks and conferences to lobby for officer-related legislation and collective bargaining rights.

MANAGEMENT RIGHTS AND COLLECTIVE BARGAINING: A DILEMMA

The most crucial factor facing the police administrator—managing the agency—arises from the emergence of collective bargaining and police union-ism. Union contracts today contain a variety of clauses affecting police opera-tions. For example, the union contract may specify that two troopers must be assigned to patrol vehicles during the midnight watch. Decisions of this nature would appear to be the prerogative of management. Yet there are two general reasons why such clauses appear in union contracts.

First, the police management role in collective bargaining in the 1960s was generally characterized as either negligent or nonexistent. Because of the multilateral nature of the process, negotiations often were carried on by a member of the state or municipal personnel office who may or may not have advised the police agency affected by the outcome of the contract. On the other side of the table, union negotiators were generally better prepared to argue their demands, strengthening their position with the use of outside consultants for expertise on issues and tactics.

Second, not all infringements on managerial prerogative occurred through the collective bargaining process. In some cases, police departments were forced to comply with union demands via binding arbitration rulings or court litigation. Arbitration and legal rulings forced many law enforcement administrators to undertake participatory management in the formulation of policy within their agencies. In many cases, grievance and litigation proceed-ings may be avoided in having union input as a part of the policy decision-making process. On the other hand, militant unions may harass management through their use of grievances at every turn.

The first step in hindering union infringement on managerial rights lies with a management-rights clause in the contract. A model clause prepared by the National League of Cities states (Rynecki, Cairns, and Carnes, 1978: 7):

> The parties agree that all subjects not specifically listed here are retained by the city, and the union further agrees to waive its rights to grieve concerning the con-templation, approval, application, implementation or adoption of any manage-ment rights, whether heretofore listed, regardless of the frequency of exercise.

In simple terms, this contract language states that management has certain rights that may not be grieved by the union even if such rights are not exercised frequently. Such rights include the right to do the following (Geller, 1991: 303):

1. Establish departmental rules and procedures
2. Schedule shifts, tours of duty, and work assignments
3. Discipline and discharge for cause
4. Lay off employees if the need arises
5. Transfer employees and governmental operations

6. Consolidate the operations of two or more departments or reorganize the operations within a department
7. Set hiring and promotional standards
8. Set education and training standards

Nevertheless, the union should be consulted on important matters affecting the operations of the department simply because it is good administrative procedure. The existence of a management-rights clause is not the final solution in the problem of managing without union interference. Unpopular decisions still may be the basis for a lawsuit or for resistance by personnel. Yet there remains the need for such a clause, as it is the first line of defense if a decision is grieved and reaches arbitration. Management can point to this clause as part of the contractual agreement.

THE COLLECTIVE BARGAINING PROCESS

The goals and objectives of police management and labor in the collective bargaining process are similar, although they may differ somewhat in detail and substance and substantially in the means to obtain these goals.

Management Goals	**Labor Goals**
1. Provide fair and adequate pay for all employees, including a reasonable and competitive compensation package for management	1. Provide fair and adequate pay for all employees in the bargaining unit, along with a solid fringe benefit package
2. Maintain managerial efficiency, producing an efficiently run police department	2. Respect police officers as individuals and as part of an efficiently run police department
3. Preserve the public interest in policing the community	3. Preserve the public interest in policing the community
4. Have employees identify with managerial and departmental objectives, along with a positive esprit de corps and high morale	4. Have a positive esprit de corps, with high morale and the creation of departmental objectives that are mutually beneficial to both the department and the sworn officers
5. Have adequately trained officers who respond in a professional manner to management's needs, objectives, and specific orders	5. Have adequately trained officers who have good working conditions and who respond in a professional manner to reasonable requests by management personnel

These objectives are complex because police personnel relations are complex and often not as clear as this chart would indicate (Klotz, 1978).

The language of the goals for management and labor differs, along with some of the meaning of this language. The matter of definition is paramount for good management-employee relations. The municipality setting wages and fringe benefits may differ considerably in what it considers to be adequate and fair pay; this may well be below what the union considers fair and adequate and even below what management considers fair and adequate. The same holds true for (1) conditions and benefits of employment, (2) reasonable orders or requests, (3) mutually beneficial objectives, and (4) an efficiently run department. A major problem is the existence of three groups—police management, sworn officers and other police department members of the bargaining unit, and municipal politicians and governmental officials—using differing definitions.

Although bargaining has been likened to horse trading, certain preparations must be made before the horse trading begins. Effective use of the collective bargaining process means that the police management team has an organization that collects data and does extensive homework on a year-round basis. The basic issues that are normally reviewed are as follows (Klotz, 1978):

1. A review of prior contracts with key administrative personnel to see what items need to be updated or revised. Special attention should be given to items that have poor language or have been the source of problems or grievances with the union.
2. A review of current union agreements with other area police agencies and agencies of similar size facing similar problems. This should be looked at in terms of remaining competitive in the market, keeping the officer's morale high, and being able to make reasonable offers in light of union demands.
3. Collection and analysis of economic data concerning what the municipality can afford to pay and is willing to pay given political and economic realities. This could include informal discussions with local decision-making leaders concerning what they feel is a reasonable increase in wages and benefits.
4. A thorough study and analysis of arbitration decisions awarded under the current contract or awarded to police unions.
5. Checking out rumors informally as to what items are important to the union and to members of the bargaining unit and what areas of dispute might be unknown to management. By checking informally before bargaining is begun, management may offer compromises, and settlement may be possible before either party takes a solid position.

The next step in the bargaining preparation is the selection of the bargaining team. The key person of this team, the chief **negotiator,** has the authority and prestige to represent the department with credibility. The negotiator has to be able to have frank discussions with the chief concerning all issues, especially those deemed undesirable or contrary to management's best interest. He or she also has to enjoy the chief's confidence. Assisting the chief negotiator are other members of the team who generally provide two major services: (1) information retrieval and research and (2) expertise in areas with which the chief negotiator might not be familiar.

In small police agencies with limited budgets and personnel, the chief often takes an active role in the bargaining process. While it is imperative that police management be represented at the bargaining table, it is *not* recommended that the chief become a chief negotiator. By becoming personally involved in the bargaining process, the chief may foster future morale and personal repercussions that would be detrimental to management. For example, if the chief is seen as not supporting his or her people on the issue of higher wages, this could be a blow to morale.

Some municipalities have been hiring professional negotiators, and most have found them well worth the expense. These negotiators are familiar with the labor laws and the expenses of such items as health and dental insurance. They have gone through the process thousands of times and are familiar with the rituals and customs of collective bargaining in relation to the membership, the government, and the press. National unions often send professional negotiators to unions in the field when a contract is about to end. Since literally millions of dollars and the basic welfare of the department are involved, the negotiating process is no place for amateurs.

Contract Administration

The signing of the contract is only the continuance of the collective bargaining relationship. The contract reflects new guidelines between the employer and the union that will be subject to future review by both sides. The most important aspect of administering the contract involves the dissemination of information to all members of the agency on policies, programs, and equipment affected by the new agreement. Those items affected by the contract will still have to be worked out between management and union representatives. For example, while the contract may specify that all officers will receive a new caliber of weapon, the actual issuance of the weapon will not occur overnight.

Between the signing of the new contract and the initiation of the next round of negotiations, a chief portion of contract administration by union and management involves handling and monitoring formal and informal deviations arising from situations and interpretations not covered in the existing document. The most effective manner in which to work out these disputes is to have one person or officer administer the contract and keep records concerning these differences or disagreements. What often happens is that over the life of the contract, these differences become agenda items for the new contract negotiations. Unresolved issues often become agenda items during the next round of bargaining or may become major grievance items. These issues can be summarized as follows:

Seniority. **Seniority,** meaning the number of years or days that an officer has served, remains the cornerstone of collective bargaining agreements for such items as shift and special detail assignments. Grievances that arise over this issue are, in fact, very complicated in terms of the calculation of seniority time. For example, depending on the locality, "time on the job" may begin the first day the person walks through the front door, after graduation from the training academy, or after the probationary period. From the management view, seniority is a hindrance in terms of assigning the best person to the best job, and seniority often interferes with the administration of the daily operation of the agency.

After September 11, 2001, efforts in Massachusetts to create an elite antiterrorism team at Boston's Logan Airport became stalled as the union for state police officers wanted this assignment made on the basis of seniority (Daniel, 2002). In another agency, a major grievance emerged over training school assignments based on management decision rather than the existing seniority list. The calculation of the seniority list is most important in those police agencies facing employee layoffs, as it is well known that the last hired is the first fired.

Grievance Procedures.   The reasons and guidelines for a grievance procedure have been discussed in detail. Grievances can arise from disputes over administration of the contract relating to wages, benefits, and conditions of employment. Conditions of employment pose an open-ended arena for grievances. Police officers in states with comprehensive collective bargaining statutes can grieve anything and everything, and they do! A typical batch of grievances in one large state agency for a six-month period includes the following:

- Lack of interior or writing-light replacement bulbs in patrol vehicles
- Administration of first aid to a person suspected of having AIDS
- Transportation of prisoners by only one officer in an uncaged vehicle
- Responding to fires without proper equipment and going inside to locate the cause of the alarm before the arrival of fire-service personnel
- Not being allowed to wear leatherlike athletic shoes in place of the prescribed leather shoes
- The presence of rats in a locker room

The reader, no doubt, will ask why these items could not have been settled by open, face-to-face communication. The reality is that mundane and seemingly simple issues should be worked out either through informal communication or formal labor-management meetings. Although necessary and important, formal grievances take time and bruise egos in terms of win-lose-or-draw outcomes between management and labor. Most of these issues could and should be worked out with direct and frank discussion.

Improper Labor Practices.   Known in the field as an IP, an **improper practice** occurs when an employer does one or more of the following:

- Interferes with, restrains, or coerces employees who wish to form or join a labor union

- Dominates or interferes with the formation or administration of a labor union
- Discriminates against any employee for the purpose of encouraging or discouraging membership or activity in the union
- Refuses to negotiate in good faith with the recognized or state-certified representatives of the union
- Assigns work performed by union employees to nonunion employees

Charges of improper practices can also be alleged against employees for similar reasons: (1) failing to negotiate in good faith with management, and (2) interfering, restraining, or coercing fellow employees from exercising their rights as union members, for example, seeking new representation from another labor organization. In most cases, IP complaints are handled at the local administrative level up to a final resolution at a state employee relations hearing.

Charges of improper practices by both labor and management often occur when contract negotiations reach a stalemate. They also seem to arise when officers of a department begin to organize a union under prevailing legislative guidelines. Invariably, in these situations, there are outright or implied threats by command personnel or the civilian administration about abolishing jobs, cutting back on existing benefits, and sometimes abolishing the entire department! It is best in these situations for police and civilian administrators to back off before it is too late. When previously nonunionized police officers desire to form a union, it normally means that there are serious, unresolved problems relating to wages, benefits, and conditions of employment. Time and effort would be better spent by administrators in taking a training course on collective bargaining and contract administration rather than dirtying the arena with threats, lawsuits, counterlawsuits, and so on.

Another rich area for IP complaints involves instances when management attempts to hire or use outside consultants or employees for work that is normally done by police union members. Two common IP complaints are the use of civilians for dispatching or for writing parking tickets. The basis for these complaints is the contention that management is discriminating against union employees by having civilians do the jobs of sworn officers.

Discipline Procedures.   In states with comprehensive collective bargaining statutes, disciplinary procedures invariably appear in the collective bargaining agreement. Contract language often defines the process by which discipline is imposed in terms of written charges, the parameters for interrogation, and union representation during interrogation. An important element is the time frame by which the employer should have known that a rule or law was violated.

Contracts often have prohibitions against the use of chemical or polygraph tests unless voluntarily agreed to by the suspect employee. Employees may also demand a review by an outside arbitrator on the punishment that the agency has imposed or seeks to impose. As with IP complaints, employee-discipline procedures follow a grievance-type process involving a local hearing and then review of the charges and punishment by a state labor relations board. The desire by the employee to dispute either the notice of discipline and/or the punishment must be made within a specified period.

Union contracts vary with regard to representation of members by union-paid attorneys for charges filed by other police agencies and civilians. With some contracts, the union defends all officers against charges, while in other jurisdictions, paid-for legal defense is optional or nonexistent. As discussed in Chapter 10, the police administrator must know by heart the rules and conditions for discipline that appear in the union contract and the relevant civil service law. The police manager needs to follow the common law that evolves through the administration of a contract or contracts over time. Although many say that every case is different, state arbitrators have dismissed charges because of the following:

1. Lack of proper and complete investigations and proper documentation
2. Too severe punishment in relation to the offense (e.g., suspension for failing to wear the uniform)
3. Lack of just cause in initiating discipline (e.g., a personality clash rather than a legitimate issue)
4. Lack of consistency in enforcing department rules

Thus, a labor agreement is not a static document but, rather, changes as the organizational needs change. Also, conditions change and fringe benefits are looked at differently from one year to the next. One general rule: It is easy to add a benefit to a contract but extremely difficult to take one away, even if the benefit proves too costly.

Fair Labor Standards Act

An important element in the collective bargaining relationship is the payment of money for work performed. The Fair Labor Standards Act (FLSA), passed by Congress in the 1980s with strong support from police union groups, proscribes that employees must be paid overtime at a rate of one and one-half times the regular wage rate for over 40 hours of work. For many years, state work practices exempted law enforcement agencies because operational needs required personnel to work shifts that would fill 24 hours without any gaps. However, in 1986 this concept was tested in *Garcia v. San Antonio Metropolitan Transit Authority*; the Supreme Court ruled that FLSA was applicable to state and local law enforcement agencies.

Since that time, police unions and employers have addressed a number of complicated issues related to the law, either through labor/management discussions or lawsuits. Law enforcement officers must be compensated for overtime, with either pay or compensatory time off, at a rate of not less than one and one-half hours for each hour over 43 hours per week, or 171 hours for a 28-day work period. The notion of work performed includes all activities that provide a benefit to the employer, such as preshift briefing, finishing reports from the previous tour, and travel to and from training courses. The rules for overtime apply to investigators who may work for days on one case. When the FLSA is violated, law enforcement officers may sue for back wages, attorneys' fees, and punitive damages.

There are exceptions to these standards. As McCormack (1995: 29) discusses, the FLSA does not cover law enforcement agencies that employ fewer than five officers within a workweek. Elected officials, such as the sheriff, or volunteers or management officials who are paid on a yearly salary are FLSA exempt. Those who are attending a training academy may not be covered because they are not considered regular employees. The issue of who is an exempted employee is always problematic for law enforcement managers who hold command rank. For example, if the manager can have hourly wages deducted based on a fine imposed by the department, then he or she is not FLSA exempt.

THE POLICE STRIKE

Even though most states prohibit strikes or work slowdowns by police, police **strikes** (stoppages of work) sometimes do occur. Short of a strike, police unions may resort to job actions such as blue flu (not reporting to work for alleged sickness), slowdowns, and the initiation of "Fear City" campaigns over police cutbacks.

There have been fewer police strikes and job actions in the 1980s and 1990s than in the 1970s. A major reason for this is the economics of local municipalities that have suffered decreased tax revenue along with cutbacks in federal and state aid. In the light of the many austerity budgets, there has been a new tendency for many police unions to cooperate with administrative and legislative leaders and managers in order to retain job security.

What has arisen in many contracts is the concept of givebacks, where the union gives back certain benefits negotiated and won in the past. There have also been many cases where unions have agreed to wage freezes or to work free for a specific number of days in order to continue job security.

While the Boston police strike remains an important historical event, but a strike in Montreal in 1969 should also be considered. Soon after it was realized that police were not on the streets, there was a rash of robberies and looting in the central area of the city. The absence of police led many observers to conclude that perhaps there was some validity to the "thin blue line" philosophy in that the police are the last defense against total anarchy.

Even though most contracts and state statutes forbid strikes by police and firefighters, it is important that all agencies have prepared plans to maintain essential police services. Most police agencies rely on outside assistance and the use of supervisors and nonstriking officers to fill this need. While services are being maintained, it may become the duty of the chief to be the mediator between the striking union and the political administration. As Burpo states, "The issues precipitating the strike are usually economic and cannot be unilaterally resolved by the chief, therefore the chief becomes the go-between" (1977: 416).

A court **injunction** is often used in halting a strike. Because of the no-strike clauses in labor contracts and state legislation, the injunction forces the officers back to work under the threat of contempt of court. In some strikes, court injunctions have been successful, and strikers have returned to work under threat of jail or huge fines levied against the union treasury.

After the dust has settled and the police officers return to work, there are the follow-up issues of disciplinary proceedings against the strikers. There are no precise answers to this dilemma simply because each strike has different variables. However, a no-penalty or no-punishment clause in some contracts helps to stop petty punishments that serve only to damage morale and undermine employee-employer relations. A general rule that might be applied is that punishments do not deter future strikes and do a great deal of damage to the organization in terms of creating resentment among the employees.

POLICE UNIONS AND THE POLITICAL PROCESS

As police union contracts are tied to local and state economic issues, it is no surprise that local, state, and national politics often becomes enmeshed with union activity. Politicians running for office routinely request the endorsement and sometimes the economic support of police unions. The candidate's views on crime control and his or her previous support for police-sponsored bills become an important consideration before political support is given.

Police unions often present themselves as good community citizens by sponsoring community events, crime-prevention programs, and sports teams for youth. Community activity is often devoted to fund-raising to augment fiscal resources obtained from member dues. Fund-raising can lead to a number of issues and concerns. It is not uncommon for local unions to contract with national fund-raisers to conduct phone campaigns for money. In one month, the author received two requests from telemarketers to support local police benevolent associations and their anti-drug education. Further investigation found that less than 10 percent of the money raised actually went to the union.

Another related activity is the police union yearbook, which consists of police activity photos, crime-prevention tips, and many advertisements. It's the advertisements that often become a sore spot. When businesses are asked to buy space for advertising, some observers complain that this may become a form of shakedown if there is any hint of reprisals for not supporting the campaign.

Major police unions, or confederations of local unions, maintain offices in state capitals and Washington, D.C., to monitor legislation and to lobby for support of union-sponsored bills. For example, the Fraternal Order of Police is urging all its members to write to their elected representatives to urge Congress to pass a bill that would allow police officers to carry firearms on or off duty anywhere in the United States. The rationale for this legislation is that current homeland security efforts may require emergency mobilization of off-duty and retired police officers who may have to cross state lines. When this occurs, officers do not have official police status or authority to carry a weapon (Young, 2002: 1).

If anything, police unions have become more active in defending their members, especially those who have been arrested for crimes. It is not unusual for the local union or the national group to set aside funds for the legal defense of officers accused of criminal misconduct, as contracts do not, as a rule, provide legal indemnification for union members who are accused of a crime.

CONCLUSION

Collective bargaining is an important process for law enforcement agencies throughout the nation. Professionals who manage police departments see it as a step toward easing some of the strain between employees and employer, as written contracts help to eliminate misunderstandings. A fair grievance procedure, one that is fair both to management and to labor, if used as intended, can settle disputes before they worsen. Disputes settled at the informal stage of the grievance procedure can help a department grow and adapt to changing times and conditions. However, disputes that go through the formal machinery assure all officers that they can have their day before a neutral hearing officer.

In all, collective bargaining is seen as a generally powerful force in upgrading police agencies. However, contracts do give management less flexibility in exercising the necessary authority to administer an agency. This problem will be met when management is willing to use the civil service and/or contract machinery to fire undesirable employees. Many managers feel that it is not worth the trouble; however, inaction means that the department will have to live with that undesirable employee for many years.

One new concept concerns givebacks, that is, returning or giving up certain benefits that have been previously earned at the bargaining table (e.g., agreeing to give up uniform cleaning). This stems from the dire economic state in which many municipalities find themselves because of budget cuts and a declining tax base.

Overall, there is nothing that has dramatically changed with collective bargaining and police over the past 20 years. The majority of officers in states where collective bargaining is allowed belong to local police unions that focus on the terms and conditions of employment for their city, town, or county members. The idea of a national police union for all officers remains abstract.

Nationally, unionism in the private sector appears to be declining due to (1) the transformation of a manufacturing economy into a service economy; (2) growth of economies in nonunionized states, particularly in the South; and

(3) competition by companies with unions in granting job security, benefits, and a say in company operations without employees paying union dues. According to the Bureau of Labor Statistics (2003: 1), union membership in the United States dropped from around 20 percent in the workforce in 1980 to 13.2 percent in 2002. Nearly four in 10 government workers were union members in 2002 compared to 1 in 10 for private sector industries. The highest membership for the public sector is with "protective service occupations" which includes police and fire fighters.

QUESTIONS FOR REVIEW

1. What are the major issues surrounding the rise of collective bargaining for police in the United States?
2. Define the following terms: *blue flu*, *arbitration*, and *management rights*.
3. Identify four major national police unions in the United States. Why are many local police unions reluctant to join national organizations?
4. Define *collective bargaining*. How does public-sector collective bargaining differ from that found in the private sector?
5. Explain the significance of the following strikes: Boston (1919) and Montreal (1969).
6. Give three reasons why police should have the right to strike. Give three reasons why police should not have the right to strike. Give one reason why you choose one side or the other.
7. List what you feel are the major issues in collective bargaining for police today, and explain their importance.

CLASS PROJECT

The city of Jonesville will be negotiating a contract with the newly formed Jonesville Police Benevolent Association. At present, the overall conditions of employment for Jonesville officers are as follows:

1. Salaries are $30,000 for patrol officers, $35,000 for sergeants, and $40,000 for lieutenants. All personnel receive a $500 pay increase every two years.
2. The following holidays are allowed: July 4, Christmas, Thanksgiving, and Memorial Day.
3. There is one week of paid vacation for all personnel.
4. All officers must contribute toward their own pension fund.
5. All officers receive major health and dental care benefits from the city.
6. Uniforms are provided, except for leather and handguns.
7. There is no pay for overtime or call-in time.
8. All grievances are handled by the chief of police.

The city of Jonesville might be located anywhere in the United States. As with many American cities, Jonesville is showing a deficit, in this case $2 million, for this fiscal year. There is talk of layoffs for municipal workers. General unemployment for the area runs roughly 6 percent.

Game Plan

The class will be divided into two teams. One team will represent the Jonesville Police Benevolent Association; the other, the city of Jonesville. We suggest that teams be limited to eight students each. Each team must select a chief negotiator. The chief negotiator will then assign each member specific research tasks. For example, one team member might be assigned to research the costs of pension programs for municipal employees, another member would deal with the issue of salaries, and so on.

Roles of Negotiators

The instructor will assign various team members to play specific roles. During one role-play session, one of the authors had the following characters:

For Jonesville PBA

Bill Griffith—recently elected as chief negotiator. Bill has promised to "bring home the bacon" and improve working conditions.

Wayne Freeman—a veteran patrol officer who sees this whole process as "chicken s—t" stuff. Freeman advocates the use of blue flu and strikes.

Linda Tomley—the first female officer in the department. Officer Tomley wants such things as lockers for female personnel and paid family leave.

Jack Smith—presently serves as public relations officer for the PBA. Among other things, he feels that the PBA should go "national" and get some clout to improve salaries and working conditions.

For City of Jonesville

Bill White—recently hired as director of personnel for the city. This is his first job since graduating from the School of Labor Relations at the state university. White has promised the mayor and the city council to "kick ass and take names" when it comes to increasing personnel costs for any group of city employees. White hopes to make a name for himself here in Jonesville before moving on to a larger city.

Susan Brown—deputy director of personnel relations. She has great concern for the role of women and minorities in city personnel practices. Brown also handles complaints filed against city workers, including the police. She feels that too many members of the police department are overpaid and are unfit to be police officers.

James Castle—city councilman who is assigned to the Public Safety
Committee. Castle received an endorsement from the PBA in the last election.
He is known as a "cop lover" by other politicians.

Objectives

The Jonesville PBA must try to improve its present wages, benefits, and other
conditions of employment. The city of Jonesville must attempt to keep the status quo lest it plunge itself deeper into debt.

Playing the Game

Both sides must organize and prepare themselves for the bargaining session.
Review this chapter and follow the processes presented by the authors. There
should be enough time to complete the game, but your instructor may have to
impose some time constraints. In one bargaining session, the class spent over
40 hours and still was at an impasse before the role play was terminated.

BIBLIOGRAPHY

"Bargaining Preparations for the Negotiator." *Police Law Reporter*, 5 (1978), pp. 10–13.

BOPP, WILLIAM J. "The Detroit Police Revolt." In William J. Bopp, ed., *The Police
Rebellion*. Springfield, Ill.: Charles C. Thomas, 1971, pp. 162–172.

BOWERS, M.H. "Contemporary Police Employee Organizations and the Labor Relations
Process." In *Crucial Issues in Police Labor Relations*. Gaithersburg, Md.: International
Association of Chiefs of Police, 1973.

BUREAU OF LABOR STATISTICS, "Union Members in 2002." Washington, D.C.: United
States Department of Labor, February 2003. Web posted at www.bls.gov.cps.
Accessed May 12, 2003.

BURPO, J.H. "The Legal and Management Aspects of Police Strikes." In R. Ayres and
T. Wheelen, eds., *Collective Bargaining in the Public Sector*. Gaithersburg, Md.:
International Association of Chiefs of Police, 1977.

DANIEL, MAC. "Massport Hoping to Create Elite Police Unit at Logan." *Boston Globe*, re-
trieved from Lexus/Nexus, September 4, 2002.

FALLON, DENNY. "Police Labor in the '80s." *National Centurion*, 2, no. 5 (June 1984),
pp. 38–45.

FLIPCZAK, BOB. "Unions in the '90s: Cooperation or Capitulation?" *Training*, May 1993,
pp. 25–34.

GAMMAGE, A.Z., and S.L. SACHS. *Police Unions*. Springfield, Ill.: Charles C. Thomas,
1972.

Garcia v. *San Antonio Metropolitan Transit Authority*, 29 U.S.C. Sections 201–262 (1986).

GELLER, WILLIAM A. *Local Government Police Management* (3rd ed.). Washington, D.C.:
International City Management Association, 1991.

INTERNATIONAL ASSOCIATION OF CHIEFS OF POLICE. *Crucial Issues in Police Labor
Relations*. Gaithersburg, Md.: International Association of Chiefs of Police, 1977.

JURIS, H.A., and P. FEUILLE. *Police Unionism: Power and Impact in Public Sector Bargaining.* Lexington, Mass.: D.C. Heath, 1973.

KLOTZ, R. "Ground Rules." *Police Law Reporter,* 5 (1978), pp. 13–16.

"Labor Notes." *Police Magazine,* July 1979, p. 21.

The Law Officer, August/September 1979, p. 1.

Lehnert v. *Ferris Valley Faculty Association,* 111 S.Ct. 1950 (1991).

MCCORMACK, WILLIAM U. "Law Enforcement and the Fair Labor Standards Act." *FBI Law Enforcement Bulletin,* 64, no. 5 (May 1995), pp. 28–32.

RYNECKI, STEVEN, D.A. CAIRNS, and D.J. CARNES. *Police Collective Bargaining Agreements: A National Management Survey.* Washington, D.C.: National League of Cities, 1978.

SWANSON, CHARLES R., LEONARD TERRITO AND ROBERT W. TAYLOR. *Police Administration: Structures, Processes, and Behavior* (5th ed.). Upper Saddle River, N.J.: Prentice Hall, 2001.

WALKER, SAMUEL. *The Police in America* (3rd ed.). Boston: McGraw-Hill, 1999.

YOUNG, STEVE. "Nationwide Concealed Carry: Is It a Priority for You?" *The Journal— Fraternal Order of Police* (fall 2002), pp. 1–2.

THE FUTURE OF PROACTIVE POLICE MANAGEMENT

A SCENARIO FOR THE FUTURE

Captain Ryan Ortega put on his virtual helmet as his command vehicle came to a stop. His partner, Mary Fung Kan, looked at the swirling crowds. Stealth helicopters transmitted clear pictures of the housing project directly to Ortega's helmet. The computer screen in the car was alive with probability curves of potential crimes and disturbances in the 10-block area surrounding the car. Lieutenant Kan was doing an asset array, including undercover assets and firepower potential, on her laptop. Ortega opened the command channel, which included a digitized encrypted line to the community police section headquarters.

Captain Ortega calls the sergeant for the community policing unit in the area and requests information on the causes for the gathering. According to Sergeant Anthony Smith, a rumor has started that the project is scheduled to be closed because of the collapse of federal and state housing funds. The project, which used to be a brick city in the 1990s, was turned into a neighborhood with townhouses, trees, and gardens. The majority of the population here is over 50 years old. According to the rumor, everyone will be forced to move, and the area will be turned into a manufacturing site owned by a multinational corporation. What has sparked this event is that private police officials from the Euro-Pacific and Space Transportation Company have been doing crime-prevention surveys to see whether the area can become a repair station for earth and space transport ships.

Smith asks Ortega to contact the mayor's office and ask representatives to come and talk to the crowd. "The organizers have promised not to hurt the public community police officers, but they will take out property owned by Euro-Pacific that is in the area," Smith reports.

The information is transmitted directly to the executive team at headquarters and becomes part of a database for the district community policing team. A riot is forming. Riot-control dispersal experts are called in while the burglary-prevention team secures the majority of homes in the project. A notification via the 3-D video goes to a computer-generated address list in the neighborhood, overriding all other broadcasts.

All these events and actions have been anticipated by the central police agency planning team, which works out of the regional planning, hiring, training, and laboratory center. The metropolitan department had just been given high marks for its training/education, community involvement, and police service. The rapid response team was one of the department's highlights.

ANTICIPATING THE PROACTIVE POLICE UNIVERSE

While the above excerpt is fictional, current economic and political trends in the United States and the global environment give the scenario a great deal of reality for police managers. These trends include the following:

- Increased costs for medical services and drugs
- Growth of inexpensive technology with instant communication through smart cell phones and miniaturized personal computers
- Increasing economic and social division and barriers between rich and poor individuals and countries
- Changes in population demographics, with the increase in the cultural and ethnic diversity of the population creating ethnic, lifestyle, and social-class enclaves and neighborhoods throughout the country
- Career equity regardless of gender, race, and ethnicity pushed, in part, by the immigration into North America of highly educated professionals from Third World and former Soviet countries
- Increased multinational organized crime activity preying on individual neighborhoods and businesses through illegal drugs, extortion, and theft of major goods and services, partially sponsored by Third World governments
- Decline in the overall crime rate but increased concern with offenses committed by violent juveniles and individuals with modern weapons, terrorism, and threats against the infrastructure, such as the disruption of communications by cybercrime
- Increases in planning and allocation of domestic resources for homeland security and protection from terrorist groups

- Increasing powers of multinational corporations, many of which are based in the United States, and the mix of competition and cooperation from private police controlled by these same corporations. Target hardening and executive protection become major concerns.
- Increasing professionalization of public and private police. Community involvement with public police but the growing numbers of private police who protect only certain people in the community by contract.
- Universal smart credit cards based on imbedded microchips, DNA identification, and global positioning system (GPS) technology, with data transmitted to central banking and public databases, which can be used to track the movements and transactions of almost everyone

The Proactive Police Response

The proactive police response is a series of strategies that includes cost-effective concentration of administration, human resources, laboratory services, corruption and police brutality intervention, and training services for police departments. It includes the following:

- Deployment of community policing, including giving more authority to remote unit supervisors; human service/communication training for officers, supervisors, and police managers
- Proactive planning to anticipate planned and unplanned events, including critical incident and hot spot management; centralized rapid-response teams with maximum equipment and human relations experts organized for instant deployment
- Greater dependence on private police, auxiliary police, and community volunteers; major corporation private police begin to have more public police powers
- Major police executives who are highly educated and professional and move from one major police department to another throughout the country

All this is the extrapolation of current trends. This is done by becoming thoroughly familiar with current police management data, policies, and concepts. Ours is a rapidly changing society. Adults from the World War II and Korean War generations can still remember a childhood without electricity. The car became important to policing in the 1920s, before television. Anomalies exist. As we did in the nineteenth century, we still use horses for effective crowd control. Computers became available to the general public only during the last two generations.

The global world is here to stay with instant communication and rapid transportation. The pace of change for the postindustrial generation is staggering. This is a scenario for America and other industrial and postindustrial countries. The overwhelming majority of the world's population lives in preindustrial conditions, with access to modern communications. Thus, we must never forget that policing is global and both private and public. That globe is shrinking every day. The overlooked power and authority of private police is growing all over the world.

The human condition will always be with us despite the rapid changes. Law enforcement is still a human service agency, a people agency. Let's examine how we plan proactively to involve the community in the future. Of course, the realistic view is that the future is now.

What does the future hold for law enforcement managers? Given current trends, it is expected that police departments may be changed or organized along the lines presented in this chapter by the year 2010. We believe that this will result in effective policing given the socioeconomic, political, and technological realities of the future. The major thrust for change will be the demands made by cost-conscious municipal governments to continue to provide the wide array of police services demanded by citizens.

POLICE DEPARTMENT CONSIDERATIONS

This abundance of forces is the historical result of our federal system of government and the wish of local communities to have control over their police. These realities of a democratic republic produce common problems of concurrent jurisdiction and duplication of effort. While citizens in cities can generally identify their police department, citizens of the many townships across the country have two or more options when they need the police. The selection includes the state police, town police, county sheriff's department, or village police. As a result, there exist these organizational realities in American policing today:

1. Active competition between police organizations for calls, resources, and, at times, personnel
2. De facto spheres of influence arranged by formal and informal agreements between agencies. For example, while the state police have statewide jurisdiction, many will normally not answer calls in a village that has a police department; the village police, in the same light, will not go outside municipal limits except in pursuit of an offender.
3. Informal relationships, usually based on how well certain officers or agency heads get along, determine the distribution of intelligence information, assistance to other departments during emergencies, and the success or failure of interagency projects

Some economists and social scientists might argue that this is healthy since it allows for competition, selection, and other market variables used by consumers for private-sector products. Some feel that police services can be provided by private contractors as long as the legal questions and cost-for-services formulas are worked out.

The number of law enforcement organizations would undoubtedly continue to increase were it not for the recent sharp demand for cost-effective police services. As municipal and police managers dealing with annual budgets know, costs for police personnel, equipment, and buildings have escalated in the last decade. Most of the funding is derived from taxation, and taxpayers are generally angry over the prospect of future tax increases at the federal, state, or local level. Political officeholders know that if taxes escalate in their communities, they will be out of jobs. The message to "hold down costs" has been relayed to all municipal department heads. This includes police commanders, who are told that their jobs will be jeopardized if they cannot balance their budgets. And so the story goes all over the country.

This financial crisis has reached new proportions created in part by policies on the federal level, which have reduced aid to state and local municipalities. When funding is tight, vehicles are overhauled rather than replaced, plant maintenance and rehabilitation are deferred, and wage and benefit increases are forestalled either by contract or by mutual agreement. All in all, proactive police managers of the future will have to offer police services in an effective and economical way; that is, they will be required by their citizenry and elected officials to do more with less. State and federal governments may have to respond with creative ways of raising money for policing. For example, we may see a tax on certain services, such as responding to home or building alarms in private businesses. Already, parking fines are returned either directly or indirectly to police budgets; other forms of revenue may be generated outside of the tax structure.

The Jurisdictional Dilemma

The existence of too many police departments results in duplication of services for many areas in the United States. Many argue for this, especially small-town politicians and police chiefs, who use the **home rule** argument to keep this jumbled, inefficient system intact. We predicted in our first edition that many municipalities would merge their police department with other governmental units or abolish the department outright. This has not occurred, mainly because of home rule.

Many local schools have been closed or merged because of the decline in the numbers of children who have to be educated. When such an action is announced, there is often community protest and some delay, but usually the change is effected. Police departments are now subject to similar action, but there are some alternatives available for communities that wish to retain their local police. One common way is to share centralized services; for example, computerized recordkeeping, communications, vehicle acquisition and repair, supplies, equipment, and even laboratory and training facilities. In many instances, this type of sharing results in an upgrade of the present system of equipment currently in use by the local department.

A trend that we see increasing is police **consolidation,** as when two or more departments are disbanded and merged into an area or county metropolitan police department. Departments that have undergone this process include those in Nassau and Suffolk Counties in New York; Riley County, Kentucky; Jacksonville, Florida; and Toronto, Ontario. While this may sound easy, consolidation can be a very arduous process.

Although there is potential for increasing police efficiency by reducing duplication of effort, consolidation does not always result in economy. From the outset, it can be expensive. Officer and command officials of previously existing departments are given new pay raises based on the highest wage scale paid in one of the "older" departments. New equipment has to be purchased on a mass scale for distinctive uniforms, vehicles, and weapons. New station houses have to be rented, purchased, or constructed. Aside from implementation, there are some other long-term managerial ramifications. Regarding the collective bargaining issue, smaller police unions are eliminated and reformed into one or more powerful union(s) because of increased membership. Former chiefs of police are "demoted" to ranking administrative officers. New organizational charts and duties have to be prepared. Interestingly enough, departmental subculture is revised with the creation of a consolidated police force, which results in new patrol zones, shifts, and duty assignments. But for lower-ranking administrators and patrol officers, consolidation presents all kinds of opportunities for professional and career advancement.

What this all means is that the concept of consolidation can be feasible where there are high concentrations of people or businesses that create a single socioeconomic municipality. Consolidation, moreover, may reflect another trend whereby municipalities merge as political entities resulting in a merger of police, fire, and other public services.

Another form of consolidation is combining police and fire departments. This has met with mixed success. Generally, it works best with small departments within a limited geographic area. For example, communities that have consolidated are Clifton, New Jersey, population 90,000; Flagstaff, Arizona, population 26,000; El Dorado, Kansas, population 13,000; Glencoe, Illinois, population 10,000; and the largest population and area, Sunnyvale, California, population 106,000 with 22 square miles of jurisdiction. According to Rubin (1984: 225), the cities of Peoria, Lincoln, and St. Petersburg adopted public safety programs combining fire and police and later abandoned them. In all cases, Rubin (1984: 226) concludes, "Labor-management cooperation is imperative."

Consolidation of fire and police services has been around the United States since 1911 and may work in some communities with fairly small populations. There has been both partial and full consolidation. It is a difficult process with many legal, personnel, and organizational problems, but it is tempting to mayors and city managers hoping for cost savings. Cost savings may or may not come about, and any fire/police consolidation should be carefully thought through, especially in terms of analyzing the different missions of the police and fire departments.

Many communities in the United States contract for police services from another municipality. The basic considerations in determining contractual services are the following:

1. Statutory provisions related to contract agreements
2. Formulas to be used in charging for such services as patrol, traffic, criminal investigations, and so on
3. Planning and resolving various issues that come with normal policing (e.g., interruption of services, liability, physical plant needs, personnel requirements)
4. Determining performance criteria for continuance of the contract (e.g., lower crime rate, citizen satisfaction with services)

Since the 1970s, a number of feasibility studies were undertaken on the issue of contractual services. According to the National Sheriff's Association, there are the following types of contractual arrangements:

City to city. Police service is provided by one city to another.

County to city or county to region. Perhaps the most common contractual arrangement in the United States occurs when a county sheriff or police department provides police services to municipalities in the county on a shared-expense or contributory-expense arrangement. Such situations exist in Cook County, Illinois; Los Angeles County, Orange County, and Riverside County, California; Decatur County, Iowa; Brown County, Wisconsin; and Penellas County, Florida.

Resident officer program. Small towns that do not have a police department may contract for one or more full-time police officers from the state police or county sheriff's department. Expenses paid for these officers by the township are usually one-half the total cost of each person. In some cases, the officers receive a bonus if they reside in the contractual area.

Technology

If anything, the technological revolution continues to revise police practices. Even the smallest of departments have embraced microcomputing systems and workstations. We see no end in sight to the various adaptations that can be accomplished. Nevertheless, police managers have to be informed consumers of this new **technology**.

Although managers are not expected to know how to tear apart a computer terminal system, they should know the strengths and weaknesses of implementing a computerized records system for a department or division. They need to know about basic programming to experiment with new methodologies that deal with budgets, crime trends, personnel records, and so on. The same is true for other forms of technology, such as video units, which can be used for long-term surveillance of target areas, thereby freeing personnel for other duties.

As we talk about technology and policing, we must not lose sight of the need for greater interaction between citizens and their police officers. One program that has assisted in this endeavor is bicycle patrol (some might say a rather low-tech program), which on college campuses and in densely populated areas has received high marks for increasing visibility and officer-citizen interaction.

Patrol methods may change dramatically from the preventive brand that is employed today. It is now possible for every patrol vehicle to be equipped with a miniature computer-augmented mobile radio that relays an automatic signal back to the communications center giving the location of the vehicle on an electronic map of the metropolitan area. Computerized crime analysis also permits this map to be keyed to show a great variety of characteristics to facilitate planning. Some of these are the following:

1. Street and map response time grid
2. Modus operandi grid related to demographic characteristics and time of crime commitment
3. Time, place, and nature of crimes shown by number and color for easy identification. Listings of burglaries, robberies, traffic deaths, juvenile crimes, and other grids would be available at the punch of a button.
4. Demographic vehicles: density, distribution, and vital statistics of population
5. Trend-analysis grids for traffic control, civilian disasters, and energy blackouts would be available for planners if a disaster or traffic stoppage occurred.
6. All this available on encrypted, hand-held palm computers.

Reflecting the state of the art for cable television, all homes and businesses can be linked to a central dispatch system in a police-approved, computer-based, remote linkage system. This would combine burglar and fire alarms operating through land lines and cable television circuits.

Personnel Practices

Given the current trends in positive personnel selection, it is possible that we may see the following in the future:

1. Associate's or bachelor's degree demanded of all recruits
2. Men and women being assigned to all facets of the police mission and promoted to specialty units and command and supervisory positions—all on an equal basis.

3. The police recruit selection process placing less emphasis on pencil-and-paper tests and more emphasis on testing by role play, interview, aptitude, and other assessment-center methods.

More lateral entry between police departments on a state and national level would increase the pool of available candidates for line, staff, and managerial positions. If this becomes a reality, there will be renewed emphasis on the quality selection of police managers since the available pool will increase competition.

While running the risk of criticism for being too general, it can be said that the "typical police chief" of today has the following characteristics:

- Is 45 to 52 years of age
- Has worked through the ranks of a department
- Has had little experience in either public or private administration prior to appointment or selection as chief. Training consisted of some police academy seminars and learning by the ropes. Formal education was limited to high school, augmented by courses taken at the local community college, or an associate's degree.
- Was selected as chief by written civil service examination, political appointment, or election

With the organizational and milieu changes that we see occurring in American policing, it comes as no surprise that the credentials of future managers will also be undergoing some change. Reflecting current trends in patrol officer selection, police managers of the future will also be the products of advanced managerial training and higher education. In the future, the selection of police managers will correspond to that already practiced by many private-sector enterprises for executive talent. Psychological testing, role plays involving managerial problems, and oral review boards will be the rule for selection rather than the exception. This cadre of police executives will be highly mobile in that a police executive could be "chief" at a number of departments during a law enforcement career, with minor or extended excursions into industry and teaching.

Selection for supervisors and administrative staff members will also reflect some changes. Again, less reliance will be placed on pencil-and-paper tests and years of experience. Requirements for future hiring might be the following:

- A master's degree in police administration or a related field
- Three years of experience in police planning, patrol, or investigations
- Successful completion of the state-certified training academy for police patrol officers and supervisors. Some states may be issuing licenses by this time that have to be renewed on a timely basis.

Individuals who show administrative talent would be "tracked" into a departmental executive-development program that would provide for future executives a rational combination of in-class training and field exposure to all facets of the police mission.

WHAT WORKS AND EVIDENCE-BASED POLICING

Twenty-first-century technology gives the proactive police manager the tools to control events. This technology is being improved and becoming less expensive almost on a daily basis. The first proactive principle is that police management is always in charge of technology. Technology should never be allowed to drive police management policy.

Police management in the twenty-first century will be both data driven and based on the rapid communication of information. This means that all justifiable policies and procedures will be computer based. Police officers deal with human beings, often in stressful situations. Officers will need to be grounded in the social sciences and human behavioral studies.

Let's take a look at the state of affairs that meet professional proactive standards for the twenty-first century. As a community-based criminal justice social service, police departments and police management need the latest in technology for both communications and planning. With scarce resources, the police manager needs to keep doing what works and stop doing what does not work.

Unlike the rigid computer mainframe technology of the past, the twenty-first-century approaches, focused on the individual officers and field units, are changing rapidly and are extremely flexible. To make full use of this new technology, police management will have to decentralize daily decision making down to the line officers, their immediate supervisors, and individual field units. Centralized communications, a solid feedback system, and proactive, flexible written departmental rules will make this system work.

Written rules and records include stored electronic communications and some limited use of hard copy. Laptop technology will be built into every police car. Individually compatible palm-type communication and recording devices will be carried by every officer in the near future.

A proactive department is a data-driven department, with its human side being provided by community policing. This department (1) lowers crime through good management and the proactive use of technology and (2) has the community set the agenda for the police department. A community-based problem-solving approach will create the twenty-first-century proactive police department. This department will be goal oriented, focusing on the same goal as the first nineteenth-century professional police department. The 1829 Metropolitan London Police Department's goal was the prevention of crime rather than just the apprehension of criminals. Prevention is proactive, while apprehension is reactive because apprehension comes after the crime has been committed.

The major proactive police management and technology tools to bring about this successful approach involve crime mapping. The New York City Police Department's Compstat program is the most successful use of crime mapping. It is available to other departments now, and it will work even more effectively in the future when combined with the newest laptop and palm information technology with continuing feedback.

Crime-mapping approaches can also enhance community policing when community policing guidelines are added. Crime maps can be made available to citizen groups to provide crucial information to crime problems in specific neighborhoods, towns, and villages. In Hartford, Connecticut, a local crime-prevention community organization was provided with basic mapping tools to "analyze incident level calls for service, crime and arrest data" (Rich, 1999). It was said to have improved communications between residents and police since they shared the same database on neighborhood crime.

Two major documents published in 1998 by Larry Sherman help set the stage for this new approach: *Preventing Crime: What Works, What Doesn't, What's Promising* and *Evidence Based Policing*. This approach, which is enhanced by computer mapping, is to base crime-reducing strategies on hard data and scientific evidence.

Preventing Crime (Sherman, 1998b) was based on a review of 500 prevention programs using standard data-based scientific criteria. Some of the nonpolice programs that diminished criminal behavior were antibullying campaigns in schools, teaching social competence and stress-management skills, ex-offender job training for older males, and therapeutic community-treatment programs in prisons for adult drug addicts.

Going after landlords who allow drugs on their property works. Working with public housing authorities to drive out the drug dealers and penalize the landlords works. Focusing extra police presence on what Sherman calls "hot spots" works. Hot spots, or places where crime is concentrated, may be determined by the high percentage of police calls to a bar or public housing project, for example. Arresting employed suspects for family violence who live in the suburbs works, but arresting unemployed, minority suspects in the inner city increases family violence and does not work.

Some favorite police programs do not work. Mobilizing inner-city residents to stop crime, gun buy-back programs, Drug Abuse Resistance Education (DARE), neighborhood watch, storefront police offices, and police newsletters with local crime information do not work. Crime prevention that is based on data works. Crime prevention that is based on good feelings is a public relations program rather than a crime-prevention program.

This is partly what is meant by a proactive data-driven police department: Do what works based on data, not on public relations or good feelings. This also means that police departments need to evaluate police policy based on data and scientific evidence.

According to Sherman (1998a: 3–4), "Evidence-based policing is the use of the best available research on the outcomes of police work to implement guidelines and evaluate agencies, units and officers. . . . Evidence-based policing uses research to guide practice and evaluate practitioners." He wants to create a feedback loop using the evaluation of outcomes to change police practices. For example, if DARE does not work, put your limited resources into hot-spot policing. If gun buy-back programs do not work to control youth homicides, create an interagency drug task force focused on youth homicides, like the one that worked in Boston. Use some of the resources that you had to fund storefront police and instead fund programs for controlling homicide by gang members. We cannot continue to fund police programs that are documented as failures while we have police programs that have been documented as successes. This is how an evidence-based police department works to justify choices by police managers.

Sherman (1998a: 5) shows what data he would refer to in **evidence-based policing:** "offenses per 1,000 residents, repeat victimization per 100 offenders, and so on." If you complain about how an officer handles a call but have no data, it is a negative remark with negative outcomes. If you have a program that can be placed on a graph concerning call-backs by officers and units, you have, at least, one data-driven evaluation. This would have a positive effect on future police management decisions. Management would have to analyze the reasons for the call-backs and the rate of call-backs by each unit for specific events.

Sherman's evidence-based policing and proactive data-based police management focus on outcomes. If police managers want to have a police department that actually solves ongoing community problems, part of every problem-solving approach needs to include data-based evaluations (Goldstein, 1990). Sherman says that successful approaches to problem solving have to be generalized. Police management can no longer consider each problem to be unique to every police department.

Sherman (1998a: 6) says that most police practices are "still shaped by local custom, opinion theories and subjective impressions." He is looking for a new data-driven approach based on implementation evaluations as well as experimental evidence.

One study conducted by Sherman found that offenders who felt that the police did not treat them fairly committed 60 percent more incidents of family violence than those who felt that they were treated fairly. Sherman recommended creating guidelines for police procedure concerning the fair treatment of suspects in family violence incidents. The success of these guidelines and their implementation would be evaluated using county- or citywide data on family violence.

If the police management goal is to decrease repeat instances of family violence, then different procedures and policies have to be tried until police management identifies the ones that work. From time to time, the new policy will have to be evaluated to see (1) whether it is still working and (2) what may be hindering and helping the implementation of each successful policy.

GLOBAL CRIME AND THE NEED FOR A GLOBAL POLICE ORGANIZATION

Have we reached a time when there is a need for a global police organization? We already have a history of transnational police cooperation. In 1992, the European Union established Europol to combat "illicit drug trafficking, trafficking in human beings, terrorism and money laundering" (Reichel, 2002: 181). Interpol has facilitated an international exchange of criminal information since the 1920s (Footner, 1975). The International Narcotics Control Board of the United Nations has established international exchange of police information and cooperation. National police agencies now need to move beyond this sharing of information and extradition treaties to something far more universal, however.

A global police organization is the next step needed to investigate and arrest both cross-national criminals and terrorists and to destroy cross-national criminal and terrorist organizations. A global police organization would assist and train local, regional, and national police departments in investigations across national borders.

Consider the following. Conspiracies involving drugs, stolen property, illegal immigration, and terrorism with roots in other parts of the world have profound economic and political effects on the United States. For example, the attacks on September 11, 2001, continue to have an impact on the American economy in terms of homeland and transportation security costs. Terrorist and transnational crime organizations buy and sell arms and explosives throughout the world. Money laundering worldwide is an important enterprise of illegal drug cartels and international groups. It is well documented that cross-national drug enterprises are organized and supported by terrorist groups as a major source of funding. Often these groups engage in murder and kidnapping of high-ranking public and corporate officials. Right now, the current emphasis is on the Al Qaeda terrorist group, which continues to be a worldwide network reaching out from the isolated regions of Pakistan to the urban areas of Europe and the United States. While attention is focused on the training and transit of terrorists, the real dilemma is the extent to which Al Qaeda accumulated fiscal resources through legitimate businesses in Europe and the Sudan. There is even the theory that the group attempted to manipulate airline stock prices and profits before September 11.

While terrorism and narcotics trafficking gain much official and media attention, there are other important issues. On the global level, rapidly increasing population trends and civil war inevitably lead to overcrowding of urban areas, large areas of poverty and hunger, and concentrated movements of people and goods across national boundaries. These unstable conditions attract transnational criminal organizations to provide weapons for competing political factions. Conditions of this nature, as evidenced by recent events in Africa and the former communist state of Yugoslavia, can lead to state-sponsored genocide, which is the elimination of entire ethnic groups.

Adding to the problem is the issue of "rogue countries." A rogue country is one that actively supports international offenses ranging from drug smuggling to terrorism. In some cases, the country is unable to deal with criminal cartels because of civil war, as in Colombia, or because official corruption has rendered law enforcement efforts ineffective, as appears to be the case in Nigeria, Jamaica, and many other countries. Another example is Libya, which serves as a haven for terrorists and provides them with operational and financial assistance.

Another important issue is the large number of financial transactions that escape all formal foreign exchange regulations imposed by national governments. The billions generated by drugs, money laundering, and illegal arms purchases have a destabilizing effect on many countries in terms of lost tax revenue and official corruption.

The Link between Global Terrorism and Global Crime Organizations

Financing for terrorist activities is generated with the help of organized crime and involves the illicit drug trade, the smuggling of weapons, kidnapping, and extortion. These terrorist activities have reached global dimensions. There is a clear link between many terrorist organizations and cross-national crime, but there is no effective proactive global police organization available to combat this activity.

Many politicians and bankers are involved in global money laundering that escapes all formal foreign exchange regulation imposed by the national governments. Due to the nature of the transaction and the lack of any traceable records, it is very difficult to detect or prove these criminal violations. Profits generated through these transactions are often used to purchase arms across borders. These illegal transactions create political and economic instability in the country of origin and in neighboring countries. The billions generated by drugs, money laundering, and illegal arms purchasing and smuggling has had a destabilizing effect on Third World countries and regions. Law enforcement agents and practitioners working in this field emphatically argue, "Into the twenty-first century America will be increasingly confronted by international crime, including international terrorism and organized crime" (Sessions, 1990).

Obstacles to International Police Cooperation

The great rates of transnational criminality have laid the foundation for new guidelines for various forms of international police cooperation at the global level. There are, however, some major obstacles:

Language Barriers.   The lack of a universal language is a major communication problem for regional, national, intercontinental, and international levels of policing. This can range from investigative practices to arrest and apprehension of transnational criminals. Associated police agencies inevitably have to rely on interpreters. Following in the footsteps of the airlines and the World Wide Web, the adoption of English as the major language for international police cooperation would simplify communications and eliminate a major source of misunderstanding and expense.

Police Corruption.   Police personnel in many countries still lack elements of professionalism, receive meager remuneration, and are equipped with weak technology. This leads to police personnel's involvement in many direct and/or indirect forms of corrupt activities. In some situations, the corruptive practices are linked with fellow governmental officials and some political leaders. Problems of corruption and unethical behavior plague law enforcement agencies the world over. In all countries in the world, there are informal relations and the exchange of favors between the police, political leaders, governmental officials, and private citizens.

International training centers with high professional and ethical standards administered by a cross-national police service would be a major step in fostering a positive attitude toward the elimination of police corruption. A highly ethical cross-national police service would serve as a standard and model to professionalize Third World police forces.

Lack of Permanent Funding for Global Policing Activities.   Police organizations face obstacles in recruiting, training, and paying for global policing services. These factors are highly disproportionate from country to country. This has a negative impact on the quality of personnel selected for policing. Many poor countries lack appropriate electronic and other technical equipment that is needed to detect crimes, especially when investigating homicides, drug transactions, and fraudulent documents, which include illegal passports, visas, and counterfeit currency. Chemical analysis laboratory facilities are often either inadequate or nonexistent.

Political Hostility and Indifference.   It is important that politicians support the policing functionaries when compared to other social and economic problems of the respective countries. The criminals and terrorists have organized the world. The time is ripe for the legitimate countries and global corporations of the world to defend their citizens and customers against these criminals and terrorists by establishing a cross-national police service.

Favorable Conditions for the Establishment of a Cross-National Police Service

Most countries participated in international police cooperation as early as 1923 (Footner, 1975). Most countries, including those that gained independence only recently, have shared and extended various informal and formal mechanisms for apprehending crimes and criminals. Most countries confronted three major problems: illegal drug trafficking, terrorist activities, and various forms of social, political, and economic upheavals. These conditions threaten the stability of all countries.

International cooperation is crucial in addressing transnational crimes. Rapid changes in countries provide many new opportunities for transnational criminal activities. Cooperation has become functional at (1) formal and informal levels; (2) regional and national levels; (3) intercontinental levels; and (4) international levels. The process of police cooperation at the global level is continuing. A coordinated effort between developed and underdeveloped countries is required for the establishment of treaties, agreements, and conventions on extradition, legal assistance, transfer of criminal proceedings, transfer of penal sanctions, and transfer of prisoners (Anderson, 1989; Sessions, 1990; and Nadelmann, 1993).

Nevertheless, several factors favor international police cooperation:

1. Current travel facilities enhance offenders' mobility and thus their ability to escape detection of crime.
2. The present technologically advanced world of electronic transactions allows transfer of illegally obtained funds and profits to overseas financial institutions, thus reducing the possibilities of detection.
3. Transnational criminals are able to harm individuals, organizations, and neighboring countries through technological transactions without entering the victimized countries. Thus, transnational law enforcement has become enormously complex.
4. Due to the transparency of national boundaries, criminals can easily "lose" themselves, thereby making detection and apprehension difficult if not impossible. The rapid reorganization and boundary changes witnessed recently in Eastern Europe have also made it easier for fugitives to escape detection and apprehension.
5. Although many countries have developed and introduced treaties to extradite offenders, many still lack identical definitions and punishments for similar crimes (Anderson, 1989; Nadelmann, 1993).

The global economy needs a cross-national police organization that will deal with criminal problems that cross national boundaries. Economics and crime are global, while policing has remained national.

The Global Investigation of Cross-National Crime

A global police organization would provide expert personnel in various areas of cross-national crime, including drugs, money laundering, extortion, international kidnapping, terrorist organizations, banking, and computer crime. This takes sophisticated technology and personnel that many countries cannot afford. Global police services would provide access to these specialized services through treaties and private contracts by signature countries and global corporations.

Regional cross-national crime laboratories could provide both analysis of evidence and transnational criminal patterning. Communications would be both land and satellite based. Sophisticated imaging would provide digital results of chemical and other physical tests.

A global police training center is needed to focus on forensics, crime investigation, cybercrime, organized and organizational crime, tracking across borders, money-laundering techniques, banking protocols, proactive police management techniques, budgeting, hostage negotiation, and terrorist organizations and methods. Courses would be on-line and on campus. Certain courses would only be taught on campus, with limited and carefully screened enrollments for security reasons. Experienced faculty would be borrowed from national police academies to augment the training center's permanent core of full-time faculty. They would need the appropriate academic credentials and field experience.

Cross-national criminal and terrorist groups are organized with the latest technology. They are more profitable and have more money than many Wall Street corporations. They do not respect national boundaries, legitimate governments, or police agencies. Rogue nations protect these criminal and terrorist groups, providing them with safe havens and legal documentation.

It is now time for the legitimate countries and global corporations of the world to set up a counterforce to fight these criminal and terrorist groups. Crime and terrorism are global. Police organizations have to become proactive, transnational, and global.

CONCLUSION

Proactive Community Policing in the Twenty-First Century

In a society of scarce resources, police departments need to plan carefully a cost-efficient use of police resources targeting the most pressing community problems as perceived by the community. As corporate and private police become more evident, new legislation concerning professionalization of these forces will take place. Public and private police will work together using legally enforceable contracts. Increasingly, some police services will be contracted out.

The extensive use of technology makes this possible. The educated line officer will take on more responsibilities, using community enforcement as a major approach to street and neighborhood crime. Training in communication, use of technological services, and collective behavior will become most important to the proactive police officer, manager, and supervisor.

As more responsibility for anticipating events and taking proactive action is embraced by every level of command, morale will improve. Communities will take back their neighborhoods with the help of their proactive police department.

Proactive Rural Policing

Meanwhile, rural communities will become less isolated as the Internet and communications systems link them with the worldwide network of work/communications. Rural police will have to adapt to the standards of the proactive police departments in metropolitan areas. Regional academies and services for rural agencies will upgrade the professionalism of these police officers. Their enlightened communities will also demand a higher level of community policing.

In 1994, a systematic national survey of rural police was conducted with 80 percent of the departments having 20 officers or fewer. The most frequently cited crime problems were drug use, drinking and driving, juvenile crime, and drug trafficking and production. More than one-half had crime-prevention programs, officers involved as members of community organizations, volunteers in their agencies, officers assigned to elementary and secondary schools, officers engaged in problem-solving community policing, including community policing training programs, and officers on foot patrol (Thurman and McGarrell, 1997: 20–23).

Rural communities have existed in the United States since its early years as an agricultural society. Police were already part of these communities even before the idea of community policing had been formed. The sense of community that urban areas are searching for was established in small-town America. Since police in these areas are considered part of a greater community, it is a fairly simple step to establish the proactive community policing of the twenty-first century.

Technology will provide a vast communications network; distance and weather are no longer barriers to instant communication. Virtual communities have already been established. These virtual communities will welcome a professionalized proactive community police force.

The Proactive Community Policing Management Model

It will take time to establish proactive community police norms as part of police culture. Police still cherish their social isolation and their perception of public hostility. Reality and political pressure will play an important part in the transformation of the traditional police department into the technologically aware, proactive, professional police force of the future. Since the creation of the London Metropolitan Police Department in 1829, police culture has had to solidify its present subculture. It will take time and a great deal of effort to transform our police forces into a paradigm. However, it will happen. The new generation of police officers, supervisors, and managers who are reading this textbook will make it happen. But it will not be easy.

The combination of centralized administration and internal services for the police agency and remote community-based decision making will work. The extensive use of technology and communication makes this possible. The educated line officer will take on more responsibilities with community enforcement as a major approach to street and neighborhood crime. Training in communication and human services and the use of technological services and collective behavior will become of paramount importance to the proactive police officer, manager, and supervisor. As more responsibility for anticipating events and taking proactive action is embraced by every level of command, morale will improve along with responsibility. Communities will take back their neighborhoods with the help of their proactive police department.

A consultive management model is demanded by the new generation of professional police line officers and supervisors. They are college educated and are taking their place in police departments throughout the nation. These police officers and supervisors will demand more responsibility and autonomy. The promise of present and future technology, along with an attitude change brought about by the proactive community police model, will make this possible. The major characteristics of proactive community police management are the following:

1. Participatory management with more responsibility and autonomy given to supervisors in the field.
2. Centralized rapid response for critical incidents and emergencies.
3. The community sets the agenda for proactive policing in every neighborhood, town, village, and community center.
4. Police managers, supervisors, and line officers actively working with the community to prevent and contain crime, property theft and damage, and community violence.
5. Proactive, planned, and limited patrolling. The split force will have a section responding to 911 calls and a section for planning, hot-spot targeting and community policing, and so on.
6. Planning, forecasting, and anticipating events taking place in every part of every department. This will be conducted from a centralized planning unit to an individual team of officers making plans with a community neighborhood. Anticipatory planning will be central to the proactive community police department.
7. Training and education will take place side by side. After extensive background checks and testing, including psychological testing, the college-educated police officer will enter a highly professional training program. This program will emphasize police ethics, community involvement, technological and communications expertise, and human service skills along

with the traditional subjects. In-service and clinical training will persist throughout an officer's career, including supervisory and management training at promotion. Human resources will include stress management for all levels from line officers to major managers and their families.

8. This will be a "smart" police force that will use technology extensively. However, the educated proactive police manager will use technology as a tool and never let technology drive policy. Human beings will be in charge of technology, which will be extensively used in a community-oriented human service department.

9. This proactive department will use this planning and technology to reduce crime and to solve crimes for their communities. Solid investigative work will use the latest techniques, including DNA identification and hair/drug testing. Departments will employ their own lawyers to make cases prosecutable and to protect them against unreasonable plea bargains. Everyone, from line officer to police manager, will take a proactive approach to creating the best prosecutable cases possible.

Will this happen? This is the model that we reach for. If we reach for it, it can happen. If we do not reach for it, it will never happen. It can and will happen as the new generation of police managers, supervisors, and line officers work with the communities they have sworn to protect.

QUESTIONS FOR REVIEW

1. Do you agree or disagree with the societal changes for the twenty-first century that appear at the beginning of this chapter? Add two changes to the list.

2. Is the proactive police response realistic or just science fiction?

3. State the pros and cons of police consolidation. What do you think will happen in the future, and why?

4. What would you add to personnel practices for the future, and why?

5. Analyze the characteristics of the proactive community police model, and explain why you think it will or will not work.

BIBLIOGRAPHY

AMERICAN BAR ASSOCIATION, PROJECT ON STANDARDS FOR CRIMINAL JUSTICE. *Standards Relating to the Urban Police Function*. Chicago: American Bar Association, 1972.

ARMSTRONG, KAREN. "Was It Inevitable? Islam through History." In James F. Hoge Jr. and Gideon Rose, eds., *How Did This Happen?* New York: Public Affairs, 2002, pp. 53–70.

BALLARD, JAMES DAVID, JOSEPH G. HORNICK, and DOUGLAS MCKENZIE. "Technological Facilitation of Terrorism." In Harvey W. Kushner, ed., *Cyberterrorism in the Twenty-First Century*.

BANTON, MICHAEL. *The Policeman in the Community*. New York: Basic Books, 1964.

BARD, MORTON. *Training Police as Specialists in Family Crisis Intervention.* Washington, D.C.: U.S. Government Printing Office, 1970.

BRODEUR, JEAN-PAUL, ed. *How to Recognize Good Policing.* Thousand Oaks, Calif.: Sage/Police Executive Research Forum, 1998.

CRANK, JOHN. "The Community-Policing Movement of the Twenty-First Century: What We Have Learned." In John Klofas and Stan Stojkoic, eds., *Crime and Justice in the Year 2010.* New York: Wadsworth, 1995, pp. 107–127.

GARY, EILEEN M. *Performance Measures: What Works.* Washington, D.C.: National Institute of Justice, 1997.

GOLDSTEIN, HERMAN. *Problem-Oriented Policing.* New York: McGraw-Hill, 1990.

A Guide to Developing Performance Measures in Result-Based Budgeting. Washington, D.C.: Finance Project, 1997.

KELLING, GEORGE, and MARK H. MOORE. "The Evolving Strategy of Policing." In Victor Kappler, ed., *The Police and Society.* Prospect Heights, Ill.: Waveland Press, 1995, pp. 3–28.

KLOFAS, JOHN, and STAN STOJKOIC. *Crime and Justice in the Year 2010.* New York: Wadsworth, 1995.

MCDONALD, THOMAS D., ROBERT A. WOOD, and MELISSA A. PFLUG. *Rural Criminal Justice.* Salem, Wis.: Shieffield, 1996.

RICH, THOMAS. E. *The Use of Computerized Mapping in Crime Control and Prevention Programs.* Washington, D.C.: National Institutue of Justice, 1996.

RUBIN, RICHARD. "Consolidation of the Police and Fire Services." *Journal of Police Science and Administration,* 12, no. 2 (1984), pp. 58–69.

SHERMAN, LAWRENCE. *Evidence Based Policing.* Washington, D.C.: Police Foundation, 1998a.

―――. *Preventing Crime: What Works, What Doesn't, What's Promising.* Washington, D.C.: National Institute of Justice, 1998b.

STEPHENS, GENE. "Crime in Cyberspace: The Digital Underworld." In Edward Cornish, ed., *Exploring Your Future.* Washington, D.C.: World Future Society, 1996.

STRECHER, VICTOR G. "Revising the Histories and Futures of Policing." In Victor Kappler, ed., *The Police and Society.* Prospect Heights, Ill.: Waveland Press, 1995, pp. 83–94.

THURMAN, QUINT C., and EDMUND F. GARRELL. *Community Policing in a Rural Setting.* Cincinnati: Thomas, 1997.

INDEX

A

Academies, police, 355
Accreditation for law enforcement agencies,
    384–386
Activating, process of, 6
ADA (Americans with Disabilities Act), 311,
    312–315, 365
Adarand Constructors v. *Pena*, 307
Administration (administrative/staff functions),
    67–70, 76, 237–266
    budgeting, 69–70
    case study, 239–240
    community relations, 240–247
    coordinating, 69
    department rules and collective
        bargaining agreements, 253–254
    directing, 69
    disciplinary actions, 252–253
    legal adviser, 247–249
    line/staff conflict and cooperation,
        238–240
    organizing, 68
    patrol officers and, 160, 164–165
    planning, 68
    police misconduct, 259–266
    proactive control of police violence and
        deviance, 254–259
    professional standards and, 249–252
    reporting, 69
    staffing, 68

Advanced Regional Justice Information
    System, 144
Advanced training, 368
Aerobic power, 311
Affirmative action, 304–308
AFIS (Automatic Fingerprint Identification
    System), 292
African-American officers, 35–37
Age Discrimination in Employment Act of
    1974, 310
Age limits, for selection of personnel,
    310, 325
Agency shop, 428
Aggressive cynicism, 21
AIDS (acquired immunodeficiency syndrome),
    training and, 361
All-channel communication, 117
Amber Alert system, 208
American Federation of State, County, and
    Municipal Employees (AFSCME), 431
Americans with Disabilities Act (ADA), 311,
    312–315, 365
Ancillary public safety services, 295–296
Animal control, 296
Annual report, 136
Arbitration, 429
Argot, 20–21
Assessment center, 321–322
Assumptions about messages, 118
Athletic programs for juveniles, 218
Audits, internal, 261

Automated Regional Justice Information System (ARJIS), 142–143
Automatic Fingerprint Identification System (AFIS), 292
Automatic vehicle monitoring (AVM), 139–140
Auto-related crime, 417
Auxiliary functions, 76–77, 271–296
    ancillary public safety services, 295–296
    building maintenance, 285–287
    communications, 271–275
    crime laboratories, 287–295
    licensing, 287
    property control, 280–282
    records division, 275–280
    vehicle maintenance, 282–285

B

Background investigation, 315–322
    college education requirements, 320–321
    interviews, 319–320
    lateral entry, 318
    polygraph testing, 318–319
    psychological testing, 317–318
    residency, 316–317
Baurney v. *Pawtucket*, 38
Behavioral management, 10–11
Benchmarking, 94
Bias motivated crimes, 364–365
Bicycle patrol, 167–168
Biven's actions, 375
Black officer associations, 431
Black officers, 35–37
Blood-borne pathogens, training and, 361
Blue flu, 426, 439
Blue minority, 24
Boston Gun Project, 220–222
Boston Police Department, 1919 strike, 424–425
Bowling Green, Kentucky, Police Department, 151
Bratton, William, 12–13, 82, 98, 147–150
Brown, Lee P., 13–14
Budget, computer applications, 136
Budgeting, 69–70
Budgets, 392
    completed, 398
    line-item, 394–395
    open-end, 393
    planned program budgeting system (PPBS), 395–399
    supplementing, 399–401
    types of, 393
    zero-based budgeting (ZBB), 397–399
Buffalo, New York, 173
Building maintenance, 285–287
Bureaucracy, 5
    primary group and, 28–31
    traditional concept of, 61–62
Bypassing, as obstacle to communication, 119

C

CAD (computer-aided dispatch), 137, 138–139, 145
CALEA (Commission on Accreditation for Law Enforcement Agencies), 384–386
Calls for assistance, 160–162, 164
    preventive patrol and, 160
Calls for service, 163–164
Canal City Police Department (case study), 42–43
Career criminals, 229
Carnivore, 151
Caseload, investigation, 227–228
Centralization, 391
Chain communication, 117
Chain of command, 117
Change agent model, 56
Channels, 112
Chaos, managing in, 86–89
Charismatic authority, 80–81
Chicago, community-oriented policing in, 180–182
Chicago's Alternate Policing Strategy (CAPS), 180–182
Child pornography, 294
Children. *See also* Juvenile crime; Youth services and juvenile aid units
    missing, 208
Chula Vista, California, 173
Citizen volunteer programs, 245–246
City of Canton v. *Harris*, 186, 376
Civilian employees, 53–54
Civil liability, training and, 371, 374–377
Civil Rights Act of 1964, 304
Civil service, 5, 52–54, 303
Civil service selection, 301. *See also* Selection of personnel
Cliques, 32

Collective bargaining, 424
 contract administration and, 435
 discipline procedures and, 437–438
 Fair Labor Standards Act (FLSA) and, 438–439
 grievance procedures and, 436
 improper labor practices and, 436
 management rights and, 432–433
 process of, 433–439
 seniority and, 435–436
Collective bargaining agreements, 253–254
College education requirements, for selection purposes, 320–321
College internships, 244
Collins v. *City of Harker Heights*, 376–377
Common culture, 9
Communications, 271–275
Communication(s), 71–72, 111–130
 all-channel, 117
 case study, 272–273
 chain, 117
 consolidated, 273
 context of, 115–116
 definition of, 112
 encoding and decoding, 114–115
 feedback and, 115
 Johari window and, 119–122
 networking approach to, 116–117
 obstacles to, 118–119
 operational, 122–125
 personal attributes of communicators, 274–275
 proactive communication model, 128–130
 typical model of, 112–113
 "Y," 117–118
Communications personnel, 273–274
Communications Workers of America (CWA), 430
Community liaison, juvenile cases and, 208
Community-oriented policing (COP), 54, 174–183. *See also* Problem-oriented policing
 Chicago, 180–182
 implementation of, 175, 177–180
 problem-oriented policing differentiated from, 172
 Seattle, 179–180
 St. Petersburg, Florida, 178–179
 traditional policing compared to, 175–177
 Weed and Seed program, 183–184

Community relations, 72, 136, 240–247
 college internships, 244
 crime-prevention programs, 244–245
 functions of the community relations unit, 242–246
 home pages and electronic newsletters, 243
 personnel for, 242
 public speakers' bureaus, 242–243
 ride-alongs, 243–244
 tours and demonstrations, 243
Community relations officer (CRO), 246–247
Completed budget, 398
CompStat, 98, 147–150, 416–418
Computer-aided dispatch (CAD), 137–139, 145
Computer and communications administrator, 277–278
Computer crimes, 204
 categories of, 293–295
 investigation of, 292–293, 366–367
Computers (computerization), 89–90, 276. *See also* Technology
 Automated Regional Justice Information System (ARJIS), 142–143
 CAD (computer-aided dispatch), 137, 138–139
 CompStat, 147–150
 crime mapping, 146–147
 cross-jurisdictional high-speed notification, 151–152
 cyberterror and cyberattacks and, 150–151
 fingerprint identification systems, 292
 imaging technology, 143–144
 information management applications, 135–153
 mobile data access, 152–153
 National Crime Information Center (NCIC), 141–142
 paperless police departments, 143–144
 proactive management-based information system (PMBIS), 145–146
 Remote Control Information System (RCIS), 144
 video simulation and, 365
Conceptual skill, 99–100
Consolidation of police departments, 451–452
Contingency plans, 406
Contract administration, 435
Contract police issues, 331–332
Control, 73

Controlling, process of, 6
Coop, 31
Cooper Institute for Aerobics Research, 311
Coordinating, 69
Corridor Safety Plan (California Highway
  Patrol), 173
Corruption, 259–260, 417
  internal norms and, 31–32
  international police cooperation and, 460
  primary group cliques and, 32
County of Sacramento v. *Lewis*, 186
Crime analysis, 165
Crime laboratories, 287–295
  computer crime investigation units,
    292–293
  fingerprint identification systems, 292
Crime mapping, 146–147, 456
Crime-prevention programs, 244–245
Crimetac system (New York City), 147
Criminal investigations. *See* Investigation
Criminalistics, 288
Critical-incident management, 372
Critical infrastructure assessment and protec-
  tion, 414–415
Cross-cultural training, 363
Culture, definition of, 18
Curfew programs for juveniles, 217
Cyberterror and cyberattacks, 150–151
Cynicism, 21

D

DARE (Drug Abuse Resistance Education),
  215–217
Databases. *See* Computers
Data gathering, planning and, 388
DCP (distributed collaborative planning)
  systems, 146
Deadly force, 372
  police use of, 257
Decentralization, 391
Decoding, 112–115
Decoy squads, 166
Delray Beach Police Department, 400
Demonstrations, 243
Department contract model, 331, 332
Department rules, 253–254
Detention facilities, temporary, 286–287
Developing others, 92, 93
Developmental training, 368–369
Deviance, police

proactive community policing and,
  263–264
  strategic interventions for, 256–257
Differential Police Response System, 159
Digital revolution, 89–90
Dipping, 306
Directed patrol, 165–167
Directing, 69, 74
Directives, 122
  general rules for writing, 124–125
Disasters, 87–89
Disciplinary actions, 252–253
  collective bargaining agreements and,
    437–438
Disparate impact theory, 306
Distributed collaborative planning (DCP)
  systems, 146
Diversity, training and, 363–364
DNA testing, 290
Doli incapax, 206
Domestic violence, 417
  training and, 361–362
Drucker, Peter F., 27, 28
Drug Abuse Resistance Education (DARE),
  215–217
Drugs, 201–202
Drug testing, for police personnel, 219,
  327–330
Due process, 264–266
Duty manual, 122, 125–128, 402

E

Early-warning (EW) system to identify problem
  officers, 258
Education, 83–84
  selection of police officers and, 325
EEOC (Equal Employment Opportunity
  Commission), 305
Effectiveness, traditional measures of, 54–55
Efficiency of police, 55
  in 1829 duty manual, 3
Electronic newsletters, 243
Emergency management, training and, 360–367
Emergency medical services, 296
Emergency mobilizations, 295–296, 407–408
Emergency-response plans, schools and, 213
EMIT (Enzyme Multiplied Immunoassay
  Technique), 328
Emotional awareness, 92
Emotional intelligence, 90–93

Empathy, 91–93, 99
Employee-assistance programs, 339–341
Empowerment, 9, 104
Encoding, 112, 114–115
Enforcers, 34
Equal Employment Opportunity Commission (EEOC), 305
Esoteric knowledge, 21
Ethics, 73, 83
Europol, 458
Evaluation, 72
Evidence-based policing, 457–458
Evidence control, 281–282
Excessive force, police use of, 258
Experience, 82–83
Explorer posts, 212
Extrapolation, 381
Eyesight standards, 312

F

Fact finding, 429
Fair Labor Standards Act (FLSA), 438–439
Family-service bureaus, 210
Fatigue management, 338–339
Federal Drug Free Workplace Act (1988), 330
Federal Emergency Management Agency (FEMA), emergency mobilizations and, 407
Feedback, 112, 115
Female officers, 37–41
Female police executives, 14
Field training, 352–354
Fingerprint identification systems, computerized, 292
Fiscal plans, 392–401
Fixed-ceiling budget, 393
Flexibility, 311
Florida Contraband Forfeiture Act (1980), 400
Follow-up investigation, 224–225
Foot patrol, 167
Forecasts, 381
Forensic science, 288
Forfeiture, budgets and, 400
Fort Lauderdale Police Department, 400
Fosdick, Raymond B., 7
Found property, 282
Fraternal Order of Police (FOP), 430
Freedom of Information Act (1974), 279
Future of proactive police management, 446–465

consolidation of police departments, 451–452
evidence-based policing, 457–458
global crime and policing, 458–462
jurisdictional dilemma and, 450–452
personnel practices, 453–455
scenario for, 446–447
technology, 452–453
trends, 447–448
what works, 455–457

G

Gang Resistance and Education Training (GREAT), 217–218
Gangs, youth, 210, 211, 214, 217, 218, 221
Garbriel v. *City of Plano*, 376
Garcia v. *San Antonio Metropolitan Transit Authority*, 438
Gates, Bill, 89, 90, 152–153
Gay and lesbian police officers, 41
Gemeinschaft group, 28
General area surveillance, 166
Generalist-specialist controversy, 195–197
General orders (GOs), 123
Gesellschaft, 29
Global crime and policing, 458–462
Goods, theft of, 293
GOs (general orders), 123
Grant preparation, juvenile cases and, 208
Grass eaters, 32
Great Britain, origins of the modern police force in, 1–4
GREAT (Gang Resistance and Education Training), 217–218
Grievance procedures, 436
Grievances, 429
Griggs v. *Duke Power Company*, 306

H

Habits, 72
Hate crimes, 364–365
Hate groups, 412–413
Hate Watch, 412
Hawthorne Study, 27
Hazard analysis, 407–408
Helicopters, pursuits with, 187
Herzberg's eternal triangle, 98–99
Herzberg's hygiene/motivators approach to job satisfaction, 102–104

Hierarchy of needs, Maslow's, 100–102
High-speed notification, cross-jurisdictional, 151–152
High touch, 104
Hollingshead, A.B., 20–22
Hollywood, Florida, Police Department, 218
Homeland security planning, 409–414. *See also* Terrorism
Home pages of police departments, 243
Hook, 20
Hopwood v. *Texas*, 308
Horse, 21
Hostile work environment standard, 326
Hot spots, 184–185
Humanist approach to organization, 61
Human relations approach, 8, 27
Human resource management, 300–341
    affirmative action, 304–308
    civil service selection, 301
    contract police issues, 331–332
    director of human resources, 308–309
    drug testing, 327–330
    employee-assistance programs, 339–341
    essential functions of a police officer position, 315
    fatigue management, 338–339
    long-range personnel deployment, 391–392
    overtime, 332–334
    private security industry, 330–331
    public service employment, 301, 303–304
    selection of personnel. *See* Selection of personnel
    sexual harassment, 326–327
    stress management, 334–338
Human skill, 99
Hygiene/motivators approach to job satisfaction, Herzberg's, 102–104

I

Idealists, 34
Ideal types, 33
Identity, theft of, 293
Imaging technology, 143–144
Implementation, 72–73
Improper labor practices, 436–437
Incident management, 372
Increase-decrease analysis, 393
Industrial Revolution, 1, 2
Inference, 118

Informal group structures, 26–30
Informants, 230
Infrastructure, terrorism and, 414–415
Injunctions against strikes, 440
In re Gault, 206
In-service training, 355
Inspection, 72
Inspections, 261
Instrumental planning, 382
Intelligence, emotional, 90–93
Intelligence gathering, 230–231
Intermediate training, 368
Internal affairs, 256
Internal audits, 261
Internal norms. *See* Peer group norms police corruption and. *See* Corruption
Internal sanctions, police subculture and, 22
International Association of Chiefs of Police (IACP), 83–84
International Brotherhood of Police Officers (IBPO), 431
International Brotherhood of Teamsters, 430–431
International Union of Police Associations (IUPA), 430
Internships, 244
Interpol, 458
Interviews, for selection purposes, 319–320
Intuitive approach, 383
Invasion of privacy, 294
Inventory, 136
Inventory control, 280–281
Investigation (investigations divisions), 222–231
    computer crime, 292–293
    of computer crimes, 366–367
    of cross-national crime, 462
    follow-up, 224–225
    issues and concerns regarding, 229–231
    of juvenile cases, 207
    managing, 227–229
    preliminary, 223–224
    Rand study of, 226
    traditional structure of, 225–226
Investigation(s), 75
Investigative checklists, 228
Isolation, social, 19–20
    norm of, 255–256
    police subculture and, 23–24
Item-by-item control, 393

J

Job satisfaction, Herzberg's hygiene/motivators approach to, 102–104
Johari window, 119–122
Joyce v. *Suffolk County*, 313–314
Justice, U.S. Department of, Weed and Seed program, 183–184
Justice Technology Information Network (JUSTNET), 144–145
Juvenile aid divisions. *See* Youth services and juvenile aid units
Juvenile court, preparation of cases for, 207
Juvenile gangs, 210, 211, 214, 217, 218, 221
Juvenile record keeping, 208–209
Juveniles, 76

K

Kansas City Experiment, 51
Kansas City studies, 158
Kansas City Study, 160–161
Kerr v. *City of West Palm Beach*, 377
Kibbe v. *City of Springfield*, 376
King, Rodney, 258
Kirkham, George, 20
KITA (kick-in-the-pants approach), 102
Klanwatch, 412
Knapp Commission, 31, 32, 259
Krocka v. *Reigler*, 314–315

L

Laptop computers, 134, 143
Lateral entry, 318
Law enforcement agencies, as big business, 51–52
Law Enforcement Assistance Administration (LEAA), 7
Law Enforcement Television Network (LETN), 366
Leaders (leadership)
    definition of, 80
    proactive, 79–84
    reengineering and, 97
Legal advisers, 247–249
Legal authority, 81
Legalistic style of policing, 34
Lehnert v. *Ferris Valley Faculty Association*, 428
LETN (Law Enforcement Television Network), 366
Licensing, 287

Line functions, 74–76, 194–232
    generalist-specialist controversy and, 195–197
    investigation, 222–231. *See* Investigation
    traffic, 197–201
    vice, 201–204
    youth services and juvenile aid units, 205–222
Line-item budgeting, 394–395
Line-item control, 393–394
Line organizations, 50
Line/staff conflict and cooperation, 238–240
Live scan, 292
Local control, principle of, 3–4
Lockup, 286–287
London Metropolitan Police, 125
Los Angeles Police Department, excessive force used by, 258
Los Angeles Police Department (LAPD), 6–7

M

McGregor's Theory X and Theory Y, 8, 104–105
McGruff national media campaign, 245
McNamera v. *City of Chicago*, 308
Macroforecasting, 381
Magic Lantern, 151
Main man, 21
Management, 85–108
    behavioral, 10–11
    Blake and Mouton's managerial grid and, 106–108
    emotional intelligence and, 90–93
    Herzberg's eternal triangle and, 98–99
    Herzberg's hygiene/motivators approach to job satisfaction and, 102–104
    Katz's three skills approach, 99–100
    McGregor's Theory X and Theory Y and, 104–105
    participatory, 8–10
    principles of, 57–60
    proactive, 11–14
    reengineering and, 96–98
    scientific, 4–5
    systems-behavioral, 10–11
    total quality (TQM), 10, 93–96
Management skills, 84–85
Management training, 372–374
Managerial grid, 106–108
Mapping, computer, 134

Maslow's hierarchy of needs, 8, 100–102
Maximum strength, 311
MDC (mobile digital communications), 137, 139
Meat eaters, 32
Mechanical approach to organization, 61
Mediation, 428
MEMOs (memorandums), 123–124
Metropolitan Police Act, 1, 3
Metropolitan Police (London), 125
Miami Police Department, 258–259, 399
Military model, 256
Military Training and Moral Training, 2
Militias, 412–413
Minority group structures, 35–43
Misconduct, police, 259–266
Misconduct review, 262–263
Missing children, 208
Mobile digital communications (MDC), 137, 139
Mobile digital terminal (MDT), 137, 139
Mobile neighborhood watch, 211
Mobile radio district (MRD), 273
Model youth programs, 211
Modus operandi, 142–143
Monell v. *Department of Social Services*, 375
Money, theft of, 293
Morale, 73
Morrisey v. *Brewer*, 264
Motivation, 91
    Herzberg's hygiene/motivators approach to job satisfaction, 102–104
    Maslow's hierarchy of needs and, 100–102
Muscular endurance, 311

N

Narcotic Investigation Tracking of Recidivist Offenders (NITR), 148
National Association of Women Law Enforcement Executives (NAWLEE), 14
National Crime Information Center (NCIC), 141–142
National Treasury Employees Union v. *VonRaab*, 328
Neighborhood-oriented policing (NOP), 13
Neighborhood Watch, 60, 245
Networking, 408–409
Networking approach to communication, 116–117
Neutral zones, 211

New Haven, Connecticut, Police Department, 217
Newport News, Virginia, Police Department, 171, 172
New York City Police Department (NYPD), 20, 30, 36, 39, 98
    CompStat, 147–150
    Crimetac system, 147
New York City Police Foundation, 400
Niederhoffer, Arthur, 21
911 system, 134, 140–141, 158
    hot spots plan, 184–185
Normative planning, 382–383
Norms, definition of, 19
Northwestern University Traffic Institute, 60

O

Oakdale Police Department, 219
Obesity, 312
Obscenity, police use of, 257
Officer contract model, 331
Officer-initiated activities, 160
Oklahoma City v. *Tuttle*, 375
Omnipresent police officer, 50–51
Open-end budgets, 393
Operational communications, 122–125
Operational planning, 402
Operation Identification, 244
Operations, 67, 74–77
Orders, types of, 122–124
Organization(s), police
    concept of, 60–62
    as line organizations, 50
    reality-based, proactive purposes of, 56–57
    traditional concept of bureaucracy and, 61–62
    traditional purposes of, 54
Organized crime, 201, 203–204
Organizing, 68
Outdoor adventure programs, 218–219
Overgeneralization, 119
Overtime, police, 332–334

P

Panic stop, 168
Paperless police departments, 143–144
Parens patriae, 206
Parent networks, 211
Parker, William H., 6–7

Parking enforcement, 197
Participatory management, 8–10
Patrol, 74–75
Patrol allocation plans, 402
Patrol cars, 134
    automatic vehicle monitoring (AVM),
        139–140
    personal, 284–285
Patrol officers, investigative role of, 227
Patrol operations, 158–188. *See also*
        Community-oriented policing
    administrative tasks, 160, 164–165
    bicycle patrol, 167–168
    calls for service, 160, 163–164
    case study, 168
    community policing, 174–183
    directed patrol, 165–167
    foot patrol, 167
    hot spots plan, 184–185
    Kansas City Study, 160–161
    officer-initiated activities, 160
    preventive patrol, 159–163
    problem-oriented policing, 170–174
    pursuit policies, 185–187
    rethinking the traditional model,
        161–168
    specialized patrol, 166–167
    tactical patrol, 170
    team policing, 169–170
    traditional model of, 159–160
Patrol staffing model, 402–404
Payroll, 136
Peel, Sir Robert, 1, 55
Peer group norms, 30–31
Peer group pressure, 22
Pendleton Act, 303
Pendleton Act (1870), 4
Performance, 57, 72
Personal patrol car, 284–285
Personnel
    future of personnel practices, 453–455
    selection of. *See* Selection of personnel
Personnel costs, 301
Peters, Tom, 9–10
Phase approach to training, 367–374
Physical fitness, selection of personnel,
        311–315
Physical requirements, for selection of
        personnel, 325
Planned program budgeting system (PPBS),
        395–399

Planning, 68, 72–73
    case study, 389
    Compstat and, 416–418
    contingency, 406
    definition of, 382–383
    emergency mobilizations, 407–408
    fiscal, 392–401
    homeland security, 409–414
    instrumental, 382
    long-range administrative/management
        plans, 390–392
    need for a planning officer or a planning
        unit, 386–387
    normative, 382–383
    operational, 402
    patrol staffing, 402–404
    process of, 6
    rapid response, 404–406
    response to special populations
        (networking), 408–409
    short-range operational/tactical plans,
        401–411
    significance of, 383–384
    steps in, 387–390
    types of plans, 390–409
Police Administration (Wilson), 5
Police corruption. *See* Corruption
Police deviance
    proactive community policing and,
        263–264
    strategic interventions for, 256–257
Police misconduct, 259–266
Police organizations
    concept of, 60–62
    as line organizations, 50
    reality-based, proactive purposes of,
        56–57
    traditional concept of bureaucracy and,
        61–62
    traditional purposes of, 54
Police probation counseling center, 219
Police subculture. *See* Subculture, police
Police typologies, 33–35
Police unions, 424–431. *See also* Collective
        bargaining
    political process and, 440–441
    strikes and, 439–440
Police violence and deviance, proactive control
        of, 254–259
Policy, 67
Political process, police unions and, 440–441

Polygraph testing, background investigation for selection purposes and, 318–319
Pornography, child, 294
POSDCORB, 67
Power slide, 168
PPBS (planned program budgeting system), 395–399
Preliminary investigations, 223–224
Preparatory training, 354
Preparedness, 57
Preventive patrol, 159–163
     calls for assistance and, 160–162, 164
Primary groups, police bureaucracy and, 28–30
Priority listing, 393
Private security industry, 330–331
Proactive communication model, 128–130
Proactive community policing, police deviance and, 263–264
Proactive homeland security, 409–414
Proactive leadership, 79–84
Proactive management-based information system (PMBIS), 145–146
Proactive planning, 381–418. See Planning
Proactive police management, 11–14
     future of. See Future of proactive police management
Problem officers, early-warning systems to identify, 258–259
Problem-oriented policing (POP), 13, 170–174
     model program and examples of excellence, 172–174
Professionalization of policing, 5
Professional standards, 249–252
Progressive discipline, 253
Progressiveness, 57
Project STAR (System and Training Analysis of Requirements for Criminal Justice Participants), 355–357
Project teams, 10
Promotions, 52–53
Property control, 280–282
Prostitution, 202–203
Pseudo-cynicism, 21
Psychological distance, police subculture and, 24–26
Psychological testing, 317–318
     selection of police officers and, 317–318
Public speakers' bureaus, 242–243
Purchasing, 136
Purposes of policing, 56–57
Pursuit policies, 185–187

Q

Quality teams, 10

R

Rabbi, 20
Racial discrimination, 35, 36
Racial profiling, 198–201
Random patrol, 51
Rand study of investigative divisions, 226
Rapid response, 404–406
Realism, 21–22
Realists, 34
Receiver, 112
Record-management systems (RMS), 145
Records division, 275–280
     categories of records, 275–276
     computer and communications administrator, 277–278
     computerization of, 276–277
     security, sealing, purging, and public access to records, 278–280
     storage of records, 278
Recovery, as principle of management, 59
Recruitment of police officers, 322–326. See also Selection of personnel
Recruit training, 367–368
Reengineering, 96–98
Regional communication system (RCS), 141
Regulation, as principle of management, 58
Reinforcement, as principle of management, 60
Remote Control Information System (RCIS), 144
Reporting, 69, 71–72
Repression, as principle of management, 59
Residency, selection of police officers and, 316–317
Resigned cynicism, 21
Resource utilization, 73–74
RESPECT approach to supervision, 71–74
Response, as principle of management, 57–58
Response time, crime rate and, 161
Restraint, as principle of management, 58–59
Result and performance measures, 55–56
Reverse discrimination, 306–307
Ride-along programs, 219
Ride-alongs, 243–244
RMS (record-management systems), 145
Road rage, 197
Rogers County, Oklahoma, 174
Role entrapment of female officers, 40

Rolling dismount, 168
Romantic cynicism, 21
Rowan, Sir Charles, 2, 55
Rule of three, 301

S

Safire, Howard, 13
Sager v. *City of Woodland Park*, 375
St. Petersburg, Florida, community-oriented
    policing in, 178–179
Salt Lake City, Utah, 174
San Diego Police Department, 41
San Francisco Police Department, 41
Santos v. *Port Authority of New York and New
    Jersey*, 314
SARA model, 172–173
Scheduling of personnel, 136
School liaison programs, 212–213
School violence, 213–215, 416
Scientific management, 4–5
Screening of cases, 227
    juvenile cases, 207
Seattle, community-oriented policing in,
    179–180
Seattle Police Department, 167
Secrecy, 19
    norm of, 255
Selection of personnel, 309–322
    age limits, 310
    assessment center for, 321–322
    background investigation, 315–322
    model for, 324–326
    physical fitness, 311–315
    recruitment of police officers, 322–326
    written tests, 309–310
Self-actualization, need for, 101
Self-awareness, 91
Self-control, 92
Self-fulfillment, need for, 101
Self-regulation, 91
Selling illegal goods, 294
Semimilitary model, 3, 4, 15
Sender, 112
Seniority, 435–436
September 11, 2001, terrorist attacks, 86–88
Services, 72
    theft of, 293
Sexual abuse, 260–261
Sexual harassment, 326
Shift design, patrol operations and, 165–166

Skinner v. *Railway Labor Executives Association*,
    328
Smith, Bruce, 7–8
Social isolation, 19–20
    norm of, 255–256
    police subculture and, 23–24
Socializing, 113–114
Social skills, 91
Social utility, 399
Solidarity, 19
    norm of, 255
    police subculture and, 22–23
Sophisticated patronage, 323
SOPs (standard operating procedures), 122–123
SOs (special orders), 123
South Euclid, Ohio, 174
Spades v. *City of Walnut Ridge*, 315
Spatial and Temporal Analysis of Crime
    program, 147
Speakers' bureaus, 219
Specialist training, 369
Specialization, 195–197
Specialized patrol, 166–167
Special orders (SOs), 123
Special populations, response to, 408–409
Spoils system, 301, 303
Stacking, 164
Staff functions. *See* Administration
    (administrative/staff functions)
Staffing, 68
Stakeouts, 166
Stalking, training and, 362–363
Standard operating procedures (SOPs), 122–123
STAR (System and Training Analysis of
    Requirements for Criminal Justice
    Participants), 355–357
State of New Jersey v. *Pedro et al.*, 199
Station-house probation, 207, 219
Status offenses, 206
Sting operations, 59
Stolen property, recovery of, 163
Stranger-danger program, 219
Strength, maximum, 311
Stress management, 334–338, 372
Strikes, police, 439–440
Student intern programs, 244
Styles of policing, 34
Subculture, police, 18–43
    argot and, 20–21
    characteristics of, 20–26
    cynicism and, 21–22

Subculture, police (*continued*)
    definition of, 19, 20
    esoteric knowledge and, 21
    internal sanctions and, 22
    norms of, 19
    perception of violence and psychological
        distance and, 24–26
    solidarity and, 22–23
Subscripts, 114
Supervision, 67
Supervision (supervisors), 70–74
    RESPECT approach to, 71–74
Supervisory training, 369–370
Supporting services. *See* Auxiliary functions
Surveillance
    general area, 166
    suspect, 166
Suspect surveillance, 166
Sutton and Hinton v. *United Airlines*, 314
Syracuse Police Department (New York), 143
Systems-behavioral management, 10–11

T

Tactical operations, training and, 363
Tactical patrol, 170
Talent, 80–82
Team policing, 8, 169–170
    history of, 169
    positive aspects of, 169–170
    tactical patrol and, 170
Technical skills, 99
Technology, 133–153. *See also* Computers
    automatic vehicle monitoring (AVM),
        139–140
    CAD (computer-aided dispatch), 137–139
    future of policing and, 452–453, 455
    mobile digital terminal (MDT), 137–139
    new technologies for police managers,
        144–145
    911 system, 140–141
Teens on Patrol program (Rochester, New
        York), 217
Temporary detention facilities, 286–287
Temporary operating procedures (TOPs), 123
Tennessee v. *Garner*, 257, 375
Terrorism, 409–416
    criminal groups *versus*, 411–412
    critical infrastructure assessment and
        protection and, 414–415
    global crime organizations and, 459

intelligence gathering on, 230–231
    proactive homeland security and, 409–412
    proactive policies for combating, 413–414
    racial profiling and, 200
    training and, 360–367
Theft, computer-related, 293–294
Theory X and Theory Y, McGregor's, 8, 104–105
Theory Z, 104–106
Thin blue line, 20
    female officers and, 40
Thomas v. *City of Evanston*, 38
Title VII, 304–305
TOPs (temporary operating procedures), 123
Total quality management (TQM), 10, 93–96
Traffic, 75
Traffic enforcement, 197–201
Training, 74, 83–84, 347–377
    advanced, 368
    AIDS and other blood-borne pathogens,
        361
    Americans with Disabilities Act, 365
    civil liability and, 371, 374–377
    computer and video simulation, 365
    computer crime investigation, 366–367
    computerized records, 136
    curriculum changes (1952 to present),
        357–359
    developmental, 368–369
    diversity, 363–364
    domestic violence, 361–362
    field, 352
    general need for, 349–351
    hate crimes, 364–365
    historical perspectives on, 347–348
    historical recommendations for,
        354–355
    importance to police managers, 354
    in-service, 355
    instruction quality control, 355
    intermediate, 368
    location and timing of basic training,
        351–352
    management, 372–374
    model first-line manager's (supervisor's)
        course, 370–372
    new technologies and, 365–366
    phase approach to, 367–370
    preparatory, 354
    Project STAR (System and Training
        Analysis of Requirements for Criminal
        Justice Participants), 355–357

before promotion, 355
recruit, 367–368
specialist, 369
supervisory, 369–370
tactical operations, 363
terrorism and emergency management, 360–361
topical issues in, 360–367
Trustworthiness, 92
Turning people into things, 256
Two-minute limit for talking on duty, 113, 127
Typologies, 33–35

U

Understanding others, 92, 93
Uniform Crime Reports, 51
Union brokerage model, 331
Unions, 424–431. *See also* Collective bargaining
political process and, 440–441
strikes and, 439–440
Unit costing, 393
United Steel Workers v. *Weber*, 306
U.S. v. *North Carolina*, 38
USA PATRIOT Act (2001), 151, 360

V

Vanguard Justice Society v. *Hughes*, 38
Vehicle maintenance, 136, 282–285
Vice, 75–76
Vice crimes, 201–204
Vice units, 203–204
Victimless crimes, 75
Video simulation, 365
Violence, perception of, police subculture and, 24–26
Virtual reality, 366
Viverette, Mary Ann, 14
Volunteer programs, 245–246
Voutour v. *Vitale*, 375

W

Wambaugh, Joseph, 23
Ward's Cove Packing v. *Atonio*, 307
Webb v. *City of Chester, Ill.*, 38
Weber, Max, 4, 28, 29, 33
on charismatic authority, 80–81
traditional concept of bureaucracy from, 61–62

Weber case, 306
Weed and Seed program, 183–184
Wellness program, 371
Whitefield v. *Board of Commissioners of Eagle County, Colorado*, 200
Wilkins v. *Maryland State Police*, 199–200
Williams v. *City of Charlotte, North Carolina*, 314
Wilson, O.W., 5–6, 50, 55
Wincanton (Reading, Pa.) protection system (case study), 33
Women
as civilian employees, 53
police officers, 37–41
Work community, 27–28
Work measurement, 393
World Wide Web, 134
Wright v. *Universal Maritime Service Corp.*, 314
Written tests, 309–310

Y

Yale University Child Center, 217
"Y" communication, 117–118
Youth gangs, 210, 211, 214, 217, 218, 221
Youth services and juvenile aid units, 205–222.
See also Juvenile crime
case studies, 219–222
current programs, 217–219
DARE (Drug Abuse Resistance Education), 215–217
juvenile record keeping, 208–209
model youth programs, 211–213
organization of, 209–210
personnel selection for, 209
role of, 207–208

Z

Zero-based budgeting (ZBB), 397–399